Poetry
for Students

National Advisory Board

for *Poetry* *Students*

Presenting Analysis, Context, and Criticism on Commonly Studied Poetry

Volume 24

Anne Marie Hacht and

Ira Mark Milne, Project Editors

Foreword by David Kelly

THOMSON

━━━━━★━━━━━ ™

GALE

Detroit • New York • San Francisco • New Haven, Conn. • Waterville, Maine • London • Munich

THOMSON

GALE

Poetry for Students, Volume 24

Project Editors
Anne Marie Hacht, Ira Mark Milne

Rights Acquisition and Management
Shalice Shah-Caldwell, Kim Smilay,
Andrew Specht

Manufacturing
Drew Kalasky

Image Research & Acquisition
Robyn Young

Imaging and Multimedia
Lezlie Light, Mike Logusz

Product Design
Pamela A. E. Galbreath

Vendor Administration
Civie Green

Product Manager
Meggin Condino

ISBN 0-7876-6963-6
ISSN 1094-7019

Printed in the United States of America
10 9 8 7 6 5 4 3 2 1

Table of Contents

Guest Foreword
  "Just a Few Lines on a Page"
  by David J. Kelly ix

Introduction xi

Literary Chronology xv

Acknowledgments xvii

Contributors xxi

All I Was Doing Was Breathing
(by Mirabai) *1*
  Author Biography 1
  Poem Summary 2
  Themes 3
  Style 5
  Historical Context 5
  Critical Overview 7
  Criticism 7
  Further Reading 13

Always
(by Guillaume Apollinaire) *14*
  Author Biography 14
  Poem Text 15
  Poem Summary 15
  Themes 16
  Style 17
  Historical Context 18
  Critical Overview 20
  Criticism 22
  Further Reading 34

At the Cancer Clinic
(by Ted Kooser) 35
   Author Biography 35
   Poem Summary 36
   Themes 38
   Style 39
   Historical Context 40
   Critical Overview 40
   Criticism 41
   Further Reading 50

The Chambered Nautilus
(by Oliver Wendell Holmes) 51
   Author Biography 52
   Poem Text 52
   Poem Summary 53
   Themes 54
   Style 56
   Historical Context 56
   Critical Overview 58
   Criticism 58
   Further Reading 65

For the Sake of Strangers
(by Dorianne Laux) 66
   Author Biography 67
   Poem Summary 67
   Themes 68
   Style 70
   Historical Context 70
   Critical Overview 71
   Criticism 72
   Further Reading 82

Kindness
(by Naomi Shihab Nye) 83
   Author Biography 84
   Poem Text 84
   Poem Summary 85
   Themes 87
   Style 88
   Historical Context 89
   Critical Overview 90
   Criticism 91
   Further Reading 99

The Litany
(by Dana Gioia) 100
   Author Biography 100
   Poem Text 101
   Poem Summary 102
   Themes 103
   Style 104
   Historical Context 104

   Critical Overview 105
   Criticism 106
   Further Reading 118

Monologue for an Onion
(by Sue (Suji) Kwock Kim) 119
   Author Biography 120
   Poem Text 120
   Poem Summary 121
   Themes 121
   Style 123
   Historical Context 123
   Critical Overview 124
   Criticism 124
   Further Reading 133

Not like a Cypress
(by Yehuda Amichai) 134
   Author Biography 134
   Poem Text 135
   Poem Summary 135
   Themes 137
   Style 138
   Historical Context 139
   Critical Overview 141
   Criticism 141
   Further Reading 156

One Is One
(by Marie Ponsot) 157
   Author Biography 157
   Poem Text 158
   Poem Summary 158
   Themes 159
   Style 161
   Historical Context 162
   Critical Overview 163
   Criticism 164
   Further Reading 175

Our Side
(by Carol Muske-Dukes) 176
   Author Biography 176
   Poem Text 177
   Poem Summary 177
   Themes 180
   Style 181
   Historical Context 182
   Critical Overview 184
   Criticism 184
   Further Reading 192

A Poison Tree
(by William Blake) 194
   Author Biography 195

Poem Text 195
Poem Summary 196
Themes 198
Style 198
Historical Context 200
Critical Overview 201
Criticism 202
Further Reading 212

Portrait of a Couple at Century's End
(by Sherod Santos) *213*
Author Biography 214
Poem Text 214
Poem Summary 215
Themes 216
Style 218
Historical Context 218
Critical Overview 219
Criticism 220
Further Reading 231

The Room
(by Conrad Aiken) *232*
Author Biography 232
Poem Summary 233
Themes 234
Style 236

Historical Context 237
Critical Overview 238
Criticism 239
Further Reading 242

Seeing You
(by Jean Valentine) *243*
Author Biography 244
Poem Text 244
Poem Summary 245
Themes 246
Style 247
Historical Context 248
Critical Overview 250
Criticism 250
Further Reading 262

Three To's and an Oi
(by Heather McHugh) *263*
Author Biography 264
Poem Text 264
Poem Summary 264
Themes 266
Style 268
Historical Context 268
Critical Overview 269
Criticism 270
Further Reading 276

Glossary 277

Cumulative Author/Title Index 297

*Cumulative Nationality/Ethnicity
Index* 305

Subject/Theme Index 313

Cumulative Index of First Lines 319

Cumulative Index of Last Lines 325

Just a Few Lines on a Page

I have often thought that poets have the easiest job in the world. A poem, after all, is just a few lines on a page, usually not even extending margin to margin—how long would that take to write, about five minutes? Maybe ten at the most, if you wanted it to rhyme or have a repeating meter. Why, I could start in the morning and produce a book of poetry by dinnertime. But we all know that it isn't that easy. Anyone can come up with enough words, but the poet's job is about writing the *right* ones. The right words will change lives, making people see the world somewhat differently than they saw it just a few minutes earlier. The right words can make a reader who relies on the dictionary for meanings take a greater responsibility for his or her own personal understanding. A poem that is put on the page correctly can bear any amount of analysis, probing, defining, explaining, and interrogating, and something about it will still feel new the next time you read it.

It would be fine with me if I could talk about poetry without using the word "magical," because that word is overused these days to imply "a really good time," often with a certain sweetness about it, and a lot of poetry is neither of these. But if you stop and think about magic—whether it brings to mind sorcery, witchcraft, or bunnies pulled from top hats—it always seems to involve stretching reality to produce a result greater than the sum of its parts and pulling unexpected results out of thin air. This book provides ample cases where a few simple words conjure up whole worlds. We do not ac-

tually travel to different times and different cultures, but the poems get into our minds, they find what little we know about the places they are talking about, and then they make that little bit blossom into a bouquet of someone else's life. Poets make us think we are following simple, specific events, but then they leave ideas in our heads that cannot be found on the printed page. Abracadabra.

Sometimes when you finish a poem it doesn't feel as if it has left any supernatural effect on you, like it did not have any more to say beyond the actual words that it used. This happens to everybody, but most often to inexperienced readers: regardless of what is often said about young people's infinite capacity to be amazed, you have to understand what usually does happen, and what could have happened instead, if you are going to be moved by what someone has accomplished. In those cases in which you finish a poem with a "So what?" attitude, the information provided in *Poetry for Students* comes in handy. Readers can feel assured that the poems included here actually are potent magic, not just because a few (or a hundred or ten thousand) professors of literature say they are: they're significant because they can withstand close inspection and still amaze the very same people who have just finished taking them apart and seeing how they work. Turn them inside out, and they will still be able to come alive, again and again. *Poetry for Students* gives readers of any age good practice in feeling the ways poems relate to both the reality of the time and place the poet lived in and the reality of our emotions. Practice is just another word for being a student. The information given here helps you understand the way to read poetry; what to look for, what to expect.

With all of this in mind, I really don't think I would actually like to have a poet's job at all. There are too many skills involved, including precision, honesty, taste, courage, linguistics, passion, compassion, and the ability to keep all sorts of people entertained at once. And that is just what they do with one hand, while the other hand pulls some sort of trick that most of us will never fully understand. I can't even pack all that I need for a weekend into one suitcase, so what would be my chances of stuffing so much life into a few lines? With all that *Poetry for Students* tells us about each poem, I am impressed that any poet can finish three or four poems a year. Read the inside stories of these poems, and you won't be able to approach any poem in the same way you did before.

David J. Kelly
College of Lake County

Introduction

Purpose of the Book

The purpose of *Poetry for Students* (*PfS*) is to provide readers with a guide to understanding, enjoying, and studying poems by giving them easy access to information about the work. Part of Gale's "For Students" Literature line, *PfS* is specifically designed to meet the curricular needs of high school and undergraduate college students and their teachers, as well as the interests of general readers and researchers considering specific poems. While each volume contains entries on "classic" poems frequently studied in classrooms, there are also entries containing hard-to-find information on contemporary poems, including works by multicultural, international, and women poets.

The information covered in each entry includes an introduction to the poem and the poem's author; the actual poem text (if possible); a poem summary, to help readers unravel and understand the meaning of the poem; analysis of important themes in the poem; and an explanation of important literary techniques and movements as they are demonstrated in the poem.

In addition to this material, which helps the readers analyze the poem itself, students are also provided with important information on the literary and historical background informing each work. This includes a historical context essay, a box comparing the time or place the poem was written to modern Western culture, a critical overview essay, and excerpts from critical essays on the

poem. A unique feature of *PfS* is a specially commissioned critical essay on each poem, targeted toward the student reader.

To further aid the student in studying and enjoying each poem, information on media adaptations is provided (if available), as well as reading suggestions for works of fiction and nonfiction on similar themes and topics. Classroom aids include ideas for research papers and lists of critical sources that provide additional material on the poem.

Selection Criteria

The titles for each volume of *PfS* were selected by surveying numerous sources on teaching literature and analyzing course curricula for various school districts. Some of the sources surveyed included: literature anthologies; *Reading Lists for College-Bound Students: The Books Most Recommended by America's Top Colleges*; textbooks on teaching the poem; a College Board survey of poems commonly studied in high schools; and a National Council of Teachers of English (NCTE) survey of poems commonly studied in high schools.

Input was also solicited from our advisory board, as well as educators from various areas. From these discussions, it was determined that each volume should have a mix of "classic" poems (those works commonly taught in literature classes) and contemporary poems for which information is often hard to find. Because of the interest in expanding the canon of literature, an emphasis was also placed on including works by international, multi-cultural, and women poets. Our advisory board members—educational professionals—helped pare down the list for each volume. If a work was not selected for the present volume, it was often noted as a possibility for a future volume. As always, the editor welcomes suggestions for titles to be included in future volumes.

How Each Entry Is Organized

Each entry, or chapter, in *PfS* focuses on one poem. Each entry heading lists the full name of the poem, the author's name, and the date of the poem's publication. The following elements are contained in each entry:

- **Introduction:** a brief overview of the poem which provides information about its first appearance, its literary standing, any controversies surrounding the work, and major conflicts or themes within the work.

- **Author Biography:** this section includes basic facts about the poet's life, and focuses on events and times in the author's life that inspired the poem in question.

- **Poem Text:** when permission has been granted, the poem is reprinted, allowing for quick reference when reading the explication of the following section.

- **Poem Summary:** a description of the major events in the poem. Summaries are broken down with subheads that indicate the lines being discussed.

- **Themes:** a thorough overview of how the major topics, themes, and issues are addressed within the poem. Each theme discussed appears in a separate subhead and is easily accessed through the boldface entries in the Subject/ Theme Index.

- **Style:** this section addresses important style elements of the poem, such as form, meter, and rhyme scheme; important literary devices used, such as imagery, foreshadowing, and symbolism; and, if applicable, genres to which the work might have belonged, such as Gothicism or Romanticism. Literary terms are explained within the entry, but can also be found in the Glossary.

- **Historical Context:** this section outlines the social, political, and cultural climate *in which the author lived and the poem was created.* This section may include descriptions of related historical events, pertinent aspects of daily life in the culture, and the artistic and literary sensibilities of the time in which the work was written. If the poem is a historical work, information regarding the time in which the poem is set is also included. Each section is broken down with helpful subheads.

- **Critical Overview:** this section provides background on the critical reputation of the poem, including bannings or any other public controversies surrounding the work. For older works, this section includes a history of how the poem was first received and how perceptions of it may have changed over the years; for more recent poems, direct quotes from early reviews may also be included.

- **Criticism:** an essay commissioned by *PfS* which specifically deals with the poem and is written specifically for the student audience, as well as excerpts from previously published criticism on the work (if available).

- **Sources:** an alphabetical list of critical material used in compiling the entry, with full bibliographical information.

- **Further Reading:** an alphabetical list of other critical sources which may prove useful for the student. It includes full bibliographical information and a brief annotation.

In addition, each entry contains the following highlighted sections, set apart from the main text as sidebars:

- **Media Adaptations:** if available, a list of audio recordings as well as any film or television adaptations of the poem, including source information.

- **Topics for Further Study:** a list of potential study questions or research topics dealing with the poem. This section includes questions related to other disciplines the student may be studying, such as American history, world history, science, math, government, business, geography, economics, psychology, etc.

- **Compare and Contrast:** an "at-a-glance" comparison of the cultural and historical differences between the author's time and culture and late twentieth century or early twenty-first century Western culture. This box includes pertinent parallels between the major scientific, political, and cultural movements of the time or place the poem was written, the time or place the poem was set (if a historical work), and modern Western culture. Works written after 1990 may not have this box.

- **What Do I Read Next?:** a list of works that might complement the featured poem or serve as a contrast to it. This includes works by the same author and others, works of fiction and nonfiction, and works from various genres, cultures, and eras.

Other Features

PfS includes "Just a Few Lines on a Page," a foreword by David J. Kelly, an adjunct professor of English, College of Lake County, Illinois. This essay provides a straightforward, unpretentious explanation of why poetry should be marveled at and how *Poetry for Students* can help teachers show students how to enrich their own reading experiences.

A Cumulative Author/Title Index lists the authors and titles covered in each volume of the *PfS* series.

A Cumulative Nationality/Ethnicity Index breaks down the authors and titles covered in each volume of the *PfS* series by nationality and ethnicity.

A Subject/Theme Index, specific to each volume, provides easy reference for users who may be studying a particular subject or theme rather than a single work. Significant subjects from events to broad themes are included, and the entries pointing to the specific theme discussions in each entry are indicated in **boldface**.

A Cumulative Index of First Lines (beginning in Vol. 10) provides easy reference for users who may be familiar with the first line of a poem but may not remember the actual title.

A Cumulative Index of Last Lines (beginning in Vol. 10) provides easy reference for users who may be familiar with the last line of a poem but may not remember the actual title.

Each entry may include illustrations, including a photo of the author and other graphics related to the poem.

Citing Poetry for Students

When writing papers, students who quote directly from any volume of *Poetry for Students* may use the following general forms. These examples are based on MLA style; teachers may request that students adhere to a different style, so the following examples may be adapted as needed.

When citing text from *PfS* that is not attributed to a particular author (i.e., the Themes, Style, Historical Context sections, etc.), the following format should be used in the bibliography section:

"Angle of Geese." *Poetry for Students.* Eds. Marie Napierkowski and Mary Ruby. Vol. 2. Detroit: Gale, 1998. 5–7.

When quoting the specially commissioned essay from *PfS* (usually the first piece under the "Criticism" subhead), the following format should be used:

Velie, Alan. Critical Essay on "Angle of Geese." *Poetry for Students.* Eds. Marie Napierkowski and Mary Ruby. Vol. 2. Detroit: Gale, 1998. 7–10.

When quoting a journal or newspaper essay that is reprinted in a volume of *PfS,* the following form may be used:

Luscher, Robert M. "An Emersonian Context of Dickinson's 'The Soul Selects Her Own Society.'" *ESQ: A Journal of American Renaissance* Vol. 30, No. 2 (Second Quarter, 1984), 111–16; excerpted and reprinted in *Poetry for Students*, Vol. 1, eds. Marie Napierkowski and Mary Ruby (Detroit: Gale, 1998), pp. 266–69.

When quoting material reprinted from a book that appears in a volume of *PfS,* the following form may be used:

Mootry, Maria K. "'Tell It Slant': Disguise and Discovery as Revisionist Poetic Discourse in 'The Bean Eaters,'" in *A Life Distilled: Gwendolyn Brooks, Her Poetry and Fiction*. Edited by Maria K. Mootry and Gary Smith. University of Illinois Press, 1987. 177–80, 191; excerpted and reprinted in *Poetry for Students*, Vol. 2, eds. Marie Napierkowski and Mary Ruby (Detroit: Gale, 1998), pp. 22–24.

We Welcome Your Suggestions

The editor of *Poetry for Students* welcomes your comments and ideas. Readers who wish to suggest poems to appear in future volumes, or who have other suggestions, are cordially invited to contact the editor. You may contact the editor via E-mail at: *ForStudentsEditors@thomson.com.* Or write to the editor at:

Editor, *Poetry for Students*
Thomson Gale
27500 Drake Rd.
Farmington Hills, MI 48331–3535

Literary Chronology

c. 1498 Mirabai (sometimes written as Mīrā Bāī) is born into a minor royal family in Merta, in northwestern India.

1530: Mirabai's "All I Was Doing Was Breathing" is published.

1546: Mirabai dies, although some scholars consider 1547 or 1550 to be a more likely date.

1757: William Blake is born on November 28 in London.

1793: William Blake's "A Poison Tree" is published.

1809: Oliver Wendell Holmes is born on August 29 in Cambridge, Massachusetts.

1827: William Blake dies on August 12 in London and is buried in an unmarked grave in Bunhill Fields, a Dissenters' cemetery.

1858: Oliver Wendell Holmes's "The Chambered Nautilus" is published.

1880: Guillaume Apollinaire is born (most likely with the name Wilhelm Apollinaris de Kostrowitzky) on August 26 in Rome.

1889: Conrad Aiken is born on August 5 in Savannah, Georgia.

1894: Oliver Wendell Holmes dies of respiratory failure on October 7 in Boston.

1918: Guillaume Apollinaire dies of influenza on November 9, two days before Armistice Day, which will end World War I.

1918: Guillaume Apollinaire's "Always" is published.

1921: Marie Ponsot is born in Queens, a borough of New York City.

1924: Yehuda Amichai is born on May 3 in Wurzburg, Germany. He will come to be considered one of Israel's greatest poets.

1930: Conrad Aiken's "The Room" is published.

1934: Jean Valentine is born on April 27 in Chicago, Illinois.

1939: Ted Kooser is born in April in Ames, Iowa.

1945: Carol Muske-Dukes is born on December 17 in Saint Paul, Minnesota.

1948: Sherod Santos is born on September 9 in Greenville, South Carolina.

1948: Heather McHugh is born on August 20 in San Diego, California.

1950: Dana Gioia is born (Michael Dana Gioia) on December 24 in Los Angeles, California.

1952: Dorianne Laux is born on January 10 in Augusta, Maine.

1952: Naomi Shihab Nye is born on March 12 in St. Louis, Missouri.

1958: Yehuda Amichai's "Not like a Cypress" is published.

1968: Sue (Suji) Kwock Kim is born.

1973: Conrad Aiken dies on August 17 in Savannah at the age of eighty-four.

1980: Naomi Shihab Nye's "Kindness" is published.

1990: Jean Valentine's "Seeing You" is published.

1994: Dorianne Laux's "For the Sake of Strangers" is published.

1998: Marie Ponsot's "One Is One" is published.

1999: Sherod Santos's "Portrait of a Couple at Century's End" is published.

1999: Heather McHugh's "Three To's and an Oi" is published.

2000: Yehuda Amichai dies on September 25 in Jerusalem.

2001: Dana Gioia's "The Litany" is published.

2003: Sue (Suji) Kwock Kim's "Monologue for an Onion" is published.

2003: Carol Muske-Dukes's "Our Side" is published.

2004: Ted Kooser's "At the Cancer Clinic" is published.

Acknowledgments

The editors wish to thank the copyright holders of the excerpted criticism included in this volume and the permissions managers of many book and magazine publishing companies for assisting us in securing reproduction rights. We are also grateful to the staffs of the Detroit Public Library, the Library of Congress, the University of Detroit Mercy Library, Wayne State University Purdy/ Kresge Library Complex, and the University of Michigan Libraries for making their resources available to us. Following is a list of the copyright holders who have granted us permission to reproduce material in this volume of *Poetry for Students (PfS)*. Every effort has been made to trace copyright, but if omissions have been made, please let us know.

COPYRIGHTED MATERIALS IN *PfS*, **VOLUME 24, WERE REPRODUCED FROM THE FOLLOWING PERIODICALS:**

American Book Review, v. 26, May–June, 2005. Copyright © 2005. Reproduced by permission.—*American Libraries*, v. 35, December, 2004. Copyright © 2004 by the American Library Association. Reproduced by permission.—*American Literature*, v. XXXVI, January, 1965. Copyright, 1965, Duke University Press. All rights reserved. Used by permission of the publisher.—*Antioch Review*, v. 58, spring, 2000; v. 60, winter, 2002. Copyright © 2000, 2002 by the Antioch Review Inc. Both reproduced by permission of the Editors.—*Booklist*, v. 97, March 15, 2001; March 1, 2003. Copyright © 2001, 2003 by the American

Library Association. Both reproduced by permission.—*Boston Sunday Globe*, August 3, 2003 for "On Unions, Sundered or Enduring," by Liz Rosenberg. Copyright © Liz Rosenberg 2003. Reproduced by permission of the author.—*Christian Science Monitor*, November, 2004. Copyright © 2004 The Christian Science Publishing Society. All rights reserved. Reproduced by permission from *Christian Science Monitor, (www.csmonitor .com).*—*Commonweal*, v. 125, September 25, 1998. Copyright © 1998 Commonweal Publishing Co., Inc. Reproduced by permission of Commonweal Foundation.—*Georgia Review*, spring, 2004, for a review of "Notes from a Divided Country," by Amy Schroeder. Copyright © 2004 by Amy Schroeder. Reproduced by permission of the author.—*Gettysburg Review*, v. 12, winter, 1999, for "Transience and the Lyric Impulse," by Floyd Collins. Copyright © 1999. Reproduced by permission of the author.—*Judaism*, v. 45, summer, 1996. Copyright © American Jewish Congress Summer 1996. Reproduced by permission.—*Los Angeles Times*, May 29, 2002, for "A Poet's Progress," by Allan M. Jalon. Copyright © 2002 by *Los Angeles Times*. Reproduced by permission of the author.—*Louisiana Review*, v. 4, fall– winter, 2004–05. Reproduced by permission.— *MELUS*, v. 26, winter, 2001. Copyright *MELUS: The Society for the Study of Multi-Ethnic Literature of the United States*, 2001. Reproduced by permission.—*Midstream*, v. 47, May, 2001. Copyright 2001 Theodor Herzl Foundation. Reproduced by permission.—*Midwest Quarterly*, v. 46, summer, 2005. Copyright © 2005 by *The Midwest Quarterly*, Pittsburgh State University. Reproduced by permission.—*Nation*, v. 243, December 6, 1986. Copyright © 1986 by The Nation Magazine/The Nation Company, Inc. Reproduced by permission.—*National Public Radio: All Things Considered*, October 13, 2003. Copyright 2003. Reproduced by permission.—*Ploughshares*, v. 27, spring, 2001, for "About Heather McHugh," by Peter Turchi. Copyright © Ploughsares 2001. Reproduced by permission of the author.—*Poetry*, v. 177, January, 2001; v. 186, June, 2005. Copyright © 2001, 2005 by the Modern Poetry Association. Both reproduced by permission./v. 179, February, 2002, for a review of "Interrogations at Noon," by Bruce F. Murphy; v. 185, February, 2005, for "Delights and Shadows," by Brian Phillips. Copyright © 2002, 2005 Modern Poetry Association. Both reproduced by permission of the respective authors.—*Publishers Weekly*, v. 248, June 18, 2001. Copyright © 2001 by Reed Publishing USA. Reproduced from *Publishers Weekly*, published by the Bowker Magazine Group of Cahners Publishing Co., a division of Reed Publishing USA, by permission.—*Western American Literature*, v. xxxi, fall, 1996. Copyright © 1996 by the Western Literature Association. Reproduced by permission.—*Women's Review of Books*, v. 12, November, 1994, for "What We Carry," by Alison Townsend. Copyright © 1994 by Alison Townsend. Reproduced by permission of the author./v. 16, October, 1998, for "The Bird Catcher: Poems," by Sandra M. Gilbert. Copyright © 1998 Sandra M. Gilbert. Reproduced by permission of the author.—*World Literature Today*, v. 71, spring, 1997 ; v. 78, September–December, 2004. Copyright © 1997, 2004 by *World Literature Today*. Both reproduced by permission of the publisher.—*Yale French Studies*, 1964. Copyright © Yale French Studies 1964. Reproduced by permission.

COPYRIGHTED MATERIALS IN *PfS*, VOLUME 24, WERE REPRODUCED FROM THE FOLLOWING BOOKS:

Alston, A. J. From an Introduction to *The Devotional Poems of Mirabai*. Motilal Banarsidass, 1980. Copyright © Motilal Banarsidass. Reproduced by permission.—Amichai, Yehuda. From "Not Like a Cypress," in *The Selected Poetry of Yehuda Amichai*. Edited and translated by Chana Bloch and Stephen Mitchell. University of California Press, 1996. © 1986, 1996 by Chana Bloch and Stephen Mitchell. Republished with permission of University of California Press, conveyed through Copyright Clearance Center, Inc.—Apollinaire, Guillaume. From *The Self-Dismembered Man*. Translated by Donald Revell. Wesleyan University Press, 2004. Copyright © 2004 by Donald Revell. Reprinted by permission of Wesleyan University Press. www.wesleyan.edu/wespress—Brenkman, John. From "The Concrete Utopia of Poetry: Blake's 'A Poison Tree,'" in *Lyric Poetry: Beyond New Criticism*. Edited by Chavia Hoser and Patricia Parker. Cornell University Press, 1985. Copyright © 1985 by Cornell University. Used by permission of the publisher, Cornell University Press.—Gioia, Dana. From *Interrogations at Noon*. Graywolf Press, 2001. Copyright © 2001 by Dana Gioia. Reproduced by permission of the publisher, Saint Paul, Minnesota.—Housden, Roger. From *Ten Poems to Last a Lifetime*. Harmony Books, 2004. Copyright © 2004 by Roger Housden. Used by permission of Harmony Books, a division of Random House, Inc. In the United Kingdom by the author.—Kim, Suji Kwock. From *Notes From the Divided Country*. Louisiana State University Press, 2003. Copyright © 2003 by Louisiana State University Press. All rights reserved. Reproduced by permission.—McHugh, Heather. From *The Father of the Predicaments*. Wesleyan University Press, 1999. Copyright © 1999 by Heather McHugh. Reprinted by permission of Wesleyan University Press.www.wesleyan.edu/wespress—Muske-Dukes, Carol. From *Sparrow*. Random House, 2004. Copyright © 2003 by Carol-Muske-Dukes. Used by permission of Random House, Inc. In the United Kingdom by the author.—Nye, Shihab Naomi. From *Words Under the Words: Selected Poems*. The Eighth Mountain Press, 1995. Copyright © 1995 by Naomi Shihab Nye. All rights reserved. Reprinted with the permission of Far Corner Books.—Ponsot, Marie. From *The Bird Catcher*. Alfred A. Knopf, 2002. Copyright © 1998 by Marie Ponsot. Used by permission of Alfred A. Knopf, a division of Random House, Inc.—Santos, Sherod. From *The Pilot Star Elegies*. W. W. Norton, 1999. Copyright © 1999 by Sherod Santos. Used by permission of W. W. Norton & Company, Inc.—Valentine, Jean. From *Door in the Mountain: New and Selected Poems, 1965–2003*. Wesleyan University Press, 2004. Copyright © 2004 by Jean Valentine. Reprinted by permission of Wesleyan University Press. www.wesleyan.edu/wespress—Valentine, Jean, and Richard Jackson. From *Acts of Mind: Conversations with Contemporary Poets*. University of Alabama, 1983. Copyright © 1983 The University of

Alabama Press. All rights reserved. Reproduced by permission.

COPYRIGHTED EXCERPTS IN *PFS*, VOLUME 24, WERE REPRODUCED FROM THE FOLLOWING WEBSITES:

Laux, Dorianne, and Michael J. Vaughan, "An Interview with Dorianne Laux," *http://www.themonserratreview.com/interviews/DL_interview.html*, Reproduced by permission.—Ponsot, Marie, with Meghan Cleary, "Marie Ponsot: Interview," *Failbetter.com*, summer–fall, 2002. Reproduced by permission.—Rother, James, "A Star to Pilot By," *http://www.cprw.com/members/Rother/star.htm*, 2001. Reproduced by permission.—Santos, Sherod, and James Rother, "Sherod Santos: The Refining Instrument of Poetry (An Interview)," *http://www.cprw.com/members/Rother/santos.htm*, 2001. Reproduced by permission.

Contributors

Bryan Aubrey: Aubrey holds a Ph.D. in English and has published many articles on contemporary poetry. Entry on *All I Was Doing Was Breathing*. Original essays on *All I Was Doing Was Breathing* and *Monologue for an Onion*.

Jennifer Bussey: Bussey holds a master's degree in interdisciplinary studies and a bachelor's degree in English literature, and she is an independent writer specializing in literature. Entries on *For the Sake of Strangers* and *Monologue for an Onion*. Original essays on *For the Sake of Strangers*, *Monologue for an Onion*, and *Seeing You*.

Joyce Hart: Hart is a published author and former writing instructor. Entries on *Not like a Cypress*, *One Is One*, and *Our Side*. Original essays on *Not like a Cypress*, *One Is One*, *Our Side*, and *Seeing You*.

Neil Heims: Heims is a writer and teacher living in Paris. Entries on *A Poison Tree* and *The Room*. Original essays on *Monologue for an Onion*, *A Poison Tree*, and *The Room*.

Pamela Steed Hill: Hill is the author of a poetry collection, has published widely in literary journals, and is an editor for a university publications department. Entry on *Kindness*. Original essays on *For the Sake of Strangers* and *Kindness*.

Anna Maria Hong: Hong has published poems in numerous journals and is the editor of the fiction and memoir anthology *Growing Up Asian American* (1993). Original essay on *Kindness*.

David Kelly: Kelly is an instructor of creative writing and literature. Entries on *At the Cancer Clinic*, *Portrait of a Couple at Century's End*, and *Three To's and an Oi*. Original essays on *At the Cancer Clinic*, *Our Side*, *Portrait of a Couple at Century's End*, and *Three To's and an Oi*.

Lois Kerschen: Kerschen is a school district administrator and a freelance writer. Entry on *Seeing You*. Original essay on *Seeing You*.

Wendy Perkins: Perkins is a professor of American and English literature and film. Entries on *Always* and *The Litany*. Original essays on *Always* and *The Litany*.

Lisa Trow: Trow is a published poet and journalist, and she has been an instructor of creative writing. Original essay on *At the Cancer Clinic*.

Scott Trudell: Trudell is a doctoral student of English literature at Rutgers University. Entry on *The Chambered Nautilus*. Original essay on *The Chambered Nautilus*.

All I Was Doing Was Breathing

Mirabai

1530

The sixteenth-century Indian poet Mirabai was a controversial figure during her lifetime. She was revered by many, but others regarded her as dangerous because she rebelled against the narrow social codes of her day, particularly those relating to gender roles. Her most controversial act was refusing either to immolate herself or to live the circumscribed life of a widow upon her husband's death. Instead, she devoted herself to worship of the god Krishna.

In "All I Was Doing Was Breathing," Mirabai describes what may have been one of her first encounters with Krishna, who is one of the best-loved gods in Hinduism. Although she writes in a way that suggests a meeting of human lovers, the relationship is, in fact, a spiritual one, conducted between the individual soul and God. Mirabai's experience of Krishna had such a powerful effect on her that she cast aside her former life completely, believing that she could not live for a moment outside the presence of the god. The exact date of composition of "All I Was Doing Was Breathing" is unknown. A modern version of the poem is in *Mirabai: Ecstatic Poems* (2004), a book that contains fifty poems attributed to Mirabai, which are freely translated by Robert Bly and Jane Hirshfield.

Author Biography

Mirabai (sometimes written as Mīrā Bāī) was a sixteenth-century Indian saint, poet, and devotee of the god Krishna. Devotion to Krishna is at the heart of "All I Was Doing Was Breathing." The facts of her life that can be established beyond doubt are few, and traditional accounts of her life are embroidered with many legends. Mirabai was born into a minor royal family in Merta, in northwestern India, in approximately 1498. It is probable that her mother died when she was very young and that she was raised by her grandfather, Rao Duda, in a spiritual and devotional atmosphere. When Mirabai was still in her teens, possibly in about 1516, she married Bhoj Raj, a crown prince of the neighboring kingdom of Mewar.

Bhoj died of wounds received in battle five years later, in 1521. But instead of following the Hindu custom of immolating herself, or burning herself, on her husband's funeral pyre, Mirabai embraced her widowhood and dedicated her life to worshipping Krishna, the god to whom she had been devoted since childhood. This refusal to follow the traditional custom upset her late husband's family. According to one legend, they sent Mirabai a basket of flowers with a deadly cobra inside, but when Mirabai saw the snake, it turned into a small statue of the god Vishnu. Another legend has it that her husband's family demanded that she drink poison in front of them; she drank it but remained unharmed.

Undeterred by the opposition she faced, Mirabai continued her public singing and dancing in praise of Krishna. The more traditional elements in society found her behavior shocking, particularly for a woman from an aristocratic family. At some point, Mirabai returned to her childhood home of Merta. For a while, her life appears to have been peaceful, but according to some accounts, she faced more persecution from her uncle, who had taken power in the kingdom following the death of Mirabai's father in battle. Mirabai left Merta and seems to have spent some time in her thirties as a wandering ascetic, or holy person. She eventually traveled to Vrindavan, a sacred city associated with Krishna. While in Vrindavan, she met a renowned holy man, Jiva Goswami (1486–1533), and stayed in close touch with him. In about 1542, Mirabai left Vrindavan for Dwarka, another city in which the worship of Krishna was well established.

During her lifetime, Mirabai composed many untitled devotional songs and poems to Krishna in Hindi. These are known as *padas* and *bhajans*. Scholars do not know how many poems she composed, since she made no effort to preserve them. Some 450 years later, there are as many as 1,300 poems attributed to Mirabai, but it is likely that

Mirabai herself composed only a fraction of those, perhaps between 100 and 200. The others were written by her followers in similar style and form. She is revered in India and has had an enormous influence on the culture of the country.

Mirabai remained in Dwarka until a delegation of priests from her late husband's family arrived to take her back to Rajasthan, threatening to fast to death if she refused to accompany them. According to legend, Mirabai asked permission to consult with Krishna in the temple. She entered the temple and was never seen again, because in her devotion she had been absorbed with the image of Krishna. Mirabai's death is usually considered to have occurred in 1546, although some scholars consider 1547 or 1550 to be a more likely date.

Poem Summary

In the first line of "All I Was Doing Was Breathing," the poet explains that she has been, so to speak, taken hold of by a force she identifies at first only as "something." The process is mysterious. The "something" actively reaches out and seemingly absorbs into itself some essence of the speaker that emanates, or radiates, from her eyes ("the beams of my eyes"). The light from the eyes is presented as a tangible, or concrete, thing that can be taken in by another being. Some as yet unspecified spiritual exchange has been accomplished.

In the second line, the poet reveals how she longs for this "something," although she does not say, "I have a longing." Her phrase, "There is a longing," is impersonal, which suggests that the desire may be more universal than the desire of one individual. This longing may be part of the fabric of life in which the finite creature longs for contact with and absorption in the infinite.

In this line, the poet also makes it clear that the object of her longing is the god Krishna, who is traditionally known as the "dark one" and is depicted in pictorial representations as having dark skin, like the color of a rain cloud. Thus, the poet longs for every hair of his "dark body." The image is a very physical one, suggesting the physical intimacy of lovers, but the poet intends this in a spiritual sense. The poet wants to know the divine intimately, in all its manifold aspects.

In line 3, the poet emphasizes her own passivity, as if what happened to her was none of her own doing: "All I was doing was being." It was the god who took the initiative and came calling on her or at least passed by her house. Another interpretation of this phrase might suggest, however, that the poet was well prepared to receive the divine; she was in a state of spiritual readiness, in which she was simply aware of "being," to the exclusion of all sense impressions and physical or mental activities. In this line, Krishna is described as the "Dancing Energy." The image suggests the subatomic world revealed by modern physics, in which subatomic particles interact in a ceaseless flow of energy. Some have likened this view of the world to Indian spiritual thought, in which there is one underlying reality behind all the changing forms of life.

In line 4, the poet says that Krishna was smiling as he passed her house. She saw his face in profile, and she says that it looked like the moon. This unusual image conveys the idea of Krishna's cosmic dimension. Although he lived a life on the earth, he is also the lord of the universe. In Hindu scriptures, Krishna is presented as containing everything in the universe within himself, including the sun and the moon. A simpler interpretation of this line, however, would be that Krishna's face sheds light, like the moon.

The poet explains in line 5 that her family is worried about what they see as her excessive devotion to Krishna. They warn her not to see him again. Perhaps they are concerned that she will neglect her worldly duties and bring dishonor on the family. They whisper about her, perhaps implying that she is mad.

The poet dismisses her family's concerns in line 6. The family has no control over her, because she is now living in a different dimension of life, in which the old rules do not apply. Such rules even seem absurd, something to be laughed at. The poet as devotee has her eyes firmly fixed on the divine, and this is her life now.

In line 7, she shows how confident she is in her new life and understanding. She does not care what others say about her; she is strong enough to bear any burden, because she has surrendered her life to the Dark One.

The poet implies in line 8 that she has no choice now. Her entire existence depends on the god. Describing Krishna as "the energy that lifts mountains," she knows that he is the foundation of her life. The reference is to one of the stories about Krishna's childhood. As a boy, Krishna persuaded the people in the village of Vrindavan, which was

Media Adaptations

- *Poems of Mirabai* (1997) is an audiocassette published by Audio Literature. The poems are read by Robert Bly, David Whetstone, Marcus Wise, Bruce Hamm, Manda Venkata Ramanamma, and Nirmala Rajasekar.

suffering from a drought, to stop offering prayers and sacrifices to Indra, the god of the heavens who was responsible for rainfall. This angered Indra, who caused torrential rain to fall for countless days on the village. Rivers burst their banks, houses collapsed, and the whole village turned into a lake of mud. Krishna saved the people from drowning by holding up the Goverdhana mountain with his little finger and using it to protect the villagers from the rain. After seven more days of rain, during which the entire village kept dry under the mountain, Indra relented, and the storm ceased. In the original Hindi, the name given to Krishna at this point in the poem is *Giridhara*, which comes from two Sanskrit words meaning "hill" and "holding." According to A. J. Alston in *The Devotional Poems of Mirabai*, the word "means 'He who held aloft the Mountain.'"

Themes

Spiritual Devotion

The poet writes within the Hindu tradition of bhakti, which represents the devotional path to union with God. Bhakti is an attitude of the heart rather than the mind, of feeling rather than intellect. In the bhakti tradition, devotees surrender themselves completely to God, the object of their devotion, and God responds by allowing them to share his infinite love and his infinite consciousness. (Alston points out that in Sanskrit, "the word 'bhakti' comes from the root 'bhaj,' meaning 'to share.'") For devotees, loving commitment to God is absolute and total; it is more important than anything else in life. Motivated by love, the devotees

Topics For Further Study

- Write your own devotional poem. It does not have to be addressed to a religious figure or to God. You could write such a poem to anyone you love or even to your dog or cat. What is important is the sincerity and depth of the feelings conveyed.

- What is meant by the term *Hinduism*? What are the main gods in Hinduism? Is Hinduism a polytheistic religion? Prepare a class presentation on the main elements of Hindu belief, including brief explanations of such topics as reincarnation, karma, and the caste system.

- Read as many poems by Mirabai as you can find on the Internet or in books, and explore her life story, including the many legends that surround

her life. In what sense might Mirabai in her life and work be considered a role model for women? Write a letter to a friend explaining who Mirabai was and why your friend should read and study her work. Be sure to emphasize two or three main points and support them with reference to Mirabai's life and work.

- Read some poems by the medieval Sufi poet Rumi, who is in many ways similar to Mirabai. Prepare a class presentation in which you bring out the similarities and differences between the two poets. What are the characteristic themes of these two poets, and how do they present those themes?

---

lose their individual selves in order to find themselves in God, the universal consciousness. They are like small rivers of love that flow to the vast, eternal ocean of pure and universal love, where they find their fulfillment. In the ocean of God-consciousness, they are one with God; there are no longer any distinctions between God and the devotees. For the devotees, their path of love and devotion is one of ever-increasing joy and bliss, and they feel in their hearts that they cannot live for a moment without the presence of the divine.

The poem gives the impression that it is recording the very first time in which the poet was caught up and embraced by the divine. It carries a note of surprise, as if the poet was overwhelmed by some irresistible force that came to her suddenly and unexpectedly, without any doing on her part. This is conveyed first in the title, "All I Was Doing Was Breathing." (Mirabai's poems were untitled; this title is supplied by Robert Bly, who adapted the poems.) The same effect is echoed in line 3, in the phrase "All I was doing was being." These two similar phrases convey the idea that the divine might make itself known at any moment in a person's life, whether the person is preparing for it or not. Perhaps significantly, the incident did not happen in a temple, where the presence of the god

might be expected, but in a seemingly chance moment, in the street outside the poet's house.

"All I was doing was breathing" and "All I was doing was being" might also, however, carry another meaning, quite different from the notion that the poet was merely going about her daily business when the god, suddenly, chose to make himself known to her. These two phrases could suggest that the poet was in a state of spiritual readiness, in which she was receptive to the influx of the divine "energy." She was not distracted by any activity of body or mind. She was not engaged in the activities of the senses. In a passive, simple state of being, a kind of emptiness, she was ready to experience the fullness of the god.

Spiritual Life versus Worldly Life

There is a stark contrast between the call of the spiritual life, in which the poet declares that she is entirely devoted to Krishna, and the demands of family and worldly life. Choosing the former, the poet rejects the ties of family and custom. Her family's opposition to her seems fierce and is emphasized by the only words in the poem that appear in direct speech ("My family says: 'Don't ever see him again!'"). But the poet is responding to what she sees as a higher calling, one that transcends her duties and responsibilities to family and society. She rejects her culture and upbringing, as contained in all the "rules" that are laid down for a woman to follow—rules that she now derides as petty and meaningless. Human laws, relationships, and customs are a product of the earthly life, whereas now she is beholden only to the god, who embodies infinity. The ground of the poet's being has shifted from the temporal to the eternal. Behind this notion of transcending human ties in favor of union with the divine is the idea that there is an essential opposition between the world of the flesh and the world of the spirit. All human and worldly pleasures and responsibilities only lead a person away from the divine; they must be cast aside if a person is to gain enlightenment and become permanently at one with the divine consciousness.

Style

Imagery

Some of the effect of the poem comes from its contrasting images. Line 2 emphasizes the minute aspects of the divine being that the speaker worships; she yearns for "every hair of that dark body." In line 4, however, the image of the minute gives way to a vast, cosmic image, of the face of the divine being that is "like the moon." By swinging the reader's awareness from the tiny to the immense, the poem conveys the entire range of the divine.

A somewhat similar swing between opposites can be seen in the direct references to the god. Krishna is represented clearly in human form. He possesses a human body, and he walks past the poet's house. But he is also represented in abstract, rather than concrete, terms as the "Dancing Energy," which describes not a human form but something more immense and fundamental, the dynamic consciousness that is the underlying reality of all things in the universe. Once again, the reader's awareness switches between a localized point—a human body—and the infinity of the "Dancing Energy."

The poem also contains significant imagery about eyes and seeing. The poet looks directly at her beloved with her eyes, not through some inner process of contemplation, of considered thought. It is through the beams that emanate from her eyes that the divine takes hold of her. She also sees his face; it is the visual image of him that is important to her, not his speech or anything else about him. And she describes her life now that she is devoted

to the divine in terms of her eyes: "my eyes have their own life."

Historical Context

The God Krishna

Krishna is worshipped by Hindus as an incarnation of the supreme god, Vishnu. Little is known for certain about the historical Krishna, but scholars suggest that he was a spiritual teacher and a member of the warrior caste who fought on the side of the Pandava clan in a great battle recorded in the Indian epic the Mahabharata. Legends grew up about him, and he came to be worshipped as a divine being who took human form. The cult of Krishna goes back to at least the fourth century B.C.E.

There are many legends about Krishna's birth and life. The story goes that Kansa, an evil king, heard a prophecy that he would be killed by the eighth son of Devaki, his sister. Kansa had Devaki's first six sons killed at birth; the seventh was stillborn, and the eighth, who was Krishna, escaped. Krishna, the divine infant, was raised by the daughter of a cowherd, who loved him as her own. Krishna became a mischievous, charming boy, known for playing pranks on the milkmaids (as the young women who tend the cows are called in Hindu tradition), such as stealing their cream and upsetting their milk pails. According to one story, when the girls went bathing in the river, Krishna took their clothes and refused to give them back until the girls came out and showed themselves to him one by one.

As a child, Krishna possessed supernatural powers and was able to rid the country of demons, which won him the love of all the milkmaids. His favorite milkmaid was named Radha, and she became his lover, even though she was a married woman. In later interpretations of this aspect of the myth, the love between Radha and Krishna became an allegory for the love between the individual soul and God. In manhood, Krishna returned to his place of birth and killed his wicked uncle, restoring righteousness to society. He acquired many wives and continued to slay demons.

The spiritual teachings of Krishna are contained in the Bhagavad Gita (meaning "Song of the Lord"). The Gita, one of Hinduism's most sacred and popular texts, was written probably in the second century B.C.E. or later. Krishna gives his teaching to the warrior Arjuna on the battlefield. His

Compare & Contrast

- **1600s:** In India, women have no independent legal rights. They are given in marriage, often to create alliances between royal families. Widows are expected to immolate themselves on their husbands' funeral pyres (a practice known as suttee, in which a widow allows herself to be burned on the pyre), although not all of them do so. Widows occupy very low social status in society. They are required to dress in drab clothes and are shunned by others. Also, they are not allowed to take part in Hindu festivals. Some widows who commit themselves to suttee do so in order to escape being carried off by Muslim soldiers as slaves or concubines.

  Today: Many laws exist in India to protect women's rights, including the Equal Remuneration Act, the Prevention of Immoral Traffic Act, and the Dowry Prohibition Act. The practice of suttee is illegal. However, according to a report issued by the U.S. State Department in 2004, the Indian government is often unable to enforce these laws, especially in rural areas in which traditions are deeply rooted. Suttee continues to be practiced in some areas; there was such an incident in Madhya Pradesh in 2002.

- **1600s:** Portuguese, Dutch, and British explorers establish trading posts in India, but Hindu spiritual practices and philosophies are virtually unknown in Europe. This is because Indian scriptures are written in Sanskrit, and translations will not be made until near the end of the eighteenth century.

  Today: After some two centuries of dissemination of Indian religious and philosophical ideas in the West, Hinduism and Buddhism are part of the American cultural landscape. Indian gurus popularize meditation techniques adapted

from Indian tradition, and the Hindu philosophy of the underlying unity of all things is the bedrock of spiritual beliefs and practices associated with the New Age spiritual movement. In the United States, the International Society for Krishna Consciousness, founded in 1965 and known as the Hare Krishna movement, disseminates knowledge of Krishna and his teachings.

- **1600s:** The Mogul Empire grows in India throughout the century and by 1700 extends to most of the Indian subcontinent. Muslim rulers vary in their attitudes to Hindus. In some cases, the Muslims destroy Hindu temples and impose taxes on non-Muslims. But some Muslim rulers display a more enlightened attitude and allow Hindu culture to flourish. There is also interchange between the two religions. Elements of the Hindu caste system enter Muslim society, and Hindus adopt the Muslim practice of purdah (keeping women secluded, away from men or strangers).

  Today: India is an independent, predominantly Hindu country, while its neighbors Pakistan and Bangladesh are Muslim. India has a secular government and is the largest democracy in the world. However, tensions exist between the Hindu majority and the Muslim minority. The holy city of Ajodhya is a frequent source of religious strife. In 1992, Hindu nationalists tear down a sixteenth-century mosque in Ajodhya. Hindus believe the mosque was built on the site of a temple marking the birthplace of the Hindu deity Lord Rama. In 2002, seventy people are killed in Gujarat province, as Hindu mobs attack Muslims in retaliation for the firebombing by Muslims of a train carrying Hindu nationalists back from Ajodhya.

teachings include the essence of bhakti, or devotion, promising that if a person is sincerely and intensely devoted to Krishna, Krishna will return that love and grant the devotee spiritual salvation.

India in the Sixteenth Century

Mirabai's birthplace, Merta, was the capital city of the independent and fairly prosperous state of Merta, although it was less powerful than the neighboring state of Mewar, where Mirabai lived after her marriage. (Both states became part of the modern state of Rajasthan.) There was traditionally much rivalry between the two states, and there were also constant internal feuds and dissension within the ruling clans. Because of these internal conflicts and because these states were often fighting each other, they were ill prepared for the threat posed by the Muslim Turks, who wanted to expand their rule into India.

In 1527, Merta and Mewar managed to put aside their differences and combine to fight the invading Turks, who were led by Bābur. However, the Indian states were defeated in the battle of Khānua, in which Ratan Singh, who is said to be Mirabai's father, was killed. This battle marked the establishment of Muslim rule in India, which was continued by Bābur's son Humāyūn following Bābur's death in 1531. The Mogul Empire was further extended under the rule of Akbar the Great, who reigned from 1556 to 1605, by which time the empire had expanded from Afghanistan across most of northern India.

The Warrior Ideal

Mewar was one of the Indian states that became known for resisting Mogul domination. Its ruling ethos, according to Parita Mukta in her book *Upholding the Common Life: The Community of Mirabai*, was that of the Rajput, the warrior class. The Rajputs glorified militarism and war. Dying in battle was considered a noble death, and some of the fallen warriors were worshipped as gods by large numbers of the lower classes. One of the reasons Mirabai faced persecution was that she rebelled against the warrior code and everything it involved. As Mukta explains, the society in which Mirabai lived was a patriarchal one, a brotherhood based on concepts of loyalty and honor. Feudal ideas of duty and service to the master and lord were the standards of behavior that held society together. For a woman, this meant accepting the authority of her husband. Since Mirabai, according to the legends, placed her love for Krishna above her duty to her husband and also refused to sacrifice herself on her husband's funeral pyre, she was denounced as a destroyer of the clan, a threat to the entire structure of society. The path of bhakti (devotion) that she followed ignored traditional hierarchies based on caste or gender and created a new type of community founded on shared beliefs and forms of worship.

Critical Overview

Mirabai is one of the leading figures in Indian devotional poetry, a tradition associated with the bhakti religious movement. This type of devotional poetry dates from the sixth century C.E. and flourished particularly between the fifteenth and seventeenth centuries. Other devotional poets from this period include Kabīr, Tulsīdās, and Sūrdās. During her lifetime, Mirabai's songs were preserved through an oral tradition. They were not recorded in writing. This accounts for the fact that it is impossible to identify poems that the historical Mirabai may have composed, since hundreds of poems attributed to her appeared in later centuries. These were written by her followers, in similar style and form. Mirabai has had an immense influence on Indian culture. According to her adapter Robert Bly, "There is no one else exactly like her in the whole history of poetry. . . . Mirabai's genius encouraged thousands of people in her time to compose ecstatic poems and to sing and to dance them."

Mahatma Gandhi, leader of the movement for Indian independence in the twentieth century, frequently mentioned Mirabai in his speeches and writings and even translated and sang some of her poems when he was jailed in Yervada Central Prison in 1930. Mirabai thus became, through Gandhi, part of the Indian nationalist consciousness, although Mukta argues in *Upholding the Common Life* that Gandhi distorted her message in order to do so.

Mirabai remains a popular and revered figure in India as the foremost of women bhakti poets and saints. According to John Stratton Hawley, in his afterword to *Mirabai: Ecstatic Poems*, "Her story is told from one end of India to the other, and more or less unceasingly in her native Rajasthan." At least fifteen films have been made in India about her life, from 1932 to the 1990s, and her life story appears in a popular comic book. Mirabai is also an internationally known figure. Hawley points out that an international conference, held at the University of California at Los Angeles in 2002, hailed her as "Hindu Saint for a Global World."

Criticism

Bryan Aubrey

Bryan Aubrey holds a PhD in English and has published many articles on contemporary poetry. In this essay, he discusses Mirabai's poetry in the

> *In the eyes of the world, the complete immersion of the devotee in the object of his or her love may look like a kind of madness. Indeed, madness is a theme in a number of Mirabai's poems."*

context of the bhakti tradition, as exemplified in the teachings of Krishna in the Bhagavad Gita.

In the fifty adaptations by Robert Bly and Jane Hirshfield that appear in their book *Mirabai: Ecstatic Poems*, it is as if Mirabai's poetry attains a new lease on life. "All I Was Doing Was Breathing," titled with such subtle resonance by Bly, makes previous English versions of this poem seem flat by comparison. Bly's adaptation is a free one, and indeed the poems are described as "versions" of Mirabai rather than translations. As John Stratton Hawley points out in his afterword to the book, the word *energy,* which Bly employs twice in different contexts in this poem, does not appear in the original. But, he says, "Robert Bly must have felt that the whole motif of a divine adolescent lifting a mountain ought to suggest the displacement of matter into its dynamic counterpart: $E = mc^2$." Hawley suggests this may be "misleading," but it may be that the first connection a reader makes regarding the word *energy* is not so much with Einstein's famous equation but with the parallels between subatomic physics and Indian spirituality that have been popularized in books such as Fritjof Capra's *The Tao of Physics* (1975).

Physicists now understand that the universe is made up of dynamic patterns of energy created by the interactions of subatomic particles, and this fact has reminded some people of the representations in Hindu mythology of the god Shiva, who embodies the eternal cosmic dance of creation and destruction as the underlying basis of all existence. As Ninian Smart puts it in *The Religious Experience of Mankind,* "Shiva is god of the dance—as Lord of the Dance he dances out the creation of the world . . . as an expression of his exuberant personality."

Capra identifies the dance of Shiva with "the dance of subatomic matter" discovered by modern physicists. When Bly has Mirabai describe Krishna as the "Dancing Energy," he is drawing on this idea and relying on the reader to make the connection. Bly is untroubled by the fact that it is Shiva, not Krishna, who is portrayed as the cosmic dancer, because the phrase supplies him with the metaphor he wants, which presents the divine as an infinitely dynamic, infinitely powerful mode of consciousness. It is this perception of Krishna that has seized hold of Mirabai in the poem; she has felt the all-attractive power of the god, before which everything else pales in comparison.

It is in the Bhagavad Gita—which for Hindus has an authority not unlike that which the New Testament has for Christians—that Krishna is presented in his most majestic form. In the eighteen short chapters of the Bhagavad Gita, Krishna is no longer the divine child who slays demons and flirts with milkmaids. He is now the all-knowing incarnation of the supreme god Vishnu, "the beginning and the middle / Of beings, and the end as well." He describes himself to the warrior Arjuna as "infinite Time"; he is at once death and "the origin of those things that are to be." He is the sun and the moon. (The latter is echoed in the image of Krishna's face "like the moon" in "All I Was Doing Was Breathing.") Everything that exists can do so only through him; he is the fundamental power in the universe: "I support this entire universe constantly / With a single fraction of Myself." This statement recalls Krishna as the "energy that lifts mountains" in Mirabai's poem, which itself recalls the story of Krishna as a boy holding up the mountain with his finger.

In book 11 of the Bhagavad Gita, Krishna presents Arjuna with a vision of himself in his fullest glory. In verse 12, the awestruck warrior sees the whole universe as a manifestation of Krishna in dazzling light:

If there should be in the sky
A thousand suns risen all at once,
Such splendor would be
Of the splendor of that Great Being.

The vision, of which this verse forms only a fraction, is so amazing that it makes Arjuna's hair stand on end.

Approximately seventeen centuries later, Mirabai well understood what Arjuna saw on the battlefield of Kurukshetra, where Krishna's communication took place. It is because Mirabai had such a deep understanding of the true nature of her divine lord that she had so little regard for things

What Do I Read Next?

- *For Love of the Dark One: Songs of Mirabai* (1998), translated by Andrew Schelling, includes a short introduction and a glossary. Schelling's translations bring out the passionate and erotic quality in Mirabai's devotion to Krishna.

- *Rumi: The Book of Love: Poems of Ecstasy and Longing* (2003), translated by Coleman Barks, is a collection of poems by the thirteenth-century Sufi poet whose absolute devotion to God resembles that of Mirabai. These poems tell of Rumi's deep desire to lose himself in love for the divine.

- *The Gift: Poems by the Great Sufi Master* (1999) is a collection of poems by Hafiz, translated in colloquial language by Daniel Ladinsky. Like his predecessor Rumi, Hafiz was a fourteenth-century Sufi mystic who wrote short, ecstatic, devotional poems to God.

- *Kabir: Ecstatic Poems* (2004), versions by Robert Bly, is a collection of the verse of a near contemporary of Mirabai. Kabīr (1440–1518) was an important influence in the formation of the Sikh religion. He was a Muslim weaver from Benares, India, who became influenced by Hindu ideas. Kabīr condemned the caste system and disliked the dogmas and rituals that divided one religion from another. He wrote many poems and hymns, and his followers today form a distinct sect within Hinduism. John Stratton Hawley's introduction places Kabīr's work firmly in modern times.

---

such as family duty and accepted social roles, which others thought were so important. For Mirabai, their rules were as nothing when compared with the majesty of the god. Krishna offers salvation and incorporation in the oneness of all things; society offers nothing but the dull round of petty obligations, small-minded values, and short-lived pleasures.

It is also in the Bhagavad Gita that Krishna sets out the influential idea of bhakti, that salvation can be attained not only through knowledge but also through devotion. The key passages come toward the end of book 9. In verse 26, for example, Krishna tells Arjuna:

He who offers to Me with devotion
A leaf, a flower, a fruit or water,
That offering of devotion
I accept from him whose self is pure.

In the same book, Krishna promises those who worship with devotion that "They are in Me, and I also am in them." Even if a man is evil, if he worships Krishna with "undivided devotion," he will be considered virtuous and will go to "everlasting peace." In the final verse of the book, Krishna makes a promise to Arjuna:

With mind fixed on Me, be devoted to Me;
Sacrificing to Me, make reverence to Me.
Thus steadfast, with Me as supreme aim,
Thou thyself shalt come to Me.

In Hindu tradition, devotion can take many forms. Krishna P. Bahadur in his book *Mīrā Bāī and Her Padas*, cites a scriptural text that lists nine kinds of devotion, including listening to the praises of the Lord, community singing, remembering God's name ("The name of the Dark One has entered my heart," writes Mirabai in "Mira Swims Free"), ritual worship, complete dependence on God ("I can't live without him," says Mirabai in "The Dagger"), and self-surrender ("And seeing his beauty, I offered him all that I am," Mirabai states in "Not Hiding Not Seeking"). Bahadur cites another scripture in which activities such as keeping company with holy men and saints, cultivating attitudes like simplicity, and being content with what one has and not finding fault in others are also aspects of devotion, as is an expanded perception in which the devotee "see[s] the whole world pervaded by the Divine." Devotion therefore involves an all-encompassing orientation of the entire being of a person. It is not possible to be a part-time devotee or a devotee who retains

---

allegiance to anything other than the lord—in this case, Krishna.

In the eyes of the world, the complete immersion of the devotee in the object of his or her love may look like a kind of madness. Indeed, madness is a theme in a number of Mirabai's poems. She is quite direct about how others regard her: "'Mira is insane,' strangers say that. 'The family's ruined'" ("Ankle Bells"). It is a characterization that does not upset Mirabai in the slightest. In fact, she embraces it, describing herself in several poems as mad. In "The Dagger," she tells what happened when Krishna threw a glance in her direction. It felt to her like a thrust with a dagger. She says, "Since that moment, I am insane; I can't find my body. / The pain has gone through my arms and legs, and I can't find my mind." In "The Fish and the Crocodile," when Krishna's face appears to her, she says, "I forgot about the world and its duties. I went out of my mind." The last phrase is especially resonant, since it suggests both madness and a kind of ecstasy.

The word *ecstasy* comes from the Greek word *ekstasis*, which literally means "a being out of its place." Religious ecstasy means to stand outside oneself in a state of heightened awareness. It is the great paradox of all mystical literature that in standing outside the ordinary day-to-day self, the devotee or mystic discovers the true self in larger measure. She or he comes home to the god, so to speak, just as Mirabai says, "I'll sing about him; then I will be home" ("The Gooseberry Patch"). Mirabai has left her material home, in terms of her family and all her worldly ties, and has discovered her spiritual home, in Krishna. She has gone into him "As the polish goes into the gold" ("Polish into Gold"). In doing so, she has realized the eternal truth of Krishna's words in book 10 of the Bhagavad Gita, that he "abid[es] in the heart of all beings." This is clear from her poem "Not Hiding Not Seeking": "Friends, let those whose Beloved is absent write letters— / Mine dwells in the heart, and neither enters nor leaves." Like all the great seers in all religious traditions, Mirabai has gone beyond the "world's five fabrics" (that is, the five senses), as she calls them in "Not Hiding Not Seeking," and knows the ultimate, unchanging reality that lies beyond all the shifting phenomena of this world.

Source: Bryan Aubrey, Critical Essay on "All I Was Doing Was Breathing," in *Poetry for Students*, Thomson Gale, 2006.

A. J. Alston

In the following introduction to The Devotional Poems of Mirabai, *Alston discusses the Padāvalī.*

Mīrā's poetical works are conventionally referred to as her "Padāvalī". The word Padāvalī means a series of padas. The term pada was used by the popular preachers of the Siddha and Nātha schools who preceded Kabīr. The pada in its more mature form was a short song conveying instruction on the spiritual life, usually rhyming and composed in simple rhythms, adaptable for singing. The melody (rāg) to which they should be sung is specified, and they would usually have a Dhruvak or refrain for their opening or second line. The author's name is incorporated in the last line as a kind of signature.

The great Sanskrit poet Jai Dev refers to his Gīta Govinda as a Padāvalī in the poem. Here the word "āvalī" or series has a special significance, as the work is conceived as suitable for dramatic production. But this is not the case with the Padāvalīs of the popular religious poets of mediaeval India. They did not write their poems, but just composed and sang them from time to time. In some cases, for example in the case of Kabīr, Guru Nānak, Sūr and Dādu, attempts were made to reduce their work to writing fairly soon after their death. But this was not so in the case of Mīrā. Her songs simply survived in the mouths of itinerant singers who learned them, sang them, sometimes altered them and added to them, and passed them on.

Various attempts have been made from the latter part of the last century on to collect and print Mīrā's poems and some manuscript collections as well as printed editions exist. A modern edition of Mīrā's poems cannot be anything more than a miscellaneous collection of songs that have come down under her name, pruned of extraneous material by the editor so far as he is able and arranged in whatever order seemed to him good. Āchārya Chaturvedī's edition of the Padāvalī first appeared well over thirty years ago, but on the occasion of the fifteenth edition in 1973 he subjected the text to considerable revision, partly in the light of material published in the intervening years and partly in the light of manuscript material made available to him by friends.

Shrī Chaturvedī's 1973 edition comprehends 202 songs, plus eighteen songs which include the use of the terminology of the Sant school, considered by him to be doubtful and placed in an Appendix. No attempt to translate this latter group has been made here. He also considers the songs containing conversations between Mīrā and her relatives inauthentic. He accepts the poems in which Mīrā threatens to become a "Jogin" or pictures Krishna as a Jogī, while remarking that they should not be made a ground for supposing that Mīrā was an initiate of or subscribed to tenets of the Jogīs of the Nāth school. Shrī Chaturvedī's edidition does not aim to be all-inclusive. Svāmī Ānanda Svarūp's *Mīrā Sudhāsindhu* contains 1312 songs and Padmāvatī Shabnam's *Brihad Pada Sangraha* 590. The last-named, in her *Mīrān Vyaktitva aur Krititva* (1973), has collected more material and suggested new methods of classification of the songs and comparison of the different versions. Eventually a new picture of the Padāvalī may emerge, but for the present the edition of such an experienced hand as Shrī Chaturvedī may be allowed to constitute a kind of standard version.

Everyone agrees that Mīrā's songs have been much tailored and altered by the singers who sang them. They are mostly in Rājasthānī or Braj Bhāshā, but also contain material in Gujarātī, Panjābī or even Eastern Hindī. On the whole, the linguistic forms that have come down in the Padāvalī seem to correspond with geographical data of Mīrā's life as reconstructed by modern scholarship. Her childhood and youth in Rājasthān would account for the Rājasthānī base. Her travels to Braj and Dvārak and her mingling with holy men would account for the sprinkling of other dialects.

Mīrā's songs, being eminently popular and "singable" in style were evidently much sung in different places, and the versions of them which have come down to us owe part of their linguistic colouring to the local dialects of the singers who have sung them. In many cases, what have come down to us as different songs are really only different versions of one song made at different times by different singers. The more popular the song, the more numerous the alternative versions are apt to be. Where there are several alternative versions of one song, the extra verses in the longer versions are inclined to be suspect, especially if any element of "modernity" is betrayed by their linguistic forms. No doubt this helps to account for the absence of familiar lines in several of the poems as printed in Chaturvedī's text. (See e.g. Poems 12, 18, 154, 193)

The spiritual teaching in Mīrā's Padāvalī, which is what most interests the person who reads her songs in English, may be summarized as follows, drawing largely on Āchārya Chaturvedī's work. Mīrā's experiences of death and bereavement in a Rājpūt family taught her the flimsiness of all worldly supports. Life is short. The body will soon mingle with the dust. (Poem 156) Whatever mode of human life be adopted, it will be like the sporting of sparrows that will end at nightfall. (195) Committing suicide at a

> *At the beginning of her love she might have restrained it. But once she was in mid stream there was no turning back. She follows the guidance of her Lord wherever it leads her, like a puppet attached to the thin thread of love."*

holy place or the formal adoption of the life of a monk will not help, as without the intervention of the Lord one remains caught in the net of rebirth. (195) The spectacle of the way people live in the world when bereft of associationship with holy men evokes tears. (18) Without worship, man's life is a poor thing, (160) a mere burden.

Mīrā cherished visual images of the beauty of the Lord in His manifest form as an adolescent boy (Kishor) in Gokul. She sings of his divine sports. She dances before His image in the temple. (36, 37) She drinks His footwash after Pūjā in the temple. (31) She ensconces His image in her heart. She longs to embrace His feet and be His personal servant. (94, 154, etc.) Whatever He clothes her in, that she wears. (20)

The path of devotion is difficult and the devotee finds unexpected obstructions. (54) Desire comes like a cur and imposes his fetters. (158) Pride is like a mountain on the slopes of which water will not settle. (158)

Mīrā was loyal to her aristocratic lineage in the very courage with which she rejected its customs. Her love was hidden at first, but later it expanded, like the seed of a banyan tree, for all to see. At the beginning of her love she might have restrained it. But once she was in mid stream there was no turning back. She follows the guidance of her Lord wherever it leads her, like a puppet attached to the thin thread of love. (173) She accepts praise or blame with equal humility and passes on. (13)

In one sense, Mīrā is ever conscious of the presence of her Lord within her heart. "Only she whose Beloved is abroad needs to write letters: my

Beloved rests ever in my heart." (23) She has actually *seen* Him, present in her heart. (darasa lahyām sukha-rāsī, Poem 194) Hence her every act is an act of worship. Wherever her feet touch the earth she is dancing in love of her Lord. (21) Yet the paradox holds that as long as worldly-life lasts He is both present and absent. The lover of God is he who, being awake to the presence of God, feels His absence, hidden by the world of multiplicity, all the more keenly. Shrī Chaturvedī quotes the Indian Sūfī poet Jāyasī, "The nectar of the sense of absence abides in love like honey in the honeycomb." Mīrā loves the Lord with the fidelity and loyalty of a young wife faced with the absence of her husband. (66) Only those who have felt the gash know the pain of love wounds. (70 and 102) The sights and sounds of nature in spring or the rainy season only add to the pain.

Both the sense of the absence for the Lord and the awareness of His presence are capable of filling the devotee with such emotion that he is reduced to impotence. In the absence of her Lord, Mīrā wishes to write Him a letter, but her hand trembles and she is unable. Love is a state which reduces one to silence. The Gopīs distributing curds in pots are so carried away by the sight of Krishna that they cannot remember the word for curds. (177) But Mīrā dwells with particular insistence on the effect of the sense of the *absence* of the Beloved. It is felt so keenly as to induce a kind of madness (dīvānī, 70, 97, 130), involving an indifference to all worldly objects and values. A grain of Sufism seems to be detectable in Mīrā's mysticism, perhaps derived from her associationship with holy men of the Sant school, who themselves mingled with the Muslim mystics. She several times refers to her "darad", which prompts recall of a certain later Indian Sūfī poet (who was indeed known as "Dard") who said:

> dard i dil ke wāste paidā kiyā insān ko
> varanah tā'at ke liye kuch kam na the karūbiyām
> He created man to suffer agonies of the heart:
> If it had only been a question of obedience,
> There was not a scarcity of angels.

Mīrā predominantly worshipped God "with form" (saguna), and cannot without qualification be classed among the Sants. But her love is of the kind that demands and presupposes identity with its object, and when she emphasizes the identity-aspect her lines remind us not only of the Sants but sometimes even of the Upanishadic sages. Adoration of the beautiful Shyām is the dominant theme in her poetry, but the Beloved is Himself said to be "like the Indestructible Principle." (26) Mīrā is conscious of her identity with and separation from God at the same time. She can say "Thou and I are one like the sun and its heat" and "Come to my house, Thy coming will bring peace" in the same song. (114) She speaks mysteriously of an "impenetrable realm, that Death himself trembles to look upon." The phrasing of some lines in Mīrā suggests familiarity with and willingness to reproduce the teachings of Kabīr. (See Note 165 to Poem 158) In lines like "I care neither for Ganges nor Jumna, I am making my way to the sea" (Poem 24) we hear an echo of the ancient Upanishadic wisdom, through which the soul loses its individuality and unites in perfect identity with the supreme Spirit. She speaks of the body as a smock of five colours (the five elements) in which she is playing hide and seek with the Lord. Taking into account the traditions of Mīrā's childhood passion for the image of Krishna, and combining this with what we find in the Padāvalī, it is possible to think of Mīrā's devotion as developing through three stages. It can be seen as beginning with plain image-worship, progressing to the celebration of the glories of the Holy Avatāra Shrī Krishna in song and culminating in vision of Him as the Absolute beyond form. (Chaturvedī, Prem Sādhanā p. 139)

It seems that, throughout the history of the Indian spiritual quest from the Upanishads on, three tendencies can be noted. The first (with Shankara) locates the beginning of the path in devotion but tends to insist on the sole reality of the Absolute beyond all form and plurality and to preach knowledge as the only road to final release; the second insists on the validity of distinctions within the one all-comprehending reality, placing the ideal of perpetual adoration of God above the path of knowledge and tending to conceive the latter (with Vallabha) as a mere dissolution into the impersonal "unmanifest" aspect of the Lord (akshara, avyakta); the third insists that when either the path of devotion or the path of knowledge is followed to perfection the God to which they lead is the same. Āchārya Chaturvedī considers that Mīrā belonged to this last category, and quotes the following lines of Tulsī Dās as evincing a similar attitude. "There is no difference between (the Lord) with form and beyond form. So sing the Vedas and Purānas, the sages and enlightened souls. He who is attributeless, formless, unborn, transcendent—He it is who assumes manifest form, constrained by the love of His devotees." (Rāma Charita Mānasa I. cxv.1)

Source: A. J. Alston, "Introduction," in *The Devotional Poems of Mirabai*, translated by A. J. Alston, Motilal Banarsidass, 1980, pp. 27–32.

Sources

Alston, A. J., trans., *The Devotional Poems of Mirabai*, Motilal Banarsidass, 1980, pp. 9, 122.

Bahadur, Krishna P., trans., *Mīrā Bāī and her Padas*, Munshiram Manoharlal Publishers, 1998, pp. 34–35.

Bly, Robert, and Jane Hirshfield, eds., *Mirabai: Ecstatic Poems*, Beacon Press, 2004, pp. xi, 3, 4, 8, 9, 12, 16, 18, 19, 57.

Capra, Fritjof, *The Tao of Physics*, Fontana/Collins, 1978, p. 259.

Hawley, John Stratton, Afterword, in *Mirabai, Ecstatic Poems*, translated by Robert Bly and Jane Hirshfield, Beacon Press, 2004, pp. 67–68, 91.

Mukta, Parita, *Upholding the Common Life: The Community of Mirabai*, Oxford University Press, 1994, pp. 49–66.

Sargeant, Winthrop, trans., *The Bhagavad Gītā* edited by Christopher Chapple, State University of New York Press, 1984, pp. 396, 402, 405, 406, 407, 410, 420, 443, 444, 449, 452, 464.

Smart, Ninian, *The Religious Experience of Mankind*, Fontana, 1970, p. 158.

Further Reading

Archer, W. G., *The Loves of Krishna in Indian Painting and Poetry*, Dover, 2004.

Archer gives the entire story of Krishna as presented in different historical texts. His purpose is to shed light on Indian paintings that represent Krishna, and he shows why the figure of Krishna is still enchanting to modern Indians. The book includes thirty-nine black-and-white plates.

Bhaktivedanta, Swami, *Krsna, the Supreme Personality of Godhead*, Vol. 1, Bhaktivedanta Book Trust, 1996.

This is a commentary on the tenth canto of the Srimad-Bhagavatam, which tells the story of Krishna's early life, by the Krishna devotee who founded the International Society for Krishna Consciousness. The book includes a two-page message from the rock star George Harrison and thirteen color plates showing incidents from Krishna's life in Indian art, including one in which the child Krishna holds up the mountain with one finger.

Hawley, John Stratton, *Three Bhakti Voices: Mirabai, Surdas, and Kabir in Their Times and Ours*, Oxford University Press, 2005.

Hawley's study of the literature of bhakti includes four chapters on Mirabai that discuss what is known of Mirabai as a historical figure and how her work has been received from her time to ours. Also included are Hawley's translation and analysis of twenty-two of Mirabai's poems.

Levi, Louise Landes, *Sweet on My Lips: The Love Poems of Mirabai*, Cool Grove Publishing, 1997.

This volume includes translations of Mirabai's poems, a glossary, and several short personal essays by Levi. Among other topics, Levi discusses her own spiritual experiences in studying Mirabai and the bhakti tradition and the art of translation. She also offers musical notation for a Mirabai song in Indian and Western notation.

Rosen, Steven J., ed., *Vaisnavi: Women and the Worship of Krishna*, Motilal Banarsidass Publishers, 1997.

This book includes an essay on Mirabai by Andrew Schelling, in which he examines the differences between Mirabai and earlier religious poets. It also contains an essay by A. K. Ramanujan on the lives of women saints in India, including Mirabai.

Taft, Frances, "The Elusive Historical Mirabai: A Note," in *Multiple Histories: Culture and Society in the Study of Rajasthan*, edited by Lawrence A. Babb, Varsha Joshi, and Michael W. Meister, Rawat Publications, 2002, pp. 313–35.

Taft analyzes the primary sources and other evidence available that give a picture of the historical Mirabai. She argues against the view held by some that no such person as Mirabai ever existed.

Always

Guillaume Apollinaire
1918

"Always" appears in Guillaume Apollinaire's second volume of poetry, *Calligrammes*, which was published in 1918 and is thought to contain some of his best and most experimental poems. The poem was reprinted in *The Self-Dismembered Man*, published by Wesleyan University Press in 2004.

"Always" reveals the influence of cubism, an art movement that emerged between 1908 and 1912. Apollinaire was fascinated by the way such modern painters as Pablo Picasso and Georges Braque were able to imaginatively reconstruct reality in their work. He applied their methods to "Always" as he examined the nature of poetic inspiration and construction. In a series of separate but related images, the poem focuses on the process of exploration of the universe, from its celestial to its terrestrial boundaries, by such diverse figures as Christopher Columbus and the legendary lover Don Juan. Through creative contradictions and ambiguities, Apollinaire investigates in "Always" the poet's desire to create fresh visions of the world.

Author Biography

Guillaume Apollinaire is considered one of the most important literary figures of the early twentieth century. His use of direct language and unconventional poetic structure had a great influence on his fellow exponents of the avant-garde, his literary descendants, and modern poetic theory, especially cubism and surrealism.

Apollinaire was most likely born with the name Wilhelm Apollinaris de Kostrowitzky in Rome on August 26, 1880. It is difficult to determine his exact name, because his mother, Angeliska Alexandrina Kostrowitzky, a Polish aristocrat, recorded several names for him. Apollinaire's father was probably Francesco-Constantino-Camillo Flugi d'Aspermont, an Italian army officer and gambler. After Flugi d'Aspermont broke off his relationship with Apollinaire's mother, she moved with her children to the French Riviera. Apollinaire was a successful student at Collège Saint-Charles in Monaco, where he often entertained his friends with his imaginative stories. He neglected his studies at the Lycée de Nice in favor of poetry writing and so failed to graduate.

After he moved with his family to Paris in 1899, Apollinaire worked as a copyist, a secretary, and a writer for the newspaper *Le matin*. One of his stories, *Que faire?* (What to Do?) was published serially in the paper and later, in 1950, as a novel. The story mixes romance, fantasy, and inventiveness into a style that characterizes Apollinaire's later work.

The revenue from his writing did not provide enough income, so Apollinaire in 1901 went to Germany to work as a tutor, a position that allowed him time for extensive reading and writing. The next year, after being rejected by a woman with whom he had fallen in love, Apollinaire returned to Paris and took a position in banking. During this time, he began his association with literary and journalistic circles, which included the poets Stuart Merrill and René Ghil. Apollinaire also started *Le festin d'Esope* (1903–1904), a small literary magazine that published many of his stories and musings.

Apollinaire supplemented his small income by distributing and selling pornography, some of which he wrote himself, including *Les exploits d'un jeune Don Juan* (The Exploits of a Young Don Juan) and *Les onze mille verges* (The Eleven Thousand Rods), both published in 1907 and later considered classics of erotic literature. After his introduction to the Spanish cubist painter Pablo Picasso in 1904, Apollinaire became intrigued with modern art and became one of its most ardent supporters. He promoted cubism in his articles and lectures on art and coined the term *surrealism*.

Apollinaire's literary reputation was cemented by the publication in 1910 of his collection of short stories *L'Hérésiarque et cie* (translated as *The Heresiarch and Co*, 1965), which was a runner-up for the Prix Goncourt in 1910. Apollinaire's two collections of poetry, *Alcools: Poèmes 1898–1913* (1913; translated as *Alcools: Poems, 1898–1913*, 1964) and *Calligrammes: Poèmes de la paix et de la guerre, 1913–1916* (1918; translated as *Calligrammes: Poems of Peace and War (1913–1916)*, 1980), which includes "Always," are considered his finest work.

In 1914, when attention in Paris shifted from the fine arts to the war, Apollinaire enlisted in an artillery regiment at Nîmes. His experiences in World War I influenced the poetry of *Calligrammes*. On March 17, 1916, Apollinaire was severely wounded during battle. After recovering, he returned to Paris, where he continued to write. On November 9, 1918, two days before Armistice Day, Apollinaire died of influenza.

Poem Text

Always
We'll go even further never advancing

From planet to planet
Nebula to nebula
Never leaving the ground   5
The Don Juan of 1003 comets
Seeks new forces
Takes spooks seriously

So many universes forgotten
Yet where are the truly great forgetters   10
And whoever will teach us to forget this or that
        corner of the world
And where is the Christopher Columbus to forget
        entire continents

    To lose
Really to lose
To make room for the windfall   15
To lose
    Life to Victory

Poem Summary

Stanza 1

The first stanza of "Always" consists of only two lines. The first line is the word "Always." The second line introduces the speaker and his or her audience ("we"), neither of whom is initially identified. This line contains a contradiction in its prediction. The "we" on whom the speaker is focusing will go further, to an unidentified place, but will not advance. This contradiction separates the concepts of going further and advancing. The word "even" suggests that the process of going further has already begun.

Stanza 2

The second stanza introduces celestial imagery, including planets, nebulae, and comets. Planets are the large bodies that revolve around the sun in a solar system. A nebula is an area of astronomical dust and gas appearing as a hazy bright patch. A comet is an astronomical mass of ice and dust that produces a long, bright tail of vaporized particles when orbiting close to the sun. The three types of celestial bodies are similar in that they are bright objects in the sky. "The Don Juan of 1003 comets" is apparently traveling to and from these objects, seeking "new forces."

In Spanish legend, Don Juan was a nobleman who seduced many women. He has become a popular hero of plays, poems, and operas. Don Juan in "Always" could be a persona of Apollinaire himself and so of a poet. Apollinaire, who enjoyed many amorous relationships with women, liked to envision himself as a Don Juan. In this stanza, then, the speaker becomes the poet who is "going further," perhaps to new poetic territory. The ghosts are similar to the hazy nebulae, which do not appear clearly. They also may represent something to fear as the explorer seeks "new forces."

Stanza 3

In the third stanza, the speaker pulls the focus from specific objects in the universe to the universe or universes in general, focusing on the relationship between the explorer and the explored. The tension is between finding new universes and forgetting them. The speaker suggests that many places have been forgotten by "truly great forgetters." The speaker also suggests that Christopher Columbus is one of these forgetters, because he thought he had found a new passage to the East Indies (later called Indonesia) and Asia when he landed in what came to be called the Bahamas. In this sense, Columbus's discovery is fleeting, like the hazy nebulae or ghosts in the previous stanza.

Stanza 4

In the last stanza, the speaker focuses on the loss of something that makes "room for the windfall," which is defined as a bonus or a benefit. In the final line, the speaker clarifies that the loss is loss of life, which can result in a sense of victory.

Themes

Exploration

Exploration emerges as the dominant theme of "Always," as Apollinaire presents his view of the creative process. The poet links scientific inventions with literary creations through explorations of the boundaries of the world. The first explorer in the poem, Don Juan, imaginatively investigates the cosmos, hopping from "planet to planet," "nebula to nebula," while "never leaving the ground." During his explorations, Don Juan seeks "new forces" that can replace the old, an important principle in Apollinaire's aesthetic. Christopher Columbus's explorations of the terrestrial world extend this process. He forgets old worlds (Asia and the East Indies) while in search of the new. This ability to "lose" the old in order to "make room for the windfall" (that is, the new) will result in a "victory" for the explorer.

Contrast and Contradiction

Apollinaire's interest in cubism can be seen in his use of contrast and contradiction in "Always." When they visually fractured objects into pieces on their canvases, the cubists presented contrasting points of view that often contradicted accepted notions of reality. Apollinaire uses this technique in the poem when he juxtaposes contradictory words and images. He forces readers to view the world from different perspectives and, in this way, participate in the creative process.

The first contradiction presented in the poem is between the notion of progressing and that of advancing. The juxtaposition of these two words suggests that there are different ways to view the concept of progress, forcing readers to reexamine traditional values. As it relates to the literary world, a poem would be valued by how successfully it follows poetic conventions. Yet Apollinaire, who rejected traditional methods of prosody, or metrical structure, insisted that creative progress can be measured only by the inventiveness of the work, thereby resisting conventional notions of advancement.

The contradictions continue in the second through fourth stanzas of "Always," in which the legendary lover Don Juan becomes a celestial explorer and Columbus one of the "truly great forgetters." As the reader examines these juxtapositions, which initially appear incomprehensible, new points of view relating to the creative process open up. As a result, the contrasts and contradictions express an underlying sense of unity.

Victory

The sense of victory in "Always" does not rely on traditional notions of success. Apollinaire offers a new definition of success in the opening stanza when he notes that going "further" does not necessarily mean advancement. In the second stanza, he proposes celestial exploration as a way to "go even further," but the type of exploration he describes would be readily rejected by the scientific community. The explorer the poet envisions traveling from planet to planet and nebula to nebula does not appear at first glance to be qualified for the job. Yet by placing Don Juan in this role, Apollinaire suggests that the heavens could be effectively viewed from a different perspective.

Don Juan's legendary amorous adventures would have prepared him to embark on such a journey not from the detached perspective of the scientist but instead from the view of one who seeks connections, albeit previously personal ones. He perhaps would note the "new forces," including the "spooks" in the universe that might be missed by traditional explorers. In the sense that he would discover multiple perspectives of reality, Don Juan would be victorious.

Apollinaire views terrestrial explorations in new ways. Usually commended for his discovery of the New World, Columbus in this poem is praised for what he has forgotten—for his imaginative ability to see the Old World in the New, concluding that he discovered a new passage to the East Indies and to Asia. This oversight becomes a victory. In the final stanza, Apollinaire challenges his readers to see the world in new ways, to be open to the possibility of failure in order to make room for "the windfall." Only in this sense can one ultimately be victorious.

The Process of Interpretation

Apollinaire's vision of the relationship between author and reader stems from his view of the role of the creator. Apollinaire insisted that the poet is not a recorder of experience, taking a picture of it much as a photographer would do. A poet is instead a creator of experience through his imaginative representation of it. The new visions of reality the poet creates require more active participation from readers. Readers are required to use imagination when reading a poem in order to comprehend it. In this sense, the reader participates in the creative process of the work of art.

In "Apollinaire and the Modern Mind," Anna Balakian explains the process of interpretation by

Topics for Further Study

- Read another of Apollinaire's poems from *Calligrammes* and prepare to lead a class discussion comparing and contrasting it to "Always."

- Investigate the symbolist school of poetry and write an essay discussing its influence on Apollinaire's poetry.

- Write a poem of three or four stanzas of self-contained images that as a whole express thematic unity.

- Rearrange the lines of your poem into a picture that expresses its meaning. Use some of the more visual poems in *Calligrammes*, such as "Fan of Flavors" or "Cotton in Your Ears," as models.

noting that the reader must reject the passivity of the traditional method of reading—"of absorbing and feeling the message of the artist"—and assume "the more creative role of relating the sensations of the artist to his own experiences and his own faculties of imagination and association." As a result, the "flexibility of the visions of the artist are set to a perpetual motion of interpretations, which may in themselves be a form of creative activity." This technique, according to Balakian, became one of the dominant principles of the dadaists and surrealists.

Style

Ironic Contradictions

A sense of irony is produced by the contradictory imagery and language in "Always." Apollinaire's juxtapositions become ironic as he obscures in order to communicate. He achieves this effect by contrasting images in each stanza. In the first stanza, Apollinaire contrasts going further to never advancing, a contradiction that becomes the main thematic thrust of the poem. This contradiction is reinforced by the juxtapositions in the second stanza, in which, without ever leaving the ground, Don Juan explores the cosmos, contrasting solid objects (planets) to transitory ones (nebulae). The contrast of the realistic (comets and planets) to the fantastic (legends and ghosts) adds an element of playfulness. In the third stanza, Columbus both forgets and discovers, and in the last stanza, loss becomes a gain.

Apollinaire achieves a delicate sense of irony in the shifts of tone across the contradictions. The serious often turns mischievous. Scientific exploration is contrasted to amorous adventures in the second stanza, and the somber condition of forgetting turns into a celebration of forgetting entire continents in the third stanza. The poem ends with the loss of life, ordinarily a sad experience, but transformed through contrast into a victory.

Apollinaire extends the irony to the use of language. He uses free verse and a conversational style to address serious topics. This technique adds to the playfulness of tone. The poet's opaque contradictory language makes demands on readers that force them to slow down and examine each word instead of racing to the end of the stanza or poem to find meaning.

Balakian, writing in her *Yale French Studies* article, notes that Apollinaire "believed that words could make and unmake a universe." As a result, the poet used his creative imagination to "string side by side images often logically disconnected, demanding of the reader leaps and bounds of the imagination to keep pace with his self-characterized 'oblong' vision." Balakian concludes that Apollinaire's "dislocations of temporal and spatial perspective defy ordinary reality but are of this earth in their tactility, colors and scents."

Cubism

Apollinaire structures "Always" into stanzas that present four distinct images that can be viewed from different perspectives, much as a cubist painting is viewed. The poet carries this method over into his line construction. In his introduction to *Selected Writings of Guillaume Apollinaire*, Roger Shattuck concludes that Apollinaire maintains "an integrity of line, a desire to make each line a partially self-sufficient unit which does not depend too greatly upon the succeeding line. This integrity of line extends to an integrity of stanza and of the poem itself." This technique is most evident in the third stanza, in which each line forms a complete thought.

Shattuck notes that Apollinaire's lack of punctuation illustrates this integrity, for "his lines are

sufficiently end-stopped to make each a unit." Apollinaire's use of free verse with its conversational tone causes him to end a line at a natural pause. The use of language and the design of the poem in this sense add to its directness.

Historical Context

World War I

World War I was triggered by the assassination of Archduke Francis Ferdinand, the heir to the Austro-Hungarian Empire, on June 28, 1914, in Sarajevo, Bosnia. The war started a month later, when Austria-Hungary declared war on Serbia. Other European countries soon made their own declarations of war. Great Britain entered on August 4, 1914, after Germany began its invasion of France. The war between the Allied and Associated powers (France, Russia, Great Britain, and the United States as well as numerous other nations) and the Central powers (Germany, Austria-Hungary, and Turkey) raged until 1918. The number of total casualties was extraordinary, estimated at ten million. France lost more soldiers than did Great Britain or Germany. One tenth of the French population was killed or went missing during the war. The French economy suffered as industrial and agricultural production fell to less than half of prewar levels.

In the aftermath of World War I, European society went through a period of change. Traditional beliefs in God, country, and humanity were shaken as Europeans faced the devastation of war. The feelings of confusion and dislocation that resulted led to a questioning and often a rejection of conventional morality and beliefs.

Cubism

Cubism, an art movement that emerged between 1908 and 1912, was led by the Spanish artist Pablo Picasso and the French painter Georges Braque. Artists who followed this movement were influenced by African tribal art and the work of the French impressionist Paul Cézanne. The movement lasted only until about 1920, but it helped generate new ideas about art and literature and influenced later movements, such as expressionism and imagism.

Cubists believed that an object could be expressed only by revealing it from multiple points of view presented simultaneously. Objects were

Compare & Contrast

- **1910s:** Cubism, one of the most influential art movements in the early twentieth century, presents multidimensional views of reality. Cubist painters render these views by incorporating cylinders, spheres, and cones in abstract visions of the human form or of landscapes or still lifes.

  Today: Contemporary art often engages political and social themes, such as human rights or gender issues. Artists do not limit themselves to traditional artistic techniques but instead experiment with performance and multimedia works.

- **1910s:** Poetry often presents an austerely pessimistic view of contemporary society as a reaction to industrialization and war. Poets such as T. S. Eliot ("The Love Song of J. Alfred Prufrock") and William Butler Yeats ("The Second Coming") express pessimism most often through the depiction of general, social experience rather than in specific, personal terms.

  Today: Poets such as Sharon Olds ("Taking Notice") and Margaret Atwood ("They Eat Out") continue what has come to be considered the pessimistic zeitgeist, or moral and intellectual trends, of the twentieth century. Pessimism is most often expressed in a personal style that reflects the author's own experience and point of view.

- **1910s:** World War I begins in 1914 and lasts until 1918 and is the largest war to date. Approximately ten million people are killed, and twenty million are wounded. Poets such as Wilfred Owen ("Dulce et Decorum Est"), Siegfried Sassoon ("The Power and the Glory"), and Apollinaire express the devastation of the war in their work. Their poetry does not always engage in a protest of this war. More often, these writers question in a general sense the motives for war and the glorification of the soldier.

  Today: The United States, with aid from thirty-four other countries, invades Iraq in 2003, initiating a war plagued by controversy. Soon after the invasion, the poet Sam Hamill calls on approximately fifty of his peers to express their views about the war in their poetry. Fifteen hundred poets respond immediately with poems of protest that Hamill forwards to the White House. Poets from around the world, including Julia Alvarez ("The White House Has Disinvited the Poets") and Robert Bly ("Call and Answer"), join Poets against War and write poems that voice their opposition.

---

thus broken up on the canvas and reassembled in abstract forms, often made up of cylinders, spheres, and cones. Picasso and Braque incorporated open-edged planes into their work that slid into each other. Color was limited and muted, and elements such as letters, musical notes, and sand added interest and texture. Later works were made with vibrant colors, often in collages created with a jumble of glued paper and objects such as playing cards and tobacco packets.

Balakian notes that Apollinaire's involvement with and support of the cubist movement made him "a better apologist for the new art than the painters themselves could have been." As a result, she says, stronger links were forged between art and literature,

"a relationship which was to prove so significant and influential in the development of dadaism and surrealism."

Dada

Dadaism, a movement in art and literature that was characterized by irrationality and anarchy, was started in Zurich, Switzerland, in 1916 by the Romanian poet Tristan Tzara, along with the French artist and poet Hans Arp (also known as Jean Arp), the German writer Hugo Ball, and the German physician and poet Richard Huelsenbeck, in response to the widespread disillusionment brought about by World War I. The founders meant dadaism to signify total freedom from ideals and traditions concerning aesthetics and behavior. The most important concept of dada was the word "nothing."

In art, dadaists produced collage effects as they arranged unrelated objects in a random manner. In literature, dadaists produced mostly nonsense poems consisting of meaningless, random combinations of words and read them in cafés and bars. These constructions in art and literature stressed absurdity and the role of the unpredictable in the creative process. The dadaists came into vogue in Paris immediately after World War I. Tzara carried the school to England and the United States, where dadaist influence became apparent in the poetry of Ezra Pound and T. S. Eliot. By 1921, dadaism as a movement had modified into surrealism. The influence of dadaism, however, continued for many years in literature and art.

Surrealism

The surrealism movement originated in France in the second decade of the twentieth century and was promoted by Apollinaire, who coined the term; by the French poet André Breton; and by the Spanish painter Salvador Dali. In 1924, Breton wrote the first of three manifestos defining the movement. Influenced by Freudian psychoanalysis, which looked at the subconscious mind of a patient, surrealists rejected traditional, rational artistic renderings of reality that called for reason, morality, and intention and instead promoted the removal of all constraints to creativity. Surrealists often worked with automatic writing, which was written expression of the unconscious mind, dreams, and hallucinatory states. Surrealists believed that the true source of creative energy could be found in the unconscious, where the seemingly contradictory elements of daily life were resolved. That energy, surrealists claimed, could be focused by the conscious mind into art.

Painters such as Max Ernst and Picasso and writers such as Louis Aragon and Paul Éluard became involved in the surrealist movement, which often had links to revolutionary political and social groups of the age. The movement continued to influence writers throughout the twentieth century, especially such American writers as Henry Miller, William Burroughs, and Allen Ginsberg and playwrights like Eugène Ionesco and Samuel Beckett, who experimented with free expression of thoughts not tied to formal poetic or dramatic conventions.

Imagists

The poets of the early decades of the twentieth century experimented with new forms and styles in their concern with the truthfulness of language. A group of poets prominent during this period, the imagists, had an important effect on modernist poetry in this sense, modernism being a style that reflected the social and philosophical fragmentation of modern life. Imagist writers rejected traditional clichéd poetic diction, or the choice and arrangement of words, and regulated meter in favor of more natural expressions of language written in free verse. *Des imagistes*, an anthology by Ezra Pound, one of the leading proponents of the movement, was published in 1913. The anthology contained examples of what Pound considered imagist verse by James Joyce, H.D. (Hilda Doolittle), William Carlos Williams, Frank Stuart Flint, Ford Madox Ford (also known as Ford Madox Hueffer), and Amy Lowell, among others. Pound included in the work his imagist doctrine, which insisted on a direct treatment of what the poet is expressing, the discarding of any language that does not contribute to the presentation of this essence, and an emphasis on a sequence of musical phrases rather than on consistent, regulated meter.

Critical Overview

Reviews for *Calligrammes*, which includes "Always," are positive for the original edition and remain so for subsequent editions. M. B. Markus, in his review of the 1980 edition for *Library Journal*, cites the "ebulliency and epic vision of the poems," which "demonstrate Apollinaire's acceptance of World War I as a new realm of experience and creative possibility." Markus notes that the poet "abandoned punctuation, syntax, linear and discursive style for free verse . . . and contemporary idiom."

In her commentary on "Always," Anne Hyde Greet concludes that the poem is one of Apollinaire's "prophetic" works, revealing "his old love of science-fiction imagery." The paradoxical nature of the first two lines, Greet argues, is made clear in the philosophy of his lecture "L'Esprit nouveau et les poetes," given in 1917. Greet writes that in this lecture Apollinaire declared that progress, "which is limited to the manipulation of external phenomena, exists on the level of scientific invention; newness, which man can find within himself, exists, apart from progress, in science and especially in art."

Margaret Davies, reviewing the 1980 edition of *Calligrammes* for *Modern Language Review*, determines the collection to be a "fascinating labyrinth" of "very diverse material" that switches "from the inward turning of *Alcools*," a collection of Apollinaire's poems published in 1913, to an extroverted "enthusiasm." Davies identifies in *Calligrammes* "the radical dislocations and discontinuities that were the result of [Apollinaire's] search for simultaneity" and "the new type of 'lecture' which is solicited from the reader." She finds within the poems "the inevitable and continued Apollinarian ambiguities, which culminate in the final choice of anxiety and conflict as the essential condition of his aesthetic." The poems reveal the "interesting effects which can arise when the visual form actually contradicts the semantic message of the words."

In the introduction to the 1980 volume, S. I. Lockerbie concludes that *Calligrammes* is "the second major volume of poetry on which rests Guillaume Apollinaire's reputation as one of the great modern poets in French literature," *Alcools* being the first. The poems reveal "a novelty of accent and composition which clearly rests on aesthetic assumptions different from those underlying" his previous works. The assumptions "can conveniently be drawn together under the concept of modernism." Lockerbie states that the mood in these poems "reflects much greater confidence and enthusiasm for life" than those in *Alcools*, showing a change that resulted from "the rapid technological advances of the early years of the twentieth century and the general widening of horizons brought about by such inventions as the motorcar, the airplane, radiography, cinematography, and radio communications." Lockerbie concludes that "now [Apollinaire] seemed the triumphant master of his own destiny."

Anna Balakian, in her article on Apollinaire for *Yale French Studies*, writes that the poet's importance "lies not so much in being the originator of an attitude as in having stated it more provocatively and held to it more persistently than his contemporaries." Balakian argues that Apollinaire's "ideas on art did not remain in the realm of theories but were illustrated consciously in the major part of his poetic work."

In her review of *Calligrammes*, Balakian concludes that the collection "is a more striking example of [Apollinaire's] inventive approach to writing" than is his earlier collection, *Alcools*. Balakian finds that in *Alcools*, the poet displays a "vigorous imagination" that "often accepted the challenge of new vistas revealed by the inventions pertaining to the war." She adds that in *Calligrammes*, Apollinaire effectively uses "juxtaposition and discarded

A monument to Guillaume Apollinaire in Vallauris, France © Gjon Mili/Getty Images

symmetry and order much more than in his previous works." The poems in *Calligrammes* are "circumstantial in the sense that their point of departure is a factual event or concrete detail of the color of the times." Balakian argues that the poems "fearlessly" illustrate Apollinaire's theory that symbolism should sometimes contain contradictions and so set "a new relationship between the artist and his audience." Balakian concludes that this theory had a profound influence on other poets.

Scott Bates, in his book-length study of Apollinaire, writes that the collection is "strikingly freer, the freest in Apollinaire's poetry since his first adolescent experiments." Bates believes that Apollinaire noted "the need of bringing even more of the twentieth century into his simultaneous vision of it in order better to influence it in return." As a result, Apollinaire "adopted a synthetic style, incorporating various techniques of European art and poetry around him."

In his afterword to his translated edition of selected poems from *Calligrammes*, including "Always," Donald Revell writes that the "vivid and witty" poems express "the fullest and most beautiful horizons of Apollinaire's combat, contoured to sweet reason and to new, new music." They are, he claims, the "final, finest of his poems."

Criticism

Wendy Perkins

Wendy Perkins is a professor of American and English literature and film. In this essay, she examines Apollinaire's focus on the creative process.

Anna Balakian, in her article on Guillaume Apollinaire in *Yale French Studies*, notes that in the early decades of the twentieth century, a rift that had emerged at the end of the nineteenth century between art and science was growing wider. Artists concluded that "science seemed to be the destroyer of the marvelous and the mysterious." In addition, after scientific inquiry produced inventions such as the electric light, the cinema, and the subway, "the supremacy of the scientist in the history of human progress" appeared assured.

Unlike others, who felt challenged by the supremacy of the scientist, Apollinaire was fascinated by the new world scientists were creating. As a result, Balakian states, Apollinaire "sought conciliation between the work of the scientist and of the modern artist." This conciliation becomes the main focus of his poem "Always," which explores the role of the poet as a creator of new worlds.

Like the modernist authors of his age, Apollinaire rejected forms of art that were attempts to imitate reality, such as photography. Balakian explains that Apollinaire determined reality to be "dependent not on physical nature but on the mind's creativeness." As a result, Balakian writes, "he found in the cubists the truest competitors of the imaginative technologists." In an effort to fuse creatively with reality, cubists expressed objects by breaking them up on canvas and presenting them from multiple points of view simultaneously.

In his introduction to the 1980 edition of *Calligrammes*, S. I. Lockerbie writes that Apollinaire "had the creative genius to transform aesthetic concepts that were in general circulation into powerful and appealing poetry." Lockerbie explains that "central among these aesthetic ideas was the notion that the modern work of art must adequately reflect the global nature of contemporary consciousness."

In the twenty-first century, people are continually bombarded with different kinds of information transmitted in different forms. Lockerbie claims that Apollinaire knew that in order to "mirror such a multiple form of consciousness, the work of art had to abandon linear and discursive structures, in which events are arranged successively."

The simultaneity that Apollinaire proposed would necessitate "a type of structure that would give the impression of a full and instant awareness within one moment of space-time." This arrangement, according to Apollinaire, created a fresh view of reality, a process that becomes the subject of "Always."

In "Always," Apollinaire links the worlds of scientific and poetic invention in his exploration of the poet's creation of new worlds through conflict and contradiction, a process that encourages multiple points of view. As he juxtaposes contrary, often obscure images, Apollinaire forces readers to see in different ways and thus take part in the creative process. He does not insist on any absolute visions of reality but instead, through his playful juxtapositions, suggests that anyone can become an explorer and an inventor.

Each of the four stanzas contains a separate statement that the reader must derive from the text. Balakian notes that Apollinaire tries "to infuse his work with unexpected sparks: visions concretely resplendent and limitless, meant to surprise and mystify the reader" in order to involve the reader in the interpretative process. The surprise begins in the first stanza with the seeming contradiction of its two lines. The "we" is most likely the poet and the reader, both taking an active part in the exploration and interpretation of the world. In Apollinaire's aesthetic, the reader contributes to the creative process begun by the poet by gathering together the fragments of the poem in an effort to discover meaning.

The speaker confounds the search for meaning by claiming that when "we" go even further, we do not advance. Still, a careful examination of the apparent contradiction of this line helps the reader understand the speaker's point. Apollinaire suggests that the discovery of different perspectives does not necessarily mean advancement in the traditional sense of progress. The new vision that may be achieved through the collaboration of poet and reader may not be accepted as a realistic vision of the universe, but it can be an accurate vision.

The second stanza appears as a separate unit of the poem, focusing on Don Juan's exploration of the universe. This stanza, however, contributes to the underlying unity of the poem's focus on the creative impulse through its linking of cosmographic explorations of new forces and the construction of art. Apollinaire blends realism and fantasy as he confounds the reader with his inclusion of the paradoxical Don Juan, an odd choice for a cosmological explorer. The legendary lover may be Apollinaire's persona, and this hypothesis is supported by the poet's biographical details. The "1003" shooting comets may be an image of war, which Apollinaire experienced firsthand. In this sense, the imagery suggests that the experience of war taught the poet to view the world in new ways.

Don Juan becomes an appropriate explorer in a universe that Apollinaire suggests must be viewed from diverse perspectives for it to be understood in its fullest sense. Unlike traditional space explorers, who view the cosmos from an objectively analytical position, Don Juan focuses on personal connections, because they form the basis of his experience. Don Juan takes any "spooks" he encounters seriously, refusing to find rational explanations for them.

An avid reader, Apollinaire could have used "1003" to represent the year the Norse mariner Thorfinn Karlsefni left Greenland with three ships for a three-year exploration of the western continents. Karlsefni did not establish any settlements, therefore not making progress in the traditional sense, but his explorations would have provided him with new visions of his world.

This theme of exploration is carried over into the third stanza, which focuses on Christopher Columbus. Apollinaire confounds the reader's attempts to find meaning when he characterizes Columbus as a forgetter. Looking at the concept of forgetting in a new way, however, the reader may be able to understand Apollinaire's odd image. The stanza appears to begin with a complaint, because on the surface forgetting an entire universe does not seem to be a preferable state. In the second line, Apollinaire gives the condition of forgetting a positive quality, insisting that the reader must study the "truly great forgetters," because they have so much to teach about forgetting "this or that corner of the world." If the reader considers the history of Columbus's exploration, an interpretation can be derived.

When he reached what came to be known as the Bahamas, Columbus believed that he had found a new passage to the East Indies and Asia. In this sense, his discovery is an act of forgetting an old continent or universe and discovering a new one. The image of forgetting can be linked to the hazy nebulae or ghosts in the previous stanza, which suggest an ephemeral, or fleeting, state of matter. In a sense, Columbus did not "advance" in a traditional way, but his explorations resulted in the discovery of a new world. Columbus triggered extraordinary

> *As he juxtaposes contrary, often obscure images, Apollinaire forces readers to see in different ways and thus take part in the creative process."*

changes in the concept of the world as the people of the East began to intermingle with the West. Another way to look at the act of forgetting is to consider that the new territory Columbus claimed for Spain was eventually lost by the Spaniards. Still, the independence gained by the inhabitants of North America helped create a new world for them.

The final stanza presents another mysterious image that resists interpretation. The speaker juxtaposes the seemingly contrary words "lose" and "Victory." Yet the speaker suggests that if it is viewed in a positive sense, the act of losing can be interpreted as a victory. Losing one's life force allows a new one, a "windfall," to emerge—what Don Juan and Columbus are searching for in their cosmological and terrestrial explorations. The creative act sometimes necessitates "forgetting," or the rejection of the old in the process of constructing the new.

The final stanza links to the first and creates a harmonious whole. The contradiction between going further but never advancing is recreated in the juxtaposition of loss and victory at the end. New, sustaining visions can be created through an imaginative engagement with the universe.

Lockerbie argues that Apollinaire's conclusions about the nature of poetry in the modern world "led to a radical dislocation of poetic structure." In his efforts to encourage readers to view different perspectives simultaneously, Apollinaire juxtaposes thoughts that, taken as a whole, seem to suggest "considerable disorder." The discontinuities, Lockerbie claims, are "much more radical [than in traditional verse], forcing the reader into a greater effort of synthesis to discover the underlying unity." As a result, the reader is required "to reassemble the apparently random fragments in a new order." "Always" is a striking example of this innovative process. As he encourages readers to

What Do I Read Next?

- *Cubism* (1998), by David Cottington, is a comprehensive overview of this important art movement.

- Stanley Appelbaum's *Introduction to French Poetry* (1991) is a collection of poems by several important French poets, including Voltaire, Victor Hugo, Arthur Rimbaud, and Apollinaire, that includes critical and biographical information on each poet.

- T. S. Eliot's "The Love Song of J. Alfred Prufrock" (1915), one of the most celebrated poems of the age, captures the pessimism and sense of hopelessness of the war years. It can be found in Eliot's *Collected Poems, 1909–1962* (1963).

- "Ocean of Earth," another selection in *Calligrammes* (1918), is often cited as one of Apollinaire's most inventive poems.

join his creative expeditions in the poem, Apollinaire challenges them to discover fresh and invigorating visions of the world.

Source: Wendy Perkins, Critical Essay on "Always," in *Poetry for Students*, Thomson Gale, 2006.

L. C. Breunig

In the following essay, Breunig explores the "fusion of laughter and despair" and the resulting sense of malaise in Apollinaire's poetry.

Apollinaire, like Surrealism, lives on. A decade ago it was customary, especially after Sartre's statement: "Breton is in exile among us," to tuck Surrealism neatly between the two World Wars and pronounce its obituary. C. A. Hackett, for example, assessed it in the past tense in the introduction to his *Anthology of Modern French Poetry* in 1951: "Surrealism produced few coherent poetic forms—that after all was not its purpose—but it was undoubtedly successful as a literary polemic and a perhaps necessary social irritant." And in the same vein he wrote that Apollinaire's

"achievements, like those of the Surrealists who claimed him as their immediate predecessor, are less impressive than his intentions."

Admittedly much in Apollinaire seems as passé to us as a Waco or the taxis of the Marne. Paradoxically his so-called "modernism" has perhaps aged most quickly, not because it was merely a "veneer" as Mr. Hackett claims (alluding presumably to the enthusiasm for aeroplanes, wireless telegraphy, the Eiffel Tower, the silent cinema, etc.) but rather because of its old-fashioned optimism, its hope in a bright future where the union of the spiritual and the technological would ensure the felicity of mankind.

> So don't cry over the horrors of war
> Before it came we had only the surface
> Of the earth and the seas
> But after we will have the abysses
> The subsoil and airspace
> Masters of the helm
> After after
> We will take all the joys
> Of conquerers who are relaxing
> Women Games Factories Business
> Industry Agriculture
> Fire Crystal Speed. . . .

Such lines, which for all their charm sound like a not so felicitous mixture of Whitman and Marinetti, fall on deaf ears today.

The optimism of the Surrealists, although more doctrinaire, seems no less naive. If one combines the hope expressed most fervently by Eluard, after Lautréamont, that every man can be a poet—and in the 'thirties this meant the proletariat—with Breton's belief, announced in the *Second Manifesto*, that Surrealism can lead us to a point where all antinomies disappear: life and death, the real and the imaginary, past and future, etc. one begins to realize that the Surrealists were aiming at a goal so unattainable that one wonders if they seriously believed in it at all. It is definitely not because of their hopes that Apollinaire and Surrealism remain alive today.

Mr. Hackett admits that in the work of Apollinaire "there are individual verses, refrains and short lyrics which have more than a period interest," but he concludes that the best work is "that which reflects the work of other and greater poets, such as Villon, Rimbaud and Verlaine."

Such an evaluation is based, it seems to us, upon an oversimplification, a neat classification of all Apollinaire's poetry into two categories—the two, it must be admitted, which he himself set forth in "La Jolie Rousse"—poems of "Adventure" and

poems of "Order." The first, of which "Zone" is a
good example, are then disposed of as mere "experimental" pieces having a "veneer of modernity"
and the second, poems like "Le Pont Mirabeau," as
"traditional" pieces lacking originality.

Certainly the poetry of Apollinaire is more
complex. It contains elements, it must contain elements, which account for its continued appeal a
half-century later. Without attempting in this short
essay to discuss them all we would like to examine a single but a very essential element, or rather
a tone in this poetry which would seem to have
considerable resonance in the nineteen sixties. The
contemporaries of Apollinaire, those of the "banquet years," were not particularly sensitive to it, but
thanks to Surrealism we are able to hear it more
clearly. It is the laughter of Apollinaire.

In 1940 Breton published his *Anthologie de
l'humour noir,* a collection which in addition to
such masters of "black humor" as Swift, Lichten-
berg and De Quincey includes the Surrealists
Vaché, Rigaud, Dali, Prévert and, among the few
writers of the immediately preceding generation,
Apollinaire. In his presentation Breton recalls the
sound of Apollinaire's laugh as he himself had actually heard it before the poet's death in 1918. "It
made the same noise as a first burst of hailstones
on a window pane." The implication is that this
laugh had nothing contagious about it; it caused no
merriment but rather a shudder. Was it not a sudden outburst of the more inhuman, unfeeling, destructive side of the poet's nature?

The excerpts from Apollinaire in Breton's Anthology, most of them in prose, are not among his
more significant work, and what Breton fails to
stress is that one can hear these "hailstones" not
only in many of the weird tales of *L'Hérésiarque
et Cie* or the more sinister episodes of *Le Poète assassiné* and *La Femme assise* but also in the pages
of lyric poetry upon which Apollinaire's reputation
stands, in *Alcools* and *Calligrammes.*

What is the nature of this laughter? For ears
which are attuned to it today it has a remarkable
resemblance with that which is heard less perhaps
in the novel or the poetry of the last few years than
in the theatre of the avant-garde. Indeed Breton, if
he so desired, could publish a new edition of his
Anthology for the present decade to include, in all
fairness, more of the Surrealists of his own generation such as Artaud and Vitrac (whom he had "ex-
communicated") and in addition excerpts from
Ionesco, Beckett, Genet, Tardieu, Arrabal, Obaldia,
Vian and others. He could give, for example, the

> *... as a lyric poet
speaking in the first person
Apollinaire plays the role of
both author and characters
in his own 'theatre of the
absurd.'"*

scene from Vitrac's *Les Mystères de l'amour* in
which the author, having failed to commit suicide,
comes on stage still bleeding and laughing uproar-
iously; the passage from the beginning of Ionesco's
Les Chaises where the pathetic old man and his
wife shake with laughter as he repeats the same
inane story ("Alors on arri . . .") that they have
heard every evening for the last sixty-five years;
the scene in Tardieu's *La Serrure* with the
grotesque laugh of the "madame" as she leaves
the young man alone to stare through the keyhole;
the sneering laughter of the father in the final scene
of Boris Vian's *Les Bâtisseurs d'empire* as he beats
the schmürz before falling to his death; the gay pa-
sodoble at the end of Arrabal's *Pique-nique en
campagne* as the machine gun mows down Zépo,
Zapo and the father and mother; and the laughter
and song of the two maids in Genet's *Les Bonnes*
as they decide to do away with their mistress:

> Sing out! We'll carry her off into the woods and, un-
> der the pine trees, in the moonlight, we'll carve her
> to pieces. And we'll sing. We'll bury her under the
> flowers, in our flowerbeds which we'll water every
> night with a little garden can.

The characters may be victims, they may be exe-
cutioners but in all these scenes, despite the many
differences, the laughter is on stage, not in the audience. This is not comedy in the traditional sense.
The author does not wish to elicit laughter but
rather, as Ionesco specifically indicates at the end
of *Jacques ou la soumission,* "to provoke in the audience a painful sentiment of malaise. . . ."

In his study of these playwrights in *The Theatre of the Absurd* (1961) Martin Esslin salutes
Apollinaire as a precursor, but he limits his analysis to *Les Mamelles de Tirésias.* Undoubtedly the
irrational action of this "Surrealist drama" and the
dramatic creed set forth in the prologue have influenced the theatre today, but the gay, genial

tone of *Les Mamelles* sets it quite apart. The balloons are not black. If we were looking for influences we would be the first to claim that Jarry's *Ubu* series and Artaud's "Theatre of Cruelty" have had a more direct effect on the new playwrights. Our aim, however, is merely to invite the reader to look again at the lyric poetry of Apollinaire with today's very somber laughter still echoing in his ears.

We discover first that we do not need to rely on Breton's testimony alone, for Apollinaire describes his own laugh. In "Zone" he writes:

> You make fun of yourself and like the fire of hell
> your laughter crackles
> The sparks of your laughter gild the depths of your
> life
> It's a painting hung in a somber museum
> And sometimes you go to have a close look at it.

Breton's image has changed here into that of little crackling flames, but the troubling effect is the same. The poet is speaking to himself. Heautontimoroumenos-like he is both the one laughing and the one laughed at. And as he steps up closer to himself he realizes that beneath the gentle, tender sentimental self lies the infernal, destructive force which was to chill Breton.

In some poems Apollinaire transfers this laugh to another character, usually a woman, and portrays himself as the victim. In such cases he becomes the traditional "mal-aimé," Guillaume who suffers from the perverse capriciousness of Mareye, Annie, Marie, Lou and Madeleine and who in his more grief-stricken moments sees himself as Orpheus being torn to pieces by the Maenads. This theme is of course as old as poetry itself, but the distinctiveness, the modernity, if you will, of Apollinaire lies in the very intensity of the harsh, sadistic laugh which reveals a monstrous degree of insensitivity. At times it becomes an atrocious grimace, mechanical, fixed, like a whinny, and creating between the two beings a wide, mysterious void which alienates them beyond all hope. The haunting sound of this laughter echoes throughout the work from an early poem written probably in Stavelot, containing the line:

> Et je mourais encore en entendant ton rire

through *L'Enchanteur pourrissant* where Merlin, locked in his tomb by Viviane, the Lady of the Lake, hears her peals of laughter which "awaken the echoes of the deep forest"; down to the conclusion of *Le Poète assassiné* which presents the flippant little Tristouse Ballerinette dancing with joy as she witnesses the ruthless murder of Croniamantal.

An awareness of this sound helps us to reread certain poems with a deeper sense of their meaning. The very possibility that Salome ("Salomé") is not broken-hearted over the death of John the Baptist, that her feverish burst of frivolity is perhaps authentic makes the death of her victim even more horrible. Incidentally the situation here is quite different from that in *Les Bonnes,* but the frenzied mood and the language are strikingly similar:

> We will scoop out a hole and bury him there
> We will plant flowers and dance in a circle
> Up to the moment when I'll have lost my garter
> the King his snuffbox
> the child his rosary
> the curé his breviary.

The song beginning "Ah Dieu! que la guerre est jolie . . ." ("L'Adieu du cavalier") is hardly an attempt to prettify war as has been claimed. The sinister implications of this sweet little sentiment become apparent at the end when the soldier disappears:

> He disappeared in a turn of the road
> And died down there while she kept laughing at
> the suddenness of destiny.

Once more the poet dies amidst the strange sound of a lady's laughter.

The sound is even more disquieting, however, when it emerges from the poet himself. In "Poème lu au mariage d'André Salmon" Apollinaire recalls the birth within him of his black humor. He is speaking to his fellow poet, Salmon:

> We met each other in an accursed little cellar
> In the time of our youth
> Both of us smoking and poorly dressed as we
> awaited dawn
> Smitten, smitten with the same words whose meaning needed to be changed
> Deceived, deceived, poor fellows, and not yet
> knowing how to laugh
> The table and the two glasses became a dying man
> who threw us Orpheus' last glance
> The glasses fell and broke
> And we learned how to laugh.

Here Apollinaire takes the place of the Maenads. The dying Orpheus seems to symbolize all the sorrow, and of course the self-pity within the poets themselves, sentiments which they suddenly demolish with a guffaw that bursts forth like breaking glass. Actually Apollinaire had evoked this sound in an earlier poem, "Nuit rhénane." Carried along one evening in a frenzy of despair as he sits, wine glass in hand, listening to a folk song about seven Rhineland maidens he abruptly breaks the spell with a violent final line:

> Mon verre s'est brisé comme un éclat de rire

One of the most powerful examples of these explosive outbursts comes in the middle of "La Chanson du mal-aimé." The Zaporogian Cossacks, who have just received the order to surrender to the Sultan of Constantinople, compose with a burst of mirthless laughter their foul-mouthed reply. For them the laugh is an act of defiance, but for the poet-lover it is a purge for his grief and his mortification at finding himself the victim of a passionate and impossible attachment. And indirectly through a kind of "poetic logic" the impassive young English girl who inspired the poem is splattered by the most ungallant ribaldry which follows.

Once we realize that Apollinaire chose consciously or unconsciously to laugh infernally, to stand alongside the Maenads, to become himself the destructive force we can appreciate more fully some of the incongruous juxtapositions which so puzzled his contemporaries. In an essay on Picasso he once wrote that "surprise laughs savagely in the pure light" of the artist's paintings. The technique of surprise, which he made so much of without ever defining it adequately, takes on more meaning if we associate it with the explosive quality of his own "savage" laughter. Many of the devices of surprise such as the juxtaposition of the tender and the grotesque, of gravity and triviality or, as in the example we have just seen, the sudden intrusion of obscenities into a sentimental mood seem to stem from the poet's decision to let "the fire of his laughter crackle."

This black humor is nowhere more apparent than in the war poetry which one should read keeping in mind a letter sent to André Billy from the trenches in 1915:

> I tell you André Billy that this war
> Well it's Obus-Roi
> And much more tragic than Ubu but hardly—
> believe me Billy
> Less of a burlesque—Oh, believe me, old fellow,
> it's really very funny.

Apollinaire, like Jarry, turns the tragic inside out and by making death a subject for laughter conveys more freshly all its horror. Face to face with it he can affect the most insensitive cheerfulness, a kind of amused detachment, or a puckish smile. In "Merveilles de la guerre" the bursting shells in the darkness remind him of a huge banquet:

> I feel I'm attending a great banquet illuminated a
> giorno
> It's a banquet the earth organized for herself
> She's hungry and opens long pale mouths
> The earth is hungry and here's her cannibal
> Balthasar's feast

> Who would have said that one could be so anthro-
> pophagous
> And it would take so much fire to roast a human
> body
> That's why the air has a slight empyrheumatic fla-
> vor which after all isn't so disagreeable.

Who would have said that one could be so casual, so jaunty when one is in the trenches, ready to be blown up at any moment?

In "Chant d'honneur" the poet recalls the sight of four dead soldiers still standing upright in the trench:

> J'en vis quatre une fois qu'un même obus frappait
> Ils restèrent longtemps ainsi morts et très crânes
> Avec l'aspect penché de quatre tours pisanes. . . .

Four Towers of Pisa! What are we to make of this delightful simile which derives from such detached, almost callous, indifference? This is not irony in the usual sense; Apollinaire in fact was rarely ironical. Nor can one accuse him of cynicism. Only a few lines later he will address his comrades in the most moving terms:

> Your hearts are all within me I feel each wound
> Oh, my suffering soldiers, oh, mortally wounded
> men.

It seems rather that as a lyric poet speaking in the first person Apollinaire plays the role of both author and characters in his own "theatre of the absurd." He can make the most abrupt leaps from the anguished, heavy-hearted self within him who feels as deeply as the writers of today the tragedy of man's condition, to himself as *persona,* detached, inhuman, an "image d'Epinal" soldier, "Guy au galop," a stranger as mysterious and alarming as the stylized, Guignol characters we see in the theatre today. The laughter of Apollinaire in such cases is also on stage. And like the mask-maker of Marcel Marceau, holding the two masks of Tragedy and Comedy and putting now one, now the other on his face in rapid-fire succession, the lines of Apollinaire with their sudden shifts often convey a single sentiment, neither tragic nor comic and yet containing both, the sentiment of the absurd.

The power of the Theatre of the Absurd comes from the fact that beneath the vaudeville gags, the word-play and the farcical nonsense the audience senses the author's earnestness, his deep concern before what he feels to be the "non-sense" of the world itself. Is is unlikely that Apollinaire had any clearly formulated notion of the absurd, and his own moods were undoubtedly more personal and less representative of any collective anxiety in the world of his day. Nevertheless, in its fusion of laughter and despair, whatever its causes, his poetry produces a malaise that we are perhaps more sensitive to than his contemporaries. The playwrights of today tend to hide their own anguish beneath the laughter of their characters whereas Apollinaire as a poet was more inclined to alternate the two elements within a single poem. Although the method may be different the emotional effect is nonetheless much the same.

And it is largely Surrealism that we have to thank for this affiliation. By revealing those mysterious and irrational recesses of the mind from which the "hailstones" of laughter emerge, Surrealism has attuned us to the poetic impact of a new kind of theatre and at the same time has disclosed a new tone in the poet whose signature, in black ink, was "Tout terriblement Guillaume Apollinaire."

Source: L. C. Breunig, "The Laughter of Apollinaire," in *Yale French Studies*, No. 31, 1964, pp. 66–73.

Anna Balakian

In the following essay, Balakian discusses Apollinaire's attempts to define and further the role of the artist in the early twentieth century.

An unusual experience in historical self-consciousness must have belonged to those who reached the age of reason with the turn of the century and felt compelled to express awareness of a new era. Dates are arbitrary landmarks, and the world does not change suddenly because a new figure appears on the calendar. Yet, a reading of the more personal writings of those who turned the big leaf from the eighteen hundreds to 1900 gives indications of a psychological upheaval and of a conviction on the part of these writers that if things had not changed they should,—an attitude not as readily associated with the mid-century adult. The writings of Guillaume Apollinaire, born in 1880, show that he was not only conscious of a transition but felt responsible to have a hand in heralding and shaping a new world.

Nineteen-hundred brought to France an international exposition. One of the most important gadgets peddled there was the magical electric bulb; it was also the year of the cinema, the Paris subway, and liquid oxygen. It marked the advent of the supremacy of the scientist in the history of human progress, not the pure scientist who dealt with the abstract, but the man who applied the principles of science and *produced.* Whatever else twentieth-century man was going to possess in the way of distinguishing traits, he seemed assured of a generous share of concrete intelligence, an inventive

spirit, which would provide unfathomable resources to the activity of his imagination.

This development of technical imagination seemed, however, to have no immediate parallel in artistic activities. Art suddenly appeared a weak sister. Since the end of the nineteenth century a rift had taken place between science and art which was growing wider and wider. Art, after a shortlived alliance with positivism, had soon protested, revolted, taken refuge in the dream, unsuspecting that soon science was to claim the dream itself as one of its legitimate domains of investigation. Science seemed to be the destroyer of the marvelous and the mysterious. The resentment was not untouched by a certain amount of jealousy on the part of the artist in regard to the strides made by the scientific inventor.

This conflict is vividly demonstrated by Apollinaire in his *Le Poète assassiné* (1916). Much of this Rabelaisian novelette is autobiographical. We trace the fantastically confused origin and international upbringing of the poet-hero, Croniamantal, which parallels closely the apocryphal data about Apollinaire's own early years; we see the poet making ties with the vanguard painters of his time, like Apollinaire's relations with the cubists. We are exposed to Croniamantal's conception of an extraordinary play containing in a one-paragraph description the seeds of playful irrationality which was to be more notoriously demonstrated the following year in the staging of Apollinaire's play, *Les Mamelles de Tirésias,* and was to reach fruition in the works of the surrealists:

> Close to the sea, a man buys a newspaper. From a house on the prompt side emerges a soldier whose hands are electric bulbs. A giant three meters high comes down from a tree. He shakes the newspaper vendor, who is of plaster. She falls and breaks. At this moment a judge arrives on the scene. He kills everyone with slashes from a razor, while a leg which comes hopping by fells the judge with a kick under the nose, and sings a pretty popular song.

Finally Croniamantal comes face to face with the archenemy of poets, not the smug unimaginative bourgeois, but the champion of the scientists, Horace Tograth, who demands the killing of all poets because they have been overrated and are contributing nothing valuable to present civilization:

> True glory has forsaken poetry for science, philosophy, acrobatics, philanthropy, sociology etc. Today all that poets are good for is to take money that they have not earned since they seldom work and since most of them (except for cabaret singers and a few others) have no talent and consequently no excuse.... The prizes that are awarded to them rightfully belong to workers, inventors, research men ...

Croniamantal protests furiously against this persecution of the artists, and pays with his life. Yet Apollinaire leaves an undertone of criticism not only of the rash generalizations of the glorifiers of science, but also against the artist who has partially merited the attack. The fault for this apparent impotence of poets is partly the public's, that public which demands boredom and unhappiness as the subject matter of literature instead of magic such as is expected of the modern scientist and even of the acrobat. As for Croniamantal, he is Apollinaire's concept of the authentic twentieth-century artist, one who has looked God in the face:

> I am Croniamantal, the greatest of living poets. I have often seen God face to face. I have borne the divine refulgence which my human eyes made softer. I have lived eternity.

He is killed by the science worshipper, who does not realize that Croniamantal is not a stereotype poet. His sculptor friend, cognizant of the hard times through which poets are passing, manages to build him a statue, an extraordinary one, "une profonde statue en rien," ironically symbolic of the emptiness of art and glory, also indicating that the substance of which the true poet is made is undistinguishable to ordinary eyes.

Although in *Le Poète assassiné* the conflict between science and art ends in tragedy and defeat for the artist, Apollinaire defied in his own life and writings the secondary role attributed to the artist in the world of new values. He sought a conciliation between the work of the scientist and of the modern artist. He called himself and those like him "pilgrims of perdition" because they were risking what intellectual security they had as artists to explore the uncertain and the unproven.

Although his conjectures about the potentialities of the modern mind were most precisely stated in an article, "L'Esprit moderne," which appeared in the *Mercure de France* in 1918 shortly after his death, he had been crystallizing these views since his earliest associations with the artistic and literary coteries of Paris.

The need for inventiveness to preserve the prestige of the twentieth-century artist in competition with the twentieth-century technologist was first illustrated through Apollinaire's negative reaction to the existing imitative character of early twentieth-century writings and their author's concern with autobiographical lamentations. This critical attitude is particularly apparent in his evaluation of the current novel, of which he was the principal reviewer on the staff of *La Phalange* for

> " *Perhaps art, following more and more in Apollinaire's footsteps, may rid itself of its apologetic attitude and find, as Apollinaire hoped, that after all the world is just beginning and imagination has yet to come of age.*"

a number of years early in his literary career. Even when commending the originality of a novel such as *Tzimin-Choc* by Louis-Bréon he makes of it an opportunity to chide the average contemporary novelist and expresses the hope that a change of direction is at hand:

> Wonder should be the primary concern of the novelist, we should abandon for a while—long enough to realize what reality is—all this false realism which overwhelms us in most novels of today, and which is only platitude. Under pretext of following the trend for psychological and sentimental naturalism, most authors do not even need to have recourse to their imagination any longer. Autobiography is all that is needed, and those who take the trouble to invent the most insignificant little story become famous. They have almost no competition to fear. But things appear to be changing. Imagination seems to be reclaiming its rightful place in literature.

While literature had been neglecting imagination, science had learned to make maximum use of it. It had cast aside the known patterns of matter and through ingenuity had created new ones. Science's contribution in Apollinaire's opinion was its ability to give to reality a relative meaning and thus to liberate it from its established synonymity with the *natural*. The unnatural could become a reality, as twentieth-century objects, which had no connection with nature, were proving more conclusively every day. The factory worker was all the time creating reality. The automobile had a dynamic existence which removed Apollinaire from the old world and its limited concepts; candidly he states it in his poem, "La Petite Auto:"

> Nous dîmes adieu à toute une époque . . .
> Nous comprîmes mon camarade et moi

Que la petite auto nous avait conduits dans une
époque
Nouvelle
Et bien qu'étant déjà tous deux des hommes mûrs
Nous venions cependant de naître.
Calligrammes

Why not a parallel between the creativeness of applied science and that of the arts? In his preface to *Les Mamelles de Tirésias* he fabricated the word "surreal" to designate the human ability to create the unnatural, and he pointed out that man's first surrealistic act was the creation of the wheel, which imitates the physical function of motion but creates a form entirely independent of natural entities; the wheel becomes for him a product of purely creative work on the part of man, a manifestation of unconscious surrealism. Now the magic of the telephone, the automobile, the electric bulb, the airplane,—creations in the same sense as the wheel—disproved even to a further degree the well accepted adage that there is nothing new under the sun. The same independence from natural objects, which the technologist had achieved by his inventions, and through which he revolutionized the physical appearance of the world, should be sought by the artist in the intellectual realm. To Apollinaire the acquisition of that freedom was to be the fundamental attainment of the modern mind.

One could be a poet in many fields, and the technologist had proved for the moment to be a "poet" in a truer sense than the artist, admits Apollinaire in "L'Esprit moderne":

> Poetry and creation are one and the same thing; he alone must be called poet who invents and creates, as much as it is given to man to create. . . . One can be a poet in all fields: all that is needed is to be adventurous, to be after discoveries.

In retrospect it occurred to him that the poet had until recently been the precursor of the scientific inventor. Had he not conceived of the airplane centuries before the technologist was able to materialize his legend of Icarus? But Apollinaire accepted the fact that for once the scientist had stepped ahead of the artist in the realm of magic, and he took the attitude that since the scientist had become not a destroyer of fantasy but a producer of marvels, his inventiveness should prove a challenge and an incentive to the artist:

> The wonders impose on us the duty of not letting imagination and poetic subtleties lag behind those of the artisans who improve the machine. Already scientific terminology is in deep discord with that of the poets. This is an unbearable state of affairs.

> "L'Esprit moderne"

Art's pitfall in recent times had been its imitative approach to nature. Apollinaire waged war against photography, which to him was in all its technical perfection what smoke is to fire. He made photography the symbol of imitation and the antithesis of art. Some years later Louis Aragon was to repeat Apollinaire's words against photography even more vehemently in defining his concept of the relation between reality and art. Since reality, according to Apollinaire, was dependent not on physical nature but on the mind's creativeness, all the arts had the same basic revolution to promote: that of creating rather than representing the object.

The symbolists had had a similar notion about the "interiority" of art but they had feared the object, feared the *concrete,* which to them had been synonymous with the *natural.* With this difference of attitude in mind Apollinaire had made up the word "surreal" as opposed to the word "symbolist." In his judgment art had to be terribly concrete albeit unnatural. He looked for this twofold quality in the works of his contemporaries, signaled it in the poetry of André Salmon, his companion pilgrim of perdition.

Although Apollinaire showed a certain affinity at first with Marinetti and Company, he soon noticed something superficial in the way the futurists extolled science. They were confusing speed with progress. It was the object of scientific creation which interested them rather than the process of creation. Marinetti's attitude toward science is a far cry from Apollinaire's. When in an unfriendly apostrophe to the moon the futurist praises the electric bulb and belittles the light of the moon, he is led to no adventures of the imagination by the stimulus of the newly created object of science but merely expresses a journalistic appreciation of technological progress. In much the same manner, in his *The Pope's Monoplane* the airplane is admired as a means of escape and not as an impetus to broader artistic visions.

Apollinaire's relations with the cubist painters were of a much more fundamental nature. He found in the cubists the truest competitors of the imaginative technologists. As the perfect illustration of his own theories he defined cubism in *Les Peintres cubistes* (1913) as "an art of conception which tends to rise to the level of creation." In looking back on traditional painting he found too many painters who worshipped plants, stones, water and men. Without being iconoclastic,—as some of his followers were to become—he warned the artist not to be too much attached to the dead. He foretold before José Ortega y Gasset a dehumanization in art, contended that the true artist tends to be inhuman: "They painstakingly search for the traces of inhumanity, traces which are to be found nowhere in nature."

He discovered in the works of the cubists the fourth dimension of reality, which he deemed not only an act of creation but of divinity. This new dimension was conveyed by simultaneous representations in various perspectives, giving the impression of the immensity of space which pointed in all directions at the same time and suggested the infinite. The cubists were thereby producing, according to Apollinaire, a fusion of science and metaphysics. Through his observations of the cubists' activities he was able to make a crucial distinction between the new and the old mental formation of the artist: the traditional artist is a sieve of human experiences and, stimulated by the muse of inspiration, he is a facile interpreter of life; while the new artist, like the scientist, plods from effort to effort in the process of construction, unaided by divine inspiration, but possessing himself the grains of divinity.

Apollinaire's friendship with Picasso, Braque, Picabia and the Douanier Rousseau made him a better apologist for the new art than the painters themselves could have been, thus setting a precedent for closer association between the arts of painting and writing, a relationship which was to prove so significant and influential in the development of dadaism and surrealism.

The influence of ideas is a subtle thing and an elastic one. To what extent an individual is the originator and principal propagator of concepts can be a subjective evaluation. Certainly in the writings of several early century thinkers there are to be found parallel challenges to the new artist to become concretely creative. Saint-Pol-Roux, that remarkable esthetician too long associated exclusively with symbolism, had made in his analysis of current tendencies in French literature in 1913 the same prediction as Apollinaire in regard to the viability of art under the stress of science's competition: "Not to reproduce but to produce. The whole future of art seems to be there." Similarly Max Jacob, who was Apollinaire's friend and contemporary, laid the same stress on inventiveness and the faculty of using concrete imagery in his *Conseils à un jeune poète;* and the gifted young poet, Pierre Reverdy, was seeing in cubism in 1917 much the same thing as Apollinaire and expressing it in almost the same words: "an art of creation and not of reproduction or interpretation." And strangely, in an issue of *La*

Phalange, at the time when Apollinaire was book reviewer of it, there appeared the translation of an article by the American, Gerald Stanley Lee, explaining the modern writers' fear of the machine and deploring their melancholy attitude toward it. The artist, he said, is afraid of the machine only because he has let himself be dominated by it instead of emulating the attitude of mind which created it. The examples could be multiplied; Apollinnaire's importance lies not so much in being the originator of an attitude as in having stated it more provocatively and held to it more persistently than his contemporaries. His ideas on art did not remain in the realm of theories but were illustrated consciously in the major part of his poetic work.

Apollinaire was not a suggestive artist in the way that the symbolists have been found to have developed the art of suggestion. Like the magician whom he wished to emulate, the poet tried to infuse his work with unexpected sparks: visions concretely resplendent and limitless, meant to surprise and mystify the reader in the manner of one who pulls a rabbit out of his sleeve. The old artistic aim was to arouse the emotions of the reader or spectator; now art was to be a sort of jovial game to create not pity nor empathy, but wonder—and sometimes irritation.

His earliest poetical work, *L'Enchanteur pourrissant* (1909), in which he depicts the imprisonment of the enchanter by those who exploited his power but also prophesies the magician's eventual resurrection, ends with a piece of writing called *"Onirocritique,"* which is a natural appendix to his work. It represents Apollinaire's earliest example of inventive writing: in an apocalyptic vision of the universe he combines creatures and disintegrates them into a hundred feet, eyes, in an ever-changing panorama; sounds are transformed into beings, silence into movement, trees consume stars; and each reader is left with his own interpretation of the imagery.

In *Alcools* (1913), his first collection of verse, we find instances of the same mixture of perspectives and sensations. Just as the technologist formed a new world of realities with existing matter, Apollinaire believed that words could make and unmake a universe. He attempted to use his "five senses and a few more" to string side by side images often logically disconnected, demanding of the reader leaps and bounds of the imagination to keep pace with his self-characterized "oblong" vision. His dislocations of temporal and spatial perspective defy ordinary reality but are of this earth in their tactility, colors and scents. *"Cortège"* presents one of the utmost incoherent yet challenging visions in the theme of the inverted flight of a bird and its effects on the relativity of land, sky and light:

> Oiseau tranquille au vol inverse oiseau
> Qui nidifie en l'air
> A la limite où brille déjà ma mémoire
> Baisse ta deuxième paupière
> Ni à cause du soleil ni à cause de la terre
> Mais pour ce feu oblong dont l'intensité ira
> s'augmentant
> Au point qu'il deviendra un jour l'unique lumière

"Le Brasier," "Le Voyageur," "Vendémiaire," could be called experimental poems: attempts to avoid ordinary descriptions of the world and to personalize and thus recreate the realities of fire, sun, sky, sea, heights, depths and the elixirs of human thirst. In "La Maison des morts" he goes as far as to combine the two spheres of life and death, and he allows his living and dead creatures to intermingle and coexperience not abstract but very concrete sensations.

Calligrammes (1918) is a more striking example of his inventive approach to writing. The leitmotiv of this collection of poetry is the newness of the world: new fires, new forms, new colors impatient to be given reality. The wand which has brought about the return of the "age of magic" is the war. Although Apollinaire experienced the tragedy and pathos of war first hand on the front line of action, nonetheless his vigorous imagination often accepted the challenge of new vistas revealed by the inventions pertaining to the war, and he partially at least overcame his emotional susceptibility to the catastrophe. With a prophetic eye he placed the marvels of war above its miseries. Beyond the political conflict he discerned the more fundamental quarrel between tradition and invention:

> Ne pleurez donc pas sur les horreurs de la guerre
> Avant elle nous n'avions que la surface
> De la terre et des mers
> Après elle nous aurons les abîmes
> Le sous-sol et l'espace aviatique
> "Guerre"

He felt the science of war making him at once invisible and ubiquitous; he felt that time had acquired a new flexibility which could make it vanish and be restored. He sensed that man was approaching the exploration of the lower depths not only of the physical world but also of his own consciousness.

In *Calligrammes,* Apollinaire used juxtaposition and discarded symmetry and order much more than in his previous works. These poems are circumstantial in the sense that their point of departure is a factual event or concrete detail of the color of the times. But the submarine cables, the planes fighting overhead, the bombs, the flares, the telephone or the phonograph, each serves as an impetus to new imagery surpassing its circumstantial nature and announcing to Apollinaire the need to alert and sharpen the senses.

When Apollinaire was criticized for the obscurity of the symbols in his play, *Les Mamelles de Tirésias,* he defended himself by stating that true symbolism, like the Sibylline Oracles, lends itself to many meanings, "to numerous interpretations that sometimes contradict each other." *Calligrammes* fearlessly illustrates this theory, thereby setting a new relationship between the artist and his audience: if the writer or painter is no longer to be a mere interpreter of life but a creator, then his erstwhile role of interpreter will be transferred to the reader or spectator, who loses his passive task of absorbing and feeling the message of the artist and assumes the more creative role of relating the sensations of the artist to his own experiences and his own faculties of imagination and association. Thus the flexibility of the visions of the artist are set to a perpetual motion of interpretations, which may in themselves be a form of creative activity. This same technique, called by the uninitiated the obscurity of modern art forms, was to become the *sine qua non* of the works of the dadaist and surrealist disciples of Apollinaire.

Perhaps fifty years from now the greatest mark left by Apollinaire on the current of ideas will be the break he dared to make with the *mal du siècle* attitude which, after having played the poetic strings of melancholy in the nineteenth century, had continued uninterrupted through the undetermined *inquiétude* and unease over the modern world's ills shared by the leading writers before and after the First World War,—and which has been deemed by many critics to be synonymous with profundity. Apollinaire rose like a mountain above the dejection of his times. He felt that it was time to replace "this pessimism more than a century old, ancient enough for such a boring thing." The fat, jovial, buoyant cosmopolite had had his share of the personal disappointments of life and the tragedy of war. In "La Jolie Rousse," the last poem of *Calligrammes,* he sums himself up, not forgetting his misfortunes:

> Me voici devant tous un homme plein de sens
> Connaissant la vie et de la mort ce qu'un vivant
> peut connaître

Ayant éprouvé les douleurs et les joies de l'amour
Ayant su quelquefois imposer ses idées
Connaissant plusieurs langages
Ayant pas mal voyagé
Ayant vu la guerre dans l'Artillerie et l'Infanterie
Blessé à la tête trépané sous le chloroforme
Ayant perdu ses meilleurs amis dans l'effroyable
lutte. . . .

But he has hope in the future with its challenges and surprises. In the words of his friend Philippe Soupault, who recalled Apollinaire's character some years after his death, he was "l'être le plus heureux de vivre" and although sometimes sad, languorous and melancholy, yet never a "désespéré."

Apollinaire had an unfailing faith in modern man who, according to his prediction, would be "plus pur, plus vif et plus savant." He believed more fervently perhaps than any writer of his generation in the future of art, and he announced in one of his very last writings, *Couleur du Temps,* that the resurrection of the poets was approaching. At a time when despair would have been a more natural note to strike on his lyre, he preferred to give man confidence in himself:

Mais il y a si longtemps qu'on fait croire aux gens
Qu'ils n'ont aucun avenir qu'ils sont ignorants à
jamais
Et idiots de naissance
Qu'on en a pris son parti et que nul n'a même
l'idée
De se demander s'il connaît l'avenir ou non
"Sur les Prophéties," *Calligrammes*

Having cultivated in himself the power of prophecy he saw beyond the grimness of mechanization, beyond the dumbness of uncontrolled instincts, beyond the gruesomeness of war. He was not afraid to use the word "progress" although he had inklings that a more appropriate term for what he wanted would be found perhaps in a hundred years. Beyond mechanization was to be the new world of enchanters, beyond uncontrolled instincts would be the discovery of their secret motivations and possibly the eventual improvement of man, beyond the gruesomeness of war would be the letting down of physical barriers, the broadening of the domains of man in all directions. And through all these, what primarily interested him was the possibility of new subjects for the artists' imagination: thousands of new combinations which spell progress in art, as well as in life. The hymn of the future would be "paradisiac," as he announces in his poem "La Nuit d'Avril 1915," and "victory" has for him a more basic meaning than the cessation of hostilities:

La Victoire avant tout sera
De bien voir au loin

De tout voir
De près
Et que tout ait un nom nouveau
"La Victoire," *Calligrammes*

Has Apollinaire's optimism been an anachronism so far in the intellectual history of the twentieth century? Considering the utter pessimism of established writers in most countries today, even including some of the new post-war crop, one is inclined to believe that Apollinaire's tone of hope and faith is alien to the general tenor of the times. Yet many of his contemporaries and younger *confrères* had the conviction that he would exercise great influence on art and literature. Philippe Soupault called him a "signal flare" on the artistic horizon and pointed out that Apollinaire subjected his contemporaries to a sort of contagion: "It is . . . thanks to him that poetry was revived. . . . All he had to do was to write a poem and immediately many poems would be born, publish a book like *Alcools* and all of the poetry of his time found an orientation." André Breton, who according to Soupault was one of the first to realize what a poet Apollinaire was, grants him the credit of having been the reinventer of poetry, in his article on Apollinaire in *Les Pas Perdus;* and he points to the psychological truth revealed in the apparent disorder of his writings, this disorder which through Breton was to become a major characteristic of surrealism. Awareness of Apollinaire's role as a motivator of ideas went beyond French boundaries. In his preface to Apollinaire's *Il y a,* Ramón Gómez de la Serna states that he was the poet who has suffered the least degree of death in dying.

Today, observing what used to be the initially despairing school of surrealists who borrowed so much from Apollinaire's technical concepts but rejected his tone of optimism, one notes that most of the present and past members of the coterie have undergone a change of outlook and in the midst of the tragic social and political chaos of troubled Europe have adopted the note of fortified prophecy bequeathed to them by their precursor. The war and post-war poems of Breton, Aragon, Char and Eluard abound in the same type of energetic optimism and hope as in the vigorous poems of Apollinaire written during the previous war. The enthusiasm shown on the thirtieth anniversary of his death last year, the number of memoirs appearing lately about him, and "the great enthusiasm and fervent admiration of Apollinaire which animates the youth of today," according to a letter of Madame Apollinaire addressed to me last year, may be further indication of increasing influence and even of a new trend.

For the critic to be prophetic is even more presumptuous than for the creative writer, and yet I venture to ask what can be the utter and outer limits of the pessimism of the more popular and distinguished writers of today? Silence or suicide, both literary dead ends! This brings Apollinaire's prophecy into the category of Pascal's wager. He can be right or wrong. If wrong, no matter, for the line of artists will have extinguished itself. If he is right in believing in the energy and creativeness of the modern mind, he is indeed a herald of a new age of enchantment and will loom more and more prodigious in the history of ideas as well as of literature.

Science is never pessimistic about its powers and is never ashamed to foretell beyond its existing limitations its capacity for tomorrow. Perhaps art, following more and more in Apollinaire's footsteps, may rid itself of its apologetic attitude and find, as Apollinaire hoped, that after all the world is just beginning and imagination has yet to come of age.

Source: Anna Balakian, "Apollinaire and the Modern Mind," in *Yale French Studies*, No. 4, 1949, pp. 79–90.

Sources

Apollinaire, Guillaume, "Always," in *The Self-Dismembered Man: Selected Later Poems of Guilluame Apollinaire*, translated by Donald Revell, Wesleyan University Press, 2004, p. 109.

Balakian, Anna, "Apollinaire and the Modern Mind," in *Yale French Studies*, No. 4, 1949, pp. 79, 81, 83–87.

Bates, Scott, *Guillaume Apollinaire*, Twayne Publishers, 1967, p. 111.

Davies, Margaret, Review of *Calligrammes*, in *Modern Language Review*, Vol. 77, No. 3, July 1982, pp. 730–31.

Greet, Anne Hyde, "Commentary," in *Calligrammes: Poems of Peace and War (1913–1916)*, translated by Anne Hyde Greet, University of California Press, 1980, p. 435.

Lockerbie, S. I., "Introduction," in *Calligrammes: Poems of Peace and War (1913–1916)*, translated by Anne Hyde Greet, University of California Press, 1980, pp. 1–3.

Markus, M. B., Review of *Calligrammes*, in *Library Journal*, August 1980, p. 1639.

Revell, Donald, "Translator's Afterword," in *The Self-Dismembered Man: Selected Later Poems of Guillaume Apollinaire*, Wesleyan University Press, 2004, p. 141.

Shattuck, Roger, "Introduction," in *Selected Writings of Guillaume Apollinaire*, translated by Roger Shattuck, New Directions, 1971, p. 26.

Further Reading

Berry, David, *The Creative Vision of Guillaume Apollinaire: A Study of Imagination*, Anma Libri, 1982.
    Berry traces the development of Apollinaire's theories on creativity and their application in his poetry.

Davies, Margaret, *Apollinaire*, St. Martin's Press, 1965.
    Davies explores biographical information about Apollinaire and presents analyses of his work.

Mackworth, Cecily, *Guillaume Apollinaire and the Cubist Life*, Horizon, 1963.
    Mackworth analyzes the cubist artists' influence on Apollinaire's life and work.

Steegmuller, Francis, *Apollinaire: Poet among the Painters*, Farrar, Straus, 1963.
    In this study, Steegmuller outlines Apollinaire's relationship with the artists of his age.

Themerson, Stefan, *Apollinaire's Lyrical Ideograms*, Gaberbocchus, 1968.
    Themerson concentrates on the style of Apollinaire's later poetry.

At the Cancer Clinic

Ted Kooser's poem "At the Cancer Clinic" is told from the point of view of a patient in a waiting room observing another patient. The woman the narrator describes is frail and too weak to walk on her own; she is being helped into the examining area by two women, who accompany her on either side. The patients in the waiting room, including the poem's narrator, marvel at the ill woman's determination and inner strength, as the poem tries to capture the feeling of awe that people often get when they realize that someone who is battling against unimaginable physical weakness is struggling to persevere with the little strength they have.

This poem is included in Kooser's 2004 collection *Delights & Shadows*, which was awarded the Pulitzer Prize for Poetry that year. Its plain style and clear, simple language are typical of Kooser, who has served two terms as the poet laureate of the United States. Avoiding the obvious stereotypes about infirmity that another poem might lament, "At the Cancer Clinic" invites readers to reflect on the strength of the woman and not to dwell on the illness that has ravaged her; as a result, the poem is actually a much more uplifting experience than its title might at first suggest.

Author Biography

Ted Kooser was born in Ames, Iowa, in April 1939. His father was a storekeeper and his mother was

Ted Kooser

2004

Ted Kooser © AP/Wide World

a teacher. He attended Iowa State University in Ames, receiving his bachelor's degree in 1962, the same year that he married his first wife, Diana Tressler. The couple had one son but later divorced. Kooser taught high school briefly and then enrolled in the graduate writing program at the University of Nebraska. By his own admission, he did not have the discipline to be an academic, and so his post-graduate career ended after only a year.

In 1964, Kooser took an entry-level position at Bankers Life, an insurance company in Lincoln, Nebraska; this was the start of a thirty-five-year career in the insurance industry. During the years that he worked in insurance, Kooser wrote poetry, usually in the morning, before going to the office. He also taught at the University of Nebraska as an adjunct professor of writing from 1975 to 1990.

His first collection of poetry, *Official Entry Blank*, was published in 1969. Over the next few decades, he continued to write and publish, winning several major awards, including two National Endowment for the Arts fellowships in poetry, the Pushcart Prize, the Stanley Kunitz Prize, the James Boatwright Prize, and two Society of Midland Authors prizes. He also ascended in his business life, rising to the position of vice president for public relations at Lincoln Benefit Life. In 1977, he married Kathleen Rutledge.

In the late 1990s, Kooser was diagnosed with cancer. The news forced him to change the priorities of his life. He quit the insurance industry and gave up teaching. While recuperating, he wrote poetry daily and sent it to his friend, the author Jim Harrison; these pieces were published in a book in 2001, titled *Winter Morning Walks: One Hundred Postcards to Jim Harrison*, which won the Nebraska Book Award for Poetry. As his health improved, he returned to teaching at the University of Nebraska.

Kooser was appointed Poet Laureate Consultant of the United States in 2004, a position that has brought him an international following. His reappointment for the following year came during the same week that he won the Pulitzer Prize for *Delights & Shadows*, the collection that contains "At the Cancer Clinic." In 2005, he was living on farmland in rural Garland, Nebraska.

Poem Summary

Lines 1–3

"At the Cancer Clinic" begins with a character who is identified by no other designation than "she." The body of the poem does not identify the setting, which readers already know from the title. The woman being described moves across the waiting room of the cancer clinic with the help of two other women. She is young, or at least young enough to be taken for the sister of two young women. They are helping her through the waiting room toward the examination rooms.

Readers can infer a couple of things from this brief description. For one, the woman being observed is so weak that she needs help walking: not just the extra strength of one person but, indeed, a person on each side of her, to balance her. That she is walking at all and is not chair-bound or bedridden indicates a sense of pride and inner resolve. Finally, the fact that her sisters are willing to take time to attend her doctor appointments with her shows that she has a loving family and implies that she is a person who deserves their affection. Line 3 introduces an observer, the "I" who is narrating the poem.

Lines 4–5

In the few words of these two lines, Kooser reveals much about the three sisters whom the narrator sees. The main one, the woman being helped, is apparently not too decayed from her illness: though she cannot walk without help, her body is still substantial enough to pull down on the arms that are supporting her, which bend under her weight. All three women are described as reflecting the same sort of attitude, which the poem describes with the words "straight" and "tough." Although illness is clearly a burden on them, they face it with resolve and with a unity that makes the bearing of the helpers indistinguishable from that of the person who is actually ill; even though only one body is stricken, all three are struggling with the disease.

Lines 6–8

Line 6 begins with the narrator's interpretation of the bearing of three sisters: it is courage. There are other things that it could be, other ways that readers could imagine this scene if Kooser did not describe it that way. Their "straight, tough bearing," described in line 5, might have been read as resolve, anger, resignation, numbness, or fear. Using the word "courage" spares the poem all of the description that it would have taken to get this concept across through imagery. The statement that the sisters' stance against cancer is courageous affects how readers imagine all of the rest of the actions in the poem.

Lines 7 and 8 introduce a new character, a nurse who is holding the door for the sisters as they approach the entrance to the examination area. Kooser emphasizes the difficulty that the three sisters have in moving across the room by telling readers that the trek, which cannot really be that far, must seem like a long distance to them. He reiterates that idea by having the nurse "call" to them across the distance.

The nurse is nothing but supportive: smiling, calling encouragement, and holding the door. In this poem, all of the people surrounding the cancer patient are selfless and supportive. While other poems might focus attention on the ways that hardship isolates individuals, "At the Cancer Clinic" concerns itself with the ways that people pull together with support and kindness.

Lines 9–10

After being identified by her kindness, the nurse is described in a way that contrasts with her actions. Her clothes are called "crisp white sails"; literally, this image refers to the stiff, starched points of her uniform cap, but figuratively it implies rigidity, unyieldingness, sterility, and impatience. She is, in fact, quite patient, as Kooser

Media Adaptations

- The Library of Congress's website at www.loc .gov/poetry/laureate-1990–2005.html discusses Kooser's background and his work as a poet laureate and provides several links to other websites about him.

- The page that the Nebraska Center for Writers keeps on Kooser at mockingbird.creighton.edu/ NCW/kooser.htm contains links to poetry, biography, and excerpts from book reviews.

makes a point of noting with a slight hint of surprise in line 9.

Line 10 refers to the woman being observed as "the sick woman." The word "sick" is simple and direct: Kooser does not try to intellectualize her condition with a more complex description, nor does he try to wring pathos from it by using a word that is more graphic or disturbing.

Lines 11–13

In keeping with the tone of the rest of the poem, the narrator does not try to disguise the woman's condition. She is wearing a hat, probably because, like most people who take chemotherapy to combat cancer, she has lost her hair at the same time that her white blood cell count is diminished, making her vulnerable to disease. Chances are that if it is a "funny" hat, the sick woman has not been expending much thought on her wardrobe or caring about how she looks. She might also be exhibiting a sense of humor in the face of duress.

Line 12 looks at the sick woman's movement from her point of view, as if she is an objective observer and not an active participant. This estrangement from her own body gives readers an idea of what it must be like for her to be ill with cancer. Her weakness is shown in the awkward motion of her feet: each foot swings forward, as if by chance and not by its own volition; when it lands, it has weight put on it, taking the weight off the other foot. In these few words, the poem captures the awkwardness of severe infirmity and the lack of coordination of a body that is no longer under control.

Lines 14–15

Having directly characterized as "courage" the attitudes of the sick woman and the women who are helping her in line 6, the narrator makes sure that readers understand the situation by pointing out emotions that one might expect to be involved but that are strangely absent: restlessness, impatience, and anger. The lack of these feelings is extended to include the whole range of what the narrator can see: there are other patients in the clinic's waiting room, as is implied by the poem's final line, and the narrator is crediting them with having controlled emotions as well.

Lines 16–17

The moment of watching this brave woman walk, with help, toward her examination is called a "mold" in line 16; it is an empty form, waiting to be filled with a meaning that will then take on its shape. Kooser says that this mold is filled with Grace, which he capitalizes.

This moment of Grace, with a capital "G," is not noticed just by the poet but is also palpable to all who see it. The magazines mentioned in line 17 are shuffled by people who are trying to wait their turns, impatient to see the doctor, to find out prognoses and get on with their own lives, but they fall silent as everyone there notices the sick woman accepting help. They all feel the Grace, and it takes them away from their small, ordinary concerns.

Themes

Illness

The woman described in "At the Cancer Clinic" is clearly at odds with her body. She does not have the strength to walk on her own, struggling with each step. The narrator describes her as staring at her feet as she walks, as if they are independent of her and she is interested in what they are doing. Her body is not under her control.

Cancer is a state in which cells grow without control. As opposed to normal cells, which reproduce in an orderly fashion and limit themselves, cancer cells are inclined to keep growing, creating tumors and blockages that impede the body's normal functions. It is plain to see that the woman described in this poem is very ill. One of the ironies of treating cancer is that some of the

most effective treatments, most notably chemotherapy and radiation therapy, weaken the body; they have to attack the cancer cells and kill them while trying to do as little harm to the good cells as possible. Someone like the woman in the poem might be more weakened by the treatment than by her disease, even though the treatment will eventually make her stronger. The point of the poem, though, is that she has surrendered neither to her illness nor to the suffering that she must go through to eradicate the illness.

Dignity

Despite the fact that she is weakened, there is no sign that the woman described here feels any loss of dignity; in fact, the case is quite to the contrary. Kooser gives the detail of the "funny knit cap" to let readers know that this is a person who is not concerned with what people think of her weakened appearance. Although the narrator of the poem never talks to her or hears her talk, he can tell from her behavior that the illness that has weakened her body has not damaged her sense of pride.

The poem plays off of the common perception that a person in as diminished a physical condition as this woman is would be expected to feel a loss of dignity. The more that readers expect her to feel the indignity of her weakness, the more heartening it is to see that, regardless of her trouble, she can hold her head up. The other people in the room respond to the woman's sense of dignity by according her even more respect; her dignity creates respect for her.

Compassion

The narrator does not have any direct contact with the woman, so he cannot say whether the two women helping her walk are her sisters, but there is something in their interaction that makes this likely. Kooser uses the idea of familial relationship as an abbreviated way to express the patience and concern that they show toward her. They walk slowly, bearing the weight of the sick woman between them and giving her the kind of compassionate care that an onlooker would assume comes from a family bond.

Having set the scene with the compassion of the two helpers, the poem goes on to show that this woman's dignified bearing elicits compassion from all who see her. The nurse holds the door for her and waits patiently, even though it is clear that the woman is taking a long time to cross the room. A person with a physical infirmity could bring out the

Topics For Further Study

- The narrator of this poem assumes that the people who are with the sick woman are her sisters. Read about people who care for terminally ill patients and make a chart to compare the characteristics that they have in common.

- Kooser uses the phrase "crisp white sails" to describe the nurse's uniform. Members of the medical profession have come to purposely shun the idea of wearing clothes that convey the ideas of severity and sterility. Look through catalogs of medical uniforms and present the best ones to your class in a discussion of why you think they would be effective.

- Rewrite this scene as a poem or short story from the point of view of one of the women accompanying the sick woman. Be sure to focus on what she thinks of the poet who is watching them.

- As the U.S. population ages, medical facilities, such as cancer clinics, have become viable commercial ventures. Write a song that could be used in a television or radio commercial for such a place, taking care to be tasteful as well as memorable. Perform it for your class.

---

worst in some people, but the people at this particular cancer clinic have nothing but compassion as they watch this woman. Kooser makes a point of going beyond describing a few compassionate people to make the blanket statement that "there is no restlessness or impatience / or anger anywhere in sight." There may be people in the world who could face this woman's problems coldly, but not at the cancer clinic.

Grace

There are many different understandings of the word "grace," which holds a special relevance at the end of "At the Cancer Clinic." In the Catholic religion, there are two distinct types of grace, both of them pertaining to this poem. "Sanctifying grace" is the supernatural life that exists in a person, the soul. The sick woman in this poem behaves with dignity, showing herself to be full of sanctifying grace. "Actual grace," on the other hand, exists outside a person: it is God's recognition of a good life. This is the kind of grace that fills the room of the poem—a recognition that the situation, and not just any one person, has achieved unity with the Almighty. By using such a word, Kooser elevates the situation described in the poem from one that is extremely moving in a common way to one that is transcendent and supernatural.

Style

First-Person Narrator

Although the focus of this poem is on the sick woman, the women helping her walk, and the nurse, there is another important character who is neither discussed nor described: the person referred to, just once in the third line, as "I." Readers who know that Kooser, the author, went through a bout with cancer around the time that he wrote this poem will be tempted to assume that Kooser is talking about himself, probably even relating an experience that he once had. It is, however, very possible that the incident described was entirely formed within his imagination. It is also possible that the "I" speaking to the reader could be any type of person: young or old, male or female. The first-person narrator is a persona that the author wears, a mask, and not necessarily the author himself. By using a first-person narrator, Kooser reaches a level of intimacy that would not come out if the poem were entirely descriptive. Readers are asked not only to experience the event itself but also to experience what it would be like to be there and see it unfold.

Imagery

In some places, this poem conveys its ideas with abstract terms, as when the narrator describes the sick woman and her helpers as having "the straight, tough bearing of courage." Words like these do not represent the physical world with objects that readers can understand experiencing with their five senses. More often, "At the Cancer Clinic" conveys its ideas by presenting concrete images. A concrete image is one that appeals to the reader's sense of smell, taste, touch, sight, or sound.

Concrete imagery is often visual: human beings experience the world visually, for the most part, and so poems present the world visually. In this poem, there are visual images in "the crisp, white sails" of the nurse's uniform, the patient's knit cap, and the swing of the foot, which the patient experiences as a visual event rather than a feeling. The poem also has the audible image of the sound of shuffling magazines, and the tactile, or touch, image of the two women feeling the sick woman's weight. Concrete images like these help readers feel that they are in the scene, experiencing the event the narrator is talking about, and also help communicate the poem's main themes.

Historical Context

Midwestern Poetry

When Kooser's poetry is discussed, reference is usually made to the fact that he has spent his entire career in Nebraska. He is characterized as being a midwestern poet. Midwestern poetry is thought of as poetry that uses plain language and simple structure. To some extent, such a generalization is excessively broad, as most generalizations are. The Midwest is a wide range, encompassing the Great Plains, the areas around the Great Lakes, and the eastern fringes of the Rocky Mountains. It would be highly improbable that the same sensibilities exist in all writers in that geographic terrain, from Detroit, Michigan, to Bismarck, South Dakota, from the Germans who founded Milwaukee to the relatively new Vietnamese population of the Quad Cities at the Illinois-Iowa border. Even if there are differences within the region, though, the basic characteristics are still thought of when talking about midwestern writing.

The tendency toward directness and simplicity in literature is often linked to the physical environment of the area. The northern United States is known for difficult, freezing winters and blistering summers. Unlike other northern areas, the Midwest has the additional drawback of being mostly flat. The area has fertile farmland—soil enriched by the glaciers that drained toward the center as they

created the Mississippi River—but the temperature extremes make farming a struggle. It is the constant battle with nature and the bleakness of the mostly flat landscape that is said to make up the character of the Midwest, and literary critics often see these influences in the writing of the region's authors, who tend to produce works that cling tenaciously to difficult subjects without much stylistic embellishment. Sherwood Anderson, one of America's great short-story writers and a son of Indiana and Illinois, noted in his essay "An Apology for Crudity": "The awakening to the reality of 'the life we have' has been responsible in great measure for the strength of midwestern poetry as well as prose."

"At the Cancer Clinic" has the serious, no-frills style of midwestern poetry. While southern literature is often associated with the faded antebellum tradition, northeastern writing with the cultural refinement that America has developed since its inception, and West Coast writing with the optimism of a people who traveled as far as they could to seek the promise of something more, midwestern writing generally refers to a steadily modulated style without any social pretenses. It is a culture that speaks plainly and determinedly, much as this poem does.

Critical Overview

Kooser built his poetry career quietly over the course of thirty years, from the 1960s through the 1990s, with little recognition beyond the small inner circle of poets and poetry teachers from whom he earned universal respect. That changed in 2004, when he was appointed to the position of poet laureate of the United States: almost overnight, his name was elevated to international attention.

Most reviews of his work make a point of mentioning Kooser's Nebraska upbringing, placing his poetry into a larger context of midwestern poetry. As Ray Olson puts it in his review of *Delights & Shadows* (Kooser's first collection after the announcement of his appointment as poet laureate), "Kooser is a poet of place." In part, he attributes this label to the fact that Kooser's poetry is more concerned with immediate, at-hand issues than with trying to cope with political or social trends. Olson explains, "Kooser is less big-C culturally concerned, less anxious about the destiny of nation and world," than other poets.

Brian Phillips, reviewing the collection for *Poetry*, notes that the Nebraska connection sometimes has led reviewers to use words like "heartland" and "homespun" derogatorily in their reviews. This, he theorizes, has less to do with Kooser's writing than with those critics' preconceptions. "There is some quaintness in Kooser's new book," he says of *Delights & Shadows*, but "it comes more from Kooser's outlook than from any particular flaw in his use of rural Nebraska settings or his plainspoken register." Phillips goes on to point out that Kooser's "poems are written from the perspective of a man who has resolved his life's pressing conflicts, who now moves familiarly among the larger, lasting uncertainties." What reviewers take to be regional traits are actually aspects of the poet's personality.

Writers also have drawn attention to Kooser's visual sense, as displayed in this collection. In a 2005 review in *Midwest Quarterly*, Kathleen De Grave notes that "opening Ted Kooser's collection of poetry, *Delights & Shadows*, is like walking into an art gallery, each poem a painting or photograph, sometimes a sculpture." After describing the book's four distinct sections, De Grave says in summary that "the common threads are the bright image, the compassionate tone, and the insight into human nature."

Criticism

David Kelly

David Kelly is an instructor of creative writing and literature. In this essay, he makes the case that a poem as plain and direct as this one can be read for a richer meaning by paying attention to the line endings.

Kooser's poetry is clearly an example of midwestern folk art; like all folk art, it sometimes seems simple, the kind of work that could be accomplished by earnest but underskilled people who are guided by what their hearts tell them is right. In poem after poem, Kooser's work focuses readers' attention on the subject he is talking about and away from the poet or the poet's style.

Poets use the techniques that critics identify and explain, such as rhyme and rhythm, for emphasis: to polish the meanings embedded in their words and to make the situations described in their works clearer. Technique and poetic style are tools for taking their poems to a level of meaning beyond that which the words can reach on their own. There is another school of thought, though, that treats such structural elements as distractions or even as useless decorations, which call too much

> *'Grace' is certainly the most important single word in the poem: it is a metaphysical, spiritual concept, an intangible thing that becomes tangible in one clear, lucid moment.*

attention to themselves and away from the central points they are supposed to be assisting in making.

An example of one extreme of this view is prose poetry, which uses none of the physical elements that are usually associated with poems; prose poems focus on the meanings and sounds of words, but they do not make use of their arrangement on the page. Kooser's poetry is not as unadorned as prose poetry, but it comes close. A typical piece from his 2004 collection *Delights & Shadows* tends to run down the middle of the page in a large, blocky rectangle, each line approximately the same length, often in one continuous piece with no stanza breaks.

With so little going on in the way of technique, critics have characterized Kooser's style as "plain." There is still an undeniable structural element to Kooser's poems. The very fact that the poems do run down the center of the page means that they are products of design. Unlike prose or prose poetry, in which the ends of the lines are determined by the size of the paper and the size of the type, it is clear, in even the plainest of poems written in Kooser's style, that care has been put into determining where each line should end (and, conversely, where each following line should begin).

Assuming that the poet has chosen his line endings, an examination of the end words should reveal something about the poem's priorities. As with any critical examination of structural elements, this is not meant to reveal a secret code embedded by the poet only for those who hold the answer; rather, it is a way of appreciating the dynamics that already exist in the piece. For example, the main idea in a poem like Kooser's "At the Cancer Clinic" is not difficult for the average reader to understand. The poem depicts a scene in the waiting room of a

What Do I Read Next?

- Kooser's book *The Poetry Home Repair Manual: Practical Advice for Beginning Poets* (2005) outlines his philosophy of poetry for students and the theories by which he lives.

- Kooser has published his postcards to his friend Jim Harrison in *Winter Morning Walks: One Hundred Postcards to Jim Harrison* (2001), written while undergoing treatment for cancer.

- Kooser cowrote with Jim Harrison *Braided Creek* (2003), about his diagnosis with cancer.

- Jim Harrison's novella *Tracking* is a long, twisting, semi-autobiographical account of his own life. It is included in the collection *The Summer He Didn't Die* (2005).

- Many of the poems in *The Cancer Poetry Project: Poems by Cancer Patients and Those Who Love Them* (2001), edited by Karin B. Miller, are by nonprofessional poets, people drawn together by a similar life experience, but they resemble Kooser's work in their emotional focus.

- The fiction writer Ron Hansen has a prose style that is as controlled and yet plain as Kooser's is in poetry. Hansen's story "Wickedness," from his collection *Nebraska: Stories* (1995), is a fine, poetic work of haunting imagery.

- Lisel Mueller is another midwestern writer whose style is often associated with that of Kooser. Her poetry is informed by personal history, such as immigrating to the United States at an early age and experiencing the death of her mother. Her poem "Curriculum Vitae," from the 1995 collection *Alive Together: New and Selected Poems*, is a wonderful introduction to her work.

---

medical facility, describing, with awe and admiration, the progress of a woman weakened by disease, while, with the help of two women the narrator takes to be her sisters, she crosses the room. The action in the poem is this: the woman and her aides walk tentatively; a nurse holds the door to the examination area and waits, patient and smiling, for the sick woman; sensing the miracle of her struggle against affliction, the onlookers bring an end to the small distractions that characterize life in a waiting room. Kooser does nothing to obscure or hide these actions.

The scene itself has enough inherent power to earn its readers' attention, and there is a very good possibility that any more stylistic technique would have done harm, drawing attention to the poem and the poet and away from the touching humanity of the situation. The plain style works, but, as mentioned earlier, a plain poem is certainly not one that is free of style. What little Kooser has done to shape the material on the page does have some, if only the most subtle, effect on what the poem has to say.

"At the Cancer Clinic" contains seventeen lines. Without a rhythm or a structure, the poet is left to make the decision about where each of those lines should end. In five of the seventeen, the answer is simple: they end at the natural break in the language, with punctuation, either a period or comma (any other punctuation marks, such as the dash, semicolon, colon, or ellipsis, would be a bit flamboyant amid such plain language). The seventeen lines end with these words: "door," "rooms," "sisters," "arms," "bearing," "be," "door," "encouragement," "sails," "woman," "cap," "forward," "weight," "impatience," "Grace," "moment," and "still." Each of these words is significant: collectively, they reveal some telling patterns.

When these words are listed on a page, it is hard not to notice some basic similarities. For one thing, there is the preponderance of nouns, thirteen in all. This makes the poem even more plainspoken than Kooser's basic rhetorical style, even though it might seem that such a thing would not be possible. Along with verbs, nouns are the basic building blocks of the English language. They could be considered even more basic than verbs because of what they stand for. Nouns represent tangible things, often things that one can wrap hands around and hold, while verbs represent actions, which have no physical presence. Verbs are, by their nature, more ephemeral, more intangible, more conceptual. A reader might have trouble imagining an action that is described, but a noun speaks for itself. Speaking for themselves is especially true of the nouns on this list. Most of them are simple, direct, one- or two-syllable words describing concrete objects: "door" (twice), "cap," "women," and "sails." This is *very* plain language.

A few of the nouns that the poem uses are slightly more complex. "Sisters," for example, describes the same basic object as "women" but includes within it a reference to a specific social relationship. "Bearing" is used as a gerund here, a noun derived from a verb form: in itself, this transformation is not very complicated, but it is complicated by comparison to the other nouns. "Encouragement" is completely abstract: it is a thing, but not a tangible thing. The same holds true for "impatience."

Near the end of the poem, there are two lines that end with words that, taken together, capture the sense of what "At the Cancer Clinic" has to say, in a sort of summary. "Grace" is certainly the most important single word in the poem: it is a metaphysical, spiritual concept, an intangible thing that becomes tangible in one clear, lucid *moment*. This "moment" happens to be the word ending the following line. These stand out because they are so appropriate to the overall point, which is to take readers into a moment of Grace (capitalized by Kooser). It is such a sacred idea that using language any more complex than that which Kooser uses here would be almost blasphemous, but there is certainly nothing wrong with his giving emphasis to the very words that convey his meaning.

If the words that end the individual lines are assumed to carry special weight in a poem, then the words that end the entire poem must resonate that much more. "Grace," important as it is, is not the final word. That honor goes to "still." It is a word with multiple meanings, at least two of which are relevant here. The concept of immobility is one of them, as the poem says that people, sensing the room fill with Grace, fall still. There is, however, no denying the sense of "still" as a situation that is continuing, as something that has existed before and remains so moment by moment. Each of these dual meanings works with the word that precedes it in the poem, the verb: "growing still" means slowing to a condition of immobility, and "growing still" means continuing to grow. Again, both

meanings fit the people in the waiting room, who are just starting to apprehend the presence of Grace in the room as the poem reaches its conclusion.

A poem like "At the Cancer Clinic" is accessible to most readers. Using simple language and few poetic techniques, Kooser makes poetry look easy, taking readers into the heart of emotional situations without making them feel the presence of the poem. Even after examining the words that end his poem's lines and seeing just how *right* they all are, it still is not too clear whether Kooser arranged these end words with much deliberation. It would not take much of a stretch of the imagination to believe that they just rolled off his pen and landed in the right places, a result of divine inspiration. Keeping alive the belief that such might be the case is what good writing is always about.

Source: David Kelly, Critical Essay on "At the Cancer Clinic," in *Poetry for Students*, Thomson Gale, 2006.

Lisa Trow

Lisa Trow is a published poet and journalist and has been an instructor of creative writing. In this essay, she discusses the use of free verse in allowing careful word choice to express meaning.

Kooser's poetry is so easy to read and understand that readers might assume that anyone could have written it. But its simplicity is really an aid to the reader in reaching for the poem's deeper meanings. By refraining from using complicated and formal poetic devices that might have driven away the average reader, Kooser has cleared the way for readers, allowing them easier access to the poem. There is no rhyme scheme, no singsong cadence, and no flowery language that many of us associate with the poets we have been assigned to read in literature classes. Kooser's simple poetry, like the work of many contemporary poets, relies on its ability to create an image. It depends on carefully chosen words to give us the key to the poem's meaning.

Formal style, with prescribed line endings, line length, and rhythm, creates poetry that is part literature and part engineering. Rhyme and form work together to support the poem's main idea. The poet should not, however, allow form to intrude jarringly on the reader's appreciation of the poem. Formal poetry offers the poet one traditional way to integrate all the tools at his or her disposal—the sound of the words spoken together and the shape they form on the page—using universal poetic principles. The artistry in using such formal devices in this way is apparent in its subtlety.

> *The artistry in free verse often lies in the ability of the poet to choose words that most powerfully convey the poem's meaning. In contrast to formal poetry, the effect of free verse is sensual rather than intellectual."*

Some modern poets, such as Theodore Roethke and Anthony Hecht, have used form successfully. Although some modern and contemporary poets have continued to employ formal verse forms, many contemporary poets have avoided form for the freedom to write without constraints. The reader who is drawn to poetry but challenged by the conventions of more formal types of verse may enjoy reading Kooser's uncomplicated free verse for that reason.

Formal verse typically requires the poet to write to fulfill the rules of the chosen poetic form. For example, in an English sonnet the poet must write exactly fourteen lines of poetry. Each line of a sonnet contains a certain number of unstressed and stressed syllables, which gives the poem a singsong quality when it is read aloud. In the sonnet form, the poet must rhyme the words ending every other line until the closing couplet, made up of two rhyming lines. Poets attempting a sonnet may feel as though they must "fill in the blanks" to meet the requirements of the form and must choose words that work with the set rhyme scheme. With free verse, poets can select whatever words they wish. The artistry in free verse often lies in the ability of the poet to choose words that most powerfully convey the poem's meaning. In contrast to that of formal poetry, the effect of free verse is sensual rather than intellectual.

Critics have called Kooser's poetry homespun and plainspoken and likened it to the work of such other American poets as William Carlos Williams and Edgar Lee Masters, and they have praised his ability to choose exactly the right words to create powerful images. Kooser's conscious and deliberate use of specific nouns, adjectives, and verbs in describing the simple scene in "At the Cancer Clinic" give clues to its meaning.

In the seventeen lines of "At the Cancer Clinic," Kooser describes the slow, arduous procession of a gravely ill woman and two companions to an examining room, where a smiling nurse is waiting for the patient. There is no discussion of the sick woman's history, no clue about what she was like before she became ill with cancer, and no epilogue to let the reader know what became of her. The language of the poem, however, is suggestive of death. This feeling begins with the first line: "She is being helped toward the open door." In the passive voice, Kooser is telling us that the sick woman in the poem is past activity; she must be acted upon. Two young women, who the narrator assumes are the sick woman's sisters, are each bearing "the weight of an arm" as they help her down the hall. "Weight" is used again in association with the sick woman in line 13, emphasizing the dead weight her body has become.

There are four women in the poem—the sick woman, her two sisters, and the nurse waiting at the door of the examining room. Kooser devotes many adjectives to describing them, to contrast their stations in life. The young women are comparatively vital and strong, bearing up under the weight of their sister's ravaged body with toughness and courage. The nurse is good-natured and patient, and Kooser's comparison of her white, crisp aspect to "sails" suggests that she has a stately, ceremonial role in this important procession.

In contrast, Kooser uses no personal adjectives to describe his cancer victim, mentioning only a "funny knit cap" that she is wearing, presumably to cover a head denuded by chemotherapy. In fact, the sick woman is barely more of a personal presence than the unnamed onlookers watching her. She is even divorced from the functioning of her own body, watching her feet "scuffing forward" down the hall as though she had nothing to do with motivating them. Instead, the sick woman's role seems to be to function as a symbol of death and to elicit reactions from those touched by it. In this way, her courage is skillfully implied.

The lack of any mention of what the sick woman feels helps to create the transcendent mood of the experience that so impresses the poet: "There is no restlessness or impatience / or anger anywhere in sight." Then the poem pivots on its most important word, "Grace," which Kooser emphasizes by ending the line there, in mid-phrase. In this way, Kooser makes us feel the awe of the moment and gives us the very word we need to describe it. Formal poetry might not have allowed him to make such a fluid choice.

Because of the poem's lack of artifice, anyone will find "At the Cancer Clinic" accessible and its meaning clear. It would be a mistake for the reader to dismiss this free-verse poem as simple because of its lack of formal structure, however. Many poets have used traditional poetic forms to create powerful works of poetry, enhanced rather than inhibited by the requirements of the form. Still, free verse opens up the craft to a wider audience of readers who may not have the literary sophistication to appreciate the flourishes of rhyme and meter. Kooser's use of free verse shows his respect for the average reader and implies his respect for their deeper emotional sensibilities. Free verse also allows Kooser a varied palette of nouns, verb forms, and adjectives in painting this indelible portrait of bravery. The economy of language he uses in "At the Cancer Clinic" perhaps best suits the nature of the poem.

Source: Lisa Trow, Critical Essay on "At the Cancer Clinic," in *Poetry for Students*, Thomson Gale, 2006.

Jo McDougall

In the following essay, McDougall explores how Kooser "finds his crossroads in the mystery and eternal truths of the plain folk and unpretentious subjects of the Great Plans" in Delights & Shadows.

In her enlightening essay about Southern literature, "The Regional Writer" in *Mystery and Manners,* Flannery O'Connor makes a fascinating and well-known comment: "The writer operates at a peculiar crossroads where time and place and eternity somehow meet. His problem is to find that location." Although her essay is primarily about Southern writers, her comments apply to all writers who use regional details to transmit what they believe to be eternal, abiding truths to a univeral audience.

O'Connor found the location for her fiction, her "triggering town" (in Richard Hugo's words), in and around Milledgeville, Georgia. Poet Ted Kooser finds his in Garland, Nebraska. At first glance, these writers could not seem more disparate. By native ground, temperament, and chosen genre, they are distinctly apart. But in one endeavor they are united: both recognize the "mystery" of the human condition and both delight in the "manners"—the community

> *But Kooser has discovered, and conveys by way of that 'accessible' language, the perplexing mysteries at work in the world."*

of a shared culture and past, a time and place—of their peculiar regions.

While O'Connor finds her crossroads in the deeply human, flawed, sometimes grotesque characters who, as she notes, "lean away from typical social patterns"—a wondrous understatement—Kooser finds his crossroads in the mystery and eternal truths on the plain folk and unpretentious subjects of the Great Plains. In that world, where his community and larger, eternal truths meet, Kooser works the alchemy of his poetry.

That transmutation is startlingly evident in the poem "Old Cemetery" from *Delights & Shadows.* Here lowly mowers and bindweed and gravestones take on a luminosity that calls us to awareness, that transcends the phenomenological and the mortal:

> Somebody has been here this morning
> to cut the grass, coming and going unseen
> but leaving tracks, probably driving a pickup
> with a low mower trailer that bent down
> the weeds in the lane from the highway,
> somebody paid by the job, not paid enough,
> and mean and peevish, too hurried
> to pull the bindweed that weaves up
> into the filigreed iron crosses
> or to trim the tall red prairie grass
> too close to the markers to mow
> without risking the blade. Careless
> and reckless, too, leaving green paint
> scraped from the deck of the mower
> on the cracked concrete base of a marker.
> The dead must have been overjoyed
> to have their world back to themselves,
> to hear the creak of trailer springs
> under the weight of the cooling mower
> and to hear the pickup turn over and over
> and start at last, and drive away,
> and then to hear the soft ticking of weeds
> springing back, undeterred, in the lane
> that leads nowhere the dead want to go.

Much has been written about Kooser's clean, clear, "accessible" style. It is true that, in Kooser's poems, high school dropouts and Rhodes scholars alike can feel a flash of recognition in the haunting details, transporting images, and metaphors doing their right and inexplicable work. But Kooser has discovered, and conveys by way of that "accessible" language, the perplexing mysteries at work in the world. That mystery gives his work its tough complexity and force.

We read a poem like "Old Cemetery," then, with pleasure and a sense of peril. For here, as in most of Kooser's poems, we face the inevitability of time lost, of our own extinction. We are brought face to face with mystery. It's a tribute to Kooser's superb handling of tone that the revelation of such truths is subtle, never labored. He is cognizant of an intelligent reader capable of making leaps of imagination, of finding the truth of a poem on his own.

How Kooser brings the reader to realization by his handling of a poem's elements is remarkable. Consider in "Old Cemetery" his nuanced control of sound imagery. The reader is led to imagine the harsh sounds of the mower operated by somebody "mean and peevish" who leaves "green paint/ scraped from the deck of the mower/on the cracked concrete base of a marker." Then the mower cools, the pickup drives away, and we are left with the "soft ticking of weeds." We are not told that the mower's engine has also ticked as it cooled; the poet leaves that important conclusion to the reader.

Kooser's mastery of language is at full power in this poem. The delicate image of the "filigreed iron crosses" contrasts with the harshness of the invading mower and suggests the age of the markers. The "ticking" of the weeds and the "cooling" mower are potent metaphors, reminders of our mortality.

To my eye and ear this is a seamless poem. Nothing could be added, nothing taken away. To paraphrase it would mar the magic; it demands to be read word by word, detail by detail. Kooser's enjambed lines and strategic line breaks serve the poem's conversational but deliberate pace. The scattered slant rhyme (mean/peevish, grass/tracks, close/mow) give a nod to the formal feeling we hold toward the poem's subject. The silences—the fulcrums—inform the meaning: a major fulcrum between lines fifteen and sixteen marks a significant turn, a pause; we note that the human, noisy presence has been superceded by the "undeterred" weeds and the dead. As the poem closes with the sobering image of the "lane that leads nowhere the dead want to go," a silence lingers. And lingers.

In "Old Cemetery," Kooser stands firmly at that crossroads of time, place, and eternity of which O'Connor speaks. Midwestern readers will readily connect with this cemetery. They hold in common a metaphorical and physical community of time and place—small, rural towns, reverence for the weathered and the unadorned, sad knowledge of the ticking and erosion of time. They know the land; they've seen firsthand how weeds and nature triumph. Kooser shepherds the reader beautifully in this poem, as he does in most of his work, through that shared time and place to a universal truth, a mystery—mystery being what I think O'Connor meant by "eternity."

And there is something else, something that gives this poem its authority and authenticity. To write such a poem as "Old Cemetery," one must have looked into the abyss, accepted the inevitable, and decided to go on, affirming life with whatever time and talents are left. In mystery lies paradox; in "Old Cemetery," Kooser leads us to realize that, in Death's finality, we are offered the power of acceptance. We are offered—and I believe O'Connor would have approved—a moment of grace.

Source: Jo McDougall, "Of Time, Place, and Eternity: Ted Kooser at the Crossroads," in *Midwest Quarterly*, Vol. 46, No. 4, Summer 2005, pp. 410–13.

Brian Phillips

In the following review, Phillips finds a limited range in Kooser's celebration of "daily life and his memories" in Delights & Shadows.

If there is something maddening about Ted Kooser's success—something about the abridgement of a region into seventy-five synonyms of "homespun"; something about the way the word "heartland" seems to embroider itself in six-inch sampler letters across the covers of his books—then in all fairness, it has as much to do with the way his work has been received by critics as with the work itself. (Edward Hirsch in the *Washington Post Book World:* "Something about the Great Plains seems to foster a plain, homemade style, a sturdy forthrightness with hidden depths, a hardwon clarity chastened by experience. It is an unadorned, pragmatic, quintessentially American poetry of empty places, of farmland and low-slung cities. The open spaces stimulate and challenge people. One's mettle is tested." I grew up in Oklahoma, where we also had the Internet.) There is some quaintness in Kooser's new book; there are lines about "small hope" and "the ones who got away" and a staggeringly unsuccessful attempt to use creamed corn as a metaphor for race relations. But it comes more from Kooser's outlook than from any particular flaw in his use of rural Nebraska settings or his plainspoken register. His poems are written from the perspective of a man who has resolved his life's pressing conflicts, who now moves familiarly among the larger, lasting uncertainties. The range of his book is the mild emotional fall and swell of livable contentment: Kooser looks forward quietly to death (the old people in one poem "are feeling their way out into the night, / letting their eyes adjust to the future") and celebrates his daily life and his memories, without probing much beyond his confidence in everyday grace. Some lovely images ("the wind turns the pages of rain") provide a few more animated moments in the placid stasis of the rest.

Source: Brian Phillips, Review of *Delights & Shadows*, in *Poetry*, Vol. 185, No. 5, February 2005, p. 396.

Kathleen De Grave

In the following review, De Grave finds "bright image, . . . compassionate tone, and. . . . Insight into human nature" across Kooser's collection, Delights & Shadows.

Opening Ted Kooser's collection of poetry, *Delights & Shadows* is like walking into an art gallery, each poem a painting or photograph, sometimes a sculpture. Kooser is the Poet Laureate of the United States, has ten books of poems published and has received numerous awards, including two NEA fellowships, and this book lives up to that reputation. The collection of poetry is broken into four parts, each with its theme or motif. But common threads are the bright image, the compassionate tone, and the insight into human nature.

The first section, "Walking on Tiptoe," is in some respects indeed like an art gallery, a hall of portraits. Each poem is a brilliant moment in the life of a child, an old man, a student. The poems rise from image to insight, as if, as the lead poem of the section says, we are "suddenly able to see in the dark." Stereotypes turn human, as in "Tattoo," which gives us a man in a tight black T-shirt with "a dripping dagger held in the fist / of a shuddering heart" on his arm. By the end of the poem, the man has shown his age as he picks among the trinkets at a garage sale, "his heart gone soft and blue with stories." Sometimes a poem develops a subterranean metaphor, as in "Student," in which we suddenly realize we are not watching merely a student, hung over, trudging up the steps of the library, but humanity in evolution, as the student "swings

his stiff arms and cupped hands." A key line is the one in the center of the poem: "backward as up he crawls, out of the froth." It is his baseball cap that is backward and it is the "froth / of a hangover," but the evolutionary tie is clear by the last line, when the student "lumbers heavy with hope" into the library. Kooser has commented on this poem in his guide for beginning poets, *The Poetry Home Repair Manual,* explaining the genesis of the poem: He saw a connection between the student and a turtle. But the poem takes an extra step, growing beyond Kooser's own intentions.

These poems often resonate beyond the image and do, in fact, much more than portraits can, making us question our assumptions about human life and our own natures. One of the most evocative poems of this section is "The Old People," with its image of the old walking into a "cold river of shadows," hearing us calling, sometimes, sometimes not, because "They are feeling their way out into the night." All of these poems are short and intense, and some uneasily beautiful. "A Rainy Morning," for instance, compares a woman in a wheelchair to a pianist: she "strikes at the wheels, then lifts her long white fingers," "her wet face beautiful in its concentration." It takes the mind and art of a master to turn disability into music.

The second section, titled "The China Painters," is about memory and family, on an Iowa farm. The speaker of "Memory" imagines that he has used his pen as a tornado, that "peeled back" the roof, "reached down and snatched up / uncles and cousins, grandma, grandpa" and then "held them like dolls, looked / long and longingly into their faces." The poems in this section give the long look—at the speaker's mother who recently died. She taught him "to see the life at play in everything"; at his grandmother throwing out dishwater, creating "a bridge that leaps from her hot red hands" turning into "a glorious rainbow / with an empty dishpan swinging at one end"; and at his father who thankfully did not live into old age, a "fearful hypochondriac" following "the complicated, fading map of cures." This section holds the longest poem of the book, "Pearl." The speaker goes to tell a 90 year old woman that his mother, her friend, has died. Pearl is frail herself and has "started seeing people who aren't here." The speaker's futile effort to save her helps us understand his grief at his mother's death.

As if the art gallery metaphor holds true, section three, "Bank Fishing for Bluegills" has a series of poems based on "Four Civil War Paintings by Winslow Homer," which contain such beautiful images as "mules [that] graze on light" and "his white shirt / the brightest thing in the painting" and "he mows his way into the colors of summer." In "At the Country Museum," we see a horse-drawn hearse, "its oak spokes soberly walking," as it "carefully unreeled / hard ruts the wheels could follow home." This section deals with a vaster memory than section two. It is about history: The hearse has a "top like a table / from which a hundred years have been cleared," and in the poem "Casting Reels," the fishermen, grown old, "felt the line go slack / and reeled the years back empty."

The collection ends with a series of poems on love and loss. "Tectonics" puts it best: "After many years, / even a love affair, / one lush green island / all to itself, / . . . / may slide under the waves / like Atlantis, / scarcely rippling the heart."

Delights & Shadows is a book that can be read more than once, for the immediacy of the color and line, and then again, for the generosity of its vision.

Source: Kathleen De Grave, Review of *Delights & Shadows*, in *Midwest Quarterly*, Vol. 46, No. 4, Summer 2005, pp. 439–40.

Elizabeth Lund

In the following essay, Lund profiles Kooser's career upon his being named poet laureate of the United States.

Ted Kooser isn't embarrassed to say that the poems he wrote in grade school were decidedly ordinary: "I love my dog/ his padded paws/ at Christmas he's my/ Santa Claus." He doesn't try to hide the fact that as a teenager "my impulse toward poetry had a lot to do with girls." Mr. Kooser, a retired insurance executive, even admits to knocking the sideview mirror off his car after being named poet laureate of the United States in August. He was so excited, he says in a phone interview, that he didn't pay attention as he backed out of his driveway in Garland, Neb.

Some poets might not mention those stories, cultivating instead a more worldly image. But for Kooser, the first US laureate from the Plains States, ordinary moments are the impetus for art. His poems are like flashlights illuminating small dramas: a father watching his son get married; a tattoo that has faded; a brown recluse spider walking inside the bathtub. The setting may be rural America, but the scene is universal. That resonance, along with his clear, graceful style, have earned him numerous awards, including two NEA fellowships and a Pushcart Prize. Yet what really makes Kooser a "thoroughly American laureate"—as predecessor Billy Collins has called him—is not just his approach but the way his perspective seems to mirror that of "average" Americans.

"Most of us would prefer to look at cartoons in a magazine than read a poem," says Kooser, noting the common complaint that poetry is hard to decipher or full of elusive, hidden meanings. "In the real world, if you come across a poem, who says, 'Study it'? If it doesn't do anything for you, you just move on."

Kooser wants readers to linger, of course, which is why he works so hard to make his poems clear—sometimes going through 40 or 50 drafts. One of his best critics, he says, is his wife, Kathleen Rutledge, editor of the *Lincoln Journal Star*.

A few years ago at Lincoln Benefit Life, he showed poems to his secretary. If she didn't understand them, he'd revise. "I never want to be thought of as pandering to a broad audience," he says, "but you can tweak a poem just slightly and broaden the audience very much. If you have a literary allusion, you limit the audience. Every choice requires a cost-benefit analysis."

Kooser has done several "risk analyses" regarding his career choices, too, each of which pushed him toward a literary life, albeit in a circuitous way.

The first came during his undergraduate years at Iowa State, where he majored in architecture until his junior year. That's when the math and the physics "killed me," he says. He switched into classes that would allow him to teach high school English.

After a year of teaching high school, he began a master of arts program at the University of Nebraska, but again there was an unexpected detour. The problem: He was so focused on his studies with poet Karl Shapiro that he let his other classes slide. The solution: he began working in the insurance industry, a career that lasted 35 years.

Such decisions might sound more practical than poetic. But in his life, as in his work, the extraordinary stems from the ordinary. "I liked the money and the benefits. I liked the structure, too," he says of the corporate world. He began writing at 4:30 or 5 A.M. each day, a habit he still continues, often with dogs Alice and Howard by his side.

His teaching career resumed at the University of Nebraska in the 1970s, when he taught creative writing to nontraditional students. He returned as a visiting professor after retiring from his insurance company in 1999.

But his experience in the corporate world influences his literary work in surprising ways. His book *Sure Signs* (1980) opens with a poem called "Selecting a Reader." In it, Kooser describes the kind of audience he wants: a woman who weighs the choice of buying one of his books or having her dirty raincoat dry cleaned. The coat wins.

Now, years later, the poem reveals much about the new laureate. "I am still interested in acknowledging that the people who read books have other priorities, and I want to consider those. I want to write books of poems interesting enough and useful enough that they can compete with the need to get a raincoat cleaned."

Some might snicker at that, but Kooser has never been afraid to say what he feels or to express deep emotion. When he battled cancer a few years ago, poetry provided an important anchor.

Each day he'd write a short poem—on a postcard—to a close friend. Those poems, which celebrated the heartbreaking loveliness of life, eventually became *Winter Morning Walks: 100 Postcards to Jim Harrison,* which won the Nebraska Book Award in 2001.

"The kind of poem I like very much looks at the world and shows readers its designs and beauty and significance in a new way," he says. "it's like a type of kaleidoscope, only I don't have colored glass chips, I just have [words as] mirrors, mirror patterns to make ordinary things look attractive."

Those "mirrors" wouldn't work nearly as well without Kooser's keen observation. "If you pay attention to the ordinary world, there are all sorts of wonderful things in it," he says. "But most of us go through the day without noticing."

Some reviewers have complained that Kooser writes sentimental poems, but he shrugs off such comments. "Sentimentality is a completely subjective word," he notes.

"If I don't take the risk, I'll wind up with a bloodless poem. I have to be out there on the edge." He likens the process to the movie *Modern Times,* where Charlie Chaplin roller skates on a department store balcony to impress a woman. "You have to run the risk of falling down into ladies ready to wear."

Kooser has given several readings since his installation last month, and the response has been encouraging, he says. "I have had many letters from people who said that they don't usually read poetry but have been trying mine and finding that they like it. My work seems to present an example of a kind

> ❝ *But for Kooser, the first US laureate from the Plains States, ordinary moments are the impetus for art.* ❞

of writing that a wider audience might use as a point of entry into poetry."

Still, he is realistic about how much he can accomplish in a one-year term as poet laureate. "If I could convince a few people who don't read poetry that it's worth reading, that would be enough, really."

Source: Elizabeth Lund, "Retired Insurance Man Puts a Premium on Verse," in the *Christian Science Monitor,* November 16, 2004, pp. 15–16.

Ted Kooser and "American Libraries"

In the following interview, Kooser discusses what his approach to being poet laureate will be and the importance of libraries and poetry.

You'll never be able to make a living writing poems," Ted Kooser cautions beginning poets in *The Poetry Home Repair Manual,* due out in January from the University of Nebraska Press. "But look at it this way: Any activity that's worth lots of money, like professional basketball, comes with rules pinned all over it. In poetry, the only rules worth thinking about are the standards of perfection you set for yourself." While Kooser speaks from experience—for 35 years, he supported himself with a job in the insurance business, rising at 4:30 or 5:00 A.M. to put in a few hours of writing before heading to the office—he also speaks with authority, having published 10 collections of poetry, earned numerous awards, and now, taken on the role of the 13th U.S. poet laureate. Kooser officially began his new post as the Library of Congress's consultant in all things poetry by opening LC's annual literary series October 7 and speaking at the National Book Festival October 9.

[American Libraries]: How did you find out about your appointment? Was it a surprise? [Ted Kooser]: I received a phone call, and it was,

indeed, a complete surprise. I am still a little surprised, two months later.

What do you see as the role of the poet laureate? To try to expand the audience for poetry. I intend to do that largely by showing people that there are poems that don't turn readers away by their obscurity and difficulty.

What will you be doing for LC in the next year? Do you have a specific project planned, such as Robert Pinsky's Favorite Poem Project? It's still too early to go on record with my ideas, but I do plan to undertake a project or two.

What is the value of libraries in your work? My first job, as a boy of 12 or so, was making the posters for the glass cases in front of our Carnegie Library in my hometown of Ames, Iowa, and I have been devoted to public libraries ever since. I once wrote a novel, not a very good one and unpublished, set in a library in a small town. I have served on the board of the Lincoln, Nebraska, library system and raised money for a special collection there. I recently read my poems at the dedication of a Carnegie Library Museum in Perry, Iowa, a stop I would recommend to anyone crossing the country. In short, libraries are a big part of my life, and a big part, I'd guess, in every writer's life.

Why is poetry important, and what can librarians do to help people see its value? Poetry can make our lives brighter and more interesting. The challenge is in overcoming people's fear of poetry, learned in public schools where poems were taught as if they were algebra problems with one right answer. We need to show readers that there is a wealth of poetry that is not intimidating and formidable.

You're the first poet laureate from the Great Plains. How will that affect the way you approach your duties? I intend to bring some poets from out here in the great middle of things to the library to read their work, and I will be traveling and speaking in the general area.

Will you participate in the National Book Festival if there is one in 2005? I greatly enjoyed the 2004 celebration and would certainly attend again if it worked out. It would be fun to go at a time when I could just listen to the authors and look at the books and was not so caught up in interviews, etc.

How has your new schedule affected your own work? Are you able to devote much time to writing? I have done very little writing thus far, and very little reading, which is just as important.

There's been lots of correspondence to answer and places to be. Perhaps as the year goes on I can find some quiet time to read and write, but I can afford to do this work and let the other rest for a while. It's not like there are people holding their breath till I write the next poem.

Source: $@American Libraries$$, "Straight Answers from Ted Kooser," in *American Libraries*, Vol. 35, No. 11, December 2004, p. 31.

Sources

Anderson, Sherwood, "An Apology for Crudity," as quoted in *Heartland: Poets of the Midwest*, edited by Lucien Stryk, Northern Illinois University Press, 1967, p. viii.

De Grave, Kathleen, Review of *Delights & Shadows*, in *Midwest Quarterly*, Vol. 46, No. 4, Summer 2005, pp. 439–40.

Olson, Ray, Review of *Delights & Shadows*, in *Booklist*, Vol. 100, No. 15, April 1, 2004, p. 1342.

Phillips, Brian, Review of *Delights & Shadows*, in *Poetry*, Vol. 185, No. 5, February 2005, p. 396.

Further Reading

Kelvin, Joanne Frankel, and Leslie B. Tyson, *100 Questions and Answers about Cancer Symptoms and Cancer Treatment Side Effects*, Jones and Bartlett Publishers, 2005.
   This book is not meant for medical professionals but is easy for a person researching the topic to understand.

Kooser, Ted, "Lying for the Sake of Making Poems," in *After Confession: Poetry as Autobiography*, edited by Kate Sontag and David Graham, Graywolf Press, 2001, pp. 158–61.
   Kooser rejects the idea of making up events from one's life, finding life itself rich enough to sustain poetry—a position that is clearly evident in "At the Cancer Clinic."

Solomon, Deborah, "The Way We Live Now: 9-12-04: Questions for Ted Kooser; Plains Verse," in the *New York Times Magazine*, September 12, 2004, p. 21.
   This interview was conducted soon after Kooser became poet laureate. He gives his views on such diverse subjects as the value to writers of unhappy childhoods and his own unfamiliarity with European poetry.

Woessner, Warren, "Let Us Now Praise Rusty Tractors—Ted Kooser and the Midwest Poetry Renaissance," in *Midwest Quarterly*, Vol. 46, No. 4, Summer 2005, pp. 434–38.
   The author describes a resurgence of quality literature coming out of the Midwest since the 1960s and details Kooser's place in the center of this literary growth.

The Chambered Nautilus

Oliver Wendell Holmes

1858

With its rich imagery and ringing verse, "The Chambered Nautilus," by Oliver Wendell Holmes, is one of the most enduring nature poems of the mid-nineteenth century. Its subject is the nautilus, a sea creature that lives inside a spiral shell. As it grows, the nautilus makes new, larger chambers of its shell in which to live, closing off the old chambers and gradually forming a spiral. Holmes compares the nautilus to a "ship of pearl" sailing through enchanted but dangerous waters until it is wrecked. The speaker or narrator of the poem uses the nautilus as a metaphor for the human soul, stressing that its example provides a "heavenly message" of how people should grow and develop through their lives. At the end of the poem, Holmes emphasizes the idea that humans expand their horizons until they achieve the spiritual freedom of heaven or the afterlife.

Although it may appear abstract or timeless, "The Chambered Nautilus" is grounded in the world of mid-nineteenth-century Boston, sometimes called the American Renaissance because of its flowering in literature, philosophy, and culture. Holmes—a medical doctor, poet, novelist, travel writer, scientist, essayist, philosopher, lecturer, and conversationalist—was a prominent figure in the literary and philosophical circles of his era. "The Chambered Nautilus" was originally published in the new magazine *Atlantic Monthly* as part of a series combining poetry and prose that derived from Holmes's many stimulating conversational groups in Boston's intellectual society. In 1858, this series,

Oliver Wendell Holmes The Library of Congress

called *The Autocrat of the Breakfast-Table*, was published in book form, and it was widely received as a witty and insightful work. "The Chambered Nautilus" is available in collections such as *The Poetical Works of Oliver Wendell Holmes*, published by Houghton Mifflin in 1975, as well as in reprint editions of *The Autocrat of the Breakfast-Table*, such as that published by J. M. Dent & Sons in 1960.

Author Biography

Oliver Wendell Holmes was born on August 29, 1809, in Cambridge, Massachusetts. His father was a Congregationalist minister, and his mother was a member of what would become the Unitarian Church. After years of private schooling, Holmes attended Harvard College, where he began to translate and write poetry. He started to have his poetry published after college, while he was studying law. One of his most famous poems, "Old Ironsides," was published in 1830. A response to the news that the famous Revolutionary War ship USS *Constitution* was to be taken apart and used as scrap, the poem gained Holmes a wide audience and garnered the necessary public support to have the ship preserved.

Holmes quit studying law in 1831 in favor of a degree in medicine, and, in 1833, he traveled to France to continue his medical education. During his studies and upon his return to the United States, Holmes refused requests that he have more poetry published and dedicated himself to practicing medicine. In the late 1830s, however, Holmes became involved in a variety of pursuits that included lecturing and gathering in prominent conversation circles. In 1840, Holmes married Amelia Jackson. In 1841, their first child, Oliver Wendell Holmes, Jr., a future U.S. Supreme Court justice, was born. A variety of Holmes's important articles about medicine were published, and he continued lecturing until his position on issues such as the abolition of slavery, which he opposed, drew too much criticism. In 1857, installments of Holmes's *Autocrat of the Breakfast-Table* were published in the first edition of the magazine *Atlantic Monthly*. Posing as the record of a lively discussion group, *Autocrat* mixed prose with poetry; it contained some of Holmes's best poems, including "The Chambered Nautilus,"; and was very well received. Holmes wrote further installments of the series under the title *The Professor at the Breakfast-Table*, which was published in book form in 1860.

A collection of Holmes's medical essays and his novel *Elsie Venner* were published in 1861, and both received mixed reviews. During the Civil War, Holmes wrote patriotic poetry and twice traveled to Philadelphia, because his son had been wounded in combat. Holmes's novel *The Guardian Angel* was published in 1867, and Holmes afterward focused on his medical research. His works on determinism and the brain were published in 1871 and 1875. After he retired from Harvard Medical School in 1882, Holmes concentrated on his literary work, editing his collected writings and writing a biography of the American essayist and poet Ralph Waldo Emerson, a novel dealing with women's rights, a travel narrative titled *Our Hundred Days in Europe*, and a prose work titled *Over the Teacups*. Holmes died of respiratory failure on October 7, 1894, in Boston.

Poem Text

This is the ship of pearl, which, poets feign,
 Sails the unshadowed main,—
 The venturous bark that flings
On the sweet summer wind its purpled wings
In gulfs enchanted, where the siren sings,   5

And coral reefs lie bare,
Where the cold sea-maids rise to sun their
    streaming hair.
Its webs of living gauze no more unfurl;
    Wrecked is the ship of pearl!
And every chambered cell,   10
Where its dim dreaming life was wont to dwell,
As the frail tenant shaped his growing shell,
    Before thee lies revealed,—
Its irised ceiling rent, its sunless crypt un-sealed!

Year after year beheld the silent toil   15
    That spread his lustrous coil;
    Still, as the spiral grew,
He left the past year's dwelling for the new,
Stole with soft step its shining archway through,
    Built up its idle door,   20
Stretched in his last-found home, and knew the old
    no more.

Thanks for the heavenly message brought by thee,
    Child of the wandering sea,
    Cast from her lap forlorn!
From thy dead lips a clearer note is born   25
Than ever Triton blew from wreathed horn!
    While on mine ear it rings,
Through the deep caves of thought I hear a voice
    that sings:—

Build thee more stately mansions, O my soul
    As the swift seasons roll!   30
    Leave thy low-vaulted past!
Let each new temple, nobler than the last,
Shut thee from heaven with a dome more vast,
    Till thou at length art free,
Leaving thine outgrown shell by life's un-resting   35
    sea

Poem Summary

Stanza 1

The title "The Chambered Nautilus" refers to a sea creature that lives in the western Pacific and the Indian oceans and has a hard external shell, or exoskeleton. The creature lives in and is able to withdraw into the outermost compartment of its shell, which consists of sealed sections and is one of nature's best examples of a logarithmic spiral, one that grows at an exponential rate and appears to expand while it grows. Line 1 calls the nautilus a "ship of pearl," which combines a comparison to a human-made sailing vessel with a description of the pearly finish of the nautilus shell. The speaker then notes that "poets feign," or pretend, that the nautilus "Sails the unshadowed main," or the wide-open waters.

Lines 3, 4, and 5 continue the conceit, or extended comparison, of the nautilus to a ship, creating an image of a "venturous," or adventurous, wooden ship whose "purpled wings," or sails, fly

on the "sweet summer wind." This description sounds like some kind of magical fairyland, and the speaker notes that the ship, or nautilus, sails to enchanted "gulfs." A gulf is a large, partially enclosed body of water, and the word *gulf* has a secondary meaning of "chasm" or "abyss." The speaker notes that "the siren sings" in these gulfs. This image refers to the beautiful and seductive water nymphs of ancient Greek mythology that sang so beautifully as to lure sailors to be destroyed on the rocks surrounding their island. Lines 6 and 7 continue this imagery, describing coral reefs that "lie bare." This image refers to the beautiful yet dangerous reefs that can destroy a ship but is also vaguely suggestive of the nude "cold sea-maids" who lie in the sun and dry their "streaming hair."

Stanza 2

Stanza 2 discusses the nautilus's wreckage and death in the past tense. In line 8, the speaker's conceit continues and expands as the nautilus is said to have "webs of living gauze," or sails. It is important to consider which part of the nautilus refers to the sails and which indicates the "ship of pearl." Logic would suggest that the sails, or "purpled wings" and "webs of living gauze," are the tentacles and head of the creature and that the pearly ship is the shell. In this stanza, however, the sails do not "unfurl," because the ship is "Wrecked" and the nautilus is presumably dead.

In lines 10 through 14, the speaker describes the nautilus's empty shell, continuing to use the comparison of a ship. The speaker discusses "every chambered cell," referring to the compartments and rooms of a ship as well as the sections of the nautilus's exoskeleton, which it makes as it grows larger, closing off old compartments and moving into new ones. The speaker describes these abandoned cells as expired locations where the nautilus's "dim dreaming life" used to dwell. Line 12 refers to the nautilus as a "frail tenant" constructing "his growing shell." Line 13 refers to the reader as "thee," suggesting that the empty shell lies directly in front of the reader. Line 14 describes the inside of the empty shell as having an "irised," or rainbow-colored, ceiling that has broken open and let the elements into what used to be a "sunless crypt," or coffin.

Stanza 3

Stanza 3 backtracks from the preceding description of the nautilus's death to describe in the past tense its lifelong "silent toil" to create protective compartments in its spiral shell. In this description, the speaker seems to abandon the comparison of the nautilus to a ship, although Holmes's choice of words is characterized by terms of human construction, such as "coil," "archway," "door," and "home."

Lines 15 and 16 emphasize the laborious repetition of creating the "lustrous" shell, and the following two lines state that each year the nautilus abandons its previous chamber in favor of a new one that it has created to accommodate its larger size. Line 19 describes this process as stealing, or moving sneakily, "with soft step" through the "shining archway" that divides the chambers, as though the nautilus were human. This process of personification, or assigning human qualities to an animal or object, continues in lines 20 and 21. The speaker describes the seal that the nautilus forms to block off its old chamber as an "idle door" ("idle" probably means "unused" in this context, as opposed to "useless" or "unproductive"). In line 21, the speaker explicitly compares the nautilus to a person, describing it as "Stretched in his last-found home" and noting that it "knew the old no more," or has shut out its past.

Stanza 4

In stanza 4, which changes to the present tense, the speaker addresses the nautilus directly and describes its effect on him. Line 22 thanks the nautilus for the "heavenly message" it has brought, and line 23 describes the creature as a "Child of the wandering sea," which is a mysterious image because it is difficult to envision the sea itself as wandering. Line 24 suggests that the nautilus is wandering or "forlorn" and has been cast from the lap of the sea as though the sea were its mother.

In line 25, the speaker reminds the reader that the nautilus is dead, but at the same time, he produces an image of a "note" coming from its "dead lips." The next line continues this thought by stating that the note born from the lips of the nautilus is clearer than that which "Triton" has blown from his "wreathèd horn." Triton is an ancient Greek demigod—or a being more powerful than a human but less powerful than a god—whose father is the sea god, Poseidon. Triton is usually portrayed as a merman, or a creature with the upper body of a man and the tail of a fish, although the name "Triton" came to be used for a host of other mythological mermen and mermaids. The "wreathèd horn" refers to Triton's great conch shell, which he blows like a trumpet to command the waves. In line 27, the speaker says that he listens to the clear note of the nautilus ring in his ear. In line 28, the speaker states

that he hears the sound of the nautilus as a "voice that sings" in "deep caves of thought," which is an interesting image that ties to the description of the nautilus's many chambers.

Stanza 5

In the fifth stanza, the speaker addresses himself instead of addressing or describing the nautilus. In line 29, the speaker urges his "soul" to "Build thee more stately mansions," implicitly comparing the nautilus's chamber-building to the process of building expensive houses. Line 30 exclaims that the speaker should build the mansions amid the swiftly changing seasons, or because time rolls along rapidly. In line 31, the speaker tells himself to leave the "low-vaulted," or low-ceilinged, "past," and in the next line he wishes that "each new temple," a new and important metaphor suggesting the religious holiness of the chamber or house, be "nobler than the last."

Line 33 uses the phrase "Shut thee from heaven," which emphasizes the separation of the house or temple from the elements and from God, but the speaker paradoxically goes on to describe the ceiling as "a dome more vast" that increases until the speaker is "free." Line 34 suggests that the speaker achieves this ultimate freedom by releasing himself into heaven, or dying. The final line reinforces this interpretation, noting that the speaker, like the nautilus, will leave his "outgrown shell," which refers to the speaker's body as well as a house, "by life's unresting sea," as though the speaker's spirit will rise out of the shell of his body and into heaven.

Themes

Development and Mobility

The discussion in *The Autocrat of the Breakfast-Table* that precedes "The Chambered Nautilus" focuses on the various stages of life and the importance of making progress by moving on from what one previously knew. In a sense, the poem is an elaboration on this idea, because it focuses on the concept of sealing off one's previous boundaries to create new and larger spaces in which to live and develop. In the paragraphs before the poem, the autocrat of the breakfast table says that "grow we must, if we outgrow all that we love," stressing the need to keep moving and developing as one ages, even if it means that one leaves one's old relationships behind. Holmes envisions a process of

Topics For Further Study

- Research the characteristics of the chambered nautilus and give a class presentation about its biological and environmental significance. How does the species survive? What is its place in evolution? How and why does it build its shell in a logarithmic spiral? What was its status and contact with humans in the mid-nineteenth century, and what is its status today? Does Holmes's poem accurately portray the biological characteristics of the nautilus? Why or why not?

- Holmes was renowned for his conversational skills. Read *The Autocrat of the Breakfast-Table* and use it as an inspiration for leading a class discussion about philosophical, scientific, artistic, and other issues. You do not need to focus on the themes of the book, and you can include issues that are pertinent and topical to you and your classmates, but make sure that you address the universal and philosophical significance of these issues. Make an effort, like the autocrat, to discomfort and even shock your classmates in order to stir debate and conversation.

- Write a poem that uses an animal or sea creature as a metaphor for a person or some kind of human endeavor. Try to tailor your description of the animal to emphasize the particular qualities of the person or endeavor that are the object of the metaphor, and try to use the technique of personification. For example, if you were using a particular dog to represent a vicious person or quality, you could dwell on the color and the points of its teeth that are in perfect order because it had braces when it was young.

- Research the cultural climate of mid-nineteenth-century Boston and write an essay discussing its intellectual atmosphere. What were the major factions or groups of thinkers, and how were they important and influential? Describe the key philosophical debates of the period. What was the significance of the Boston renaissance to the rest of the country? Describe some of the factors that sparked this movement and how it came to an end. What writings of the period have endured, and why have they endured?

---

spiritual and personal progress in which one constantly challenges oneself to become a better person.

"The Chambered Nautilus" expresses this idea of progress, particularly in stanza 3, which describes the nautilus's practice of living only in the outermost and largest chamber of its shell, completely dividing itself off from the chambers that it outgrows. The poet depicts the nautilus's chambers as sealed, enclosed spaces, stating that they are like a dim "cell" or a "sunless crypt," although they have rainbow ceilings and are "lustrous," or glowing. Stanza 5 compares the chambers (or what they will become) to noble, "stately mansions" while noting that the previous chambers are "low-vaulted." This contradiction emphasizes that life is in a constant state of flux and that it is necessary to seal off the past in order to better oneself.

Holmes seems to imply that completely sealing off one's old relationships has its problems in the sense that this action can be considered turning one's back on one's friends. This may be why the speaker notes that the nautilus must sneak away "with soft step" to its new dwelling, soon taking the attitude that it "knew the old no more." If people go through such a process, they may find that they are "forlorn" like the nautilus and are children "of the wandering sea." Because life itself is an "unresting sea," however, Holmes also suggests that the process of spiritual and personal growth facilitated by leaving one's previous situation is a necessary act and an altruistic method of self-improvement.

Death and the Afterlife

Because the nautilus's building of its shell is an extended metaphor for the speaker's spiritual life, "The Chambered Nautilus" can be interpreted as an allegory about death and the journey toward the afterlife. The idea that the human body is a ship or shell containing its spirit is not a new one, and Holmes clearly suggests that the nautilus's shell represents the physical covering of the human body and that the living creature itself represents the human soul or spirit. As early as stanza 1, Holmes hints that he is discussing dualism, the idea that the immortal soul is a separate entity from the mortal body, when he characterizes the ship with "purpled wings" like those of an angel. Holmes also suggests in stanza 4 that the nautilus provides a "heavenly message" as though it were an immortal spirit providing advice to the living.

The most explicit discussion of the idea that the nautilus is a metaphor for the human spirit comes in stanza 5. The speaker instructs his "soul" to build increasingly "nobler" temples until he becomes free like the dead nautilus, whose shell has been pierced. Although the domes of the chambers of the speaker's soul "shut [him] from heaven," the last dome appears to break away when he leaves the "outgrown shell" and ascends into the afterlife. The nautilus's journey toward immortality is somewhat perilous, given the deadly sirens, and it is a "forlorn" and "frail" creature resigned to "silent toil." This journey seems justified, however, because it creates the "heavenly message" of the shell. Similarly, the soul's hard work on earth is seemingly rewarded with the "free[dom]" of heaven.

Style

Personification

"Personification," or the attribution of human qualities to nonhuman objects or creatures, is an important literary technique in "The Chambered Nautilus." One of the poem's main extended metaphors compares a nautilus to the human soul, and the success of this metaphor depends on imagery that associates the nautilus with a human. Examples of this personification include the idea that the nautilus has a "dreaming life," its description as a "tenant," its stealing with "soft step," its ability to stretch out in a home, and the notion that it is a "child" with "lips." All of these characteristics are not literally possible in a shelled aquatic creature, and they implore the reader to imagine that the nautilus is human. Holmes uses this technique to develop the idea that the nautilus is a metaphor for the human condition, because personification makes it easier for readers to imagine themselves as a nautilus.

Symmetrical Rhyme Scheme

"The Chambered Nautilus" contains five stanzas, all of which follow the same rhyme scheme consisting of a rhymed couplet (group of two lines), followed by a rhymed tercet (group of three lines), followed by another couplet. Also written *aabbbcc*, this rhyme structure makes the verse flow musically by adding rhythm and musicality to the poem. Rhyme can also serve other functions, including linking words and associating them thematically, although Holmes does not seem to use it for these purposes.

Alliteration and Diction

Holmes carefully uses language to develop the meaning, rhythm, and structure of his poem. He uses alliteration, or the repetition of consonant sounds such as the use of *d* in "dim dreaming life was wont to dwell," to draw attention to the words that are alliterated and provide a pleasing or musical sound. Holmes's diction, or choice of vocabulary, is also carefully selected for various purposes; for example, it sounds somewhat antiquated (even for 1858) in order to make the poem seem more eloquent or authoritative. Finally, the poet uses diction to develop his thematic agenda, using spiritual terminology when he wishes to discuss the human soul and mythological references when he wishes to strike a fanciful or "enchanted" note.

Historical Context

The 1850s were a period of dangerous and rising tensions in the United States, but it was also a time of great intellectual progress and a flourishing of intellectual development in cities such as Boston. In a sense, therefore, it was a decade of contradictions and debate, and the great divide in values and patriotic sentiment would cause the country to erupt in civil war in 1861. This divide was between southeastern states, which were based on a cotton- and tobacco-producing plantation system, and northeastern states, whose economy was largely industrial. Although slavery had been outlawed in the North, it was legal in the South, and slave labor remained the basis of the southern economy. Much of the debate in the 1850s was about the destiny of the large middle and western sections of the country, to which settlers were moving in great numbers. Congress decided whether new states would be slaveholding, and this designation largely determined whether they would assume Southern or Northern values.

Compare & Contrast

- **1850s:** The United States is an increasingly divided country. Tensions flare between Southerners and Northerners, and two presidents fail to ease the conflict over slavery and ideology that is building steadily toward civil war.

  Today: The United States appears to be a divided country once again. Republicans and Democrats have deep ideological differences, and the administration of President George W. Bush is known for rewarding its ultraconservative base and refusing to take a moderate stance.

- **1850s:** Boston is the literary and intellectual hub of the United States, boasting the greatest thinkers and scholars of the American Renaissance.

  Today: Although Boston remains a center of American intellectual life, home to many of the best universities in the country, New York is a larger hub of literary and philosophical thought.

- **1850s:** In the United States, slavery is legal in Southern states, African Americans throughout the country are impoverished and segregated from white society, women cannot vote, and discrimination against immigrants is widespread.

  Today: The United States guarantees equal rights for all adult citizens under the law, but discrimination against minorities continues to exist.

The question of slavery, therefore, was an extremely important and divisive issue of the day, hotly debated by politicians, writers, intellectuals, and ordinary people. Holmes and other figures lectured and wrote about the possible abolition of slavery in the territories, which Holmes opposed because he feared the consequences of the building conflict between the South and the North. American intellectuals also spoke and wrote about other major issues of the day, such as women's rights (women were barred from voting and experienced severe discrimination) and new, large-scale immigration. Massive numbers of immigrants, particularly from Ireland because of the Great Famine there, settled in the United States in the 1850s.

Holmes's hometown of Boston was famous in the 1850s for its vibrant intellectual culture full of social reformers and literary figures, and historians often characterize this period as a renaissance of literature and philosophy with Boston at its hub. Influential figures, including Ralph Waldo Emerson, Henry David Thoreau, Margaret Fuller, and James Russell Lowell, lived and wrote in Boston, which was a commercially successful and rapidly expanding city at this time. Emerson was the chief proponent of transcendentalism, a post-Romantic literary and philosophical movement that stressed the unity of all things and the revelation of deep truths to be found in personal experience as well as in reason. Thoreau (an influential early environmentalist) and Fuller (who helped found the American feminist movement) also were transcendentalists, and they met in conversation circles to develop their theories and inspire each other.

Also of great importance in Boston in the 1850s were the elite members of the white male Protestant ruling class, who gathered in places like Harvard College. As a prominent member of the faculty at Harvard Medical School (although he upset the Harvard elite by speaking against its Calvinist doctrine in various public addresses), Holmes was a member of this class. He was also one of Boston's leading intellectual figures, famous for his conversational skills, and he met in conversation circles that debated issues ranging from art to science. A practicing physician and medical researcher, Holmes was interested throughout his life in advancing medical science and promoting awareness in the public. He was instrumental in encouraging the widespread use of microscopes by physicians and in alerting the public to a contagious condition found in women during childbirth. Although he was not a transcendentalist and even spoke out against its doctrines, Holmes later came to appreciate Emerson's ideas and wrote an influential biography of the philosopher.

Critical Overview

"The Chambered Nautilus" has been popular and critically acclaimed since its publication in Holmes's prose work *The Autocrat of the Breakfast-Table*. It is one of Holmes's most famous poems and one of the most popular poems about a sea creature in American literature. *The Autocrat of the Breakfast-Table*, in general, was an immediate success. Rowland E. Prothero writes in the *Quarterly Review* (1895) that it is by this work that "the name of Holmes will live." Prothero goes on to state that "The Chambered Nautilus" is one "of the best representatives of [Holmes's] poetic gifts." John Macy notes in *The Spirit of American Literature* that it is "Holmes's most ambitious poem, the one which he was most eager to have remembered as poetry." Macy, however, finds the poem "an elaborate conceit, pretty but not moving," and favors other examples of Holmes's verse.

Holmes has lost much of his prestige and readership in the twentieth century, in great part because of his old-fashioned views on issues such as slavery and women's rights. Many readers in the late twentieth and early twenty-first centuries have found the topical points in his prose and philosophical works, such as *The Autocrat of the Breakfast-Table*, quite dated. In her article "Sex, Sentiment, and Oliver Wendell Holmes," Gail Thain Parker argues that Holmes is a more complex thinker about gender than he may appear but nevertheless is "[eager] to believe in fundamental differences between the sexes." In the early twenty-first century, Holmes's poems, including "The Chambered Nautilus," are the most popular of his writings, although critics such as Peter Gibian continue to analyze all of Holmes's works and his place in the nineteenth-century intellectual scene.

Criticism

Scott Trudell

Scott Trudell is a doctoral student of English literature at Rutgers University. In the following essay, he discusses the didactic, or moral, emphasis on productivity in "The Chambered Nautilus," arguing that Holmes is ambivalent about his own moral message.

Immediately before "The Chambered Nautilus" is recited in *The Autocrat of the Breakfast-Table*, the autocrat asks, "Can you find no lesson in this?" In this way, he emphasizes that the poem will have a didactic, or a moral or instructional, quality. It is clear from the surrounding context that the poem's "lesson" will relate the ideas Holmes has been developing throughout the fourth chapter of his breakfast-table conversation series, which focuses on age, memory, productivity, personal development, and the spiritual journey through life's various stages. The autocrat's comments toward the end of the chapter about the "direction we are moving," the importance that "we outgrow all that we love," and the "race of life" in which a person must make his or her imprint on the world are intended to relate to Holmes's didactic message in "The Chambered Nautilus."

As the autocrat promises, the chambered nautilus serves as a didactic metaphor for the journey of the soul through life. The poem's speaker compares the nautilus to a ship in much the same way that the autocrat compares life's developmental progress to a sailing voyage: "To reach the port of heaven, we must sail sometimes with the wind and sometimes against it,—but we must sail, and not drift, nor lie at anchor." The poem reinforces this idea of personal agency when it dwells on the idea of leaving "the past year's dwelling for the new." For the speaker, the chambered nautilus is an ideal metaphor for the progress of the human soul through life. The nautilus achieves a kind of perpetual progress by leaving the old behind it and speeding through the race of life that the autocrat describes earlier.

The allegory in the poem is clearly Christian, guaranteeing an escape from the "silent toil" of "low-vaulted" and "dim dreaming" life, with its dangerous sirens besetting the "frail tenant" of mortality's shell. Although the nautilus, or the metaphor for the human soul, brings a "heavenly message," it is a "Child of the wandering sea, / Cast from her lap, forlorn!" It must endure life's trials with humble Christian patience, creating the perfect shell of a life's work in the process. When he reaches the end of life's voyage, the subject departs from life and into spiritual freedom, leaving this "outgrown" but beautiful shell behind as a mark of his achievement.

The poem reinforces the center of the autocrat's conversational argument and develops Holmes's idea of the noble process of development. It is not, like "Contentment" in chapter 11 of *The Autocrat of the Breakfast-Table*, an ironic poem that playfully and purposefully undercuts the autocrat's moral message. This is not to say that the poem is an entirely straightforward or simple allegory, however. Holmes's "lesson" dwells on a variety of preconceptions about productivity, personal development, and social mobility, and it subtly suggests potential pitfalls, dangers, and inadequacies in this worldview.

The primary preoccupation of "The Chambered Nautilus" is an obsession with productivity and industriousness. Here and throughout *The Autocrat of the Breakfast-Table*, Holmes suggests that it is necessary to work constantly, steadfastly, and earnestly throughout one's life. The nautilus, compared to a "venturous" ship that "Sails the unshadowed main," is characterized by its "silent toil" as "year after year" it builds its shell. The main lesson the speaker extracts from the sea creature is not to float aimlessly in a protective shell, enjoying life's "gulfs enchanted," but to build continuously and productively "As the swift seasons roll!"

The demanding work ethic suggested in the poem relates to the drive to increase the world's scientific, artistic, literary, and philosophical knowledge. Holmes was a prolific scientist, physician, writer, and scholar, and he was dedicated to the wide advancement of human intellectual achievement as he saw it. Well respected as an intellectual authority by his critics and friends alike, Holmes was consulted on a wide variety of matters, acquainted with nearly all of the major writers and intellectuals of his time, and continually urged to publish and speak in Boston and throughout the country. *The Autocrat of the Breakfast-Table*, like much of Holmes's work, stresses that truth is an "eternal flow" (as it is called in the poem "What We All Think"), and it is the obligation of humankind to pursue it vigorously.

The demand for industriousness extends to Christian virtue, which is framed as a sort of natural extension of a productive and laborious life. As Holmes states in "What We All Think," the "one unquestioned text" around which all human study and achievement revolves is "God is Love!" This statement emphasizes that the pursuit of heavenly virtue is also the pursuit of scientific and philosophical truth. Holmes stresses that the pursuit of religious truth results in "All doubt beyond, all fear above" because, to him, it is another of the noble or necessary aims of human toil. "The Chambered Nautilus" reflects this idea in the sense that the nautilus's, or soul's, everyday toil to make its beautiful iridescent shell on earth is also its toil to build

> *Whether or not it can be said to include transcendentalist ideas, 'The Chambered Nautilus' reveals significant ambivalence about its moral that a person is obligated to work industriously, ceaselessly, and rigorously year after year."*

new temples, and with each larger chamber it comes closer to the "free[dom]" of heaven.

Holmes's moral of industriousness also extends to social mobility, a version of the American dream in which work results in monetary rewards. The line "Build thee more stately mansions, O my soul" in "The Chambered Nautilus" suggests that productivity applies not only to the pursuit of knowledge and Christian virtue but also to the accumulation of wealth. This suggestion is somewhat curious, because "stately mansions" are not a typical image of the humble Christian home, but the poem seems to include this kind of upward social mobility in its moral as the speaker leaves his "low-vaulted," presumably impoverished, past in exchange for the most stately of mansions, heaven. This idea is reinforced by the fact that the nautilus continually abandons its previous associations, which are no longer worthy of it. The autocrat develops this idea more explicitly in the paragraphs that precede the poem when he says, somewhat ironically, "So you will not think I mean to speak lightly of old friendships." Whether he speaks of them "lightly" or not, the autocrat values old acquaintances not for their virtues or by any sense of loyalty but only because they allow him to measure his progress in life. The nautilus is an appropriate metaphor for this kind of thinking because, as the speaker emphasizes, the shelled sea creature shuts its doors on its past and locks it away in compartments.

The poem's moral of constant, relentless productivity in the pursuit of knowledge, spirituality,

What Do I Read Next?

- Holmes's "Old Ironsides" (1830), available in books of his collected poetry, such as *The Poetical Works of Oliver Wendell Holmes* (1975), is a famous poem about the USS *Constitution*, a Revolutionary War ship that was scheduled to be dismantled. Because of the emotion that Holmes's poem stirred in the general public, the ship was preserved.

- *Woman in the Nineteenth Century* (published in 1845 and reprinted in 1999), by Margaret Fuller, is a striking, impassioned, and important prose work of feminism that criticizes male hypocrisy and discrimination against women and proposes a variety of solutions to improving women's rights.

- Nathaniel Hawthorne's novel *The Scarlet Letter* (1850) is about a child born outside wedlock in mid-seventeenth-century Boston and the cruel response to the mother by the rigidly Puritan community.

- Phillis Wheatley's poem "On Being Brought from Africa to America" (ca. 1767) uses Christianity to compel whites to have compassion for the former and current black slaves in the United States.

- "The City in the Sea," by Edgar Allan Poe (1831), is a mysterious poem about a doomed underwater city. It is based on a Bible story from the book of Genesis.

---

and wealth reflects a typical outlook in its historical period. In the United States, as in Britain, the middle to late nineteenth century was a period in which many extremely prolific writers were obsessed with adding to the world's catalogue of truth and knowledge. Because of transcendentalist or post-Romantic thinking, however, the Boston renaissance did not always emphasize a logical scientific process as the ideal means by which to uncover truth. Knowledge, according to Emerson, was to be found within the human mind, and personal insight was the chief tool for uncovering what he and other transcendentalists considered the innate and universal truth of the world. It would be a mistake to imagine that Holmes entirely subscribed to logic and science over personal insight, although Holmes was often known to criticize the central tenets of transcendentalism.

Whether or not it can be said to include transcendentalist ideas, "The Chambered Nautilus" reveals significant ambivalence about its moral that a person is obligated to work industriously, ceaselessly, and rigorously year after year. The best example of Holmes's mixed feelings about a straightforward, logical, and productive work ethic is the fact that the nautilus is so dour as it labors endlessly in its chambers. A "frail" and "forlorn"

creature confined to a "cell" or "crypt," the nautilus is continually displaced from its origins in a kind of tragic, circular toil. It is not allowed to dwell in the "gulfs enchanted" because of the alluring but deadly sirens, but it ends up wrecked on the rocks anyway. The nautilus must steal away with "soft step" as though to avoid the old friends and acquaintances it has left behind in its vigorous drive to produce. Because its final product is a beautiful but cracked-open shell, the "note" from its "dead lips" is not necessarily as clear a "heavenly message" as the speaker claims.

The speaker is certainly not aware of grim ambivalence in the portrayal of industriousness, but Holmes seems to be considering it sincerely. Ceaseless and unhappy toil may be a kind of necessary result of productivity, as it is portrayed in the poem, and the beauty of the nautilus's broken shell is, in part, a kind of signal that the labor was worthwhile. Holmes implies at the same time, however, that this tragically broken shell is a warning that the nautilus has pushed itself too hard and for rewards that it never enjoys. Although it develops a moral that urges the reader to engage in the laborious process of intellectual, religious, and financial productivity, "The Chambered Nautilus" leaves a strong hint of tragedy and resignation in the creature or person that follows this advice.

Source: Scott Trudell, Critical Essay on "The Chambered Nautilus," in *Poetry for Students*, Thomson Gale, 2006.

Eleanor M. Tilton

In the following essay, Tilton examines the influence of Holmes's friend, the historian John Lothrop Motley, on Holmes's writing, asserting that Motley's influence affected the quality of Holmes's work negatively.

In the spring of 1857, Oliver Wendell Holmes sent to the historian John Lothrop Motley a private printing of a long poem written two years earlier for the opening of the 1855 lecture season of the Boston Mercantile Library Association. In 1857 Holmes seems to have had no plans for publication of the poem, but evidently felt the need of more discriminating criticism than the newspaper reporters had been in the habit of giving him. By then his friendship with Motley had reached that degree of intimacy that made him willing to ask for criticism that Motley felt willing and free to give.

Motley went through the private printing carefully, annotating his marks of praise and blame, and in his covering letter of May 3, he adumbrated his critical principles. His marginal notes and his letter provide a revealing illustration of mid-nineteenth-century sensibility. What would have been regarded in 1857 as the finest taste is recognizably moribund, an amalgam of elements drawn from the eighteenth century through Blair's *Lectures on Rhetoric* and of ingredients diluted from German sources. Blair was known to every American college student, and Motley had not escaped him at Harvard; with some of the principal German sources he had been familiar from his school days at Joseph Green Cogswell's Round Hill School.

Deferring to his friend's taste, Holmes revised the poem carefully before its first publication in 1862 in *Songs in Many Keys*. Except for the deletion of matter appropriate only to the original occasion, nearly all the changes were directed by Motley's marginal notes and his letter. For this criticism Holmes remained loyally grateful all his life. In 1889 he wrote to Morley's daughter Lily: "I believe your father is the only friend to whom I ever submitted a manuscript for criticism, though Edward Everett sent and borrowed one and made some more or less wise suggestions. But everything your father said, had meaning for me."

Introduced by the portion later entitled "The Old Player" and closing with the section later

> *Had Holmes resisted this imposition of a standard alien to his temper and his talent, he would have been a wiser and possibly a better poet than he was."*

entitled "The Secret of the Stars," this discursive sentimental poem belongs essentially to the same genre as Crabbe's "The Borough," although in those places where he allows his wit to rule, Holmes's manner is more nearly that of Pope. The poem deals with five figures—a recluse, a banker, a lover, a statesman, and a mother—each of whom cherishes a secret he fears to reveal. What Holmes called his "simple thread" was not so simple as he supposed, for the several "secrets" have no very close relation to one another. Motley, however, appeared to have no difficulty finding his way about the untitled private printing and was not disturbed by the juxtaposition of Daniel Webster and the Virgin Mary.

Of the seven parts of the poem, Motley without hesitation selected as the best the portion now entitled "The Mother's Secret." In his letter he said of this part: "The pictures are finished with an artistic delicacy of touch & a piety of feeling, which remind me of the Florentine painters of the 14th & 15th centuries." In the text against the lines describing the Nativity he wrote: "This is a picture worthy of Fra Angelico." In his letter, Motley went on to speak of sections he did not like: the recognizable portrait of Daniel Webster ("The Statesman's Secret"), the embezzling banker's farewell dinner-party ("The Banker's Secret"), and the mystery of the recluse of Apple Island ("The Exile's Secret"), although for the last of the three he was willing to make concessions. Motley's letter provides the grounds for his preferences:

> The Webster photograph is bold, shadowy and imposing—but would probably elicit more hearty applause from a public audience, than from some of us who have perhaps pondered too much the unheroic & the unpoetical elements which constituted so much of that golden headed & clay footed image—

The same remark I shd be inclined to make upon the fraudulent banker. You have painted a very vigorous picture, but there is something in the details which are too inharmonious with the ideal—I suppose that you will not agree with me, and very likely it is some narrowness on my part or over squeamishness—but the particulars of a modern dinner party, refuse to make poetry to my imagination—The more life like they are (and nothing can be more vivid than your sketch) the more does my mind rebel at them—At the same time, I beg you to believe that I feel as warmly as anyone can do the genial flow of the atmosphere & the genuine ring of the verse, even in the passages which I put below the other parts of the poem in comparison—

Indeed the description of the ruined home on Apple Island, is *almost* the best thing in the poem. . . .

Underlying the preferences here—aside from political disapproval of Webster—is the familiar opposition of the Ideal and the Actual. Having as its subject the mother of Jesus, "The Mother's Secret" could not escape being satisfactorily Ideal; an American politician, with or without feet of clay, and a banker, even an honest one, were bound to be grossly Actual. Motley was less sure of himself when he came to "The Exile's Secret." For reasons shortly to be noted, he was pleased with a passage clearly "beautiful" but put off by the fact that he could call the rumored exile by his actual name, William Marsh, and could identify the island, although Holmes had refrained from naming either and had idealized the location by referring to Boston as St. Botolph's town. So fixed in Motley's mind was the opposition of the Ideal and the Actual that he found "inharmonious with the ideal" any detail that seemed to speak or even to hint of actuality. With few exceptions, Motley's marginal protests and injunctions to "omit" or "change" are directed against such details as "refuse to make poetry" to an imagination instructed by Blair and a sensibility nurtured on the assumed opposition of Ideality and Actuality. The kind of picture Motley wanted was a Claude Lorrain. From Eckermann's *Gespräche mit Goethe* he could have taken a text for his criticism:

These paintings have the highest Truth, but no trace of Actuality. Claude Lorrain knew the real world by heart down to the smallest detail, and he used it as the means to express the world of his beautiful soul. And this is the true Ideality: in knowing how to use realistic means to reveal the True and make it create the illusion of the Actual.

For his criticism Motley did not need a text; the paired opposites, disassociated from their philosophical and literary sources, had become cant by 1857; as catchwords, they had been frequently evoked to praise Schiller as the poet of the Ideal and to disparage Goethe as the poet of the Actual. Longfellow exclaimed:

But who has told them [Goethe's admirers] that books are to be nothing more than an exact reflexion of what passes in real life? There is enough misery in this world to make our hearts heavy;—in books let us have something more than this—something to strengthen and elevate and purify us. Schiller—the beautiful Schiller does this. He is the prophet of the ideal—Goethe the prophet of the real.

Emerson made the same judgment: "Goethe, then, must be set down as the poet of the Actual, not of the Ideal; the poet of limitation, not of possibility; of this world, and not of religion and hope; in short, if I may say so, the poet of prose, and not of poetry."

The adored Schiller had offered the paired opposites as to indicate a standard for the artist's aspiration: "But how does the artist protect himself from the corruptions of his time, which beset him from all sides? By disdaining its judgments. He should look upward to his dignity and divine law, not downward to Fortune and material need. . . . He should relinquish to the Understanding, which is here at home, the sphere of the Actual; he should strive instead to effect the birth of the Ideal from the union of the possible and the necessary."

In Carlyle's prefatory comments on the writers he translated for his *German Romance,* the opposition is implied in his final judgment of the humoristic Musäus: "His imagination is not powerless: it is like a bird of feeble wing, which can fly from tree to tree; but never soars for a moment into the æther of Poetry, to bathe in its serene splendour, with the region of the Actual lying far below, and brightened into beauty by radiance not its own. He is a man of fine and varied talent, but scarcely of any genius."

Motley could not have expected Holmes always to reach the heavenly "æther of Poetry," but his criticism shows that he wished his friend to make the attempt. Wherever he found Holmes "spiritualizing the grossness of this actual life," Motley was content. We borrow the phrase from Hawthorne, for in Hawthorne's vein is a passage in "The Exile's Secret" that Motley marked with parallel lines of approval "as Channing used to do our themes":

Who sees unmoved,—a ruin at his feet,—
The lowliest home where human hearts have beat?
Its hearth-stone, shaded with the bistre stain
A century's showery torrents wash in vain;
Its starving orchard, where the thistle blows
And elbowed spectres stand in broken rows;
Its chimney-loving poplar, never seen

Save next a roof, or where a roof has been;
Its knot-grass, plantain,—all the social weeds,
Man's mute companions, following where he leads;
Its dwarfed, pale flowers, that show their straggling
heads,
Sown by the wind from grass-choked garden-beds;
Its woodbine, creeping where it used to climb;
Its roses, breathing of the olden time;
All the poor shows the curious idler sees,
As life's thin shadows fade by slow degrees,
Till nought remains, the saddening tale to tell,
Save home's last wrecks,—the cellar and the well!

Motley questioned the phrase "elbowed spectres"
and asked "can a shadow fade?", but approved of
the whole, . . . Not strictly speaking "Ideal," the
picture is "beautiful" according to standards supplied by Blair:

> There is, however, another sense . . . in which Beauty
> of writing characterizes a particular manner; when it
> is used to signify a certain grace and amenity in the
> turn either of style or sentiment. . . . In this sense, it
> denotes a manner neither remarkably sublime, nor
> vehemently passionate, nor uncommonly sparkling,
> but such as raises in the reader an emotion of the gen-
> tle placid kind, familiar to what is raised by the con-
> templation of beautiful objects in nature; which
> neither lifts the mind very high, nor agitates it very
> much, but diffuses over the imagination an agreeable
> and pleasing serenity.

Blair had earlier used as an example of the "beautiful" the movement of a bird in flight, contrasting
that with flashes of lightning, which he clearly took
for "sublime." The passage quoted is followed by
a grudging admission of the pleasure afforded by
novelty, an admission made in such a way as to
discourage the student from trying to achieve it and
the reader from admiring it. The faithful pupil of
Blair was encouraged to provide the mixture as before. It is noticeable that Motley nowhere criticized
his friend for being trite; the acceptable ideality
of picturesque ruins made him content with
stereotypes.

Pleasing to Motley and also "beautiful" according to the standards of Blair are lines from the
introductory section, "The Old Player."

> From groves of glossy beech the wood thrush fills
> In the dim twilight with his rapturous trills;
> From sweet still pastures, cropped by nodding kine,
> Their noon-tide tent the century-counting pine;
> From the brown streams along whose winding shore
> Each sleepy inlet knows my resting oar;
> From the broad meadows, where the mowers pass
> Their scythes slow-breathing through the feathered
> grass;
> From tawny rye-fields, where the cradler strikes
> With whistling crash among the bearded spikes;
> Fresh from such glories, how shall I forget
> My summer's day-dream, now the sun is set?

The critic apparently found ll. 5–10 especially satisfying, for he gave them two sets of approving parallels. Again Motley was sufficiently taken with the
ideality of the subject to be indifferent to the quality of the language, to the grotesque effects of the
personifications, and to the haphazard arrangement
of the details.

Employing the same standard of the "beautiful," Motley gave his accolade to the pseudo-
Homeric catalogue of ships in "The Exile's Secret";
but when human beings appear on the scene he had
complaints. He did not like an "old skipper" who
"curses," an "excursion crew" of fishermen, a
"slightly tipsy" sailor, and a group of "clam-
adventurers." Here Motley appears to be obeying
the injunction of Blair against the use of "such
allusions as raise in the mind disagreeable, mean,
vulgar or dirty ideas."

Anxious to meet his friend's standards,
Holmes frequently diluted his original matter.
Lines of the *Private Copy* reading:

> We stand a moment on the outstreched pier;—
> Ho! lazy boatman, scull your dory here!
> The tide runs fast;

became in *Songs in Many Keys:*

> So fair when distant should be fairer near;
> A boat shall waft us from the outstretched pier.
> The breeze blows fresh;

The change was dictated by Motley's protest
against the imperative: "Scull your dory here!"
That in quest of the Ideal and in evasion of the Actual, one might come upon the insipid—this consequence the exponents of the favored opposition
failed to perceive. Holding to the principle, Motley pushed Holmes toward an alien style. He brack-
eted and questioned these lines:

> Pilots, with varnished hats and shaggy coasts;
> Fishers, with scaly oars and slippery boats;
> Boys of rude speech, who spread a ragged sail
> On courtesying skiffs that want a crew to bale;
> Sires of the town who quit the cushioned chair
> On some bright morning when the breeze is fair,
> And tempt the dangers of the tossing brine
> To learn how paupers live,—and guardians dine;

The critic's marginal note is: "I would omit this—
It is very good & Crabby, but I like your heroic style
best particul[arl]y in this poem." Not Holmes at his
best certainly, these lines are nevertheless in his best
vein, and Motley did him no service by trying to
shift his attention from a Crabbe to a Schiller. The
whole of "The Exile's Secret," alternating between
the "beautiful" and the "Crabby," did not give Motley the same satisfaction as "The Mother's Secret,"
with its clearly Ideal theme. The incongruity of the

styles did not disturb Motley; what disturbed him was any intrusion of the Actual. "Artistic feeling" required the avoidance of Actuality; here Motley did not trust Holmes. In his letter he wrote: "To the *morally* pure & noble, there is no need of my exhorting you—To that you are always instinctively and unerringly true—To the intellectually beautiful & sublime you are equally loyal—It is only to the artistic feeling that you are sometimes false, and so far, false to your own nature. . . ."

In the section now called "The Statesman's Secret," with its unheroic and unpoetical subject, Daniel Webster, Motley found two passages that he evidently regarded as notably "false" to "artistic feeling."

> The cheated turncoat shakes his broken chain,
> The baffled spoilsman howls, "In vain! In vain!"
> The whitening bones of trampled martyrs strew
> The slippery path his sliding feet pursue.
> Go, great Deluded! Go and take thy place
> With thy sad brethren of the bovine race, frenzied
> The herd of would-be quadriennial kings
> The white-house gad-fly crazes when he stings!

Motley wanted both deleted, explaining why in a marginal note to the first:

> a presidential election is in its details so vulgar & unpoetical, that you must soar as high as possible into the *general* empyrean of poetical ambition—This you have done very skilfully, & if you will omit as above suggested, the picture is grand & solemn—it ought in no sense to be comic

Deleting the first passage, Holmes revised the second:

> Shake from thy sense the wild delusive dream!
> Without the purple, art thou not supreme?
> And soothed by love unbought, thy heart shall own
> A nation's homage nobler than its throne!

Avoiding the democratic Actual, Holmes could reach for the Ideal only by resorting to an inappropriately royal diction.

Bankers, like politicians, similarly tempted the poet toward the vulgar Actual, and the embezzler's dinner-party displeased Motley in proportion as it evoked Holmes's sense of the comic. The critic did what he could with the offending subject. The Hostess who thinks of her "vexed cuisine" is "too bourgeois"; there are "too many" extra dinner guests; the amount of drinking is "too strong for a ladies' dinner party." The "Blairish" objection to the "mean" shows in protests against such words as "sweating," "slink," "lugs out," "slow-coach," "slap on," and "jolly," offenses that Holmes amended or deleted.

A far safer subject was that of "The Lover's Secret." From Motley's standpoint a love-sick ancient Roman was Ideal in his condition, his time, and his place. Although Motley found a few inelegant words, he considered the "whole episode . . . classic, original, & brilliant," and marked the first eighteen lines with the parallels:

> What ailed young Lucius? Art had vainly tried
> To guess his ill, and found herself defied.
> The Augur plied his legendary skill,
> Useless; the fair young Roman languished still.
> His chariot took him every cloudless day
> Across the Pincian Hill or Appian Way;
> They rubbed his wasted limbs with sulphurous oil
> Oozed from the far-off Orient's heated soil;
> They led him tottering down the steamy path
> Where bubbling fountains filled the thermal bath;
> Borne in a litter to Egeria's cave,
> They washed him, shivering, in her icy wave.
> They sought all curious herbs and costly stones,
> They scraped the moss that grew on dead men's bones
> They tried all cures the votive tablets taught,
> Scoured every place whence healing drugs were bought,
> O'er Thracian hills his breathless couriers ran,
> His slaves waylaid the Syrian caravan.

Thirty-one additional lines received Motley's approving parallels. He asked for the omission of one couplet, pointed out the redundancy in "hired sicarius," and objected to "The maid of lion step," because "lion is too masculine," suggesting "panther" as a substitute. The maid is she who "bade black Crassus 'touch her if he dare!'" Motley protested in the margin: "I don't like 'touch her if he dare!'— too prosaic and the passage is very poetical & romantic." The whole, however, pleased Motley because he saw in it the ideal qualities of "classic elegance" and "tenderness & truth."

In "Ideality," however, it could not match "The Mother's Secret." In that section, Motley was able to mark nearly half the poem with the parallels; and here he saw little to complain of. Combining religion and domestic affection, "The Mother's Secret" nowhere tempted Holmes toward the gross actualities Motley wanted him to avoid. Motley saw not only Fra Angelico; he found in the description of the elders in the Temple "a vivid picture in 2 Rembrandt strokes":

> They found him seated with the ancient men,—
> The grim old swordsmen of the tongue and pen,—
> Their bald heads glistening as they clustered near,
> Their grey beards slanting as they turned to hear,
> Lost in half envious wonder and surprise
> That lips so fresh should utter words so wise.

Consistent in his major criticisms and in certain minor ones not here noted, Motley holds to the standard of the opposed Ideal and Actual as if by

1857 it were second nature to do so. As a directive for both the critic and writer, this standard carried weight well into the late nineteenth century. Extracted from their philosophical ground, the concepts of the Ideal and the Actual had degenerated into trite maxims for the selection of subject-matter and the choosing of words. The conspicuous insipidness of much American writing and painting of the period is traceable to this critical formula, not to the so-called "genteel tradition." Notions of gentility no doubt affected social behavior, but such notions cannot clearly be related to literary taste. Reference to the habit of condemning the Actual and demanding the Ideal will provide a better explanation of much nineteenth-century criticism—e.g., objections to the "realism" of William D. Howells—then loose of an assumed "tradition" of gentility. As for Victorian prudery too often charged to the Puritans, it operated to rule out entirely from the range of selection certain subject matter; but, as our illustration of taste shows, considerations of prudery need not be evoked at all. Here the magic formula provides the only standard except for those recollections of Blair not inconsistent with it.

A usable, or at least not damaging, directive for a writer of Hawthorne's interest and talents, the formula was scarcely the right one for Holmes. Using it, Motley was led to discount—perhaps was blinded to—his friend's gift for satire. For example, he enjoined Holmes to omit from "The Exile's Secret" the sharp couplet:

I dress the phrases of our tarry friend,
As lawyers trim the rascals they defend.

Apparently assuming that his friend's taste was superior to his own, Holmes accepted all Motley's criticism, except two trivial verbal ones. Had Holmes resisted this imposition of a standard alien to his temper and his talent, he would have been a wiser and possibly a better poet than he was. However successful a venture into the Ideal "The Chambered Nautilus" (1857) may be and may have seemed to its author (or to Motley), "The Last Leaf" (1831) is a better indication of where Holmes's real, if slight, talent lay. Finally, our illustration of taste suggests that a question possibly worth investigation is how far other writers (e.g., Henry James) were deflected from their courses by explicit or implicit exhortations to soar into the heavenly æther of the Ideal.

Source: Eleanor M. Tilton, "Holmes and His Critic Motley," in *American Literature*, Vol. 36, No. 4, January 1965, pp. 463–74.

Sources

Holmes, Oliver Wendell, *The Autocrat of the Breakfast-Table*, J. M. Dent & Sons, 1960, pp. 88–90, 92.

———, "The Chambered Nautilus," in *The Poetical Works of Oliver Wendell Holmes*, Houghton Mifflin Company, 1975, pp. 149–50, 152.

Macy, John, "Holmes," in *The Spirit of American Literature*, Doubleday, Page & Company, 1913, pp. 155–70.

Parker, Gail Thain, "Sex, Sentiment, and Oliver Wendell Holmes," in *Women's Studies*, Vol. 1, No. 1, 1972, p. 49.

Prothero, Rowland E., "A Review of *The Writings of Oliver Wendell Holmes*," in *Quarterly Review*, Vol. 179, No. 359, January 1895, pp. 189–206.

Further Reading

Emerson, Ralph Waldo, *Nature and Selected Essays*, Penguin, 2003, originally published by J. Munroe and Company, 1836.
   Emerson's first and most influential work on the post-Romantic philosophy of transcendentalism, *Nature* is a crucial work in the historical context of mid-nineteenth-century Boston.

Gibian, Peter, *Oliver Wendell Holmes and the Culture of Conversation*, Cambridge University Press, 2001.
   In this important book about Holmes's place in American history, Gibian provides a literary and historical analysis of Holmes and his intellectual circle.

Hawthorne, Hildegarde, *The Happy Autocrat: A Life of Oliver Wendell Holmes*, Longmans, Green, 1938.
   Hawthorne's biography of Holmes sketches the historical context surrounding "The Chambered Nautilus" and provides a useful overview of the poet's life and career.

Traister, Bryce, "Sentimental Medicine: Oliver Wendell Holmes and the Construction of Masculinity," in *Studies in American Fiction*, Vol. 27, No. 2, Autumn 1999, pp. 203–25.
   Although it does not discuss "The Chambered Nautilus," Traister's article provides an interesting commentary about Holmes's views on gender relations, particularly his idea of male medical authority and its approach to women.

For the Sake of Strangers

Dorianne Laux

1994

Dorianne Laux's "For the Sake of Strangers" first appeared in her second poetry collection, *What We Carry* (1994). It was included in *Ten Poems to Last a Lifetime* (2004), a collection of thought-provoking poems compiled by Roger Housden. The poem is about the experience of continuing through daily life despite feeling immense grief. By using the word "we," Laux demonstrates that she is writing about a universal experience shared by many of her readers. Much of Laux's poetry strives to reflect shared universal experiences. She is often praised for the way she manages to incorporate detail into poems that explore such shared experiences. Although "For the Sake of Strangers" is about an individual who is struggling with emotional pain, Laux creates a picture of hope as she describes strangers, unaware of the speaker's pain, showing kindness. The poem depicts a remedy to loneliness and hopelessness. The pain felt by the poem's speaker is a common problem, but the solution is somewhat unexpected.

"For the Sake of Strangers" is written in free verse, which gives it a modern appeal and informal tone. Laux uses few literary devices, choosing a straightforward approach to her expression instead. Still, a careful reading of the poem reveals a sophisticated use of subtlety that adds layers of meaning and insight. By describing a series of strangers and their treatment of the grieved person, Laux creates an uplifting picture of the power of the kindness of strangers. She draws understated connections between the people in the poem, pointing to the

universality of human experience. The people are strangers to the speaker in the poem, but they are not strangers to the speaker's pain. They have compassion for her because they, too, have felt grief.

Author Biography

Born on January 10, 1952, in Augusta, Maine, Dorianne Laux is the daughter of Alton Percy Green, an Irish paper mill worker, and Frances (Comeau) Green, a nurse. Frances left her husband and sons, taking her daughter to California. She remarried, and the child took her stepfather's surname, Laux. In her twenties, Laux worked at an assortment of jobs, including gas station manager, maid, and donut maker. As a single mother to a daughter named Tristem, Laux struggled to continue her education but managed to take only occasional classes and writing workshops at a local junior college. She moved to Berkeley, California, in 1983. As she started to take her writing more seriously, she sought scholarships and grants that made it possible for her to return to school when her daughter was nine years old. Laux graduated with honors from Mills College in 1988. She married Ron Salisbury in 1991, but the marriage ended three years later. In 1997, she married the poet Joseph Millar.

Laux's career has been spent writing and teaching. Her poetry was first published in *Three West Coast Women* (1983), which featured her work and the poetry of Laurie Duesing and Kim Addonizio. Subsequent collections featured only Laux's poetry; *Awake* was published in 1990, *What We Carry* (in which "For the Sake of Strangers" first appeared) was issued in 1994, *Smoke* was put out in 2000, and *Facts about the Moon* was released in 2005. Laux also collaborated with Addonizio to write *The Poet's Companion: A Guide to the Pleasures of Writing Poetry* (1997). Additionally, Laux's poetry is included in numerous anthologies and has been published in such publications as *Ploughshares*, *American Poetry Review*, and *Kenyon Review*. To date, her work has been translated into French, Italian, Korean, Romanian, and Brazilian Portuguese.

As a teacher and professor, Laux has been on the staffs of the California College of Arts and Crafts, the University of Minnesota, and the University of Oregon, where, in 2005, she was an associate professor in the Creative Writing Program. In addition to being a guest lecturer at various colleges, including Antioch University and California

Dorianne Laux Photograph by Tristem Laux. Reproduced by permission of Dorianne Laux

State University, Laux has been the writer in residence or visiting writer at the University of Arkansas, University of Memphis, University of Idaho, and Hamline University.

Laux's poetry has earned her critical recognition. She won a Pushcart Prize in 1986, her first poetry collection was nominated for a San Francisco Bay Area Book Critics Award, and *What We Carry* was a National Book Critics Circle Award finalist for poetry in 1995. She has also been the recipient of fellowships from such organizations as the MacDowell Colony, Yaddo, the Guggenheim Foundation, and the National Endowment for the Arts. In 2001, the poet laureate Stanley Kunitz invited Laux to read at the Library of Congress.

Poem Summary

"For the Sake of Strangers" describes the daily life of a person trying to carry on despite the heavy weight of grief. Throughout the poem, Laux uses the pronoun "we" to show that the experience she is describing is a universal one. Dealing with grief and trying to reenter the flow of life in the midst of it are experiences shared by the speaker and the reader.

Laux begins by stating that no matter how difficult it is to carry the weight of grief, it has to be done. The speaker says that by rising and gathering momentum, the "dull strength" is found to be in crowds of people. Laux then describes a young boy enthusiastically giving the speaker directions, which indicates that the speaker reached out to him first to ask for help. Rather than wandering around lost, she found the strength to ask for what she needed. This is relevant on a literal and figurative level. Next, Laux describes a woman who kindly opens a door for the speaker and then waits patiently as she goes through it. The speaker does not sense that the woman holding the door is in a rush to get on with her own business, but rather that she is content to extend this small kindness. That the speaker describes herself as an "empty body" passing through the door, however, suggests two things. First, it suggests that the woman holding the door is unaware of the speaker's emotional state. Second, it suggests that the speaker feels numb to the pain of her own loss. This is a common feeling for those working through grief.

The speaker then remarks, "All day it continues, each kindness / reaching toward another." The speaker goes through the entire day feeling that the kindness that total strangers show to her becomes a sort of chain that gets her from the beginning of the day safely to the end. She feels that the comfort and support she receives are ongoing. When she gives the example of a stranger singing to no one as she passes, trees offering their blooms, and the smile of a "retarded child," the reader understands that the speaker has started to see her world through a particular lens. The speaker now sees the world as a place where everyone and everything reach out to her to ease her pain and bring her small joys. Of course, she is personalizing things that are not necessarily meant for her benefit, but that is not as important as the fact that the speaker chooses to embrace the world because she feels that it embraces her. She has adopted a very optimistic perspective.

When Laux next adds that "they" always find her and seem to be waiting on her, she reveals how the speaker has come to believe that the world is not only kind to her but also actually waits on her and pursues her in order to protect her from her own despair. She sees the world not just as a temporary escape or distraction but indeed as her only hope for healing. She perceives the world as reaching out to her to save her from the pain that would drive her off the edge of her own grief. She rationalizes this idea by concluding that "they" (the

strangers) must have once been in her situation and therefore know what it is like to be summoned by pain, grief, and loneliness. The speaker feels that her despair tries to pull her away from the world and "off the edge," while the world tries to save her from herself. She describes the intangible nature of this tug-of-war when she writes about "this temptation to step off the edge / and fall weightless, away from the world."

Themes

Powerlessness and Weakness

The poem begins with the statement that regardless of the kind or size of grief, there is no choice but to carry it. The speaker then describes reengaging the world by simply rising and allowing momentum to build. Although momentum can produce speed and be powerful (especially when something heavy is gaining momentum), it is not an image of personal power. Momentum is not speed that is controlled or guided. When it is used as a metaphor in the poem, it depicts speed acting on its own. The momentum in the speaker's life is an unknown, as the rest of the poem indicates. Whether the momentum will build and take the speaker hurtling deeper into despair or lift her out of despair and back into normalcy and contentment remains to be seen. Regardless, the speaker is not in the driver's seat.

The speaker seems very clear about how she thinks and feels and how she perceives the world, but she understands her own powerlessness to direct her path to healing. She uses "dull strength" to get through crowds, and she is in an "empty body" that is "weightless" at the end of the poem. She finds herself in a world that pursues her to save her, while at the same time she feels the pull of despair and destruction. Despite being in the middle of this tug-of-war, she makes no apparent effort to move in one direction or another. She seems to be at the mercy of her own struggle, destined to go to whichever side is ultimately the stronger of the two.

Hope and Support

The main idea of "For the Sake of Strangers" is that deep despair can be cured by the kindness of strangers. The speaker describes interactions with a series of strangers who, despite knowing nothing of the pain of her emotional struggles, show her enough kindness to give her hope that she can pass through her pain as surely as she passes

Topics For Further Study

- Research the five stages of grief and determine at what stage the speaker is in at the time of the poem. What is the next stage? Write a poem expressing the speaker's feelings in the next stage. Determine what stylistic elements of "For the Sake of Strangers" you think might still be appropriate for your poem and which should be changed to make your poem the best possible expression of the speaker's emotional progress.

- In the poem, the speaker is in the midst of grief. Think of a time when you had to carry the weight of grief. Write about your experience of grief in a way that is most comfortable for you, telling how you felt when you were among people as you carried your private pain. For example, you may choose to write a poem, an essay, a song, or a monologue.

- Using pictures from magazines, photocopies from books, or other items, create a collage depicting the people described in the poem. Arrange the images in a way you feel captures the spirit of the poem. Be sure to include a copy of the poem in your collage.

- Take a walk in your community in an area where there are lots of different people. Take note of how many people are friendly to you and how many people do not seem to notice you at all. What is your general impression of strangers, based on this walk? How similar to or different from the experience of the speaker in "For the Sake of Strangers" is yours? If you were taking the same walk during a time of personal struggle, would you be uplifted or further depressed? Using a camera and music you have chosen, create a visual presentation of your experience and show it to your class. Discuss your conclusions.

- Read about depression to gain a better understanding of what sufferers experience. Look for at least five works of art that depict depression in different people, different times, or different settings. Make photocopies of the artwork you have chosen and compile them in a folder. Whenever possible, include information about the artists' motivations in creating the particular works.

- The kind of emotional distress endured by the speaker in the poem is often described in literature. Find three examples of literary characters burdened by grief. Your examples should be drawn from varying time periods, cultures, and social circumstances. Write brief plot summaries of their stories, with character sketches. Recruit two friends for a dramatic presentation in which each of you plays the part of one of the characters. Your three characters will be engaged in discussion about their commonalities and their differences.

---

through the glass door held open by the patient woman in lines 6 and 7. The speaker also encounters a boy who gladly gives her directions, a singing stranger, a smiling child, and even a blossoming tree. In the speaker's mind, all of these people and things regard her as someone deserving of kindness, and they make an effort to reach out to her in her time of need. This feeling of being supported and embraced by the world gives the speaker hope. Without that sense of support and embrace, she is certain that she would be so consumed by her own despair that she would give in to the "temptation to step off the edge / and fall weightless, away from the world." To her, the world itself holds her close, encouraging her to stay with it. In fact, the world is so committed to holding on to her and keeping her from the edge that it pursues her and waits for her (lines 13–15). The world and its inhabitants are protective of the speaker and seem to have a stake in her recovery from her grief.

Emotional Healing

Although the poem ends before the speaker has healed from her grief, Laux gives the reader some indications about the first steps to take. The speaker moves toward her recovery both passively and actively. Passively, she accepts the help of strangers and interprets their actions in a way that makes her feel loved and supported. Before she can benefit from what strangers offer her, however, she must actively choose to reenter her community and interact there. In the third line, Laux says, "We rise and gather momentum." Although the momentum may be involuntary, the choice to rise is not. The speaker makes a decision to get up and be among other people. The first person with whom she feels a connection is a boy giving her directions. This implies that she asked him for directions rather than choosing to wander aimlessly. Her decision to ask for directions is a decision not only to engage a person in an interaction but also to make a choice about where she wants to go. Without the speaker's active and passive steps toward her own healing, she would be doomed to "step off the edge / . . . away from the world."

Style

Conversational Tone

Laux maintains a conversational, emotionless tone in "For the Sake of Strangers" despite the subject matter. She achieves this tone by using a stream-of-consciousness flow, few literary devices, free verse, and informal language. This casual tone indicates that the speaker is aware of her difficult situation but is numb to the painful emotions associated with it. Whether she is speaking to someone or merely recording her thoughts, she comes across as more of a narrator than a person struggling through grief. This reveals a great deal about the speaker's emotional state.

Stream of Consciousness

"For the Sake of Strangers" is written in a stream-of-consciousness style that gives the poem a very spontaneous, honest feel. Readers feel that they are listening in on the speaker's private thoughts and are given a special insight into how she perceives the world. As her perception of the world changes, her language and observations reflect that in a very honest, believable way. This type of writing also makes it easy for readers to relate to the speaker and move into the flow of the poem without the hindrances of formality, structure, or carefully chosen words. A stream-of-consciousness poem gives readers the speaker's unedited thoughts and feelings, and it is therefore both honest and personal.

Free Verse

"For the Sake of Strangers" is written in free verse, which is unrhymed verse without metrical constraints. Free verse sounds like everyday conversation. The use of free verse is more common in modern poetry, and many readers find it less formal and more accessible. In "For the Sake of Strangers," the use of free verse allows the speaker to express herself in a straightforward manner that has a spontaneous, natural quality.

Historical Context

Security, Stability, and Contentment in the Early 1990s

In America, the early 1990s were years of general economic and political stability, technological and medical progress, social stability, and vibrant culture. President George H. W. Bush held office from 1989 to 1993. Bush and Soviet President Mikhail Gorbachev held a summit in 1991, officially ending the cold war. Military efforts were made by American troops in other parts of the world, including the Middle East and Somalia, but people were safe at home and supportive of the troops abroad. The Gulf War (1990–1991) protected Kuwait from the Iraqi leader Saddam Hussein's invasion and liberated the small nation. The 1990s began with the reunification of Germany and the end of apartheid in South Africa, so people felt that things were improving globally as well. Although Bush's popularity was strong during and after his military endeavors, it waned when the recession of the late 1980s failed to improve.

Famous Americans of the early 1990s included Steve Jobs and Bill Gates as the faces of the rapidly progressing computer industry, Martha Stewart as the face of lavish entertaining at home, Ross Perot as the face of capitalism, and Michael Jordan and Andre Agassi as the faces of elite athletics. Popular music included grunge, rap, and hip-hop, and young people became more involved in their communities.

The 1990s had its share of tragedy, including the 1992 riots in Los Angeles following the acquittal of police officers who had been filmed beating a black man, Rodney King, after a traffic stop and the 1993 bombing of the World Trade Center in New York City. Although life in America was certainly not perfect, the early 1990s were years of general well-being, security, opportunity, and contentment.

Compare & Contrast

- **1994:** Most interaction between people is either in person or by telephone. Because people relate to each other through direct communication, most of the accepted rules of courtesy still govern interaction.

  Today: With tens of millions of people using e-mail to do everything from keeping in touch with family members to selling their cars, the rules of social interaction are changing. The faceless nature of e-mail, coupled with the fact that communication does not take place in "real time," often makes people less inclined to adhere to traditional rules of courtesy and conduct.

- **1994:** During the 1990s, awareness of psychological depression and its treatment make significant progress. In 1994, particular emphasis is given to research into the genetic causes of manic depression, or bipolar disorder. As a result of research and public education, depression carries less of a stigma than it did in the past, and people suffering with it are given more hope. Millions of patients approach their primary care physicians for help; about half are treated by their physicians, with the other half ultimately treated by psychotherapists. Treatments include therapy and prescribed antidepressant drugs.

  Today: Being diagnosed with depression is rarely a shameful thing, and sufferers are offered psychological and medical support. Many antidepressants are available for prescription, and most licensed therapists have experience in this area. In addition to medication, patients are encouraged to make lifestyle changes to support their recovery.

- **1994:** Americans enjoy a general sense of well-being. The economy in 1994 is stronger than it has been in years, and there are no international threats on American soil. Overseas, genocide begins in Rwanda as the Hutus begin to decimate the Tutsis, and American troops are sent to Haiti in an effort to end human rights violations and restore democracy. Many Americans are concerned about global tragedies but feel safe from threats at home.

  Today: Having suffered the tragedy of September 11, 2001, in New York City, Washington, D.C., and western Pennsylvania and then the horrors of Hurricane Katrina in the Gulf Coast, Americans feel more vulnerable than they did in decades past. They feel the anxiety that comes with uncertainty and insecurity. Although these events remind Americans that they are not invincible, they do serve to bring them together with a stronger sense of community, charity, and compassion for each other.

Critical Overview

Critics often describe Laux's poetic voice as strong and convincing. In the *Women's Review of Books*, Alison Townsend looks at *What We Carry*, the collection in which "For the Sake of Strangers" was first published. Townsend comments, "Laux's voice is taut, tough, sensuous. . . . Her medium is the autobiographical lyric-narrative poem, but one so thoroughly grounded in the real world that it becomes a kind of transparent container, transmitting experience with uncanny immediacy." In *Ploughshares*, Philip Levine recommends *What We Carry* to readers, describing it as "gritty" in its realistic depiction of modern life. Laux's reviewers often applaud her clarity of expression and her ability to bring to life an image or an experience. Townsend expresses a similar admiration when she comments that Laux gives "scrupulous attention to detail" and "locates her poetry in the things of this world—the physical, the real, the daily." This is what is so appealing to many of Laux's readers; they can relate to her experiences as expressed in her poetry, because they tell the stories and describe the feelings of many women.

Laux's forthright style is so characteristic that, in a review of Laux's and Kim Addonizio's book *The Poet's Companion: A Guide to the Pleasures of Writing Poetry*, Molly Bendall of the *Antioch Review* writes, "The passion toward poetry that these two writers/editors feel is certainly evident. What is also evident is their bias. They prefer the plain-spoken, direct, and easily explainable poem based on personal experience." Townsend finds *What We Carry* to be a particularly strong collection of Laux's poetry: "Laux's voice has always been wise, deep and completely unself-pitying. But there is in this collection a certain fullness of spirit."

Criticism

Jennifer Bussey

Jennifer Bussey holds a master's degree in interdisciplinary studies and a bachelor's degree in English literature and is an independent writer specializing in literature. In this essay, she follows the psychological journey of the speaker in Laux's poem.

As Laux's "For the Sake of Strangers" opens, the speaker tells the reader that she is burdened by the weight of grief. The opening statement sets the stage for the poem that follows, emphasizing the speaker's emotional burden as the axis on which the rest of the poem will spin. In effect, the speaker introduces herself to the reader by identifying herself as a grief-stricken person. She does not tell the reader anything about the cause of her grief, how long she has been suffering, or how she feels about her difficult situation. Instead, she states matter-of-factly that people must carry painful burdens in life. As she continues, describing a day among strangers, she takes the reader on her psychological journey from pain to hope and healing.

In her first statement, the speaker explains that grief is a burden that is not only universal but also inescapable. She further suggests that grief comes in many packages, some small and some large. She says, "No matter what the grief, its weight, / we are obliged to carry it." By saying that it does not matter what the grief is or what its weight is, the speaker reveals that not all griefs are the same but they are all burdensome. From this, the reader understands that the speaker begins her psychological journey feeling trapped and burdened, with no way to free herself.

Despite her burden, the speaker manages to "rise and gather momentum" as she ventures out in public. She has come to a point in her grief where she is motivated to muster what little energy and "dull strength" she has to reenter society. At first, she sees the world as a place populated by faceless crowds (line 4). Because she sees only crowds through which she is pushing, she most likely feels as invisible to them as they are to her. She does not see any individuals, and because she makes no connection, she must feel that those in the crowd do not see her as an individual either. At this point in the poem, the speaker feels as lonely and isolated as she did in her own home. She is experiencing one of the ironies of human experience, feeling alone in a crowd.

Line 5 marks a turn with the words "And then." A change is taking place, and it happens in the form of a young boy who gives her directions "so avidly." The shift happens very subtly. First, strangers have changed from a crowd of indistinct people into a particular, enthusiastic young boy. Second, the reader can infer that since the young boy is giving directions, the speaker must have asked for them. In other words, it was she who first made the effort to reach out to interact with someone, rather than continuing to push through the crowd. Her effort is rewarded with the friendly, energetic help of a boy.

Next, a woman patiently holds open a glass door. The speaker realizes, as a result, that she is not invisible and that she is considered worthy of common courtesy. A stranger takes the time to hold open a door for her and then waits patiently as she goes through it. The speaker describes her "empty body" going through the door, but this is merely a description of how she feels, not how the woman sees her. Because she feels burdened by her grief and is depleted by it, she feels empty and numb, but she is discovering that feeling empty inside has not made her disappear altogether in the eyes of others. Just as she does in the interaction with the young boy, the speaker makes a decision to take action to engage the world. Here, she goes through a door, which seems a fairly passive thing to do—except for the fact that the door is glass. This means that she can see through the door, see what is on the other side, and she makes a choice to move knowingly from one place to another. On a literal level, this is a small but important step for someone so emotionally burdened. On a figurative level, however, this is a much bigger step, because it represents the speaker's willingness and ability to make choices that change her situation. Even though she does so cautiously (it is a door through which she can see, after all), the decision indicates that she is ready to take hold of her life again and choose to move in new directions.

In lines 8 and 9, the speaker claims that the rest of the day passes as a chain of kindness extended to her by strangers. The reader can safely assume that the speaker is recalling the day with a bit of selective memory, bringing her new perspective to her memory. She has come to see the world as a loving and supportive place; thinking back on the day, she recalls only the random acts of kindness that worked together to lift her spirits. The fact that her perception has become skewed toward her newfound optimism is clear in lines 9 through 12. In these lines, the speaker claims that "a stranger singing to no one," "trees offering their blossoms," and "a retarded child / who lifts his almond eyes and smiles" are all offering love and kindness to her. The reader, of course, recognizes that the singing stranger is, in fact, singing to no one (including the speaker), the trees are merely obeying the laws of nature, and the child is probably smiling as an expression of his own contentment, not at being happy to see the speaker. These lines describe an important new phase of the speaker's psychological journey, because instead of seeing bleakness and isolation everywhere, the speaker sees optimism and caring—although here, too, the speaker's perceptions are subjective, emotional, and probably inaccurate. In short, the speaker has found a way to hope.

The speaker's newly hopeful outlook is carried a step further when she perceives the world not only as caring but also as protective of her. She remarks, "Somehow they always find me, seem even / to be waiting, determined to keep me / from myself." Unable to save herself from her own despair and uncertainty, she finds hope in believing that the world will take care of her, protecting her even from herself. The world of loving strangers finds her, waits for her, and seeks to guard her. She explains that they know about her innermost struggles, about "the thing that calls to me," because have been in the same situation and heard the same call. Because they have survived their grief, they recognize it and know how to protect her from it. This is comforting to her because, at this point, she feels incapable of protecting herself in her grief. Notice how Laux creates subtle tension in the poem, reflecting the tension in the speaker's mind, by describing how the speaker "pushes" herself through crowds in line 4 and is simultaneously pulled by the call of her despair in line 15. Because the speaker feels

The opening statement sets the stage for the poem that follows, emphasizing the speaker's emotional burden as the axis on which the rest of the poem will spin."

summoned by "the thing that calls to me" to "step off the edge," it is little wonder that she is so relieved to find that the world is peopled with strangers anxious to guide her to safety.

At the end of the poem, the speaker hints that her grief has driven her almost to the edge, where she is tempted to step off "and fall weightless, away from the world." This sounds as if the speaker has considered suicide as an antidote to her emotional suffering. The way she describes her feelings suggests that falling away is making a choice to step into a great unknown, which is frightening. Finding that strangers are so friendly and caring is certainly a relief, and even though she adds layers of fantasy to her encounters with the world, her decision to embrace a world that seems to embrace her is a step toward healing. She finds a way to feel less alone, less hopeless, and less vulnerable because complete strangers value her enough to reach out to her.

Given the course the poem takes, there is new insight in the speaker's first statement. It is interesting that she uses the word "obliged." This word carries two meanings and points to the two forces in the poem. From the speaker's point of view, "obliged" means "obligated." Faced with a devastating experience, there is no escape but to feel grief and somehow to muddle through it. But "obliged" can also mean "grateful," and this reflects the point of view of the strangers. As the speaker concludes, the strangers she has met throughout the day have actively pursued her in order to protect her from the devastation of grief that they have themselves managed to survive. They have already completed the psychological journey on which she finds herself, and they have the wisdom and perspective to see her situation more clearly than she does.

What Do I Read Next?

- Kim Addonizio's *Tell Me* (2000) contains deeply personal poetry that strives to show the darkness and light of her own experiences. Her subjects include family, love, heartbreak, and confession.

- Written by Addonizio and Laux, *The Poet's Companion: A Guide to the Pleasures of Writing Poetry* (1997) is the poets' effort to share their wisdom and encouragement with would-be poets. They offer chapters on subject matter, the elements and craft of writing, and the life of a poet.

- Compiled by Richard Ellman, *The Norton Anthology of Modern Poetry* (2nd ed., 1988) offers anyone interested in sampling modern poetry a wide range of writers, styles, and subjects. The introduction to each poet's section gives the reader background and context that helps to better understand and appreciate the poet's work.

- Laux's *What We Carry* (1994), is considered by critics to be a good representation of her work in general. In it, she explores themes of femininity, sexuality, struggle, and everyday life.

Consequently, they are obliged to help her. In the opening line, the strangers are also "we." Read it again: "No matter what the grief, its weight, / we are obliged to carry it." The strangers are compassionate and insightful, and they are grateful to carry some of the speaker's burden for her. Perhaps the word "we" indicates that, someday, the reader will heal from her pain and be able to extend kindness to others in their suffering, so that she can lighten their load as strangers have done for her.

Source: Jennifer Bussey, Critical Essay on "For the Sake of Strangers," in *Poetry for Students*, Thomson Gale, 2006.

Pamela Steed Hill

Pamela Hill is the author of a poetry collection, has published widely in literary journals, and is an editor for a university publications department. In this essay, she examines the hopefulness in Laux's poem, made all the stronger by its close association with despair, isolation, and grim determination.

The first four lines of Laux's "For the Sake of Strangers" suggest a generic "everyman" persona—a voice common to all humankind in describing the "weight, / we are obliged to carry." The pronouns "we" and "us" imply the bond that runs throughout humanity. It is a bond that links the reader to the poet as well, as she relays her message about something "we" all share: grief,

heaviness, and the "dull strength" that somehow gets us through.

These opening lines also appear to set the tone of the poem—somber, bleak, resigned. They depict a world in which people are burdened by sorrow and must accept that the best they can hope for is to find the will to "rise and gather momentum" in order not to falter completely. One source of the weariness seems to be the "crowds" that the individual must push through, implying that each of us is only one drop in a big sea or only an insignificant part of the masses. Interestingly, the idea of crowds points to strangers, and strangers are at the core of this poem's meaning.

The turning point in "For the Sake of Strangers" comes early, in the fifth line of an eighteen-line poem. Here, the speaker takes center stage, and the generic "we" persona is lost in the immediacy of one person's individual experience. The way Laux begins the line—"And then"—suggests a continuation of the sentiment already established, but the only thing that continues is the bond between human beings, and it grows stronger as the poem progresses.

Line 5 not only turns the "we" into "me" but also begins the introduction of strangers into the speaker's life. Here, a "young boy" is helpful in giving directions—a seemingly simple, uneventful task, but he does it "so avidly." This description suggests an *intentional* act of kindness, a courtesy performed by someone anxious to do a good deed. The woman who holds open the door is portrayed as patient and, apparently, courteous and thoughtful. Notice, though, that the speaker describes herself—her "body"—as "empty." This self-evaluation is important in the poem, and the fact that it is presented rather subtly makes the personal appraisal all the more interesting.

Much of the remainder of the poem addresses the strangers whom the speaker encounters and the pleasant surprise she experiences at their unwarranted kindness. She even feels the warmth of "a retarded child" who seems to connect with her with "his almond eyes." All day long, she passes by strangers who give new meaning to the wearisome "crowds" that the speaker has always felt a need to shove her way through. The word "Somehow" that begins line 13 implies that she does not know why her feelings of anonymity and emptiness are contradicted by the generous acts of strangers who make her feel special and not like just another face in the crowd.

The latter part of this work draws the speaker further into herself, and, at the same time, strengthens the bond between her and the strangers who, in a sense, come to her rescue. She reveals the emotional struggle and the inner turmoil that she carries as a "weight"—the "thing that calls" to her, apparently from inside herself, where she cannot be free of it. The speaker does not, however, feel completely alone in her battle to resist the negative urges that haunt her. Instead, she reasons that the "thing" that will not leave her alone "must have once called" to the strangers as well. Again, she recognizes a bond between human beings, although a frightfully depressing one that tempts "us" to "step off the edge" and give up on life altogether.

The beginning and the ending of "For the Sake of Strangers" are misleading in their grim tones and sorrowful messages. In a sense, they misrepresent the very core of the poem, disguising its deeper theme of hopefulness, kindness, and unity among the most unlikely people—total strangers. The connotations that surround grief, weight, dull strength, and the notion of stepping off the edge do not leave much room for considering anything positive, yet there is *something* that keeps the speaker going, something that prevents her from making the final "fall . . . away from the world." It is this element alone that points to the poem's central message of hope and survival.

None of the strangers whom the speaker encounters does anything particularly remarkable—

> *Overall, Laux presents a twofold poem. The speaker recognizes individual and personal human despondency but also concedes a general human bond that derives its power from the fact that it is shared."*

they hold open a door, sing joyfully, smile at her. But she enhances these common, chance meetings by including an encounter of a different sort, one that would be truly remarkable, if taken literally: "trees / offering their blossoms" just to make her feel better. Obviously, the trees are not doing anything intentional, but the speaker's perception of their desire to comfort her insinuates her own wish to be comforted. It also speaks to her finding such purpose and consolation in simple acts of strangers, acts that may commonly go unnoticed.

One may argue that the ending of a poem reflects its true sentiment, and that is a valid point to consider. In this case, however, the meatier part of the work lies in its middle lines. And if that is not enough to convince the skeptic, then the title itself needs to be pondered. The word "sake" can mean both "behalf" (welfare, interest, regard) and "purpose" (reason, goal, aim), and, here, the latter is most pertinent. The strangers who pass by the speaker—actually acknowledging her existence—seem to be there for a reason. It is as if they are "waiting" for her, "determined" to keep her safe from her own despairing thoughts. By their sake, she is alive and even daring to be optimistic.

Overall, Laux presents a twofold poem. The speaker recognizes individual and personal human despondency but also concedes a general human bond that derives its power from the fact that it is shared. Yes, she carries the heavy weight of grief and, yes, she must often "rise and gather momentum" in order to force herself to make it through the day. But her burdensome effort is then rewarded by an unexpected return effort from the "crowds" she typically considers so taxing. Her ultimate assessment is that there is enough common good in humanity to outweigh the load of individual grief.

The idea of bearing a weight plays heavily in "For the Sake of Strangers," as it does in the collection in which the poem appears. Laux titled the book *What We Carry* to imply an overall theme of human burden, and in some of the volume's works the weight is too much to bear. This poem, however, is at least one exception. Surely, the weight is heavy here, but it is mollified by a greater force—simple human kindness. It is a kindness made all the more special by the fact that it comes from strangers who could just as easily have ignored the speaker or even been rude to her, as the idea of "crowds" often suggests.

While this is an admittedly brief poem, it is packed with both obvious messages about dealing with grief and more subtle notions on overcoming sorrow. The greatest difference lies in the smothering effect of self-absorption and the relief of opening oneself up to the bonds that tie the human race together. The word "strangers" may connote a detached feeling by itself, but Laux has managed to bring it around to the same nuance as "friends." That alone says there is an overall spirit of *hope* in the poem.

Source: Pamela Steed Hill, Critical Essay on "For the Sake of Strangers," in *Poetry for Students*, Thomson Gale, 2006.

Dorianne Laux and Michael J. Vaughn

In the following interview, Laux and Vaughn discuss her poem "Abschied Symphony" and Laux's approach to structure, organization, and theme in her poetry.

Dorianne Laux is one of the best of the West Coast poets. She was a finalist for the National Book Critics Circle Award for her 1994 book, *What We Carry,* and with long-time cohort Kim Addonizio (herself a recent National Book Award finalist), she co-authored *The Poet's Companion: A Guide to the Pleasures of Writing Poetry* (1997, W.W. Norton). Laux teaches in the Creative Writing Program at the University of Oregon in Eugene.

When Laux read recently in my adopted hometown of Tacoma, Washington, I interviewed her for my column in the *Tacoma News-Tribune.* Considering the paper's lay audience, I thought it would be nice to get away from the constant generalized philosophizing of poetry articles, and instead use the opportunity to hone in on a single poem: "Abschied Symphony," from Laux's book, *Smoke*

(2000, BOA Editions). Because of space limitations, I had to use only excerpts of the poem, and cut out large parts of the interview. Here at the *TMR* website, however, we have no such limitations—and we have the luxury of a poetry-savvy audience. That said, let's begin with the poem itself (which Ms. Laux has graciously given us permission to reprint) and then proceed to the interview.

Abschied Symphony

Someone I love is dying, which is why,
when I turn the key in the ignition
and the radio comes on, sudden and loud,
something by Haydn, a diminishing fugue,
then back the car out of the parking space
in the underground garage, maneuvering through
the dimly lit tunnels, under low ceilings,
following yellow arrows stenciled at intervals
on gray cement walls and think of him,
moving slowly through the last
hard days of his life, I won't
turn it off, and I can't stop crying.
When I arrive at the tollgate I have to make
myself stop thinking as I dig in my pockets
for the last of my coins, turn to the attendant,
indifferent in his blue smock, his white hair
curling like smoke around his weathered neck,
and say, Thank you, like an idiot, and drive
into the blinding midday light.
Everything is hideously symbolic:
the Chevron truck, its underbelly
spattered with road grit and the sweat
of last night's rain, the Dumpster
behind the flower shop, sprung lid
pressed down on dead wedding bouquets—
even the smell of something simple, coffee
drifting from the open door of a cafe;
and my eyes glaze over, ache in their sockets.
For months now all I've wanted is the blessing
of inattention, to move carefully from room to room
in my small house, numb with forgetfulness.
To eat a bowl of cereal and not imagine him,
drawn thin and pale, unable to swallow.
How not to imagine the tumors
ripening beneath his skin, flesh
I have kissed, stroked with my fingertips,
pressed my belly and breasts against, some nights
so hard I thought I could enter him, open
his back at the spine like a door or a curtain
and slip in like a small fish between his ribs,
nudge the coral of his brains with my lips,
brushing over the blue coil of his bowels
with the fluted silk of my tail.
Death is not romantic. He is dying. The fact
is stark and one-dimensional, a black note
on an empty staff. My feet are cold,
but not as cold as his, and I hate this music
that floods the cramped insides
of my car, my head, slowing the world down
with its lurid majesty, transforming
everything I see into stained memorials
to life—even the old Ford ahead of me,

its battered rear end thinned to scallops of rust,
pumping grim shrouds of exhaust
into the shimmering air—even the tenacious
nasturtiums clinging to a fence, stem and bloom
of the insignificant, music spooling
from their open faces, spilling upward, past
the last rim of blue and into the black pool
of another galaxy. As if all that emptiness
were a place of benevolence, a destination,
a peace we could rise to.

[*Michael J. Vaughn*]: *Is there a strategy to the stanzaless style (and is there an academic term for "stanzaless")? Driving the narrative forward? Or perhaps just taking out one poetic element to simplify, as in a prose poem? I notice Kim Addonizio likes to do that, too. Or is it just something you do instinctually?*

[Dorianne Laux]: No, no term for the stanzaless style, at least not one I know. Yes, stanzas do stop the reader for a moment, allow for a rest, as in music, or often are used to signal a transition of some kind. But in a poem like this, the relentlessness of the forward movement is a way to keep the reader in the thrall of the poem's subject, which is death, and which rests for no one and gives no one rest. It was instinctive, though you can look to other stanzaless poems to see where that instinct was developed—Whitman comes to mind, and later, Sharon Olds and C. K. Williams.

I notice in your stanza'd poems, you often organize your lines into twos, threes, and fours. Is there an organizational need there?

Yes, the need to organize, to separate one movement from another, scenes, ideas, images, times and locations, the stanza can help with all these things and more. But this poem takes place on a drive from a parking lot to somewhere. Though we don't know the final location, we can assume it's home. The narrator never gets home though, except in her imagination, which also makes sense in terms of how we respond to death, the pain of grief—it's an endless ride for the living, at least until their own death releases them.

The giveaway first line. There's got to be a term for this, too ("confessional prelude"?), but I did the exact same thing in a novel. Pretty much you're telling the reader, "This is what the poem's going to be about," "Someone I love is dying . . ." I love the feeling of expectation that this sets up in the reader's mind; it makes them read the poem (or the novel, or the play) entirely differently, hungry for explanations and details. Again, intentional or just "what happened"?

> *Language is a way to help our vision of the world match up to its reality. It can also release us from that other world we have to live in, with all its protective fantasies and denials, so we can survive.*"

No, no term for this one either. It's just one of those lines that, as you say, announces itself rather boldly. I think death gives us this boldness of speech. You see the bravery of those facing death and you too become brave in the face of it. I received an email recently from a woman, an ex-student I'd met briefly a few years ago. Her sister's husband died in the Twin Towers on September 11. She said when speaking of her sister: "I worry about her and miss him so much—she of course is deep in the beginning stages of grief; I just hope she makes it to the stages. I feel as if I can be blunt with you, somehow." Death gives us permission to be blunt, as does poetry. Our defenses are stripped from us, which is why she could speak of the worst when telling me about her sister, and why she could speak to me so openly. What is there to lose when all has been lost? And yes, it was again an intuitive move, but in light of what we know about death, an appropriate move. Something in me said: Just say it. And when I did, the poem began to emerge. Isn't that how we comes to terms with the inevitable, with reality? I have another poem in that section in which the narrator never really accepts the death until she says the actual words, out loud: "He's dead. He's not coming back." It's the first time she believes it. Language is a way to help our vision of the world match up to its reality. It can also release us from that other world we have to live in, with all its protective fantasies and denials, so we can survive. We break out of that psychological world, too. And sometimes, it's poetry that helps us to do that. Poetry that can help us to go on living.

I love the stabs of simple sentences near the end: "Death is not romantic. He is dying." Great rhythmic interruption there. Do you write by musical mandates sometimes? Especially in a "symphonic" poem?

Yes, rhythm and rhyme; in my case, internal rhyme (there's a term for you!) is always of utmost importance. In this poem, I had the symphony playing in my head and that helped me to find a rhythm for the poem. I tried to be symphonic in my approach, another reason, possibly for the lack of stanzas. In terms of those specific lines, they act as a different kind of rest, as well as an introduction for what's to come. Think of Beethoven's, 5th Symphony for example, the power in those first notes: dum-dum-dum-DUM. The last note deeper to give it even more power: He is dying. Then, what follows, is this lovely high fast sweet music—but it derives its power and texture from those first strong, ponderous, grief-stricken, enraged notes which play in your mind as a backdrop. I hear such suffering behind those sweet desperate notes of his—life is always sweeter when set against death. Or, as one great poet said, "Death is the mother of beauty."

Nasturtiums. Lots of poems with nasturtiums in them. Is there something about nasturtiums? I had a friend who used them so much I started calling him "Nasturtium Boy." He switched to Daturas.

I had no idea there were so many poems with nasturtiums in them. What are they? I consider them to be my personal flower! I grew up in San Diego where we had nasturtiums growing in front yards all over town. I love them. They're a tough little pinwheel of a flower. And the circular shaped leaves are so beautiful—little green umbrellas. Lilies are the flower of death so I knew I needed another kind of flower, something small and seemingly insignificant, but that had this tenacious upward movement about it. Not quite a vine, but almost. Abundant. Colorful. Relentless.

Ending the poem on a dangling preposition. I love it! 'Bout time we bury that grammatical myth once and for all. And how stilted and British it would be to say, ". . . a peace to which we could rise."

Yes, sometimes you have to break the rules to get the sound right, to get the motion into the words. There was a last line I deleted after that line. It was ". . . a peace we could rise to, if we could rise." I realized I didn't want the poem to be endstopped like that, to conclude on a visually downward motion—the image of someone on the floor in sorrow, unable to rise—but the motion of rising, that yearning we all have to find some explanation,

some solace. And maybe, to end somewhere in the realm of possibility, looking up to the universe with a desperate hope.

I know from your booknotes that "abschied" is German for "farewell," but tell me about the symphony itself.

Haydn had been commissioned to compose music and play for a king in some northern province. He was given a full orchestra and the contract was for a month. The king kept asking them to stay on longer which was a great honor, and even if it wasn't, I guess you don't say no to a king. Months passed. The orchestra members were getting tired and cold as winter came on, and were missing their families who they had left behind. Haydn, unable to bear their suffering any longer, decided to write a symphony to help them leave without offending the king. In succession, each member played their last solo and then left the stage until only a lone violinist remained. When he finished the piece he walked off the stage, leaving it empty. The king then turned to Haydn and said something to the effect of, "I get the message," promptly called them a carriage and they all packed up and went home. Haydn called it his Farewell Symphony. (Absolutely true story. I saw it on PBS.)

Source: Dorianne Laux and Michael J. Vaughn, "An Interview with Dorianne Laux," in http://www.themonserratreview.com/interviews/DL_interview.html, 2005, pp. 1–4.

Roger Housden

In the following essay, Housden analyzes Laux's poem "For the Sake of Strangers," finding that Laux "is asking us to immerse ourselves in the full experience of our humanity."

This poem is a tribute to the survival of the human spirit in the face of all adversity, to our capacity to continue living even when it would seem easier to lie down forever and let life go on without us. It is a tribute, too, to the way we can support one another unknowingly through the smallest, apparently insignificant of acts. It is a reminder that anything and everything can matter in this world in which everyone is joined through the current of life to everyone else.

> No matter what the grief, its weight,
> we are obliged to carry it.

A failed relationship, a death in the family, the loss of our livelihood, the loss of our health, loneliness: If they have not done so already, one or more of these events will come to all of us sooner or later. Or perhaps no such calamity has touched your life, and your spirit is heavy for no apparent reason. For no reason at all, there can be long periods when life can seem not worth living. And yet, for the great majority of us, the sheer will to survive, to go on, will prevail over the wish to take our own life and be apparently free of it all for ever.

> We rise and gather momentum, the dull strength
> that pushes us through crowds.

The dull strength: It's true, how dulling depression is, yet something in us can take over, click into automatic, push one foot in front of the other, despite ourselves. We trudge through life like a ghost in times like these. Dorianne Laux captures it exactly in these four lines of her poem, and rescues the feeling from any hint of shame. Neither afraid nor ashamed of her feelings, however socially unacceptable they may be, she has obviously been down there, in that dark dank hole.

And she has also climbed out, no doubt more than once. A single mother with a family history of violence and abuse, she did every kind of casual labor, from being a gas station manager to a doughnut holer. Then, when she was thirty, she moved from her home state of Maine to the west coast, where, supported by scholarships and grants, she graduated with a B.A. degree in English. Her first book of poetry, *Awake,* was published in 1990 and nominated for the Bay Area Book Reviewers Award. "This is a poetry of risk," Philip Levine wrote of Laux's first collection; "it will go to the very edge of extinction to find the hard facts that need to be sung." He could have been speaking of this poem, "For the Sake of Strangers," which is to be found in her second collection, *What We Carry*—itself a finalist for the National Book Critics Circle Award. Since then, she has been awarded various prizes and fellowships and has become an associate professor of creative writing at the University of Oregon. Poetry, and the poetic vision, have remade Dorianne Laux.

Laux writes, she has said (in a web interview for *Perihelion*), "for the ones who are unable to write, for the heroes of my life: my family, my friends, the woman on the corner with a baby on one hip and a bag of groceries on the other, the child rapt in her joy, the man standing on his porch smoking a cigarette and feeling useless. I don't do this because I'm a great humanitarian, I simply can't help writing about these people—I see myself in them. And what I want most is to communicate to them that I have seen them standing there, and how, exactly, they have moved me. I am not ashamed of my love for them, or my pity, or my

. . . Dorianne Laux listens to the big breathing world, and steps back from the edge willing to bear the weight of her own pain and the gravity of existence."

fear." These are the people who fill this poem; a poem that is, in essence, one of gratitude.

Ten years or so ago, my wife's daughter Hannah died of cancer just before her fourth birthday. In her book, *Hannah's Gift,* Maria tells the story of the lessons she was taught on her way through that fire. After Hannah's death, Maria writes, "it was as if I had been lowered into a vat of slow-drying cement; I had become immobile gradually, and now felt almost completely paralyzed by grief." A few months later, she was standing by the side of the road.

"By the sound of its engine, I knew the car was coming fast. I stood on the curb, and with a sense of calm detachment, rolled the image around in my mind. Before the unsuspecting speeder could slam on his brakes, I would throw myself in front of him. . . . A white sedan crested the hill and roared past. I turned my head and closed my eyes as a whirl of dust blew into my face. My body started to shake. Stepping back from the curb, I collapsed in a heap on the grass."

Gradually, Maria came back from the edge, began to notice again the ripeness of melons in the market, laughed out loud at a joke, or bent down to wipe a scuff mark from the toe of her shoe. Then, within sixteen months of Hannah's death, she had given birth to two more daughters, Margaret and Madelaine. Her son, Will,

> had learned to read, Margaret had walked, Claude [Maria's husband at the time] had raised money for cancer research, and Madelaine had swallowed her first gulp of the world. I no longer felt willing for life to continue on without me. . . . The grief that once threatened to swallow me up had found a home in my bones. My suffering wasn't something I was going to have to let go of; it had become part of what I had to offer, part of who I am.

The world had called to Maria, and she had responded. As Dorianne Laux responds in this poem.

> And then the young boy gives me directions
> so avidly. A woman holds the glass door open,
> waits patiently for my empty body to pass through.
> All day it continues, each kindness
> reaching toward another . . .

There is a tiny gap in Laux's depression, the smallest aperture that allows her to look up and notice what, on an even darker day, would be hidden from her eyes: that the world goes on; that life is full to the brim in the person of a young boy; that generosity, kind-heartedness, is still at large in the world, in the person of a woman who does something as small and yet as significant as holding a door open for her *empty body to pass through.*

Something similar once happened to me in, of all places, the Sinai desert. I was traveling on foot with two guides and their camels through the great stretches of silence and sand. We had been traveling for a week already, and the emptiness of the desert had begun seeping into my mind and imagination. My own life felt empty. My feet were sore, my legs were aching, the wind was whipping through me. Was this what I wanted? Plodding head down through a bare and featureless land for no other reason than for the sake of it. Fear was already at my elbow; it filtered in with the awareness of my limited resources and how easily I could be swept from existence.

We pushed on for hours until we finally reached the far side of a great plain. Selman, one of my guides, had gone on ahead, and we caught sight of him now in the distance. He was crouching by a fire among some rocks below us. He had already made camp and hobbled the camels. We clambered down to join him, my legs barely holding. I threw all the clothes in the bag on my back and lay down by the flames like a child, teeth chattering, vital force gone. Selman took his only blanket and gently covered me with it. I mumbled some thanks.

"We are all brothers in the desert," he said, without affectation. I felt tears well up as I took in our simple human kinship. No great emotion, the passing of a blanket and a cup of tea. Our shared human frailty, the ceaseless wandering together on the road from birth to death, and maybe beyond.

Of course you don't need to go to the desert to know kindness like this: A stranger calls to Laux in her poem, merely through the song that she is singing to no one. Even the trees speak to her, offering her their blossoms; a retarded child smiles.

The whole world is speaking, if only we can listen, even for a moment. The whole world is trying always to find us, to rescue us from ourselves, from our own self-absorption; from the despair that lives in everything and everyone. From

> this temptation to step off the edge
> and fall weightless, away from the world.

It is not empathy that Laux is seeking in this poem, it is immersion. She is asking us to immerse ourselves in the full experience of our humanity. In this beautiful elegy of hope and gratitude, Dorianne Laux listens to the big breathing world, and steps back from the edge willing to bear the weight of her own pain and the gravity of existence. The world calls, and she responds. She returns from the brink willing to affirm the worth of her own life. Remember, finally, what Mary Oliver says in her poem "Wild Geese": that

> Whoever you are, no matter how lonely,
> the world offers itself to your imagination,
> calls to you like the wild geese, harsh and
> exciting—
> over and over announcing your place
> in the family of things.

Source: Roger Housden, "Back from the Edge," in *Ten Poems to Last a Lifetime*, Harmony Books, 2004, pp. 59–64.

Alison Townsend

In the following excerpted review of What We Carry, *Townsend calls Laux's voice "taut, tough, sensuous" and asserts that the poems in this collection "teach us how to give ourselves up to the world, how to love."*

Often when I read women's poetry I realize that I am trying to understand what kind of ethos or personal mythology the poet is creating. What is her relationship to time, place, history? How does this intersect with home, work, love, family? What kind of self-portrait has the poet created, and how does this reflect her self-image and her relationship with the outside world? . . . Dorianne Laux writes a poetry of gritty and tender self-disclosure that documents life as a creative woman in late twentieth-century America. . . .

I read Dorianne Laux's first book, *Awake,* with enormous pleasure, and have eagerly awaited the publication of her second, *What We Carry.* Laux's voice is taut, tough, sensuous. Her province is the ordinary world as it reveals itself to be miraculous, whether in a rainbowed pool of oil at a gas station, the sight of her daughter leaning into the side of a horse, a car full of women friends singing, or the mystery and beauty of her husband's body. Her medium is the autobiographical lyric-narrative poem, but one so thoroughly grounded in the real world that it becomes a kind of transparent container, transmitting experience with uncanny immediacy.

Laux achieves this transparency through scrupulous attention to detail. More than any other poet I know, she locates her poetry in the things of this world—the physical, the real, the daily. Her long stanzas pulse with energy, moving toward the next revelation, sometimes before we're even ready:

> Today, pumping gas in my old car, I stood hatless in the rain and the whole world went silent—cars on the wet street sliding past without sound, the attendant's mouth opening and closing on air—as he walked from pump to pump, his footsteps erased in the rain— nothing but the tiny numbers in their square windows rolling by my shoulder, the unstoppable seconds gliding by as I stood at the Chevron, balanced evenly on my two feet, a gas nozzle gripped in my hand, my hair gathering rain.
>
> And I saw it didn't matter who had loved me or who I loved. I was alone. The black oily asphalt, the slick beauty of the Iranian attendant, the thickening clouds—nothing was mine. . . . ("After Twelve Days of Rain,")

Laid out as carefully as cards, meticulously controlled through enjambments and pauses, the details are the emotion in this poem. In this most unlikely of settings, she hears her "actual, visceral heart," before the sounds of things going on around her come through again, ". . . the slish of tires / and footsteps, all the delicate cargo / they carried saying thank you. . . ." Her only choice is to to go on, climbing into her car "as if nothing had happened— / as if everything mattered. . . ."

Laux's voice has always been wise, deep and completely unself-pitying. But there is in this collection a certain fullness of spirit. In poem after poem she recognizes and celebrates her ability to survive and enjoy life. In "Singing Back the World" a careful of women Mends bursts into spontaneous song:

> I don't remember how it began. The singing. Judy at the wheel in the middle of "Sentimental Journey." The side of her face glowing. Her full lips moving. Beyond her shoulder the little houses sliding by. And Geri. Her frizzy hair tumbling in the wind wing's breeze, fumbling with the words. All of us singing as loud as we can. Off key. Not even a semblance of harmony. Driving home in a blue Comet singing "I'll Be Seeing You" and "Love Is a Rose."

A deep celebration of female friendship, "[no]thing but [their] three throats / beating back

> *"Her medium is the autobiographical lyric-narrative poem, but one so thoroughly grounded in the real world that it becomes a kind of transparent container, transmitting experience with uncanny immediacy."*

the world," the poem is both praise song to and an example of the ways creativity makes it possible to go on.

In the sequence of poems about family that makes up the central section of the book, Laux muses on having a teenage daughter, on her own mother's ebony piano, on the adult world's incursions and intrusions into her childhood, in language that is fierce, precise and loving. One of the things I admire most about Laux's work is that knowledge, though it often comes painfully, is always modulated by awareness that is somehow transformative: a twelve year-old looking at a sexually explicit magazine simultaneously dusts off his baby brother's pacifier each time it falls into the dirt. And always there is the redemptive power of love. In "Family Reunion," having suddenly realized there is no film in her camera, Laux writes:

> . . . I smile at my family, ask them to stay where they are just a few minutes longer as I press the blank shutter again and again, burning their images into my own incorruptible lens, picture after picture, saving them all with my naked eye, my bare hands the purest light of my love.

I had the feeling as I read this poem and others that the speaker has moved out from beneath some burden—that she is, in some way, more fully, more joyfully inhabiting the world.

The book opens with the speaker out in her back yard at midnight, chasing away fighting cats ("forty-one years old . . . / broom handle slipping//from my hands, my breasts bare, my hair / on end, afraid of what I might do next"), and closes with an immensely celebratory series of poems on the mysteries of the body, love and marriage. Laux, whose first collection contains what are probably some of the most significant contemporary poems about incest, here turns her attention to the joys of the body. As in all her work, she is both tender and fierce, able to evoke "the dark human bread" of flesh and the sweetness of lovers kissing, "their faces like roses crushed / together and opening."

In my favorite poem from this section, "The Thief," a tender seduction takes place. The speaker is torn between "not wanting to interrupt his work" and being unable to "keep [her] fingers / from dipping into the ditch in his pants, / torn again with tenderness / for the way his flesh grows unwillingly / toward [her] curved palm, toward the light." Speaking for the beauty and necessity of union, this poem takes the lover and her husband into the "other world he cannot build without [her]." That "other world" is what Laux gives us. "It took me so long to learn how to love, / how to give myself up and over to another," she says near the end of "For My Daughter Who Loves Animals." Luckily for us, these poems teach us how to give ourselves up to the world, how to love.

Source: Alison Townsend, *"What We Carry,"* in *Women's Review of Books*, Vol. 12, No. 2, November 1994, pp. 19–20.

Sources

Bendall, Molly, Review of *The Poet's Companion: A Guide to the Pleasures of Writing Poetry*, in *Antioch Review*, Vol. 56, No. 2, Spring 1998, p. 246.

Housden, Roger, "For the Sake of Strangers," in *Ten Poems to Last a Lifetime*, Harmony Books, 2004, pp. 57–64.

Laux, Dorianne, "For the Sake of Strangers," *What We Carry*, Boa Editions, 1994, p. 23.

Levine, Philip, "Editor's Shelf," in *Ploughshares*, Vol. 21/1, No. 66, Spring 1995, p. 202.

Townsend, Alison, Review of *What We Carry*, in *Women's Review of Books*, Vol. 12, No. 2, November 1994, pp. 19–20.

Further Reading

Ellmann, Richard, and Robert O'Clair, *Modern Poems: A Norton Introduction*, Norton, 1989.
    One of the most respected publishers of literary anthologies offers this collection of works by 119 poets, along with essays about the poets and about reading poetry. The styles and perspectives of the poets are wide-ranging, giving the reader a grasp of modern poetry.

George, Don, ed., *The Kindness of Strangers*, Lonely Planet, 2003.
    This book contains excerpts from the writings of various travel writers who find that their journeys around the world often bring them in contact with warm, generous people who offer help and encouragement. Collectively, these stories point to the basic goodness of people regardless of culture or situation.

Kowit, Steve, *In the Palm of Your Hand: The Poet's Portable Workshop*, Tilbury House, 1995.
    Kowit offers numerous exercises and examples to help students understand what makes poetry good and how to write it. The lessons are meant for beginning and experienced poets alike.

Kübler-Ross, Elisabeth, and David Kessler, *On Grief and Grieving: Finding the Meaning of Grief through the Five Stages*, Scribners, 2005.
    Kübler-Ross originally established the five stages of grief for the dying, but her life's work led her to realize that they were also useful for the surviving loved ones. In this book, Kübler-Ross elaborates on her findings, offering research and wisdom to comfort the hurting.

Laux, Dorianne, *Awake*, BOA, 1990.
    This was the first collection of poetry that featured only Laux's work. Consistent with her later collections, her style here is straightforward and strong, and her subject matter includes the best and worst of human experience.

Kindness

Naomi Shihab Nye
1980

Naomi Shihab Nye's poem "Kindness" appears in her first collection of poems, *Different Ways to Pray*, published in 1980. The tone, themes, and ideas presented in this inaugural volume establish Nye's core message as a poet and as a human being: All of humanity is worthy of respect, deserving of consideration, and in need of kindness. "Kindness" is reprinted in Nye's 1995 collection *Words under the Words*, which compiles selections from her first three books: *Different Ways to Pray*, *Hugging the Jukebox* (1982), and *Yellow Glove* (1986).

The poet's many travels have taken her to some of the world's most prosperous countries and thriving cities as well as to some of the harshest and poorest lands, where violence, hunger, and injustice are common. One such place is Colombia, a country in northwestern South America. In Colombia, the natural beauty of a lush landscape with mountains and rivers is sometimes overshadowed by the ugliness of social oppression, government corruption, drug trafficking, and violent crime. Somewhere within this ironic blend of nature's magnificence and society's decadence, Nye finds a reason to believe in the power of simple acts of kindness. This belief is the inspiration for her poem of the same name, which signs off with the single word "*Colombia*" below the work's final line. In the original version in *Different Ways to Pray*, the poem ends with "(Colombia, 1978)."

Despite its attention to loss and desolation, "Kindness" is a positive poem with an optimistic ending. It acknowledges the unavoidable presence of sorrow in human life but points out that one must understand and accept the bad in order to appreciate and achieve the good. The speaker's perspective is based on both personal observation and philosophical musing.

Author Biography

Naomi Shihab Nye was born on March 12, 1952, in St. Louis, Missouri. Her father, Aziz Shihab, was a Palestinian and her mother, Miriam Naomi Allwardt, an American. Nye's upbringing in a household of differing cultures and heritages influenced not only her subsequent writing career but also her entire outlook on life. Nye became interested in reading and writing poetry at a very young age, publishing her first poems in a children's magazine at age seven. Years later, her family moved to Jerusalem, where she attended her first year of high school. More important, Nye experienced her first real connection to the homeland of her father and his Arab heritage. The Shihab family returned to the United States in 1967, settling in San Antonio, Texas.

Nye received her bachelor's degree in English and world religions from Trinity University in 1974, and in 1975, she became a poet in the schools for the Texas Arts Commission. She then held positions as a visiting writer and lecturer at various universities and worked as a freelance writer and editor. Throughout this time, Nye continued to write poetry, both for adults and for young readers. Her first full-length collection, *Different Ways to Pray*, in which "Kindness" first appeared, was published in 1980. Nye's collection of poetry titled *You and Yours* was published in 2005. Her two volumes for young readers, *Is This Forever, or What? Poems and Paintings from Texas* and *A Maze Me: Poems for Girls* were published in 2004 and 2005, respectively.

Nye traveled extensively, and much of the inspiration for her creative work is drawn from times she spent in the Middle East, Central and South America, and the Native American and Mexican regions of the southwestern United States. The strongest influence on Nye's writing is the wonder, beauty, and honor she recognizes in different cultures and different ethnic environments. Her poem "Kindness" is a testament to Nye's reverence for humanity, and it is representative of the themes for which Nye has become a notable contemporary American writer.

Naomi Shihab Nye © Naomi Shihab Nye. Reproduced by permission

Nye received numerous awards and honors for her publications, among them, four Pushcart Prizes, the Peter I. B. Lavan Younger Poets Award from the Academy of American Poets, a Witter Bynner fellowship from the U.S. Library of Congress, and several awards for her work in children's poetry and literature, including a 2002 National Book Award finalist nomination in the young people's literature category for *Nineteen Varieties of Gazelle: Poems of the Middle East*. As of 2005, Nye was living in San Antonio with her husband, the photographer Michael Nye.

Poem Text

Before you know what kindness really is
you must lose things,
feel the future dissolve in a moment
like salt in a weakened broth.
What you held in your hand,   5
what you counted and carefully saved,
all this must go so you know
how desolate the landscape can be
between the regions of kindness.
How you ride and ride   10

thinking the bus will never stop,
the passengers eating maize and chicken
will stare out the window forever.

Before you learn the tender gravity of kindness,
you must travel where the Indian in a white poncho   15
lies dead by the side of the road.
You must see how this could be you,
how he too was someone
who journeyed through the night with plans
and the simple breath that kept him alive.   20

Before you know kindness as the deepest thing
        inside,
you must know sorrow as the other deepest thing.
You must wake up with sorrow.
You must speak to it till your voice
catches the thread of all sorrows   25
and you see the size of the cloth.

Then it is only kindness that makes sense anymore,
only kindness that ties your shoes
and sends you out into the day to mail letters and
        purchase bread,
only kindness that raises its head   30
from the crowd of the world to say
It is I you have been looking for,
and then goes with you everywhere
like a shadow or a friend.
Colombia.   35

Poem Summary

Lines 1–2

The first two lines of "Kindness" establish a premise that runs throughout the poem: Before a person knows one thing, he or she must know something else. (The "you" in this work refers simply to the universal "you," or people in general, not to a specific person.) In this case, the real meaning of kindness, which seems easy to understand, is shown to be more complex than one may realize. The speaker suggests, ironically, that to "know what kindness really is," first "you must lose things."

Lines 3–4

Instead of explaining what the opening lines mean right away, the speaker relies on an intriguing metaphor to make the point. (A metaphor is a figure of speech that compares an intended concept or thing to something unrelated as a way to clarify the original intention.) The speaker wants to describe how the future can "dissolve in a moment," so she compares it to "salt" dissolving "in a weakened broth." The notion of losing all of one's tomorrows is a frightening prospect, and likening it to something as easy as salt blending into soup

Media Adaptations

- In 1995, Nye appeared on *The Language of Life with Bill Moyers*, an eight-part series on PBS featuring interviews with poets. The interviews are available on a single audiocassette from Random House Audio.

makes it all the more chilling. The first thing "you must lose" to know true kindness, then, is a hefty loss indeed.

Lines 5–9

Lines 5 through 9 provide further examples of what one must lose to know kindness. "What you held in your hand" may be an infinite number of items, but the implication is that it is something significant enough and dear enough that someone would want to hold it close. The subject of line 6 is clearer. "What you counted and carefully saved" refers to money, a vital commodity in most people's lives. Even these precious items "must go" before one can comprehend "how desolate the landscape can be / between the regions of kindness." In other words, one must give up the good things in life to understand how bad and how barren living can be during times of hardship and sorrow.

Lines 10–13

Line 10 connects directly to line 8, beginning with "How" and developing the idea that only total loss can remove the blinders that many people wear when it comes to seeing reality as it is. The bus rider is guilty of ignoring the suffering and injustice that others endure by "thinking the bus will never stop" and believing that the other passengers will continue their pleasant and endless journey while "eating maize and chicken" and gazing benignly "out the window forever." The word "maize" insinuates that the other bus riders are natives of the land, because it is a word for corn derived from an extinct Latin American language and translated by the Spanish. Maize is sometimes referred to as "Indian corn."

Lines 14–16

Throughout the first three stanzas, lines 1 to 13, examples of the opposite side of kindness grow more serious and more depressing: from the future as dissolving salt, losing something once held dear, and forfeiting a life's savings to the lonely, haunting death of an unknown Indian who "lies dead by the side of the road," seemingly of no concern to those who pass by. The phrase "tender gravity" implies the fickle and fragile nature of kindness, and it is this deepest level that one needs to reach to understand kindness. The word "tender" also is a startling opposite of the senseless inhumanity in letting the dead lie in the street without the benefit or respect of proper treatment.

Lines 17–20

Lines 17 through 20 are perhaps the most poignant in the poem. They make a remarkably strong human-to-human connection between the forgotten dead Indian and every person who passes by—the "you" in general. The vital message is that what happens to the Indian can happen to anyone in the world. The words "this could be you" bring the poem's message down to the gut level: Regardless of one's ethnicity or race, economic status, nationality, educational level, or any other defining characteristic, human beings are all "someone . . . with plans / and the simple breath" that keeps them alive. This theme not only is pertinent in "Kindness" but also permeates much of Nye's work. Its reflection on her personal life as an Arab American is both unmistakable and intended.

Lines 21–22

In direct and precise language, lines 21 and 22 highlight the opposing poles of kindness and sorrow. They begin the third consecutive stanza that begins "Before you," but this stanza ties together the concrete images of the beginning of the poem—salt, broth, bus riders, maize, chicken, Indian, and white poncho—with more contemplative, philosophical aspects. Kindness and sorrow are parallel. Before one can "know kindness as the deepest thing inside," he or she must know that it has a real and formidable opposite: Sorrow is the "other deepest thing."

Lines 23–26

Lines 23 through 26 demonstrate how important it is to realize true sorrow before being able to understand true kindness. To say that one "must wake up with sorrow" implies how deep the feeling should be ingrained in a human being before he or she can appreciate the beauty of having sorrow lifted through kindness. In lines 24 through 26, Nye again relies on metaphor to convey the actual depth of sorrow's impact. The message is that everyday talk must be full of sorrow until "your voice / catches the thread of all sorrows," "thread" implying something connecting and growing. When one sees "the size of the cloth" that sorrow becomes, one knows how large a part it plays in the overall fabric of human life.

Lines 27–29

Lines 27 through 29, which begin the fourth and final stanza of "Kindness," mark a turning point in the tone and ultimate message of the poem. After all the examples of how bad ignorance, desolation, and sorrow can be, it is finally "only kindness that makes sense anymore." Kindness is tied to the simple, everyday things that the average human being can relate to: tying shoestrings, mailing letters, buying bread. The common occurrences listed may be misleading in their apparent simplicity. The actual message is that all of everyday life revolves around how people are treated on a regular basis. Sometimes the smaller things a person experiences, such as daily chores, are made possible only by the knowledge that somewhere out there someone else was kind to him or her that day.

Lines 30–32

In lines 30 through 32, Nye uses personification—the technique of bringing a concept or nonhuman thing to life by attributing to it a human form, human characteristics, or human behavior—to describe the relationship between kindness and the "you" in the poem. Kindness "raises its head / from the crowd of the world," implying its uniqueness in an otherwise cold and mean environment. Nye then gives kindness a strong and undeniable existence in human life: "It is *I* [emphasis added] you have been looking for." This line leaves no question about the importance of kindness in people's lives. Kindness purports itself to be the very thing that human beings are seeking.

Lines 33–34

The final two lines of the poem leave the reader with a positive thought, personifying kindness as a welcomed being in anyone's life. Kindness "goes with you everywhere," like a willing partner who aims only to please. At times it may be "like a shadow," something that follows a person around even when he or she is alone. At other times, kindness may be like "a friend," someone who has the person's best interests in mind. Regardless of its role at any given moment, kindness is conveyed as the perfect companion.

The poem does not actually end with line 34. One more word is added to give it a more specific identity: "*Colombia.*" Even so, identifying a country in which "Kindness" was written or that inspired it does not dilute the relevance of the poem to any nation in the world.

Themes

Human Kindness

The most obvious theme in this poem is revealed in its title: Kindness is one of the most cherished and hard-to-come-by values of the human race. As the work ultimately claims, kindness is the only thing "that makes sense anymore." This conclusion is drawn from Nye's assessment of the negative observations she has made and her firm belief that good can triumph over bad.

"Kindness" is, essentially, a poem that speaks for itself. It is not mysterious or difficult to understand, and it uses simple, straightforward language to make its points clear. The central theme, however, is played out carefully in a series of both philosophical and graphic examples. For instance, Nye theoretically writes about feeling the "future dissolve" and about the "desolate . . . landscape . . . between the regions of kindness," but she also very specifically details bus riders "eating maize and chicken" and "the Indian in a white poncho" who "lies dead by the side of the road." This juxtaposition of theory and reality does not hinder the message of the poem but actually enhances its credibility in defining human kindness.

The very nature of kindness as a desirable yet sometimes elusive trait gives it a broad range of interpretations, especially when one is trying to pin it down to a certain definition. In philosophical terms, there may be a "tender gravity of kindness," or kindness may be the "deepest thing inside." In more direct terms, however, it may be the thing that "ties your shoes / and sends you out in the day to mail letters and purchase bread." This abrupt shift between the meditative and the practical demonstrates the multiple values of human kindness.

It is no secret that one of Nye's most critical concerns—in both her writing and her life in general—is to promote compassion and fairness throughout the various populations of the world. "Kindness" unmistakably advocates for deeper human sympathy among citizens of various countries, regardless of nationality, ethnicity, or even placement within a local community. The unfortunate Indian depicted in the poem may well have died among his own people within his own town or village, but he is still unjustly ignored, as though his body is a foreign object that no one wants to acknowledge. Only kindness, the poem suggests, can prevent such wretched treatment of a fellow human being.

Balancing Opposites

A second theme in "Kindness" may not be as obvious as the first, but it is just as powerful. To grasp the full meaning and benefit of kindness, human beings must first comprehend its opposite: losing things. In doing so, one can find the delicate balance between what is truly good and what is truly bad. This idea is introduced in the first two lines, but only the subsequent specific examples bring it into clear focus.

What the "you" riding the bus must lose is the notion that the other riders will keep enjoying their maize and chicken endlessly instead of eventually reaching their less-than-desirable destinations in dilapidated homes or violent communities. What the more general "you" must learn is that no matter how pleasant or "tender" one's own life may be, somewhere in the world a forgotten soul "lies dead by the side of the road" and that he could just as easily "be you," if circumstances were only a bit different. This message is perhaps the strongest one in the poem regarding opposites: There is a very thin line between the haves and the have-nots. The former could quickly become the latter if events were to unfold a different way.

"Kindness" suggests that balancing opposites is more beneficial than simply choosing one thing and trying to squash the other. A person who decides to see only the good things in life and to ignore the bad is living with blinders on, and the real meaning of "good" is lost in a world of illusion and make-believe. On the other hand, if one accepts that bad and sorrowful aspects of life can carry as much weight as the wonderful, happy events, then the positive moments are all the more appreciated because of the very real possibility of the negative.

Topics For Further Study

- "Kindness" relies on a specific setting to give credence to its poignant message. Rewrite this poem basing it on your own community. Give descriptions that make the poem sound as though it is meant for your particular time and place. Emphasize the details that are crucial to your environment and that ultimately suggest the need for kindness.

- Nye bases many of her poems and essays on the places to which she has traveled, both near and far away from her home in Texas. Make a class presentation on a place you have visited and talk about its differences from your own environment. Do you find it easy or difficult to speak objectively about the environment of the place you visited? Explain to the class why you find it one way or the other.

- As a person of both American and Arab descent, Nye faces a particularly difficult task in blending reverence for the two cultures into her work and into her life in general, especially after September 11, 2001. Write an essay about a simi-

lar experience you have had in dealing with cultural differences and prejudices, either your own or those of an acquaintance.

- If you were running for an important political office in Colombia, what would you concentrate on in your speeches to the Colombian people? Research the history of this nation and then present a campaign speech on important national matters. Consider points such as how Colombia has become known as one of the illegal drug capitals of the world as well as one of the countries most terrorized by insurgent groups. Why has this predominantly democratic country fallen prey to these groups over and over again? What will you do to help end the cycle?

- Have you ever known of a person whose death seemed to affect no one? Write an essay on what that person's circumstances were or may have been, why he or she seemed discarded in the end, and how your own life may have been affected by this somber yet ignored passing.

Style

Contemporary Free Verse

The free-verse style of poetry began in the late nineteenth century with a group of French poets, including Arthur Rimbaud and Jules Laforgue, who balked at the long-held system of composing verse according to strict patterns of rhyme and meter. Their *vers libre*, or free verse, movement relaxed all "poetic" restrictions and allowed poets to use more natural language and voice to express common human concerns. Contemporary free verse simply takes the original free verse a step closer to even more relaxed language and voice as well as an anything-goes attitude about subjects and themes. In short, contemporary free-verse poets use direct, everyday language to address matters that affect them, regardless of how controversial the

topics may be. The concentration is more on subject than on style.

Nye uses no rhyme scheme or specific meter in "Kindness," but she creates her own pattern of language within the work to give it a subtle rhythm. There are four stanzas of varying lengths, but the first three (lines 1 through 13, 14 through 20, and 21 through 26) begin with similar or matching words: "Before you know," "Before you learn," and "Before you know" again. Each opening line follows with the overall message about kindness: Before one understands what kindness is, one must understand what it is not. Although each stanza takes a different turn in how it supports the overall themes, Nye makes general but strong use of metaphor in all of them. From the "desolate . . . landscape . . . between the regions of kindness" through "tender gravity" to the "thread of all sorrows" that makes up the total "size of the cloth," each comparison provides an interesting and revealing definition of both kindness and its opposite.

The fourth stanza, lines 27 through 34, does not begin with the same words as the first three stanzas, but it is full of metaphor, more so than the others. Kindness is described in terms of personification, or attribution of human characteristics to inanimate objects or concepts. In this case, kindness "ties your shoes / and sends you out into the day," as a loving parent may do for a child. Kindness also has a "head" to raise above the "crowd of the world" and to speak directly to "you": "It is I you have been looking for." Kindness is *like* a human being, and its characteristics are so vital to the poet that it actually *becomes* a human being.

Historical Context

Political Turmoil in Colombia

Only by the brief identifier at the end of "Kindness" in *Different Ways to Pray* can one attribute a specific time and place to both the setting and the inspiration of the poem. "(Colombia, 1978)" implies that this work resulted from one of the poet's many travels, in this case to South America. It is interesting that the date is omitted in the version of "Kindness" that appears in the later collection *Words under the Words*. This omission may simply be a matter of preference or change in editorial style, but it may also suggest that the message in the poem is timeless.

Despite the fact that Colombia has had three military takeovers and two civil wars in its history, the country has a long and enduring democratic tradition, marred sporadically by violent and effective insurgencies. During the mid-twentieth century, the second civil war cost nearly 300,000 lives and was resolved in the late 1950s with the formation of the National Front. This resolution called for a compromise between the warring conservative and liberal factions, the position of president rotating every four years between the two parties. The agreement allowed Colombia to prosper economically with increased exportation of goods such as coffee, oil, minerals, and fruit.

During the 1970s, Colombia suffered setbacks both politically and economically when a campaign of terrorism began. Various rebel groups attacked military leaders, government officials, and innocent civilians. Many outlaw groups became involved in drug trafficking and eventually made Colombia one of the world's major suppliers of cocaine. Since at least 1978, the main focus of the besieged government has been to defeat terrorist guerillas, drug lords, and reportedly Cuban-backed revolts. Both liberal and conservative leaders have shared the burden of ridding their country of violent insurgents who have weakened Colombia's overall economic and political stability. A once flourishing tourist trade has dwindled dramatically over the years, although some people, such as Nye, are willing to risk the dangers in order to experience the underlying beauty of both the land and its people.

Social Inequality in Colombia

A strict sense of class structure has existed in Colombia for centuries. The original racial groups that helped form the country—Indians, blacks, and whites—eventually melded into a mixture of these groups, adhering to a class system that dates to the one created by Spanish colonizers centuries ago.

The Spanish settlers found the native Colombian people relatively easy to conquer and take advantage of because the indigenous population was widely scattered and not united by a sense of community or shared destiny. As a result, the Indians and the black slaves brought by the Spaniards were readily cast as the lowest rung on the social ladder. Between a top and a bottom, however, there is always a middle rung, and Colombia's society eventually divided into four distinct classes that could easily be labeled by the late 1970s and early 1980s. The classes are labeled upper, middle, lower, and the masses.

White professionals dominate the upper class and traditionally hold the highest government positions as well as top careers in law, medicine, architecture, and university teaching. The middle class is made up largely of self-employed shopkeepers, clerks, and managers. These families are able to find adequate housing, food, medical attention, and a decent education for their children. The lower class typically consists of domestic servants, unskilled workers, taxi drivers, and various repair service people. Often, these families go without sufficient means to meet their housing, nutritional, medical, and educational needs.

The class distinctions in Colombia are similar to those in many other countries, and the lowest level suffers as greatly as that anywhere. In Colombia, impoverished Indians and blacks make up the "masses," and they, along with the lower class, constitute the majority of the population of the country. Even so, there is still a distinct class divide between the lower class and the masses. Whereas

Compare & Contrast

- **1970s:** Colombia becomes one of the international centers for illegal drug production and trafficking. Drug cartels virtually control the country, which provides 75 percent of the world's cocaine.

  Today: The United States invests $3 billion into "Plan Colombia," a joint U.S.-Colombia coca antinarcotics plan, which started in 2000. Officials claim that as of 2005 the program has eradicated more than a million acres of coca plants, but Colombian drug traffickers still manage to supply 90 percent of the cocaine used in the United States—the same percentage supplied when the program began.

- **1970s:** Marxist guerrilla groups organize against the Colombian government, most notably, the May 19th Movement, the National Liberation Army, and the Revolutionary Armed Forces of Colombia. They plunge the country into violence and instability.

  Today: The United Nations declares that Colombia is suffering the worst humanitarian crisis in the Western Hemisphere. More than two million people have been forced to leave

their homes, and several Indian tribes are close to extinction. Colombia now has the third-largest displaced population in the world because of guerrilla violence and the fear its population endures on a daily basis.

- **1970s:** Andean Indians such as the Guambianos weave their own clothes, grow their own food, and glean a meager income from tourists, who are eventually driven away by guerrilla and paramilitary forces waging regular shoot-outs in the region. Eventually, the Indians resort to growing poppies for the illegal cocaine industry in order to make a living.

  Today: Colombian president Alvaro Uribe promises the Guambianos that the government is taking a tough approach in combating guerrillas, paramilitaries, and drug traffickers and that the Indians will be paid well to destroy their poppy plants and return to legitimate farming. So far, unkept promises have resulted in the indigenous people's disillusionment in the government and, for some, a return to growing poppies for the drug lords who they know will pay for the effort.

members of the lower class typically hold jobs and have an increasing level of political and social awareness, the masses usually live on the fringes of society, are largely illiterate, and lack job skills and employment. Their illness and death rates are high because they lack adequate nutrition and medical attention.

Because cocaine trafficking became a dominant industry for Colombia's illegal factions in the 1970s, it has also become a deadly yet attractive source of income for many of the country's poorest people. Members of the masses who resort to cultivating coca plants are often murdered by guerrilla groups if the planters refuse to sell to the group or if they sell to a rival gang vying for drug profits. As disturbing as they are, these facts may well

account for the plight of the Indian in a white poncho, whose sorrowful death is apparently just as negligible as his life has been.

Critical Overview

Nye's work has been highly critically acclaimed from the time her poems started to appear in print. Critics praise Nye's poetry, children's literature, and essays for their pertinent social and humanistic messages and the effectiveness of the direct, unadorned language with which Nye conveys them. Although her style is straightforward and her themes readily understood, Nye is not considered a simple or unsophisticated writer. The opposite is true: Her talent lies in presenting profound and complex human emotion and behavior in a refreshingly uncomplicated manner.

In an article for *American Women Writers: A Critical Reference Guide from Colonial Times to the Present*, the reviewer Daria Donnelly notes that "*Different Ways to Pray* attends to human landscapes" and that "Nye's attention to the simple acts of human communion wherever and however they occur springs from a generosity and acuity forged by a sense of her own multifaceted identity." A poem such as "Kindness" certainly supports Donnelly's assertion, and its reappearance in the later collection attests to its continuing relevance.

In a review of *Words under the Words* for *Western American Literature*, Bert Almon claims that "Nye is one of the best poets of her generation" and that she is "always vigilant: the rhythms are sharp, the eye is keen. She excels at the unexpected and brilliant detail that underwrites the poetic vision." Almon goes on to say that "the title of her collection, *Words under the Words*, expresses a confidence in ultimate meaningfulness of our descriptions of reality. If we listen, we can hear the inner meaning." These comments are typical. As much as Nye continues to focus an ear on the pain, sorrow, kindness, and joy of humanity, her readers focus on what she hears.

Criticism

Pamela Steed Hill

Pamela Hill is the author of a poetry collection, has published widely in literary journals, and is an editor for a university publications department. In the following essay, she discusses how "Kindness" is one of the most apt examples of Nye's works because it adheres to a core principle of both the poet's writing and her daily life: The "words under the words" are of utmost importance.

When a poem from a first collection is chosen to appear in the poet's later volume of selected works, the implication is that the poem is worthy of an encore appearance. "Kindness" is one such poem. When another work from the first collection not only makes a second appearance in the selected works but also shares its title with that of the entire book, this poem must carry thematic significance or divulge some idea of the author's overall message. "The Words under the Words" is that kind of poem.

> *Sadness and desolation can darken the human spirit as much as kindness can brighten it. It is fitting, then, to consider how low one may go in order to appreciate how high one can rebound.*"

Nye is completely forthcoming about her vision of how the world should be and how human beings should treat one another. A deep concern for humanity lies at the base of nearly all she writes and all she does. She also knows, however, that not every vision or every hope or every human experience is always plainspoken and accessible. Sometimes one must pay keen attention to seemingly insignificant occurrences or conversations in order to discover and learn from the importance that lies beneath. This is the case for everyone—not just poets and other writers—as Nye points out in an interesting story about a man she met on a bus on September 11, 2001.

In an interview with Angela Elam for *New Letters*, Nye talks about her long bus ride home after the terror attacks in New York City and Washington, D.C., had closed airports across the nation. Her seatmate was a man who had been released from prison that day and who knew nothing of the attacks. The man spoke mostly to himself but occasionally commented to Nye that he did not remember buses being so crowded. Elam's response to this story is to say, "What a wonderful thing to have happen to a writer. That's almost something you couldn't even invent." Nye's reply sets the interviewer straight: "I think they happen to everybody; writers are just in the habit of listening to them in a certain way or believing there's something to hear, to pay attention to." In other words, writers look for what is not visible on the outside and listen to what is said in silence: the words *under* the words.

"Kindness" is full of these kinds of words, and its premise is based on discovering one thing by examining another. This fundamental, philosophical

What Do I Read Next?

- Nye's work as an editor demonstrates the same tireless dedication to promoting tolerance and humanity throughout the world as her own writing does. *This Same Sky* (1992) is a collection of the poems of 129 poets from sixty-eight countries with an overall theme of how much human beings have in common, regardless of different physical environments, ethnicities, and religions.

- Edited by Nathalie Handal, *The Poetry of Arab Women* (2001) is a collection of the work of more than eighty women poets translated from the original Arabic, French, English, and other languages. From work by Nye to that of relatively unknown American graduate students, this volume presents a number of views that share a common voice.

- *Arabs in America: Building a New Future* (1999) is Michael Suleiman's collection of twenty-one scholars' writings on the status of

Arab Americans in North America. Suleiman's overall contention is that this ethnic group is largely ignored, except when words like "terrorism" and "extremism" come up, yet Arab Americans have contributed to Western culture for centuries. The writers work in a variety of fields, including anthropology, economics, history, law, literature, political science, and sociology.

- *Indian Givers: How the Indians of the Americas Transformed the World* (1989), by Jack Weatherford, is a thought-provoking and easily read account of the many "gifts" that native peoples of all the Americas have given to the entire world. From gold and silver works, agricultural techniques, and medicine to economics and the concept of personal freedom, the contributions of Indians from North, South, Central, and Latin America are crucial to the development of cultures and governments worldwide.

idea is inspired in part by Nye's beloved Arab grandmother, Sitti Khadra, who lived to be 106 years old. This woman has great influence on the poet's life, even though the two spent little time together because the grandmother lived on the opposite side of the world. The poem "The Words under the Words" bears the dedication "for Sitti Khadra, north of Jerusalem" and is a reflection of the grandmother's life in Palestine and the wisdom she imparted to the poet. Sitti Khadra, however, was probably unaware of her tremendous influence on her Americanized granddaughter.

In "The Words under the Words," Nye attributes the notion of listening for hidden messages to the teachings of her grandmother. The following lines acknowledge human inadequacies when it comes to true understanding: "She knows the spaces we travel through, / the messages we cannot send—our voices are short / and would get lost on the journey." The final lines of the poem quote the grandmother directly: "'Answer, if you hear the

words under the words—/ otherwise it is just a world with a lot of rough edges, / difficult to get through, and our pockets full of stones.'"

In "Kindness," the world is definitely full of rough edges—so rough that a man can lie dead by the side of the road without anyone bothering to cover his body, much less give it a proper burial. It is a world where people ride buses to and from their squalid homes, eating their simple meals along the way. It is a world where the future can "dissolve in a moment" and where the landscape "between the regions of kindness" is bleak and barren. It is also a world where the good and the kind are matched equally by the bad and the mean-spirited. This world is the one Nye finds in her travels to Colombia, but on a deeper level it is a world that spans the globe.

Although the message in "Kindness" is obvious, its language is compelling, if not complex. Nye forces the reader to look beneath the surface of the words to find a more profound meaning of kindness than one may have ever considered. The idea that human beings should be kind to one another is simple enough, but the poet makes the point by encouraging readers to take a look at what kindness is *not*, to reach a better understanding of it by concentrating on its opposite.

In the first stanza of the poem, lines 1 through 13, a deep sense of loss is the opposite of kindness. From money to the future itself, one must experience losing things in order to "know what kindness really is." This approach provides a much more interesting perspective than simply trying to define kindness in typical terms. For instance, one may say that volunteering in the community, making donations to charities, and mowing the lawn for an elderly neighbor are all acts of kindness, and arguably everyone would agree. When people are challenged to think about all of their tomorrows fading away "like salt in a weakened broth," however, the notion of such tragedy makes the thought of kindness all the more vital. Most human beings can understand how wonderful it is to have something good happen—no matter how small—when times are otherwise difficult to handle.

Later in the poem, it is profound sorrow that is the opposite of kindness. From the concrete physical description of the Indian's body along the roadside to the more metaphoric treatment of sorrow in the third stanza, lines 21 through 26, the message again is that kindness is more explicitly defined in terms of what is not normally associated with it. Sadness and desolation can darken the human spirit as much as kindness can brighten it. It is fitting, then, to consider how low one may go in order to appreciate how high one can rebound. In this stanza, Nye suggests that people need to make sorrow a part of their daily routines so that they can grasp its full presence. "You must wake up with sorrow" implies the depth that grief and anguish must reach inside the human being in order for one to take kindness to the same depth. When both the good and the bad are capable of going the same distance, it is up to the individual to decide which will exert the greatest influence over his or her life.

In the last stanza of "Kindness," lines 27 through 34, Nye makes heavy use of personification to explain the importance of kindness in human life. She also uses it to stress the need for finding the words under the words—those that may go unnoticed if one pays attention only to what is spoken instead of what is not spoken. If kindness is the thing that "ties your shoes / and sends you out into the day to mail letters and purchase bread," what are these words really saying about the role

of goodness in everyday human life? More important, where would humanity be if charity and compassion were largely nonexistent? Certainly, the idea in the poem is that the role of goodness lies at the very base of all people do, including the simple tasks of daily living.

Nye claims that her grandmother, Sitti Khadra, acknowledged "the spaces we travel through" and "the messages we cannot send." But the elderly woman also understood that if the human race is content to let such negative impulses guide human behavior, then the world's population is doomed "with a lot of rough edges" and "our pockets full of stones." The better solution, she suggests, is to "Answer, if you hear the words under the words." *Answering* is precisely what Nye tries to do with the poem "Kindness."

The major theme of "Kindness" is obvious, but the fact that the message is made more subtle by the enticement to look deeper into it suggests that the overall idea is more complex than it appears. Nye's dedication to humanistic affairs is well known. Her ability to relay that sentiment in such an intriguing manner speaks not only to her abilities as a poet but also to her unwavering commitment to humanity in general.

Source: Pamela Steed Hill , Critical Essay on "Kindness," in *Poetry for Students*, Thomson Gale, 2006.

Anna Maria Hong

Anna Maria Hong has published poems in numerous journals and is the editor of the fiction and memoir anthology Growing Up Asian American *(1993). In the following essay, she discusses how Nye uses metaphor and personification to define what kindness is and how it is achieved.*

Nye's "Kindness" is a philosophical poem that defines kindness as a way of living life. In the poem, Nye proposes that rather than being a random and discrete act, kindness is a mode of being arrived at through a series of basic human experiences. The poet argues that kindness is also the inevitable conclusion of feeling one's life deeply, as she elucidates three essential steps to achieving kindness. Throughout the poem, Nye uses metaphor and personification to emphasize her ideas.

Nye begins each of the first three stanzas with similar phrases, each stating that one must know or learn something before knowing what kindness is. In the first stanza, the speaker proposes loss as a prerequisite to understanding what kindness is. The poem opens with the speaker saying, "Before you know what kindness really is / you must lose things, / feel the future dissolve in a moment / like salt in a weakened broth." In these lines, Nye suggests that a sense of great loss is necessary to knowing what kindness is. The simile "like salt in a weakened broth" powerfully conveys a sense of sudden and final dissipation. The speaker follows this line by adding that one must lose everything in order to understand how bleak life is in the absence of kindness. The speaker notes that one should lose those things that one took precautions to save.

In line 9 of this opening stanza, the speaker defines kindness as a kind of place, as she refers to "regions of kindness." She concludes the stanza by comparing the feeling of loss without kindness to riding a bus that you think will never stop, as you believe "the passengers eating maize and chicken / will stare out the window forever." This metaphor underscores the sense of helplessness and isolation that accompanies loss, with the words "maize and chicken" conveying the sense of riding a bus in a foreign country. The feeling of being different in a strange land is compounded by the fact that people going about their daily business do not pay attention to one another but instead look out the window. In this opening stanza, Nye establishes the idea that a sense of intense loss without relief is the first step toward kindness.

In the next stanza, Nye asserts that empathy is the second prerequisite to knowing kindness. In lines 14 to 16, she continues the bus metaphor, as the speaker states, "Before you learn the tender gravity of kindness, / you must travel where the Indian in a white poncho / lies dead by the side of the road." By describing it as "tender gravity," the poet introduces the idea of kindness as a powerfully attractive force. She also casts kindness once again as a place that one travels toward, as on a journey in an unfamiliar land.

Following her description of the stark, somewhat transcendent image of the dead Indian in a white poncho, the speaker says that the reader must see how that person could be him or her and how the Indian was once also a person "who journeyed through the night with plans / and the simple breath that kept him alive." In these lines, Nye suggests that one must feel empathy in order to feel kindness. Since the Indian in the white poncho is an iconic figure, presumably different from most readers of the poem, the poet also implies that one must learn to be empathetic to all people, no matter how distant they seem from oneself. In particular, she proposes that one must understand that death comes to all of us and that the knowledge of one's own

> *In personifying kindness, Nye describes it as a type of salvation and emphasizes kindness as a crucial aspect of humanity."*

death is also a prerequisite to achieving kindness. She suggests that this knowledge paves the way to recognizing others as fellow travelers in life.

The experiences of loss, empathy, and recognition of death as a universal experience are connected with the final prerequisite to embracing kindness, sorrow, which is the subject of the third stanza. In lines 21 to 22, the speaker invokes the opening refrain of each stanza by saying, "Before you know kindness as the deepest thing inside, / you must know sorrow as the other deepest thing." Here, Nye asserts that sorrow or an intense sadness is the deepest or most basic part of human experience. Since sorrow follows loss and empathy with another's death, the poet suggests that sorrow comes from experiencing loss in a deep and profound way.

The speaker goes on to personify sorrow as someone who must be lived with every day and spoken to until "your voice / catches the thread of all sorrows / and you see the size of the cloth." In these hopeful lines, Nye implies that by really grappling with sorrow, by experiencing one's sense of loss and sadness fully, one can break through and feel how universal suffering is. One can see that one's own sorrow is part of a larger scheme, whose size is all-encompassing. By personifying sorrow and using everyday images such as thread and cloth, Nye also suggests that sorrow is not an aberration but a part of normal daily life.

In the fourth and final stanza, Nye concludes the poem by casting kindness as the inevitable outcome of the experiences of loss, empathy, and sorrow. In line 27, the speaker says that after living through these things, "Then it is only kindness that makes sense anymore." In the previous stanza, Nye intertwined kindness with sorrow by positing both as the deepest human emotions, the things that remain inside in the wake of loss and death. Here, she asserts that after recognizing the inevitability of one's own death and the universality of sorrow, one will logically conclude that kindness is the only mode of being that makes life bearable.

Here again, she personifies kindness, this time as a force that animates people to go about their daily tasks, as kindness "raises its head / from the crowd of the world to say / It is I you have been looking for, / and then goes with you everywhere / like a shadow or a friend." In personifying kindness, Nye describes it as a type of salvation and emphasizes kindness as a crucial aspect of humanity. Rather than describing a simple act with no motives, she portrays kindness as the ultimate companion against loneliness, a way of being that abates the sense of helplessness and desolation we would otherwise feel. She argues that by embracing kindness, and only by embracing it, we are never alone.

Although the poet never spells out what kindness is, she suggests that it is a mixture of all the things she illuminates in the course of the poem: the recognition of personal loss, the inevitability of one's death, and the magnitude of sorrow that results in empathy. She defines kindness not as selfless act but rather as a rational mode of living, as only generosity and gentleness toward others can provide a sense of solace in our solitary journeys through life.

Source: Anna Maria Hong, Critical Essay on "Kindness," in *Poetry for Students*, Thomson Gale, 2006.

Ibis Gomez-Vega

In the following essay, Gomez-Vega explores how Shihab Nye uses storytelling in her poetry to evoke themes such as family connections and displacement.

When Naomi Shihab Nye says in "For Lost and Found Brothers" that "Facts interest me less than the trailing smoke of stories" (*Words under the Words*), the essence of her work becomes clear. As a poet she is, at heart, a storyteller, one who focuses on the lives of everyday people, especially her own relatives, to understand the world around her. She is neither a "New Formalist" nor a "Language" poet, the terms that define the work of some of the most critically revered contemporary poets. Instead, she writes free verse in what is, by most standards, fairly accessible language. Like most poets, Shihab Nye is enamoured of words, but her free verse poems tell stories which seem to emerge from that "boundary [that] becomes the place from which *something begins its presencing*

in a movement not dissimilar to the ambulant, ambivalent articulation of the beyond" (5) that Homi K. Bhabha defines in *The Location of Culture*. Often, the stories become a tool for survival, the only way to make sense of difficult moments in a harsh world, and nowhere is this more evident than in "How Palestinians Keep Warm," a poem about the subtle changes that have taken place in the lives of contemporary Palestinians who huddle together in a war-torn city. The poet says, "I know we need to keep warm here on earth / and when your shawl is as thin as mine is, you tell stories" (*Red Suitcase* 26).

Naomi Shihab Nye's first collection of poems, *Different Ways to Pray* (1980), marks the beginning of her exploration of what will become recurrent themes through the body of her work. Her concern with family connections is the subject of many of her poems because, as she states in *Fuel* (1998), "If you tuck the name of a loved one / under your tongue too long / without speaking it / it becomes blood," so "No one sees / the fuel that feeds you" ("Hidden"). The family must be acknowledged; it must be recognized, but so must the fact that families have been torn asunder by the displacement created by war. For this reason, the sense of loss so prevalent in the work of exile or immigrant writers also runs through Shihab Nye's poetry even though she is herself not an exiled poet.

Born to a Palestinian father and a mother of European ancestry, Naomi Shihab Nye was born and raised on a farm in St. Louis where she learned to love animals and appreciate her father's love for the land. At the age of twelve, she spent a year in Palestine getting to know her father's family, an experience that filled her with a deep sense of belonging and, thereby, displacement. Lisa Suhair Majaj points out that Shihab Nye's poetry "explores the markers of cross-cultural complexity, moving between her Palestinian and American heritages" because Shihab Nye's poems document the differences as well as the similarities between two very divergent peoples, although Suhair Majaj also claims that Shihab Nye "is heir to an Arab essence passed down across generations." Regardless of her "Arab essence," Naomi Shihab Nye's work lies well within the American tradition of story-telling poets like Robert Frost.

Whether she is writing about her father's Palestinian family or her own connections with people in other parts of the world, Shihab Nye's poems are acquainted with the pain of displaced people. In "Brushing Live," she writes about an unexpected

> *Often, the stories become a tool for survival, the only way to make sense of difficult moments in a harsh world, . . ."*

meeting between her father and a Palestinian man in Alexandria.

> In a shop so dark he had to blink twice
> an ancient man sunk low on a stool and said,
> 'You talk like the men who lived in the world
> when I was young.' Wouldn't say more,
> till my father mentioned Palestine
> and the gentleman rose, both arms out, streaming
> cheeks. 'I have stopped saying it. So many years.'
> My father held him there, held Palestine, in the dark,
> at the corners of two honking streets.
> He got lost coming back to our hotel.
> (*Red Suitcase*)

The encounter is awkward and casual, but it taps at the pain of the exiled, the displaced, the pain of a people adrift in a violent world. Gregory Orfalea, when asked to discuss the Palestinian connection in Shihab Nye's work, points out that "her work is faithful to the minute, but essential tasks of our lives, the luminous in the ordinary."

Because so much of her work harks back to her memories of the Shihab family home in Palestine, a picture of her Palestinian grandmother, Sitti Khadra, graces the cover and half title page of *Words under the Words,* a volume that brings together three of her early books: *Different Ways to Pray* (1980), *Hugging the Jukebox* (1982), and *Yellow Glove* (1986). The photograph was taken by Michael Nye, Naomi Shihab's Swedish American husband, which seems appropriate because much of Shihab Nye's work focuses on the moments recovered from family connections. She writes in *Never in a Hurry* that when she visits Palestine, "feelings crowd in on" her, and she reasons that "maybe this is what it means to be in your genetic home. That you will feel on fifty levels at once, the immediate as well as the level of blood, the level of uncles, . . . weddings and graves, the babies who didn't make it, level of the secret and unseen." She tells herself that "maybe this is heritage, that deep well that gives us more than we deserve. Each time I write or walk or think, I drop a bucket in."

The influence of the Shihab family on the Palestinian American poet evolves through the years. In "My Father and the Figtree," one learns about the time when the poet, at age six, eats a fig and shrugs, unaware of what the taste of a fig means to her Palestinian father:

> 'That's not what I'm talking about!' he said,
> 'I'm talking about a fig straight from the earth—
> gift of Allah!—on a branch so heavy it touches the
> ground.
> I'm talking about picking the largest fattest sweetest fig
> in the world and putting it in my mouth.'
> (Here he'd stop and close his eyes.)
> (*Words under the Words*)

The six-year-old child, raised in a country where figs are exotic, not as common as apples or even oranges, fails to understand her Palestinian father's appreciation for the fruit, even if the taste of figs functions in the poem like Proust's madeleine to bring back the past. The father's longing for the memory of the fig's taste reiterates the poet's concern with her father's displacement and her own sense of inadequacy as a Palestinian who does not share her father's memories.

In "The Words under the Words," Shihab Nye remembers her grandmother, Sitti Khadra, who lived north of Jerusalem and impressed her with her silence and wisdom. Because she lives in a war-torn country, "my grandmother's voice says nothing can surprise her. / Take her the shotgun wound and the crippled baby. / She knows the spaces we travel through, / the messages we cannot send" (*Words*). For the grandmother, affected by war, the one constant is Allah. Her "eyes say Allah is everywhere, even in death. . . . / He is her first thought, what she really thinks of His name." The grandmother reminds the poet to

> 'Answer, if you hear the words under the words—
> otherwise it is just a world with a lot of rough
> edges,
> difficult to get through, and our pockets full of
> stones.'

Her grandmother's words remind her to look for meaning in life, to look for the words under the words, which is exactly what the life of this poet is about, creating a context for understanding through story telling.

Because meaning can only spring from what she knows, Naomi Shihab Nye also writes about what it means to be "different" in America. Her most poignant poem on this subject is "Blood," published in *Yellow Glove* in 1986. In it, she remembers how

Years before, a girl knocked,
wanted to see the Arab.
I said we didn't have one.
After that, my father told me who he was,
'Shihab'—'shooting star'—
a good name, borrowed from the sky.
Once I said, 'When we die, we give it back?'
He said that's what a true Arab would say.

That she tells the girl that they "didn't have" an
Arab in the house reiterates Shihab Nye's own
sense of inadequacy. Although she shares her father's Palestinian ancestry, she does not recognize
it as a marker.

Although the child in the poem does not know
that she does in fact have an Arab in the house, the
adult poet refuses to forget him or her own connection to his ancestry. In the same poem, Shihab
Nye confronts the disturbing news emerging from
the Palestinian struggle for self determination.

I call my father, we talk around the news.
It is too much for him,
neither of his two languages can reach it.
I drive into the country to find sheep, cows,
to plead with the air:
Who calls anyone civilized?
Where can the crying heart graze?
What does a true Arab do now?

The Arab American who can see both sides of the
story in the Israeli/Palestinian struggle is torn between her desire for justice and her love for her ancestral country. The struggle, however, leads the
poet to recognize her ethnicity and her own place
as an "other" in America.

In "Speaking Arabic," a short essay in *Never
in a Hurry,* Shihab Nye ponders the need for ethnic identity as she wonders why she could not "forget the earnest eyes of the man who said to [her]
in Jordan, 'Until you speak Arabic, you will not
understand pain.'" She considers his statement
"ridiculous" and remembers how he goes on to say
"something to do with an Arab carrying sorrow in
the back of the skull that only language cracks."
As in the case of her father's earlier longing for the
taste of figs, the man's statement leads her to remember yet another man's statement when,

At a neighborhood fair in Texas, somewhere between
the German Oom-pah Sausage stand and the Mexican Gorditas booth, I overheard a young man say to
his friend, 'I wish I had a heritage. Sometimes I
feel—so lonely for one.' And the tall American trees
were dangling their thick branches right down over
my head.

Words from a zealot and from someone who has
lost his heritage are juxtaposed in an attempt to understand what it means to have a heritage, to come

from a place so deeply ingrained in the mind that
figs savored in childhood retain their taste forever.

As an Arab American, Naomi Shihab Nye
writes in English even as she frets over her inability to understand Arabic as well as she would like.

I thought pain had no tongue. Or every tongue
at once, supreme translator, sieve. I admit my
shame. To live on the brink of Arabic, tugging

its rich threads without understanding
how to weave the rug . . . I have no gift.
The sound, but not the sense. (*"Arabic,"
Red Suitcase*)

She associates speaking Arabic with her father and
with relatives who live far away, and, probably because she is a poet who values words, she wants
the gift of that language.

The power of words to renew and uplift the
spirit is another theme that runs through Naomi Shihab Nye's work, and it is manifested in her appreciation for the work of other poets. Through the
years, she has written many poems to her mentor
and teacher, William Stafford, of whom she says
in "Bill's Beans" that "He left the sky over Oregon
and fluent trees. / He gave us our lives that were
hiding under our feet, / saying, You know what to
do" (*Fuel*). Shihab Nye also maintains close relationships with many contemporary poets, In "You
Know Who You Are," words from one of these poets sustain her. She claims that "Because sometimes
I live in a hurricane of words / and not one of them
can save me. / Your poems come in like a raft, logs
tied together, / they float." Then, after observing
the behavior of fathers and sons together and wandering "uselessly in the streets I claim to love," she
feels "the precise body of your poems beneath me,
/ *like a raft,* I felt words as something portable
again, / a cup, a newspaper, a pin" (*Words under
the Words*). Words move her, sustain her, connect
her to the world in ways that only words can explain, which is why she attempts to teach one of
her students in "Valentine for Ernest Mann" that

poems hide. In the bottoms of our shoes,
they are sleeping. They are the shadows
drifting across our ceilings the moment
before we wake up. What we have to do
is live in a way that lets us find them.
(*Red Suitcase*)

For Naomi Shihab Nye, poems hide everywhere,
and her task as a poet has been to write ordinary
poems in an accessible language, what Vernon
Shetley calls the "colloquial free-verse lyric that
occupies the mainstream." There is no "'unread-
ability'" as "a goal in itself" in Naomi Shihab Nye's
poetry. If anything, her work aims for clarity and

achieves it because the poet herself is consciously trying to reach readers and non-readers alike, anyone who can make the time to hear a good story.

Living "in a way that lets us find" the poems suggests that people, as poets or simply as citizens of this world, must live a life committed to other people and all of creation. This is another one of Shihab Nye's themes, and one that speaks volumes for the soul of this poet. In "Kindness," she reminds her readers that

> Before you know what kindness really is
> you must lose things,
> feel the future dissolve in a moment
> like salt in a weakened broth.
> What you held in your hand,
> what you counted and carefully saved,
> all this must go so you know
> how desolate the landscape can be
> between the regions of kindness . . .
>
> Before you know kindness as the deepest thing
> inside,
> you must know sorrow as the other deepest thing.
> You must wake up with sorrow.
> You must speak to it till your voice
> catches the thread of all sorrows
> and you see the size of the cloth . . .
> (*Words under the Words*)

Kindness emanates from Naomi Shihab Nye's work. The five volumes of her work reveal a deep understanding of our weaknesses, our humanity, as the stories that she creates define her ties to a people who endow her with an appreciation for heritage and a strong sense of what she has lost and what she has gained as she defines her own place in the world.

Source: Ibis Gomez-Vega, "The Art of Telling Stories in the Poetry of Naomi Shihab Nye," in *MELUS*, Vol. 26, No. 4, Winter 2001, pp. 245–52.

Bert Almon

In the following review of Words under the Words, *Shihab Nye's collection of poetry, and* Never in a Hurry, *her collection of essays, Almon asserts that "readers will find similar satisfactions in both books: memorable language, lively imagination, and deep human sympathies."*

Naomi Shihab Nye's selected poems, *Words under the Words*, represents her first three books: *Different Ways to Pray, Hugging the Jukebox* (a National Poetry Series selection for 1982), and *Yellow Glove*. Nye is one of the best poets of her generation, a fact underlined by her prominence in two recent PBS series on poetry: *The Language of Life* and *The United States of Poetry*. Readers can find

a very full selection of her work in *Words Under the Words*.

The most popular poetic mode of our time, the free verse lyric rooted in personal experience, has come in for criticism because it is so often practiced without commitment. This poet is always vigilant: the rhythms are sharp, the eye is keen. She excels at the unexpected and brilliant detail that underwrites the poetic vision. The image of a skillet appears in three of the poems, and that seems typical of Nye's perceptions: a notoriously solid and practical object, brought into poetry. Her vision takes in the ordinary and extraordinary: there is a poem here about sending a beloved cat in the cargo hold of a plane, and others that focus with clarity and anguish on the *intifada*. Nye has a Palestinian-born father, and she explores her loyalties with great tact, revealing the rich humanity of people who are often demonized. She has other loyalties: to the American side of her family, to the formative scenes of her childhood, and to the pressures and dramas of the people in her largely Mexican-American neighborhood of San Antonio, Texas. Like William Stafford, whose poems she admires, she is a writer with allegiances. Allegiances, not prejudices or animosities.

For all her interest in other people, one theme that runs through the poems is the formation of the self and the subtleties of its development. Here she shares a great deal with William Stafford. For both poets, "world" is a favorite term, and they avoid narcissism by stressing the ways that the mind of the individual makes its way in the world: being nurtured or injured, reaching out in sympathy or closing in a little to protect itself. Nye and Stafford both favor reaching out, but they dramatize a whole range of responses. They invite us to understand our own stories by telling theirs with memorable details. One of the best poems, "White Silk," takes off from a Zen meditation—"Try to be a piece of white silk." After a stunning series of dream images of silk, we find the poet in a general store, examining a bolt of white silk with smooth brown lines at the creases: we return to the world of iron skillets, but feel extended by the imaginative journey. The title of her collection, *Words Under the Words*, expresses a confidence in ultimate meaningfulness of our descriptions of reality. If we listen, we can hear the inner meaning.

The essays in *Never in a Hurry* share much with the poetry. They have the openness to experience and the flexibility of development that we value in the essay form. The variety of the book is one of its pleasures: the essays range from long narratives to vignettes to prose poems. The places of her subtitle include Palestine, Oahu, Rajasthan, Maine, and Oregon. She is most compelling when she writes about her complex heritage. She grew up in St. Louis, Missouri, Jerusalem, and San Antonio, Texas, and makes those diverse places familiar to us.

Perhaps the finest essays are the ones dealing with the Palestinian village where her father began his life: the figure of her grandmother, who died at 106 and lived her whole life in one place, is unforgettable. It is not easy to speak for Palestinian villagers in present-day America. Nye conveys the reality of their lives, practicing a politics of sympathy—we can surely think of "politics" in a broad sense, as the ways in which people deal with one another in this world. The essays about San Antonio remind us that there are many villages, some of them within large American cities. She writes about the poor and the immigrants in those villages without condescension, because she has a conviction of their value.

Readers will find similar satisfactions in both books: memorable language, lively imagination, and deep human sympathies.

Source: Bert Almon, "Poetry of the American West," in *Western American Literature*, Vol. 31, No. 3, Fall 1996, pp. 265–66.

Sources

Almon, Bert, "Poetry of the American West," in *Western American Literature*, Vol. 31, No. 3, Fall 1996, pp. 265–66.

Donnelly, Daria, "Nye, Naomi Shihab," in *American Women Writers: A Critical Reference Guide from Colonial Times to the Present*, 2d ed., Vol. 3, edited by Taryn Benbow-Pfalzgraf, St. James Press, 2000, pp. 212–13.

Elam, Angela, "The Subject Is Life: An Interview with Naomi Shihab Nye," in *New Letters*, Vol. 69, Nos. 2/3, 2003, p. 147.

Nye, Naomi Shihab, "Kindness," in *Different Ways to Pray: Poems by Naomi Shihab Nye*, Breitenbush Publications, 1980, p. 55.

———, "Kindness," in *Words under the Words: Selected Poems*, Eighth Mountain Press, 1995, pp. 42–43.

———, "The Words under the Words," in *Words under the Words: Selected Poems*, Eighth Mountain Press, 1995, pp. 36–37.

Further Reading

Bushnell, David, *The Making of Modern Colombia: A Nation in Spite of Itself*, University of California Press, 1993.

Bushnell contends that there is much more to Colombia than the drug trafficking, kidnappings, and terrorism that have dominated the news about the country over the past few decades. While acknowledging the prolific cocaine trade, violence, and unjust class system, Bushnell highlights a steady economic growth, a democratic government, and Colombia's artists and writers.

McBryde, John, Elaine Smokewood, and Harbour Winn, "Honoring Each Moment: An Interview with Naomi Shihab Nye," in *Humanities Interview*, Vol. 22, No. 1, Winter 2004, pp. 1, 14–17.

In this lengthy interview, Nye focuses on the important role that poetry plays in her everyday life. As the title suggests, she contends that poetry has the ability to slow down people's daily lives if they will take the time to read a little and to pay attention to and "honor" each moment as it comes.

Nye, Naomi Shihab, *Never in a Hurry*, University of South Carolina Press, 1996.

This collection of autobiographical essays provides a solid look at Nye's perspective on her childhood, adolescence, and adulthood. From her Arab American heritage through living in Jerusalem as a teenager to settling in Texas as a wife, mother, and poet, these writings offer many interesting insights on the author.

———, *Yellow Glove*, Breitenbush Publications, 1986.

Several of the poems from this volume are included in *Words under the Words*, and the overall theme of the work is closely tied to that of the later collection. Nye contemplates the tragedy of a world in which people hate one another without even knowing one another. She addresses the Palestinian-Israeli conflict specifically in some of the poems, calling for peace, kindness, and humanity in very inhumane times and places.

The Litany

Dana Gioia

2001

Dana Gioia's collection of poetry *Interrogations at Noon* (2001), which includes his poem "The Litany," has been praised for its lyricism as well as its classic sense of subject and theme. One of the strongest poems in the collection, "The Litany" makes a powerful statement of love and loss and of the search for a way to comprehend the nature of suffering. These became common themes in Gioia's poetry after the tragic death of his son at four months of age. Gioia's verse collection *The Gods of Winter* (1991) expresses his pain over his son's death; his later work is less personal but still focuses on the subject of loss.

In "The Litany," Gioia makes a confessional investigation of the nature of life and death and the universal design of that nature. Each stanza lists things the speaker has lost. These losses include someone he has loved as well as his faith in his religion, which had taught him to believe in the rightness of the cycle of life and death. His questioning of this cycle becomes an expression of grief.

Author Biography

Michael Dana Gioia was born on December 24, 1950, in Los Angeles, California, to a tightly knit family headed by his Italian father, Michael, and his Mexican American mother, Dorothy. His father was a cabdriver and store owner, and his mother was a telephone operator. Gioia rose from these humble beginnings through the academic world by earning a scholarship to Stanford University and obtaining a bachelor of science with honors there in 1973, as well as winning an award for the best senior essay. He went on to earn two master's degrees, one from Harvard University in 1975, where he studied with the poets Robert Fitzgerald and Elizabeth Bishop, and one from Stanford University in 1977.

Gioia's initial course of study was music, but he soon turned to literature. At Stanford, he had book reviews published in the *Stanford Daily* and served as editor of the campus literary magazine, *Sequoia*. His time at Harvard helped him cement his poetic aspirations, but he began to doubt whether academia was the best place to foster his talents. As a result, after completing course work for a PhD, but without finishing the degree, he left for Stanford Business School.

After graduation, Gioia joined General Foods Cooperation and made his way up the corporate structure, first as manager of business development (1977–1987), then as marketing manager (1988–1990), and finally as vice president of marketing (1990–1992). He continued to write poetry during these years, and, after he began to receive national recognition for his work, he left the business world to devote himself full time to writing.

Gioia married Mary Hiecke on February 23, 1980; the couple had three sons, one of whom died in infancy. His verse collection *The Gods of Winter* is dedicated to this son. Gioia established himself in the literary world first as a critic, with such essays as "The New Conservatism in American Poetry," published in *American Book Review* in 1986, and "Notes on the New Formalism," which appeared in the *Hudson Review* in 1987. His first collection of poems, *Daily Horoscope* (1986), won acclaim in America and Britain.

Gioia's literary reputation was firmly established with the publications of *The Gods of Winter* in 1991 and *Interrogations at Noon* in 2001, which includes "The Litany." His work earned him the Frederick Bock Prize in Poetry in 1985 and the American Book Award in 2002 for *Interrogations at Noon*. He became more famous, however, for his essay "Can Poetry Matter?," published in the *Atlantic Monthly* and available in *Can Poetry Matter?: Essays on Poetry and American Culture*. In this essay, Gioia complains that the public's lack of interest in reading poetry is a result of the genre's growing inaccessibility.

In January 2002, President George W. Bush appointed Gioia chairman of the National Endowment

Dana Gioia   © AP/Wide World

for the Arts following the untimely death of Michael P. Hammond after only one week in the office. Gioia's appointment came at a time of Republican attacks on the NEA that were part of the wave of culturally conservative views sweeping the United States.

Poem Text

This is a litany of lost things,
a canon of possessions dispossessed,
a photograph, an old address, a key.
It is a list of words to memorize
or to forget—of *amo, amas, amat,*   5
the conjugations of a dead tongue
in which the final sentence has been spoken.

This is the liturgy of rain,
falling on mountain, field, and ocean—
indifferent, anonymous, complete—   10
of water infinitesimally slow,
sifting through rock, pooling in darkness,
gathering in springs, then rising without our
        agency,
only to dissolve in mist or cloud or dew.

This is a prayer to unbelief,   15
to candles guttering and darkness undivided,
to incense drifting into emptiness.
It is the smile of a stone Madonna
and the silent fury of the consecrated wine,

a benediction on the death of a young god,   20
brave and beautiful, rotting on a tree.

This is a litany to earth and ashes,
to the dust of roads and vacant rooms,
to the fine silt circling in a shaft of sun,
settling indifferently on books and beds.   25
This is a prayer to praise what we become,
"Dust thou art, to dust thou shalt return."
Savor its taste—the bitterness of earth and ashes.

This is a prayer, inchoate and unfinished,
for you, my love, my loss, my lesion,   30
a rosary of words to count out time's
illusions, all the minutes, hours, days
the calendar compounds as if the past
existed somewhere—like an inheritance
still waiting to be claimed.   35

Until at last it is our litany, *mon vieux,*
my reader, my voyeur, as if the mist
steaming from the gorge, this pure paradox,
the shattered river rising as it falls—
splintering the light, swirling it skyward,   40
neither transparent nor opaque but luminous,
even as it vanishes—were not our life.

Poem Summary

Stanza 1

"The Litany" begins with the speaker calling attention to the poem as "a litany" in the first stanza, repeating the title phrase. The word *litany* can have two meanings: a series of prayers spoken or sung at a Christian worship service, asking for God's blessing, or a long, repetitious list of items that are usually considered complaints or problems. Both would be appropriate definitions here, since the poem is about "lost things," as noted in the first line.

The speaker finds another way to describe the litany in the second line, as a "canon." There are several definitions of this word, too, but the most relevant ones—which would suggest another term for litany as it is used in the first line—would be a body of religious or artistic works; the most solemn part of the Mass, or Holy Communion; and a list of Catholic saints.

The speaker notes that he has lost possessions, that they have become dispossessed (expelled or ejected) without his consent. He lists the things lost: a photograph, an old address, and a key, perhaps all relating to the same person. The litany then becomes a list of words to memorize or forget. The words could be part of a liturgical prayer or a list of the things lost. He then adds to the list the Latin words "*amo amas amat,*" which is the conjugation

of the verb "to love": "I love; you love; he or she loves." The speaker is not sure whether he should memorize or forget these words. The "dead tongue" refers to Latin, which is considered to be a dead language. In the last line, he declares that "the final sentence" of that language "has been spoken."

Stanza 2

In this stanza, the speaker moves from a personal focus to a description of landscape, listing different types on which rain falls. The rain falls to the earth indifferently, apathetically. It completes the cycle of life as it rises up again "without our agency" (that is, without our help) to the clouds.

Stanza 3

In this stanza, the list becomes the speaker's "prayer to unbelief," to "guttering" candles, and to incense drifting emptily. The prayer is likened to "the smile of a stone Madonna," to "the silent fury of the consecrated wine," and to "a benediction on the death of a young god." All the items in the stanza are found in Christian worship services.

Stanza 4

Here the litany becomes a list or a prayer to "earth and ashes," to dust, to fine silt, "a prayer to praise what we become." This wasteland, with its dusty roads and vacant rooms and silt settling "indifferently" on the objects in the rooms, is the backdrop for the scripture that the speaker quotes: "Dust thou art, to dust thou shalt return." The cycle of life and death, which in the second stanza was the cycle of rain falling and evaporating, now becomes focused on human death, as the body turns to ashes and dust after going into the grave. This cycle tastes bitter to the speaker.

Stanza 5

The first line in this stanza again insists that the poem is a prayer but that it is "inchoate" (unclear or unformed) and "unfinished." For the first time, the speaker identifies the person to whom the poem is addressed. This "you" is loved by the speaker and apparently lost to him. The reference to "lesion" suggests that the memory of this person is like a painful wound. The prayer becomes a "rosary" of words, a series of prayers, like a litany or like the string of beads used to count the prayers recited. But these words "count out / time's illusions." The illusions the speaker refers to are that the "past / existed somewhere" and that it could be "claimed," suggesting that the person that he had loved is gone.

Stanza 6

The first line in the final stanza continues the thought from the last. The prayer now becomes "our" litany, which is the poem itself. The speaker apparently shifts from speaking to the one who was lost, the "you," who died, to a different person, whom he calls "*mon vieux*" (my old one). This new person is a reader and a voyeur, looking in on the speaker's suffering.

In the final lines, the speaker refers back to the cycle of the rain falling to earth and then rising again but finds a more positive way to view it. The water falls down into a gorge and the mist steams upward. This process becomes a "paradox" of rising and falling, life and death. As the mist swirls skyward it becomes luminous—a symbol of "our" life, our litany, our death.

Themes

The Artistic Impulse

The impulse to communicate artistically becomes a dominant theme in the poem. The speaker reveals this need from the first line, when the poem becomes a "litany of lost things." All but the final stanza begin with the word "this," which refers to the poem itself and continually calls attention to it. This structure helps reinforce the confessional tone of the poem, as the speaker addresses first the lost loved one and then the reader of the poem.

The act of constructing the lists in the poem appears to help the speaker sort out his responses to the loss of the loved one and the subsequent loss of faith in his religion's ability to help ease his suffering. The development of his thoughts can be followed, as he moves back and forth from the universal focus on nature's cycle of life and death to his personal response to the death of someone he loved. Each list that he constructs for the poem helps him clarify and communicate his point of view.

The power of art to provide a sense of unity becomes apparent in the final stanza when the speaker addresses the reader, who shares in the universal nature of his suffering. The acknowledgment of this sympathetic understanding between poet and reader appears to trigger the speaker's more unified and therefore more satisfying vision of nature's cycle. What had previously appeared to be an "indifferent" world now becomes a paradoxical one that unites contrasting images of life and death in

Topics for Further Study

- Read Gioia's "Notes on the New Formalism" and investigate the responses to it. Lead a class discussion and assessment of his vision of the future of poetry.

- Gioia uses the technique of listing in the poem, much as Walt Whitman does in his poetry but with different effects. Read one of Whitman's poems, such as "Out of the Cradle Endlessly Rocking" or "When I Heard the Learn'd Astronomer," and compare in an essay his lists with those in "The Litany." Consider why each author chose the objects in the list and how they help express the poems' themes.

- Investigate the stages of grieving that a person goes through when a loved one dies. Chart these stages and any appearance of them in the poem in a PowerPoint presentation.

- Write a short story or poem about the speaker in "The Litany," envisioning him twenty years from now.

the rising and falling of the river. After the speaker has successfully communicated his vision to his reader, he can then turn to the living world of the present.

Influence of the Past

The powerful influence that the past can have on the present is reflected in the suffering the speaker experiences. The poem begins with the sense of loss, reinforced by memories of a loved one who has died. The speaker feels dispossessed when he looks at a photograph, an address, and a key, objects that somehow relate to the person he has lost. One of the central questions of the poem centers on whether the speaker should remember or forget the love ("*amo, amas, amat*") he has experienced in order to lessen the pain of remembrance.

He is unable to escape the past, however, as it colors his vision of the present and of the future. Because his memory has become a painful "lesion," his vision of the world has darkened. Nature imposes a cycle of life and death that is indifferent to the sufferings of humanity. Time appears to stop in the vacant rooms as mortals return to the dust of the grave. This world seems to offer no salvation for the dead or for the living.

The overwhelming presence of the past becomes most obvious as the speaker directly addresses the loved one, trying to construct a prayer that will not be "inchoate and unfinished." He struggles to find the language that will offer his loved one a clear benediction and himself a respite from his pain. He realizes that the past can never, unlike an inheritance, be claimed. It is only through the acceptance and expression of suffering that the speaker can find any relief from the burden of the past.

Style

Repetition of Word or Image

The poem uses repetition of the same word at the beginning of several verses for thematic emphasis. Five of six stanzas begin with "This is" followed by either "litany," "liturgy," or "prayer"—all used in a similar way to emphasize the loss of a loved one as well as the loss of faith. The variation in the three words reflects the dual nature of the loss. A litany could be a series of prayers or a list, having both a religious and a secular connotation. Yet the repetition of the word and its variations implies that the one loss, that of a loved one, has caused the other loss, that of faith in the rightness of the cycle of life.

Images are also repeated in stanzas 2, 4, and 6 to reinforce the focus on this cycle. In stanza 2, the life-giving part of the cycle emerges as rain falls on a mountain, a field, and an ocean and then rises to become clouds that will eventually turn into rain. In the fourth stanza, the speaker focuses on death as the body returns to the earth, to the dust from which it was formed. The final stanza reveals the entire cycle of life and death as the river rises and falls, "luminous" as it "vanishes."

Repetition of Sound

Gioia also uses the repetition of speech sounds for emphasis throughout the poem. In the first stanza alone, there are several instances of both consonance, the repetition of consonants, and assonance, the repetition of vowel sounds. Examples of consonance are "litany" and "lost"; "*amo, amas, amat*"; "is" and "list"; and "sentence" and "spoken." The

linking of "litany" and "lost" reinforces the poem's main focus: things lost. The repeated sounds in the Latin conjugation of the verb "to love" emphasizes that the most painful loss is that of a loved one. The consonance in the last example in this stanza alludes to the loss of faith, which has prevented the speaker from finding a vocabulary to describe his loss.

Assonance occurs with the vowel sounds in "this" and "litany"; "it," "is," and "list"; and "photograph" and "old." The repetition of the vowel sounds in the first two words points out the relationship between the construction of the poem ("this," meaning the poem itself) and the speaker's feelings of loss (his "litany"). The last example of assonance links details relating to the one lost. The words "possessions" and "dispossessed" contain both consonance and assonance and connect the fact of loss to the emotional response to it. Gioia's repetition of sounds also creates a musicality that adds a sense of unity and pleasure to reading the poem.

Confession

The poem creates a controlled confessional tone. Confessional poetry, a term first linked to Robert Lowell's lyric collection *Life Studies* (1959) and later to the poetry of Sylvia Plath and Anne Sexton, expresses intimate details of the poet's life. This poetry differs from that of the nineteenth-century Romantic poets like William Wordsworth and Percy Bysshe Shelley in that it explores the poet's experience with more candor. Typical subjects for the confessional poet include sexual encounters and extreme emotional states, often involving mental instability, drug use, and suicide.

In "The Litany," Gioia alternates between a confessional and an investigatory style. He expresses a personal sense of loss when he identifies the litany of the poem as a prayer to an unidentified "you," a "young god" who has died and is "rotting on a tree," most likely referring to both his infant son and the crucified Jesus. Yet he couples his sorrow with an investigation of the nature of the cycle of life and death and the ability of faith to ease suffering. This duality helps the poem achieve a more universal status.

Historical Context

The New Formalists

New formalism is a poetic movement, led by Gioia, that rejects the dominance of free verse (poetry that is not organized into recurrent units of stressed and unstressed syllables) in contemporary poetry. New formalists promote, instead, a return to traditional poetic meters (recurring regular units of speech sounds in a poem), rhymes, and stanza forms. Gioia, along with other new formalists like Charles Martin, Tom Disch, Phillis Levin, and Frederick Turner, has generated a sometimes heated discussion on the importance of prosody (the study of meter, rhyme, and stanza form) and the influence of past literary values. The theories of these poets are outlined in essays like Alan Shapiro's "The New Formalism," in *Critical Inquiry*, and Gioia's "Notes on the New Formalism," published in *Conversant Essays: Contemporary Poets and Poetry* (1990), edited by James McCorkle. In his discussion, Gioia insists that attention to form does not limit a poet but, in essence, frees the poet to expand the impact of the poem.

The new formalists emerged from a group called the "Movement," formed during the 1950s by British poets, including Philip Larkin, Kingsley Amis, John Wain, and Elizabeth Jennings. Like their formalist predecessors, they stress a unity of emotion and language in poetry rather than the intellectual exercises they claim are being taught in academia. The new formalists take as their model the lyric of the nineteenth-century British writer Thomas Hardy, which is a carefully metered lyric stanza that contains direct, common language rather than poetic diction. The members of this movement have sparked important debates about the future of poetry and its relationship to the reading public.

New Oral Poetry

In Gioia's essay collection *Disappearing Ink: Poetry at the End of Print Culture* (2004), he explores, in the title essay, the ways in which popular culture can help revive the public's interest in poetry. He argues that hip-hop and cowboy poetry and events like poetry slams, which depend on the oral presentation of verse, have become important new cultural forms. In an assessment of Gioia's title essay for *Wilson Quarterly*, the reviewer notes that "new popular poetry uses modern-day media such as radio, CDs, video, and the Internet . . . to attract a general audience that is less and less inclined to devote time to reading."

Hip-hop developed in the 1970s with the emergence of artists like the Last Poets, whose songs contained a mixture of spoken word and jazz background rhythms that expressed the African American experience. Gioia insists that hip-hop's fixed rhythms and rhyme schemes resemble those of English oral poetry, from Anglo-Saxon verse to Rudyard Kipling's ballads. The genre was promoted by Cool Herc, an influential disc jockey in New York City. Hip-hop artists like LL Cool J and Grand Master Flash have helped hip-hop maintain its popularity.

Poetry slams, which give poets a venue where they can perform their poetry in front of live audiences, first appeared in the mid-1980s. They may have been inspired by the open-microphone sessions for poets in a Chicago bar started by the poet Marc Smith. Slams are held in bars and cafés where poet-performers compete for top honors, awarded by a panel or the audience. In 2002, Russell Simmons, owner of Def Jam Records, reflected the popularity of the events when he opened a poetry slam on Broadway.

Cowboy poetry, which became a popular form during the settlement of the American frontier, reemerged in 1985 at a meeting of poets led by the folklorist Hal Cannon in Nevada. This poetry, which began as tall tales and folk songs told and sung around a campfire, expresses the culture and lifestyles of the West. It is also characterized by its regional dialects, its traditional ballad form (a sung narrative that contains quatrains with alternate four- and three-stress lines, with the second and fourth line rhyming), and its combination of realism (a literary movement that stresses accuracy in the representation of life) and romanticism (a movement that represents a world more picturesque and adventurous than real). Among the most famous cowboy poets are Buster Black and Clayton Atkin.

Critical Overview

Gioia's collection *Interrogations at Noon* has been well received for its technical artistry as well as its thematic import. Bruce F. Murphy, in his review of the collection for *Poetry*, praises the poet's "fluency and passion" and concludes, "In terms of lyricism, Dana Gioia is a virtuoso, it seems. Tones are augmented or diminished with great care. The poems are lyrical, fluid, assured; this is a poetry free of mistakes." Murphy insists that Gioia "embraces not only traditional measures, but traditional philosophy. The world exists independently of our thinking/speaking about it, and so the role of language is mimetic [something that mimics], not constitutive [something that constructs]."

Ned Balbo, in his review of the collection for the *Antioch Review*, claims that the poet is "a master of subtle registers" and insists that "elegiac in his outlook, Gioia is more likely to lower his voice than shout." He "sees the metaphors we live with every day."

In a discussion of theme, Murphy writes that Gioia "hints at the moral dimension of poetry." In all of the poems, Murphy finds a "sense of conscience, of being held to account." He argues that "behind its surface brilliance and the sometimes casual, occasional subjects, it is a very somber book. There are depths of sorrow that are refracted through form, and sometimes fully unveiled." Gioia's verse, Murphy claims, is a "public poetry that retains a sense of privacy, and a feeling for the limits of language." The "bottled-up suffering, when it finds an opening, comes out in a fierce jet. Death is everywhere present, as a desire for release from the unendurable."

Balbo concludes that Gioia speaks "with impressive gravity and range about what lies at the dark heart of human affairs," yet he "can lighten a dark moment or finely shade a lighter one." His poems are "superb in their blend of toughness and vulnerability, their quest for solace before loss, their measured yet memorable voice." Balbo concludes that though the collection "often speaks of death and absence, it offers the consolation of uncommon craft."

In his review of the collection for *Booklist*, Ray Olson notes that Gioia has obviously studied the classics of Greek and Roman literature, which teach that "the human heart is never satisfied." He argues that Gioia reveals a "formal dexterity" in his verse and has "learned the turbulent heart in the content" of his poems. Gioia "draws on Greek and Roman motifs, stories, and attitudes" and "conveys to us the acceptance of mortality and the celebration of beauty that have made the classics perdurably [long-lastingly] relevant." His "true" rhymes, "correct and musical" meters, and "fresh" diction suggest, Olson claims, that "he is well on the way to becoming a classic poet himself."

Criticism

Wendy Perkins

Wendy Perkins is a professor of American and English literature and film. In this essay, she explores the interplay of the subjects of love, loss, and faith in the poem.

In his poem "Design," Robert Frost chooses as his subject nature's cycle of life and death and examines its design. The poem is focused on a seemingly insignificant event: the death of a moth. Frost describes how the moth is attracted to a flower where a spider is lying in wait for its breakfast. He notes that this scene can be viewed as an illustration of the life cycle, an illustration that the moth must die so that the spider can live. In his description of the event, Frost questions whether this cycle has been consciously designed or is the result of random occurrence. His questioning comes from his awareness of the suffering that is a consequence of this cycle. Frost often explored the subjects of death and suffering in his poetry, especially after his son committed suicide.

Gioia also turned to the subject of death in his poetry after his infant son died. His work focuses on the suffering associated with death but does not question whether the cycle of life and death is part of a universal design. In "The Litany," one of his most compelling explorations of this theme, Gioia centers on the experience of death for those left behind.

In "Design," Frost's struggle to come to terms with death is evident in the juxtaposition of positive and negative imagery in the first stanza. The three participants in the event—the flower, the moth, and the spider—become "assorted characters of death and blight" in one line and "mixed ready to begin the morning right" in another. In these two lines, Frost contrasts the rightness of nature's cycle with the recognition that death and blight are a part of that cycle. In the next line, the three characters become "the ingredients of a witches' broth," suggesting a "design of darkness to appall." Here, Frost implies that the creator of this cycle may have had a sinister intent.

Gioia's speaker never doubts that the universe has been designed by God or suggests that God's intentions were disturbing. His focus instead is on the suffering caused by death and the role faith plays in relation to that suffering. The poem's juxtaposition of secular and religious images calls into question the ability of faith to help alleviate the pain of loss.

The speaker begins his thoughtful probing in the first stanza, which reveals him to be engaged in an investigatory process while, at the same time, isolated as a result of his loss. Here he starts to question and reevaluate his experience in order to comprehend and cope with it. He first defines his loss as a litany of "things." The use of the word "litany," which means either a list of complaints or prayers spoken at a Christian service, highlights the dual nature of his focus: the loss and the question of whether faith can help one cope with that loss.

The speaker's tone contains a touch of bitterness as he declares that his possessions have been "dispossessed," taken against his will. This word also suggests that, as a result of the loss, he has become dispossessed, or homeless. The two losses that the speaker has experienced, a loved one and the power of his religious faith to ease his suffering, have caused this sense of homelessness. These losses are revealed in the second half of the stanza, where the speaker notes the influence of the past on the present when he wonders whether he should remember or forget the conjugation of the verb "to love." The following stanzas illustrate the pain caused by the memory of the loved one, who is now lost, and the inability of faith to relieve that pain. At this point, the language of his religion, expressed in litanies, liturgies, and prayers, has become "a dead tongue / in which the final sentence has been spoken."

Like Frost's speaker in "Design," the speaker in "The Litany" turns to a description of nature's cycle, moving from a personal to a universal focus as he describes the process of rain falling on the landscape and then evaporating back into the clouds. Yet, like the speaker in Frost's poem, he is unable to keep from including his response when he determines that the rain, which engages in a "complete" process of life and death, is nevertheless "indifferent" to the sufferings that the process causes. He recognizes that we are unable to stop this cycle, which continues "without our agency."

The personal tone gains intensity in the third stanza when the speaker's sadness combines with unrestrained bitterness. Here, the speaker reveals the failure of his faith to ease his pain. At this point, he does not believe that the ceremonial candles will conquer the darkness or that the incense will carry his prayers to heaven. The Madonna, who has previously offered him comfort, is now silent stone, and the consecrated wine expresses not salvation through the blood of Christ but fury over "the death of a young god," a reference to a loss of faith as well as the loss of the loved one.

Gioia turns from scriptural to allegorical allusions in the next stanza, which help add a universal as well as personal focus. The wasteland imagery in the fourth stanza reinforces the speaker's sense of desolation in the face of an indifferent world. Nature's cycle is again described, but here the imagery is darker. All life seems to have ended in the vacant rooms that contain an

> *The poem's juxtaposition of secular and religious images calls into question the ability of faith to help alleviate the pain of loss."*

eternal silence, reflecting "what we become" as we return to the dust that we are. This prayer tastes of "the bitterness of earth and ashes."

The confessional intimacy of the fifth stanza adds a sad poignancy to the poem. The speaker admits that his prayer for conciliation is "inchoate and unfinished," because his suffering has not abated. For the first time, he speaks directly to the lost one and to the memory that has become a painful "lesion." His rosary cannot offer benediction, because the words he recites in prayer only "count out time's / illusions." As he recognizes that the past can never be reclaimed, the speaker turns to a new audience, the reader of his poem, and to the "litany" of loss that is universally shared.

The reader is a voyeur who shares in the speaker's suffering, an acknowledgment that appears to offer some comfort to the speaker. When he returns to a description of nature's cycle, he now seems to find a paradox in the rising and falling of the river. The cycle of life and death represented by the river not only shatters and splinters but also becomes "luminous" in its inevitable progress "skyward," bringing with it a suggestion of salvation for the dead as well as for the living. In his rendering of the speaker's need in "The Litany" to come to an ultimate acceptance of death as part of God's design, Gioia creates an eloquent statement of the often-suffocating aftermath of loss and the intense desire to comprehend it.

Source: Wendy Perkins, Critical Essay on "The Litany," in *Poetry for Students*, Thomson Gale, 2006.

Dana Gioia and Christina Vick

In the following interview, Gioia recounts his early love of reading and his influences, and expounds on methods of writing poetry.

What Do I Read Next?

- *A Death in the Family* (1957), by James Agee, is a tragic tale of the effect of a man's death on his family.

- For a comparative study of American poetry, read Richard Howard's *Alone with America: Essays on the Art of Poetry in the United States since 1950* (1980).

- Gioia dedicated *The Gods of Winter* (1991) to his son who died from sudden infant death syndrome. Several of the poems in the volume deal with the subject of death.

- Gioia's essay "Can Poetry Matter?," published in *Can Poetry Matter?: Essays on Poetry and American Culture* (2002), presents his controversial views of the status of poetry in America in the early part of the twenty-first century.

[*Christina Vick*]: *When did you first conceive a love for literature?*

[Dana Gioia]: I can't ever remember a time when I did not love poems and stories, but who knows how it all began? Oddly, I don't recall my parents ever reading books to me, but my mother often read or recited poems. I remember hearing hundreds of poems as a child. As soon as I learned to read, I devoured books. We had—because of political graft—an enormous library in my otherwise rundown hometown. I used to go there after school and wander the shelves. No one ever advised me on what to read, so I sampled everything. On the same visit I might bring home a book of Roman history, another of horror stories, and a third of Italian paintings. Reading was in many ways more real to me than my daily life. It opened up a world of possibilities beyond the dreary limits of working-class, urban Los Angeles.

Were there any special circumstances in your childhood that made books so important to you?

I spent a great deal of time alone. Both of my parents worked. My first brother wasn't born until I was six, and except for my cousins next door there

were almost no children in my neighborhood, which was made up mostly of small cheap apartments. Our home, however, was full of books, records, and musical scores from my uncle, Theodore Ortiz, who had served in the Merchant Marines before dying in a plane crash in 1955. He was an old-style proletariat intellectual who spent all of his money on music and literature. His library lined nearly every room and spilled over into the garage. There were books in six languages and hundreds of classical LPs. My parents never read the books or played the records, but they kept them for sentimental reasons. The books were not especially interesting to a child—the novels of Thomas Mann, the plays of George Bernard Shaw, Pushkin in Russian, Cervantes in Spanish—but growing up with this large library around us exercised a strong magic on me, and later on me brother Ted.

At what point in your life did you know that you wanted to be a poet?

I remember quite exactly when I decided to become a poet. I was a college sophomore studying in Vienna on a Stanford exchange program. I had gone to Europe as a decisive gesture to figure out if I really wanted to be a composer. Living abroad for the first time and speaking a foreign language, I brooded a great deal in my room or else wandered the labyrinthine streets of the inner city in a fever of loneliness. Soon I found myself constantly reading and writing poetry—both in English and German. By the time I returned to America, I had decided to be a poet.

Who or what do you read for pleasure or inspiration?

I read all the time—newspapers, magazines, journals, and books—usually several books at once. I don't read as many novels now as I did when I was younger, though I still read forty or fifty a year. Now I tend to read more biographies and history. I also read theological and philosophical books. And, of course, I read—and reread—poetry all the time. I find myself habitually rereading certain books and authors, especially Virgil, Horace, St. Augustine, Shakespeare, and the Bible. I read science fiction for fun at bedtime. I also devour classical music and opera magazines. I sometimes worry if I have spent too much of my life reading, but how much narrower my life would have been without books.

Who are your favorite authors?

I have too many to list, especially poets. Some of my favorite novelists include Stendhal, Balzac, James, Cather, and Nabokov. I have a special passion for the short story, which seems to me perhaps the greatest single achievement of American literature, and I adore the short work of Poe, Cheever, Hemingway, O'Connor, Faulkner, Porter, Welty, Malamud, and Carver—though I would award Chekhov top international honors in the form. Philosophers and theologians like St. Augustine, Albert Schweitzer, Dietrich Bonhoeffer, Thomas Merton, Friedrich Nietzsche, Miguel de Unamuno, Mircea Eliade, Marshall McLuhan, Jacques Maritain, and Georg Lukacs have all been important to me.

Who have been your mentors? What influence have they had on your professional and personal life?

I have moved around a great deal in my adult life and changed my profession three times—from academies to business to writing. No one person served as a mentor across all those changes, but at particular points in my life certain people had a crucial influence. The older writers who helped me the most—not so much in terms of external assistance but in internal clarification—were Robert Fitzgerald, Elizabeth Bishop, Donald Davie, Howard Moss, and Fredrick Morgan. Each helped me in a different way sometimes just for a short but critical period. There have also been some important relationships with older writers who were not so much mentors as dear friends—like Donald Justice, John Haines, Daniel Hoffman, X. J. Kennedy, William Jay Smith, Janet Lewis, William Maxwell, and Anne Stevenson.

What influence have these mentors had on you?

They provided useful models of what a writer's life might be like. Their work also kept my standards high. Each relationship was necessarily different. Elizabeth Bishop, for example, encouraged me, whereas Donald Davie discouraged me. Both interventions helped me develop as a writer. Robert Fitzgerald taught me essential things about poetic craft. He also provided me with a model of a modern Catholic man of letters. Frederick Morgan quietly encouraged me to write in my own way. I should also add that these writers were all remarkable human beings. Knowing them confirmed my sense of the importance of friendship, generosity, and integrity in literary life.

Do you compose a poem in longhand or on a computer? What is the reason for your choice? Do you think the electronic age has helped or hindered creative writing?

My methods are quite primitive. My poems begin as words in the air. I talk to myself—usually while pacing the room or walking outside. (Any observer would assume I was mad.) After I coax a line or two aloud, I jot it down. Very slowly and

To understand a poem it helps to have lived at least a little of its contents."

painstakingly I shape those lines and phrases into a poem. I pay equal attention to the way the poem sounds and how it works on the page. Only after many handwritten drafts do I type the poem up. That transition allows me to see the poem differently and revise it further. Since I believe that poetry not only originates in the body but also communicates largely through physical sound, I am skeptical of the putative advances of the electronic age. Though computers offer great convenience, they cannot substitute for direct physical embodiment of one's medium.

Mark Twain, famous for his prose style, once said, "The difference between the right word and the nearly right word is the difference between lightning and a lightning bug." How do you know when you have the found the "right" word for a poem?

This is an excellent question because so often the expressive effect of a line or stanza depends upon a single word. In poetry no effect is too small to matter. I revise a great deal and often focus on a particular word or phrase which I instinctively feel is crucial to the poem's impact. I like to combine words in a way that initially seems slightly odd but also oddly appropriate. I hope to discover a new combination that the language was waiting to have happen.

When you begin work on a poem, what is your method? Do you have the poem, or the concept of the poem, in its entirety in your mind before you set it down in words, or is writing the poem a process of discovery?

My poetic method is best described as confusion, followed by madness, exhilaration, and despair. I advise others to avoid my conspicuously bad example. For me, a poem begins as a powerful physical sensation. I can feel the poem in my throat and temples—a sudden illumination that is mostly beyond words but which is also partially embodied in a few specific words. That line or phrase suddenly opens a doorway. I usually have no idea what the final poem might be beyond its opening line. Writing the poem is discovering what one meant to say. People who aren't poets have trouble understanding how mysterious the process is.

Many of your poems seem so heartfelt and personal, particularly the poems in your recent collection, Interrogations at Noon. *I'm thinking especially the title poem, which discusses "the better man I might have been, / Who chronicles the life I've never led," as well as "Curriculum Vitae," "A California Requiem," and certainly "Pentecost" seem to speak to the reader about the author. To what extent do you chronicle your own experiences, and to what extent do you adopt a persona in your poems?*

My poems are personal but almost never entirely autobiographical. I combine my own experiences with observations from other people often adding elements of pure fantasy to create situations and stories that feel true. I deliberately try to eliminate myself in literal terms from the poem. The speaker of the poem may resemble me, but he or she is also a surrogate for the reader. Paradoxically, I find that the more I invent the more candid and truthful I become.

How does the audience affect your poetry? By that I mean, when you give a reading of your poems, does that situation dictate your choice of poems to be read?

When I write poetry, I don't consider the audience except in the most general terms—as fellow human beings who share the English language. But when I give a public poetry reading, I always consider my immediate audience. I don't worry much about its level of literary sophistication. If a poem is good enough, it should communicate at some essential level to most audiences. What I consider mostly is each audience's range of life experience. To understand a poem it helps to have lived at least a little of its contents. I take readings seriously. The sort of poetry I love best is meant to be spoken aloud and heard.

Does the act of reading in public transform the experience of those poems for you? What do you wish your audience to receive or take away from a reading?

Yes, over time the act of giving poetry readings has gradually transformed my attitude toward my own poems. Now that the finished poems exist independently of me in print I find that I am merely one of their readers, and I begin to see them very differently. They often mean things I never initially realized or intended.

In the title essay of your 1992 collection, Can Poetry Matter?, *you lamented the fact that "most poetry is published in journals that address an insular audience of literary professions." Nine years later, do you see any reasons for optimism about the dissemination of good and accessible poetry to a large reading public?*

A great deal has changed since the publication of *Can Poetry Matter?*—some for the good, some for the worse, the most important development has been the astonishing growth of the poetry world outside the university. There has been an explosion of poetry readings, festivals, broadcasts, and conferences based in libraries, bookstores, galleries, and communities. (I like to think my original essay had something to do with inspiring academic outsiders to build these new enterprises since many people have written me letters saying so, but perhaps I unduly flatter myself.) These new poetry venues range from the sublime, to the ridiculous, but collectively they have had the effect of democratizing our literary culture. Most of this activity happens on a local basis, so it has hardly challenged the established reputation-making power of New York and the Northeast, but this new bohemia does allow poets to speak directly to a broader and more diverse audience than ever before.

Writing has been called a lonely profession because it is performed of necessity in solitude. Do you have a support system—family, friends, colleagues—people who offer encouragement in your practice of what is generally considered, in America at least, an unorthodox profession?

Writing is mostly a solitary endeavor—sometimes terribly so. For many years I wrote after work and on the weekends. I had to give up a great many things to make the time for poetry. That decision exacted its price in human terms, but I paid it gladly because I felt most truly myself, most intensely alive when writing or reading. Now my life is even more solitary. I no longer work in a busy office but alone in a studio across the hill from my house. Many days I see no one except my family—and a great many animals. If things go badly, my life can become very lonely. I accept that loneliness as a necessary part of who I am. I should be lost without my friends, even though I seldom see them. Solitary people feel friendship deeply. There are a few fellow poets I love quite deeply. They sustain me.

In your experience, can writing poetry be a therapeutic exercise as well as an imaginative, creative endeavor? Do you sometimes turn to writing poetry as a means of coping with difficulties in life, past and present?

I associate therapeutic poetry with bad writing—especially my own. I guess there is some therapeutic aspect in much poetry, but it also seems to me that it concerns the emotional impulse behind the poem rather than the poem itself. I have often sat down and poured my suffering soul onto some innocent piece of paper, but surrendering to a powerful subjective emotional state does not create an imaginative structure that will replicate the experience in the reader's mind. A poem is a mysterious verbal device, a sort of magic spell, directed not at the author but the reader. If a poem is therapeutic, then the patient must be the reader not the writer.

In your experience, how much of writing poetry is art, and how much is craft?

All art depends on craft. Without proper technique a poet, however talented, can amount to very little. Despite the proliferation of graduate writing programs—perhaps because of them—our age has seen both a denigration and ignorance of poetic craft. Today any poet who wants to master versecraft must do it mostly on his or her own. Technique is the necessary beginning, but it is only a means to an expressive end. Having something genuinely compelling to express is essential. That gift can't be taught.

Your considerable background in the business world might come as a surprise to readers familiar only with your poetry. Could you comment on this background?

I originally went to graduate school in literature, but it seemed a bad place for me as a writer. I liked it too much. Harvard aggravated my inherent tendency to be overly intellectual and self-conscious. Working in business gave me a chance to construct a different sort of writing life—more private, independent, and contemplative. I went to Stanford Business School, and in 1977 I joined General Foods in New York. When I resigned fifteen years later, I was a Vice President. I still miss the people I worked with. They were smart, friendly, and funny. There were a few idiots, scoundrels, and egomaniacs, but no more than I've encountered in literary life.

Were you engaged in creative writing at the same time that you were involved in a business career?

Yes. I went into business to be a poet. For me, business was always just a job, even though I ended up doing quite well. I would work ten or twelve hours a day at the office, and then I tried to squeeze two or three hours of writing in each night at home. It wasn't easy, but I managed—mostly by giving up other things.

Did you consider these pursuits antithetical or complementary to each other?

I never considered business as either antithetical or complementary to my writing. Business and poetry were simply different occupations.

In your essay "Business and Poetry," in which you create an intriguing exploration of such poets as T. S. Eliot, Wallace Stevens, James Dickey, and others who sustained themselves and their families in business careers, you pose the question: "How did their business careers affect the lives and works of these poets?" This issue has personal relevance to you. Would you answer the same question you posed in your essay? How has your experience in the business world affected your literary work?

My years in business offered at least two advantages. First, they allowed me to develop as a poet at my own pace and in my own way. I had no pressure to publish or need to conform to any academic or intellectual fashion. I made my own necessary mistakes and discoveries. Working in isolation, my most intense literary relationships were with the great dead, the most demanding and yet attentive colleagues. Had I stayed at Harvard I would have been too vulnerable to the many captivating influences around me. Neglect, obscurity, and loneliness are the necessary nourishment of a young poet.

Second, working in business greatly broadened my life experience. It permitted me—indeed forced me—to see the world and literature from a different angle than I had in graduate school. Working with intelligent but non-literary people for nearly twenty years made me conscious of the cultural elitism I had acquired at Stanford and Harvard. I no longer took certain assumptions for granted. Most important, I understood the importance of writing in a way that does not exclude intelligent people.

Could you discuss your writing life outside the university?

It is an odd enterprise in our society to make a living as a poet outside academia. It's definitely not a career for the faint of heart. The poems—no matter how good—won't pay the bills. I work seven days a week. I travel constantly giving readings and lectures—always working on airplanes and in hotel rooms. I edit anthologies, write for BBC Radio, review books and music, and collaborate with composers. The practical challenge is to pay the bills, which I've gradually learned how to do. The deeper challenge is primarily spiritual—how to create and sustain a passionate sense of living the right life. That is far more difficult. Loneliness, exhaustion, disappointment, and despair are always nearby.

You have recently published an intriguing libretto for the opera Nosferatu *based on the silent German expressionist film directed by F. W. Murnau. What drew you to this particular retelling of the Dracula myth?*

The subject chose me. I was looking for an idea for a libretto, and by lucky coincidence I happened to read an essay on Murnau by my friend Gilberto Perez. By the time I had finished the piece I knew that this was the subject, the only possible subject for the opera the composer Alva Henderson and I were planning. What drew me to *Nosferatu* was the depth and complexity of the heroine, and the symbolic possibilities of the vampire myth. Opera is the last surviving form of poetic theater, and I wanted a subject that would allow my imagination a wild freedom.

To what extent did your background in musical composition influence your decision?

I knew I wanted to write a libretto that revived and explored traditional musical forms—arias, duets, trios, choruses, and ensembles. I also wanted the language and the dramatic structure to be inherently lyrical. I had no interest in writing a prose drama to be set to music. I tried to give every scene a dramatic shape embodied in musical and poetic structures.

When can we hope to see a staging of your opera?

Rimrock Opera will mount the world premiere in Billings, Montana and Boise, Idaho. Meanwhile two concert performances are being staged in Chattanooga. Two groups in New York also want to stage *Nosferatu*—Verse Theatre Manhattan and the Derriere Guard Arts Festival—but it remains to be seen if they can raise the money. Opera is an extraordinarily expensive art form. When we began the project, I told Alva that I wanted to perform excerpts of our work-in-progress because even successful new operas achieve so few productions. We have already produced showcases in Georgia, California, Texas, Illinois, Connecticut, Colorado, and Pennsylvania—and portions of the music have been broadcast by the BBC, KPFA, and several NPR affiliates—so a surprising number of people have heard some of the music.

You have published a number of college textbooks, including Literature: An Introduction to Fiction, Poetry, and Drama *co-edited by X. J. Kennedy, an anthology I have used for a number of years. Has this been a rewarding experience for you?*

Editing anthologies has been enormously interesting and rewarding. It has also been exhausting. To edit them responsibly, I must constantly read and reread poems, stories, plays, and scholarship to make the right selections. I am also perpetually writing critical overviews, historical notes, author biographies, and commentaries. In the dozen or so anthologies I have published in the last decade, I have published well over a million words of critical prose. I sometimes feel I am living in an eternal finals week. My private goal has been to manage this task without ever letting the writing become dull or insipid—in other words never to let it sound like most textbooks.

Why do you work so hard on textbooks?

Because they are so important. A great anthology can change a student's life. A dull one can turn him or her away from literature forever. I take anthologies seriously because they represent the logical extension of my concerns as a poet and critic. What better way is there to correct, improve, and expand literary taste? I also love to bring new or neglected writers to a broader audience.

On what current projects are you working?

I have too many projects. Graywolf Press will publish a tenth anniversary edition of *Can Poetry Matter?* in late 2002, and I am writing a special introduction about the reception and impact of the book. I am also putting together a new collection of critical essays. I am now just finishing up two large anthologies on twentieth century American poetry and poetics. I'm co-editing these ambitious and comprehensive books with David Mason and Meg Schoerke. The critical apparatus is itself several hundred pages long, and it gives me the opportunity to discuss writers and issues I have not written on before. I also plan to edit an anthology of California poetry with Chryss Yost for Heyday Books, as part of the California Legacy Project. I am also writing a second opera libretto—a phantasmagoric one-act work that mixes comedy and tragedy—for the composer Paul Salerni. And I hope to finish a few new poems. No rest for the wicked.

You recently won the American Book Award for Interrogations at Noon. *Has the prize changed your life in any way?*

The award made me slightly more respectable in official circles. More important, it greatly impressed my nine-year-old son, Mike, who likes the gold-foil sticker that went on the cover of my book. I was pleased to win a prize for my poetry since my criticism so often dominates my public image. I was also delighted to win an award given by a jury of writers, who were all strangers. Mostly, I consider the event sheer good luck, which should be enjoyed but not taken too seriously.

What advice do you have for poets who are relatively new to their craft but who want to pursue it as a serious endeavor?

Read widely and memorize the poems that move or delight you. Immerse yourself in the medium. All writers begin as readers. I also recommend spending your twenties lonely, broke, and unhappily in love. It worked for me.

Source: Dana Gioia and Christina Vick, "Interview with Christina Vick," in *Louisiana Review*, Vol. 4, Fall–Winter 2004– 2005

Bruce F. Murphy

In the following review, Murphy analyzes Gioia's form of lyric poetry and finds "fluency and passion."

Samuel Johnson said that we would worry less about what people think of us if we knew how little time they spent doing it. I was reminded of this humbling quip by a recent essay by Billy Collins (*Poetry,* August 2001), in which he explored the problems of "memory-driven" poetry—that is, all poetry written since the great Romantics that deals with, to put it crudely, stuff that happened to the poet. The appeal of memory to the rememberer is self-evident; but why a memory should appeal to anyone else is another matter. Collins dared to say what everybody already knows, that most contemporary poetry in the personal vein fails to reach "escape velocity," and never achieves lift-off into "another, more capacious dimension." The poem remains a resume of stuff that happened to the poet, tempting the guileless, and those who haven't been given a warning kick under the seminar table, to respond with a Johnsonian So what? The missing link, too often, is imagination, which would take the poem "beyond the precincts of ordinary veracity."

Collins is right, but there is more to the story than getting the tinder of memory somehow to light. Imagination also takes us beyond ordinary language. It isn't always the case with dull autobiographical poems that the author is stuck in the world of fact; sometimes he or she is stuck in the world of prose. I don't mean that the prose deck of words should be shuffled and a new, more "interesting" hand dealt, as if (to use a Collins example) "The raspberries used to hang dark and moist / in our neighbor's woods" should become "Dark and moist used they to hang, / The raspberries in our neighbor's woods"—though that is how much of the boring poetry of the nineteenth century seems to have been written. True lyricism, on the other hand, language inspired with music, is as different from

> *This bottled-up suffering, when it finds an opening, comes out in a fierce jet. Death is everywhere present, as a desire for release from the unendurable."*

merely formal sing-song as Bach is from a school fight song. Collins's moment of lift-off is when language becomes lyrical, incandescent, when the filament stops being a piece of metal.

Real poetry makes something happen. Now, in the moment of reading it. Lyricism is a kind of electricity that hums in the poem—humming being the threshold, maybe, of music—and at the very least it gives you a shock. "Lyric poetry" as a term, however, has become as stretched out of shape as an old sweater. Contemporary American poetry may be a "house of many rooms," but "lyric" is always underfoot, a term that gets stuck to poets at opposite ends of the spectrum, like Dana Gioia and Carl Phillips. Sometimes it seems lyric means merely "short"; sometimes it's just a mood (the brown study in the house of many rooms); or it's a reference to subject matter—the poet's corner in the heartbreak hotel.

All these poets have embraced—however coldly or ambivalently—lyricism in some form. Carl Phillips's lyricism is elliptical, mellifluous, and interrupted. His most recent collection begins, "What we shall not perhaps get over, we / do get past"—a pithy statement of the themes of loss and endurance. This poem, "Luck," has the dazed clarity of summer afternoons; some men pitch horseshoes in a field while another mows. But whereas William Carlos Williams would have told you, "They were pitching horseshoes!", Phillips's lyricism can be read either as an encryption of the "facts" (a la Stevens), or as a vision that pierces the everyday and reaches some "more capacious" dimension:

> How did I get here,
> we ask one day, our gaze
> relinquishing one space for the next
>
> in which, not far from where
> in the uncut grass we're sitting
> four men arc the unsaid

between them with the thrown
shoes of horses, luck briefly as a thing
of heft made to shape through

air a path invisible, but there . . .

The "thing unsaid" is luck, is the "insubstantial," the realization of the role of chance in our lives—here symbolized by the game of horseshoes. The poem makes us feel the heft of the iron shoe, and the weightlessness of air; what could have been merely an idyll somehow (that is, lyrically) becomes an evocation of the raw contingency that surrounds even the quietest, most serene moment. It is hardly necessary to note that the poem is not about being Carl Phillips; it's about being alive.

But Phillips does not always, it seems to me, trust his own intuitions, and the traces remain in the syntactically broken lyricism: "It is for, you see, eventually the deer to / take it, the fruit // hangs there." Here we are back in the raspberry patch, a kind of strange pastiche of seventeenth-century diction (as a teacher once put it to me, "I threw my horse over the fence / some hay"). In some of these poems, it is the idea that's lyrical, not the poetry. For all his penetrating brilliance, Phillips does succumb to what I would call the Jorie Graham effect, a poetry of temporizing self-interruption:

Of course, of course,
the doomed crickets. The usual—as if
just let go on their own
recognizance—few birds acting
natural, looking guilty.
Gray black gray.
You were right, regarding

innocence. A small pair of
smaller moths rising
parallel, simultaneous, ascent
itself seeming axis for
what rotation? sex? combat?

"This, The Pattern"

These poems are dramas of thought, but they are existential, not classical dramas; they avoid their own iterative tendency. One of the hallmarks of this poetry is that it constantly refers to what lies outside, beneath, behind the poem; another is the profound remark stumbled upon like a coin, as in "Lustrum," which begins inauspiciously "Not less; only— different. Not / everything should be visible. / Wingdom: // doves. Not everything / can be. There are many parts / to the body." And then, the poem says, "To begin // counting is to understand / what it can mean, to / lose track." At last, we are getting somewhere, I think, betraying my own perhaps retrograde desire to hear the chords resolve. What has been subtracted from lyricism is its urgency. A big word like

"truth"—over whose definition millions have fought and died—is now a kind of Roman candle set off in the poem, dazzlingly, but with no pressure to see where it lands. Hence, "I became tired, as / who doesn't, having always // the truth, and not saying." As though the truth were so obvious as to be not worth bothering with; instead, we have "less the truth, than a way to frame it," as Phillips says elsewhere.

At its best, the poem is a series of snapshots in which the taker's thumb has been caught over the lens:

Splendor:
nothing priceless. To believe

anything, to want anything—these,
too, have cost you. Flame,
and the beveled sword, set

inside it. This one,
this—what did you think
body was? What did you

mean when you said
not everything should
be said? The light as a tipped

cone, searching.

The body pops up the way God used to in devotional verse, tethering the poem to something that everyone can relate to, the crossroads of materiality and sexuality being the only serious subject our culture can any longer imagine. But truth and apparentness are not exactly the same thing. If the body is self-evident, what of the self? Could the body be, I wonder, not the end of lyricism, but the beginning?

Peter Balakian made his reputation as a poet with work that explored his own experience, but probed through it to the bedrock of the Armenian experience and the genocide of 1915 ("at last, poetry about genocide that is truly, in every thrust, pause, and detail, real poetry," as James Dickey wrote of Balakian's 1983 collection, *Sad Days of Light*). But it isn't quite accurate to say Balakian's work was "about" genocide, though there may be a door in the big house of American poetry with that word written on it. There were poems, like "The Claim" (containing documents from the poet's grandmother's human rights suit against the Turkish government), in which the personal element shrank beside the enormous shadow of history, but it was always there. And Balakian went beyond the poem of the body to the poem of the flesh, the human (and animal, for history reduces us to animals) flesh which has faced steel and fire and lime in the past century. In his best poems, the self was a lamp to illuminate world memory. The lyrical force of "For My Grandmother, Coming

Back," transcends categories like personal/historical even as it fuses them:

> For the purple fruit
> for the carrots like cut fingers
> for the riverbed damp with flesh,
> you come back.
>
> For the lips of young boys
> bitten through,
> for the eyes of virgins brown
> and bleating on the hill,
> for the petticoat of your daughter
> shivering by the lake,
> for the yarn of her arms
> unwinding at her father's last shout.
>
> For the lamb punctured
> from the raw opening
> to his red teeth,
> for the lamb rotating
> like the sun
> on its spit . . .

For a time, Balakian seems to have been overtaken by such images of offal, which in a peculiar way allow us to identify with the dead, for example in "Mussel Shell" ("I must come when the sky is burnt / the color of a mussel shell—/ my head bloated as the stomach of a clam") and "Fish Mouth" ("There's an imprint of scissored / teeth bound into my head / like fins that turn behind my eyes"). Sometimes it seems that the poet wants to get down into the earth with the dead to find out what our living and dying means, a drive typified by the title "I Wish Us Back to Mud".'

> I wish us back to mud
> for love that asks us
> to be free of nothing
> and nothing to be free of us.

Undeniably there is something violent in these lyrical, sometimes nightmarish poems; but undoubtedly there is something violent in cell division, as there is in genocide, war, and hunger. The poet is so carried away by his vision that he forgets to step back, or it is no longer possible. Memory is not a storehouse of material; it's a kind of diver's belt you could use to sink yourself into the past, history, the darkness—that is, if you thought there was something down there that was worth the risk.

In some of the recent poems in this collection, Balakian seems to have gone too far down. "In Armenia (1987)" contains a deep or Jungian image of a cave, a "basalt cavern," in which the self is sloughed off; "Down there I felt my name / disappear." In "Yorkshire Dales" Balakian remarks, "I came to forget the limestone anyway, / and my name given to me by history." Still haunted by history, the poet seems worn down by its horrors, past

and present. The lyricism is still there, but now ironic and satirical, for example in his labs at Fifties America and its grotesque refusals and rituals: "We're the streaks of the ICBMS / as they tethered / over Iowa, // where a box top of Cheerios / gets you a plastic A-bomb ring." Although Balakian may be tired of his imprisonment in history—everyone is—he still tries to reach across. Balakian is one of the few who have realized that memory is useless if none of us remembers the same things.

Alongside Balakian's visionary history one can place Derick Burleson's documentary one. This extravagantly praised volume grows out of Burleson's experience in Rwanda teaching English in the two years prior to the genocide. Unlike ambulance-chasing "committed" poetry, Burleson's is a modest voice and a personal one; having been there, Burleson knows that history happens to people you know—suddenly, shockingly, irreversibly: "A year / from now they'll use hoes and machetes / to harvest their neighbor's heads." Burleson faces squarely the fact that his friends may have found themselves on either or both sides of the divide, which he expresses in typically spare rhythms in "Home Again":

> President Habyarimana's plane
>
> is still in flames on the runway,
> and all the next month we watch
> as our friends are murdered,
> or murder.

There is a deftness to the syncopation, ending the poem on an upbeat while leaving the reader hanging on that terrible word.

Burleson has absorbed many African elements into his poetry, including language, the folktale, humor, magic, and the fabliau. But he also acknowledges his own position: "Safe at home we eat fast food / each night and channel-surf / until sleep takes us on the sofa, // blue tides of TV light lapping / our knees." He has an eye for the most brutal ironies of the West's self-serving interventions, whether military or humanitiarian:

> Relief planes bomb refugees
> with food, and a few more perish
> under the crashing crates of manna.

"One Million One"

Sometimes the irony is heavy-handed ("Maggots bloom out of bellies. / Crows whet beaks on bones, such glee!") as it is reiterated over and over in "One Million One." The poem circles the scene, looking for a place to land, but there is none. There's nowhere to go.

Burleson's lyric poems are journalistic rather than mythic; he sticks mostly to the major keys, his words forming pictures more than images. But these are pictures that ought not to be forgotten. Burleson reminds us that most of the world goes to sleep worrying not if tomorrow will bring greater happiness, success, and ego satisfaction, but whether they will wake up at all. Whether they too will be swept over the falls by history:

> a pile of machetes and hoes
> higher than your head most bloodstained
> and every thirty seconds or so
> another body pounds
> down Rusumo Falls in the pool
> at the bottom they bob
> back and forth so
> bloated and gray
> you might think
> massacre had created
>
> a new race

"At the Border"

Though this ironic voice, the phrasing, and the arrangement on the page seem learned from Zbigniew Herbert's *Report from the Besieged City,* Burleson has poured his own powerful memories into the mold.

In terms of lyricism, Dana Gioia is a virtuoso, it seems. Tones are augmented or diminished with great care. The poems are lyrical, fluid, assured; this is a poetry free of mistakes (though that is not the same as perfection). "Words" is an ars poetica of sorts:

> The world does not need words. It articulates itself
> in sunlight, leaves, and shadows. The stones on the path
> are no less real for lying uncatalogued and uncounted.
> The fluent leaves speak only the dialect of pure being.
> The kiss is still fully itself though no words were spoken.

There's more to Gioia's revival of formalism than meets the eye, or ear; here he embraces not only traditional measures, but traditional philosophy. The world exists independently of our thinking/speaking about it, and so the role of language is mimetic, not constitutive. Gioia also hints at the moral dimension of poetry in the title poem:

> Just before noon I often hear a voice,
> Cool and insistent, whispering in my head.
> It is the better man I might have been,
> Who chronicles the life I've never led.

"Interrogations at Noon"

Throughout this book, there is a sense of conscience, of being held to account. Behind its surface brilliance and the sometimes casual, occasional subjects, it is a very somber book. There are depths of sorrow that are refracted through

form, and sometimes fully unveiled, as in "Pentecost, after the death of our son":

> We are not as we were. Death has been our pentecost,
> And our innocence consumed by these implacable Tongues of fire.
>
> Comfort me with stones. Quench my thirst with sand.
> I offer you this scarred and guilty hand
>
> Until others mix our ashes.

Gioia's is a public poetry that retains a sense of privacy, and a feeling for the limits of language. As he says in "Corner Table," "what matters most / Most often can't be said." The theme is repeated in "Unsaid," which is preoccupied with and perhaps justifying this holding back; that it is the final poem in the book underscores the point that "So much of what we live goes on inside—/ The diaries of grief, the tongue-tied aches / Of unacknowledged love are no less real / For having passed unsaid." This bottled-up suffering, when it finds an opening, comes out in a fierce jet. Death is everywhere present, as a desire for release from the unendurable. Hence the evocation of "The End of the World," the "Song for the End of Time," and the dark prayer of "Litany":

> This is a litany to earth and ashes,
> to the dust of roads and vacant rooms,
> to the fine silt circling in a shaft of sun,
> settling indifferently on books and beds.
> This is a prayer to praise what we become,
> "Dust thou art, to dust thou shalt return."
> Savor its taste—the bitterness of earth and ashes.

This is an eerie picture of a depopulated world, after the end of time—the eternal silence in which nothing happens but the accumulation of dust.

Peter Sirr shares Gioia's fluency and passion, but it is for a world of vivid colors and rooms not vacant but stuffed to bursting. It is the lyricism of life rather than of the afterlife. A Dubliner, Sirr has a Joycean sense of the city's quotidian majesty:

> At night I open the cupboard:
> voices and stones arrive
> fruit and fish from the market
> a hand whisking tobacco
> from an inside pocket
> the floating
> greened copper of a dome
> ingredients for The City
> which is not the city
> but the grocery of an eye.

"Domes of the City"

Many poets seem to shy away from the treacherous territory of enthusiasm. This is why the poem about desire is often about the disappointment of desire. Sirr's *The Ledger of Fruitful Exchange,* on the other hand, contained one of the most powerful erotic poems of the last twenty years, about desire's fulfillment. Here, the object of desire is—everything:

Not an expedition exactly, or a journey; say then a
walking out, a meandering, an inclination towards
dust
and bustle, a putting of ourselves among buildings
and
people, which is how we found ourselves in that
city,
walking along the narrow streets on a fair day,
admiring
the stalls, running our fingers along bright fabrics,
sniffing
cheeses, wandering wherever the crowd took us;
and half expecting to be blurted eventually into the
square, the columned hall, the wide theatre where
the
city is saved or the trial proves more complex than
had
been imagined and the day grows long, where
hucksters
come to show the latest miracle, and prophets
unload
their dark freight . . .

"Gospels"

Here the lyricism works just as well within the prose technique; there is a tricky fusion of meditation and material reminiscent of Seferis or Seifert. The underlying implication is the solace that what is fully realized—"The table, the chair, / look, are utterly here"—is never entirely lost. There is a faith in connection, both of language to the world ("Sometimes you can say it and it stays") and of consciousness to existence. But all is water, as Thales said, including us; and yet we can find a kind of ecstasy in dissolution and merging; "as we approach each other / our bodies slip their ropes and drift, / how lightly, without hesitation or inquiry, / one steps into another, and stays there." But it's profoundly disturbing. Hence Sirr says, humorously, "Morning returns the world / We are gathered here / to refuse it." Luckily, things know nothing of our ideas, and "the fork in my hand, the glass at my lips / and the water in my mouth // have not learned silence. / Their language is everywhere."

Being is for tourists, becoming is for poets. Sirr understands that experience is something one devours and is devoured by—gladly, in his case, perhaps sadly in Gioia's. One can even marvel at the fading of one's own dust. Sirr echoes Whitman's "I stop somewhere, waiting for you" in the beautiful "Song":

Look for me
in the galaxy of stone,
in the ashes of the sun,

in the stubborn notes
of the servant's song
as she works through the night,
her voice filling
the empty rooms;

in the charity of the moon
above this town,
distinguishing equally
the assassin's knife,
the solitary life;

in all
that is pitiless and beautiful;

where earth meets water and water meets light.

Source: Bruce F. Murphy, Review of *Interrogations at Noon,* in *Poetry,* Vol. 179, No. 5, February 2002, pp. 238–49.

Ned Balbo

In the following review, Balbo calls the poems in Interrogations at Noon *"superb in their blend of toughness and vulnerability, their quest for solace before loss."*

Tireless essayist, librettist, and anthologist, Gioia is a poet first and foremost, as his third collection decisively confirms. A master of subtle registers, elegiac in his outlook, Gioia is more likely to lower his voice than shout, as when a husband, his wife in the shower, calls himself "the missing man . . . surrounded by the flesh and furniture of home" ("The Voyeur"). Gioia sees the metaphors we live with every day: in "New Year's," for example, "A field of snow without a single footprint" suggests our need to look toward an always unfolding future, while "Words" weighs the admission that "The world does not need words" against the recognition that "To name is to know and remember." Gioia includes two poems freely adapted from Seneca, "Descent to the Underworld" and "Juno Plots Her Revenge"; both allow him to speak with impressive gravity and range about what lies at the dark heart of human affairs.

Gioia can lighten a dark moment or finely shade a lighter one, as in "Elegy with Surrealist Proverbs as Refrain." With its arresting refrains and effortless syntax, the poem is a tour de force, a lively whirl among eccentrics; still, it remains, at bottom, a catalogue of loss, of bluster in the face of death, among minds petty, brilliant, frail: "Breton considered suicide the truest art, / though life seemed hardly worth the trouble to discard." "Words for Music," a separate section, takes a lighter touch, though here, too, death is present: the vampire Nosferatu's dactylic "Serenade," for example, summons us to an eternal idyll. (*Nosferatu,* Gioia's complete libretto, is also currently out from Graywolf.) Finally, "My Dead Lover" is a moving tribute to a loss, its anguish understated yet plain, its language charged with a sad music: "And now you are nowhere. You are nothing, / Not even ashes. How very like you, love, I To slip away so skillfully. / You didn't even leave behind a grave. . . ." Gioia's poems are superb in their blend of toughness and vulnerability, their quest for solace before loss, their measured yet memorable voice, and though *Interrogations at Noon* often speaks of death and absence, it offers the consolation of uncommon craft.

Source: Ned Balbo, Review of *Interrogations at Noon*, in *Antioch Review*, Vol. 60, No. 1, Winter 2002, p. 167.

Ray Olson

In the following review, Olson praises Gioia's incorporation of classical elements into Interrogations at Noon *and asserts that Gioia will become "a classic poet himself."*

The ancient Greeks and Romans created European civilization, and studying their literature—the classics—has long been considered a civilizing activity. But the classics also teach plenty about chaos, not least that the human heart is never satisfied. Gioia and Slavitt, each of whom has translated classical literature (Slavitt prodigiously), show that they have learned civilization in the formal dexterity of their verse, that they have learned the turbulent heart in the content of their poems.

Gioia is, at midlife, full of regrets. He writes about the youthful intellectual sparring partner, never seen since, who he learns has died of AIDS; about the child who grows ever "more gorgeously like you" but whose likeness is also "not a slip or a fumble but a total rout"; and about "the better man I might have been." Most affectingly, he writes about his son who died in childhood. "Comfort me with stones," he prays. "Quench my thirst with sand." In those desolate lines, he echoes the *Song of Songs,* a masterpiece of the third classical tongue, Hebrew, whereas in many other poems, he draws on Greek and Roman motifs, stories, and attitudes. He finds in the classics and conveys to us the acceptance of mortality and the celebration of beauty that have made the classics perdurably relevant. And his rhymes are true, his meters are correct and musical, his diction is fresh—he is well on the way to becoming a classic poet himself.

Fifteen years Gioia's senior, Slavitt has largely shaken off regrets and assumed the great Jewish obligation and passion for arguing, maybe not always with God but always with the way things are said to be. If "an instant's sin endures forever," he asks, why not a moment of grace or of beauty? And why must time flow in one direction only? He questions beauty and its satisfactions, whether the beauty produced by

honed talent in "Performance: An Eclogue," or the beauty descried by honed perceptions in "Against Landscape." He speculates that Moses was barred from the promised land because by bringing down the Torah, he "did not / diminish heaven so much as elevate earth." Slavitt complements his querulous querying with rancorous humor (see "Spite"); bittersweet resignation (see the self-scouring "Culls"); wordplay ("Cake and Milk," for instance, consists entirely of cliches); classical references and translations from Greek, Latin, Hebrew, French, and German; and a grandfather's love. He has written many civilized books, but has he written any more broadly and deeply civilized than this one?

Source: Ray Olson, Review of *Interrogations at Noon*, in *Booklist*, Vol. 97, No. 14, March 15, 2001, p. 1345.

Sources

Balbo, Ned, Review of *Interrogations at Noon*, in the *Antioch Review*, Vol. 60, No. 1, Winter 2002, p. 167.

Frost, Robert, "Design," in *The Norton Anthology of American Literature*, Vol. D, 6th ed., edited by Nina Baym, Norton, 2003, p. 1196.

Gioia, Dana, *Disappearing Ink: Poetry at the End of Print Culture*, Graywolf Press, 2004.

———, *Interrogations at Noon*, Graywolf Press, 2001, pp. 10–11.

"Hip-Hop Bards," in the *Wilson Quarterly*, Vol. 27, No. 4, Autumn 2003, pp. 105–106.

Murphy, Bruce F., "Music and Lyrics," in *Poetry*, Vol. 179, No. 5, February 2002, pp. 283, 290, 291.

Olson, Ray, Review of *Interrogations at Noon*, in *Booklist*, Vol. 97, No. 14, March 15, 2001, p. 1345.

Further Reading

Bawer, Bruce, "The Poet in the Gray Flannel Suit," in *Connoisseur*, March 1989, pp. 108–112.
    Bawer presents a comprehensive overview of Gioia and his work.

Kübler-Ross, Elisabeth, *On Death and Dying*, Scribners, 1997.
    This important study explores ways to cope with the end of life.

McPhillips, Robert, "Reading the New Formalists," in *Sewanee Review*, Vol. 97, Winter 1989, pp. 73–96.
    McPhillips examines the doctrines of the new formalists, including Gioia.

Turco, Lewis, "Neoformalism in Contemporary American Poetry," in his *The Public Poet: Five Lectures on the Art and Craft of Poetry*, Ashland Poetry Press, 1991, pp. 39–56.
    Lewis adds to the discussion his interpretations of this new school of literary criticism.

Monologue for an Onion

Sue (Suji) Kwock Kim

2003

With her 2003 collection *Notes from the Divided Country*, Suji ("Sue") Kwock Kim became the first Asian American to win the Walt Whitman Award of the American Academy of Poets. In this volume, Kim explores themes of family, nation (the title refers to Korea), isolation, community, emotion, and politics. While her poetic voice is influenced by her experience as an Asian American woman, she strives to write about universal human truths. She draws those truths from the strangled and war-torn history of her family and their native Korea. To add authenticity to her telling of history, she takes on the voices of her parents and ancestors. Kim's poems describe the horrors of war, the struggle to overcome extreme circumstances, and the pain of loss.

One of the poems in *Notes from the Divided Country* is "Monologue for an Onion." In this poem, an onion expresses its thoughts and feelings while a person goes about cutting it up. In the hands of other poets, this premise would be a setup for a humorous poem; in Kim's hands, it is serious and even disturbing. Exploring themes of appearance, essence, truth, and seeking, Kim finds an unlikely speaker in an onion. Because of this poem's accessibility and its unusual subject matter, it is appealing to students who are new to poetry. More advanced students will be rewarded by a close study of the poem that reveals its depth of style and content.

Author Biography

Born in 1968, Sue (Suji) Kwock Kim received her bachelor's degree from Yale University in 1995 and her master of fine arts degree from the prestigious University of Iowa writer's program in 1997. Kim also attended Seoul University. She began writing poetry at the age of twenty-one, when she decided to try a poetry workshop in college. She was drawn to the rhythm and the music of poetry, and she loved refining the craft of writing poetry despite the intensity she often feels when she writes. Her Korean heritage and its culture, language, and art influence her poetry, although she resists categorizing her work as strictly ethnic in theme and content.

In 2002, Kim received a Stegner Fellowship from Stanford University. In 2003, she accepted a position as an assistant English professor at Drew University in Madison, New Jersey. Her first poetry collection, *Notes from the Divided Country*, was published the same year. This debut collection won the 2002 Walt Whitman Award from the American Academy of Poets. Prior to its publication, Kim received the *Nation*'s Discovery Award.

Kim has had her poetry published in numerous journals, including *Poetry*, the *Paris Review*, the *National Review*, the *Nation*, *Ploughshares*, the *Threepenny Review*, the *Southwest Review*, *Michigan Quarterly Review*, *DoubleTake*, the *Yale Review*, the *Harvard Review*, the *New England Review*, and *Salmagundi*. Her poetry was selected to be in the anthology *Asian American Poetry: The Next Generation* (2004). Kim has also been the recipient of a National Endowment for the Arts Fellowship (2001), a California Arts Council grant (2002), a Fulbright scholarship in Korea, and a fellowship from the Fine Arts Work Center of Provincetown. Her poetry has also earned her grants from foundations such as the Blakemore Foundation for Asian Studies, Korea Foundation, Washington State Art Trust, and the New York Foundation for the Arts. While her preferred genre is poetry, Kim also cowrote a multimedia play titled *Private Property*, which was produced in Edinburgh, Scotland, at the Edinburgh Festival Fringe and appeared on BBC-TV.

Sue (Suji) Kwock Kim Photograph by Jill D'Allessandro. Reproduced by permission of Susan Kim

Poem Text

I don't mean to make you cry.
I mean nothing, but this has not kept you
From peeling away my body, layer by layer,

The tears clouding your eyes as the table fills
With husks, cut flesh, all the debris of pursuit.   5
Poor deluded human: you seek my heart.

Hunt all you want. Beneath each skin of mine
Lies another skin: I am pure onion—pure union
Of outside and in, surface and secret core.

Look at you, chopping and weeping. Idiot.   10
Is this the way you go through life, your mind
A stopless knife, driven by your fantasy of truth,

Of lasting union—slashing away skin after skin
From things, ruin and tears your only signs
Of progress? Enough is enough.   15

You must not grieve that the world is glimpsed
Through veils. How else can it be seen?
How will you rip away the veil of the eye, the veil

That you are, you who want to grasp the heart
Of things, hungry to know where meaning   20
Lies. Taste what you hold in your hands: onion-juice,

Yellow peels, my stinging shreds. You are the one
In pieces. Whatever you meant to love, in meaning to
You changed yourself: you are not who you are,

Your soul cut moment to moment by a blade   25
Of fresh desire, the ground sown with abandoned skins.
And at your inmost circle, what? A core that is

Not one. Poor fool, you are divided at the heart,
Lost in its maze of chambers, blood, and love,
A heart that will one day beat you to death.   30

Poem Summary

"Monologue for an Onion" is written in tristichs (three-line stanzas). The structure gives the poem a sense of order, although each stanza does not always contain a complete or self-contained thought. The lines often extend from one tristich to another. As "Monologue for an Onion" opens, the speaker is established to be an onion. It speaks in the first person to someone who is busily cutting it up. The onion tells the person, "I don't mean to make you cry." The onion then adds that it means the person no harm, and yet the person continues to peel its skin away. The onion cannot help but notice that this process of peeling away the skin and cutting up the onion's "flesh" brings tears to the person's eyes.

The onion says, "Poor deluded human: you seek my heart" (line 6). The onion believes that the person's act of peeling and cutting is a search for its heart, apparently not realizing that this is simply how people prepare onions for cooking or eating. The onion then tells the person to keep looking and peeling, but the person will find only more of the same layers as are on the outside. It says, "I am pure onion—pure union / Of outside and in, surface and secret core" (lines 8–9). This means that the onion knows that it is the same all the way to the center. It is not wearing a false exterior of any kind, and it is not keeping any secrets.

In the fourth stanza, the onion begins to express hostility and judgment toward the person. Because chopping the onion makes the person cry, the onion deems the person an idiot for continuing. Then the onion generalizes the person's behavior, wondering if the person goes through life using his or her mind as a knife that never stops cutting as it looks for a "fantasy of truth" (line 12) that it will never find. The onion says that this approach to life is destructive, leaving only ruin and tears as "signs / Of progress" (lines 14–15).

The onion suggests that the person stop the useless cutting and searching, telling the person that "the world is glimpsed / Through veils" (lines 16–17). Kim uses the onion as a voice of wisdom, revealing truths about the world. The onion notes that seeing the world is possible only through veils, even if they are the veils of the eye and the perceiver.

The seventh and eighth stanzas acknowledge that the person who is cutting the onion is a seeker, "hungry to know where meaning / Lies." But the onion suggests that the person survey what she has done; it tells the person to taste the onion juice on her hands and look at the onion peels and pieces. Then the onion says, "You are the one / In pieces" (lines 22–23). The onion tells the person that an insistence on seeking truth that was not there has changed the person. According to the onion, it is the person whose soul has been cut by relentless desire, surrounded by abandoned remnants of the effort to quench the desire.

For all the person's efforts to get to the essence of the onion (or of anything), the person has no core. The person's own heart is a divided organ without a center, and, metaphorically, the heart will beat the person to death by continuing to create desire that cannot be fulfilled.

Themes

Elusiveness of Truth

According to the onion, the person is peeling and cutting it in an attempt to get past the layers to understand what is at the heart of the onion. The onion states, "Poor deluded human: you seek my heart." Although the onion insists that it is hiding nothing and that it is simply an onion through and through ("Beneath each skin of mine / Lies another skin: I am pure onion—pure union / Of outside and in, surface and secret core"), the person keeps chopping. From the onion's perspective, truth is very elusive to the person, because she refuses to acknowledge the actual truth in favor of finding the desired truth. The onion accuses the person of being obstinate: "Is this the way you go through life, your mind / A stopless knife, driven by your fantasy of truth." Because the person lives in denial and seeks a fabricated truth, truth will continue to be elusive.

The onion also articulates a related theme of appearances and veils. While the person may appear to be one way but actually be another way, the onion insists that it is pure onion from the outside to the inside. The onion wears its essence for all to see, but it understands that people are not like that. Because the person peeling and cutting the onion is a perpetrator of misleading appearances ("you are not who you are"), she perceives that the rest

Topics For Further Study

- Write a companion poem for "Monologue for an Onion" that presents the other side of the story. What are the thoughts and intentions of the person who is peeling and cutting the onion? Are the tears merely the result of cutting the onion, or do you imagine something else going on in the person's mind?

- What characteristics of an onion make it a good choice for Kim's poem? Can you think of anything else that would have worked? Organize your thoughts on these questions and prepare a lesson for a poetry workshop about choosing suitable subject matter for poetry.

- Throughout "Monologue for an Onion," Kim introduces startling and sometimes violent imagery. Look for pictures from magazines, newspapers, and books to create a slideshow or PowerPoint presentation, combining the text of the poem with visual images to bring it to life. If you are artistically inclined, you may include

original drawings, but your artwork should not make up more than half of the project.

- Research the history of Korea, with particular attention to the division of North Korea and South Korea. Be sure to read about the Korean War, the political struggles in both nations, and the cultural consistencies and differences. Take what you know and interpret the poem as a political piece. Write an essay about the role of literature as a reflection of a nation's history, using this poem as your primary example. You may include other works but only to illustrate specific points.

- Choose one other poem from *Notes from the Divided Country* as a contrast to "Monologue for an Onion." Look for differences in content, themes, language, form, or voice. Lead a small-group discussion about the two poems, focusing on what you learn about Kim as a poet and what you learn about poetry in general through the two poems.

of the world (and everything in it, including an onion) also wears facades. To find the truth of something, then, requires peeling away the layers of veils to see truth laid bare. The onion ultimately reveals that there is no other way to perceive the world except through veils, meaning that it is impossible to encounter truth in a vacuum. The onion remarks, "You must not grieve that the world is glimpsed / Through veils. How else can it be seen?" The onion not only says that all things must be seen through veils, but it also goes so far as to tell the person that things can only be glimpsed through them. The person will never be able to encounter the truth with a long, unblinking gaze. There are always veils, if at no other level than that of the perceiver. Everything has a context of some kind.

Determination

Despite the onion's warnings to stop pursuing the truth so diligently (and violently), the person

continues relentlessly peeling and cutting the onion. While it is safe to assume that Kim does not intend for this poem to depict an onion actually speaking to a person who hears the onion, the fact remains that the person presses on with the mission to peel and cut up the onion completely. The tears that try to fight off the sting in the person's eyes do not slow the person down at all, and the depiction of the counter littered with onion peel and bits of onion suggests that the person is relentlessly at work. In the second stanza, Kim writes, "the table fills / With husks, cut flesh, all the debris of pursuit." The eighth stanza calls attention to the "Yellow peels, my stinging shreds." It is a picture of utter carnage and determination.

The onion begins the poem by telling the person that it means no harm at all, and yet the person methodically peels away the onion's layers. The onion says, "I mean nothing, but this has not kept you / From peeling away my body, layer by layer."

In the fourth stanza, the onion reveals that the person is not slowed down by the teary eyes; the person continues chopping. In the ninth stanza, the ground is sown with "abandoned skins." Once the object of pursuit, the skins that yielded nothing are merely tossed aside. At the very end of the poem, the onion offers the person a prophecy. Describing how the person's own heart is itself divided into chambers, the onion declares that it lacks a core. The onion believes that the person is driven by the need for a center that will give stability, peace, and reassurance. But the person's own heart does not have such a center, and thus, according to the onion, the heart will one day beat the person to death.

Style

Irony

Kim interjects irony in "Monologue for an Onion" to illustrate the human being's struggle with truth. The onion points out ironies in the person's motives and behavior. For example, the onion notes that while the person peels, cuts, and chops at the onion to get to its heart ("Poor deluded human: you seek my heart"), it is really the person's own heart that the chopper so desperately seeks. The person cutting the onion strives to find the center of something, even if it is just an onion, because the person lacks a center but does not realize it. The onion explains, "And at your inmost circle, what? A core that is / Not one. Poor fool, you are divided at the heart, / Lost in its maze of chambers, blood, and love."

The onion also points out that the person, after peeling and cutting the onion, is the one who is "in pieces." Having cut the onion, left its pieces of skin on the counter, and forced out its juices, the person is now covered in the smell, taste, and feel of the onion. Further, the onion adds, in trying to change the onion into what the person wanted, the person ended up being the one who was changed. This is another instance of irony.

The onion fails to notice the irony of its own condition. It claims that it is not guilty of having an exterior different from its interior and that peeling away its layers will only reveal more of the same layers. In other words, its argument goes, the person should stop peeling and cutting altogether, because there is no more truth in the middle of the onion than there is on its outside. The momentum of the poem, however, disproves this. As the person continues the relentless dismantling of the onion, the onion reveals more and more to the person about truth, veils, and desire. If the person had stopped after the first layer, these truths would never have been revealed. It is ironic that the onion is so perceptive about the flaws and ironies of the person, yet so blind to its own.

Metaphor

Kim uses metaphor liberally throughout "Monologue for an Onion." The entire poem is a metaphor, with the onion representing anything that is pursued and destroyed as a means to an unattainable end. The person represents stubborn, relentless, and often misguided determination. This poem could be read as if the onion and the person were people in an unhealthy relationship, or it could be read as any situation involving sacrifice for a perceived greater good. In the context of the rest of *Notes from the Divided Country*, the onion could be Korea and its people, and the person could be a political system, a war, or an ideology. In such contexts, the peeling away of layers, the cut flesh, the "stopless knife," and every other image take on new meaning.

Monologue

Kim chooses to use personification and give a humble onion a voice with which it can verbally fight back against its attacker. She chooses to use the form of a monologue to reveal the onion's thoughts and feelings about its situation and the person peeling and cutting it. A monologue is a dramatic form, which gives the reader a strong cue that this is not a humorous piece but one that will present serious, thought-provoking comments. A monologue gives the discourse of only one speaker, so the reader also knows that everything in the poem comes from the onion. Kim gives no insight into the person's thoughts, intentions, or emotional reactions. A monologue differs from a soliloquy in that a monologue reveals what would be told to an audience, whereas a soliloquy reveals the speaker's private thoughts, not intended for listeners. In the case of "Monologue for an Onion," the intended audience is the person cutting up the onion. Kim establishes this from the first line, where the onion says "you" in reference to the person whose eyes are watering from cutting the onion.

Historical Context

North and South Korea

"Monologue for an Onion" is included in Kim's *Notes from the Divided Country*. The title refers to Korea, from which Kim's family originally came. Since the end of World War II, Korea has been divided into two separate countries, North Korea and South Korea. When the two countries were formed, the Soviet Union occupied the north and the United States occupied the south. In 1950, tensions about political legitimacy between the two countries reached a head when the Korean War erupted. The war between the Communist-controlled north and the United Nations–supported south went on for three years, until an armistice was signed in 1953. North Korea continued to be governed by the Communist leader Kim Il Sung, who ruled from 1948 until his death in 1994. Upon his death, his eldest son, Kim Jong Il, assumed leadership of the country.

After the Korean War, South Korea struggled to secure its political stability, enduring a number of rulers, governments, and coups. In 1987, a more democratic form of government was established with the election of a president. During the 1990s, South Korea grew into a major economy. Despite some setbacks, most notably the Asian financial crisis of 1997, South Korea is, in the early twenty-first century, a stable democracy with a healthy economy.

Although tentative efforts have been made to reunify North and South Korea (beginning with a summit in 2000), it does not seem feasible. Relations between the two nations have grown less hostile, but concerns about North Korea's nuclear weapons capabilities made South Korea, and other nations of the world, cautious. In 2005, North Korea confirmed that it had nuclear weapons.

Korean Americans

Like most immigrant groups, Koreans arrived in the United States in waves. The first wave of Koreans entering the United States began in 1903. Most of them went to Hawaii to work on sugar plantations, although a smaller group went to the continental United States. Another immigration wave came after the end of the Korean War in 1953, when numerous war brides and children adopted by American military personnel came to the United States. Reports estimate that one-quarter of Korean Americans can trace their lineage to a war bride. The last major immigration wave came after the Immigration Act of 1965. As of 2005, there were more than one million full-blooded Korean Americans (as many as twice that number when part-Koreans are included), representing a 35 percent increase between 1990 and 2000. Asian Americans make up 3.6 percent of the American population,

with 11 percent being Korean Americans. Well-known Korean Americans include the ABC news anchors Ju Ju Chang and Liz Cho, the comedienne Margaret Cho, the writer Leonard Change, the Grammy Award–winner Joseph Hahn, and the comic actor Bobby Lee.

Critical Overview

Notes from the Divided Country has been well received by critics who review and study it. Critics praise the poems for their eloquence and their balance of wisdom and pain. They regard Kim's poetic voice as fresh and promising, based on her first published collection. Carol Muske-Dukes of the *Los Angeles Times*, for example, calls the volume an "important debut" that "deserves close and celebratory attention." Muske-Dukes finds the poems "unforgettable." Similarly, Frank Bidart of *Ploughshares* hails the book as "brilliant," adding that it is "one of the most remarkable debuts" he has read. He writes that the poems in this collection "surprise not only by their ambition and ferocity but by their delicacy, their sudden reserves of stillness and contemplation."

Kim's readers find that the struggle and pain described in her poems are equaled by the restorative power of the verse expressing them. The *Georgia Review*'s Amy Schroeder remarks that Kim's "goal is to shape-change trauma into art without losing emotional ferocity, and she does accomplish this in the majority of her poems." Schroeder praises Kim's introduction of other voices in her poems as a way to express other perspectives. Although Schroeder finds that *Notes from the Divided Country* weakens toward the end, losing its momentum and focus, she ultimately concludes that the volume is an "achievement; she [Kim] manages, almost throughout, to unite the divided countries of personal experience and political truth without relying on the easy bridge of sentimentality."

Criticism

Jennifer Bussey

Jennifer Bussey holds a master's degree in interdisciplinary studies and a bachelor's degree in English literature and is an independent writer specializing in literature. In the following essay, she discusses the hostility and violence in Kim's poem.

What Do I Read Next?

- Edited by Marilyn Chin and Victoria Chang, *Asian American Poetry: The Next Generation* (2004) includes not just the work of Kim but also the work of other young Asian American poets.

- *O Taste and See: Food Poems* (2003) is edited by David Lee Garrison and Terry Hermsen. This anthology is a collection of poems about food and its meaning, rituals, and roles in everyday life.

- The Asian American journalist Helen Zia shares her personal memories and her research of Asian American history in *Asian American Dreams: The Emergence of an American People* (2001). With this book, Zia hopes to fill in the gaps in American history and give Asian Americans better insight into the experiences of their forebears.

- Amy Tan's second novel, *The Kitchen God's Wife* (1991), is the story of a Chinese woman, Winnie, and her strained relationship with her American-born daughter. As the novel unfolds, Winnie reveals the terrible struggles of her past in China and how she overcame them.

In Kim's "Monologue for an Onion," the unlikely speaker is an onion that is being peeled and chopped by an unnamed person. The onion pleads with the person to stop, citing the irrationality of the person's actions. While, on the surface, this may seem like a humorous premise for a poem, Kim's monologue is actually quite violent and disturbing. The person and the onion are at war, and they are using very different weapons; the person uses brute force, while the onion tries to defend itself with philosophy. The metaphorical landscape of this poem is rich and deep, but without the dark, violent tone of the poem, the reader is less likely to delve deeper into it. Because of the context, the violence of the poem is so surprising that readers are caught by surprise and are driven to look at the poem more closely.

Both the person and the onion are hostile figures. They are truly at war with each other, and they have no common ground on which they can end the violence. With nothing in common, they both press on with their preferred weapons; for the person, it is a knife, and for the onion, it is reason. Because they each want something from the other that they will not get, the poem ends with the realization that neither will find satisfaction or even peace. According to the onion (who, as the poem's only speaker, is the reader's only source of information), the person is peeling, cutting, chopping, and hacking at the onion in order to get to the heart of the onion. The person seeks the truth and the essence of the onion, driven by the belief that there is much more to it than the surface layers of onion skin. The person is willing to endure stinging eyes and onion juice on his or her hands in the interest of acquiring the elusive truth of the onion. The person will never get what she wants from the onion, however, because she seeks something that does not exist. Even though the onion assures the person that there is nothing more to it than more layers of the same onion, she continues this relentless and destructive pursuit.

As the person's pursuit gains momentum and she fails to get what she wants from the onion, the violence toward the onion becomes more severe. The violence perpetrated is physical, the exercise of brute strength and power over the onion. The verbiage Kim uses to describe what the person does to the onion is startling. In line 3, the onion describes having its body peeled away "layer by layer." Two lines later, the onion describes "husks, cut flesh, all the debris of pursuit." In line 13, Kim uses alliteration to bring special emphasis to the violence: "slashing away skin after skin." She adds in the next two lines, "ruin and tears your only signs / Of progress? Enough is enough." Near the end of the poem, in line 26, the onion comments on the "ground sown with abandoned skins." Kim's use of imagery in describing the destructive wake of the person's pursuit is disturbing. Many of the words Kim uses, such as "body" and "skin," call to mind human suffering. The reader may be surprised at feeling not only compassion but even empathy for the onion. In its trials, the adept reader sees the suffering in human history.

Just as the person who is cutting will not get what she wants from the onion, the onion will not get what it wants from the person either. The onion's desire is simple and, despite its bent for philosophy, no deeper than basic survival. The onion only wants the person to stop peeling and cutting. The sum of the onion's desire is mere survival. Although it has the ability to understand and recognize ideological and psychological motives, its only concern is existence. Just as the person will not get from the onion what she wants, the onion will not get what it wants from the person. The person will not stop dismantling the onion, and the onion is powerless to stop the dismantling.

Although the onion is powerless to defend itself in any physical way, it still displays its own brand of violence. Where the person is physically violent and uses power to subdue the onion, the onion uses philosophical and intellectual power to try to defend itself. The only physical defense the onion has is its ability to sting the person's eyes and make the person weep. This is significant, because it is a passive defense (the onion does not will itself to release the chemicals that make the person's eyes water), and it is an inadequate defense. The person's eyes may water, but that is not nearly a strong enough defense to make the person stop peeling, cutting, and chopping. Faced with its basic weakness, the onion fights back with sarcasm, berating and belittling the person for the pointless violence. Positioned as the intellectually superior

figure, the onion hopes to ridicule the person into stopping the attack. When that does not work, the onion ultimately strives to teach the person the errors of her ways. By helping the person understand herself better, the onion hopes to help itself survive the attack.

The onion never fully acknowledges its own powerlessness but perseveres in its verbal attacks. Again, Kim uses startling language, putting harsh words in the mouth of the onion as it tries in vain to defend itself. At first, the onion's language is gentle and understanding. Its first appeal to the person is that it means no harm and does not deserve to be attacked. Then the onion says, "Poor deluded human: you seek my heart" (line 6). This seems genuinely compassionate and insightful. But when this approach does nothing to stop the attack, the onion becomes more angry and judgmental. By the fourth stanza, the tone has changed: "Look at you, chopping and weeping. Idiot. / Is this the way you go through life, your mind / A stopless knife, driven by your fantasy of truth, / Of lasting union." The onion resorts to name-calling and revealing the person's personal failings and ignorance. The onion criticizes the person's entire approach to life, accusing her of seeking unity and truth based on lies and self-delusion. The ideological attacks continue, and the imagery remains violent, as when the onion tries to make the person realize that there is no way to perceive the world without veils. The onion says, "How will you rip away the veil of the eye" (line 18). Then the onion points out to the person that for all of the cutting, she is "the one / In pieces" (lines 22–23), "Your soul cut moment to moment by a blade / Of fresh desire" (lines 25–26). In revealing to the person how insistence on destroying the onion has brought about the person's own destruction, the onion uses violent imagery. This is appropriate, because the situation is hostile. Throughout the poem, the onion tries to reach the person by speaking truth.

The layers of metaphor in "Monologue for an Onion" are deep. Within the context of Kim's work, it is appropriate to apply a reading of this poem as a metaphor for a people being savaged by their own rulers. Kim's family is from Korea, and much of her poetry preserves the struggles of her family and her nation as it has endured war, social strife, and political instability. In "Monologue for an Onion," these themes are clear. The person cutting the onion represents an unjust ruler, motivated by an ideology that is doomed to fail because of its own confusion and lies. The onion represents the people, basically powerless to defend themselves and yet trying to survive by fighting back with truth. Oppressive governments almost universally sacrifice their own people on the altar of their ideology. The people become the means to an elusive end, and they suffer greatly as a result. There are many incidents in history in which the cutting and slashing has been literal, and there have been many in which it has been figurative. The "onion-juice" on the person's hands in line 21 represents the blood on the hands of dictators and murderous regimes. As with the person cutting the onion, the governments generally find themselves destroyed in the end.

In the poem, the person desperately pursues a core, a center of stability. But the onion reveals to the person that even her own heart, her own core, is divided and unstable. The same can be said of unjust regimes; lacking truth and goodness at their core, they are doomed to instability, division in the ranks of the power-hungry, and an eventual loss of focus. Within this context, Kim suggests that true wisdom is readily available among the people, who long to guide and correct their rulers. The violence and hostility of "Monologue for an Onion" is a chilling reminder of the lengths to which rulers have gone to oppress their own people. And the people, for all their anger and hostility, have the ability to respond with wisdom and insight. They possess the ability to understand just power, and their suffering does not have to be meaningless.

Source: Jennifer Bussey, Critical Essay on "Monologue for an Onion," in *Poetry for Students*, Thomson Gale, 2006.

Neil Heims

Neil Heims is a writer and teacher living in Paris. In this essay, he argues that the poet represents her feelings by comparing herself to an onion.

Because onions do not talk, it is reasonable to deduce that "Monologue for an Onion," which features a talking onion, is using the onion as an imaginative substitute for a person, who can talk. Consequently, there is a central utterance that, despite the title, has been left unsaid. It is implicit and essential: "You make me feel like an onion when it is being peeled." The poet is saying, using the metaphor of an onion, "I feel as if you are tearing me apart." The feelings that the onion being peeled and the speaker comparing herself to an onion being peeled experience are rage and contempt for the person doing the peeling and tearing.

Although the poem is a monologue, it is a two-character poem. There is the speaker, and there is the person to whom she is speaking, the "you," silent throughout the poem, who is the cause of the

> *The sentences of the poem are like a winding layer turning around upon itself. Each successive word seems to be a peeling torn from previous words."*

monologue. This "you" has, presumably, just finished speaking, and the poem is a response. The reader must reconstruct his previous words and his behavior from what the speaker says. The speaker's monologue, indeed, reveals as much about her interlocutor as it does about her.

"I don't mean to make you cry," undoubtedly is uttered in response to the other person's tears. As with an onion, his tears come not from what she is doing to him but from what he is doing to her: tearing her apart. Tears, although they often genuinely express grief and sadness, often also can be, even when genuine, used in an attempt to manipulate. Tears can express the demand that someone else capitulate to us, give in to our wish. They can express frustration and anger as well as grief. Tears can be aggressive, even if sincere. The silent crying person in "Monologue for an Onion" is demanding from the speaker, by those tears, that she yield herself to him, that she be as he wants her to be. But the speaker is like an onion with regard to her suitor. She has nothing to show him but the surface he is tearing at as he tries to find something solid and deeper. She is not, at bottom, his idea of her. She is only herself. He finds only layer under layer of the same thing as he tries to penetrate to her depths. Her defiant assertion is that there is no depth. She is what she seems to be, not what he wishes to find in her.

"I mean nothing," she says, backing away from an undesired involvement. "But this has not kept you / From peeling away my body, layer by layer," she reminds him. You are looking, she says, for something in me that is not there, something you want to get from me that I do not wish, that I do not *have*, to give. The "lasting union" he desires she calls a "fantasy." When he cannot find what he wants in her, he keeps "slashing away skin after skin," tearing at her, deluded by the belief that if he tears off one more layer of her being, he will find what he wants, her heart, and possess it. But an onion has no heart, no center, no core. There are only the spiraling layers of skin that he discards in the "hunt" for the heart. An onion is only surface straight down to its nonexistent center. The speaker of the monologue is nothing more than what she appears to be.

As the monologue develops, protest becomes accusation. Your pursuit of me is an assault against me, the speaker says. The peeled-off skin of the onion is likened to chunks of the speaker's flesh, "all the debris of pursuit." The pursuer is depicted as "chopping and weeping." The self-centered aggressor appears to feel that he himself is the victim. The actual victim of his attack, the speaker of the monologue, can preserve herself only by practicing something like the martial arts strategy of using the force of the attack against the attacker rather than exerting force against him. The speaker turns accusation into instruction:

> Is this the way you go through life, your mind
> A stopless knife, driven by your fantasy of truth,
> Of lasting union—slashing away skin after skin
> From things, ruin and tears your only signs
> Of progress? . . .

The questions are reproaches. Seeking his idea of union and progress, her tormentor creates only "ruin and tears."

In the sixth stanza, the metaphor of the onion is extended. The layers of onion skin become veils, and the idea that there is something deeper and truer underneath, which is being hidden by what is on the surface, is explored and exploded. The veils, the layers of onion skin, the surface of the person who is encountered, these the poet says constitute reality and constitute their own real meaning. They hide nothing; they are the textures of being. What her interlocutor wishes to do—"to grasp the heart / Of things, hungry to know where meaning / Lies"—is a mistake. His aggression does not yield what actually is, what things mean. Ripping off the veils does not get to the heart of the matter, to a place of one essential truth. Rather its end is a place where—the poet suggests by the way words are distributed on the lines—meaning "lies," that is, deceives. Meaning is not an attribute of the onion or the speaker but the fantasy of the person who tears at the speaker as if she were an onion. Like an onion, the speaker does not *mean*; both merely *are* and can yield nothing more than what they are.

In "Monologue for an Onion," the idea that existence is a transparent absolute is reinforced by the structure of the poem itself. The sentences of the poem are like a winding layer turning around upon itself. Each successive word seems to be a peeling torn from previous words. This effect of layering and unwrapping is accomplished primarily by a combination of rhyme, assonance (the repetition of similar vowel sounds), and consonance (the repetition of similar consonants). The rhymes do not come in their traditional place at the end of lines, and they do not provide the customary stopping point or give a sense of completed individual units. Instead, the rhymes appear inside the poem and roll into each other. In the lines "Is this the way you go through life, your mind / A stopless knife, driven by your fantasy of truth," the rhymes "life" and "knife" have been removed from their generally accepted position at the end of the lines and placed in each line where the caesura (the pause that divides a line of verse into two sense and breath units) occurs. The end word, "truth" resonates as a slant rhyme, an imperfect rhyme. It recalls the "f" sound in "life," "knife," and "fantasy" distorted in the "th," and it recalls the "oo" sounds in the word "through," which precedes "life" on the first line.

A similar dislocation of rhyme occurs in an earlier tercet (a group of three lines of verse): "Hunt all you want. Beneath each skin of mine / Lies another skin: I am pure onion—pure union / Of outside and in, surface and secret core." The first line begins with the slant rhyme of "hunt" and "want," making it seem as though the word "want" is being peeled off the word "hunt." The repetition of the word "skin" in the first and second lines does not make for a rhyme, but it does give a hint of something diaphanous, especially because of the intervening end of the line, "mine," and the aural similarity "Lies" has to "mine." The echo in the language suggests the transparent skin of an onion and the phenomenon of surface revealed beneath surface. The word "in" coming right at the caesura of the third line, however, provides a true rhyme with the word "skin" in the middle of the line above. Between those two rhyming words twisted into the circle of the poem (between "skin" and "in"), Kim twice lets the "in" sound reverberate in the words "onion" and "union." Each echoing sound seems to lie beneath a preceding similar version of that sound like the layers of skin that make up an onion.

Establishing the authenticity of the onion by constructing the poem like an onion, Kim contrasts the seamless unity of the onion with the divided character of the monologist's silent interlocutor. "Whatever you meant to love, in meaning to / You changed yourself: you are not who you are." He is "divided at the heart." He demands to have the speaker be the way he wants her to be, not really as she is. He wants her, but he does not want *her*. That sets him apart from himself as well as from her. It divides him into the person who thinks he loves but who actually does not love. He loves the one he is set on having only if she conforms to his image, his truth, of how he wants her to be and takes on the meaning and, consequently, the identity he has assigned her despite herself. Her last words to him, consequently, that his heart "will one day beat you to death," do not just state a fact of life but also express an angry wish.

Source: Neil Heims, Critical Essay on "Monologue for an Onion," in *Poetry for Students*, Thomson Gale, 2006.

Bryan Aubrey

Bryan Aubrey holds a PhD in English and has published many articles on contemporary poetry. In this essay, he discusses "Monologue for an Onion" as a metaphysical poem about the human quest for knowledge, fulfillment, and love.

Kim's "Monologue for an Onion" is a witty and biting critique of the ways in which humans seek to know and to love, their earnestness matched only by the ignorant stupidity with which they go about their task. The poem does not present any optimism at all about the human condition, and its tone is relentlessly mocking. Humans are viewed as lost creatures, wandering in a maze, divided against themselves, seeking understanding but unwittingly ensuring that they will never find it.

Those who read the entirety of Kim's collection of poems *Notes from the Divided Country* will not be surprised to find the poet presenting such a bleak picture of human folly and blindness. For the most part, the book is a long song of suffering, conveyed with a visceral immediacy that scalds the mind and heart. The divided country of the title is Korea, and in many of the most powerful poems, the poet imagines herself back into the turbulent history of her country of origin, including the period of the Japanese occupation, from 1932 to 1950, and the Korean War of the early 1950s. These are poems that record, to use the Scottish poet Robert Burns's phrase, "man's inhumanity to man"; reading them is like stepping into a war zone and hearing the cries of the wounded, seeing the rotting corpses of the dead, and feeling the anguish of survivors who have lost their loved ones. The images are harrowing, and the poet refuses to flinch or to turn away from sights that, once burned into the retina, will not easily be removed.

Lost and floundering, people do not know who they are. They have become ignorant of their own selves, torn apart by one conflicting desire after another."

It is this kind of imagery—of mutilation and torn, broken bodies, of the anguish of separation and loss—that carries over, in a rather different context, to "Monologue for an Onion," which is really a metaphysical poem about the human quest for knowledge, fulfillment, and love. The human mind is presented, like the knife that cuts the onion, as a "stopless knife," cutting and slashing, crudely violating the very things it is trying to understand: the nature of human experience and the meaning of life. It is also making a mess of the attempt to love, to forge that elusive union with another human being.

Although one would not describe Kim as a Romantic poet, there is nonetheless something in this aspect of the poem that suggests the romantic rebellion against reason. Romanticism was a nineteenth-century literary movement that decried the overreliance on the rational intellect at the expense of intuition and the unifying values of the heart. Reason, the capacity of discrimination, fragments life into compartments but misses the wholeness of things. It knows differences but not unity. William Wordsworth, in his poem "The Tables Turned," called it the "meddling intellect." This is perhaps what is suggested in the poem's image of a person peeling an onion as a metaphor for the desperate but fruitless search for knowledge. The mind "slash[es] away skin after skin / From things" but produces only "ruin and tears" instead of progress. Humans flail away at life, "hungry to know where meaning / Lies," seeking frantically to understand. But like a man standing in quicksand, whose every struggle to escape only pulls him deeper into trouble, the more they try to attain knowledge, the more profound their ignorance becomes. Read with some of Kim's other poems in mind that tell of horrific events endured by people helpless to avert their fate, these mocking lines in "Monologue for an Onion" become particularly telling images of the smallness of humans, their frailty and inadequacy as actors in a cruel universe, trying to understand the mystery of why things happen as they do but succeeding only in constantly adding to their misery and bewilderment.

At one point in this grim indictment of the folly of humans, the poet seems to offer a piece of advice: "You must not grieve that the world is glimpsed / Through veils. How else can it be seen?" She seems to suggest that the essence of things and people is unknowable, and that this should not be cause for distress. She counsels acceptance. It is as if she is saying, Be content with the way things are. Do not try to penetrate beyond the veil, for it is the human condition to see only in part. Restless seeking and striving, in an effort to "grasp the heart / Of things," will never yield the desired result. Instead, they serve only to bind a person's chains tighter and leave them even more confused.

If the aforementioned lines might be construed as a piece of well-meaning advice, it is the only such example in the poem, which is otherwise a merciless assault on what the onion—in the poet's witty conceit—regards as a misguided, pitiable creature. Humans not only do not find the knowledge or the love they seek, they fragment themselves in the process ("You are the one / In pieces"). Lost and floundering, people do not know who they are. They have become ignorant of their own selves, torn apart by one conflicting desire after another. The poet sounds an almost Buddhist sensibility when she writes, "you are not who you are, / Your soul cut moment to moment by a blade / Of fresh desire, the ground sown with abandoned skins." At the core of Buddhism are the Four Noble Truths. The first is that life is suffering; the second, that the suffering is caused by attachment to desire. Every moment of a person's life, the wheel of desire turns. Fulfillment of each desire leads to only a moment's satisfaction before the next desire arises in a never-ending chain. There is neither peace nor rest.

For the Buddhist, however, there is hope, because the third and fourth Noble Truths state that freedom from suffering comes when attachment to desire ceases and that this freedom can be achieved through the Eightfold Path. But "Monologue for an Onion" offers no such hope. It is not a religious poem. It offers no prospect of salvation or transcendence. There is no nirvana existing beyond the senses. On the contrary, humans are presented as embodiments of a kind of blind desire, forever reaching out in the darkness but never attaining what they seek. Unlike the onion, which is "pure union / Of outside and in, surface and secret core," humans are divided against themselves and possess no stable center from which self-knowledge might emerge: "At your inmost circle, what? A core that is / Not one."

The masterly last three lines of the poem make clear, however, that humans are not empty at the core; on the contrary, they are too full; they cannot cope with all that courses through their hearts: "Poor fool, you are divided at the heart, / Lost in its maze of chambers, blood, and love, / A heart that will one day beat you to death." These lines artfully combine the physical characteristics of the human heart and the role it plays in the body with the emotional qualities associated with it. The assonance (repetition of similar vowel sounds) in the words "blood" and "love" links them ominously together. The heart is the source of innumerable connections with other people and their fates; it is the mysterious seat of life, its pathways secret and unknown and its passions unruly, divisive, often painful, and ending only in death. The heart, too, is a "divided country."

Such is the verdict of Kim's metaphorical onion, and there cannot be many poems in the English language that interrogate the human mind and heart with this degree of cool, detached ruthlessness. "Monologue for an Onion" may be grimly pessimistic, but its assault on human folly has a kind of uncompromising purity to it, like a sheet of clear ice.

Source: Bryan Aubrey, Critical Essay on "Monologue for an Onion," in *Poetry for Students*, Thomson Gale, 2006.

Amy Schroeder

In the following review, Schroeder notes that Kim's efforts to "shape-change trauma into art without losing emotional ferocity" are mostly successful in Notes from the Divided Country.

In her debut collection, Suji Kwock Kim—notably the first Asian American to win the Walt Whitman Award—essays the vexed and vexatious landscape of identity, attempting to unite the divided countries of lyric poetry and poetry of origin. The literal subjects of *Notes from a Divided Country* are easily ascertained: warfare, occupation, racial assimilation, family tragedy—in other words, the scourges of the twentieth century. But Kim attempts to sculpt these events into lyric; her goal is to shape-change trauma into art without losing emotional ferocity, and she does accomplish this in the majority of her poems. By skipping back and forth from the flat diction of factual truth to lusher figurative language, she unites the worlds of narrative and lyric: "immigrants driving to power plants in Jersey, / out of meadowsweet and oil / the chaff of unlived lives blowing endlessly . . ."

Form and content meet in this juxtaposition of dictions, and the use of multiple voices mirrors the effort to construct multiple perspectives. Kim seems interested in investigating legions of subjectivities: the immigrant self, the child self, the victim of war, the lover, the mother, and others. "I've never been one soul," she writes in a poem styled after the Korean poet Ko Un.

Kim's technique of colliding voices enlarges as the book goes on; in later sections, she alternates poems of lyric intensity with poems of plain speech. The latter works particularly well in her persona pieces, written variously in the voices of parents, grandparents, and great-grandparents. These are arguably the most powerful poems in the book, as Kim settles her gaze on a century's worth of war in Korea to offer witness: "Remember the coal miners ordered to war in Manchuria / . . . Remember the 'Comfort Corps' raped forty times a day, / the woman screaming who could not scream because she was on fire." In these works, she thoroughly avoids the temptation of easy redemption, of easy reconciliation, even when she does employ metaphor: "At night a sickle glinted in the sky, sharp and pure. What did it reap? / Summer wind sang through the corpse-forest." Summer winds may blow, and sickle moons may shine, but there is no quick healing in this damaged landscape.

Notes from a Divided Country founders in its final pages. Perhaps not coincidentally, we find here the poems most removed from the fields of war. Kim's subjects and voices begin to veer out of control, seeming totally unrelated to one another: a poem about sparrows (the most formally disjunctive piece in the book) is followed by several cityscapes, which are followed by a Frank O'Hara-like dream poem.

Kim ends with a poem set in a garden, and its final lines sound the one wrong note in the collection: Addressing the growing plants Kim writes, "May I, and their gardeners in the old world, / who kill for warring dreams and warring heavens / who stop at nothing, see life and paradise as one." After a tour through the killing fields and "Comfort Corps," a prayer for paradise on earth seems willfully naïve. Kim may have chosen to go this route in the desire to have a happy ending; a happier ending, stylistically, might have been a poem that maintained the tonal and emotional convictions of the rest of the volume.

That said, Kim's book does represent an achievement; she manages, almost throughout, to unite the divided countries of personal experience and political truth without relying on the easy bridge of sentimentality.

Source: Amy Schroeder, Review of *Notes from a [sic] Divided Country*, in *Georgia Review*, Spring 2004, pp. 198–99.

Ray Olson

In the following review, Olson calls Notes from the Divided Country *"impressive" and the first section "punch-in-the-guts powerful."*

The four parts of Kim's impressive first collection contain poems of family, history, love, and vision, respectively. The first part is punch-in-the-guts powerful. After opening with the spiritually virtuosic "Generations," tracing the poet's journey from before conception to implantation in the womb, the poems lay out a painful familial scenario, the soul-searing climax of which comes in "ST RAGE," in which sadistic white boys torture the poet's handicapped brother. Anguish also pervades the second section's preoccupation with the half-century of horror Kim's ancestral homeland, Korea, endured, first under Japanese occupation, then in the Korean War; members of Kim's family played historic roles then, and they figure as actors and dedicatees here. The third section's poems on love are analytic, personal, and sensual, though seldom all at once; whereas pain predominated in the first two sections, emotional intensity preoccupies these poems. In the last section, Kim applies that intensity to observation of art and nature, so strikingly that, for instance, having read "On Sparrows," you may never regard those common birds as commonplace again.

Source: Ray Olson, Review of *Notes from the Divided Country*, in *Booklist*, March 1, 2003, p. 1141.

Sue Kwock Kim and Robert Siegal

In the following radio interview, Kim discusses her Korean background and how she is able to channel the greater Korean experience into her work.

[*Robert Siegel, host*]: *This is* All Things Considered *from NPR News. I'm Robert Siegel.*

Poet Suji Kwock Kim remembers when her nursery school teacher told her Korean immigrant

But at the same time, I think because of that particular isolation, my parents were even more eager to make sure that the stories about their relatives who didn't survive either the Japanese occupation of Korea or the Korean War—they were even more determined that I know about that."

mother to speak more English in their upstate New York home. That way, Suji could learn to speak English, which she did. She also lost her knowledge of Korean. Regaining it became a project when she was in college at Yale, and later, on a fellowship in Seoul, also regaining a connection to Korea. Much of her poetry is about Korea, about war, bloodshed, division.

[Ms. Suji Kwock Kim (Poet)]: "Occupation." 'The soldiers are hard at work building a house. They hammer bodies into the earth like nails. They paint the walls with blood. Inside, the doors stay shut, locked as eyes of stone. Inside, the stairs feel slippery; all flights go down. There's no floor, only a roof where ash is falling. Dark snow, human snow, thickly, mutely falling. "Come," they say, "this house will last forever. You must occupy it, and you and you and you and you. Come," they say, "there is room for everyone."'

"Occupation" is one of the poems in Notes From the Divided Countries, *Suji Kwock Kim's first book. The poet Yusef Komunyakaa chose it for the Walt Whitman Award, given to an outstanding young poet. Suji Kwock Kim's poems reflect a Korean heritage passed on to her in the unlikely environs of Poughkeepsie, New York. That's where her father, a doctor, found work and took the family. This was in the 1970s, just as Korean immigration to the US really started to take off.*

This was definitely the very beginning of it. And especially since this was upstate New York, this was not like growing up in New York City or Los Angeles where there are really large Korean-American and Asian-American communities. But at the same time, I think because of that particular isolation, my parents were even more eager to make sure that the stories about their relatives who didn't survive either the Japanese occupation of Korea or the Korean War—they were even more determined that I know about that.

Well, some of those stories, it seems, are the substance, the stories behind poems that you've now written, and I wonder if you could read one of them for us.

Of course. I'd love to. This is a poem called "Borderlands," and it's dedicated to my grandmother. Now the context of this poem is that, of course, the Japanese occupied Korea starting in 1910 in a formal way, but they actually had arrived in Korea in 1905. And the Japanese occupation went on until, really, the American liberation in 1945, and, of course, it was quite brutal. So this comes out of that particular context and it's called "Borderlands."

Crush my eyes, bitter grapes, wring out the wine of seeing. We try to escape across the frozen Yalu to Chientao or Harbin. I saw the Japanese soldiers shoot. I saw men and women from our village blown to hieroglyphs of viscera, engraving nothing. River of never, river, the opposite of Lethe, the opposite of forgetting; dividing those who lived from those who are killed. Why did I survive? I wondered at each body with its separate skin, its separate suffering. My childhood friend lay on the boot-blackened ice. I touched his face with disbelief. I tried to hold his hand, but he snatched it away as if he were ashamed of dying, eye grown large with everything it saw, everyone who disappeared. Pupil of suffering. Lonely O, blank of an eye rolled back into its socket. I was afraid to see you. Last thoughts, last dreams crawling through his skull like worms.

How do you summon these horrific battlefield images, which, while obviously the experience of your extended family, seem, I assume, a world apart from Poughkeepsie, New York, in the 1970s and '80s?

Very much so. In fact, that's interesting. The whole epigraph to that section is one that I took from Brecht. And it has something to do with what I believe is very important in terms of the responsibility that one has in terms of using the imagination as a means of compassion and understanding things that one couldn't have experienced. The Brecht epigraph is, 'It is the crudest form of empathy when the actor simply asks: What should I be like if this or that were to happen to me?' And, of course, in that epigraph, in the context, he is critiquing this sort of received idea of empathy, that it works merely through the emotions rather than also through the intellect.

Then you have some poems obviously inspired by the time you've spent in Seoul yourself in South Korea, and there's a poem, "Montage with Neon, Bok Choi, Gasoline, Lovers & Strangers," which includes, for me, the very remarkable line, 'I can't help feeling giddy. I'm drunk on neon, drunk on air, drunk on seeing what was made almost from nothing. If anything's here, it was built out of ash, out of the skull rubble of war.' Seoul was a remarkable place to finally see, I assume, after hearing all these stories of Korea all your life.

It was the most remarkable thing to see how vibrant and thriving the contemporary city is; I mean, especially after hearing all these stories first. It was amazingly moving that people recovered in such an astonishing way.

Suji Kwock Kim, before you go, perhaps you can read something else to us, picking up with more of the "Montage with Neon, Bok Choi, Gasoline, Lovers & Strangers."

OK.

I wonder about the grocer who calls me daughter because I look like her, for she has long since left home. Bus drivers hurtling past in a blast of diesel fumes. Dispatchers shouting the names of stations. Lovers so tender with each other, I hold my breath. Men with hair the color of scallion roots, playing paduk or Go, old enough to have stolen overcoats and shoes from corpses in the war, whose spirits could not be broken, whose every breath seems to say, "After things turn to their worst, we began again, but may you never see what we saw, may you never do what we've done. May you never remember and may you never forget."

Suji Kwock Kim, thank you very much for talking with us today.

Thank you so much.

Suji Kwock Kim, Korean-American poet and author of the collection, Notes from the Divided Country.

You're listening to All Things Considered *from NPR News.*

Source: Sue Kwock Kim and Robert Siegal, "Interview: Poet," in *National Public Radio: All Things Considered*, October 13, 2003

Sources

Bidart, Frank, "Editor's Shelf," in *Ploughshares*, Vol. 29, No. 4, Winter 2003, p. 223.

Burns, Robert, "Man Was Made to Mourn," in *The Works of Robert Burns*, Wordsworth Editions, 1994, p. 112.

Kim, Suji Kwock, "Monologue for an Onion," in *Notes from the Divided Country*, Louisiana State University Press, 2003, pp. 51–52.

Muske-Dukes, Carol, "Poet's Corner," in the *Los Angeles Times*, April 27, 2003, Section R, p. 17.

Schroeder, Amy, Review of *Notes from a [sic] Divided Country*, in the *Georgia Review*, Vol. 58, No. 1, Spring 2004, pp. 198–99.

Wordsworth, William, "The Tables Turned," in *Lyrical Ballads*, edited by R. L. Brett and A. R. Jones, Methuen, 1971, p. 106.

Further Reading

Doran, Geri, *Resin: Poems*, Louisiana State University Press, 2005.
  Doran's collection is the 2004 winner of the Walt Whitman Award and contains poems of grief, struggle, and perseverance. She visits the devastation of such places as Chechnya and Rwanda, bringing the pain of modern history to her poetry.

Kerber, Linda K., and Jane Sherron De Hart, eds., *Women's America: Refocusing the Past*, Oxford University Press, 2003.
  In this widely consulted anthology of women's history in America, Kerber and De Hart offer almost one hundred essays and documents relating the events and experiences of this particular historical perspective. The editors include selections that give insight into a wide range of experiences from colonial to modern times and include factors such as race and class.

Lim, Shirley, ed., *Asian-American Literature: An Anthology*, NTC, 1999.
  By compiling poetry, memoirs, plays, and short stories by Asian American writers, Lim introduces readers to this unique segment of writers. Especially for students new to studying the literature of this American ethnic group, this anthology serves as a good introduction.

Myers, Jack, *The Portable Poetry Workshop*, Heinle, 2004.
  This spiral-bound book guides beginning and intermediate writers through the process of writing poetry. Because it uses a workshop format with lots of exercises, the text engages writers and helps them take steps toward writing better poetry.

Xun, Lu, *Wild Grass*, Chinese University Press, 2003.
  Xun is acknowledged as one of the preeminent voices of modern Chinese literature. After abandoning a career in medicine in favor of writing, he has concentrated his efforts on short fiction and prose poems that address China's problems. Xun is pained by the struggle of his fellow Chinese and explores its meaning in his writing.

Not like a Cypress

Yehuda Amichai

1958

"Not like a Cypress" was first published in 1958 in *Two Hopes Away*, a collection of poems by Yehuda Amichai; it also appears in the 1996 collection *The Selected Poetry of Yehuda Amichai*. The poem at first appears to be a work through which the speaker examines various facets of himself, describing himself first as what he is not and then providing a contrasting image that comes closer to what he is. The self that Amichai describes initially appears to be a personal description, but because he digs deeply into the truths about himself, the speaker touches the universal elements that make up all people.

Close reading of the poem reveals the element of death in it. Whether this poem was written as a reflection on the poet's own mortality or about his experiences with war and killing or the loss of his beloved father is not clear. The word "exit" is present in both the first and the last stanzas, so it is difficult to dismiss the theme of death or loss. That Amichai has hidden this theme, embedding it creatively so that readers must search for it, adds to the power of the poem.

Author Biography

Yehuda Amichai, considered one of Israel's greatest poets, was born in Wurzburg, Germany, on May 3, 1924. His family had lived in that part of Germany since the Middle Ages. When the Nazis came

Yehuda Amichai © Nina Subin

into power, Amichai's family left Germany for Palestine and then settled in Israel. Amichai studied Hebrew and, after receiving a religious education, taught Hebrew literature in secondary schools. He later served for many years in the Israeli army, an experience that is often reflected in his writing. As he grew older, Amichai became an advocate of peace and worked with Palestinians toward that goal.

Although he wrote short stories, novels, and plays, Amichai is best known for his poetry, which he began writing in 1949. Amichai was the first poet to write in colloquial Israeli Hebrew. His first collection of poems, *Achshav Ubayamin Na'acherim* (Now and in Other Days), was published in 1955. Amichai's poem "Not like a Cypress" appeared in his second collection, *Bemerchak Shetey Tikvot* (Two Hopes Away), published in 1958. In 1982, Amichai was awarded the Israel Prize for Poetry. Four years later, he became a foreign honorary member of the American Academy of Arts. After establishing himself as a major poet, Amichai was invited to the United States to teach as a visiting professor. During the 1970s and 1980s, he often taught at such schools as New York University and the University of California, Berkeley.

Known for his focus on love and loss, whether it was a love of other people or of his country, Amichai wrote eleven volumes of poetry in Hebrew.

Many of them became bestsellers. Amichai's poems often are read at weddings and funerals, and some have been set to music; they have been translated into thirty-seven languages. His last collection, *Open Closed Open*, was published in the United States in 2000. Married twice and the father of three children, Amichai lived his entire adult life in Israel, where he died in Jerusalem on September 25, 2000.

Poem Text

Not like a cypress,
not all at once, not all of me,
but like the grass, in thousands of cautious green
    exits,
to be hiding like many children
while one of them seeks.   5

And not like the single man,
like Saul, whom the multitude found
and made king.

But like the rain in many places
from many clouds, to be absorbed, to be drunk   10
by many mouths, to be breathed in
like the air all year long
and scattered like blossoming in springtime.

Not the sharp ring that wakes up
the doctor on call,   15
but with tapping, on many small windows
at side entrances, with many heartbeats.

And afterward the quiet exit, like smoke
without shofar-blasts, a statesman resigning,
children tired from play,   20
a stone as it almost stops rolling
down the steep hill, in the place
where the plain of great renunciation begins,
from which, like prayers that are answered,
dust rises in many myriads of grains.   25

Poem Summary

Lines 1–5

In the first line, "Not like a cypress," the use of the negative keeps readers in suspense. They know more is to come. Because the speaker is stating that he is not like something, readers know, or at least imagine, that the speaker must be preparing to tell them what he is like.

In the second line, the speaker qualifies the first line with "not all at once, not all of me." In other words, he catches his readers by surprise. In this line, the speaker limits the image of the first line. He is somewhat but not completely like a cypress.

Again, Amichai arouses the curiosity of his readers. What parts of the cypress are like the speaker? What parts of the speaker are like the cypress?

In the third line, the speaker does not attempt to answer specific questions about the cypress but moves to another image that offers clues to what the speaker is like. He is "like the grass, in thousands of cautious green exits." This image is offered in contrast to the cypress tree. Readers are led to compare the two images. A tree is stiff; grass is willowy and soft, more reflective of the changes in the atmosphere in which it exists.

The second part of the line is puzzling. The introduction of the word "thousands" offers a sense of comfort, as in protection by sheer mass, as in a field in which there are thousands of blades of grass. The speaker transforms that feeling with the word "cautious," which implies danger that may be real or merely perceived. In addition, the caution is applied to the phrase "green exits," which symbolizes a sense of leaving or getting away.

Lines 4 and 5 carry a similar feeling of caution but a more playful one: "to be hiding like many children / while one of them seeks." With these lines, the speaker introduces the childhood game of hide-and-seek, carrying with it a sense of caution but without a sense of danger. The caution is gentle because it is encapsulated in the desire to win a childhood game.

Lines 6–13

The pattern of the poem is set in the first stanza, in which the speaker establishes what he is not like and then provides the reader with an image that better defines him. This pattern is repeated in the second stanza: "And not like the single man, / like Saul, whom the multitude found / and made king." The story of Saul appears in the Bible. Saul was the first king of Israel, a mighty warrior, handsome and popular, who ruled from 1020 to 1000 B.C.E. According to some stories, however, Saul was also weak and was eventually defeated. The speaker in the poem insinuates that he does not want to be like Saul.

The poem continues by replacing the image of Saul with that of something more natural, more neutral, and more nourishing.

> But like the rain, in many places
> from many clouds, to be absorbed, to be drunk
> by many mouths, to be breathed in
> like the air all year long
> and scattered like blossoming in springtime.

Saul, in contrast, was a soldier who fought and killed for more land. There are suggestions that he was also greedy and jealous. The speaker likens himself not to Saul and his weaknesses but to something more giving. There is also the contrast between the phrase "the single man" in line 6 and the references to the "many" later in the same stanza. There is mention of "many places," "many clouds," and "many mouths." There are also references to the air and the breathing of it "all year long," which provides a sense of the almost eternal. The confines of the image in the beginning of this stanza are contrasted to the boundlessness of rain and air.

Lines 14–17

In the third stanza, the speaker states that he is "Not the sharp ring that wakes up / the doctor on call,"; there is an abruptness, a sense of emergency, and a disruption of sleep in these lines—all uncomfortable notions. Awakening a doctor from sleep can mean that a life is in danger. The speaker, however, is not a "sharp ring" but is a "tapping, on many small windows / at side entrances, with many heartbeats."

The sound, in other words, is soft and so far away as to almost be inaudible, like a heartbeat. Yet the mention of a heartbeat adds depth to the sound, for it is the sound of life. It is, in contrast to the call in the night, an image of the soft continuance of health rather than the fearful scream of emergency.

Lines 18–25

In the final stanza, the speaker quiets the images to almost a whisper, beginning with "the quiet exit, like smoke." The going away is carried over from the first stanza with the use of the word "exit." The almost quiet images continue with the mention of the lack of "shofar-blasts," which in Hebrew belief announce a great event. The exit to which the speaker refers is not a great event that needs to be emphasized. It is merely like

> . . . a statesman resigning,
> children tired from play,
> a stone as it almost stops rolling
> down the steep hill. . . .

It is quiet, almost a missed event and yet at the same time something very expected and natural.

The "quiet exit" occurs

> . . . in the place
> where the plain of great renunciation begins,
> from which, like prayers that are answered,
> dust rises in many myriads of grains.

Topics For Further Study

- Mimicking the pattern and form of "Not Like a Cypress," write a poem using similes that state what the subject is not followed by similes that state what the subject is. Choose any theme or subject, but try to follow Amichai's lead as much as possible.

- Research various poetic devices, such as alliteration, assonance, and personification. List at least ten devices and provide definitions for each. Then find examples of these devices in poems you have read. Make up creative examples of each device. Turn the research into a class discussion and exercise.

- Amichai was the first Israeli poet to write in colloquial Hebrew, the common language one might hear spoken on the streets. Note how your vocabulary changes when you are talking to your friends as opposed to how you might talk

to a teacher, a parent, or an authority figure in your community. What words do you use with your friends that are not in your vocabulary when you talk to someone (other than a peer) you are trying to impress? Ask a few classmates to help you demonstrate to the class the various ways you alter your language. Have one of your classmates play the role of a distinguished adult you are trying to impress. Another person should pretend to be your best friend. A third might be a parent figure.

- Choose and `read another poem from *The Selected Poetry of Yehuda Amichai*. Read both poems in front of the class and then lead a discussion on how the two poems are similar and how they differ from each other. Examine the meaning, structure, and themes of the two poems to find their similarities and differences.

The last lines suggest a death and rebirth. Someone has quietly left, having renounced all connections to his material life, and has become ethereal, like prayers. From that leaving point, however, arises a great sign of life as the dust, possibly the dust of the departed, rises once again in the form of "grains," which are a symbol of food and thus of life.

Themes

Death

Hidden in "Not like a Cypress" is the sense of death. This sense is very subtle but is at the same time unavoidable. There has to be a reason for the speaker's using the words "exits" and "exit." The poet's experiences in war and the death of his father influence much of his poetry. The "thousands of cautious green exits" can be interpreted as gravesites. The rain "to be breathed in like air" may be an allusion to tears. And the "sharp ring

that wakes up the doctor on call" sounds like an emergency—someone in pain, someone critically ill, someone dying. The "quiet exit" mentioned in the last stanza must be a reference to the last breath of life of someone who is dying. Clearer is the allusion to the "great renunciation," a reference to the final giving up of all things material.

Rebirth

Paralleling the theme of death is the theme of rebirth. This theme is offered in two places. In the second stanza is the mention of springtime. The speaker refers to rain that must be "drunk by many mouths" and then "scattered like blossoming in springtime." The rain, whether it is a literal reference to rain or a figurative reference to tears, is transformed or reborn as flowers. Springtime is representative of the rebirthing of the seasons, when the things that have died in the winter come back to life. In the last stanza, the theme of rebirth is offered in "dust rises in many myriads of grains." Dust is a lifeless form of soil; it is also a biblical reference to bodies turning to dust when they die. Grain, on the other hand, is a sign of life. Bread is made from grain, and in the Bible grain represents the basic form of food, the staff of life.

Nature

It is clear that nature is important to Amichai. In "Not like a Cypress," he uses similes to create images that deepen the poem, and all the similes are related to nature. The title and the first line refer to the cypress tree, a resilient conifer that grows in the Mediterranean region. In the third line, Amichai uses grass to build an image. Other natural forms include rain, clouds, air, blossoms, springtime, and grains. Nature grounds the poem, the central message of which is abstract and difficult to explain. The fact that all readers can relate to trees, clouds, and rain helps to create a universal understanding, for which Amichai's poetry is known.

Self-Insight

In the first stanza of "Not like a Cypress," Amichai uses the word "me," which leads the reader to consider the poem an offering of self-insight. To know both what he is and what he is not, the speaker has to be introspective. He has to know himself so well that he understands himself and can produce the words to expose himself and the images that explain what he has discovered about himself. No reader can definitely make clear what Amichai has truly discovered, but through his exploration of self, the poet exposes elements that are common to all people. In exploring himself, the poet inspires his readers to entertain their own explorations of what they are and what they are not.

Religion

Saul, the first king of Israel and a figure in the Bible, plays a minor role in "Not like a Cypress," as do other religious images. The mention of Saul brings to mind the details of his reign and his challenges. The name Saul also stirs a sense of religion classes, which teach the ancient history of the Bible. Using Saul as a reference is not the same as using the name of a politician or an athlete. Saul is chosen purposefully for the religious connotation. "Shofar-blasts" is also a reference to religion, because the shofar is related to several sacred Jewish ceremonies. Shofar blasts are used to remind people of their connection to their religious beliefs. The final stanza contains a reference to prayer.

Style

Simile

"Not like a Cypress" is written almost entirely as a simile. Similes are figures of speech in which one subject is likened to another. A sign that a simile is in place is the use of the word "like." The poem begins with a negative simile: "Not like a cypress"; what follows is "but like the grass." This pattern continues throughout the poem, offering readers verbal images of what the subject is and what the subject is not. The use of similes adds depth to a poem by painting pictures with words. For example, without trying to decipher the meaning of these words, the reader can enjoy the following lines for the impressions they give: ". . . to be breathed in / like the air all year long / and scattered like blossoming in springtime."

Echo

An echo in poetry refers to the repetition of particular sounds, syllables, words, phrases, or lines. It can be used for various reasons, among them intensifying rhythm and emphasizing meaning. In "Not like a Cypress," echoes are used throughout, beginning with the first line. The concept of "not like" begins the first three stanzas, tying the poem together linguistically and rhythmically. Answering "not like" is another repetitive concept, "but like," which introduces the contrasting images.

The word "exits" in the first stanza is echoed with "exit" in the final stanza, creating an emphasis that illuminates some of the meaning of the poem. The word "hiding" in the first stanza and the word "found" in the second stanza create a mirror-image echo. The word "children" appears in the first and last stanzas. Readers should pay attention to echoes. Poets have many choices when writing, and choosing the same word more than once is a way to make a point.

Enjambment

Enjambment is a poetic device in which the sense and grammatical construction of a phrase are carried to the next line of a verse. Enjambment is present in every stanza of "Not like a Cypress" and is used to change meaning. The first stanza contains the enjambment "to be hiding like many children." Stopping at the end of the line gives the impression, especially after the word "cautious" in the previous line, that the children may be hiding out of fear. The poet is playing with words to alter the reader's perceptions. A surprise appears in the next line, which reveals that the children are playing a game of hide-and-seek. Only reading the two lines together gives the full meaning: "to be hiding like many children / while one of them seeks."

In the second stanza, enjambment delivers an altered message. Line 7 reads "like Saul, whom the multitude found." If one stops reading at the end of the line, the impression is that Saul is discovered, as if he were hiding (a subtle joke, because in the biblical story, Saul's reaction on hearing he would be made king is to hide). However, there is much more going on than a mere game of hide-and-seek. The eighth line supplies the real message. Saul not only was found but also was made king.

In the last stanza, enjambment is used to suggest a complete change in vision. "A stone as it almost stops rolling" produces an image of a stone that is almost stationary. Motion is all but nonexistent. The speaker does something clever in the next line by adding to the image of the rolling stone the picture of a steep hill and the idea of momentum. In line 21, the stone is almost stopped, and because of the enjambment, the reader all but eliminates the possibility that the stone is still moving. Line 22 reveals that the stone is rolling down a steep hill and probably is moving faster rather than slowing. The speaker has tilted the picture.

Modulation

Modulation in poetry is the harmonious use of language related to changes of stress and pitch. Although it may be present in any good writing, modulation is emphasized in the writing of poetry, in which the sounds of words are almost as important as their meanings. Reading Amichai's poem aloud, readers can hear and feel the modulation of his carefully chosen words, phrases, and lines.

Most of "Not like a Cypress" follows the rhythm of natural speech, which in English tends to swing back and forth between a stressed syllable and an unstressed one, almost as if one were taking in breath and then releasing it. The first line of this poem has two stressed syllables followed by an unstressed syllable, a stressed one, and an unstressed syllable: "Not" and "like" are equally stressed; the voice drops on "a" and then rises on the first and falls on the second syllable of "cypress." This pattern is not repeated in the second line, but it recurs at the beginning phrase of the third line, "but like the grass." The pattern is close enough to give the reader a sense of sandwiching the first and third lines around the second line. This

pattern is repeated throughout the poem, layering tone and pitch on top of rhythm and meaning.

Historical Context

Hebrew

Although he had studied classical Hebrew since childhood, when he wrote poetry, Amichai chose to do so in colloquial Hebrew, the language spoken on the streets and in homes. Hebrew is a Semitic language with linguistic roots in the Afro-Asiatic language family. It is similar in many ways to Aramaic and south-central Arabic. Hebrew is an ancient language. Preserved writings of Hebrew date to 3000 B.C.E., but the language ceased to be spoken around 200 C.E. and was used only in its written, classical form. Hebrew was used to write religious texts as well as legal, scientific, literary, and business documents. In the latter part of the twentieth century, Hebrew was revitalized as a spoken language.

The most influential person in the revival of spoken Hebrew was Eliezer Ben-Yehuda (1858–1922), who was also instrumental in the Jewish national movement. Before the revival, most Jews were brought up speaking the languages of the various countries in which they lived. As people began moving back to what would become the state of Israel, the use of a modern form of Hebrew reconnected the Jews, giving them a single language with which to communicate. As modern Hebrew evolved, influences from languages such as German, Russian, and English found their way into the ancient language. Thus, the spoken and more common, or colloquial, Hebrew differs from the classical form used in much writing.

Israel

Some literary critics often consider Amichai's poetry a reflection of the history of his adopted home of Israel. Amichai not only wrote about his country but also served in its military. Israel is in the Middle East along the shores of the Mediterranean Sea and bordered by Lebanon, Syria, Jordan, and Egypt. Israel's occupation of the Gaza Strip, the West Bank, and the Golan Heights caused tension between Israel and her neighbors. For more than 3,000 years, Jews had lived in this area, but then they were forced to flee by the rulers of the Roman Empire. In 638 C.E., the area around present-day Israel was conquered by Arab nations. Although some Jews remained in the vicinity, their

Compare & Contrast

- **1950s:** The Law of Return is established in Israel, allowing Jews from other countries to immigrate to Israel and become citizens. More than 100,000 Jews living in Iraq immigrate to Israel.

  Today: Fewer than one hundred Jews live in Iraq.

- **1950s:** Great Britain recognizes Israel as a state.

  Today: Great Britain helps to broker a cease-fire between Palestine and Israel.

- **1950s:** Between 1950 and 1956, more than 1,300 Israelis are killed by terrorist raids.

  Today: Between 2000 and 2005, more than 600 Israelis are killed by terrorist raids.

- **1950s:** Israeli forces defeat Arab forces to establish the state of Israel.

  Today: Israeli forces remove Israeli settlers from the Gaza Strip to return the land to the Palestinians.

numbers dwindled drastically. In the 1800s, a new wave of Jewish immigrants began to arrive. Zionism, a national movement to reinstate a Jewish presence in Palestine, was established. By the 1920s, almost 40,000 Jews had moved into the area.

After World War I, the British government helped establish a Jewish homeland in Palestine. As the power of Nazism spread, the numbers of Jews immigrating to Palestine intensified. By 1940, almost half of the population of Palestine was Jewish. By the end of World War II, more than 600,000 Jews were living in the area. The British government continued its influence on Palestine, trying to avert conflicts between the Arab and Jewish cultures by attempting to put a quota on Jewish immigration and to give Arabs and Jews equal rule. However, Great Britain became fully engaged in a fight for its own survival during World War II, and laws that reflected the concepts of shared rule and an immigration quota were not fully enforced.

In 1947, attempts to divide Palestine between Arabs and Jews failed, and war ensued. One year later, the state of Israel was established. The Arab nations surrounding Israel rejected the establishment of the new country, and more fighting took place. During the battles, Israel captured more land, and many Arabs fled. Israel signed peace treaties with many neighboring Arab nations, but fighting over the right to the territory continued. Israel ended its occupation of the Gaza Strip in 2005.

Biblical Story of Saul

According to the Bible, Saul was the first king of Israel. He was appointed king by the prophet Samuel after public pressure demanded that the country have its own king. Before this time, sections of the country had been ruled by various judges, including Samuel, but the people wanted a centralized figurehead, someone who would rule the entire country and protect them.

Saul was a man of great size and was very handsome, which helped make him a popular choice. He was a reluctant appointee, however. He hid when he found out that he was to be made king. Nonetheless, when he learned that the country was threatened by invading troops, Saul rose to the occasion, brought together an army, and saved the country. Saul's heroic acts gave him a sense of pride, and from then on, he took his role as king seriously and faced it without fear.

Saul is believed to have been more of a military king than a ruling monarch. He led victorious armies in many battles. Because Saul did not always listen to the advice of Samuel, who apparently received his words of wisdom from God, Samuel denounced him. Saul eventually was killed in battle. Some interpreters believed that on realizing that he was about to lose a battle against the Philistines, Saul committed suicide.

Shofar Blasts

A shofar is an ancient instrument made from the horn of a ram. It is used in ritualistic ceremonies, such as the announcement of a coronation, which can be symbolic, as in the coronation of God as king. A shofar also is used to communicate with God. Prayers are sent with the blast of a shofar. Some people believe shofar blasts are a way to chase away evil or weakness. In modern times, shofar blasts are used to announce important events. There are three types of shofar blasts. One is called a *Tekiah*, which is one long sound. The second is the *Shevarim*, or three wails. The third type of blast is the *Teruah*, or nine sobs. One of the symbolic messages sent by shofar blast is a reminder that one has not been abandoned. Another is a signal for people to wake up, not physically but spiritually.

Critical Overview

"Not like a Cypress" was written and published early in Amichai's career. No reviews focus specifically on this poem, but Amichai's poetry in general is often studied. In an article written for *Judaism*, Chana Bloch points out the easy readability of Amichai's poems, which "lend themselves to translation because they speak clearly and directly, and because Amichai's striking metaphors carry the burden of his meaning." Bloch continues by explaining that this statement is not meant to imply that Amichai's language is simplistic. "His language is far more dense and inventive than this may suggest," Bloch writes. For example, there are biblical and liturgical allusions "on every page" of Amichai's texts.

After interviewing Amichai, N. Tamopolsky, writing for *Forward*, explains that "Amichai has become a human representation of Israel itself, a sort of national testimonial." When Amichai writes about Israel, however, it is through his personal experience. "He writes about things so personal and universal that they are public experiences," Tamopolsky writes. "He is known as a poet of love and Jerusalem, and seems to embody both."

Gila Ramras-Rauch, in a review of *The Selected Poetry of Yehuda Amichai* for *World Literature Today*, states

> Yehuda Amichai's simple, beguiling, and challenging poetry continues to fascinate readers and translators alike. He is recognized in Israel and abroad for his seeming simplicity of tone, image, and syntax. The centrality of a speaker in Amichai's poetry inevitably reflects the man himself: a gentle, often self-effacing man whose soft voice is frequently in contrast with the bold statements his poems make.

In a review of *The Selected Poetry of Yehuda Amichai*, which includes "Not like a Cypress,"

Mark Rudman, writing for the *Nation*, states that "Yehuda Amichai is by now one of the half-dozen leading poets in the world. He has found a voice that speaks across cultural boundaries and a vision so sure that he can make the conflicts of the citizen soldier in modern Israel stand for those of humankind."

In a *Booklist* review of Amichai's *A Life of Poetry: 1948–1994*, Elizabeth Gunderson writes, "In stark, beautiful language, Amichai shares with us a worldview sustained by verbal power, irony, and resonance." A *Publishers Weekly* review of the same collection refers to Amichai's poetry as "elegant, spacious and perfectly accessible." In a review of this collection for *World Literature Today*, Ramras-Rauch finds Amichai's poetry to be "a curious mix of an active dialogue with the surrounding world mingled with a contemplative mood." Ramras-Rauch continues, "His ironic tone, alluding to the basic incongruity inherent in everyday existence, also maintains a certain serenity. He is a poet of prolonged implosion that reverberates around his deceptively simple poems."

Criticism

Joyce Hart

Joyce Hart is a published author and former writing instructor. In this essay, she examines "Not like a Cypress" to find the meaning that lies in the middle of the contrasts presented in the poem.

From the first line or even from the title of the poem, readers know that Amichai's "Not like a Cypress" is going to be about contrast. If the speaker is "not like a cypress," then what is he like? This question automatically comes to mind as the poem begins. This line sets the pattern of contrasting statements throughout the poem. The contrasts are like boundaries around a field. By providing contrasts—elements that he is not like followed by elements that he is like—the speaker offers readers not only room for their imaginations to fill in the space but also a broad and creative image. By exploring the field that lies between the contrasts, readers become more involved in the poem and are rewarded with an understanding of what the poet is trying to communicate.

The speaker states that he is not like a cypress, "not all of me." Parts of him, however, may be like a cypress, a tree that, in Israel, thrives in harsh conditions—dry and windy. Another interesting fact about the cypress is that millions of cypress

What Do I Read Next?

- Amichai's *Open Closed Open* (2000) is the last collection of poems published before the poet's death. The themes that run through many of the poems are love and mortality. Amichai reflects on his life, his children, and his own childhood.

- Amichai's first poems are in *The Early Books of Yehuda Amichai* (1988). The poems in this collection were very popular in their time and influenced many Israeli poets because Amichai was the first to use Hebrew as it was spoken in private and on the streets.

- Written almost as letters from one culture to another, *Voices from Israel: Israeli Poets Speak to America of Life and Home, Anguish and Sorrow, Joy and Hope* (1998) is a collection focused on exchanging ideas. The poems are by poets who live in Israel but who speak English.

- *A Tale of Love and Darkness* (2004) is a memoir by Amos Oz, an Israeli author of many novels. This book is a glimpse into life in Israel through the eyes of a sensitive man who became an important writer.

---

trees were planted in the Martyrs Forest in Israel as a memorial to children who had died in the Holocaust. Because the poem also mentions "thousands of cautious green exits, / to be hiding like many children," a connection can be made between the cypress and death. The speaker, however, says that not all of him is like a cypress, at least "not all at once." If the cypress, in the speaker's mind, represents death, that is not all he is. He is also life and playfulness, exemplified by his allusion to children playing hide-and-seek. Taking all this information and trying to form a picture, one might read into the first stanza that the speaker is like a cypress in that he stands tall in the face of challenge. He is mindful of the sorrow that surrounds him, but he is also supple, like the grass.

The speaker uses the word "cautious," which is connected to the phrase "to be hiding." It is not simply that the children are playing a game of hide-and-seek in a field of grass. Something else is going on. By using "to be hiding like many children," the speaker is suggesting that he, too, is hiding. What might be inferred is that sometimes the speaker stands up tall. At other times, however, he does not want to face his challenges, at least not immediately. He sometimes wants to hide, "while one of them seeks." The speaker wants to wait until someone or something finds him. Sometimes he is a man; at other times, he prefers to be like a child.

The second stanza begins with "And not like the single man," giving the impression that the

speaker does not want to stand up straight in an open field and be immediately recognized. The speaker implies that if he does not want to be like "the single man," he wants to be in a crowd. This notion links to "to be hiding like many children" in the previous stanza, but even in that stanza the speaker does not want to be the only child. He wants to be included in a group. The speaker also states that he does not want to be like Saul, who is the speaker's example of what it would be like to be "the single man," someone who is responsible for the "multitude." The speaker does not want to be "made king." Saul was a powerful and charismatic man and a popular choice for king. In standing out as he did, however, Saul exposed his strengths as well as his weaknesses. Saul became greedy and disobedient. In some versions of the story, Saul commits suicide. This end, the speaker claims, is not for him.

What contrast to Saul does the speaker offer? He wants to be "like the rain." How does rain differ from the image of Saul? To answer this question, the reader needs to look at the similarities between the first stanza and the second, which contains words that imply large quantities. The speaker not only wants to be like the rain but also wants to be in "many places." He wants to be rain "from many clouds," and he wants to be "drunk by many mouths." These amounts contrast to the quantity in the first line of the stanza, in which the speaker says that he is not like "the single man." It is also similar to the comparison in the first stanza, in which the speaker states that he is not like "a cypress"—one tree.

How else does rain contrast to a man? Rain has no emotion, no ego, no strengths or weaknesses. There is no personality to rain, no name, no history, and no responsibility. Yet rain is essential to life. Air also is essential to life, and that is the next element the speaker mentions. He not only wants to be like rain that quenches the thirst of the multitudes but also wants to be "like the air" that people breathe in "all year long." There is an interesting comparison between a king and natural elements such as rain and air. People depend on their king to make rules for a civil society, to protect them in war, and to provide for them when they are in need. People also depend, even more substantially, on rain and air. The greatest contrast, however, is not to look at a king or rain or air through other people's eyes but to look at the basic characteristics of king or rain or air. A king is well known and has many benefits in undertaking his role, but the task can be overwhelming. Rain and air, in contrast, merely exist. Both are natural, circular processes that constantly refresh themselves. If people are thirsty, rain does not care. If people are suffocating, air is not to blame.

Another contrast between king and rain and air is that a king must do battle, and King Saul was a notorious warrior. Wars imply death. Rain and air imply life. The poet makes sure that his readers get this point. He ends the second stanza with the image of rain and air "scattered like blossoming in springtime." Spring is a time of rebirth. Blossoming stands in stark contrast to the image of kingly wars, or wars of any kind.

In the third stanza, another contrast pits images of life and death against each other. There is the "sharp ring" that wakes up a "doctor on call." This situation sounds like an emergency. In contrast to this possible death situation, the speaker ends the stanza with the word "heartbeats," the image of life.

In the final stanza, the speaker no longer states what he is not like in contrast to what he is like, but the stanza still contains contrast—that between life and death. The stanza begins "And afterward," which may refer to the afterward that comes with death. There is "the quiet exit," the speaker continues, during which everything all but stops, like "children tired from play" and "a stone as it almost stops rolling."

At the moment when everything is stopping, something also is starting, the "plain of great

> *If the speaker is 'not like a cypress,' then what is he like?"*

renunciation begins." This great renunciation may be the giving up of the world and all its physicality, its memories, and one's connection to people and cherished goods. It may be the renunciation of ego and self-identity. Renunciation also may be another reference to death. Is the speaker talking about a physical or an emotional or psychological death?

The poem ends, ". . . great renunciation begins, / from which, like prayers that are answered, / dust rises in many myriads of grains." This image is similar to the earlier image of the rain and the air "scattered like blossoming in springtime." Once again, there is the feeling of rebirth—one thing turning into another. In this final image, dust turns into grain. Dust, which is lifeless, is turned into food, which represents life.

The main contrasts offered in "Not like a Cypress" are that the speaker is not a puffed-up ego, like a king. He is, in contrast, like the unnamed rain. He is not a taker. He is a giver, whether giving means that he is a grassy field in which children play or the basic staples of life—water, air, and food. The speaker does not want to do anything alone but wants to be among the multitudes. Most of all, he is not like death. Rather, he is like life giving birth to itself.

Source: Joyce Hart, Critical Essay on "Not like a Cypress," in *Poetry for Students*, Thomson Gale, 2006.

Esther Fuchs

In the following essay published shortly after Amichai's death, Fuchs analyzes the major themes in his writing, including religious skepticism, disillusionment with love, and classical allusions.

Yehuda Amichai is known as one of Israel's leading poets. He is credited with pioneering a new idiom, a new poetic trend in Israeli poetry along with Natan Zach and Amir Gilboa. In general terms, Amichai can be said to have created a secularist, skeptical reinterpretation of traditional Judaism and an ironic reassessment of normative Zionism. Amichai is recognized for his penetrating

> *Amichai's poetic signature, his ability to deflate sacral pieties, and to celebrate mundane experiences and ordinary reality also requires some interpretive effort."*

critique of religious and nationalist pieties, and for his sharp questioning of conventional, self-aggrandizing collective beliefs.

It may be best to begin this assessment of Amichai's work by focusing on his ironic approach to traditional faith and his representations of God. In one of his early poems, published in the early 1960s, Amichai writes: "God has mercy on Kindergarten Children / less so on schoolchildren. / And for adults he has no mercy at all / he leaves them alone. / And at times they must crawl on all fours / in the burning sand / to get to the aid station / and they are gushing blood." God who is said to have compassion for kindergarten children does not seem to be responsive to wounded adults—a clear metonymy for soldiers in battle who are left to fend for themselves. If God is compassionate toward kindergarten children, why does he not care about the wounded soldiers? After all, they too must crawl on all fours, like children, having been cut down in battle. Should not God have mercy on the bleeding soldiers, should he not care even more for the wounded who are crawling on "burning" sand? After all, their anguish is much greater. Amichai's God is distant, detached, inscrutable, indifferent, authoritarian, cynical, even ruthless. Amichai refers to God in mechanical terms, at times, labeling God as "the police" that maintains order among various religious groups. His representation of God suggests a secular critique of the traditional conception of God as the redeemer of the chosen people. In Amichai's poetry, God stands for world order, a principle of morality and humanity—God is a metaphor for meaning. But again and again the human quest for meaning is futile, because in much of Amichai's poetry aggression and hostility rule the world.

This poem raises doubts not only about the Jewish religious approach but also about the nationalist interpretation of war. By focusing on the wounded casualties of war, Amichai emphasizes the high price of war. Where the previous generation of Natan Aherman and Avraham Shlonsky presented Zionism as a new secular religion, Amichai rejects the grand pieties of Zionism. Where Shlonsky presented the Zionist endeavor in metaphysical, even mystical terms, Amichai presents this endeavor in prosaic, routine, quotidian terms, dragging the lofty formulas down to earth and examining the underside of each ideological proclamation. For Amichai, the true meaning of Judaism is expressed in the ability to recognize the humanity and religious dimension of the national enemy. To say that Amichai rejected Judaism and Zionism would then amount to a fundamental misunderstanding. What he rejects is the heroic and exclusive aspects of Judaism and Zionism.

In his Jerusalem 1967 cycle, written after the Six-Day War, Amichai questions the consensual "othering" of East Jerusalem's Palestinians. In a poem entitled "Yom Kippur," Amichai describes his encounter with an Arab shopkeeper in East Jerusalem. On Yom Kippur, the poetic "I" dons "dark holiday clothes," a symbol of mourning, and proceeds to stand in front of the Arab shop by Damascus Gate. The poet identifies with the shopkeeper, comparing him to his own father, who had a similar shop in Europe, a shop that was "burned there"—in Germany. Not only does the poet empathize with the Palestinian shopkeeper, he perceives the buttons, zippers, and threads as sacred objects: "A rare light and many colors, like an open Ark." This epiphany becomes the core experience of Yom Kippur. The traditional prayer in the synagogue is replaced by a silent meditation on the human bond between enemies, the conventional ark is replaced by a revelation, the revelation is that the enemy is just as human as the speaker, just as persecuted as his own father was in Europe.

Amichai's pessimistic assessment of the Zionist condition complements his skeptical vision of the human quest for meaning. This quest is bound to fail because the world is torn asunder by hatred and distrust. "Half the people in the world love the other half / Half of the people hate the other half./" Hatred is endemic not only to the Arab-Israeli conflict but to the world at large. "Must I because of these people and those people / Go and wander and change unceasingly / Like rain in its cycle, and sleep among the rocks / And be rough like olive trunks / and hear the moon barking over at me?"

Amichai questions the meaning of political factionalism in the name of the individual. Because two groups of people declare war on each other, should then the individual have to resign him/herself to a life of military discipline and deprivation in the natural roughness of an inimical landscape? Later on in the poem, Amichai makes use of an allusion to the Passover Haggadah. The individual "I" finds himself caught between the "stick" and the "fire," between the "water and the ox," and between the "angel of death and God"—the familiar stations of the Had Gadya. While the Haggadah, however, presents God's victory over the various obstacles as a justification of human toil and tribulation, Amichai's poem leaves the reader with the sense of encumbrance and hardship. For Amichai, there is no respite from the awful trial by fire and water; there is no sense of redemption or resolution in the modern day trials imposed on modern Israel. Neither is there any hope for peace or meaning in the world in general for the individual who aspires to privacy and personal contentment.

The question that raises the right of the individual versus the demands of the group is at the very heart of Amichai's novel *Not of This Time, Not of This Place* (published in Israel in 1963 and in English in 1968). This novel represents the Israeli condition after the Holocaust and the War of Independence as an impossible nightmare. The protagonist Yoel, an archeologist who tries to find a place in his secular Jerusalem community finds himself increasingly alienated from both his friends and his Israeli wife, Ruth. He searches for love and meaning in his childhood past, in memories of pre-Holocaust Germany, specifically in his childhood love for a Jewish girl who was murdered by the Nazis. In addition to his escape from Israeli time, Yoel flees from Israeli culture and discourse by attaching himself to an American lover, Patricia. The vortex of confusion and dissolution into which the protagonist sinks reflects a post-Zionist and post-Holocaust reality in which ideals are no longer possible. The archeologist whose profession is to reconstruct the past is unable to deal with his own personal past, nor is he able to face his present. On the one hand, Amichai seems to imply that individual life in Israel is impossible because of the collective pressures of the immediate Jewish past and the present demands of the new state. The individual cannot find a coherent space or time where he may find a meaningful life, because the collective seems to supersede all individual quests. Amichai's novel was defined by the critic Gershon Shaked as one of the major breakthroughs of the New Wave generation, a generation of writers like A. B. Yehoshua, Amos Oz, and Amalia Kahana-Carmon. This generation sought to give voice to the individual and personal perspective, over against the collectivist desideratum of the previous Palmach generation of the 1940s and 1950s.

This sketch of Amichai's public or critical "persona" was strongly challenged by Amichai when I met him in person in 1981. I met Amichai in Jerusalem and completed my interview with him for my book, *Encounters with Israeli Authors,* in Austin, Texas, where I taught Hebrew literature as an assistant professor at the department of Oriental Studies. Certain biographical details seem to challenge the perception of Amichai as a native Israeli secularist author. For one thing, he was born in Wurtzburg (Bavaria) and immigrated with his parents to Israel at the age of 12, in 1936, during Hitler's ascent to power. He received an Orthodox education; his father, who appears as a central subject in his poetry, was an observant Jew. Amichai joined the British Brigade, and fought with the Haganah during the War of Independence of 1948. After that war, he was graduated from the Hebrew University in Jerusalem, having majored in Hebrew Literature and Bible. He taught in various colleges in Jerusalem and the US for over 40 years. Amichai has been widely translated, and he represented Israel in numerous international forums. In 1975, he won the Bialik award for literature, and in 1981 he was awarded the coveted Israel prize. In my interview with Amichai, I was struck by his consistent rejection of his public and critical persona. He insisted that he did not consider himself part of any aesthetic trend, or poetic coterie. He shied away from the critical consensus about his novel. He told me that the surrealistic juxtaposition of Germany and Israel, the past and the present, was a result of a simple personal experience. He was in love, he told me, with his childhood friend from Germany and as well as with the girl he describes as American. Because in reality one cannot love two women at the same time, he chose to bring the two together in fiction. Amichai dismissed his representation as a secularist ironic writer, arguing instead that he makes constant use of the Bible, Midrash, Siddur, and other traditional sources. Amichai refused to discuss his poetry as an art form. He argued that his poetry is neither a skill nor an art, but rather an expression of a basic need, the need for self-expression. He insisted that he was no poet, but rather "a man who writes poems." Amichai described his poetic activity as a sort of reporting on basic emotional responses to daily events. Just as children describe their emotions in terms of the outside world ("I love you like the whole world"), so he too has the need to describe his emotional responses in metaphoric terms, by using objective correlatives in the outside world.

When I pointed to the despair displayed in his so-called love poems, to a kind of disillusionment with heterosexual love as such, he told me that he usually wrote his poems as a summary of a particular phase in his life. When a person is in love, he told me, he does not analyze or reflect on it. He is too busy experiencing it. When the relationship is over, it is time to think about it and write about it.

Indeed, many of Amichai's love poems refer to the physical remains of love, to an impending separation, or to the results of an actual separation. In "What's it like to Feel a Woman," Amichai refers to the remains of seminal fluids in the body of a woman, and to the woman's remains on the male body. These remains "augur the hell" and the "mutual death" that awaits the lovers. Is the hell the yearning for the full erotic moment, the moment of love that is gone? Amichai does not usually offer information about the circumstances leading to the "mutual death" of the lovers, or to the termination of love relationships, because love in his poems seems ephemeral by definition. In "Once a Great Love," Amichai describes the termination of a love relationship as a violent cutting, which leaves half his body writhing and "twisting like a snake cut in two." The second stanza describes the abandoned lover as a man lost in the "Judean desert." The man remembers the woman, like one who notices the sign "Sea Level" in the middle of the desert. There is no sea, no sign of water or life, just like the woman's face that is no longer there. All that is left is a sign recalling another geological level, or a memory corresponding to another existential and experiential level. The metaphor of a violent cutting recurs in yet another love poem. But whereas this poem alludes to a voluntary separation, "A Pity, We Were Such a Good Invention" alludes to separation as a violent imposition by an outside social intrusion. "They amputated your thighs off my hips. As far as I am concerned they are all surgeons. All of them." The couple's divorce is depicted as a violent surgery. "They" is a general reference to other people who may have meddled in the couple's affairs, or who may have completed the legal transaction. "They" refers to a collective pressure that caused the couple to break up. Amichai indicts the separators as "surgeons" and "engineers"—the practical and lucrative professions that are here indicted for

their blindness to the more subtle expressions of love. Amichai uses the unlikely metaphor of a plane to capture the united couple, and the experience of flight to express their erstwhile happiness: "A pity. We were such a good and loving invention. / An airplane made from a man and a wife. / Wings and everything. / We hovered a little above the earth." The couple's divorce is presented in this poem as a violent cutting off of body parts from each other.

Love, whether marital or casual, is bound to end in Amichai's poetry, is bound to die. But its transitory nature cannot obscure its force. The metaphor for love here is an airplane; in another memorable poem, love is compared to the human struggle with a divine force. In "Jacob and the Angel," Amichai uses a Biblical allusion, Jacob's struggle with the mysterious messenger who changes his name from Jacob to Israel to frame a poem about casual love. The process of making love is described as a kind of struggle for playful supremacy. The lover does not know the girl's name, which he learns only when she is called "from upstairs." Jacob, in Genesis 32, is also named twice—his name is changed by the angel who wrestles with him. The use of the Biblical allusion serves a double purpose: on the one hand, it translates the heterosexual encounter into sacral terms. For the lovers, their fleeting moment is indeed sacred, despite its anonymity. On the other hand, the Biblical allusion undercuts the heterosexual encounter by juxtaposing it with a truly momentous encounter between the nation's progenitor and a divine emissary.

In the 1970s and 1980s, Amichai showed a continued predilection for privacy, pensiveness and sensuality, preferring a colloquial insularity to figurative and allusive discourse. The female love object in his poems nevertheless proclaims Amichai's belief in the validity of personal-subjective expression.

In my interview with Amichai, the poet insisted that he wrote poems because they gave him joy. He insisted that he was no professional poet. He objected to the tendency among other poets to philosophize about the poetic process, and to analyze or theorize upon it. He assured me that his poems were spontaneous responses to his personal experiences. Amichai objected to the modernist tendency to use difficult and figurative language. Nevertheless, as Chana Kronfeld demonstrates, Amichai's poetics of simplicity is often combined with aesthetic sophistication and artistic complexity. On the one hand, Amichai succeeded in "generating a truly popular poetic voice able to reach people in the work-a-day world." On the other hand, Amichai's iconoclastic and ironic approach to the traditional idiom and his use of classical allusion and syntactic fragmentation demonstrate his indebtedness to Anglo-American modernism. Amichai's poem "Once a Great Love" reflects the poet's use of incongruous imagery. The image of the snake in the first stanza does not correspond to the metaphor of the Sea Level sign. The juxtaposition of incongruities is even more salient in his poem "Half the People in the World." For the most part, Amichai uses paradigmatic sequencing in order to expose the irrational, arbitrary, and chaotic nature of modern life. In this sense he follows the modernist tradition, even when the break-up of logical progression renders his poems less readable.

Amichai's use of classical allusion also establishes him as a modernist poet. In his poem "Young David" he all but eliminates the story of David and Goliath recounted in 1 Samuel 17. Amichai's David is lonely among the fighters who celebrate his victory, fighters whose masculine swagger and vulgar camaraderie are reminiscent of the Palmach military camp. Where the Biblical David brings Goliath's head to King Saul as concrete proof of the victory he has accomplished, Amichai's David is at a loss about what to do with Goliath's head. Amichai's David is tired and despondent after his victory. The death of his enemy bothers him. He finds no joy in his military accomplishment. Amichai rewrites the Biblical David from a modern, Israeli, secular pacifist perspective. Amichai's David gives voice to the disenchanted individual soldier who remains alienated among his compatriots. Goliath's head lies heavy and superfluous in David's hands. The only literal allusion to the Biblical text is evoked in the "birds of blood" flying away from the battle scene, a subtle echo to the birds Goliath mentions in his taunting speech to David before their confrontation. As David Jacobson notes, "Yehuda Amichai challenges the adequacy of the David and Goliath myth as a basis for understanding the experience of fighting as a soldier in the Arab-Israeli wars." Amichai's Biblical allusions serve as a political critique of Israeli politics. These allusions, however, are multivalent and not always accessible.

In his poem "The Real Hero of the Sacrifice of Isaac," Amichai, contrary to the numerous traditional and modern interpretations of the Akedah, argues that the real hero of Genesis 22 is the ram. Neither Abraham, nor Isaac, nor the angel, nor even God is the true hero of the story. The shift from both human and divine agents to the animal is disconcerting. "The real hero of the sacrifice was the ram / Who had no idea about the conspiracy of the others. / He apparently volunteered to die in place of Isaac." How can a ram "volunteer" to die? The personification of the ram is extreme, and the detailed description of his killing and the production of "shofars" out of his horns deflate the sacral apotheosis that is usually associated with Rosh Hashanah. But to the religious artifact Amichai ties a military context. The "shofars" in the poem "sound the blast of their war"—in the famous antiwar poem of Amir Gilboa, "Isaac," it is the young generation of Israeli warriors who speak through Isaac's voice. Gilboa questioned the sacrifice of Israel's young generation by their fathers, the Zionist political elite that hailed from Europe. Amichai pushes this antiwar poem to further limits. The date of the poem's publication gives us a clue. The year 1982 was the date of the Lebanon war, the most controversial war in the history of the nation. Amichai uses the ram as a metaphor for the many innocent youths sacrificed during that war. If a ram can hardly "volunteer" to be sacrificed, so could the many young fighters hardly have volunteered to die. This volunteer-ism was imposed on them. "Thus, here Amichai is ironically undermining the Israeli army value of volunteerism in a war such as the Lebanon War which does not seem to be justified." Amichai transforms Abba Kovner's famous reference to Jews in the Holocaust who went to their deaths like "sheep to slaughter"—only in his poem the ram is the one who is slaughtered. "The angel went home / Isaac went home / And Abraham and God left much earlier. / But the real hero of the sacrifice / Is the ram."

Amichai's classical allusions are not easily accessible. Neither are his paradigmatic sequences, his combination of incongruities, his dissonant metaphors. Amichai's poetic signature, his ability to deflate sacral pieties, and to celebrate mundane experiences and ordinary reality also requires some interpretive effort. His use of modernist poetics suggests that he is indeed a self-conscious "poet"—the very label he was trying so hard to dispute. We may argue that Amichai is a marginal modernist, or even an anti-modernist, but he is a modernist nonetheless, and one of the leading Hebrew modernist poets of our time.

We began then with Amichai the "persona," we proceeded to investigate this "persona" through the medium of Amichai the "person," and proceeded to examine the "person" through the poet. How then should we approach Amichai, or, who is the "real" Amichai—the persona, the person, or the poet?

We have lost Amichai the person, but we have not lost the important critical corpus that has established him as one of Israel's most important poets. Above all, we have not lost the poet: Amichai's poems continue to be taught in Israeli schools, and selections from his books are required reading in the academe.

Amichai the poet then is not dead, and so while we mourn the death of the person, we give tribute to his lasting legacy and celebrate his poetic art.

Source: Esther Fuchs, "Remembering Yehuda Amichai: Homage to an Israeli Poet," in *Midstream*, Vol. 47, No. 4, May 2001, p. 27.

Gila Ramras-Rauch

In the following review of an updated version of The Selected Poetry of Yehuda Amichai, *Ramras-Rauch describes how Amichai "seduces his reader with . . . simplicity," while opening "a way into a more complex world."*

Yehuda Amichai's simple, beguiling, and challenging poetry continues to fascinate readers and translators alike. He is recognized in Israel and abroad for his seeming simplicity of tone, image, and syntax. The centrality of a speaker in Amichai's poetry inevitably reflects the man himself: a gentle, often self-effacing man whose soft voice is frequently in contrast with the bold statements his poems make.

Amichai uses known and familiar materials for his poetry: the images of Jerusalem, his parents, his loves, his children, the marketplace—all act as a storehouse of raw materials for his verse. These familiar materials however, are often left behind when his poetry, without warning, soars into a new verbal reality where paradox, irony, and a certain wonder coexist. In a way, Amichai seduces his reader with his blatant declarative simplicity. The almost prosaic opening allows for a way into a more complex world. His world of analogies, metaphysical conceits, images, and paradoxes changes proportions while still using everyday imagery.

Among other things, is Amichai a political poet? Is there a hidden agenda under his well-turned verse? Are political issues alluded to in his innocent apolitical poems? Amichai's antiwar sentiment has been there from the inception of his writing. On a personal level, for instance, his basic experience in the 1948 war and the death of his close friend Dicky mark Amichai's strong antiwar feeling. In the short cycle "Seven Laments for the War Dead" from *Behind All This a Great Happiness Is Hiding* he writes: "Dicky was hit. . . . But

he remained standing like that / in the landscape of my memory." The landscape of memory is but one resource for Amichai's warehouse inventory of images. Memory, time, history, people, smells—all float in his poetic orbit. Amichai is a perennial observer. As he says, his verse is haunted by hollow memories.

Amichai's poetry rejects his work as a guide to the perplexed. Love, a constant presence in his lyric work, touches on intimacy and his familiarity with the man-woman bond. At the same time, love is a concept tied to the Platonic idea of Love: Love that overcomes the physical, Love that transcends time, space, and causality. Amichai is bounded by the physicality of experience. Simultaneously, he aches to break away from the very matter that gives him his voice.

In this vein, in the attempt to transcend the expected and the causal, Amichai rejects a continuity of idea or stanza and opts for contiguity as a liberating mode. Simple words and complex notions merge. His poetry is strewn with road signs. The reader who is traversing the lines will, like a child in a drawing book, connect the dotted lines and thus create his or her own poetic map.

Amichai is fortunate to have had excellent translators into English—from Asia Gutman, to Chana Bloch, to Stephen Mitchell, to Benjamin and Barbara Harshav and others. The comprehensive selection *A Life of Poetry 1948–1994* appeared three years ago (1994; see *WLT* 69:2, p. 426). The current volume was first published in 1986 by Harper & Row. Updating that original, the present edition adds several excellent translations from Amichai's 1989 book *The Fist Too Was Once the Palm of an Open Hand and Fingers* (see *WLT* 65:1, p. 180), giving the reader another occasion to enjoy the work of a poet whose complex simplicity continues to challenge lovers of poetry.

Source: Gila Ramras-Rauch, Review of *The Selected Poetry of Yehuda Amichai*, in *World Literature Today*, Vol. 71, No. 2, Spring 1997, pp. 448–49.

Jeredith Merrin

In the following essay, Merrin provides an overview of Amichai's works, focusing on amalgamation and accessibility.

The contemporary Israeli poet Yehuda Amichai is enjoying renewed popularity in this country. What his widening readership can find in the poetry as well as Amichai's ventures into fiction' is a deliberate jumbling of the public and the private, the past and the present, this country and that country, the exalted and the mundane. In his world, wars become mixed up with love affairs; Isaiah mingles ironically with modern technology "the man under his fig tree telephoned the man under his vine"; the dead of Wurzburg, Germany (where Amichai was born in 1924) are seen again in contemporary Jerusalem; and, in one particularly startling move, the injunction of Genesis to "Be fruitful and multiply" gets absurdly associated, by way of sexual "sticky business," with "shaving cream." Here we have a writer of impurity, amalgamation, admixture. In this way, he is the opposite of the writer as alchemist, ceaselessly laboring in an hermetic cell to transmute base metals into gold. Amichai's work rejects preciousness in all senses committing itself to motley, unrefined reality. The poetry is strong as iron alloy is strong, and meant for everyday use.

Because of his conversational voice and his visual metaphors, Amichai translates well. His eleven books of poetry have been rendered into no fewer than twenty-nine languages including Afrikaans, Catalan, Chinese, Drentish (a Dutch dialect), Esperanto, German, Slovak, Urhobo (a Nigerian dialect), and Yiddish. My own Hebrew being limited, for the most part, to the Sabbath and Festival Prayer Book, I have had to rely on English versions. Comparing English versions of Amichai can be a frustrating task: many have tried their hands, and individual poems may make separate appearances under different titles in books more often than not out of print. On the whole, the most powerful and shapely renditions have been produced by (or in collaboration with) the English poet Ted Hughes, and by the American poets Chana Bloch and Stephen Mitchell in the *Selected Poetry of Yehuda Amichai,* which has just been reissued with new translations by the University of California Press. Quotations that follow are drawn primarily from Bloch and Mitchell—some of their translations along with Amichai's original Hebrew are included in this issue. When poems do not appear in *Selected Poetry,* or when lines have seemed to me arguably more forceful in Benjamin and Barbara Harshav's *Yehuda Amichai: A Life of Poetry, 1948–1994,* I have instead quoted from their more compendious collection.

Characterized by abrupt turns of thought and metaphors so far-fetched that they can recall Samuel Johnson's antipathetic description of English metaphysical poetry ("the most heterogeneous ideas are yoked by violence together"), Amichai's poetry nevertheless stays socially engaged and readily accessible. A story circulates that when

Amichai's work rejects preciousness in all senses committing itself to motley, unrefined reality. The poetry is strong as iron alloy is strong, and meant for everyday use."

Israeli university students were called up in the 1973 Yom Kippur War, each packed up his gear, a rifle, and a volume of Amichai's poems. And one can understand the ethics and emotional appeal of a writer just old enough to be a teenage soldier's father, who stands with impeccable pre–World War II Zionist credentials, and whose poetry speaks with an uneffete, commonsensical authority, particularly about the dilemmas and losses of war. It is not surprising to learn, then, that Amichai's books have been best sellers in Israel since the nineteen fifties; nor that he has shunned Tel Aviv cafe society, choosing to live instead in less arty, historically layered Jerusalem, where he is often seen carrying bags of fruits and vegetables from the marketplace. His stance is perhaps best summed up in one of his favorite expressions of value—used by him to describe the sort of language he prefers as well as to praise his favorite authors (among these, the Prophets; the medieval rabbi-poet Samuel Hanagid, who wrote out of a mixed Jewish and Arab culture during the Moorish reign in Spain; and the urbanely ironic and colloquial W. H. Auden): Yehuda Amichai is "down to earth." "God's hand is in the world / like my mother's hand in the guts of the slaughtered chicken / on Sabbath eve," he tells us; and "doubts and loves / dig up the world / like a mole, a plow."

In a 1992 Paris Review interview, Amichai tells a story about how, during his World War II service in a Palestinian unit of the British army (his family having immigrated to Palestine in 1936), he first came into contact with modern English poetry—an incident quite literally "down to earth":

> Between 1944 and 1946 we did a lot of underground work—smuggling arms and Jewish immigrants into what was then Palestine. We began preparing, on a small scale, for a Jewish state—we were actually

preparing for a new conflict while the one we were in was fading away. One event in Egypt had an extremely important impact on my life. It was in 1944, I think, we were somewhere out in the Egyptian desert. The British had these mobile libraries for their soldiers, but, of course, most of the British soldiers, being from the lower classes and pretty much uneducated, didn't make much use of the libraries. It was mostly us Palestinians who used them—there we were, Jews reading English books while the English didn't. There had been some kind of storm, and one of the mobile libraries had overturned into the sand, ruining or half-ruining most of the books. We came upon it, and I started digging through the books, and came upon a book, a Faber anthology of modern British poetry—the first time I read Eliot and Auden, for example, who became very important to me. I discovered them in the Egyptian desert, in a half-ruined book. The book had an enormous impact on me—I think that was when I began to think seriously about writing poetry.

With this episode the older Amichai, retrospectively proud of his military exploits and upper-class education, presents for the literary/historical record a self-epitomizing image: a young Zionist soldier-reader, groping in foreign sand for the secular, poetic word. And the text unearthed is not in Egyptian hieroglyphics or ancient Hebrew, but self-consciously modernist, twentieth–century English. Ironically (and Amichai is a great relisher of ironies), this digging excavates a future instead of a past: Amichai will produce his own brand of modern poetry—a mixture that stirs together Biblical Hebrew and phrases from the diasporan siddur with a newly evolving, spoken Hebrew suddenly called upon to accommodate the new nouns and new realities of cars and ketchup, Pepsi-Cola and tanks:

> Caught in a homeland-trap: To talk now in this tired tongue, Torn out of its sleep in the Bible: blinded, It totters from mouth to mouth. In a tongue that described Miracles and God, now to say: automobile, bomb, God.

Amichai's self-described "mixed sensibility," then, merges with and emerges from the historical occasion that was the birth of the modern Jewish state and the reawakening of the Hebrew tongue. It is Amichai's genius as a writer to have seized this moment in Jewish history as a literary opportunity and to have seen in his own personal history a microcosm of Israeli national experience:

> When I was young, the whole country was young. And my father was everyone's father. When I was happy, the country was happy too, and when I jumped on her, she jumped under me. The grass that covered her in spring softened me too, and the dry earth of summer hurt me like my own cracked footsoles. When I first fell in love, they proclaimed her independence, and when my hair fluttered in the breeze,

so did her flags. When I fought in the war, she fought, when I got up she got up too, and when I sank she began to sink with me.

In its egocentricity, exuberant and unabashed, its revolutionary energy, and its evocation of youthful accord with a responsive, feminized Nature, these opening lines of "When I Was Young, the Whole Country Was Young" recall, of course, Wordsworth's Romantic posture—and particularly Book XI of *The Prelude,* in which Wordsworth, recounting the optimism and excitement surrounding his first exposure to the French Revolution, famously exclaims, "Bliss was it in that dawn to be alive, / But to be young was very Heaven!" Yet the overall arc of Amichai's lyric is not Wordsworthian but self-consciously anti-Romantic, swerving as it does from the heroic to the humdrum, from the blithe to the blighted, with an unmistakable ironic undertow and with characteristic insistence on prosaic, pathos-deflating ordinariness. Here is the poem's final stanza:

> Afterward I bought myself some non-kosher salami and two bagels, and I walked home. I managed to hear the evening news and ate and lay down on the bed and the memory of my first love came back to me like the sensation of falling just before sleep.

Anti-heroism, reduced expectations, undercutting of what at first had seemed universal and absolute, with a sense of fragmentation and individual isolation: this poem, so self-consciously about "sinking" and "falling," is very much in line with Western iconoclastic writing of the nineteen fifties. "When I was young" is at the same time a markedly idiosyncratic and local incarnation of modernist tropes and dilemmas, a specifically Jewish work that takes stock of four decades of life in the "Promised Land."

The poem is enriched if one has read Amichai's earlier writing, where the analogy is repeatedly drawn between his beloved orthodox father (dead of a heart attack at sixty-three, at the very commencement of Amichai's writing career) and God the Father; or if one is aware that, like so many of his generation of pioneer Zionists, the young Amichai repudiated orthodoxy; or if one happens to know that when the family immigrated from Germany, Amichai's father and uncle opened a small factory in which they made salami sausages. What is ironically evoked in the last stanza, then, as the speaker goes home with his solitary meal of "non-kosher salami," is not only a dissolution of the original, Edenic reciprocity of speaker and country, but also a personal cum national turn away from kashrut and religious orthodoxy, as that orthodoxy was embodied by the previous, largely European generation ("my father was everyone's father").

Religious rebellion is never, however, a settled issue. And it reenacts itself throughout Amichai's poetry, which obsessively conjures up the figure of the simultaneously revered and rebelled-against father, and which repeatedly alludes to sacred texts in order to expose—sometimes with nostalgia, more often with some blend of worldly cynicism and good-natured humor—the gap between what we might think of as the Old Word and the New World. As just one example of this allusive practice, here from another poem is this soldier-poet's sardonic commentary on a phrase from the traditional Memorial Service:

> God-full-of-Mercy, the prayer for the dead. If God was not full of mercy, Mercy would have been in the world, Not just in him.

Irreverent as they are, Amichai's frequent textual commentary and reinterpretation are in the tradition of Rashi and other Talmudic commentators. His ambivalent and argumentative stance puts him, as Amichai himself acknowledges, squarely in the tradition, too, of Abraham and Job: "I think my sense of history and God, even if I am against history and God, is very Jewish. I think this is why my poems are sometimes taught in religious schools. It's an ancient Jewish idea to fight with God, to scream out against God."

The unresolved family quarrel throughout "When I was young" is not only with God the Father, but also with the modern Jewish nation that for Amichai's generation seemed to promise a utopian community, but that ended up—as of course it had to end up—as one more morally culpable nation among other culpable nations. When this advocate of the land-for-peace settlement (and former Haganah commando) writes, "I managed to hear the evening news," he is evoking the commonplace close of an ordinary day; but he is also inviting his reader to imagine hearing what he no doubt heard: the next in what seems to be an interminable series of news reports about Arab-Israeli mutual mistrust and violence. Since the early, heady days of socialist idealism, Israel and her writers perforce have dealt with guilt and with all the grubby pragmatics of nationhood; reluctantly, they have had to come down to earth. It is a resigned, world-weary, but residually romantic speaker who goes to sleep at the end of the poem with only "the memory" of his first love.

Amichai has written a remarkable number of poems having to do with the erotic life: it is almost (as others have remarked) as though, having given up on religion, the poet made an absolute value out of love. Almost, but not quite—because nothing in Amichai's gallimaufry of a world is allowed to stand as absolute or unadulterated. The love poems are elegiac as well as earthy; the speaker looks back, sad-eyed yet ruefully smiling, on sexual experiences now inextricably intertwined for him with limitation and loss. Here, for example, from his 1963–1968 volume *Now in the Din Before the Silence,* is the brief love poem "Pity, We Were a Good Invention":

> They amputated Your thighs from my waist. For me they are always Surgeons. All of them.
>
> They dismantled us One from another. For me they are engineers. Pity. We were a good and loving Invention: an airplane made of man and woman, Wings and all: We soared a bit from the earth, We flew a bit.

Some cruel and unspecified "They" have sundered the harmless lovers, but there is in any case something endearingly impossible about the lovers' hopeful "Invention," just as there is something endearingly impossible about every lover's dream of overleaping all obstacles. Even before the baneful interference, these two managed to get off the ground only "a bit"—the counterforce of reality always tugging their quixotic flying machine back down to earth, toward disillusion and dissolution. The scientific or technological language—"amputated," "surgeons," "dismantled," "engineers," "Invention," "airplane"—is fresh and unsettling in the context of sexual love; the poet seems something of a surgeon himself as he cuts up syntax into neat, brief units. This extreme terseness is a little frightening, suggesting both the zombie-like numbness of the victim and possibly even identification to some extent with the oppressor. The result here as elsewhere in Amichai is a complex tone, mixing helplessness and assertiveness, feyness and frisson, affection and anger, woefulness and whimsy.

From the beginning of his writing career Amichai's love poetry has inclined toward the pessimistic and worldly. In this, if not in sexual preference, Amichai follows his most important English model, W. H. Auden, who also composed modernist love poems in a wartime setting—among them the beautiful and frequently anthologized "Lullabye" (1937), which begins: "Lay your sleeping head, my love, / Human on my faithless arm." Amichai has composed a number of Audenesque lullabies. His "Lullaby 1957" borrows Auden's ballad-like stanza and incorporates colloquial language and everyday urban imagery reminiscent of Auden. Here is its concluding quatrain:

Let us fall asleep. In the dark corridor The electric
meter will go on Keeping score, all night, Always
awake, and we shall not worry.

In Auden's case (in "Lullabye" and elsewhere), the use of present tense is a means of holding on to the ephemeral moment and drawing a
wishful, charmed circle around the lovers—
threatened from within by the expectation of ho-
mosexual infidelity and from without by social
disorder and hostility. Amichai tries, much less successfully, for a similar effect: his "Keeping score"
has a forced cleverness, and the uncharacteristic
present and future tenses give him trouble. Amichai
in his own voice is almost always a love poet of
the past tense, of "we were" rather than "we are."
But it must also be noted that "Lullaby 1957"
clearly suffers in translation, as do others of
Amichai's earlier and more formally traditional
verses, and that the Hebrew text has a wider effective range of tenses.

A predilection for the distant perspective is
bound up with Amichai's most telling difference
from Auden: his use of love poetry as a field for
specifically Jewish reenactment, rebellion, and ru-
mination on history. Frequently juxtaposing erotic
descriptions and religious texts, Amichai tweaks
the law of the father(s) and brings the spiritual
realm abruptly and often shockingly down to earth.
At the same time, he points to the ephemerality of
sexual bonding, its flimsiness as a substitute for religious belief. Here, for instance, is a passage describing a sensual, skewed Sabbath (black instead
of white, despairing rather than renewing) from
Amichai's longest poem (some forty-two pages),
"The Travels of the Last Benjamin of Tudela."
Words in quotation come from Lecha Dodi, the familiar, beautiful hymn for welcoming the Sabbath
as a metaphorical bride:

> This could have been a song of praise to the sweet,
> imaginary God of my childhood. It happened on Fri-
> day, and black angels filled the Valley of the Cross,
> and their wings were black houses and abandoned
> quarries. Sabbath candles bobbed up and down like
> ships at the entrance to a harbor. "Come O bride,"
> wear the clothes of your mourning and your splen-
> dor from the night when you thought I wouldn't come
> to you and I came. The room was drenched in the
> fragrance of syrup from black, intoxicating cherries.
> Newspapers, scattered on the floor, rustled below and
> the flapping wings of the hemlock above. Love with
> parting, like a record with applause at the end of the
> music, love with a scream, love with a mumble of
> despair at walking proudly into exile from each other.
> Come O bride, hold in your hand something made of
> clay at the hour of sunset, because flesh vanishes and
> iron doesn't keep. . . .

Amichai's intermingling of the sensual and
spiritual recalls strategies of metaphysical poets
such as John Donne, but the Anglican metaphysical and the Jewish modernist own very different
poetic projects. In his early love poems, Donne
spiritualizes sex; his later, religious poems sexual-
ize the sacred, making religious subject matter concrete and apprehensible. Donne's transposition of
phrases and images may be lewd or pious, silly or
psychologically tortured: always, Donne is showy,
and always his work situates itself within an orthodox Christian context. Amichai's admixtures of
the sacred and the sexual can be as flamboyant, but
they are un-Donneish in their post-existential reg-
istration of both religious and romantic inadequacy.

Perhaps because Amichai is underscoring a
philosophical point, in his love poetry whom we
meet is not so much this or that woman as all
women, the abstract Female. Whether or not
Amichai's poems echo individual encounters, dis-
concertingly, the women encountered remain on
the whole voiceless and faceless, the speaker's
emotions not much different toward each one, and
each subsumed under the rubric of Love-That-Had-
To-Be-Lost. Here are the concluding lines of a lyric
from Amichai's 1989 book, *From Man You Came
and to Man You Shall Return:*

> I'm still inside the room. Two days from now I will
> see it from the outside only, The closed shutter of
> your room where we loved one another And not all
> mankind.

And here are lines from a poem in his
1963–1968 collection:

> And to be alone is to be in a place Where we were
> never together, and to be alone is To forget you are
> like this: to want to pay for two In a bus and travel
> alone.

We know in each case that the speaker is feeling woebegone, yet his voice participates in, even
precipitates, the distancing that pains him. Because
we are allowed to see his experience "from the outside only," the grief in these poems remains iconic,
generalized, at some emotional remove; nor do we
know anything in particular about the woman
whose presence the speaker mourns. This tonal
sameness and this blurring of otherness arise from
Amichai's more or less conceptually constant, if
metaphorically various, treatment of love. It makes
sense, of course, to internalize God as a concept to
be turned over and over in the mind while the concept remains essentially unchanged; it likewise
makes sense that a dead father would become in-
ternalized and fixed in time, so that scenarios re-
play or repeat with limited variation. But there is

something discomfiting about this recording of one lost love after another in which the speaker never (or hardly ever) appears to come into contact with a separate and unique individual as densely specific as himself. To harp on this last point might become dreary, humorless (the last things one wants to appear in the presence of a master of tragicomedy), but it remains a disappointment in work otherwise marked by uncompromising complexity.

The voice of an Amichai poem—we might be able to spot even an unattributed Amichai—comes to us with a tone at once funny and sad, fanciful and commonsensical, sweet and bitter, fluid and laconic. What makes the diverse elements cohere is a somehow recognizably Jewish and Israeli variety of irony, at once lugubrious and tough-minded. If Amichai quarrels with his diasporan fathers, he does so—ironically—by borrowing their method of coping and their tone of voice. Indeed, he sees himself as adopting the voice and view of his own father: "Irony is integral to my poetry. Irony is, for me, a kind of cleaning material. I inherited a sense of humor and irony from my father, who always used humor and irony as a way of clarifying, clearing, cleaning the world around him. Irony is a way of focusing, unfocusing and focusing again always trying to see another side. That's the way I see, that's the way I think and feel, that's the way I live—focusing and refocusing and juxtaposing different shifting and changing perspectives."

A capacity for entertaining multiple perspectives and an attempt "to see another side" may be, in the end, the only hope for peace, in the Middle East, or anywhere—which is why Amichai's particular deployment of humor and irony carries a certain amount of political as well as poetic freight. In section five of "Jerusalem, 1967," a long poem emerging from the experience of the Six-Day War, Amichai (whose father, previous to his Israeli incarnation as a sausage-maker, had been a wholesale distributor of tailoring goods in Germany) shows us how possible and yet impossible it is to make a human connection with someone on "another side":

> On Yom Kippur in 1967, the Year of Forgetting, I put on my dark holiday clothes and walked to the Old City of Jerusalem For a long time I stood in front of an Arab's hole-in-the-wall shop, not far from the Damascus Gate, a shop with buttons and zippers and spools of thread in every color and snaps and buckles. A rare light and many colors, like an open Ark.
>
> I told him in my heart that my father too had a shop like this, with thread and buttons. I explained to him in my heart about all the decades and the causes and

> the events, why I am now here and my father's shop was burned there and he is buried here.
>
> When I finished, it was time for the Closing of the Gates prayer. He too lowered the shutters and locked the gate and I returned, with all the worshipers, home.

This long noncommunication, which conjoins the incompatible elements of irony and prayer, takes place in a surprising and generous image in front of a homely "Ark of the Covenant," a cluttered Arab tailor's shop in the Shuk. The phrase "all the worshipers" may be read as wishful thinking, encompassing Arab and Jew alike, humanity in general. Yet the speaker here, in spite of his somewhat self-congratulatory and sentimental assertion that he stood "For a long time," comes across as someone realistic, someone who regretfully concedes the division between Arab and Jew brought about by "all the decades" of irrevocable "causes and events." He returns to his home in the still-embattled city together with the worshipers who are Jewish. What the shop/"Ark" has on display, we notice, are small, assorted inventions for closing more easily repaired rents or gaps than that between the shopkeeper and the Yom Kippur worshiper: needles and thread, buttons and zippers and snaps. But the poem reminds us that wishful thinking alone cannot join what history has separated.

The refusal to proffer simplistic solutions: Amichai's speaker here and in most poems is a man who, despite wide-ranging experience and an astringent intelligence, finds himself, like most of us most of the time, morally troubled and perplexed. And the most perplexing subject for this poet/speaker is the significance of Jewish history. On the one hand, history is clearly the wellspring of his humane art and the source of his most effective metaphors. On the other hand, history is, as Amichai himself acknowledges, the ultimate cause of the ongoing inhumanity that he abhors. In the following passage, for instance, the poet's wry genealogical metaphors come out of and comment on an extensive history of sufferings and reprisals (the phrase "eye to eye" wearily echoing the Old Testament edict of "an eye for an eye"):

> Joy has no parents. No joy ever learns from the one before, and it dies without heirs. But sorrow has a long tradition, handed down from eye to eye, from heart to heart.

"I hate war," Amichai has said, "So I hate history."

It is unsurprising, then, that one of Amichai's most accomplished volumes of poetry is entitled simply *Time;* unsurprising, too, that one of his best single poems takes up the time-obsessed book of

> *It is no accident that the psalmic strains of his poetry translate as well as they do."*

Ecclesiastes, which Amichai has praised as "a great, great poem of human despair." In "A Man Doesn't Have Time," Amichai characteristically argues with and even parodies the passage that begins "For everything there is a season, and a time for every matter under heaven." The poem's opening lines:

> A man doesn't have time to have time for everything. He doesn't have seasons enough to have a season for every purpose. Ecclesiastes was wrong about that. A man needs to love and to hate at the same moment, to laugh and cry with the same eyes, with the same hands to cast away stones and to gather them, to make love in war and war in love. And to hate and forgive and remember and forget, to set in order and confuse, to eat and digest what history takes years and years to do.

This is as good a description of the mixed world of Amichai's poetry as we are likely to get—set down in a straightforward manner by a man of many words whose writing somehow manages to retain the authority of a man of few words; by a Jew who wrestles with his history and his God; by a poet whose aesthetic and ethical project is both "to set in order and confuse."

Source: Jeredith Merrin, "Yehuda Amichai: Down to Earth," in *Judaism*, Vol. 45, No. 3, Summer 1996, pp. 287–98.

Mark Rudman

In the following review, Rudman praises the universal reach of Amichai's voice and vision.

Yehuda Amichai is by now one of the half-dozen leading poets in the world. He has found a voice that speaks across cultural boundaries and a vision so sure that he can make the conflicts of the citizen soldier in modern Israel stand for those of humankind. What happens to the self in his poems reverberates through the body politic. Amichai's wit is also considerable; he can say virtually anything and give his words enough sting to defuse both sentimentality and hyperbole:

> if I pull out the stopper
> after pampering myself in the bath,
> I'm afraid that all of Jerusalem, and with it the
> whole world,
> will drain out into the huge darkness.
> ("You Musn't Show Weakness")

Amichai's work is governed by a single trope: the body is the world body—alive, sensual, fleshy—and in it the private and the public come together for better:

> When you do nice things to me
> all the heavy industries shut down.
> ("Poems for a Woman")

and for worse:

> They amputated
> your thighs from my hips.
> As far as I'm concerned, they're always
> doctors. All of them.
> ("A Pity. We Were Such a Good Invention")

Assia Gutmann, in her earlier translation of the poem above, had used the word "surgeons" for "doctors" ("They are all surgeons. All of them."), and the sense and syntax of her lines retain a striking accusatory music.

Translation is a matter of coincidence. Translators don't seek the right word so much as the spirit of the phrase. If they are lucky they will find a style that corresponds to that of the original text. In the case of Marquez, for instance, the immediate resource is Faulkner; in the case of Neruda and Vallejo, it is Whitman. In Yehuda Amichai's case, it is the Bible, notably the Psalms and the Song of Songs. It is no accident that the psalmic strains of his poetry translate as well as they do.

Another reason Amichai's poetry translates well is that his imagery, drawn as it is from myth, history and common experience, unlocks a world that is not the property or domain of one language: "Children move with the footsteps of someone else's grief / as if picking their way through broken glass" ("Seven Laments for the War-Dead"). But there are many layers of irony and allusion that are lost when we abandon "a language that once described / miracles and God' and is now made "to say car, bomb, God' ("National Thoughts").

Other writers have managed this transformation of the self and its language, but they have done so mainly in epic forms: Blake in the "Prophetic Books," Joyce, Williams in Paterson, Olson in the Maximus Poems. This method of metaphor in which the body becomes the world body allows Amichai to be quick, lyrical and cryptic, yet still make larger outward connections. In fact, he cannot avoid it, and envisions his life turned into a revolving door. A private man forced to wear a public mask, he sings of division. Yet the strain he feels in his life does not come across as strain in his work.

> All the days of his life my father tried to make a man of me,
> so that I'd have a hard face like Kosygin and Brezhnev,
> like generals and admirals and stockbrokers and financiers,
> all the unreal fathers I've established
> instead of my father . . .
> I have to screw onto my face the expression of a hero
> like a lightbulb screwed into the grooves of its hard socket,
> to screw in and to shine.
> ("Travels of the Last Benjamin of Tudela")

As we can see from this wry self-portrait, Amichai knows how to leaven hard truths with humor.

But Amichai embraces the public sphere only through the self. In an early poem he compares his life to Venice: everything that is streets in others is "love, dark and flowing" in him. He submits all of his experiences to the pressure and presence of love before they can make their way into a poem. In this way he has, and no mean feat this, reclaimed the genre of the love poem for serious poetry. Personal without being private, serious without being solemn, he seeks relief and ease through the balm of love, writes as a man motivated to "go out to all [his] wars" and come back on account of love.

Amichai adopts a prophetic tone with remarkable ease. "He doesn't have seasons enough to have / a season for every purpose," he writes in "A Man Doesn't Have Time." When we speak of Biblical simplicity, we are really talking about a manner of address, a certain directness. Amichai has always been able to speak directly rather than employ metaphors for his thoughts. Metaphors are contained within the body of his poems rather than serving as a casement for them. His poems begin where most poems end. He begins without a mask, with the screen torn off and the scream in its place:

> Now that I've come back, I'm screaming again.
> And at night, stars rise like the bubbles of the drowned,
> and every morning I scream the scream of a new-born baby
> at the tumult of houses and at all this huge light.
> ("Jerusalem, 1967")

Amichai has been blessed in his translators: Assia Gutmann, Ted Hughes, Harold Schimmel, Ruth Nevo and now Chana Bloch and Stephen Mitchell. They have all ably conveyed the concrete particulars of his world, but Bloch and Mitchell get inside the text and render a subtler, more complex and formally expert Amichai than we have seen before in English. Many people who know both Hebrew and English well think that the Mitchell/Bloch translation is excellent and that it supersedes the earlier translations, but those of use who have been reading Amichai since the first translations appeared find it difficult to shake off their authority. There's a world of difference in the placement of a word. Assia Gutmann translated a line in one of his most memorable lyrics as "Hair dark above his thoughts," which isolates in an uncanny way the hair from the head, locates the source of the thoughts in the brain beneath the hair, turns the physical perception into an image of the character's psychological and spiritual condition and, in doing so, interprets the "thoughts" for us:

> Out of three or four in a room
> One is always standing at the window.
> Hair dark above his thoughts.
> ("Out of Three or Four in a Room")

Stephen Mitchell's version returns us to the thing itself, "his dark hair above his thoughts." [Emphasis added.] Gutmann's image stresses displacement, isolation; Mitchell's version—and he uses a comma after the preceding line instead of a period—stresses continuity of being in the world, ordinariness.

Reading the *Selected Poetry,* it occurred to me that Amichai's poetry resembles the work of James Wright more than that of any other contemporary American poet. Both poets are able to submerge their imaginations in momentary events; both root their poems in specific places (Israel, the Midwest) and move from the anecdotal to the universal; both use a narrative voice but write lyrics rather than narrative poems; both explore the possibilities of poetry through contexts and placement. They share the capacity to speak directly while retaining an eerie edge to what they say—and unsay. In Wright:

> The carp are secrets
> Of the creation: I do not
> Know if they are lonely.
> The poachers drift with an almost frightening
> Care under the bridge.
> ("Lifting Illegal Nets by Flashlight")

> America,
> Plunged into the dark furrows
> Of the sea again.
> ("Stages on a Journey Westward")

In Amichai:

> Jerusalem, the only city in the world
> where the right to vote is granted even to the dead.
> ("Jerusalem, 1967")

Dicky was hit.
Like the water tower at Yad Mordekhai.
Hit. A hole in the belly. Everything
came flooding out.
                    ("Seven Laments for the War-Dead")

Amichai, longing to be released from the burden of memory at the end of a long incantation in "Songs of Zion the Beautiful," pleads: "Let all of them [the scrolls, the flags, the beasts, the birds] remember so that I can rest." It is our good fortune that he is not likely to be granted his wish.

Source: Mark Rudman, Review of *The Selected Poetry of Yehuda Amichai*, in *Nation*, Vol. 243, December 6, 1986, pp. 646–48.

Sources

Amichai, Yehuda, "Not like a Cypress," in *The Selected Poetry of Yehuda Amichai*, edited and translated by Chana Bloch and Stephen Mitchell, University of California Press, 1996, pp. 12–13.

Bloch, Chana, "Wrestling with the Angel of History: The Poetry of Yehuda Amichai," in *Judaism*, Vol. 45, No. 3, Summer 1996, pp. 298–300.

Gunderson, Elizabeth, Review of *A Life of Poetry: 1948–1994*, in *Booklist*, Vol. 91, No. 3, October 1, 1994, p. 230.

Ramras-Rauch, Gila, Review of *A Life of Poetry: 1948–1994*, in *World Literature Today*, Vol. 69, No. 2, Spring 1995, pp. 426–27.

——, Review of *The Selected Poetry of Yehuda Amichai*, in *World Literature Today*, Vol. 71, No. 2, Spring 1997, p. 448.

Review of *A Life of Poetry: 1948–1994*, in *Publishers Weekly*, Vol. 241, No. 35, August 29, 1994, p. 66.

Rudman, Mark, Review of *The Selected Poetry of Yehuda Amichai*, in *Nation*, Vol. 243, December 6, 1986, p. 646.

Tamopolsky, N., "Visiting the Poet of Jerusalem," in *Forward*, Vol. 97, No. 31,020, March 24, 1995, p. 10.

Further Reading

Abramson, Glenda, ed., *The Experienced Soul: Studies in Amichai*, Westview Press, 1997.

Amichai, who has taught at universities all over the world and whose work is studied at major international schools, is considered the most important Hebrew writer of the twentieth century. In this book, Amichai authorities from major universities in various countries examine the poet's work and discuss his major themes and influences. The result is a comprehensive scholarly overview of Amichai's significant body of work.

Hirsch, Edward, *How to Read a Poem: And Fall in Love with Poetry*, Harcourt Brace, 1999.

Whether readers are new to poetry or not, Hirsch's book can enlighten them about the reading of poems. Hirsch knows his material well and teaches others to recognize the beauty in poetry.

Munk, Michael L., *The Wisdom in the Hebrew Alphabet*, Artscroll, 1986.

Hebrew is an ancient language in which each letter of the alphabet contains symbolism. Letter combinations form more than words. There are hidden meanings. This book is a beginner's guide to those meanings.

Sacharov, Eliyahu, *Out of the Limelight: Events, Operations, Missions, and Personalities in Israeli History*, Gefen Publishing House, 2004.

Sacharov's book has been called the untold story of how the state of Israel was formed. Sacharov was instrumental in the foundation of the state, and he tells the story with authority.

Warren, Bargad, and Stanley F. Chyet, eds., *No Sign of Ceasefire: An Anthology of Contemporary Israeli Poetry*, Scirball Cultural Center, 2002.

Readers who want to familiarize themselves with late-twentieth-century and early-twenty-first-century Israeli poets should start with this collection. Poets include Leah Aini, Erez Biton, Admiel Kosman, and Rivka Miriam.

One Is One

Marie Ponsot
1998

The poem "One Is One" was published in Marie Ponsot's fifth collection of poetry in her more than fifty-year-long career of writing. Long spans of time seem to pass between her publications, but this does not dampen the public's interest in her work. Ponsot's fan base has been growing. A possible reason is that Ponsot's poems are very accessible, and "One Is One" is a prime example. Her themes are universal, and her language is simple and clear. As she grapples with her emotions in an attempt to control them, she reveals her vulnerability, something to which most readers can relate. The poem's uncluttered lines etch a path, leading to a destination that is not revealed until the very last phrases in the final stanza. The poem takes readers on a quiet journey that they do not even realize they are on until the poet forces them to look at themselves. "One Is One" is collected in the book *The Bird Catcher* (1998), which won one of the most prestigious poetry awards in the United States, the 1998 National Book Critics Circle Award.

Author Biography

Marie Ponsot was born in Queens, a borough of New York City, in 1921. She has said that she never thought she would be a teacher because there were so many of them already in her family. She also never thought she would be a mother. But Ponsot has spent most of her life teaching, and she is the mother of seven children. One thing that has been

Marie Ponsot © AP/Wide World

consistent in her life, however, is her love of poetry. When she was a child, her mother would scoot
her outside to play with the other children. Ponsot
has confessed that although she obeyed her mother,
her real desire was to return, as soon as possible,
to the many books of poetry that lay about the family home. Her love of poetry was encouraged by
her grandmother, who kept scrapbooks filled with
poems and often recited them for every special occasion, including the setting of the sun each day.

Ponsot published her first book of poems, *True
Minds,* in 1956. She was already the mother of five.
Thirteen years later, her husband, the French
painter Claude Ponsot, abandoned the poet and her
children. Although Ponsot continued to write poetry, her main focus during that time was on rais-
ing her children, which also meant providing the
money to buy their food. She worked as a translator for many years, having learned to speak and
read French from her years of living in that country as a newlywed. Then, despite the fact that she
thought she would never want to teach, Ponsot
landed a job teaching composition at Queens College. These were by no means poetry classes that
she taught. They were more like remedial writing
classes, but she loved them. It would not be until
many years later that she would teach poetry at Columbia University, where she maintains her adjunct
professor status in the early twenty-first century.

After Ponsot turned sixty, a friend urged her
to collect her poems and find a publisher. The result was the book *Admit Impediment* (1981). A few
years later, in 1988, she published another collection, *The Green Dark. The Bird Catcher* (1998), in
which the poem "One Is One" was published, won
the National Book Critics Circle Award for poetry.
In 2002, she published the collection *Springing*,
which contains poems that represent all Ponsot's
years of writing. Ponsot has taught writing at the
Beijing United University in China, at the Poetry
Center at the 92nd Street Y in New York, and at
New York University. She has won the Delmore
Schwartz Memorial Prize as well as the Shaugh-
nessy Medal of the Modern Language Association.
In 2005, she was awarded the Frost Medal from the
Poetry Society of America.

Poem Text

Heart, you bully, you punk, I'm wrecked, I'm
    shocked
stiff. You? you still try to rule the world—though
I've got you: identified, starving, locked
in a cage you will not leave alive, no
matter how you hate it, pound its walls,   5
& thrill its corridors with messages.

Brute. Spy. I trusted you. Now you reel & brawl
in your cell but I'm deaf to your rages,
your greed to go solo, your eloquent
threats of worse things you (knowing me) could   10
    do.
You scare me, bragging you're a double agent

since jailers are prisoners' prisoners too.
Think! Reform! Make us one. Join the rest of us,
and joy may come, and make its test of us.

Poem Summary

Stanza 1

In the first line of Ponsot's poem "One Is One,"
the speaker identifies her subject. The first word in
the poem is "heart." She refers to her heart throughout the poem in two different ways: the physical
heart that lives in her chest, the organ that is so vital in keeping her alive, and the symbolic heart that
represents her emotions.

In the first line, the heart that she speaks to is
clearly related more to her emotions, because she
is, in essence, cursing it. "You bully, you punk,"
she yells at it. This is an emotional response,

possibly stemming from the speaker's own frustrations between her emotions and her rational thoughts. The speaker feels "wrecked" and "shocked / stiff." She is shocked, but not as she might have been in any other dispute. This one has shocked her stiff. This image of a stiff body conjures up someone close to death, possibly holding her breath, her body locked as if lifeless.

In the second line, the speaker questions the heart: "You?" Of course, this could also be directed at more than just her heart. It is difficult to determine that. She could be referring to the person or thing that has caused her emotions to flare. Either way, the speaker is obviously angry at this "you." "You still try to rule the world." Her emotions sound as if they are out of control, and it is she— the rational part of her—who wants to be the ruler or, at the least, to share the rule.

At the end of the second line, the last word "though," together with a dash, promises a surprise in the next line, which the speaker is very eager to supply. "I've got you," she declares. She has identified her adversary, and she has it (her heart) "starving, locked / in a cage you will not leave alive." The cage, on a physical level, represents the ribs. The heart, of course, is encaged inside the speaker's body. But the word "starving" implies a more emotional stance. The speaker suggests that she will starve her emotions, not allowing any more circumstances that will arouse feeling.

In the fifth and sixth lines, the image is that of a prisoner who is fighting against his captors. But it is also the image of the heart beating inside a body, as the "you" in the poem pounds on the walls and thrills "its corridors with messages."

Stanza 2

The poet begins the second stanza yelling: "Brute. Spy. I trusted you." In the middle of the third line of the second stanza, she accuses her heart of wanting "to go solo." She is also aware of "threats of worse things you (knowing me) could do." In other words, the speaker knows that even though she has the heart encaged, she is still not really in control. She is vulnerable to her heart. She relies on it. On a physical level, she relies on her heart for life. On a psychological or emotional level, she relies on her emotions to bring meaning and color to her life. This vulnerability can be frightening. "You scare me," the speaker says in line 11.

The last phrase in the second stanza, "a double agent," leaves the reader hanging, as exemplified by the lack of punctuation at the end of the line and the space that is placed between it and the remaining part of the sentence that begins the third stanza. The reader is left to ponder what the speaker means by "double agent."

Stanza 3

The answer to the puzzle that the speaker presents at the end of stanza 2 is quickly supplied in the first line of stanza 3: "since jailers are prisoner's prisoners too." Jailers must all but live in the prisons they run, and they are forced to deal with criminals all through the day and night. The two elements, prisoner and jailer, are brought together as a tightly connected unit. They are at the same time separate and tied together. The speaker continues, in the second line of stanza 3, with the commands: "Think! Reform! Make us one." What is not clear, however, is to whom the speaker is referring. Is she still addressing the heart? Whomever she is talking to (possibly even to herself), the essence of the message is that two seemingly opposing sides must learn to work together.

"Join the rest of us," the speaker says at the end of the second line of stanza 3. Then she concludes the poem on the next line with "make its test of us." This test is to be administered by happiness, or "joy."

Themes

Love

If there is a theme of love in "One Is One," it is not obvious. Readers have to dig for it. Once the digging begins, readers probably will conclude that there is no other emotion that could arouse a person as much as the speaker of this poem is aroused. What other emotion could wreck and shock a person stiff? What other feeling would make the speaker of this poem want to starve her heart and lock it in a cage?

The closest the speaker comes to expressing love is when she uses the word "joy" in the last line of the poem. She challenges her heart at this point to be one with her and to be strong enough to take on the test that joy will bring. It is very likely that the speaker is reflecting, in these last words of the poem, on the trials that love can put one through. In order for two people to be successful in love, they must become one, as the speaker points out in the poem's phrase "make us one." Whether the speaker is referring to two people (lovers) or two functions

Topics For Further Study

- Research the metaphysical poets of the seventeenth century and write a paper about who they were, how their poetry differed from the more traditional poets of their day, and what their poetry was about. Then memorize one of their poems and recite it for your class.

- The twentieth century was a time of significant change for women in the United States. Choose a poem by a female poet from each twenty-year period (1900–1920, 1920–1940, and so on) for the entire century, so that you end up with five poems. Select your poems carefully to reflect the development of women over the course of the century. Then read each of the poems to the class, without telling your classmates when the

poems were written. Let them guess from which of the time periods each poem was taken.

- Research the different styles of contemporary poetry, such as free verse, concrete verse, lyric poetry, or any other type of poetry in which you might be interested. Define each form and provide an example of a poem to illustrate the style. Then present your findings to your class.

- Find the various technical tools that poets use to create their works, such as metaphors, alliteration, caesura, synecdoche, and enjambment. Provide definitions for ten of them and examples of each term and invite your classmates to join you in an exercise, creating examples of your own.

(emotion and rationality), becoming one requires a surrendering of going "solo."

Emotions

Love may not be explicitly mentioned in this poem, but almost every other kind of emotion is suggested throughout Ponsot's poem. The poem begins with angry emotions, as the speaker berates her heart. Her emotions, as embodied by her heart, have wrecked her, and she is out to get revenge. Her heart, in retaliation, will "pound" the walls of the cage in which the speaker has imprisoned it, expressing its own anger and frustration. "You reel & brawl," the speaker explains, speaking directly to her heart. But she is "deaf" to her heart's "rages." These are all very strong emotions: anger, rage, frustration, despondency. There is also mention of threats being made and fear being experienced in response.

These emotions are wild and unruly, and the poem suggests that they must be controlled. The speaker can no longer stand being ruled by her emotions. It is her emotions that have wrecked her. She must do something to regain her balance, even if it means that she must lock her emotions away and stop listening to them.

There is one option left short of imprisonment. If her emotions can manage to share the rule rather

than going "solo," then instead of the negative emotions of fear, anger, and frustration, maybe the emotion of joy will emerge. The speaker shouts to her emotions in the second to the last line in the poem: "Think!" This is, of course, ludicrous, as emotions do not have the capacity for thought. Emotions are the opposite of rationality. But the word "think" implies the concept of control or discipline. Wild emotions may find no peace and may wreak havoc, but disciplined emotions may actually bring happiness and the experience of peace.

Imprisonment

The theme of imprisonment is stood on its head in this poem. There is the image of locking something up in a cage, which would indeed be a form of imprisonment. However, the speaker points out how this fails. She brings up the idea of the "double agent," and then she immediately explains that "jailers are prisoners' prisoners too." In other words, it is not just the captive who is imprisoned but also the one who must guard the captive. Captor and captive, they are a pair, and they depend on each other. They are equally locked away.

The speaker threatens to lock away her emotions and refuse to pay any attention to them because she has grown weary of the effect they have

---

on her. However, she also realizes that in doing so, she will destroy the element that colors her life. If she ignores her emotions, she might not have to deal with the anguish they bring her, but she also will not enjoy the pleasure they provide. So she becomes a prisoner too. Looked at in another way, she cannot stop her heart from beating and continue to go on living. So in the conclusion to this poem, imprisonment is used only as a threat, since what the speaker really wants is for the unruly emotions to reform. Just as a thief may change his or her ways and be returned to society, if the speaker's emotions reform, they, too, can be set free. Therefore imprisonment would not be necessary.

Unification

The title of the poem expresses the theme of unification. Ponsot could have titled the poem simply "One," but she is making a different kind of statement here. The word *one* does represent unity, but the poet, in her choice of title, is emphasizing that she is talking about two things becoming one. The phrase "one is one" feels more like a process than a result. In other words, there is the sense in the title of two things moving toward this goal. "Make us one," the speaker demands. It is not completely clear whether she is referring to her emotions or to a wayward lover. It is clear that she is suggesting that the anger and anguish will subside when unification is successfully completed, because that is when "joy may come."

Of course, there is irony here. When the speaker addresses her heart, she is talking about something that is already a part of her. She can no more separate herself from her heart (or her emotions) than she can separate herself from her mind or her soul. She points this out very clearly when she talks about the "prisoner's prisoners." There is this feeling of being dependent and independent simultaneously. So the division is actually artificial. There is no real need for the "reform" that the speaker requests. Unification is already present and unavoidable. Possibly all that is needed in order to have unification, therefore, is the awareness that it already exists. And since it is already there— since the two elements must work together—why not make the most of it? Instead of living together in mistrust and frustration, why not live together in joy?

Control

Another theme that is portrayed with some element of irony is that of control. The speaker first accuses the heart of wanting to "rule the world."

This is the ultimate control, is it not? But with the heart in control, the speaker feels completely out of control. In order to regain her control, she must lock her heart away. If she does this, she first believes, she will be in better shape. However, upon thinking about it further, she realizes that even this may not save her. She is fearful of worse things happening than being out of control: "You scare me," she states, "bragging you're a double agent."

The concept of a double agent embodies the irony of control. The speaker seems to be asking, who is really in control? And what is control? Can the rational mind controlling the emotions produce any better results than the emotions controlling the rational mind? Is there a point at which control makes no sense? Or, to look at it in another way, are not the rational mind and the emotions under the control of something beyond them both? For example, are they not both under the influence of life's experiences? This is what the speaker suggests when she states "joy may come, and make its test of us." Joy is coming from somewhere outside her heart and her head. In addition, it will come with its own set of challenges that neither can control.

Style

Personification

In "One Is One," the speaker talks to her heart. The technique that Ponsot uses is called personification. She gives human qualities to an object. In "One Is One," the personified object is the heart, which, in this poem, is also symbolic of the speaker's emotions.

The speaker talks to her heart as if it were an acquaintance, a lover perhaps. She yells at it, curses it, and blames it for trying to defeat her. She even grapples with her heart and threatens to lock it away. If it were not for the first word of the poem (which is "heart"), readers would conclude that the speaker is talking to another person. In other words, the speaker talks to her heart as if it were separate from her, something outside her. She even accuses her heart of trying to leave her, wanting to go "solo." But the speaker is not the only one who talks. The speaker suggests that the heart is capable of using language too. She speaks of her heart's "eloquent / threats," its "bragging," and its "rages" to which the speaker attempts to turn a deaf ear.

In personifying the heart, Ponsot provides a strong image of how the speaker feels. Her heart is so much out of her control that she believes that it is no longer a part of her. Her heart feels to her as if it has a mind and a life of its own. By using personification, Ponsot invites readers inside the speaker, so that they can look out of her eyes, can feel what she is feeling by imagining what it must be like when emotions are so powerful that they seem to exist somewhere outside the person they belong to. Words alone could explain these feelings to a certain extent, but by using personification, the poet provides an image that says it all so much more clearly and more powerfully.

Symbolic Language

Symbolic language makes use of images to portray feelings. The most obvious example in Ponsot's poem is the use of the heart, which symbolizes the speaker's emotions, from love to rage or anger. Although emotions are really reflective of chemical changes throughout the whole body, the heart centralizes them. And unlike the more popular symbolic heart, such as the ones used to suggest Valentine's Day, Ponsot uses the heart to symbolize all the speaker's emotions.

Other symbolic language is presented when the speaker refers to how the heart hates being imprisoned in the speaker's rib cage. This is, of course, absurd. The heart feels quite at home and protected inside the rib cage. But when the speaker's emotions are enraged and her heart pounds in reaction to these strong emotions, it is as if the heart is pounding in an attempt to get out. Likewise, the speaker's reference to the heart's wanting to go solo is also absurd. She mentions this to symbolize the feeling she gets when her emotions take over her rational thoughts. In other words, it is as if the emotions want to be independent of her. It is not an actual truth. At the end of the poem, when she requests that the heart "join the rest of us," she is symbolically asking the heart to come back home. Of course, the heart never really left home and could not exist if it did not join the "rest of us," which is assumed to be the rest of the speaker— her other organs, on one level, and her other functions, on another. By using symbolic language, Ponsot is able to take abstract and intangible elements and create more solid images that make her message easier to understand.

Rhyme and Near Rhyme

Overall, Ponsot's poem does not follow any structured rhyming pattern. However, rhymes and near rhymes do appear in her poem. The poem is not dependent on the rhymes, but when they occur,

they tend to tie certain elements together. For example, in the first stanza, the first and the third lines rhyme, as do the second and the fourth lines. This looks like a pattern, but it occurs only in the first stanza. There are no more end-line rhymes in any other part of the poem. In the first stanza, "shocked" and "locked" are paired, as are "though" and "no." Each of these words has something else in common. They are all enhanced by the line that follows them. For example, the word "shocked" in the first line is followed by "stiff" in the second line, which emphasizes the degree of the shock. The word "though" in line 2 provides a sort of turning point that is explained in the line that follows it. So the rhyming of these words may have been purposefully done to emphasize these turning points of the poem.

In the fourth line of the first stanza is the word "cage," which provides a near rhyme with the word "rages" that appears in the second stanza, line 2. The heart, it is said, rages in its cage. Another near rhyme occurs in the second stanza in lines 3 and 5 with the words "eloquent" and "agent." These near rhymes may merely enhance the sound of the poem, without attempting to affect the meaning. After all, the sound of a poem, the way the words flow, is an important element. One more rhyme occurs between stanzas 2 and 3. The word "do" ends the fourth line of stanza 2, while the word "too" ends the first line of stanza 3. Again, this rhyme may merely be present for the sound of it.

At the end of the poem, there are two rhyming phrases, "rest of us" and "test of us." This rhyming pattern, because it comes at the end of the poem, lingers with the reader. It is rather catchy phrasing, almost like something that might be done in a commercial jingle, so the message sticks in the head. This rhyming is probably done for emphasis. It is somewhere in these rhyming phrases and around them that the real message of the poem is hidden.

Historical Context

Metaphysical Poets

When writing about Ponsot and her poetry, reviewers and literary critics tend to label her work as being closely related to that of the metaphysical poets, whom Ponsot has admitted are a great influence on her writing. Metaphysical poetry was once described by the poet T. S. Eliot (1888–1965) as bringing together reason and passion. Writers who are often classified as the metaphysical poets wrote in the seventeenth century and include John Donne (1572–1631), Andrew Marvell (1621–1628), Henry Vaughn (1621–1695), and George Herbert (1593–1633). Their poetry tends to appeal to the intellect rather than to the emotions and incorporates energetic imagery, which in the case of the metaphysical poets is called "metaphysical conceit." This is a figure of speech through which the poet creates a long, elaborate comparison between two dissimilar objects. It is used by these poets to enhance their poetry and to exhibit their wide range of knowledge of everything from commonly found objects to concepts that are more esoteric or obscure. For instance, in John Donne's poem "The Flea" (1633), the poet compares a flea bite to the act of making love.

Another characteristic of metaphysical poetry is the attention put on trying to catch readers off guard. Other poets of the same time period as the metaphysical poets follow a rather predictable path. They state what their poems are going to be about and then elaborate on those points. The metaphysical poets, however, want to surprise their readers. Also in contrast to some of the poets who came before them, the metaphysical poets do not believe in the worship of the lover as a topic for their poetry. They look at love and sex through the lens of reality. Their poetry does not place women on some unreachable pedestal. The metaphysical poets are also interested in the deeper aspects of love, such as the psychological analysis of the emotions. John Donne, one of the more important of the metaphysical poets, often sets the pattern of his poems in the form of an argument. These arguments could be with anyone, from a mistress to God. The metaphysical poets went out of fashion for a hundred years or so, but thanks, in part, to the interest of T. S. Eliot, the work of the metaphysical poets regained popularity and influenced poets of the twentieth century.

The Beat Writers

Ponsot was friends with Lawrence Ferlinghetti, one of the beat writers, who also would go on to publish Ponsot's first collection of poetry. Ponsot's collection was overshadowed by another of Ferlinghetti's publications, *Howl* (1956), by the beat poet Allen Ginsberg (1926–1997). Although Ponsot's collection did not reap the popular support that Ginsberg's book received, her friendship with Ferlinghetti and her connection to Ginsberg often causes her to be considered one of the lesser known of the beat poets.

The beat poets and fiction writers are a small group of American authors that include, besides Ginsberg, such well-known characters as Jack Kerouac (1922–1969), Neal Cassady (1926–1968), and William S. Burroughs (1919–1997). Most of the beats came from New York, but they shifted their focus to San Francisco in the early 1950s. There they started to gain the public's awareness through poetry readings, in particular, those held at San Francisco's Six Gallery.

The beats are known for their total disregard or rejection of academic verse. They wanted to transform writing as well as change their assumed roles in American culture. They sought illumination through means as diverse as drugs, sex, and Buddhism. Kerouac is best remembered for his fiction writing, especially *On the Road* (1957). Cassady's collection of autobiographical stories and essays is called *The First Third* (1971). Burroughs's classic work is *Naked Lunch* (1959), a trip through the seedier side of life, from New York to Tangiers. This book has been said to be hard to read because of its brutal honesty about American culture.

Several musicians became fascinated with William S. Burroughs's work, including the London psychedelic-scene band The Soft Machine and the 1970s rock band Steely Dan. Then, in 1992, Kurt Cobain made an album with Burroughs, *The Priest They Called Him*, in which Burroughs reads some of his writing over Cobain's music.

Short History of Free Verse

Free verse (sometimes referred to in its French form, *vers libre*) is an informally structured style of writing poetry. There are no set rules of rhyming patterns or cadence. "One Is One" is an example of free verse. Free verse was made popular in the early part of the twentieth century by such poets as T. S. Eliot and Ezra Pound (1885–1972). Since then, free verse has become even more in style in contemporary writing, although it does have its critics. More traditional poets find the lack of structure somewhat degrading to the poetic form. However, Walt Whitman (1819–1892) wrote poetry that is considered the model of American free verse and that is hardly considered unpoetic. Whitman's *Leaves of Grass* (1855) is a collection of poetry whose form was probably ahead of its time.

Critical Overview

Ponsot, who is enjoying something of a reawakening of interest in her poetry, after writing for more than fifty years, was praised in a *New York*

Times article, "Recognition at Last for a Poet of Elegant Complexity," written by Dinitia Smith. "A Marie Ponsot poem," Smith writes, "is a little like a jeweled bracelet, carefully carved, with small, firm stones embedded in it." Smith wrote this article after Ponsot had been awarded the National Book Critics Circle Award for the collection *The Bird Catcher*. Smith goes on to say that Ponsot's poems are "full of carefully thought-out rhetorical strategies," pointing out, for example, Ponsot's tendency to use ampersands (&) instead of the word "and" in order to maintain the rhythm of the words in her poems. Smith then quotes Ponsot, who says her poems "are meant to be beautiful" and adds that this is "a very unfashionable thing to say."

In a *Publishers Weekly* article about Ponsot's work, Dulcy Brainard describes Ponsot's poems as "intellectually rigorous and full of language play" and says that they "nourish the spirit." In *Commonweal*, Suzanne Keen states her fondness for the endings of Ponsot's poetry. In particular, she likes the ending of "One Is One," which, she says, points out "how accessible, how aphoristic, and even quotable Ponsot's poems can be." Keen continues: "Yet there is never anything pat about the thinking or phrasing even in the most rigorously formal of the verses" in *The Bird Catcher* collection.

Lee Oser, writing for *World Literature Today*, describes the poems in this collection as having "an exasperating brilliance." Oser says of Ponsot that she is one who "drives her poetics by adapting to people, times, and landscapes, by changing hats and sometimes—it would seem—faces as well."

Barbara Hoffert, writing for the *Library Journal*, states that Ponsot's poems "should be sampled every day" because of their "gorgeous simplicity." Another *Library Journal* reviewer, Louis McKee, remarks that Ponsot's poems are "personal but charged with science and the natural world, with history and myth." In the *Women's Review of Books*, Marilyn Hacker describes Ponsot's poetry in this way: "Her work is comprehensible as part of the ongoing enterprise of poetry as she understands it, not limited to national borders or even to the English language, but an irreplaceable part of what defines the human mind and the human community." Donna Seaman, writing for *Booklist*, finds that because so much time elapses between the published collections, Ponsot's poems are "aged to perfection: complex and concentrated." She also characterizes Ponsot's poetry as "fluid and efficient."

Criticism

Joyce Hart

Joyce Hart is a published author and former writing instructor. In this essay, she looks at the narrative behind the lines of Ponsot's poem to find just what the poet is saying about emotions.

In Ponsot's poem "One Is One," it is obvious that the speaker of the poem is upset about her emotions. She does not speak very kindly about them from the first words of the first stanza all the way through to the end of the poem, yet she does not want to completely rid herself of them. Even though she is disgusted with them, she does not want to banish them forever. Just exactly what does she want? Why does she want this? And how does she go about trying to solve the problem of her runaway emotions?

The speaker lets it be known from the first words of the poem that she considers her heart (and thus, her emotions) to be a bully. What is a bully? Is it someone who pushes another person around? Is it someone who makes another person do not what that person wants, but rather what the bully wants? If this is what the speaker means, she is saying that her emotions are beyond her control. The speaker next calls her heart a punk. The word "punk" has several different meanings, ranging from "prostitute" to an "inexperienced young man." However, in the speaker's frame of mind, readers can assume the meaning to be closer to "gangster," which again implies that her heart is forcing her do things that she does not want to do.

As a result of her heart's brutish activities, the speaker is a total wreck, but she is something more, too. She is shocked, which implies that she is surprised by her emotions. She has been caught off guard by them. Whether she is shocked by the essence of her emotions or by the strength of them is not completely clear. However, her next statement is that her heart is arrogant enough to believe that it can rule the world. What is the story behind this statement?

The speaker could be saying that she had thought her emotions could rule the world and was surprised to find out that this is not so. Or she could be saying that her emotions are stronger than she had rationally considered them to be and is therefore surprised by their strength (or by their arrogance, depending on how she looks at the situation). Since the speaker uses the word "still," as in "you still try to rule the world," the second choice seems the more likely. In other words, the

What Do I Read Next?

- Ponsot's publication *Springing* (2002) is a good place to find an overview of the poet's career. Poems from all of her previous collections, along with some that were never published before, are in this book. The evolution in her writing, as well as in her life, is evident.

- Reportedly, one of Ponsot's favorite poets is the Nobel Prize–winning Irish poet Seamus Heaney, who has published a collection of poems called *Open Ground: Selected Poems, 1966–1996* (1999). His poetry is not light reading, so it is best taken in small doses, which gives it time to sink in. It is well worth the effort.

- Josephine Jacobsen, another of Ponsot's favorite poets, is not a well-known poet, except by those who are serious about poetry. Jacobsen's 2000 collection, *In the Crevice of Time,* is a good place to start getting to know her.

- Jane Cooper, a poet of Ponsot's generation, published *The Flashboat: Poems Collected and Reclaimed* in 1999. In this collection, she writes about her eighty years of life, from nursing ailing children to pondering the lives of women artists.

- Jean Valentine won the Yale Younger Poets Award in 1965 for her first collection of poems. Those earlier poems have been likened to the work of the poet Sylvia Plath (author of *The Bell Jar* [1963]), who committed suicide. In later years, Valentine gave up her focus on the more depressing side of life and went on to write about political protest and mysticism. Her 2004 collection, *Door in the Mountain*, covers feminist topics, digging into the emotions of women in prison and the nature of the soul.

---

speaker has seen this performance or attitude before. She has experienced these emotions in the past, so the surprise is that she thought her emotions had learned some kind of lesson from past experience. It sounds as if the speaker, who in this poem tends to represent the rational side of things, has reprimanded her heart before. How could you be so stupid, the speaker seems to be saying, to think that you could get away with this again? Or, looked at in another way, the speaker might be reprimanding herself for having allowed herself to be consumed or carried away with her emotions. She might be saying to herself, How could you be so stupid as to fall in that trap once again?

What exactly does it mean for one's emotions to "try to rule the world?" It is clear that the speaker does not really mean the whole wide world. She is more than likely referring to her own private world. If her emotions are trying to rule her world, then she is saying that she has been experiencing everything through her emotions, to the exclusion of any rational thought. This could suggest that she had,

for example, fallen in love with someone who was deceitful but that she chose to ignore the facts that were staring her in the face, to disregard the data that her rational mind had collected. Another possibility is that someone had hurt her emotionally and she had allowed her emotions to depress her and had wallowed in her sorrow, losing all desire to clean the slate and move on with her life.

Then the speaker says, "I've got you." This is the gotcha statement. For whatever reason the speaker has allowed her emotions to bully her, to wreck her, to try to rule her world, she is on to them now. She has caught and fingerprinted them and slammed them into jail. That is what you do with bullies and gangsters, after all. She is going to keep her emotions locked up no matter how much they "hate it." Hate is a very powerful emotion, in direct opposition to love, another potent emotion. The speaker is not really imprisoning her emotions, but what is she doing? If she hates locking her emotions away, why is she doing this? She must, readers can assume, love to allow her emotions to run

> *When she is high on emotion, she does not want to think. When she is depressed, she cannot think. Now that she has imprisoned her emotions, however, thinking is exactly what she wants to do.*"

free. She must love living her life through her emotions, in other words. But she just cannot stand to do so anymore. Remember that she is "shocked / stiff." She cannot afford to allow her emotions to remain undisciplined; she must confine them for her own good. Although allowing one's emotions free rein could make life exciting, it could also make life miserable. There are two sides to every emotion: one positive and healthy and the other morose. Happiness, for instance, can infuse a person with almost boundless energy, but depressive emotions can weigh so heavily that the spirit of life is all but extinguished.

In the second stanza, the speaker confirms these observations. "I trusted you," she says to her heart. She thought that she could fly on the positive emotions, but it sounds as if they took her too high, and she did not notice the flaw in the wings of her emotions until it was too late. She must have been hurt, because she refers to her heart as "brute," someone who is cruel or savage. Howl as her heart may, she will not listen to it anymore. It must be calling to her, which means that she is yearning to give in to her emotions once again. The pain reminds her not to do so, to become "deaf" to her heart's calls. She has heard those calls before and remembers the threat of "worse things you (knowing me) could do." Although she remembers how high her emotions can take her, she also knows how low she can go. Her emotions know her. In other words, the speaker understands her own vulnerability, her weakness for the highs and the blindness they can cause. When she is high on emotion, she does not want to think. When she is depressed, she

cannot think. Now that she has imprisoned her emotions, however, thinking is exactly what she wants to do.

"Think! Reform!" With these words, she commands new behavior from herself. Here, she is not talking to her heart anymore. Hearts are not made to think. By the time the speaker reaches the last two lines of the poem, it appears that she is talking directly to herself—the self that she wants to become "one." "Make us one," she says. Who else could she be talking to but herself? She is realizing that she is made up of two parts: the heart and the mind, the emotions and the rational self. She wants these two parts to come together, to take her through life via both her emotions and her thoughts. She wants to find a balance. She does not want to give up her emotions; she loves them. She just does not want ever to be blinded by them again. Neither does she want to go through life merely as a rational observer, gathering data but not feeling anything. She wants to enjoy life: "joy may come," she says. Joy is the emotion that she wants. It is peace that she craves. Still, she has learned something by the end of the poem. She knows that despite the fact that joy is a positive emotion, one that can make her feel good, joy can be demanding. It can "make its test of us." Whether the "us" in this statement is directed at the two sides of her—heart and mind—or refers to the speaker and some other person is not clear. It is clear, however, that the speaker knows that it is through the rational mind, which is the disciplinarian, that she will experience the best of her emotions. She mentions the coming of joy only after she demands reform.

Source: Joyce Hart, Critical Essay on "One Is One," in *Poetry for Students*, Thomson Gale, 2006.

Allan M. Jalon

In the following essay, Jalon provides background on Ponsot's life and career, noting the critical attention her "second arrival" has received.

Right after making history by publishing Allen Ginsberg's *Howl and Other Poems* in 1956, Lawrence Ferlinghetti introduced the first book of another young poet. Her name was Marie Ponsot, and she was so different from Ginsberg that they seemed like opposites.

He was male, gay, Jewish (and increasingly Buddhist). She examined marital love and her Catholic faith. His chanting, long-lined rhythms and jazzed images hurtled across the page. She made short, lyrical poems, often in rhyme—songs more than howls. He beatified anti-conformity. Her title, *True Minds,* came from a Shakespearean sonnet about ideal commitment. He treasured Walt Whitman; she, Emily Dickinson. He became the poet-prophet of the Beats. She raised seven children and didn't publish again for 25 years.

She kept on writing, however, seemingly indifferent to whether anyone but the muse noticed. At 81, she's enjoying a second arrival that has erupted with all the fanfare the first one lacked. It started with the National Book Critics Circle Award for poetry in 1998. A few weeks ago, the Poetry Society of America made her co-winner of its Shelley Memorial Award, honoring a whole career. She arrives at Beyond Baroque in Venice on Saturday to read from her fifth volume, *Springing* (Knopf), which the *New York Times Book Review*—featuring a large picture of her on its cover, rare for a poet—recently called "a great book." It offers a selection of new poems, previously published ones and uncollected early work that illuminates the buried progress of her writing life.

One outcome of her blossoming status is that she's taken on a somewhat Ginsberg-like role as a public poet. She's been sought after as one of New York's senior poets after the attacks of Sept. 11. On Sept. 22, writer-broadcaster Kurt Andersen invited her to his nationally distributed *Studio 360* program to discuss the cultural impact of what had happened 11 days before. "What is good will endure with all the treacheries of what is dreadful," Ponsot assured listeners in the still-reeling city, her crackling voice both tough and refined. She spoke of "the subset of strength that we all have in us." Giving echoes of Winston Churchill's resolve a pacifist twist, she added that "violence begets violence begets violence. It will take us perhaps another million years to get past this. But I believe we will."

Then, she somberly read a poem called "Oceans," which starts:

Death is breath-taking. We all die young,
our lives defined by failure of the heart,
our fire drowned in failure of the lungs.
Still planning on pouring the best ripe part
of wines our need or grasp has sucked or wrung
from fruit & sun, we're stopped before we start.

Ponsot is a petite bird of a woman whose gray-white hair was wound into a bun on a recent day

> *One outcome of her blossoming status is that she's taken on a somewhat Ginsberg-like role as a public poet.*

as she stood in the kitchen of her small, bright apartment on Manhattan's Upper East Side and prepared lunch for a visitor. She has a daughter and six sons, one of whom started to renovate her kitchen but hasn't finished. Drawers function but lack final facings. A blank wall waits for cabinets. "He's busy and had to stop, but I'm sure he'll get around to it when he can," Ponsot says, sounding certain.

It could be a scene in a Ponsot poem. She might compare the kitchen ceiling to the sky, contrast internal light with sunlight, refer to Dante's *Paradiso,* tie it to an illuminated manuscript in a museum (maybe about Dante's war-plagued era), summon a phrase or two from Latin and end with a bit of dialogue between her and her son or—since she tends to see men over women's shoulders—her son's wife.

All this would occur in the 14 lines of a sonnet or another of the many traditional forms she's mastered ("Oceans" is a sonnet), plus two utterly untraditional lines just because she felt like it.

When this imitation Ponsot is suggested to her, she laughs, something her witty poems make others do quite often. She says the make-believe poem reflects the focus she puts on the importance of "a governing intention to live a perfect life in an imperfect world."

Even when she describes a New York wildlife sanctuary or a small rooftop garden (she's the enthusiastic keeper of one) her work poses the contrast between an ethical tenderness and the brutal ways human beings betray their "tremendous interconnectedness" with each other and nature.

Invited the other day to speak to honor graduates at Queens College, where she taught for many years, she read "Jamaica Wildlife Center, Queens, New York," about a beautiful but endangered corner of the borough where she was born.

Describing the "sea air off the flats and inlets of Jamaica Bay," she never makes an explicit case against developers and politicians, but it's clear what she's talking about. She notes how even a poet exploits these details, turning them into "bite-sized images" that "intelligence eats & eats eagerly."

"You can't change the major rule that death is the price of life," Ponsot says, chewing on a grape. "But there is a particularly human capacity to make choices about how to use that life. You can keep making water filthy until the water dies, or you can decide not to."

She was born Marie Birmingham, to a family that derived its relative affluence from a business supplying imported gourmet food and fine wines on a private basis to very wealthy New Yorkers. Her late stature disguises an early bloomer. She says she can't remember not writing, and found her mature poetic voice quite young. "I didn't know you were supposed to find a voice. I just wrote the poems and let them do that."

She discovered James Joyce's short story, "Ivy Day in the Committee Room," at 13, and became devoted to Joyce's work. She excelled at Latin and French by the time she graduated from public school in Queens at 15, entering a small Catholic college there called St. Joseph's. Joyce taught her to trust the power of a single creative moment to embody the whole of human consciousness. Dante's *Divine Comedy* thrilled her when she read it as an assignment as a college freshman—the last part, the *Paradiso,* most of all.

As a child, she had experienced an exultant pleasure in the most basic sensation of being alive but couldn't quite find images and words to describe the all-encompassing sensation. As she read Dante's long poem, "it was clear that the 'Inferno' was intolerable if it wasn't going somewhere pretty quickly. And it was. Beatrice leads him to the ultimate vision, and then she disappears. And, in the text, he disappears, too. And there is just this visionary moment.

"It's a sky vision," says this poet whose work brims with skies that suggest both internal and universal infinities. "It's an out-of-your-own-body, out-of-your-own-mind, out-of-your-own-sky vision. And when you see that somebody has found a story that leads to it, a kind of showing forth of that in words . . ."

She stops talking, and her clear blue eyes roll upward with an awestruck savoring of the experience. "It is the great sense of the great value of everything," she says.

In 1941, at 19, she got a master's in 17th century poetry at Columbia. The war years, during which she worked in Manhattan bookstores, seeped

into her. She found a way to think about them in the *Catholic Worker,* the Pacifist newspaper co-founded by the activist Dorothy Day. Around the war's end, a relationship with a Navy man who suffered deafness and depression from shellshock gave her insight into men who'd returned from the war.

On *Studio 360,* she read a poem about a young, World War II flier she knew who had "burned, that boy, my age, Lt. Little, / prayed for in my parish monthly thirty years . . ."

In 1947, Ponsot made her first trip to Europe, to Paris. On the ship, she first met Ferlinghetti, who'd served as an officer in the Navy. In a cafe, she met a painter named Claude Ponsot. They soon married and returned together about a year later to the United States. The marriage came apart in the 1960s, and she increasingly raised their children on her own.

Though she came from a well-off family, her marriage and subsequent life gave way to financial difficulties. She taught writing and translated French literature to support her family. Though too busy to worry about getting published, "while children slept and popovers popped," she wrote at every opportunity. "You just do it," she says. "You do it because you've got to get your focus, even if it is for only half an hour or 20 minutes."

In 1981, a poet friend urged Ponsot to submit a manuscript to Knopf, which was planning a new series of poetry books. The result, an unusually thick volume, just started to catch up with the years of unseen writing.

Her next book took eight years; the one after that, 10. She says she's a slow, painstaking writer.

Springing, with 26 new poems, took only four years to produce—an instant in Ponsot time.

Ferlinghetti, speaking from San Francisco recently, says he's not surprised at her growing impact, that he'd never met anyone with her "very acute sensibility, before or since." Ginsberg, he says, "transformed the poetry world of his time, but she is not a poet of her time. That is not one of her attributes. She is a poet out of time, in the way that is true of the best poetry." Softly, he speculated: "She may last longer than Ginsberg. Who knows? It just shows how right I was to publish her all along."

Source: Allan M. Jalon, "A Poet's Progress," in *Los Angeles Times,* May 29, 2002, Section E, p. 1.

Marie Ponsot with Meghan Cleary

In the following interview conducted by Meghan Cleary of Failbetter.com, Ponsot discusses poetry form and process and literary influences.

Native New Yorker Marie Ponsot is one of the most venerated poets writing in America today. Her collection of new and selected poems, *Springing*, just released, is already in its second printing, a mark rarely achieved by poets publishing in today's literary marketplace.

Her verse is elegant, refined, and packs a punch with a frequent twist of phrase or an unexpected revelation. She makes us feel poetry is the necessary antidote to our media-strewn culture, filled as it is, with sound bites and fragmented images. But then again, maybe it is just *her* poetry that is a cleanser and balm to our modern minds. *failbetter* editorial consultant Meghan Cleary had a chance to sit down with Marie at a tiny Italian restaurant and linger well into the espresso course. . . .

***

[*failbetter*]: *Do you think forms live naturally in language or do you think you have to summon them out somehow?*

[Ponsot]: I think there are the forms of syntax which give you part of the mental light of the poem. It is the way the mind takes in the relation of an actor or a subject *acting,* you know.

The subject and the verb together link up in some grasping way that grabs meaning for us—and that's a poem. That link between subject and predicate is a formal leap. And then there are other ways in which language is formal. Even the most colloquial truck driver cursing out a cab driver will have a structure. Usually when someone is enraged, it will have a rhetorical structure. Yes, I think language generates forms because language conveys meaning, and if there is no form holding anything together, how are you going to hand somebody the soup?

The great surviving forms of the Old Testament for example will turn up over and over again in American literature. Whitman writes in that form. Doesn't look like a form to us because we have sort of a narrow view of a form, like a quatrain, "its got to have four lines and the second and fourth line have to rhyme", and stuff like that. . . . And that kind of form is great fun to play with. It's really fun to play with because it's got to contain these other levels of formality that are here in human language and it's got to do all of that at once. And thank god for our mother's knee where we learned all the hard stuff without pain, you know.

Who do you like to read?

I love the Cavalier poets, the Renaissance poets, I love Dante. Not so much the *Inferno* but the way the *Inferno* produces the *Purgatoriam*—and then together the *Inferno* and the *Purgatoriam* produces the *Paradiso* which is one of the great works of literature. Very concrete images of the *Inferno,* extremely concrete, and the effect on the speaker of the poem and the guide and the effect among the characters of the punishment that they are undergoing and their history are all very, very concrete. Then in the *Purgatoriam,* the level of concreteness is also very sharp but it's kind of spread out through air—they keep walking, they can breathe easier, and Beatrice arrives and that makes it all still lighter, more open and then the *Paradiso* which is just this explosion of light and beautifulness. So I read that. I just finished reading it about two weeks ago.

What did you like to read as a child, what were you drawn to?

Anything in print. I was a desperate *omnilect.* . . . My mother was always, in her own adorable way, trying to send me out to play, and I did that, because I was good child, God help me, but what I was really looking forward to was getting back in there and backing into a corner with my book, and I read it all. I read sort of grown-up things, childish things. I read them over and over sitting in the corner.

I read a lot of modern poetry too. I don't read very much fiction. At the moment I'm reading a remarkable woman called Elaine Scarry, who has three books that I know of, and all three of them truly refreshing and the latest one I think every poet should read, they would really like it, they would just delectate in it. One of the words that has dropped out of writing program writing, is imagination. People don't know what it means anymore. They think that it is something Paul McCartney wrote about, and she is trying in a *really* meticulous way to look at the events the whole phenomenology of imagining something and writing it. She has a whole hypothesis about why some things are present when we are writing—not only do we get that out of our own head onto the page, but then how does the reader get it back and pick it up?

I've been reading philosophy all my life because it is so interesting to me and I never saw anybody write about imagination the way Scarry does as—as an act. Theories of the imagination in classical philosophy are interesting, they're wonderful, but they don't do this at all, they would think that is un-philosophical, but we don't think that anymore. And she *is* a philosopher, it's just wonderful. It's called *Dreaming by the Book* (Farrar, Straus and Giroux, 1999) and it's not dreaming, it's better than dreaming! It's imagining.

I believe it's the life of language in our heads, the preconscious life of language because all the language we have is in our heads. Put your hands on your head and all the language you've possibly got is in there.

Do you ever feel like you don't have enough language?

What I feel is that there are times when my access to my own language is somehow impaired, I can't get at it—"there is something there, something there"—the trickle is so thin I can't get it and that's frustrating. You just have to be unbearably patient and keep pressing. And wait.

When you sit down to write a poem, generally, do you find the poem comes out because you are writing, or do you have something in your head and it comes out then?

Occasionally, I have something in my head that's on its way. When the weather is friendly I like to go for long walks and I'm not sure but I think the rhythms of walking gives me some sort of language access. Somehow the purposeless of walking, not *going somewhere,* just going. And looking around and seeing this and seeing that, sometimes a phrase will come to my mind out of the morass of stuff that interests me enough for my mind to keep going with it, to keep thinking it, and I might come home with five or six lines and the rest of it, you know, comes out of that.

You can start anyplace and language will be your friend if you really want to work on it. You can say to yourself, "all right, the first thing I see when I open my eyes I am going use that as a subject." Ordinarily, writing about a subject is lethal. Most of the really dull stuff you get is because someone decided to write a poem ABOUT, and it comes out really wrong because every cliché in your head clusters around it and the subject attracts the cliché long before it attracts real language, and you have to work it out, you have to sweat it out, and it takes strong exercise for your sweat to cleanse you of that so that you are approaching the subject or event in itself, and can say something about it that is not a cliché and advances the theory you have about it, into some kind of light.

Writing is so weird. . . .

It *is.* It really is. Language itself does the writing. We know that we have language. That is one of the things memory is packed with, everything we know is remembered verbally, the conversation

of language, is what we store, and I think the that's not very tightly compartmentalized back there [*gesturing to the back of her head*]. I think it's all swimming around back there, you know, I think it's all swimming around, all the time.

Language itself is weird and it does some amazing things.

We don't have perfect access to all that stuff. That's why rewriting is vital. If you had to get it perfect the first time you'd die. You'd shoot yourself. You are going to have stuff coming and coming . . .

Source: Meghan Cleary, "Marie Ponsot: Interview," in *Failbetter.com*, No. 7, Summer–Fall 2002, pp. 1–3.

Sandra M. Gilbert

In the following review, Gilbert profiles the well-aged poets Ponsot and Rajzel Zychlinsky, noting the "pleasure in time's gifts of ripeness and sweetness" in "One Is One" and other Ponsot poems.

Age is not all do rot. It's never too late. Sweet is your real estate.

So declares Marie Ponsot at the end of her exuberantly witty "Pourriture Noble" ("Noble Rot"), subtitled "a moral tale, for Sauternes, the fungus ceneria, and the wild old." And indeed this contemporary fabliau tells a charming story' of the origin of the famed Chateau d'Eyquem sauternes. The grapes seemed to have grown "too old, I too soon squeezed dry" because while the lord of the manor was off carousing "rot wrapped (them) like lace"; but (for, Ponsot counsels, the "meanest mistake / has a point to make") the astonished "vintner d'Eyquem" reports that the wine issuing from these grapes has

the best bouquet you can remember of sundown summer & someone coming to you smiling. The taste has odor like a new country, so fine at first you can't take it in it's so strange.

And for people as for grapes, the poet implies, the "new country" of age can make a wine that's "thick, gold-colored" and "pours like honey"—except it doesn't taste like honey, it's more "punchy, / you've never drank anything like it."

Though they were born a little more than a decade apart, have had dramatically divergent life-experiences, write in different languages and have significantly different views of the world, Marie Ponsot and Rajzel Zychlinsky have in common a poetic intensity that seems, like the bouquet of the vintner d'Eyquem's sauternes, to have been so sharpened and refined by age that it has what

Ponsot's poem defines as a special punchiness, a kind of unprecedented zing.

Now in her seventies, Ponsot is the New York–born and –bred author of three previous collections—*True Minds* (1957), *Admit Impediment* (1981) and *The Green Dark* (1988)—who has had a long, distinguished career as a teacher of English literature and creative writing at Queens College and elsewhere. In her eighties, Zychlinsky is a Holocaust refugee who has published seven volumes of poetry in Yiddish (between 1936 and 1993, in Poland, the United States, France and Israel), but although in 1981 a collection was translated into German, until now few of her poems have appeared in English. Beyond the almost visionary fascination with what Carolyn Heilbrun has called "the last gift of time" that animates the work of both these writers, however, each has plainly spent many years honing her art to a fierce clarity as moving in its confrontation of the pain and loss associated with aging as it is illuminating in its revelation of age's unexpected pleasures.

Of the two, Ponsot is (not surprisingly) the more affirmative. Besides praising such unexpected intoxications of the quotidian as the bouquet of "Pourriture Noble," she abandons herself with warmth, indeed with a sort of comic glee, to the vagaries of sheer feeling. In the dazzlingly colloquial "One Is One," she plays with cardiology and literary history to produce an elegant sonnet that is Petrarchan in theme as well as form. Beginning with mock outrage—"Heart, you bully, you punk, I'm wrecked, I'm shocked / stiff. You? You still try to rule the world—though / I've got you: identified, starving, locked / in a cage you will not leave alive"—this witty lyric ends with a prophetic flourish of delight that concisely captures the hopefulness with which Ponsot yearns to approach change:

> Brute. Spy. I trusted you. Now you reel & brawl in your cell but I'm deaf to your rages, your greed to go solo, your eloquent threats of worse things you (knowing me) could do. You scare me, bragging you're a double agent since jailers are prisoners' prisoners too. Think! Reform! Make us one. Join the rest of us, and joy may come and make its test of us.

Similarly, in "Restoring My House" she describes the salutary purification—the release from spiritual clutter—bestowed by a voluntary bonfire of words and images. Burning old papers, longing to "clear out / the debris of keeping," she insists that the "leaves I have torn up / turn into the hum of a / budding comfort disclosing / along a tree of transforming," because, tellingly, she is "hungry / to open up images / into the presence of absence / of images, and change."

> *"For Ponsot, absence is a presence, and necessary losses can be cherished if they bring restoration and renewal."*

For Ponsot, absence is a presence, and necessary losses can be cherished if they bring restoration and renewal. When in "Trois Petits Tours et Puis . . ." a son sets out on the road of life, as in a fairytale, "She gives him paper and a fine-nibbed pen; / he discovers the world and makes a map. / She gives him boots and a Havaheart trap, / Peterson guides, tent, backpack, fish-hooks, then / rehearses the uses of the North Star." But eventually "His map omits her. His snapshots go to friends"—at which a "fresh music fills her house, a fresh air." And when "Against the Dark, New Poets Rise" (in a poem of that title) she marvels, with characteristic generosity, "Look up, / there's burning going on, / exploding old stuff into new."

Perhaps Ponsot's gravest, most musical affirmation of the "sundown summer" of age and its "new country" shapes the beautiful sestina "For My Old Self, at Notre-Dame." Here, as she contemplates the "dark madonna cut from a knot of wood" who has presided for centuries over the great cathedral of Paris, the poet prepares, also, for a confrontation with the sequential selves that slot her, too, into history. Or, rather, catching sight of a girl walking away on the Ile de la Cite she imagines this young woman as her earlier self interrogating the person she has now become, and interprets "her Who are you?" as a wild "question raised / by seeing me, an old woman, in plain view." And the serenity with which this person she has become now names the difference between these selves— "Time is a tree in me; in her it's a grain / ready to plant"—contrasts strikingly with the fear of age and aging that she knows the person she was once felt: "She dreads clocks, she says. Such dry rot warps the grain." But Ponsot wants to teach that earlier self, along with the rest of her audience, that "age is not / all dry rot," and in a resonant gesture toward the magic of matrilineage, she turns to "Notre Dame" for assistance, praying

Magic dame, cut knot, your ancient wood would reach back to teach her if it could. Spring rain. Through it I call to thank her, loud above the joy she raised me for, this softfall. Sweet time.

In a rather different way, the equally lovely "Pre-Text," apparently dedicated to a grandchild, captures a one-year-old baby's first steps ("a step a step a rush // and he walks") and places him with tender precision into the puzzles and paradoxes of time:

> Firm in time he is out of date—like a cellarer for al-
> tar wines tasting many summers in one glass. or like
> a grandmother in whose womb her granddaughter
> once slept in egg inside grandma's unborn daughter's
> folded ovaries.

For finally, as in the eloquent sonnet "Explorers Cry Out Unheard," Ponsot wants to argue that "What I have in mind"—the mysteries of time, age, growth, transformation—constitutes "the last wilderness," a new country in which simply to be is to explore:

> I sweat to learn its heights of sun, scrub, ants, its
> gashes full of shadows and odd plants, as inch by
> inch it yields to my hard press. And the way behind
> me changes as I advance. If interdependence shapes
> the biomass, though I plot my next step by pure
> chance I can't go wrong. Even willful deviance con-
> nects me to all the rest. The changing past includes
> and can't excerpt me.

The tone of acceptance in which Ponsot artic- ulates her view of the "changing past" is hard-won ("I sweat to learn"), but it also suggests the plea- sure in time's gifts of ripeness and sweetness out of which such poems as "Pourriture Noble" and "One Is One" seem to have emerged. That "joy may come, and make its test of us" is one of Pon- sot's central tenets, an axiom infusing *The Bird Catcher* with much the same delight the "vintner d'Eyquem" must have felt when he tasted the sur- prisingly "thick, gold-colored" drops of his first sauternes.

The special bouquet of age that brings sweet- ness to Ponsot has a bitterer and often more con- tradictory flavor for Rajzel Zychlinsky, who writes in one poem that

> The red brick home for the aged smiled to me early
> this morning with one bright, sunny wall—an old
> smile—that can only be smiled by old people, when
> one eye laughs and the other cries. The other walls
> of the home, with their curtained windows in shad-
> ows, closed, grieved ancient griefs deeply hidden
> amid the bricks.

Because she composes her poetry in Yiddish, non-speakers of Yiddish (including myself) will never, of course, grasp all its verbal and prosodic nuances. Emanuel S. Goldsmith, a professor of Yiddish Language and Literature at Queens Col- lege, notes in his incisive introduction to *God Hid His Face* that as "the horizons of Zychlinsky's world broadened [she] abandoned her sometime re- liance on rhyme to adorn and buttress the power of her poems and committed herself to the more dif- ficult but more rewarding paths of free verse, to the fires of poetic imagery, dream and hallucination. The moral stance of her poetry became clearer and the purity of her voice among the poets unmistak- able." This aspect of Zychlinsky's evolution can- not easily be traced by English readers. Yet the powerful understatement and fierce imagery mark- ing the verse collated in this extraordinarily im- pressive volume do indeed give her voice a "purity" that is "unmistakable," even through the scrim of translation.

Born in Poland in 1910, Zychlinsky fled to Russia in 1939, then to the United States in 1951, but her mother and all her siblings died in the gas chambers of Chelmno; as Goldsmith puts it, for more than half her life she has "lived with the Holo- caust in her house and in her heart." Thus even the America of her later years is a country far more sorrowful than sweet, more rueful than ripe. "What swims there in the Hudson / in the red light?" she asks in the poem that opens *God Hid His Face:*

> Who is crying there: Save us, we are sinking? They
> are my dead, the cremated, who are sinking again in
> my memory.

Haunted not just by the ghosts of those who died but also by the guilt of the survivor, Zychlin- sky returns over and over again to such swimmers in the river of memory, ghosts who bring with them the responsibility to seek out the truth of loss, to carry its burden everywhere, to testify about the weight of that burden and thereby to seek some measure of healing or at least atonement. In poem after poem she almost ritually re-calls—that is, in- vokes as well as remembers—the "severed lives" she wanders among. In "My Mother Looks at Me," her dead confront her with their helpless woe:

> My mother looks at me with bloodied eyes out of a
> cloud: Daughter, bind up my wounds. Her gray
> head is bowed.
> Amid the leaves of each green tree my sister
> moans. My little daughter, where is she? Rajzel,
> gather her bones.
> My brother swims in the waters—days, weeks,
> years—dragged forward by the rivers, flung back
> by the seas.
> My neighbor wakes me in the night; he makes a
> woeful sound: Take me down from the gallows—
> put me in the ground.

It is perhaps this sense of haunting that gives Zychlinsky's voice such testimonial purity, an intensity of perception that verges at times on the surreal, or at any rate the uncanny. One senses, reading her verse, that the experience of war and flight along with the trauma of the Holocaust itself have so radically defamiliarized the quotidian that even the most ordinary objects she encounters must inevitably take on strange, often frightening meanings. "At night my shoes look at me / with my mother's tired eyes—/the same goals unachieved / and happiness missed," she writes in "My Mother's Shoes"; while elsewhere she observes "the elevator operator / drowning in his cage," sorrows for "the wooden leg / that walked around all day in the rain, / and no one said to the wooden leg: / Go home, go home, / enough walking in the rain" and hears "the clocks in Times square / ring[ing] the message of death."

In material settings of such fearful resonance, the human world too takes on a terrifying cast:

> He who has not felt a knife in his back does not know what a knife is—says the taxi driver who takes me to the train.

In one of the most remarkable moments in this remarkable collection, even "The Unborn Are Feverish" with terrible knowledge:

> The unborn are feverish in the branches of September—do not wake us, let us rest in our blue, transparent shirts. Between the ashes of yesterday and the smoke of tomorrow let us sleep here, concealed, hidden, without hands, without eyes, without lips, without years, sinking, drowning in no one's memory.

As it does for Ponsot, then—but very differently—age brings Zychlinsky into a "new country" where she funds herself, as Wallace Stevens once put it, "more truly and more strange." On the one hand, the "dresses you have seen me wear—/they never get old," but on the other hand, what might have been her "real" self has been severely fragmented and fantastically transformed:

> I looked on a street into a mirror—was it me I saw in the mirror? Or was it a woman I had seen somewhere and don't remember where? When? Do you know her? I turned my head—a woman was standing near me and pointed a finger at the mirror. She asked again—do you know her? Before I could answer a word, she disappeared. I stood a long time before the mirror, which looked at me—empty.

This tension between the familiar dress and the unfamiliar image is one that has traditionally shaped much poetry of old age. But what gives special force to *God Hid His Face* is a further tension, a tension between the particular and the universal. Zychlinsky speaks for and of the overwhelming

pain of a specific historical moment that has been ineradicably fixed in her memory. Yet at the same time, as a survivor who has aged in predictable human ways, she speaks for and of a common (if uncommonly moving) experience. "The Grass Has Grown Pale" dramatizes her relationship to the terrible history of our century:

> The grass has grown pale, the sky is cold my brother, Duvid, I no longer looking for you on the earth.
> I will now follow the clouds a long time with my eyes. I will look for you, my brother, in the autumn silence.
> I walk with my son over the clay field, on the Polish roads—O let them come, the autumn nights, over the bloody roads.

There is, quite rightly of course, no acceptance here—though there is ironic resignation to what has long since, and calamitously, happened.

More serene in its recording of the inexorable transformations inherent in the human condition, the monitory and Whitmanesque "My Story Is Your Story" moves (as many of Ponsot's poems do) from the particular to the general:

> My story is your story, neighbor across from me in the subway. What you are thinking about I have long since forgotten. What will happen to you happened to me long ago. What you hope for I smile about with closed lips. My fate is shown in the blue veins on your hand, yours, you can read in the deep wrinkles on my face.

Source: Sandra M. Gilbert, Review of *The Bird Catcher: Poems*, in *Women's Review of Books*, Vol. 16, No. 1, October 1998, pp. 11–12.

Suzanne Keen

In the following review of The Bird Catcher, *Keen praises the meaningfulness of the last lines of Ponsot's poems, describing how Ponsot "uses demanding forms without making the reader feel the strain of artfulness."*

Read over time, a journal like *Commonweal* begins to feel like a friend, known well enough to be praised and abused, missed when it goes away over the summer vacation, relied upon to recommend its favorite books. Marie Ponsot's *The Bird Catcher* begs to be pressed into the hands of a friend. I know I will not be alone among *Commonweal* readers to recognize Marie Ponsot's name and poems from these pages, and I hope I will be forgiven for quoting at length, in case anyone out there has missed her. Take a gulp of this poem,

> "Underbutter"
> This house has three entrance-ways. Water flushes its hidden places.

Sun-flush slides rosily off the wall. Dusk dawns.
Cats want out. Deer nose out of the woodlot. Bats
scour the near air as it cools.
Wheel-house: the house rides a cooling land-mass.
Oceans hiding desirable continents flank it. The
round earth turns as it rides.
Its flank turned to the flank of the hill, the dog
turns off the vista and sniffs at fresh grass.
Angels fly into the fresh vat of cream & suddenly
it's butter.
Sudden awe sudden dread: the visible fontanelle
just under the scalp of the delicate new-born head.
The delicate tip of the window geranium broke
off. The root-threads pop out a strong bud, lower
down.

Let me begin by commenting on the end. Marie Ponsot writes wonderful ends of poems. This final pair of lines tells a story of loss and recovery, set in the vital miniature world of the window box. It suggests not only the burgeoning that can be induced by pruning, but the adjusted point of view that enables us to see the "strong bud, lower down." The poem has already carried its reader through a dizzying variety of perspectives—in the house, hearing the water somewhere—looking out at various times of day—suddenly spinning and dwarfed by the scale of landmass, oceans, and planet— shuffled down from earth flank, hill flank, dog flank, to the dog's nose—whisked from the ether with the angels into the interior of the churn. What could the "underbutter" be? (I don't know, but I want some!)—perhaps some of it lies through the fontanelle "just under the scalp / of the delicate new-born head." Though the poem's speaker tacitly urges adjustments in consciousness, it scarcely reveals the mind of the human person inside the container of the house. "Underbutter" is mysterious: "Sudden awe sudden dread" pulses a rare

inward interruption in the searching outward gaze, in the terse descriptions.

Close to the kennings of Anglo-Saxon verse, Ponsot's evocative word pairs comprise a bright thread running through the poem's fabric: "entrance-ways," "sun-flush," "woodlot," "wheel-house," "land-mass," "new-born," and "root-threads" evoke an archetypal pattern of arrival, dissolution, cycling back. This tale, embedded in the nouns, does not contradict the top layer of implicit story: a person (woman?) in a house considers its structure, notes both times of day and woodland neighbors, carries out ordinary tasks without dulling to their mysteries, considers two kinds of delicacy, human and vegetable. Along the way the earth gets older, cream turns to butter, and the sight or memory of an infant's skull swerves into the sublime emotions of awe and dread. The causes of these disorientingly different actions remain obscure, except for the angels who make the butter come. This gives the poem the feel of riddling, as in the first stanza: 'This house has three entrance-ways. / Water flushes its hidden places." Answer: the body? Question: Is then the underbutter the soul or the life force inside?

Marie Ponsot's poems both invite and disarm this kind of readerly questioning. Some poems are so direct that a collection of their last lines can reasonably evoke the power of their themes. From "One is One," a command addressed to a wayward heart: "Join the rest of us, / and joy may come, and make its test of us." From "Pourriture Noble," a moral: "Age is not / all dry rot. It's never too late. / Sweet is your real estate." From "The Border": "Getting married is like that. / Getting married is not like that." And from "Festival of Bread": "The widow shoves her night-time self aside, / kneads silence down into dough, and lets it rise." This sampler of conclusions suggests how accessible, how aphoristic, and even quotable Ponsot's poems can be. Yet there is never anything pat about the thinking or phrasing even in the most rigorously formal of the verses.

Ponsot risks losing some readers when she returns again and again to elaborate Provencal verse forms, sestinas and villanelles, and she ups the ante when she adds (arcanely) two "tritinas," one of which I quote below. A tritina goes the troubadours one better, evidently requiring the recycling, in decasyllabic lines, of three end words in one-two-three, three-one-two, two-three-one order, with a concluding line that employs each end word in one-two-three order. (There may be other rules I have not discerned.)

"Living room"
The window's old & paint-stuck in its frame. If we
force it open the glass may break. Broken windows
cut, and let in the cold
to sharpen house-warm air with outside cold that
aches to buckle every saving frame & let the wind
drive ice in through the break
till chair cupboard walls stormhit all goods break.
The family picture, wrecked, soaked in cold, would
slip wet & dangling out of its frame.
Framed, it's a wind-break. It averts the worst
cold.

What makes a poem in so tight and elaborate a form transcend the sense of exercise? The resolute plainness of the language helps to justify the densely packed repetitions. Perhaps also the intimation that a lapse in the performance, like the imagined crack in the pane, would "buckle every saving frame," adds to the urgency of the wordsmith's work. With anti-Romantic sentiment, this poem casually props no wind harp (Aeolian lyre) to await inspiration and let in the destructive wet. Far better, the poem suggests, to stick with a tight container, a form that acts as a windbreak and preserves home and family, averting "the worst cold." Like Elizabeth Bishop, another poet who conjured up the elemental from the homeliest of subjects, Marie Ponsot uses demanding forms without making the reader feel the strain of artfulness.

Source: Suzanne Keen, Review of *The Bird Catcher: Poems*, in *Commonweal*, Vol. 125, No. 16, September 25, 1998, pp. 23–24.

Sources

Brainard, Dulcy, Review of *The Bird Catcher*, in *Publishers Weekly*, Vol. 245, No. 4, January 26, 1998, p. 88.

Hacker, Marilyn, "The Poet at 80: A Tribute to the Aging Poet Marie Ponsot Is Full of the Imagery of Vigor and Growth," in *Women's Review of Books*, Vol. 20, No. 10–11, July 2003, pp. 12–13.

Hoffert, Barbara, Review of *The Bird Catcher*, in *Library Journal*, Vol. 124, No. 6, April 1, 1999, p. 96.

Keen, Suzanne, "Words Take Flight," in *Commonweal*, Vol. 125, No. 16, September 25, 1998, pp. 23–24.

McKee, Louis, Review of *The Bird Catcher*, in *Library Journal*, Vol. 123, No. 2, February 1, 1998, p. 89.

Oser, Lee, Review of *The Bird Catcher*, in *World Literature Today*, Vol. 73, No. 1, Winter 1999, pp. 155–56.

Seaman, Donna, Review of *The Bird Catcher*, in *Booklist*, Vol. 94, No. 11, February 1, 1998, p. 894.

Smith, Dinitia, "Recognition at Last for a Poet of Elegant Complexity," in the *New York Times*, April 13, 1999, Section E, p. 1.

Further Reading

Ciuraru, Carmela, ed., *Beat Poets*, Everyman's Library, 2002.
  Ponsot published her first book of poems in the same year and through the same small publishing house (City Lights) that Allen Ginsberg's book *Howl* (1956) was published. The publishing house fostered many of the beat poets; for this reason, Ponsot is often considered one of the beat poets herself. To find out about these poets, this collection is a good place to start. The poems of Kerouac, Ferlinghetti, and Diane di Prima are featured in this collection.

Gardner, Helen, ed., *The Metaphysical Poets*, Penguin Classics, 1960.
  Ponsot is often referred to as a metaphysical poet. This book is a good introduction to some of the metaphysical poets. There is an excellent introduction as well as copious footnotes to help readers gain insight into this form of poetry.

Hirsch, Edward, *How to Read a Poem and Fall in Love with Poetry*, Harvest Books, 2000.
  This book is a journey into poetry, including not only the poems of famous poets but also a glimpse into the poets' lives. Although he is a scholar, Hirsch makes his material very accessible as he describes his own love of poetry.

Knorr, Jeff, *An Introduction to Poetry: The River Sings*, Prentice Hall, 2003.
  Knorr not only teaches his readers how to love poetry, he also breaks down the basic elements of the poetic form and thus informs his readers how a poem is put together, what devices poets employ, and how literary theory is used to understand poetry. This introduction to poetic literature is easy to read and understand.

Schneider, Pat, *Writing Alone and with Others*, Oxford University Press, 2003.
  Schneider has taught people to write from the elementary school level to the college level. In this book, she describes some of the challenges writers must face, including the loneliness of having to work alone. In other parts of the book, she portrays the joys of encouraging one's creativity and learning to express it.

Our Side

Carol Muske-Dukes

2003

Carol Muske-Dukes's poem "Our Side," published in 2003, is about the loss of a lover. Many of the poems in *Sparrow*, the collection in which this poem appears, are about death. The collection is dedicated to the poet's husband, David Dukes, who died unexpectedly in 2000. In "Our Side," the speaker tries to call back the spirit of someone she has loved and who has died. She wants him to return in some form to "our side," the side of the living. The speaker admits that she understands that this need to see "the lost," those who have died, is one-sided. The living, the speaker says, are the ones who have the need to be remembered. This view is the opposite of the belief and practice of most people, who visit the graves of the dead in attempts to remember them, to memorialize them. Although it is about death and about longing on the part of someone who has lost a lover, "Our Side" is not morbid or melancholic. By the end of the poem, readers are much more aware of the love felt by the speaker than they are of death. The poem is a love song rather than a requiem.

Author Biography

Carol Muske-Dukes is the director and founder of the graduate program in literature and creative writing at the University of Southern California, where she also teaches poetry. She is a reviewer for the *New York Times Book Review* and the *Los Angeles Times Book Review*, for which she writes a regular

Carol Muske-Dukes   Photograph by Rex Wilder. Reproduced by permission

column called "Poets Corner." Muske-Dukes is the author of several fiction and nonfiction books, but she is best known for her award-winning poetry.

Muske-Dukes was born on December 17, 1945, in Saint Paul, Minnesota, and went to Creighton University, where she received her bachelor's degree in English in 1967. Three years later, she completed her master's degree in English and creative writing at San Francisco State University. Muske-Dukes gained her writing experience at several prestigious schools, including the New School for Social Research, Columbia University, and New York University. She has taught at the University of Virginia, the University of Iowa, and the University of California, Irvine.

Her books of poetry include *Sparrow* (2003), in which "Our Side" appears; *An Octave above Thunder: New and Selected Poems* (1997); *Red Trousseau* (1993); *Applause* (1989); *Skylight* (1981); and *Camouflage* (1975). *Women and Poetry: Truth, Autobiography and the Shape of the Self* (1997) and *Married to the Icepick Killer: A Poet in Hollywood* (2002) are her two collections of essays. Muske-Dukes has written three novels: *Life after Death: A Novel* (2001), *Saving St. Germ* (1993), and *Dear Digby* (1989).

Muske-Dukes has received many awards, including the Chapin Award from Columbia University for *Sparrow*, which also was a National Book Award finalist. *Married to the Icepick Killer* was listed as a Best Book of 2002 by the *San Francisco Chronicle*. The poet has one daughter and was married to the actor David Dukes, who died in 2000. *Sparrow* is dedicated to her late husband.

Poem Text

Disoriented, the newly dead try to turn back,
across the great expanse of water. But the distance
inside each of them, steadily growing, is what draws
    them away at last.

Tenderness and longing lose direction, all terror   5
and love in the cells slowly dissipate.
    Despite our endless calling,

their names fall away into the great canyons
of the infinite. They try to remember how to
    answer,
then turn away, distracted, from the repetitive cries.   10
    What shall I call you now, lost sailor?

This was the port, this bright uneasy harbor where
    we never
completely set anchor. I understand the implacable
    clichés now:
"Its imperfection is its beauty" and so on. How
    instinctively we

defend the poor illusions of that beauty, the   15
    limitations of the present.
These colored paper lanterns are strung along our
    side because
we like the red-gold light, the pure ornament—

and because we insist on the desire of the lost to
    remember us,
to recognize the shape of our small flames. Late-
    night walks by
dull brimming water: candles and searchboats,   20
    bright beams scanning
for faces. Unstoppable need for solace, that hunger
    for the perfect
imperfect world. Still I sometimes think that you
    are too far away now
to recall anything of our side—not even that day
    we saw human forms

suspended over the sea: the hang-gliders at sunset,
    the old beach hotel
behind us and all our shining ambivalent love   25
    airborne there before us.

Poem Summary

Stanza 1

"Our Side" begins with an attempt by the speaker to understand what it must be like to be dead. The speaker begins by describing the "newly dead" as "disoriented" because they have crossed over into unfamiliar territory. Their first reaction, according to the speaker, is "to turn back." The speaker refers to the newly dead as having crossed "the great expanse of water." This crossing may refer to the symbolic crossing of the river that is often mentioned in poems and myths about death. The crossing also may be a reference to a favorite place in which the speaker and her departed lover may have spent time—the ocean's edge, which is mentioned later in the poem.

The speaker relates the great expanse of water to another kind of distance, that which is "inside each of them," that is, the newly dead. This distance, which the speaker does not quite define, is "steadily growing" inside of them. It is also this distance that "draws them away at last." Depending on the reader's religious or spiritual background, these lines can be interpreted in many ways. The distance may represent a god or a spiritual dwelling place, such as heaven. Because the distance is inside each of the departed, it also may be a reference to the soul. In this sense, the speaker may be referring to the soul's wanting to be reunited with the source of its energy, which is what is causing the dead to be drawn away. By using the phrase "at last" at the end of stanza 1, the speaker adds an element of release, as if the living endure life and the dead finally experience a sense of the peace they have been waiting for. This feeling is emphasized in stanza 2.

Stanza 2

"Tenderness and longing lose direction," the speaker states. This notion is confusing and difficult to understand until the next phrase is added: ". . . all terror / and love in the cells slowly dissipate." The speaker imagines the release that the dead feel when they cross the great expanse of water. All worldly emotions, all connections with loved ones are finally lifted, or finally melted away. These burdens belong to the living, not the dead. The burdens are the feeling of loneliness and the emptiness that those left behind must bear. The ones who once supported them in love no longer care. "Despite our endless calling" is attached to stanza 2 by meaning as well as by structure. The dead release their emotions despite the fact that the ones whom they once loved are calling out to them. The thought is completed in stanza 3.

Stanza 3

The first line of stanza 3 completes the thought that begins "Despite our endless calling," in stanza 2. The speaker continues, "their names fall away

into the great canyons / of the infinite." Loved ones crying out to the dead, calling their names, eventually must face the fact that the newly dead cannot hear them. The names of the newly dead are like their bodies. They have become useless. A name is significant only in this life. Babies are born and given a name. The mention of that name conjures up the memories of the person the baby has become in life, all the experiences shared with the people who loved him or her. The name will always be closely followed by the image of that person. The newly dead, however, have no more need of names. They return to the place they inhabited before they were born, when they had no names. Their names "fall away" in this reality, as does everything else about their physicality on earth. The newly dead fall into the "great canyons of the infinite," a symbol of abstractions such as nothingness, eternity, the unknown, and a spiritual god or source.

By "They try to remember how to answer," the speaker means that the newly dead are unable to answer the cries of those left behind. She wants to believe that the newly dead do hear the cries, but because they have lost their physicality, the dead have lost all emotion and connection. They have forgotten how to speak, so they "turn away." In stanza 1, the speaker uses the phrase "turn back"; in stanza 3, she says "turn away." The direction has changed. In stanza 1, the newly dead appear to be contemplating coming back to earth, to life. By stanza 3, however, they turn away from life and the ones who are calling them, because they are "distracted." Something else apparently is calling to them—something that is more enticing than life on earth. The newly dead turn away "from the repetitive cries" of those left behind. The speaker, however, has not given up all hope of making contact. "What shall I call you now, lost sailor?" she asks. If the newly dead does not respond to his name, the speaker wonders, will he respond to something else? By using the adjective "lost," which corresponds to "disoriented," in stanza 1, the poet ties the stanzas together. The speaker also expresses hope, in a strange way, through the use of these two words. If the newly dead is disoriented and lost, there is still a chance that he may find his way back to her.

Stanza 4

"This was the port," the speaker says at the beginning of stanza 4. The tense of the verb is important. The speaker does not say, "this *is* the port." She speaks in the past tense, implying that she and the newly dead will not meet at the port again. The poem continues "this bright uneasy harbor where we never / completely set anchor." The word "bright" suggests happiness, but the word "uneasy" is unsettling, suggesting conflict. The couple has not "set anchor" in the port, has not put down roots, has not decided to call the port home. The speaker continues, "I understand the implacable clichés now." The word "implacable" means callous or hard-hearted. A cliché is a worn-out phrase that has lost its original impact because it has been overused. Despite the callousness and worn-out quality of the words, which the speaker insinuates she once glanced over without giving them much thought, the speaker has come to understand the meaning behind the cliché "Its imperfection is its beauty." It must relate to the harbor, because both the cliché and the mention of the harbor are in the same stanza. That the harbor is both bright and uneasy may explain its imperfection and thus its beauty. However, the speaker also may be suggesting that when someone dies, all his imperfections take on a certain element of beauty, that flaws are suddenly forgiven because one's heart longs so wildly to be reunited with the lover.

Stanza 5

Like stanza 2, stanza 5 begins with a fragmented sentence, the beginning of which, "How instinctively we," ends stanza 4. The speaker continues, "defend the poor illusions of that beauty." Because the speaker refers to the dead as "they" up to this point in the poem, her use of the pronoun "we" in this phrase must refer to the living. Therefore the living are defending the illusion of beauty. This notion may amplify the interpretation of how the living create illusions of what their now-dead loved ones were like when they were alive. The speaker adds "the limitations of the present" as if qualifying or adding to the phrase "poor illusions of that beauty." Are the limitations of the present also poor illusions? Or is it because of the limitations of the present that the living defend the poor illusions? It is not totally clear, so a leap of faith or a creative interpretation is required of the reader. What is clear is the contrast between the "great canyons of the infinite" (stanza 3) to which the newly dead have gone and the "limitations of the present" to which the living are confined. With these two statements, the speaker insinuates that the newly dead are much freer than the living. She also insinuates that the consciousness of the dead is more expanded than that of the living, who are still defending "poor illusions."

The rest of stanza 5 describes "colored paper lanterns . . . strung along our side." The lanterns are probably a reference to the Buddhist practice, especially prevalent in Japan and in Asian American communities, in which paper lanterns representing the souls of the dead are sent back to their side. The speaker once again refers to "our side," to signify the contrast between the living and the dead. The speaker explains that the lanterns are used "because we like the red-gold light, the pure ornament." The candlelight of the lanterns is warm ("red-gold"), and the "pure ornament" may be a reference to the body—warmth, red, and ornament together produce an image of flesh and blood. The living wear their bodies as ornament. The dead no longer need such things. This feeling is carried into stanza 6.

Stanza 6

The first line of stanza 6, "and because we insist on the desire of the lost to remember us," completes the explanation of the use of lanterns begun in stanza 5. The living want to be remembered by the dead. The ornament, or the body, is worn to make the living visible. The next line, "to recognize the shape of our small flames," also emphasizes this notion. The contrast of the living as small and the dead as infinite is insinuated.

The poem then repeats some of the previous images: water, which is first mentioned in stanza 1, and candles, which are suggested in the mention of paper lanterns in stanza 5. A brighter illumination is brought forward, that of "bright beams" that are "scanning." There is also the mention of "searchboats." The search boats may be metaphorical or may be imagined by the speaker, who desperately wants to find the person who has died. The bright beam may be merely a flashlight that the speaker carries.

Stanza 7

The speaker's "Unstoppable need for solace" is a reference to crying and longing and an unfulfilled need to be comforted. The need is unstoppable because it is impossible for the speaker to be reunited with her departed. This impossibility explains the next phrase, "that hunger for the perfect imperfect world." The statement is a contradiction. Nothing can be perfect and imperfect at the same time. The speaker craves something that cannot exist.

Part of the speaker, her rational side, understands the impossibility. Her emotional side, however, continues to long for the impossible. In the next line, however, some of the speaker's rationality returns: "Still I sometimes think that you are too far away now." The speaker continues to hope that the newly dead person can return, but she also rationally understands that the person is too far gone to return or "to recall anything of our side—not even that day we saw human forms," and the poet ends the stanza.

Stanza 8

Once again, the first line of the stanza is a continuation of the thought begun in the last line of the previous stanza. The speaker ends stanza 7 with "human forms" and begins stanza 8, "suspended over the sea." At first these phrases provide a strange image. Readers have been led to believe that the speaker is walking along the shore, searching for faces, looking once again for the newly dead, who have gone to the other side. The image of the speaker's searching along the shore, wanting to see a physical human form, suddenly shifts to an image of "human forms suspended over the sea." This eerie image in some ways fulfills the speaker's longing. She is searching, and suddenly physical forms appear. The poem is misleading, however. The human forms are not hanging freely over the sea but are attached to hang gliders.

In the last stanza, the speaker goes back in memory. She is no longer wandering the beach alone. She is with the person who has died, and she is remembering their love rather than being lost in her sorrow. She has turned her search around. It may be that in her search the speaker is reminded of another time, a happier time when she strolled on the beach with someone she loved. She sees the sunset and the "old beach hotel," an image that suggests that the couple was on vacation. The hang gliders are symbolic of their love, "all our shining ambivalent love airborne there before us."

Themes

Longing

The word "longing" occurs only once in "Our Side," and the word is associated with the newly dead, not with the speaker. However, even in the one instance, in the first line of stanza 2—"tenderness and longing lose direction"—the reader can feel the ache of loneliness that longing produces in the speaker. The speaker is calling out to the subject of the poem, the newly dead, and

waiting for a response. She realizes that she is calling into a void, and therefore she says that the longing has lost direction. In other words, the longing is not reciprocal. The newly dead person no longer is craving. It is only on "our side," the side of the living, that the longing still exists.

Although "longing" does not appear elsewhere in the poem, the theme continues to be represented. There is "endless calling," which would be done by people who are yearning for something. Longing is also represented in the line "and because we insist on the desire of the lost to remember us." Why would the living insist that the dead remember them? There is a craving for nostalgia, a kind of homesickness. The living want to return to a point in their lives when the dead were still alive. There is another sense of longing in this phrase and in the desire to be remembered. It is the awareness of their own mortality that people feel when they face the death of a loved one. Suddenly death, which has been only a fleeting thought, stares the person left behind in the face. The longing is a desire to stay alive, of not wanting to face a personal death. It is ironic that the feeling may also be a longing to die, to join the newly dead, assuring that the newly dead person will not forget the one left behind.

Death

Death is an inevitable unknown. Poets, philosophers, and probably all adults with an imagination try to conjure up what death means. Death is the force behind "Our Side." The speaker is trying to come to grips with where her loved one has gone. She tries to conjure up a place where his spirit dwells, and she tries to envision what it may be doing. She wants to know whether death means that the love they once shared also has died. She wants to know whether any of the emotions she shared with her loved one remain in an after-death existence.

Death is represented by the "great expanse of water" and by the "great canyons of the infinite." The "lost sailor" has set sail from the "port," or the "bright uneasy harbor where we never / completely set anchor." Life, in other words, is an "uneasy harbor" in which an anchor is never truly set. Death has proved to the speaker that life is transitory, or temporary. Death is also represented in the "colored paper lanterns," a symbol of the festival of the dead that is practiced by Buddhists.

Love

"Our Side" is about death and mourning, but its power is in what lies behind the dramatic moments—a deep love is being expressed. Without

Topics For Further Study

- Research the topic of death according to different beliefs. These beliefs can be taken from Judaism, Islam, Hinduism, Christianity, or another religion. Contrast one or more of these beliefs with those of Buddhism. Look for details about an afterlife, reincarnation, and the existence of a soul. Write a paper and present your findings to your class.

- Find pictures of the Japanese floating paper lanterns used during the Buddhist festival of the dead. Make a floating paper lantern that closely resembles the picture. Bring it to class and explain the significance of the celebration.

- Research how various cultures honor the dead and write a paper about your findings. For example, look at how the celebration of Halloween began, how the Day of the Dead is celebrated in Mexico, or how the U.S. military honors fallen soldiers.

- Write a poem about something you have lost. Practice understatement of your emotions concerning this loss. Rather than using adjectives to describe your emotions, create images that show how you feel.

that love, there would be no longing, there would be no "endless calling," and there would be no living lover calling out the name of the deceased. When she wants to be remembered by the newly dead, the speaker is not talking through her ego, wanting to be recognized in that way. She wants her love to be remembered. In particular, she wants the feeling of love to be returned. Love causes pain if it is one-sided. The speaker once had someone to love, but that someone has gone, and she wonders where he has gone. How far away is he? Can he still see and hear her? Does he still love her? What is she supposed to do with the love inside her heart? These unspoken questions are the basis of the poem.

Confusion

An element in "Our Side" is confusion. The first word in the poem is "Disoriented." The speaker is referring to the newly dead person, but all of the thoughts are supposedly coming from the speaker. Who really is disoriented? The speaker states that the newly dead are disoriented and try to turn back but cannot. This confusion may be the speaker's about an underlying hope of reincarnation, the belief that people die and are reborn in another form, a sort of turning back to life. The speaker, however, is not sure whether she truly believes in reincarnation. She wants a sign that it is

possible. The speaker senses, however, that the newly dead person, whom she addresses in this poem, is drifting farther and farther away. Nevertheless, she ceaselessly calls out to him. She is not completely sure.

Even though she calls out, the speaker states that "their names fall away into the great canyons / of the infinite." Again she is torn between two beliefs. She calls out, intuitively knowing that doing so is a senseless endeavor, but the calling out remains "endless." In an effort to reach the newly dead, the speaker asks: "What shall I call you now . . . ?" Although she feels that the practice of calling out is useless, instead of stopping it, the speaker believes that maybe she has been calling out the wrong name. Maybe if she changes the way she is calling out, the dead will finally hear.

Style

Enjambment

Enjambment is used in poetry to create a sense of tension. It occurs when the full sense of a line is interrupted because it is carried over to the next line. Sometimes enjambment leads to a change in meaning. In reading a phrase and then stopping at the end of a line, readers may gain a certain understanding of what the poet is trying to say. When the part carried over to the next line is read, the understanding changes.

Examples of enjambment in "Our Side" include the break in stanza 1. The poem begins "Disoriented, the newly dead try to turn back, / across the great expanse of water. But the distance," and the second line stops. At this point, "the distance" appears to refer to the "great expanse of water." This image is strong in the reader's mind. It suggests a sense of staring out at sea and imagining how far away the horizon is. The horizon can never be reached, so this "great expanse of water" represents a distance related to infinity. The third line offers a surprise. It is not the distance of the great expanse of water but rather the distance "inside each of them, steadily growing." In the reader's mind, the infinite sense of reaching the horizon switches to the infinite expanse growing inside the newly dead. The poet does not have to describe or explain what she means by the distance inside each of them, because she provides the reader with the image of the sea.

Visual Effects

"Our Side" is divided into stanzas of two, three, and four lines (distichs, tercets, and quatrains, respectively). Because there is no formal rhyme or meter in this poem and because the meaning of one line is often completed in the next line, there is no formal reason for the poem to be broken into stanzas of two, three, and four lines. There is also no set pattern to how the stanzas are formed. This poem is free flowing, so why has the poet divided it into distichs, tercets, and quatrains? The visual appearance of the lines on the page may be meant to enhance the meaning of the poem. An argument in favor of the poet's use of visual effects to enhance meaning is that she also alters the right-left alignment of the poem's lines. Most of the lines are aligned with the left margin. Only the last lines of the first three stanzas are aligned with the right margin. There is quite a bit of space between the left margin and the beginning of these three lines.

The variation in alignment gives the poem a look of waves, which may relate to the water that separates the newly dead from those who are alive. It also offers an effect of something being pulled away, because the type is pulled away from the left margin. An underlying tone in the poem is that of the newly dead being pulled away from the living. The three lines that are aligned with the right margin read "them away at last," "Despite our endless calling," and "What shall I call you now, lost sailor?" These lines have something in common, and that may be why the poet has set them apart. The newly dead are being drawn away, even

though the living are endlessly calling to them. They newly dead are not responding, perhaps, the speaker wonders, because she is not calling out the right name. She is also not completely sure that the newly dead person to whom she is calling is aware that he is going away. Therefore she refers to him as a lost sailor.

The foregoing interpretation can be based merely on the way the poet has placed her lines on the page, demonstrating that visual form can provide extra meaning to a poem. A poem is more than just its words, a quality that sets poetry apart from other forms of writing. Not only is each word carefully chosen for meaning, song, and rhythm, but also each work is carefully placed on the page.

Symbolic Language

Muske-Dukes uses symbolic language in an attempt to describe the abstract concept of death. She refers to the "great expanse of water" between the two sides: the side of death and the side of life. She calls the dead person a "sailor," as if death were a journey across that great expanse of water. She continues with the concept of death's being something very large when she refers to death as "the great canyons of the infinite." This image is a different type of expanse, so infinitely large that the living cannot cross it. The different kind of "distance" inside a dead person is that which "draws them away." The distance represents death but also may be a reference to a soul, which in some belief systems is humankind's connection with the infinite.

The mention of a port symbolically refers to life. Life is a port in the journey of the soul. The soul, however, never puts down a permanent anchor in life. The speaker insinuates that the journey is much more significant than life alone. In other words, the speaker believes in an afterlife, which is represented as the "infinite." Life, in comparison, is finite and small, like the "shape of our small flames." The speaker uses hang gliders as symbols of the affection and passion, the "shining ambivalent love," between her and her lover. The hang gliders, not quite in heaven and not quite on earth, are an emblem of how the speaker envisions the couple's love and how their love made her feel—elevated, or "suspended" in space.

Historical Context

Obon and Toro Nagashi: Festival of the Dead

The speaker in "Our Side" mentions "colored paper lanterns" while remembering her dead lover. In Japan, an annual holiday incorporates welcoming the spirit of the dead back to earth and then sending the spirits back to the other side. The festival, Obon, is celebrated from August 13 through August 15 and encompasses Buddhist observances that honor the spirits of everyone's ancestors. *Obon* means "festival of the souls." The observance began in China and was brought to Japan in the seventh century.

During Obon, great fires are lit, so the spirits can see their way home. Food offerings are made to entice the spirits, and traditional folk dances are performed to make the spirits feel at home. At the end of the Obon, paper lanterns are lit during a part of the festival called Toro Nagashi. The lanterns are placed on small, floating platforms, and prayers are written on papers that are then placed on the lanterns. These prayers are intentions that the spirits rest in peace. The lanterns on their floating platforms are set adrift on a river or in the ocean. The lanterns float down the river or out to sea, showing the spirits their way back to the other side. Many people in Japan believe in the supernatural powers of the dead and respect the fact that their ancestors' spirits can affect their own lives.

David Dukes

Muske-Dukes dedicates her collection *Sparrow* to her husband, David Dukes, who died in 2000. Dukes was a stage, film, and television actor in more than thirty productions, including *The Josephine Baker Story* (1991), for which he was nominated for an Emmy Award. In 1980, Dukes was nominated for a Tony Award for Best Featured Actor in a Play for his role in *Bent*. Dukes was well known for his roles in made-for-television movies and popular television series. He appeared in the miniseries *The Winds of War* (1983) and had guest roles in the television series *Ally McBeal* in 1999, *Law and Order* in 2000, and *Dawson's Creek*, playing Mr. McPhee from 1998 to 2000.

Dukes was born on June 6, 1945, in San Francisco. He began his acting career in 1971, in a Broadway production of *School for Wives*. Dukes died on October 9, 2000, while playing tennis, having taken a day off from filming the television miniseries *Rose Red*. Ironically, Muske-Dukes was only months away from completing *Life after Death* (2001), her novel about a woman who wishes her husband to die, which he does on a tennis court. Dukes died of an apparent heart attack, something he had advised his wife, while she was writing her novel, could very well happen to a tennis player because of the cardiovascular exertion that occurs during the game. Muske-Dukes has been reported as saying that she felt that her having created this scenario in her novel somehow caused it to happen to her real-life husband. The couple had one child.

Women and Poetry

The speaker in "Our Side" is a woman remembering her dead lover. Critics have often deemed women's poems too personal and overly emotional, and women have struggled to claim authenticity in the realm of poetry. Women poets have been criticized for emphasizing the domestic realm, and this point is used to demean their work. Only since the middle of the twentieth century have the frequently autobiographical and personal poems of women been sanctioned and recognized as important expressions worthy of study.

Putting the issue of women and poetry in perspective is the poet Audre Lorde (1934–1992), who wrote nine books of poetry. In her essay "Poetry Is Not a Luxury," which was published in *By Herself: Women Reclaim Poetry*" (2000), Lorde presents her view of women writing poetry and the importance of this act. She writes,

> I speak here of poetry as a revelatory distillation of experience, not the sterile word play that, too often, the white fathers distorted the word *poetry* to mean— in order to cover a desperate wish for imagination without insight.

Lorde believed that for women, "poetry is not a luxury. It is a vital necessity of our existence." For women, poetry is a form through which their fears and hopes are named. By exploring these feelings through poetry, women create "the most radical and daring of ideas." Without poetry, Lorde believed, women might not be able to put those feelings into words. She writes, "Poetry is not only dream and vision; it is the skeleton architecture of our lives."

Lorde believed that the old concept of the head's (rational thought) ruling or forming poetry was an idea that women were forced to accept. Because of this long-held concept, emotions were relegated to a lower class, one less important, less authentic than the world of thought. Lorde writes,

> For within living structures defined by profit, by linear power, by institutional dehumanization, our feelings were not meant to survive. . . . Feelings were expected to kneel to thought as women were expected to kneel to men.

Women's power, Lorde believed, was long hidden because of denial and denigration of women's emotions. It is through feelings and their exploration in poetry that women will discover freedom.

Critical Overview

"Our Side" was published in the collection *Sparrow*, which was a National Book Award finalist in 2003. In his review of the book in *Publishers Weekly*, Michael Scharf describes the collection as follows: "Longing and grief produce concentrated moments of terse, wry observations on grief." Scharf points out that "the best poems [in this collection] capture the darkly ambiguous ruminations of a partner left behind."

Most of the poems in *Sparrow* are about or are addressed to Muske-Dukes's late husband. Ken Tucker, in the *New York Times Book Review*, describes the collection as follows:

> These poems, most of them forthrightly about the death of the author's husband . . . are at once extravagantly emotional in content and tightly controlled as verse, two qualities that echo the extremes of the committed romance described throughout *Sparrow*.

Kevin Craft, in Seattle's weekly publication *The Stranger*, says that he has been a fan of Muske-Dukes's poetry over the years. Knowing that this collection of poetry is focused on the emotions the poet feels after her husband's death, Craft admits that he was not looking forward to reading the poems in *Sparrow*. Although Craft has long admired Muske-Dukes's "tough-minded, elegant lyricism," he is wary of what this collection may contain. "The title seemed, well, slight for such weighty subject matter, and I didn't relish the prospect of page after page of personal grief," Craft writes. He continues, "My initial skepticism, however, was quickly and irrevocably disarmed." Although the poems are "deeply personal," Craft finds the collection "an intricate marriage of dramatic and lyric voices, grief so acutely rendered it prefigures centuries of love and loss."

Fred L. Dings, in *World Literature Today*, also finds more than grief in Muske-Dukes's poetry. "These poems never seem to succumb to the common pitfalls of gilding sentimentality or staged public expressions of bereavement," Dings writes. Rather, Dings finds "page after page of convincingly honest, accurate sentiment pitched tonally just right." Rather than sentimentality, Dings finds the strongest emotion in these poems to be "love, always love." In terms of language and style, Dings calls Muske-Dukes's poems "carefully crafted," but that craft "never becomes self-conscious to the point of undermining the core, driving sentiment."

Barbara Hoffert, in *Library Journal*, mentions a line from one of Muske-Dukes's poems in which the poet asks about the difference between love and grief. Hoffert points out that although Muske-Dukes does not provide any easy answers to this question, readers soon discover that her poems about love and grief "bring you to tears with her evocation of both."

Criticism

Joyce Hart

Joyce Hart is a published author and former writing instructor. In this essay, she looks at how Muske-Dukes avoids sentimentality in writing about love and loss.

Muske-Dukes's "Our Side," from her collection *Sparrow*, is about love and loss, a combination that could make anyone cringe. A person who experiences love and loss is often overwhelmed by the emotional effects of the tragedy. People trying to come to grips with heartbreak can talk about it with friends, family, or counselors, or they can write about it. Writing can provide a catharsis—a purification, or purging, of the emotional tension. However, writing produced under trying conditions can be saturated with melodrama and sentimentality. These qualities may be necessary for the psychology of the person who is writing the material, but they are not easy for outsiders to digest. Because the emotions are near the surface and overpowering in most material written by authors who are suffering, the feelings in the material tend to lose their impact on people who read it. In these cases, the author is said to be too close to the material to have an objective stance. In other words, the emotions are still too raw. The emotions are true and real, but the author cannot see beyond the feelings, cannot grasp meaning from them.

Readers tend to rebel against writing that is too sentimental or overwrought with anguish. Writing of this type (overly dramatic soap operas, for example) can come across as a mockery of the emotions the material is attempting to portray, or else it comes across as too difficult or too uncomfortable to look at or to even think about. Although people outside a tragedy may want to empathize with the victim of an unfortunate event, they tend not to want to be dragged into all the deeply personal psychological distress that the victim is suffering. The critic Kevin Craft writes in *The Stranger* that when he picked up *Sparrow* as he was preparing to review it, he "was wary" of the grief

What Do I Read Next?

- In her collection of essays about women and poetry titled *Women and Poetry: Truth, Autobiography, and the Shape of the Self* (1997), Muske-Dukes reviews her own poetry written over approximately twenty years to discover her own changing attitudes about women and poetry.

- In the novel *Life after Death* (2001), Muske-Dukes tells the story of a woman who, in a fit of anger, tells her husband to die. To her horror, he does, on the tennis court. This death is hauntingly similar to that of Muske-Dukes's husband, who died on a tennis court immediately before the publication of this novel.

- Muske-Dukes's collection of essays *Married to the Icepick Killer: A Poet in Hollywood* (2002) captures moments in her life as an artist living in film-crazy Los Angeles. Muske-Dukes also writes about her marriage and the challenges two artists face in living together.

- Jane Kenyon's *Collected Poems* (2005) is a tribute to Kenyon, who died at the age of forty-seven in 1995 but whose value as a poet has increased since her death. Kenyon is known as a down-to-earth poet. She writes equally honestly of her life and her depression.

- Like Muske-Dukes, Jane Kenyon was involved in a somewhat famous marriage, to the poet Donald Hall. Hall's memoir of the marriage is *The Best Day the Worst Day: Life with Jane Kenyon* (2005).

- A collection by another prize-winning poet is Mary Oliver's *Why I Wake Early: New Poems* (2004). Oliver's Pulitzer Prize–winning poems have a spirit behind them that is full of life and focused on beauty.

---

he might find there. Craft was surprised, however, as he began reading. He and several other book reviewers have found that Muske-Dukes has been able to portray her grief objectively, without sentimentality and melodrama.

A device Muske-Dukes uses to dissipate the overwhelming feeling of loss is to create a division of realms, "our side" (of the living) and their side (of the dead). This reaction is a common one when someone suffers the death of a loved one. The dead person is gone, but where is "gone"? All the living person knows is that "gone" is not here. The separation and unknowing create the sense of loss and longing. To minimize the sense of loss, Muske-Dukes portrays the speaker as wondering whether the newly dead experience a similar emotion. Are the newly dead trying to turn back? the speaker of this poem wonders. Are they as disoriented as those they have left behind? In a strange way, as in the old saying that misery loves company, the thought that the dead also suffer passionate longing gives comfort to those who are left behind. At the beginning of "Our Side," the speaker, rather than screaming at the top of her lungs, gnashing her teeth in anguish, and pulling her hair out in frustration, imagines what death must be like. This reaction is easier for readers to take. It makes readers wonder about death rather than focus on the pain of separation.

The first stanza contains a reference to spirituality in which the concept of an afterlife is established. The speaker refers to the "distance / inside each" of the newly dead. This space is "steadily growing" inside the newly dead, pulling "them away at last." This image offers solace to the speaker. Something inside the newly dead person is taking him away from her. The speaker infers that the dead person is not leaving of his own accord. Something more powerful than the material world is calling to him, enticing him. Because the speaker and the newly dead person have shared love, the image suggests that whatever is calling the dead lover is even greater than the love the couple has shared. If the call is that strong, the speaker seems to conclude, there is nothing that she can do about it. Although she never names the distance inside the newly dead

> *Instead of turning readers away with overemphasis, the poet invites readers to fill in the gaps, to imagine what the speaker is feeling and what the readers would feel if they were in the same situation."*

lover, readers can fill in the blank with their own spiritual beliefs. The distance may be a god figure. It may be a return to the source of all energy from which life is created. The image implies that something happens beyond death, that there is another realm. The image keeps alive the speaker's hope that one day she may be reunited with her lover. It also keeps her from focusing on her anguish.

In the second stanza, instead of crying out in anger at the departed person (an anger that is often stirred in those left behind, as if a loved one's death is a curse upon the living), the speaker seems accepting of her fate. As she looks at her emotions objectively, she discovers an image that helps her to announce, "Tenderness and longing lose direction, all terror / and love in the cells slowly dissipate." The speaker understands her lover's leaving, and she accepts the fact that the tenderness and longing that once were shared are hers alone. The speaker acknowledges that the love the couple enjoyed together is slowly dissolving, as her lover's body is decomposing. The poet looks at this process not through her emotions but through her intellect. She feels the loss, but in many ways she understates what she is experiencing. Through understatement of emotions and through imagery, readers are encouraged to embellish the feelings the speaker is suggesting. Instead of turning readers away with overemphasis, the poet invites readers to fill in the gaps, to imagine what the speaker is feeling and what the readers would feel if they were in the same situation. This style is much better than pouring out emotions and drowning readers in mournful details—a style that would turn most readers away.

Although "Our Side" is about death and loss, the most prevalent theme is love—the loss of love and the celebration of love. Celebration, in this instance, is not related to giving a party, playing loud music, and enjoying food and drink (although in some cultures people celebrate death in this way). In this poem, the celebration is a quiet one. Like quiet waters, the celebration of love runs deep.

The speaker wants to be remembered, but not for herself or for what she shared with her lover. She wants to make sure that despite death, the love she shared with her lover will never be forgotten: ". . . we insist on the desire of the lost to remember us, / to recognize the shape of our small flames." The love the couple shared may be small in relation to the spirit world to which the dead belong, but for the speaker that love is all she has left. She does not want the flame to go out. Although the love and longing may be dissipating in terms of the person who has died or is being overshadowed by the unnamed experience that the dead lover is going through, the speaker tries to remind herself that she alone must keep the love alive. She is worried that her lover is "too far away now / to recall anything of our side." In her reminiscing about the day the couple saw the hang gliders, she is reminding herself of their love.

In the last two lines of the poem, the speaker is not merely reminding herself of the day at "the old beach hotel," she is also creating an image that will help her remember the love that the couple once shared. She sees, in her mind's eye, the hang gliders and relates them to the love she must newly define. The hang gliders will represent "all our shining ambivalent love." The use of the word "ambivalent" suggests the speaker's inability to fully define the love, especially because her lover is no longer available to provide his portion of it. The use of "ambivalent" also may suggest other elements present before the lover died. However, it seems not to matter at this point. The speaker appears to be able to see the "human forms / suspended over the sea" as a metaphor for where she and her lover are at this point. The love is present—suspended and undefined. Although death has interrupted the love, or redefined it, the love remains visible, at least in the speaker's heart and mind.

Source: Joyce Hart, Critical Essay on "Our Side," in *Poetry for Students*, Thomson Gale, 2006.

David Kelly

David Kelly is an instructor of creative writing and literature. In this essay, he examines two elements of the poem that Muske-Dukes uses to bridge the gulf between the living and the dead: the final couplet and the use of pronouns.

It is unlikely that a reader could make it very far into Muske-Dukes's collection of poems *Sparrow* with no awareness of the biographical story behind it: the book is built of poems about grief, raw and processed, that came out of her own experience of sudden, tragic, early widowhood. To some extent, knowing about the poet's loss enriches readers' experience, causing them to read the poems with a heightened sense of their emotional pedigree. It can, however, be distracting to focus too much on the real life story behind the works at the expense of the works themselves. These poems are crafted and emotionally complex, requiring no background to confirm their legitimacy; in fact, giving too much attention to the sorrow that brought them into being can sap them of their individual identities. Muske-Dukes is a first-rate poet who would have something important to say about any subject. After a first reading, with the initial impressions that it evokes, readers should experience the deft skill that makes it possible for Muske-Dukes to translate her experience from author to reader.

A fine example of Muske-Dukes's controlling hand as a poet can be found in one of the poems from the collection, "Our Side." In this poem, death is presented as a physical separation, with the recently deceased being ferried across a river, like the River Styx, to a distant shore. The title seems to place the living and the dead into different social groups, "us" against "them," until the poem finally comes around to a point where space and identity converge. That the poem is certainly infused with grief is beyond question, but it would be a mistake to believe that an understanding of grief, in itself, qualifies a reader to understand the poem or that a lack of loss could prevent one from seeing what Muske-Dukes has to say. This is a poem about death, life, and memory, but even these grand subjects might not command the attention they deserve if it were not for the author's canny machinations.

As with any good poem, "Our Side" has its stylistic elements so deeply embedded that it is hardly relevant to talk about form as a separate thing from meaning. There are, though, a few points that deserve to be looked at on their own, just to understand a little more clearly what makes this particular poem successful. They have to do with the poem's progression from hopelessness to despair and from the isolation that death imposes to the saving grace of memory.

Throughout the poem, Muske-Dukes refers to 'us' and 'we' in ways that change the poem's meaning, taking readers from the traditional separation of the living from the dead to an alignment of the poet with the one she lost."

For one thing, the poem ends with two lines that change the sense of the seven stanzas that preceded them. The first seven stanzas are generally three lines each, not counting a few half-lines. The brevity of the last stanza would in itself make the stanza stand out, but there is also the fact that its function has a familiar echo for poetry readers. This couplet functions in this poem in the same way that such a couplet would function in one of the world's most recognizable poetic forms, the sonnet: it brings closure to "Our Side," punctuating the poem's imagery of despair with a coda that raises it in another direction.

In English sonnets, the significance of what is discussed in the first twelve lines is counterbalanced by the last two lines; they may restate what came before, but more often they add a new dimension to the discussion by introducing a contrasting image or idea. The reader has to consider the whole thing from a new perspective after this change in direction. The focus of "Our Side" is, from the start, water, air, and ground, with the eye being drawn downward: "canyons / of the infinite," "this bright uneasy harbor," "candles and searchboats," and "bright beams scanning" not the skies but "for faces." The imagery seems to struggle to lift itself away, to draw attention upward, but it is stuck, as if too laden with sorrow.

In addition to standing alone on the page, the final couplet distinguishes itself by presenting the same ideas of air, water, and earth in a new juxtaposition: the poet remembers a time when she and the deceased were together, uplifted by the vision of hang gliders floating ephemerally over the water, unencumbered by the weight of existence. Life, which is usually thought of as the more tangible, is remembered as being no heavier than death. The issue of separation that the poem raised at the beginning, with the deceased crossing over to the other side, is reconciled at the end, as boundaries are erased and life and death, ground and air, and shores of all types are looked at as "our" side.

This transformation, which is abrupt in the poem's imagery, is brought along more gradually throughout "Our Side" by the use of pronouns. Throughout the poem, Muske-Dukes refers to "us" and "we" in ways that change the poem's meaning, taking readers from the traditional separation of the living from the dead to an alignment of the poet with the one she has lost. The fact that the "we" of the end of the poem is different from the "we" of the beginning is no coincidence.

For its first few stanzas, the poem speaks directly to its reader, functioning as a sort of lecture about the behaviors of "the newly dead." That ends, though, at the end of stanza 3, when the "I" is first referred to, bringing in the personal element. This line, which also has the first reference to the poetic "you," stands alone as a question. It is not clearly addressed to a particular person but could be taken as a meditation on the recent dead in general. This line is out of sync with the rest of the poem because it is an individual question, a self-supported sentence—an aside, or a question one might ask oneself but not say aloud. It is the last time that "I" and "you" are mentioned until the end.

Through most of the poem, the pronouns divide reality into two distinct camps: "our" and "we" or "them" and "they." The early mention of "the newly dead" establishes the identities of who these pronouns refer to. "They" are those who have died, and "we" would therefore be those who have remained in the land of the living. A line like "we insist on the desire of the lost to remember us" helps to further this distinction, drawing a line between "the lost" and "us." In the sort of nondistinct way that poetry can treat its references, living and dead are members of different social circles, and they are unable to associate. That changes, though, in the end.

In the seventh stanza, "I" and "you" are mentioned, and there is no ambiguity about whom they mean: they are the poet and the person that the poet has lost. That same line uses the title words—"our side." This "our" seems to place the speaker in opposition to the dead person, if "our" is taken to

mean the side of the living; it does not have to mean that, though. "Our" could still include both members of the couple, as "we" does, later in that same line.

The final couplet shows the two, mourner and mourned, together at some earlier time. The image conveyed is the contrast of all the images that came before: instead of being weighted down, the living are lighter than air; they fly over the water rather than being carried across it; and the source of light is not the longing lights set out along grief's shore but the sun still in the sky, though waning. There is no question whom the poet means by "us" in the final line, "behind us and all our shining ambivalent love airborne there before us": it is herself and the one who has died. Although this is a memory, it is presented at the end as such a powerful and important moment that it can negate, or at least equal, the loss of the present.

This is a poem about death, and, like any poem, it needs to make its subject abstract in order to make its meaning transferable from the writer to the reader. The fact that Muske-Dukes suffered a great loss is too often reported, as if that alone makes her meditation on death worth attention. What is more important is that she knows when to give her poem form—but not only a hint, allowing her to refer to tradition without being a slave to it—and how to use her words deftly, to make readers think about who is included.

Source: David Kelly, Critical Essay on "Our Side," in *Poetry for Students*, Thomson Gale, 2006.

Fred L. Dings

In the following review, Dings calls Sparrow *"an eloquent and beautifully written book."*

Except for one elegy about a woman who died of breast cancer (which appears mysteriously in the middle of the collection), the poems in *Sparrow* are wholly devoted to remembering, addressing, and further knowing the actor David Dukes, the recently deceased husband of the author. Although written in "fresh grief," these poems never seem to succumb to the common pitfalls of gilding sentimentality or staged public expressions of bereavement, except for the possible case of the proem, "Valentine's Day, 2003." Instead, we find page after page of convincingly honest, accurate sentiment pitched tonally just right ("a stubborn witness walks within me"). The leading emotion is love, always love, even when the poems confess residual anger about a longstanding problem in the relationship: the beloved possibly not completely committed by way of some built-in distance, some inaccessibility, some frustrating withholding of self. The artist/lover meticulously witnesses her own memories to make present the deceased and to more fully know the complicated and sometimes enigmatic person who has died. In this sense, the act of writing these poems extends and deepens a relationship that will have no end while the speaker lives, and we are left with a complicated, fully human profile of the deceased, described through eyes that have paid and are still paying very close attention.

These are carefully crafted poems, but the craft (except in the poem "Box") never becomes self-conscious to the point of undermining the core, driving sentiment. Even in the poem "Box," however, where we become conscious of the artist's joy in the artifice of the poem momentarily dislocating the core grief that is the occasion of the poem, we somehow don't mind, seeing the possible healing that awaits all of us in the transformation of grief. The transformative power of this poet manifests itself at times in poetic images that blaze into startling metaphoricity. Consider: "crystal flutes of ruined grape, we lifted them—/ afloat in the pool in the cliff hung over the sea" or "we saw human forms // suspended over the sea: the hang-gilders at sunset . . . / all our shining ambivalent love airborne there before us." *Sparrow* is an eloquent and beautifully written book.

Source: Fred L. Dings, Review of *Sparrow*, in *World Literature Today*, Vol. 78, No. 3–4, September–December 2004, pp. 101–102.

Liz Rosenberg

In the following review of Sparrow, *Rosenberg asserts that, in* Sparrow, *a collection focused on her recently deceased husband, Muske-Dukes has managed to "capture and immortalize the shifting, mortal beauty of a living being."*

In this season of summer wedding parties, it's touching to find a pair of books largely about marriage, by two highly prized American poets. Carol Muske-Dukes's heart breaking *Sparrow* catalogs the infinite faces of marriage in poems that mourn and celebrate her husband, the late actor David Dukes. Maxine Kumin's *The Long Marriage* honors her partnership to her husband, Victor, while extending "marriage" to lifelong relationships to other beloveds: poetry, poets' friends, gardens, the body, and a Noah's ark of animals, from the "scarlet tanager / who lights in the apple tree" to cattle, sheep, and horses. Both books are gorgeous,

densely layered, melancholy, comical, and moving—all the more so upon rereading.

Sparrow is almost unbearably sad in its exact recounting of loss, but I want to emphasize that "almost," since its beauty and intelligence keep both the poems and the reader pulling steadily forward. *Sparrow* circles around the vortex of a particular absence, the death of one's beloved. "On my study floor, the books were piled high. 'you stepped over them, smiling, as you came in / to kiss me goodnight." Muske-Dukes musters her considerable powers to come to an understanding of her grief— if not a victory over it, at least the momentary stay against confusion that is one of poetry's gifts.

Sparrow refuses to rest, to reside in answers. Instead the poet reexamines the past—"I lift my face, distracted, still, for your late, tender kiss"— calibrating each of her actor-husband's mercurial faces, her own shock and grief, hurling questions against herself: "Was I sleeping, while the others suffered?"; "Where did I / imagine the heart would go? To danger?"; and, in the dazzling and deadly poem "The Call": "That nurse in a distant blazing room / beginning to take shape before my eyes / paused, then put my question back to me. / Did I want to be told what was happening to you?"

In the story of this particular marriage, this early death and all its aftershocks, Muske-Dukes does for her beloved what Shakespeare in his sonnets sought to do for his—to capture and immortalize the shifting, mortal beauty of a living being. Her husband is often figured as a hawk—beautiful, swift, largely untamable, always on the verge of motion: "You turned back / once to look at me over your shoulder, opening the Stage / Door. Not yet made up, but already a stranger, the hawk staring out of your face." The poet is apparently a more domestic bird: "The sparrow I brought / home in my hand outlived you." If a sparrow in her own self-figuration, she is thrushlike in the sad beauty of her singing—a blue morpho's wings seen "stained with the color of the afterlife," the actor playing a part: "You are Algernon. You have been / Algernon before, though not tonight's / Algernon." She deeply understood her husband's art, and she deeply understands her own, rendering even deepest sorrow as lovely, as haunting as birdsong.

Source: Liz Rosenberg, "On Unions, Sundered or Enduring," in *Boston Sunday Globe*, August 3, 2003, p. 1.

Roger Gathman

In the following essay on the occasion of the publication of Muske-Dukes's third novel, Life after Death*, Gathman profiles her writing life.*

> *She was at the epicenter of the feminist surge in poetry in the '70s and '80s. But her roots are in the tradition-bound Great Plains."*

If you go south of Hollywood on LaBrea and turn east on West 3rd Street, you will travel through the heart of Hancock Park, an L.A. neighborhood built in the 1920s to accommodate the needs of non-Hollywood nabobs, like the Getty family. The street passes by massive English Tudor mansions with odd Spanish Colonial addenda, a beautiful golf course and occasional LaLa Land eccentricities (the mini-villa, for instance, with the 17 life-size reproductions of Michelangelo's David lining the driveway). On this overcast May morning, the jacaranda and magnolia trees are in full bloom along the side streets.

Poet and novelist Carol Muske-Dukes lives in the Windsor Square section of this neighborhood, in a pied-a-terre that does not, as it happens, particularly allude to the reign of King Henry VIII or the Spanish conquest of Granada. Her dogs clamor at the gate when *PW* shows up, but become a friendly welcoming committee when Muske-Dukes appears.

This must be an eerie season for the writer. On the bright side, her latest book, *Life After Death* (Forecasts, Apr. 3), an elegantly written novel of manners, will surely be well received this summer. The story centers on a St. Paul, Minn., woman, Boyd Schaeffer, whose 42-year-old husband, Russell, drops dead of a heart attack. She goes back into medicine and starts an awkward romance with a funeral home director. The book is full of marvelous throwaway pieces, prose poems of a sort. Here's Freddy, Boyd and Russell's daughter, on the playground with a book, after shooing away a playmate who smells:

> Freddy returns to her consideration of the tree and her letters, safe in her milieu. To her right, near the aquarium, grim, asthmatic Felicia batters pegs into holes, wheezing and grunting. They are all in place, all the categories and predictable social types that she will meet and remeet throughout her life. The

Aggressor throwing blocks, the Whiner sobbing in his wet plast pants, the Seducers, he and she tossing their curls, the Good Citizen preparing to report to the Teacher.

Favorable criticism might cast a retrospective glow of interest over Muske-Dukes's two previous novels, *Dear Digby* (Viking, 1989) and *Saving St. Germ* (Viking, 1993), the last of which was a *New York Times* Notable Book of the year. Both were published to critical acclaim, but neither achieved more than modest popular success.

The dark side is hinted at in the novel's dedication: "For David, who gave me constant love and encouragement in writing this book since 1994 and whom I lost on October 9, 2000." "David" is David Dukes, her husband, the actor who starred in television (*The Winds of War*), theater (*Bent*) and film (*The First Deadly Sin*). After Muske-Dukes had completed the book, her husband unexpectedly suffered a heart attack and died. It was a cruel coincidence, an instance of what Thomas Hardy called "satires of circumstance," that Boyd's fictional trauma was visited on her author.

Muske-Dukes (who uses the simple "Muske" for her poetry) has been a recognized figure in the literary world since her first volume of poems, *Camouflage,* came out from University of Pittsburgh Press in 1975. Since then her poetry has garnered her major recognition in the poetry world and the prizes and grants that go with it. She was at the epicenter of the feminist surge in poetry in the '70s and '80s. But her roots are in the tradition-bound Great Plains.

Her grandfather was "a Separator Man / harvesting the wheat / in Wyndmere." Wyndmere is a town in North Dakota, where her mother's family still owns land. "Back in the Great Depression they were land rich, but poor. My mother was a frustrated poet. She got a scholarship, but the family couldn't afford to have her go to college. So she married my father and had a family, but she always had a great store of poetry she'd memorized. I remember she would insert these asides into her bits, like 'Let me not to the marriage of true minds—put your dishes in the sink—admit impediments.' I remember it would puzzle me coming upon these poems and thinking, hey, where's the part about putting the dishes in the sink?"

More seriously, Muske-Dukes appreciates the act of memorizing poetry, which used to be a standard element of the teaching curriculum, as a way of "embodying the poem." "Joseph Brodsky," she says, "who was teaching at Columbia when I was also teaching there, used to have his graduate students memorize poems. Brodsky was the kind of poet who committed poems to heart naturally—he learned English by memorizing poetry—out of great love."

"I became one of those insufferable kids who are encouraged to produce poems on all occasions" is the way Muske-Dukes wryly sums up her early writerly drive. When she went to Creighton, a Jesuit college in Nebraska, and then to San Francisco State, she already knew, in a sense, what she wanted to do. "I wasn't very hip when I left Creighton. I just walked into the whole San Francisco scene. I took a course in directed reading under Kay Boyle. (You know, I like saying this whenever I can. Kay Boyle should be part of the canon, along with her modernist brothers.) I got my degree, went to Europe, and even played in *Hair* in Paris. Then I went to live in New York."

Muske-Dukes wrote about the poetic and political moment in New York in an autobiographical essay in her essay collection, *Women and Poetry: Truth, Autobiagraphy, and the Shape of the Self* (1997): "When I arrived in New York in 1971, I joined consciousness-raising groups, but I found it impossible to express my own sense of conflict. I eventually sought out women in prison, because their isolation and extremity reflected a dislocation I felt in my own life and writing."

"I was really inspired at San Francisco State by Kathleen Fraser, who electrified me when she read Plath's 'Daddy,'" Muske-Duke says. "Fraser seemed to be able to be both a poet and live an ordinary life. I didn't see how I could do that myself. In addition to that, the public world of poetry then was controlled by men—as it still is. What I thought would help was teaching in the Riker's Island prison, and so I was going between two enclosed places—I was teaching at Columbia, and at Riker's. Eventually I set up, through the National Endowment for the Arts, a program for this, 'Art Without Walls.'"

If her political side was active at the time, her poetry was also becoming known. "My first book was published because I'd entered these poems in a contest. I didn't win the contest—a Thomas Rabbit did. But they had enough money, they could afford to publish two books, so they published *Camouflage*."

In 1981, she went to live in Italy on a Guggenheim grant, and there she met David Dukes, in highly romantic circumstances. "I rented a house in Barbarino Val d'Elsa, outside of Florence. A beautiful house built into an ancient Etruscan wall.

My friend, Jorie Graham [the poet], was in Italy then, too. Her mother, Beverly Pepper, is world renowned for her heavy metal sculptures. Her father, Bill, is an author and journalist. They own a castle in Todi, which they built from ruins of a 12th-century fortification and tower, the Castella Torre Olivola.

"Okay. Jorie's brother, John, was an assistant director on the television miniseries, *The Winds of War,* which was shooting in Florence when I was there. Among the cast was a friend of John's—David Dukes—who was coming over to see John at his parents' place. Since Jorie had invited me to come, too, the plan was that David would pick me up in Florence and we would drive down there together. Of course, it was a setup. We drove down there, and imagine this place, with Beverly's sculptures surrounding the grounds like brooding sentinels. Jorie and I talk about poetry, John and David talk about acting. David was trained as a Shakespearean actor, he knew the classical repertoire, Moliere to Chekhov. Now, who wouldn't fall in love in those circumstances?"

Muske-Dukes shows me an album of photos of these places she made for her sixth wedding anniversary. It ends with a clip from Liz Smith's gossip column, announcing the marriage of David Dukes and Carol Muske, and a news picture of the bride and groom, looking radiantly happy.

In the early '80s, Muske-Dukes was starting to write fiction. Her first novel, *Dear Digby,* started as an epistolary goof. "I was supposed to co-write that with a friend, who was actually in the letters department at *Ms.* magazine." The friend dropped out of the project, but Muske-Dukes continued. "The letter format was really helpful for me just starting out in fiction, because it gave a natural flow to my chapters—you end a letter, or you begin one, and that provides a way of swimming from one piece of text to another." The novel is about a Lonely Hearts–style columnist at *SIS,* a feminist magazine. Digby radiates a sort of combination of the ingenue humor of Gracie Allen and the in-your-face feminism of the early Gloria Steinem. "I didn't have an agent at the time. A friend showed the manuscript to Viking, and they bought it. So I scrambled to find an agent." The book was received with critical enthusiasm and optioned, by Michelle Pfeiffer, for a movie. "It was greenlighted by Orion, but they couldn't get their screenplay together. At one point Callie Khouri—who later did *Thelma and Louise*—wanted to do it, but they turned her down." Her second novel, *Saving St. Germ,* in 1993, reflected her move to Southern California. By this time, she was teaching creative writing at USC, in the same department as T. C. Boyle. The novel is about a scientist, Esme Charbonneau, who makes a brilliant but highly technical discovery in physics.

"That novel came out of reading a very beautiful novel by Charles Baxter, *First Light.* I fell in love with that book, which is about a woman who is an astrophysicist, who has a deaf child. Baxter is great at showing how the child enters the world in a different way that really captured my imagination. I knew I couldn't just cop his idea, but I decided I'd write about a chemist who wants to be a cosmologist." That she would have to use a whole different vocabulary did not seem daunting. "I like the vocabularies of other disciplines. I had an interesting experience when I was researching this book, because I went to a scientist at USC with various questions, and before he explained things to me, he asked me, what level of calculus do you have? Or trigonometry? Or algebra? And I kept shaking my head. So he said, I'm going to have to use lay language? And it turned out that when he used 'Jay' language, he started giving me metaphors and analogies—as you would get, notoriously, in poetry." In the book, Esme's life comes apart as she tries to develop a purely theoretical insight into the origin of the universe. "I got some odd reactions to that book. A scientist from San Diego told me that I was doing a disservice to women in science by showing this woman as unstable. I tried to explain that it was fiction." *Saving St. Germ* was also published by Viking.

Her current novel was inspired by Evelyn Waugh's *The Loved One.* "I thought I might do something in a comic vein like that. So in St. Paul, I talked to funeral home directors. But the satiric impulse in the novel petered out as I got more interested in Boyd. Now that David has died, I have more perspective on her. I think maybe I didn't allow Boyd to be as shocked—as traumatized—as she would have been. This novel had nothing to do with David. He was pyrotechnically active, and you simply wouldn't have suspected that he had advanced coronary artery disease."

She has nothing but praise for her new publisher, Random House, who will also be publishing her book of essays, *Married to the Icepick Killer: A Poet in Hollywood,* next year. She likes it that her editor there, Daniel Menaker, is an author himself. When Random House took her novel, she was between agents. On the recommendation of Menaker, she went to Molly Friedrich, who has "been more than good, she's been a source of strength, a real friend." Muske-Dukes is also pleased with the look of the

novel, which features, on its cover, a reproduction of a painting by the Flemish master Joachim Patinir, *Charon Crossing the Styx,* showing a gigantic ferryman of death steering a pale, dwindled, suppliant figure across a glassy sheet of water to a shore upon which a signal fire, or funeral pyre, has been lit. The painting complements not only this novel, with its subtly woven tension between the transitions of everyday life and the aura of myth, but also the striving in her work to understand the emotional tug produced by the stubborn particularity, the finitude, of objects and persons. As she put it in a poem in *Red Trousseau:* "The rest of it, you see, / is my work: slowing the mind's quick progress / from the hypnotic of that startled world / to the empty solicitation of metaphor / the loathsome poetic moment."

Source: Roger Gathman, "Carol Muske-Dukes: The Cruel Poetries of Life," in *Publishers Weekly,* Vol. 248, No. 25, June 18, 2001, p. 52.

Sources

Craft, Kevin, "The Sparrow, the Fall; Carol Muske-Dukes and the Awful Tangle of Language and Fate," in *The Stranger,* Vol. 13, No. 31, April 15–21, 2004, p. 49.

Dings, Fred L., Review of *Sparrow,* in *World Literature Today,* Vol. 78, No. 3–4, September–December 2004, pp. 101–102.

Hoffert, Barbara, "Best Poetry of 2003: Ten Titles, Four Collections from Major Poets, and Four Anthologies," in *Library Journal,* Vol. 129, No., 7, April 15, 2004, pp. 88–89.

Lorde, Audre, "Poetry Is Not a Luxury," in *By Herself: Women Reclaim Poetry,* edited by Molly McQuade, Graywolf Press, 2000, pp. 365–66.

Muske-Dukes, Carol, "Our Side," in *Sparrow: Poems,* Random House, 2004, pp. 60–61.

Scharf, Michael, Review of *Sparrow,* in *Publishers Weekly,* Vol. 250, No. 25, June 23, 2003, p. 61.

Tucker, Ken, Review of *Sparrow,* in the *New York Times Book Review,* July 6, 2003, p. 20.

Further Reading

Ikeda, Daisaku, *Unlocking the Mysteries of Birth and Death: And Everything in Between, a Buddhist View of Life,* 2nd ed., Middleway Press, 2004.
    Daisaku Ikeda, a winner of the United Nations Peace Award, presents an easy-to-read and easy-to-understand introduction to Buddhism, which explores people's interconnectedness to one another and all things of the world.

Kübler-Ross, Elisabeth, *On Death and Dying*, Scribner, 1969, reprint, 1997.

> This book is a classic study of the stages that people go through when they know they are dying. Kübler-Ross, a psychiatrist, devoted her life to dealing with the emotions of dying. By understanding what a dying person goes through, those who experience the loss of a loved one also gain insight into how to deal with their grief.

McQuade, Molly, ed., *By Herself: Women Reclaim Poetry*, Graywolf Press, 2000.

In this collection of essays, women poets describe their creative writing and women's poetry in general.

Segal, Alan F., *Life after Death: A History of the Afterlife in Western Religion*, Doubleday, 2004.

> Every religion has its own definition or assumption of what happens after a person dies. Segal examines the beliefs about afterlife throughout the history of Western religions, from ancient Egyptian to contemporary Muslim, Jewish, and Christian beliefs.

A Poison Tree

William Blake

1793

"A Poison Tree" is one of the lesser-known of the twenty-six poems William Blake published in 1793 as *Songs of Experience*, which also contains "The Tyger," "Ah, Sun-flower," and "London." *Songs of Experience* is the companion volume to Blake's *Songs of Innocence*, published in 1789. Blake printed *Songs of Innocence* and *Songs of Experience* in one volume in 1794, adding the descriptive subtitle "Shewing the Two Contrary States of the Human Soul." One of the best sources of "A Poison Tree" is *The Complete Poetry and Prose of William Blake* (1982), edited by David V. Erdman and published by Doubleday.

In the poems of *Songs of Innocence* and *Songs of Experience*, Blake contrasts how the human spirit blossoms when allowed its own free movement, which he calls a state of "innocence," and how it turns in on itself after it has been suppressed and forced to conform to rules, systems, and doctrines, which he calls a state of "experience." The two states recall one of the principal events in the Judeo-Christian story, the fall from innocence caused by Adam and Eve when they eat fruit from the forbidden Tree of the Knowledge of Good and Evil in the Garden of Eden. The poison tree of Blake's poem suggests that biblical tree.

Although it can be read by itself, "A Poison Tree" benefits significantly from being read as a further expression of the poems immediately preceding it in *Songs of Experience*, especially "The Garden of Love" and "The Human Abstract." In the three poems, Blake criticizes the imposition of

religious and social morality on the human sensibility, suggesting that it stifles the goodness and love inherent in a spirit not fettered by such rules. In Blake's *Notebook*, the original title of "A Poison Tree" is "Christian Forbearance," which the poem criticizes as the cause of hypocrisy.

Author Biography

Poet, painter, engraver, mystic, and visionary, William Blake was born in London on November 28, 1757. His parents, James and Catherine, ran a hosiery shop and were political radicals and religious Dissenters. They opposed the tenets of the Church of England and the policies of the English monarchy, such as the war against the American colonies. They believed in the personal, mystical revelation of the Divinity through scripture and in following the dictates of conscience. Throughout his life, Blake's own interpretation of scripture; actual visions of the nonmaterial world; and a dedication to political, religious, and sexual liberty formed the foundations of his beliefs and served as the cornerstones of his work.

Blake's parents did not send him to school but allowed him to wander through the streets of London and the outlying woods. Nevertheless, Blake was not uneducated. From childhood, he read works of philosophy and literature, especially the Bible. Blake's father encouraged him to write and to draw and bought him prints of classic drawings, paintings, and sculptures. When he was ten, Blake was enrolled in a drawing school. At fifteen, he became an apprentice to an engraver. On August 18, 1782, Blake married Catherine Boucher, who was a lifelong admiring and loving companion to him and assisted him in his workshop.

In much of his work, Blake combined poetry and engraving, etching the text of his poetry onto copper plates impressed with images that he colored after printing. It was in such an illuminated book, called *Songs of Experience*, that "A Poison Tree" appeared in 1794.

To a small circle of admirers, Blake was regarded as a prophet. The visionary and subversive nature of his mystical Christianity, however, and his revolutionary politics gave him the reputation of being a madman in the influential circles of his times. So did his art. Blake's poetry is marked by a private mythology. Blake personified forces of nature, the psyche, and the spirit and gave them names such as Orc, Urizen, and Rintra. He showed

William Blake   © Corbis-Bettmann

these forces in dramatic and mortal conflict with one another. Blake's visual art represents the visions he beheld and the characters he imagined.

Blake lived all his life in poverty, indebted to several benefactors who provided him with commissions. Although he was firm in his belief that his work was appreciated in heaven, Blake often felt bitterness because lesser artists were being rewarded on earth while he was being rejected. *Songs of Experience*, for example, sold only twenty copies in Blake's lifetime. Blake died in London on August 12, 1827, and was buried in an unmarked grave in Bunhill Fields, a Dissenters' cemetery.

Poem Text

I was angry with my friend;
I told my wrath, my wrath did end.
I was angry with my foe:
I told it not, my wrath did grow.
And I waterd it in fears,   5
Night & morning with my tears:
And I sunned it with smiles,
And with soft deceitful wiles.
And it grew both day and night.
Till it bore an apple bright.   10
And my foe beheld it shine.
And he knew that it was mine.

And into my garden stole,
When the night had veild the pole;
In the morning glad I see;   15
My foe outstretchd beneath the tree.

Poem Summary

First Quatrain

On first contact with "A Poison Tree," a reader may be deceived by the apparent simplicity of the poem. It seems like one more example of the children's verses and nursery rhymes that had become popular and were being published in the later part of the eighteenth century. The most famous collection was the one attributed to "Mother Goose." Such verses were intended to teach children moral lessons through easy-to-remember rhymes and catchy rhythms.

"I was angry with my friend; / I told my wrath, my wrath did end," Blake begins. The language and sentiment are simple and hardly need to be explained even to a young child. Someone is speaking of his direct experience: He was angry at his friend. He told his friend that he was angry, and the result was that his anger went away. The whole thing is presented in a neat package tied up and resolved by the rhyme of "friend" and "end." In contrast to this way of handling anger, the speaker says, "I was angry with my foe: / I told it not, my wrath did grow." Again the verse seems clear and simple, and so, too, the lesson. When people do not say how they feel, the bad feeling becomes worse. The latter two lines of the quatrain, furthermore, seem to reinforce the wisdom of the first two: Say what you feel; do not suppress it, or things will get worse.

The analogy the reader is led to draw between the first set of two lines, or rhyming couplet, and the second couplet is not exact. The situations are different. In the first couplet, the speaker is angry at his friend; in the second, at his foe. This difference immediately makes the simple poem less simple. The lines are not really moralizing about confessing or concealing anger. They are referring to the way people classify other people as friends and foes and to the different ways people treat friends and foes. By extension, the poem considers the nature and consequences of anger, exploring how it grows and what it grows into.

Second Quatrain

The second quatrain, composed of two more rhyming couplets, seems less like a child's verse than the first quatrain. "And I waterd it in fears,"

the speaker says, "Night & morning with my tears: / And I sunned it with smiles, / And with soft deceitful wiles." In these lines, the speaker tells how he has tended and cultivated his anger, how he has made it grow. He is not suggesting a moral, as he does in the first quatrain, but he is examining a process. He is revealing the pleasure he takes in his own slyness. He also begins to speak using metaphor. Metaphor allows one thing to suggest or stand for something else. The "it" of the first line of the second quatrain refers to the speaker's wrath, but he speaks of his wrath not as if it were an emotion, which it is, but as if it were a small plant. He "waterd" his anger with his tears, and, using another metaphor, he "sunned it with smiles / And with soft deceitful wiles."

Wiles are sly tricks, strategies intended to deceive someone into trusting. The speaker is laying a trap for his foe, tempting him to desire something that seems alluring but is harmful. As he pretends to be friendly to his foe, the very act of being friendly strengthens his wrath. The false smiles he bestows on his foe act like sunshine on the plant of his wrath. The friendlier the speaker seems, the more hostile he really is, and the worse are his intentions. The clarity of innocence is gone. The speaker's behavior does not look like what it is. He is not what he seems. By using metaphor, by talking about anger as if it were a plant and about hypocrisy as if it were sunshine, the speaker represents the duplicity of his behavior in his language. He makes his behavior appear more attractive than it is.

Third Quatrain

What is a figure of speech, a metaphor, in the second quatrain seems to become the thing itself, an actual tree, in the third. "And it grew both day and night," the speaker says. The "it" must refer to his wrath, which he has been cultivating with "smiles, / And . . . soft deceitful wiles." In the second line of the third quatrain, however, "it" bears "an apple bright." The wrath has become an actual tree. Anger does not bear apples. Apple trees do. A feeling has been given so much weight that it has become a presence, an actual thing. The fruit of the speaker's wrath, then, is not *like* an apple on a tree, it *is* an apple. The speaker has made his anger seem like something else, and then it actually becomes something else. He has made something deadly become alluring and tempting to his foe.

By association, the speaker's anger, which has become a tempting apple, can remind the reader of the apple on the forbidden Tree of Knowledge in the Garden of Eden. That fruit seems as if it would offer a world of good, but in the Judeo-Christian story, it actually offers a world of woe. The apple of "A Poison Tree" is the same kind of apple. The reader may have the uneasy feeling that Blake is suggesting that in the Bible story, what is called God's love is really a form of wrath, that the God of the established Judeo-Christian religion is a god of wrath, not of love. Blake does believe that, as his longer poems repeatedly demonstrate. "A Poison Tree," a poem *using* metaphors *becomes* a metaphor. The relation of the angry speaker to his foe comes to stand for the story of an angry god and humankind.

Fourth Quatrain

The climax of "A Poison Tree" comes rushing on so swiftly that a break between verse paragraphs, which has marked movement from one quatrain to the next, no longer seems necessary. The first line of the final quatrain follows without a pause after the second couplet of the third: "And my foe beheld it shine. / And he knew that it was mine. / And into my garden stole." The repeated use of the word "and"—a poetic device called polysyndeton—at the beginning of each line shows how clearly one action leads to and follows another. Blake also accelerates the action of the poem by the way he uses the word "stole." "And into my garden stole" means that his foe came secretly into his garden. "Stole," however, also suggests thievery, what the foe sneaks into the garden to do under cover of darkness. By giving the word "stole" the strength he does, the speaker is emphasizing the culpability of his foe.

The culpability, in large part, has been created by the speaker himself. The speaker, the tempter, is the one who has laid snares for his foe and is responsible for them. The poem never reveals whether the person called the "foe" has a feeling of enmity, or ill will, toward the speaker or whether he realizes the speaker even considers him a foe. The poem tells nothing about what sort of person the "foe" is, why the speaker considers him a foe, or why he is angry with him. Stealing into the garden and eating the apple, moreover, is not necessarily an act of enmity. It is foremost an act of appetite, of desire, which, in fact, has been induced and stimulated by the speaker. The speaker, by using the word "stole," shows his own excitement at luring his foe into blameworthiness and transgression, and, unknowingly, he is indicting himself. The only thing Blake allows the speaker to say about his foe is that he "stole" into the garden

Media Adaptations

- *Famous Authors: William Blake* (1996), a documentary on the life and work of the poet, with commentary from scholars, was produced by Kultur Video.

- *Pioneers of the Spirit: William Blake* (2005), put out by Vision Video, looks at the visionary and mystical elements of Blake's art and writing.

"when the night had veild the pole." The polestar, that is, the fixed North Star, the star that mariners use to keep them on course, is obscured. In other words, the foe steals into the garden at a moment when, the metaphor of the veiled polestar reveals, his sense of moral direction has been impaired by the speaker's subterfuge.

The final couplet, "In the morning glad I see; / My foe outstretched beneath the tree," is more ambiguous than at first it may appear. How one decides to understand it determines how to understand the entire poem. The first problem of interpretation is whether "outstretched" means dead. If it does, as the reader is entitled to believe it does because the tree bears poison, then the couplet reveals the baseness of the speaker. It shows the pleasure the speaker takes at the fall of his enemy: In the morning, I am glad to see that my foe lies dead beneath the tree. If, however, "outstretched" means only outstretched—that the foe is not dead but that the apparently friendly relationship is poisoned and the foe realizes that his apparent friend is not his friend—then the problems of human confrontation, anger, and enmity remain, as they do for all people.

Another problem is that Blake's punctuation of the penultimate, or next to the last, line—"In the morning glad I see;"—allows two readings of the line. There is no punctuation until the semicolon at the end of the line. The word "glad" can be read as describing either "morning" or "I." If "glad" describes "morning," the interpretation is that in the happy morning, bright with light, as opposed to the "veiled" night, the speaker is seeing. If "glad" describes "I," the interpretation is that in the morning the speaker is happy to see the sight of his fallen foe. The first reading allows readers to see the speaker enlightened, even shocked by the effect of his anger, that it is fatal to his foe. The glad morning contrasts to the speaker's sober realization. The second interpretation allows readers to see the effect of anger on the character of the person who cultivates it. It is fatal to his innocent regard for humankind. Blake has changed the focus of the story from the Fall of human beings to the fall of God.

By making it a metaphor for the story of the Fall, Blake has constructed the poem so that the speaker's behavior, modeled on God's behavior in the Old Testament, *represents* God's behavior and the speaker represents God. Through his analysis and implicit condemnation of the speaker, Blake analyzes the vision that has created the god of the Old Testament and the attitude that this god embodies. Blake warns against that vision, that attitude, and that kind of god, identifying him as a god of wrath and cruelty rather than of love.

Themes

The Cultivation of Anger

The principal theme of "A Poison Tree" is not anger itself but how the suppression of anger leads to the cultivation of anger. Burying anger rather than exposing it and acknowledging it, according to "A Poison Tree," turns anger into a seed that will germinate. Through the cultivation of that seed, which is nourished by the energy of the angry person, wrath grows into a mighty and destructive force.

The Wrathfulness of the Old Testament God

An implicit theme of "A Poison Tree" is that the god of the Old Testament is a god of wrath, cunning, jealousy, and guile. Blake presents this theme in the poem by alluding to the story of the Fall in Genesis. The tree in Blake's poem is intended to remind the reader of the Tree of the Knowledge of Good and Evil. The bright apple represents the fruit on that tree, which God forbids Adam and Eve to eat, thus making it more appealing. The garden into which the foe steals signifies the Garden of Eden, where Adam and Eve act in stealth and disobey God. The attitude of the speaker himself is to be understood as a reflection of God's attitude. By showing the speaker of the poem acting in a way reminiscent of God, Blake is showing

God to be not a god of love but a cruel god and is thus criticizing the commonly held idea of God.

Suppression versus Expression

To the extent that "A Poison Tree" teaches a lesson and asserts a moral proposition rather than offering a critique of a theological system, the lesson is less concerned with anger than with demonstrating that suppressing the expression of feelings leads to a corruption of those feelings, to a decay of innocence, and to the growth of cunning and guile. Repeatedly in *Songs of Experience*, not just in "A Poison Tree," Blake argues that the religious doctrines intended to train people, especially children, in virtue are cruel and cause harm. In addition, Blake depicts those who implement religious discipline as sadistic.

Hypocrisy

Blake called the original draft of "A Poison Tree" "Christian Forbearance," suggesting that what is meant to appear as a gentle attitude is often a mask for disdain and anger. Furthermore, Blake believed that the attitudes of piety that adherents of conventional Christianity were taught to maintain actually led to hypocrisy, causing people to pretend to be friendly and accepting when they were not. The righteousness that the conventional religion prescribed, Blake believed, allowed people to hide evil intent and to perform evil deeds, such as stifling the healthy growth of children, under the cover of appearing virtuous.

Style

Iambic Tetrameter

Poetry is measured speech. Its words are organized in rhythmic patterns called meter. The most common pattern or meter for English poetry is the iambic foot, which is composed of two beats, the first unaccented and the second accented. Most often in English poetry, the iambic foot appears in lines of five feet called iambic pentameter, but lines can be shorter or longer. Blake's "A Poison Tree" is in iambic tetrameter, four iambic feet, but a variation on that pattern is common throughout the poem. In most of the lines, the second beat of the last foot is truncated, or cut off.

The first line of "A Poison Tree" offers an example of truncated iambic tetrameter. "i WAS / anGRY / with MY / friend" is a line with three and a half feet. The second line is a full tetrameter line.

Topics For Further Study

- In "A Poison Tree," Blake maintains that restraining anger, rather than preventing cruelty and aggression, gives extra energy to aggression and strengthens cruelty. Organize a class debate to argue whether it is better to tell other people how you feel when you are upset with them or have a difference of opinion or to keep it to yourself and try to be accommodating.

- Stated perhaps overly simply, Blake's idea of correspondences suggests that the way people imagine or think about something affects the way it actually is in the concrete world. Choosing an event from your own experience, write an essay that shows how the way you thought about or imagined something influenced how it "really" was. As an alternative, choose a social, national, or historical event and discuss how expectation influenced outcome.

- After assembling a questionnaire, conduct a series of interviews with at least ten people. Find out what they think about a widely held or controversial moral or religious value or about a current law. Try to determine whether these people believe the law or moral stance accomplishes

what it is supposed to accomplish and whether that goal is a worthy one. Make sure to interview people of different ages, races, sexes, religions, and class backgrounds. Report the results to the class, highlighting both individual differences and similarities among the respondents.

- Write a poem in rhyming couplets in which you describe a vision you have had. Using the same subject, write a poem that is unrhymed. In a paragraph, describe the difficulties writing each poem presented.

- Choose any Bible story and write a well-developed essay discussing how it is conventionally interpreted. Then show how it could be interpreted differently.

- Write a short story in which one character deceives another while pretending to be his or her friend or believes that the deception is for the other person's "own good."

- Using watercolors or pastels, draw a scene from "A Poison Tree." Afterward, try to find a copy of *Songs of Experience* with Blake's illustrations to see how he illustrates his poems.

There are four complete iambic feet: "i TOLD / my WRATH, / my WRATH / did END." The missing beat at the end of the first line signals the incompleteness of the thought. The full fourth foot at the end of the second line gives a sense of completion. The pattern is repeated for the same result in the second rhyming couplet. This pattern distinguishes the first quatrain from the ones that follow, as do the straightforward, nonmetaphorical nature of its language and the didactic nature of its content.

In the two middle quatrains and the first couplet of the last quatrain, Blake writes only in truncated iambic tetrameter lines, such as "and I / waTERD / it IN / fears" and "and HE / knew THAT / it WAS / mine." Although the recurring rhymes tie the lines of each couplet together, the missing

beat at the end of each line gives a subtle sense of process rather than resolution. In the last couplet, however, Blake returns to the pattern of the first quatrain. The first line of the last couplet, "in THE / mornING / glad I / see," lacks a complete fourth foot. The last line, "my FOE / outSTRETCHED / beNEATH / the TREE," completes the utterance, resolves the poem, and places a final emphasis on the subject and central image of the poem, the word "tree."

Metaphor, Simile, and Allusion

A metaphor is a figure of speech in which one thing represents another. A metaphor helps to make an abstract idea concrete by turning something intangible into an image. It also reveals the subtle relatedness between things that may seem unrelated to each other. In "A Poison Tree," Blake represents anger as a plant and compares the angry person's relationship to his anger to a gardener's relationship to the plants he tends. Comparison is implicit in metaphor. Blake is saying anger is *like* a plant. A person who cultivates his anger is *like* a gardener. Stating the word "like" produces a special class of metaphor called a simile. In "A Poison Tree," the metaphor of the tree, the apple, and the garden not only represents the speaker's anger, its result, and its boundaries but also *alludes* to the biblical Tree of the Knowledge of Good and Evil and the forbidden fruit that grows on it in the Garden of Eden. An allusion is an indirect reference a speaker or a figure of speech makes to something else not specifically named. By means of allusion to the story of the Fall in Genesis, Blake gives greater depth of meaning to "A Poison Tree."

Historical Context

Swedenborgianism

Religious dissent in England, which first appeared in 1662 when a group of English Puritans broke away from the Church of England, refusing to take communion in the Church or accept its doctrines and authority, took many forms. Dissenters were persecuted until 1689, when the Act of Toleration was passed. The form of dissent to which Blake was drawn in his youth was known as Swedenborgianism. Emanuel Swedenborg (1688–1772), a Swedish mystic, philosopher, theologian, and scientist, established the doctrine of correspondences, teaching that the spiritual world and the natural world were joined—that the tangible objects of the natural world were actually physical instances of spiritual realities. Consequently, Swedenborg asserted, it was possible for human beings to communicate with spirits, an experience Blake himself had on a number of occasions, most notably with the spirit of his younger brother Robert immediately after Robert's death.

Swedenborg taught that God is the source of love and wisdom and that humankind, to the degree that it manifests and is guided by love and wisdom, is the seat of the godhead. Christianity, as perverted by the tenets of the established Christian churches, Swedenborg proclaimed and Blake believed and suggests in "A Poison Tree," leads humankind away from God. That loss of touch with God is, according to Swedenborg, the Fall. The

Second Coming of Christ, similarly, is not to be thought of as a tangible historical event but as an event of the human spirit to be realized when humankind becomes, again, the source of and is guided by love and wisdom. In his later writing, Swedenborg saw God as a god of wrath and judgment, and the churches founded on his teachings began to emphasize the importance of sin. After 1790, Blake rejected Swedenborg but not all of his ideas.

Revolution

The latter half of the eighteenth century was an age of revolution. In philosophy, John Locke and Thomas Paine, among others, advocated greater individual liberty, democratic government, and human rights. In science, Isaac Newton altered the way the natural world—indeed, the universe—was understood. Rather than finding in Newton's mathematical reasoning and laws of nature grounds for enlightenment, however, Blake thought of them as a source of obscurity. Blake favored the intuitive knowledge produced by visionary revelation.

It was in the realm of politics that the beliefs of the past exploded with warlike fury. The revolutions in the American colonies in 1776 and in France in 1789 brought to an end the predominance of autocratic and monarchical government; extended among citizens the right to own property and to determine taxation; and instituted systems of representative republican democracy based on principles of liberty, brotherhood, and equality. Blake was an ardent supporter of these revolutions and celebrated them and their principles in his work. He saw them as eruptions of suppressed energy and understood their excesses as inevitable consequences of the suppression of energy.

In England, the conservative reaction to these radical events influenced the way Blake wrote, causing him to express himself symbolically to avoid political persecution. Nevertheless, in 1803, at the height of the English wars against Napoleon, Blake was brought before a magistrate on charges of sedition, against which he successfully defended himself.

The Industrial Revolution and the Factory System

During the latter half of the eighteenth century, England was transformed from a country of people who worked on the land or, if they manufactured things, such as spinning cotton or weaving cloth, in their homes, to a country where most people labored in factories using newly invented

Compare
&
Contrast

- **1790s:** In his poetry, Blake opposes the emotional repression advocated by the morality of his time and posits that it has harmful spiritual, social, and individual effects.

   Today: Conservative cultural voices call for sexual abstinence among young and unmarried people. Many people who have been influenced by psychologists such as R. D. Laing (in his books *The Divided Self* and *Knots*) argue against the defenders of conventional morality, asserting that the repression of honest emotional and sexual expression is responsible for mental health problems and for many of the problems facing society as a whole.

- **1790s:** Revolutionary upheaval against monarchy and the Reign of Terror in France causes the British government to enact measures intended to guard against attacks on English soil and limit freedom of expression.

   Today: In response to acts of terrorism by members of fundamentalist Islamic sects in the

United Kingdom, the British government seeks to draft tough antiterrorism legislation and to strengthen the power of the police.

- **1790s:** Because of the factory system, workers, including children, are confined to factories for as long as fourteen hours a day, engaging in painful drudgery that ruins their health and breaks their spirit.

   Today: Although it has been abolished in Britain, child labor exists in many third world countries, which supply the people of the United Kingdom with consumer goods. The British Broadcasting Company reports that "more than half of British workers are suffering from stress" and that "companies [are] adding to employee stress levels by demanding long hours." In the United Kingdom, one third of employees work more than forty-eight hours a week, and "three out of five people are working unpaid overtime."

---

machinery for the manufacture of goods. The Industrial Revolution and the advent of the factory system not only brought a great increase in commodities and wealth for some members of society—the owners of the factories, importers and exporters, and merchants, for example—but also turned most of the men, women, and children who toiled for pittance wages in the factories into commodities themselves. People became items bought and sold as implements of labor.

   Blake found the industrial system abhorrent. It violated the spiritual integrity of each human being and alienated workers from their work by turning them into machinery. The system also produced goods that were uniform and lacked the impression of the hands that had made them. Blake not only wrote against the evils of the Industrial Revolution and the factory system but also resisted them in the manufacture of his works by etching, printing, coloring, and binding his books in his own workshop.

Critical Overview

Blake's friends and circle of disciples published articles in praise of Blake during his lifetime and after his death. These tributes served as the sources and inspiration for the 1863 biography of Blake by Alexander and Anne Gilchrist. Their *The Life of William Blake* was received with enthusiasm by mid-Victorian poets such as Dante Gabriel Rossetti, Robert Browning, and Algernon Charles Swinburne. The enthusiasm fired the poet William Butler Yeats, who wrote the essay "William Blake and the Imagination" in 1887 and edited an edition of Blake's poetry in 1893.

   In the nearly two hundred years since Blake's death, the manner in which the poet has been regarded both has and has not changed. While Blake lived, his admirers and his detractors did not much disagree on the nature of his genius and the meaning or the quality of his work. It was over the merit

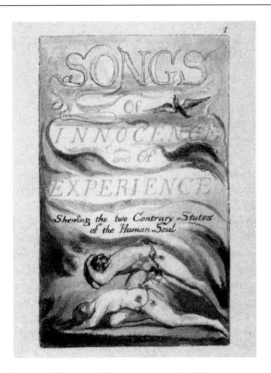

Cover of Songs of Innocence and of Experience

© 1994 The Henry E. Huntington Library and Art Gallery

of the work and whether Blake's genius was alloyed with madness that there was disagreement. The opposing factions simply differed in their valuations of Blake's work and his thought. Most were dismissive, regarding Blake primarily as a fine engraver. Some people, such as John Giles (quoted in Heims), one of Blake's young disciples, cherished Blake's work and saw him as a prophet who "had seen God . . . and had talked with angels."

Robert Southey (quoted in Heims), appointed the poet laureate of England in 1813, called Blake "a man of great, but undoubtedly insane genius." In 1830, the poet and man of letters Allan Cunningham wrote in *Lives of the Most Eminent British Painters, Sculptors, and Architects* (quoted in Heims) that Blake was "a loveable, minor eccentric: unworldly, self-taught and self-deluded." Blake's champion Henry Crabbe Robinson (quoted in Heims) did not sound a very different note when he called Blake "a Religious Dreamer" in 1811, but he made his comments approvingly. John Linnell (quoted in Heims), a painter and carver who was both a disciple and a patron of Blake's, wrote of Blake in 1818,

> I soon encountered Blake[']s peculiarities, and [was] somewhat taken aback by the boldness of some of his assertions. I never saw anything the least like

madness. . . . I generally met with a sufficiently rational explanation in the most really friendly & conciliatory tone.

Perhaps the ambiguity of attitude toward Blake is best expressed by another of his younger contemporaries, the art historian and scholar Seymour Kirkup, who met Blake and later wrote, "His high qualities I did not prize at that time; besides, I thought him mad. I do not think so now."

Essentially the same understanding of Blake exists in the early twenty-first century as existed in his time. Blake is recognized as a mystic, a visionary, an advocate of liberty, and an opponent of repression. The only difference is that the balance between regard and disdain for his work has shifted. Blake's work has been accepted into the canon of great literature and valued by such respected academic critics and scholars as Northrop Frye, Harold Bloom, and G. E. Bentley, Jr. David Erdman, in the preface to his monumental edition of Blake's written work, calls Blake "one of the greatest of English poets, and certainly one of the most original, and most relevant to us now."

As if to confirm Erdman's judgment, Blake studies are thriving in academic settings, and his work has been included in the repertoires of such popular and counterculture icons as the beat poet Allen Ginsberg, the rock musician Jim Morrison, and the writer, singer, and social activist Ed Sanders. Ginsberg released an album of himself singing his own settings of Blake's *Songs of Innocence and of Experience*, and the Fugs, the 1960s underground rock band founded by Sanders and Tuli Kupferberg, recorded their version of Blake's "Ah, Sun-flower." The American composer William Bolcom premiered his grand symphonic choral setting of *Songs of Innocence and of Experience* in 1985.

Criticism

Neil Heims

Neil Heims is a writer and teacher living in Paris. In this essay, he argues that Blake deconstructs the meaning of the Tree of the Knowledge of Good and Evil, which appears in the story of the Fall in the book of Genesis, by his use of the apple tree, which appears as a symbol of hypocrisy and cruelty in "A Poison Tree."

For Blake, intelligence—the faculty of seeing, knowing, and understanding—is a function of imagination. The word "imagination" has so weakened

What Do I Read Next?

- In *Othello* (1604), one of Shakespeare's great tragedies, Iago, who hates Othello, pretends to be Othello's friend in order to destroy him.

- In *The Scarlet Letter* (1850), Nathaniel Hawthorne's novel of New England Puritanism, Roger Chillingworth, a physician, pretends to be the Reverend Arthur Dimmesdale's friend and takes on the care of the clergyman's troubled soul in order to discover his terrible secret.

- A. E. Houseman's poem "Is My Team Plowing?" in his collection *A Shropshire Lad* (1896), is written in a rhyming pattern similar to that of "A Poison Tree." In Houseman's poem, one of the two speakers gently deceives his dead interlocutor, or the other person in the discussion, about the way things are after his death.

- In Sherwood Anderson's short story "Hands," included in the collection *Winesburg, Ohio* (1919), the fate of the gentle Wing Biddlebaum testifies to the evils of sexual repression and the force of unleashed wrath.

- In Igor Stravinsky's opera *The Rake's Progress* (1951), libretto by W. H. Auden and Chester Kallman, Nick Shadow (the Devil) befriends Tom Rakewell and tempts him with money, happiness, and fame, leading him away from a life of love and virtue to madness and death.

- In Patrick Hamilton's play *Gas Light* (1939), which was made into the film *Gaslight* (1944), directed by George Cuckor, the protagonist pretends to be a loving and caring husband, but he is actually driving his wife crazy and planning her murder.

since Blake's time that its meaning has degenerated and the word is commonly used to represent the capacity for make-believe or for pretending that things that do not exist do exist. For Blake, however, imagination signifies the organic capability to perceive the realities of the spirit world, which the eye, because its capacity to see is limited to the natural, tangible world, cannot do. The imagination is, therefore, a higher faculty than the eye. By means of imagination, for Blake, eternal things and beings, such as angels, which he holds to be real but invisible to the eye and which constitute the actual substance of the spirit, can be perceived in visions and represented by images. That Blake thought of imagination as a bodily organ and the experience of visions as the fruit of its operation is clear from the following anecdote: At a social gathering, after he had described one of his visions, Blake was asked by a woman challenging his credibility, if not his sanity, just where he had seen it. "Here, madam," he answered, pointing to his own head with his index finger.

The spiritual world, for Blake, is not independent of the natural world. Each is seamlessly a part of the other, fosters the existence of the other, and determines its quality. "Man has no Body," Blake asserts in "The Marriage of Heaven and Hell," "distinct from his Soul for that calld Body is a portion of the Soul discerned by the five Senses." Similarly, God for Blake is not an idealized, abstracted, unreachable presence in the distant heavens existing as an eternal force in a time sphere different from the one human beings inhabit, as Blake understood the Judeo-Christian God the Father of the Old Testament to be. God is a man-god, the ever-present Jesus existing as a person, in each person when each person follows the precepts of love and wisdom rather than hatred, suppression, and guile. The eternal power of God consequently becomes the ever-present capability of individuals to create the earth as a reflection of heaven rather than as a type of hell, which, according to Blake, it has been made by adherence to a Christianity perverted by belief in the repressive authority of a wrathful, beguiling father-god. Blake calls it an error fostered by "Bibles or sacred codes" to believe "that God will torment Man in Eternity for following his [Man's] Energies."

> *Blake believed that the way human beings imagine the spiritual world determines how they fashion the physical world in which they live.*

Two principles lie at the root of Blake's imaginative intelligence, are the basis for his belief system, and confirm his own visionary experience: the principle of correspondences and the principle of contraries. Blake derived the principle of correspondences from the writing of the Swedish mystic Swedenborg. Swedenborg taught that the spiritual world is represented in the natural world and can be apprehended through visions. Thus the two realms correspond to each other. According to Blake, the human being is the architect of this correspondence. Blake believed that the way human beings imagine the spiritual world determines how they fashion the physical world in which they live. Here, Blake uses the word "imagine" in its profound sense, meaning the way in which the human being forms his or her image of the world or concretely perceives that world, which is invisible to the unaided eye. Consequently, it matters greatly what conception of God humans imagine and what vision of the invisible world they behold.

The other principle, the one that provides humankind with the ability to choose, is the doctrine of contraries. According to this doctrine, there are forces and states in opposition to each other—innocence and experience, love and hate, attraction and repulsion, reason and energy. The list is Blake's own set forth in "The Marriage of Heaven and Hell," in which he writes that "without Contraries there is no progression" and that they "are necessary to Human Existence. From these contraries spring what the religious call Good & Evil." What is radical in Blake's understanding is not only that he challenges the way these two contradictory terms—good and evil—are conventionally valued but also that he identifies good and evil as lying on one continuum. Referring to how the terms are conventionally defined, Blake writes, "Good is the passive that obeys Reason. Evil is the active springing from Energy."

Blake himself believes that "Energy is the only life and is from the Body and Reason is the bound or outward circumference of Energy." Blake defines reason as the force that contains energy—in the sense of keeping it within fixed limits. The degree to which reason is a virtue depends on how reason is guided by Blake's belief that "Energy is Eternal Delight." Reason that thwarts energy, according to Blake, is evil and promotes evil. It is not for reason to determine what boundaries to impose on energy, but energy must determine the boundaries with which reason ought to surround it.

If Blake's definitions and distinctions seem confusing, perverse, or even dangerous, it is clear from them that Blake is challenging the accepted categories and values of conventional Christian morality. Conventional Christian virtues, he insists, are not real virtues. They are the result of the repression of energy and themselves are dangerous—the source of ill, not of good. In Blake's understanding, the repression of human energy, fostered by state and church, for example, during the ancien régime, or the political and social system in France before the Revolution of 1789, was the cause of the brutal and violent explosion of energy called the Reign of Terror in 1793. "Sooner murder an infant in its cradle than nurse unacted desires," Blake writes, and "Prisons are built with stones of Law, Brothels with bricks of Religion." On the foundation of this reinterpreted idea of virtue and his associated condemnation of suppressing the energy of bodily passion, which is a position in direct contradiction to the behavioral precepts and moral regulations of conventional Christianity, Blake builds the vision and derives the values that support the implicit argument of "A Poison Tree." In "A Poison Tree," Blake argues that the repression of wrath, the form energy takes in the poem, is a fault that leads to hypocrisy and cruelty. The experience or the expression of energy (in the instance of the poem, wrath) does not. The idea that repression is what passes for virtue and is actually harmful is one that Blake develops in several poems in *Songs of Experience.* In "The Garden of Love," which comes five poems before "A Poison Tree" in the collection, Blake expresses the idea directly.

The "I" of this poem is a different "I" from the "I" of "A Poison Tree," in which the "I" indicates a corrupted actor. In "The Garden of Love," the "I" indicates an observer of the world's corruption. The contrast and the conflict presented by the "I" of "The Garden of Love" are between love (energy) and repression (the priests who thwart love). In the poem, Blake has inverted the values that governed the morality of his time. The same moral inversion is at the root of "A Poison Tree" and is the source of the cruelty the poem recounts.

The central image cluster of "A Poison Tree"— the tree and the bright apple—begins as metaphor. It is a figure of speech that represents wrath and its result as a tree and the apple that grows on it. As the poem progresses, this image cluster is transformed from metaphor into concrete actuality. In "The Human Abstract," a poem coming once removed before "A Poison Tree," Blake prepares the reader for this transformation of metaphor into the thing itself and states directly the doctrine of correspondence between the spiritual and natural worlds that is effected by the mind.

In "The Human Abstract," Blake turns humility into a tree. First, he shows how "Cruelty," which Blake personifies, that is, writes of as if it were a person rather than a behavioral characteristic, "knits a snare, / And spreads his baits with care" in a way that is quite similar to the way the speaker sets his trap in "A Poison Tree." Cruelty "sits down with holy fears, / And waters the ground with tears." This is the same process as the one described in "A Poison Tree," and the same rhyming words are used to describe it. After "Humility takes its root / Underneath his [Cruelty's] foot," a "dismal shade / Of Mystery" spreads "over his [Cruelty's] head." Finally, "it [the tree grown from Humility] bears the fruit of Deceit, / Ruddy and sweet to eat." In the last stanza of the poem, Blake explains the nature of the tree itself by pinpointing its location:

> The Gods of earth and sea,
> Sought thro' Nature to find this Tree
> But their search was all in vain:
> There grows one in the Human Brain.

By constructing the two trees in "The Human Abstract" and "A Poison Tree" and showing them as visionary structures representing the negative characteristics cruel humility and deadly hypocrisy, Blake offers a reinterpretation of the Tree of the Knowledge of Good and Evil planted by the Judeo-Christian father-god of the Old Testament in the Garden of Eden, the story surrounding it, and the very nature of God himself. In "A Poison Tree," implicitly relying on the formula of correspondence presented in the last stanza of "The Human Abstract," Blake deconstructs the Tree of Knowledge and its story and re-presents them according to what he sees as their true nature. Thus, from the circumstances of the Bible story, Blake derives the contrary state, which he believes is deeply embedded in those circumstances.

What is understood in "A Poison Tree"—that the behavior of the god of Genesis is the model for cruel and unloving human behavior because of humankind's corrupt vision of virtue—is made explicit in "The Human Abstract." The Old Testament story is the cause of human evil because of the belief and value systems it instills, and the story itself is a projection of a faulty vision. The deadly tree grows in the human brain, not in nature. Taken from the imagination, the tree is planted in culture. It is transplanted from inside the mind, where it is a cruel mental image, into literature (the Bible), where it becomes a cruel concrete representation of a mental image and from there reenters the mind as a cruel religious value. Thus, through the process of correspondences, an insubstantial, mental construction is given concrete form as the poisonous tree, as Blake construes it, of the Garden of Eden. The trees Blake represents in "A Poison Tree" and "The Human Abstract," which he derives from the biblical tree, are visions resulting from a corrupted imagination, as is the Edenic tree, in his view. They are visions produced by an imagination formed by the priests who have destroyed the garden of love and installed within it both a chapel with "Thou shalt not" written over the door and the tombstones of those felled by that doctrine.

Blake's deconstruction of the story of the Fall brings the force of the doctrine of contraries into play. By implicitly opposing his vision of the story of the Fall and the nature of the tree that figures in that story to the story in Genesis, Blake endeavors to heal the imagination and restore its power. He supplants what he sees as the false vision of an imagination beguiled by repression and a false idea of virtue with a vision that plants in its stead an implied contrary model of love and wisdom expressed freely in the graceful energy of bodies, and therefore spirits, freed from the "Priests in black gowns" who bind "with briars" our "joys & desires."

Source: Neil Heims, Critical Essay on "A Poison Tree," in *Poetry for Students*, Thomson Gale, 2006.

John Brenkman

In the following essay, Brenkman analyzes "A Poison Tree" within the framework of formal social and political theory.

Preliminaries

Seldom does the question of lyric and society get beyond "extra-textual" considerations, principally the role of social and political ideas in a poet's biographical and intellectual development or in the poetry's thematic content. Marxist criticism mirrors

> *The text has generated two conflicting and irreconcilable readings, each of which apprehends the poem's status as speech event in a particular way, as a confession or moral judgment on the one hand, and as a cold statement of fact or scenario for destructive action on the other."*

this deficit by relegating poetry to the margins of its own investigations of social and aesthetic experience. William Blake's poetry encourages us to counter the habits of Marxist and non-Marxist criticism alike by recognizing that society and politics shape the very project of a poet's work and the inner dynamics of poetic language itself, its processes of figuration, its status as a linguistic act, its forms and techniques, its effects within the reading process.

Blake was a poet of the volatile decades of the late eighteenth and early nineteenth centuries, writing at the very point when the democratic revolutions were being institutionalized as the class rule of the bourgeoisie. The claims of freedom and liberation that gave impetus to poets and novelists in this period were rapidly coming up against the necessity of establishing the new economic order of capitalism. Blake's vital contribution to our cultural heritage lies in the response that his poetry made to this changing relation of art to the evolution of bourgeois society. He was also a poet who himself constantly reflected on the political and historical possibilities of the imagination. For Blake, poetry is the active imposing of imagination or fantasy in the struggles against dominant values and institutions. Casting the poet in the double role of visionary and voice of condemnation, he attributed both a utopian and a negative power to poetic language.

It is this interplay of the utopian and the negative, of imagination and critique, that makes Blake's poetry resonate with the social and aesthetic theories of thinkers like Ernst Bloch and Herbert Marcuse, Walter Benjamin and T. W. Adorno. In this paper, I will test some broad perspectives on art that have come from this tradition of "critical Marxism" against a reading of a poem from the *Songs of Experience*. The reading owes as much to hermeneutics and poststructuralism as it does to the aesthetic writings of the Frankfurt School.

From Bloch I have taken the phrase "concrete utopia." Bloch meant by this that utopian possibilities are latent in the freedom and self-organization which social groups and classes possess, intermittently and fragmentedly, in their everyday existence, political experiences, myths, and artistic endeavors. These latent tendencies have as their heritage all the unfinished or abortive efforts in history to extend justice and happiness. The heritage of utopia is thus a discontinuous history, one that must be constructed from cultural traditions and the popular struggles and revolts of the past. The question we can draw from Bloch's reflections is this: *In what ways is poetry a bearer of utopian hope, of this historical latency which is at once within and beyond society?*

From Marcuse I will borrow a thesis about art and literature that he advanced in his last published work, *The Aesthetic Dimension:* "The inner logic of the work of art terminates in the emergence of another reason, another sensibility, which defy the rationality and sensibility incorporated in the dominant social institutions." The phrase "terminates in the emergence of" suggests, first, that art is utopian insofar as it anticipates new orders of reason and sensibility that can be secured only through political action and social transformation, and, second, that this utopian anticipation is nonetheless concrete insofar as it stems from what is realized aesthetically in the artwork. Marcuse's thesis leads to a second question about lyric and society: *How does the "inner logic" of the poem at the same time manifest a counterlogic against the constraining interactions organized by society?*

While Bloch and Marcuse help to establish the aims of interpretation and to frame the questions that a socially critical study of poetry needs to address, their own aesthetic reflections rest on suppositions open to challenge from many directions in the recent theory of interpretation and art. Bloch maintains that great artworks are part ideology, part authentic utopia. The first task of analysis is to dissolve the ideological shell of the work by exposing the ways it serves particular rather than general interests and legitimates the forms of domination prevalent in its own society; once this ideological shell is dissolved, the utopian kernel of the work is supposed to shine through, a radiant core of meanings and images expressing the strivings and hopes of humanity. Bloch's conception of interpretation shares with the hermeneutics of Heidegger and Gadamer the insight that cultural meanings come forward only from historically situated works and are appropriated only in historically situated contexts, but he nevertheless tends to view the *valid* meanings of culture as a semantic storehouse that preserves itself intact across historical periods and epochs. Hence the questionable notion that interpretation can with assurance separate the valid and true aspect of a work from its ideological and false aspect. Contemporary criticism, in the wake of Heidegger and more recently of poststructuralist and deconstructive criticism, raises an inescapable problem concerning our own reception of the art and literature of the past, namely, that there is no ground of meaning or foothold in truth on the basis of which we can with certainty extract the valid significations of a work.

Marcuse's aesthetic reflections accentuate the unity of form. Throughout his work he transcribes into socially critical terms the aesthetic experience that was the basis of bourgeois aesthetics since Schiller. Marcuse attributes the utopian and negative power of art to the sharp contrast that individuals experience between the unity or harmony they apprehend in the artwork and the disharmony and conflict that characterize the social relations they encounter in everyday life. The notion of the artwork's formal harmony has been contested by an array of contemporary theories of the signifying and formal dynamics of literary texts. The transaction between writing and reading, between the poetic text and its reception, can no longer, I believe, be fruitfully described as the subject's inward appropriation of an outwardly realized harmony of sensuous and symbolic elements.

Without undertaking to solve the problem that hermeneutics and poststructuralism pose for the aesthetic thinking of critical Marxism, I have sketched the relevant problems in order to clarify the background of my reading of Blake. For my concern is to transpose the problem of lyric and society and of the negative-utopian power of poetry into a question of poetic language, of poetry as a language practice, and the interaction of writing and reading.

The reading I will present of Blake's "A Poison Tree" is guided by three sets of propositions intended to sharpen this dialogue between critical social theory and contemporary literary theory:

(1) The social dialectic of art does not come from the conflict beween a divided reality and a unified work, but rather takes the form of a conflict *within* the work. By the same token, the social counterlogic that a poem manifests results from the internal contradictoriness of the poem as *text,* not from the wholeness of the poem as *beautiful appearance.* Literature is a practice that acts upon language. The text enters into a complex but determinate relation with the actual social world because language is the very ground of social interaction. The utopian power of poetry stems from its concrete connections, as a language practice, to the social and political realities of its moment rather than from any capacity to shed those connections or set itself above them.

(2) Poetic language solicits, incites, calls for a reading, a reading which at once lets the effects of poetic condensation erupt across the poem and ties those effects to the situation or act of writing itself. Reading always entails this double movement—receptivity to a language that is multivalent and overdetermined and moments of decision in which the multivalence and overdetermination are reconnected to the place or situation from which the poem has arisen. It will be my position that this site of the poem's genesis is social. An analogy might be made between the reading of poetry and psychoanalytic interpretation. The analyst listens with what Freud called a suspended or floating attention in order to hear what reverberates within the subject's discourse and its silences; on the other side of the dialogue, the subject is pressed toward what Lacan called the "moment to conclude," where he or she feels the pressure of the unconscious and integrates it into his or her actual discourse with the analyst, allowing the unconscious to interrupt the false "conclusions" that up to then have resisted it. The two sides of reading poetry are a dialectic of this kind between floating attention and the moment-to-conclude. The reader, however, is more like the patient than the analyst, in that interpretations, usually in the name of their own coherence, tend to resist the effects of the poetic text. This is not to argue for the indefinite postponement of interpretive decisions. Such decisions always take place, even when they are masked as in the rhetoric of deconstructive criticism. Every interpretive moment-to-conclude links the interpretation and the text as the two historically—and socially—situated sites of aesthetic experience.

(3) The transaction between writing and reading is thus an encounter between the social situation of literary production and the social situation of literary reception. The problem of ideology is best focused on this encounter and transaction. Art and literature become enmeshed in the vital ideological struggles of the present through the conflict of interpretations, the contesting efforts to understand the texts of the cultural heritage concretely and reflectively. Aesthetic experience is not a given but is *formed* in the interplay of writing and reading. The cultural heritage is not a given but is *constructed.* This heritage becomes charged with significance for the present through the conflict of interpretations.

"A Poison Tree"

Let us first quote the poem in its entirety:

I was angry with my friend;
I told my wrath, my wrath did end.
I was angry with my foe:
I told it not, my wrath did grow.

And I waterd it in fears,
Night & morning with my tears;
And I sunned it with smiles,
And with soft deceitful wiles.

And it grew both day and night.
Till it bore an apple bright.
And my foe beheld it shine,
And he knew that it was mine.

And into my garden stole,
When the night had veild the pole;
In the morning glad I see
My foe outstretchd beneath the tree.

Much depends on the relation of the first stanza to the rest of the poem as it unfolds what happened to the wrath that was not told to the foe. Every time one reads the poem, I believe, the first stanza has the force of a moral statement. The past tense establishes the twin perspective of Blake's action *then* and his judgment *now.* The danger or unhappiness of a wrath that grows, as against a wrath that ends, establishes a set of values or preferences that virtually goes without saying. And all of this is then confirmed in the account of the ensuing anguish that he experienced and the harm he brought on his foe. The poem reads as a kind of confessional utterance in which Blake the speaker shares with the reader a reflective judgment on the actions of Blake in the past, anchored in the view that telling one's wrath is healthy and not telling it is harmful and even self-destructive.

Another extreme, however, emerges against this reading and contradicts its every detail. The last two lines of the poem, breaking the consistent past tense of the rest, can be taken at face value: "In the morning glad I see / My foe outstretchd beneath the tree." A transcendent joy! He has gotten his satisfaction, and his wrath has finally been expressed, yielding the sheer delight of seeing an enemy destroyed. One might try to avert this reading by arguing that the phrase "glad I see" is not really in the present tense, but rather is an elliptical construction for something like "glad I was to see." But the amoral reading of the poem draws on other aspects of its total structure. First of all, there are two oppositions in the first stanza, not only telling as against not telling one's wrath, but also the difference between friend and foe, suggesting that there is no undestructive means of expressing wrath toward a foe but that it must be enacted. Secondly, the poem's words and syntax are not particularly charged with affective connotations; the tone is flat, and this second reading leaves it so by construing the first stanza not as a moral statement but as a statement of fact: wrath can be expressed and immediately dissipated with a friend, but not with a foe. Indeed, one can take this reading to its logical conclusion and say that the poem as a whole, far from being a confessional utterance, is more like a set of instructions on how to do in an enemy and feel relief, even joy.

Either of these readings can account for itself, bringing the various details of the poem into line. In this sense, the poem generates both readings. However, neither reading can account for the possibility of the other, except to declare that it is the product of misreading; they could only accuse one another of naive moralism and amorality respectively. Nor, on the other hand, is it adequate to leave off with these results and declare that the poem is formally or logically undecidable, a pure oscillation between two mutually exclusive meanings. For this undecidability also represents two contrary experiential situations, remorse and remorselessness, condemnation and coldness, constituting an ethical impasse that the reading of the poem need not yet accept, that is, decide to affirm.

The very flatness of the poem's tone allows each reading to invest the poem with the effects appropriate to it. In the first reading, the poem acquires the solemn awe of witnessing an action that the speaker himself can hardly believe he committed. The second reading, on the other hand, takes the speaker's final joy at face value and, in turn, invests the atonal surface of the poem with the connotation of coldness. But the conjoining of coldness and joy calls into question the joy itself. The tone becomes the symptom of a joy that is derived from an altogether different emotion, namely, the wrath that has had to wend its way through elaborate detours in order to manifest itself in the fatal deception of the foe. The conceit which gives the poem its title is the image of this circuitous transformation of wrath into fear, duplicity, and finally deception:

> And I waterd it in fears,
> Night & morning with my tears;
> And I sunned it with smiles,
> And with soft deceitful wiles.
>
> And it grew both day and night.
> Till it bore an apple bright.

Without making reference to any moral judgment against duplicity and deception, we discover in the image of the watering and sunning of the wrath (tree) that there opened within the subject a split between his inner feeling (fear) and his outward show of fraternity (smiles, soft deceitful wiles), which from that moment on precludes any direct connection between emotion and action. This distortion of experience is not subject to a moral condemnation in the sense of a judgment against the speaker himself, for he had made no choice which could be judged. He has suffered the effects of an anger that cannot immediately express and resolve itself.

The conceit of the poison tree, its simplicity and completeness extending over the last three stanzas as a whole, nonetheless has at its center an indeterminate element—the "apple bright." All the other single elements of the image equating untold wrath with a tree easily find their appropriate equivalents. Within the logic of the conceit, the image of the apple is only vaguely motivated, as by the idea that it is the "fruit" of his wrath. The meaning of "apple bright" is otherwise unspecifiable from the standpoint of the conceit itself. It could be anything—an object, a situation, a person—so long as it fulfilled one general condition: that it be, in the eyes of the foe, an *enviable possession* of the speaker's. Here indeterminacy is an extreme instance of metaphorical condensation. A thousand and one narratives could be told which revolved around an episode in which a character's enemy, thinking he is about to deprive the protagonist of a valued possession, falls to his own ruin:

> And my foe beheld it shine,
> And he knew that it was mine.
>
> And into my garden stole,
> When the night had veild the pole;

These lines resist the poem's moral reading more than any other passage, for they show that this foe

could be counted on to try to rob the subject of his possession. Blake had calculated exactly what his foe's reactions and actions would be, having imputed to the other the same destructive antagonism that he had discovered within himself. This equality between protagonist and antagonist now causes the amoral reading to lose its force. The apparent difference between protagonist and antagonist has been dissolved into their essential identity with each other.

At this point, the indeterminacy of the apple and the prototypical nature of the narrative yield a significance that exceeds the grasp of either the moral or the amoral reading. The poem's story is abstract, but not in the sense that it *is* an abstraction. Rather, it unveils the form of abstraction that is historically specific to capitalist society. The prototype narrative and the image of the "apple bright" are like a vortex that pulls everything into itself. Anything could be the enviable possession around which the deadly struggle between Blake and the foe revolves. Possessiveness is not merely an element of their antagonism but its cause; possessiveness pre-forms, socially, their relation to one another as a relation of equality and envy, their mirroring of one another being so complete that the protagonist need only calculatively impute his own aims and motives to the other in order to make his scheme a success. The conditions of the central image-narrative, in other words, are in fact met only in the social conditions of capitalism, where possessive individualism is but the ideological and characterological manifestation of a practice of exchange in which every, that is, *any* object or situation or person is susceptible to an economic designation of value which is then the same for all individuals and becomes something to be possessed. Only under these conditions does the equality of individuals necessarily take the form of antagonism between individuals. Envy, a term borrowed from the ethics of precapitalist societies, is but a name for the fundamental law of interactions in capitalist society as a whole.

The unusual power of this simple poem derives from the play of the image of the "apple bright," which is at once the poem's most abstractly indeterminate and its most concretely, socially determined image. The figurative movement of the image has three distinct moments. First, as an element in the conceit, the "apple bright" stands for the *effect of unexpressed wrath,* a result arrived at in the course of the narrated events. Second, and to the contrary, as a metaphor of the social process of abstraction that forms the very interrelation and interactions of individuals, the "apple bright" stands for the *cause of the antagonism* from which the narrative originated. The conceit substitutes effect for cause. The "apple bright" is thus, at the third moment of its figuration, the trope called a metalepsis. The metalepsis here takes the form of a contradiction between *what is narrated* and *the narrative* itself, for we have discovered the social cause of the poem's narrative in the image that initially stood for the psychological effect of what was narrated, namely, the speaker's unexpressed wrath. In order to have followed this figurative swerve in the poem's language, we have made a break with the two readings, the moral and the amoral, that the text has engendered.

In "A Poison Tree," the critique of bourgeois society is expressed not thematically but in the very articulation of the text and in the dynamic that it provokes. Linguistic theory has distinguished between a text's *énoncé* ("statement") and it *énonciation* ("utterance"), that is, between what is said and the saying of it. In our context, Roman Jakobson's original terminology suffices, distinguishing the *narrated event* and the *speech event*. At the level of the narrated event of "A Poison Tree," an unexpressed wrath results in the destruction of an antagonist by ensnaring him with an enviable possession. The speech event of the poem, I am urging, should be grasped in social and indeed political terms. The text has generated two conflicting and irreconcilable readings, each of which apprehends the poem's status as speech event in a particular way, as a confession or moral judgment on the one hand, and as a cold statement of fact or scenario for destructive action on the other. Neither of these readings can be a true understanding of the text, because neither can explain or cancel the other. Our interpretation has been forced beyond the moral and the amoral reading. The poem must rather be interpreted in terms of its generation of these two partial, blind readings. It generates these readings because they correspond to the two poles of ethical consciousness through which individuals actually live the social relations of capitalist society. The moral reading corresponds to a false morality of goodwill and honesty—which would have been, by the way, the simple object of a satire had Blake kept the poem's notebook title: "Christian Forebearance"! The amoral reading, on the other hand, corresponds to that form of individualism in which individuals, having been made interchangeable with one another, are deprived of the very individuality in the name of which they act.

The dialectic of the text consists in imposing the moral and the amoral readings, which represent the two poles of ethical experience in bourgeois society, and then forcing these two readings back to the figure of the "apple bright" in order for the reader to understand the poem. Both readings are doomed to fail, since they take the "apple bright" as the effect of wrath rather than as the social cause of the antagonism between individuals. The metalepsis, in breaking our interpretation from the two readings, gives form—or figure—to the difference between this act of poetic speech and the lived ethics of bourgeois society.

Let me explain this formulation on poetic form by contrasting the results of the analysis with the position that Marcuse held. For Marcuse, aesthetic experience marks the difference between the real and the possible by presenting an image or appearance whose completeness separates it from the existing conditions and prevalent experiences of social life. Art is sublimation in the sense that it transforms the real into the beautiful appearance; accompanying this aesthetic sublimation, Marcuse argues, is a process of desublimation that occurs in aesthetic perception: "The transcendence of immediate reality shatters the reified objectivity of established social relations and opens a new dimension of experience: the rebirth of rebellious subjectivity. Thus, on the basis of aesthetic sublimation, a *desublimation* takes place in the perceptions of individuals—in their feelings, judgments, thoughts; an invalidation of dominant norms, needs, and values." Now, Blake's "A Poison Tree" does indeed invalidate dominant forms of experience and of ethical consciousness, those which are embedded in the socially organized practices and interactions of bourgeois society. But the poem accomplishes this not by means of the beautiful appearance of aesthetic wholeness but rather in the contradiction within the text between the readings it generates and its genesis of the readings. The "dominant norms, needs, and values" the poem negates are as integral to the inner workings of the text as they are inherent in actual social life. What is felt, thought, judged within the historical forms of ethical consciousness that the bourgeois subject must live are themselves a part of the poem's aesthetic dimension, here as the dynamic of the readings which corresponds to the polarity in that ethical consciousness. It is not the unity but the active division of the text which invalidates these social-ethical forms.

So, too, the utopian power of the poem lies not in its protection of an aesthetic appearance of wholeness but in its concrete act of speaking. The concreteness of utopia does not, however, as Bloch would have it, reside in the semantic storehouse of images of happiness and freedom. The utopian is more thoroughly tied to the negative. The poem announces the necessity of an ethical consciousness that cannot yet be lived or represented, but it does so in the fracture between the énoncé and énonciation. The utopian dimension of the poem is enacted in a poetic speaking which manifests the struggle between the social conditions of the poet's speech and the latent possibilities of speech. The movement of figuration, through the three moments of the trope of the "apple bright," invalidates the two readings capable of giving the narrated event (énoncé) and the conceit (tree=wrath) consistency and in this way negates those forms of ethical experience that can be lived in the social context of the poem. What the poem says is negated in the saying of it. What I have called poetic form or figure is here just this difference between énoncé and énonciation, an enactment of the divergence between the real and the possible, the lived and the utopian. "A Poison Tree" points toward a future in which its own story and its mode of telling would no longer be necessary.

The inner logic of Blake's writing is not that of a cultural monument separated from time and change. By the same token, a historicist reading of Blake, intent only on "placing" him "in his own time," would forget that the future is an indispensable dimension of Blake's poetic dialogue with time and history. The socially critical construction of the cultural heritage eschews both the idea that art is above history and the idea that art is merely bound to its own time. When Marx contrasted the bourgeois revolutions of the eighteenth century with the proletarian revolutions of the nineteenth century, he saw in each a specific disharmony of form and content:

> The social revolution of the nineteenth century cannot draw its poetry from the past, but only from the future. It cannot begin with itself before it has stripped off all superstition in regard to the past. Earlier revolutions required recollections of past world history in order to drug themselves concerning their own content. In order to arrive at its own content, the revolution of the nineteenth century must let the dead bury their dead. There the phrase goes beyond the content; here the content goes beyond the phrase.

Blake stands between the realities of the bourgeois revolutions and the possibilities of socialist revolution. Historically, he is a poet of the American and French Revolutions. Unlike the revolutions

that stirred his imagination, his poetic practice does not stop short of the goal, rigidifying the forms of freedom and destroying the contents of freedom. Blake was *not* of his time. His poetry demanded a future which the bourgeois revolutions had to resist. I conclude with this juxtaposition of Blake and Marx, of the politics of poetry and the poetics of history, not in order to place Blake within Marx's frame of reference but to situate Marx within a political and cultural process that includes, as a productive and prophetic moment, the poetry of Blake. This becomes all the more necessary in our own historical moment. What for Blake was a future that promised to free him from his present has disappeared within the fabric of our own political and cultural inheritance. We look back at Blake across a wide gap, in that we live a reality that exists because the proletarian revolutions of the nineteenth century did not succeed. We are more the heirs of Blake's restraining reality than of his imagined future. Put another way, his poetry still speaks to us because we have not yet been freed to hear it.

Source: John Brenkman, "The Concrete Utopia of Poetry: Blake's 'A Poison Tree'," in *Lyric Poetry: Beyond New Criticism*, edited by Chavia Hoser and Patricia Parker, Cornell University Press, 1985, pp. 182–93.

Sources

Blake, William, "The Garden of Love," in *The Poetry and Prose of William Blake*, edited by David Erdman, Doubleday & Company, 1965, p. 26.

———, "The Human Abstract," in *The Poetry and Prose of William Blake*, edited by David Erdman, Doubleday & Company, 1965, p. 27.

———, "A Little Girl Lost," in *The Poetry and Prose of William Blake*, edited by David Erdman, Doubleday & Company, 1965, p. 29.

———, "The Marriage of Heaven and Hell," in *The Poetry and Prose of William Blake*, edited by David Erdman, Doubleday & Company, 1965, pp. 34, 36, 37.

———, "A Poison Tree," in *The Poetry and Prose of William Blake*, edited by David Erdman, Doubleday & Company, 1965, p. 28.

Erdman, David, ed., *The Poetry and Prose of William Blake*, Doubleday & Company, 1965, p. xxiii.

Heims, Neil, "Biography of William Blake," in *Bloom's Bio-Critiques: William Blake*, edited by Harold Bloom, Chelsea House Publishers, 2006, pp. 23, 34, 35, 75–77.

"Long Hours 'Stress British Workers,'" BBC News, November 7, 2001, available online at news.bbc.co.uk/1/hi/health/1642472.stm

Further Reading

Bentley, G. E., Jr., *The Stranger from Paradise: A Biography of William Blake*, Yale University Press, 2001.
    Bentley's highly regarded biography of Blake contains more than five hundred pages of careful and profound scholarship that draws on documents from Blake's time, which Bentley weaves into a narrative analysis of Blake's life, work, beliefs, and thought.

"Book of Genesis, 2:8–19," in *The Torah: The Five Books of Moses*, Jewish Publication Society of America, 1980.
    This passage of Genesis tells the story of the Tree of the Knowledge of Good and Evil, which God plants in the Garden of Eden. The forbidden fruit, the satanic temptation, and the divine punishment appear.

Erdman, David V., *Prophet Against Empire*, 3rd ed., Dover, 1977.

Erdman, Blake's major modern editor, offers a thorough and scholarly examination of the political and historical contexts of Blake's work.

Frye, Northrup, *Fearful Symmetry: A Study of William Blake*, Princeton University Press, 1947.
    This book is a classic study of the development of Blake's religious symbolism and mysticism set in the context of the eighteenth-century background against which he rebelled.

Ruskin, John, "The Nature of Gothic," in *The Genius of John Ruskin*, edited by John D. Rosenberg, Riverside Press, 1965.
    In this excerpt from his book *The Stones of Venice*, the nineteenth-century art and social critic John Ruskin, who was a great admirer of Blake, reacts against the Industrial Revolution by analyzing the medieval workmanship and the philosophy of craftsmanship that characterized the building of the great cathedrals in the Middle Ages.

Portrait of a Couple at Century's End

Sherod Santos

1999

"Portrait of a Couple at Century's End" contrasts the private pain of contemporary life to the awareness of global strife. Its author, Sherod Santos, does not give a detailed view of the couple mentioned in the title but instead looks at their situation in only the most general terms. He presents them as the sort of anonymous people who live all over America in warm, respectable homes and commute to jobs that distract them from the fact that they are out of touch with what is important in their lives. These are people who have chosen a life of comfort over openly acknowledging the memories of bad times that haunt them. The couple live a life of quiet discontent, making small talk over dinner and pretending that past arguments have no lingering effect. Santos stands these controlled lives against the international news that streams into the couple's living room over the twenty-four-hour news network, bringing the horrors of modern urban warfare into their staid living room with the same emotional suppression that characterizes the couple's quiet lives.

A version of "Portrait of a Couple at Century's End" was published in the January 7, 1992, issue of the *Nation*. A revision of the poem is in *The Pilot Star Elegies*, which was published in 1999 by W. W. Norton and for which Santos was a finalist for the National Book Award.

Author Biography

Santos was born on September 9, 1948, in Greenville, South Carolina. His father was a pilot in the United States Air Force, and his mother was a painter. Like that of many children of servicemen, Santos's childhood was marked by constant relocation. He attended grammar school and high school in such varied locales as Germany, Switzerland, France, and Hawaii and various places in the United States.

In his late teens, Santos bought a one-way ticket to Paris, traveling with no particular plan. Without a work permit, he could not obtain legal employment, but a concierge at the Hotel Racine hired him to serve breakfast to the guests for fifty cents an hour and a room in the attic. Santos spent his mornings working at the hotel and his afternoons honing his poetry at the American Library. Having learned to love what he had once found most challenging about poetry—its difficulty— Santos returned to the United States with no doubt about what he wanted to do with his life.

Santos attended San Diego State University, from which he received a bachelor of arts degree in 1971. He went on to receive a master of arts degree from San Diego State University in 1974 and a master of fine arts degree from the University of California, Irvine, in 1978. Santos earned his doctorate from the University of Utah in 1982, having focused his dissertation on the works of William Shakespeare. After completing his education, Santos began his teaching career at California State University, San Bernadino, and in 1983 moved to the University of Missouri, where he was teaching in 2005. In 1990, Santos took the position of external examiner and poet in residence at the Poet's House in Islandmagee, Northern Ireland, holding that post until 1997. Santos was the poetry editor of the *Missouri Review* from 1983 to 1990.

Santos was the recipient of numerous awards, including fellowships from the National Endowment for the Arts and the Guggenheim Foundation. He won the Pushcart Prize for essays and for poetry, the Ingram Merrill Award, the Delmore Schwartz Memorial Award, and the B. F. Connors Prize for Poetry. For *The Pilot Star Elegies*, the book that includes "Portrait of a Couple at Century's End," Santos was a finalist for the National Book Award and the *New Yorker* Book Award and won the Theodore Roethke Memorial Poetry Prize. Santos's published works include five collections of poetry, essays, and memoirs.

Sherod Santos   Photograph by Rob Hill. Reproduced by permission of Sherod Santos

Poem Text

Impatient for home,
the after-work traffic fanning out along
      the wet streets, a jagged sound,
like huge sheets of construction paper torn
      their length, and through   5

the walls, the shudder
of the furnace, as though a hundred thousand
      bottle-flies were trapped between
the clapboards and the plaster. A gentler
      rain blows across   10

the TV screen, where
a CNN foreign correspondent tells
      how a single Serb mortar shell
just leveled the crowded terrace of a
      Tuzla café.   15

The darker crimes are
faceless in that lidless, immemorial
      eye (*a world outside, a world
within*), so summer's what they talk about,
      the meal, their work,   20

and how they quarreled
one night in Iowa. The buried longings
      such memories stir. And yet,
in what they can't express they remind us
      of something too,   25

of something we've felt
settle on our lives, in shadow-life of ours.
    So forget for a moment
the future of their monogamous hearts,
    forget the rain,   30

    the traffic, the boot-
soles pressed forever in our century's mud,
    for it's all there, whatever
they'd say, the industry of pain, the Ho-
ly Spirit of   35

    everything that's been
taken away, it's all there in the burnt match-
    head preserved into amber
by a beeswax candle pooling beside
    their dinnerware.   40

Media Adaptations

- Sherod Santos is one of the poets recorded reading at the *Robinson Jeffers Festival* in Carmel, California, on October 8, 1994. A cassette of this recording is available from the Oral Traditions Archives of Pacific Grove, California.

Poem Summary

Lines 1–5

The first stanza of "Portrait of a Couple at Century's End" establishes a commuter traffic scene. The poem starts out on a note of discomfort, beginning with the word "Impatient." The drivers of the cars are looking forward to their homes, where, presumably, they will be comfortable and feel safe from the hassles of their day. Santos compares the sound of cars on a wet street to the sound made by construction paper when it is torn. The tearing of construction paper foreshadows domestic strife.

This stanza ends with what seems like a redundancy. The sheets of paper in the audio image are said to be torn not only "their length" but also "through." This image makes more sense when "through" is joined to the following stanza, to make "through / the walls," which is where the sound can be heard.

Lines 6–10

With the second stanza, the poem shifts from outdoors to indoors, using the phrase "through / the walls" to cross the boundary, as if readers are being brought inside along with the traffic sounds. Line 7 specifically mentions the furnace to evoke the warmth and dryness of the inside of the house in contrast to the wetness of the outside. The furnace sound is identified with the simile of the sound of "a hundred thousand / bottle-flies" trapped in the walls. The sound evoked is no less unpleasant than the traffic sound. By detailing the insides of the walls, Santos implies a hidden, sinister problem in the house, referring to the domestic problems of the couple mentioned in the title.

Like the first stanza, the second stanza ends with a transition that can be misleading. Line 10

mentions a rain, but one not as harsh as the one outside. Readers are forced to question why there is rain inside until they read on to the third stanza.

Lines 11–15

Santos uses the concept of a news broadcast playing on the television to move the action to a third locale, beyond the house and the commuter traffic outside it to Tuzla, Bosnia. Tuzla was a central point of contention during the Bosnian war of 1992 to 1995, which occurred after the breakup of the former Yugoslavia. During 1995, Tuzla was hammered by mortar fire, including the single most deadly attack of the war: On May 25, 1995, a Serb mortar killed seventy-two children. The poem shows this bombing program in the context of a television report from the Cable News Network (CNN), which brings tragedy and destruction from far away into the sheltered and secluded world of an American living room.

Lines 16–20

"Eye" in line 18 refers to the television set. Line 16 mentions "darker crimes" in the context of the war, but the ominous sound shuddering through the walls of the house also foreshadows the suggestion that there are things going on domestically that can be considered dark and shameful. The parenthetical phrase *"a world outside, a world within"* serves as a membrane between the television report of terrors far away and the couple's awareness that there are terrors within their own marriage.

After the parenthetical phrase, the poem's focus shifts to the couple mentioned in the title. Readers can see that the poem is no longer talking about the news anchor, because it mentions personal matters such as the summer, the meal the couple are sharing, and the work they do. Presenting the topics of dinner conversation in a list such as this trivializes them, showing that, following the horrors presented on the television, the couple's discussion is actually very banal.

Lines 21–25

The conversation about uncontroversial topics leads to an unpleasant topic: an argument the couple has had in another place. Their memory of that argument awakens repressed feelings. Santos presents these feelings as positive ones, referring to them as longings that have been stirred up by the memory of the argument. The poem implies that even the negative emotions of an argument are preferable to living with no emotions at all.

In line 24, the focus of the poem changes again, from "they" to "us." Just as the argument has opened up the couple in the poem to the emotions they have once known but have suppressed, the poem tells the reader that observing the couple's transformation can have the same effect on the reader, awakening suppressed feelings. The subject of recognizing buried emotions is referred to in a deadpan way, as a simple reminder.

Lines 26–30

Line 26 repeats the word "something" from line 25, indicating that the meaning of the memory is slowly dawning on the poem's speaker. This technique of rephrasing an idea is repeated in line 27, in which "our lives" is refined to the idea "shadow-life of ours." The difference between the two phrasings is that the first uses the plural word "lives," indicating the separate lives lived by separate people, whereas the use of the singular "life" in the iteration indicates that a plurality is involved even in a common life.

In lines 28 to 30, the poem reverses direction. Readers are told to "forget" about the hypothetical couple living in the house on the rainy day and to ignore any speculation about what their life is going to be like in the future. The couple's hearts are called "monogamous," which means that they are true to each other and that their problem is not unfaithfulness to each other. However, the poem is no longer interested in exploring the couple's real problem after it has finished using them to raise the broader issue of people living with each other but harboring discontentment.

Lines 31–35

In erasing the importance of the couple that have been the focus of most of the poem, Santos

indicates that they are never going to change. The poem uses the image of a boot stuck in mud to indicate that their lives (and, by inference, "our" lives) are not going to be appreciably different in the future. The relationship they have established, which continues to create dissatisfaction, is referred to as "the industry of pain," as if producing pain is the work that these people have set for themselves.

Lines 36–40

The poem's final stanza addresses the emptiness of the couple's lives and the lack of hope that their lives will change. The couple are people of some refinement who eat dinner by candlelight, but their problems are so deeply ingrained that their refined exteriors are used only to deflect emotions. Santos uses the image of a burnt match—a spent article, destroyed, with no further hope that it will have any good use. He extends the visual image of the match head stuck in wax, referring to its being "preserved into amber." Amber is tree resin that has become fossilized, usually dating back thirty million to ninety million years. Scientists sometimes find stuck in amber the remains of an insect that is completely intact. These fossils are used in the study of anatomical forms that have not changed for thousands of centuries. The novel and film *Jurassic Park* (1990 and 1993, respectively) are based on the idea of being able to revive dinosaur DNA found in the blood of a mosquito that has been embedded in amber. The poem therefore indicates that the couple's relationship will not grow or improve when the new century comes in, that it will never change—these people are set in their unhappy relationship, like an insect in amber, unmoving for eons.

Themes

Empathy

In the fifth stanza, in line 24, "Portrait of a Couple at Century's End" changes direction. Lines 1 through 23 focus on one continuous scene: a suburban home with cars going by in the rain and the news on the television while a couple eat their dinner and placidly discuss their day. In line 24, however, the speaker intrudes on the story. "They remind us / of something" draws attention to the fact that the poet is describing a scene and that the reader is observing it. In lines 24 through 32, the poem uses the words "us," "we've," "our," and "ours" to make readers see how the poem is talking not only about the lives of theoretical people but also about readers' lives.

Topics For Further Study

- Conduct a survey of people who watch television while they eat dinner. Determine which programs are watched most while people eat. Write an analysis of how you think watching television while eating dinner affects people's moods.

- Write the story of an argument that you once had with someone who is still your friend but that neither of you mentions anymore. Include as many details as you can remember.

- Although it was widely covered by the news media, the Bosnian war did not gain the attention of Americans that other international conflicts have drawn. Research news reports of the biggest stories of 1995 for mentions of the bombing of Tuzla. Write an essay comparing the war in Bosnia with any current event that you think Americans are not noticing.

- What are the chances that you will be alive at the end of the twenty-first century? Research the latest advances in the science of aging and produce a chart that shows the factors that will affect your long-term survival.

- In line 34, "Portrait of a Couple at Century's End" mentions the "industry of pain." Research the condition of the world at the end of the nineteenth century and write an essay comparing it with major events at the end of the twentieth century. Was there more or less suffering at the close of the twentieth century? Why?

The poem counts on the fact that readers will empathize with the couple described. Unlike sympathy, which entails understanding another's suffering, empathy requires one to put oneself in the other person's place and to feel his or her situation from the inside rather than from the outside. When he switches the focus to "our lives," Santos forces readers to accept the couple's situation as their own.

Bourgeois Life

"Bourgeois" is a word that comes from the French and means "a middle-class person." It is often used derogatorily and usually while discussing opposition between social classes. "Bourgeois" is used to indicate a comfort with materialism and a conformity with middle-class values that makes a person wish for nothing more than continued financial stability. In this "Portrait of a Couple at Century's End," Santos depicts a couple locked up in their bourgeois values. The signs of their prosperity include the house, the television they watch during their meal, their dinnerware, and the beeswax candles on their dinner table. The couple is financially comfortable but not independently wealthy, because not one but both of them work. Santos contrasts the couple's placid middle-class life to life in war-torn Bosnia.

The couple is evidently so comfortable with their life that they want to avoid thinking about things that might upset them, such as an argument that they once had. Given such little information, readers cannot help but assume that the couple would rather keep their lifestyle consistent than explore the things that really matter in life, such as having an honest relationship. It is characteristic of the bourgeois lifestyle that the couple would put material comfort over spiritual growth.

Permanence

The imagery used in the final stanza, lines 36 to 40, of "Portrait of a Couple at Century's End" is fatalistic in that it tells readers that the situations described in the poem will never change. The situations are indeed grim. The television describes war overseas; thousands of commuters sit stuck impatiently in traffic; and in the living room of one house, a couple talks about the summer in order to avoid acknowledging their unhappy situation. When it comes up, the quarrel in Iowa is seen as an opportunity to let emotions flow again, but by the final stanza, the couple, as well as everyone else mentioned or referred to in the poem, including the speaker and the reader, are said to be stuck in the maddening patterns they have lived in, presumably doomed to stay dissatisfied forever. The images that Santos uses to imply this state of suspended animation are the boot stuck in the mud, the amber that has been known to imprison life forms for millions of years, and the candle wax that solidifies around the burnt matchstick.

Optimism

The end of the century is used in "Portrait of a Couple at Century's End" to imply a turning point, a time when the wrongs of the past can be set right. It is mentioned in the title, but after that this cause for hope is left to linger in the back of the reader's mind while the poem goes on to concentrate on other matters, such as traffic, the international news, and the tension in the couple's living room.

The idea of the passage of time and its ability to clear up old, lingering wounds is raised in the fifth stanza, lines 21 through 25, in which Santos alludes to a past quarrel. The quarrel is presented as a good thing, bringing up longings, leading readers to hope that the resurrection of buried emotions can mean that the wounds can be healed once and for all. The wounds are not healed, though. The poem reminds readers of how such moments reflect their own "shadow-life" and tells them that the future of the couple's "monogamous hearts" is to be forgotten. Lines 31 through 35 return to the century's end of the title, using a metaphor to indicate the unpleasant fact that the turn of the century will not, in fact, free the couple from the unpleasantness they have buried. The century is mentioned in terms of one hundred years of accumulation of mud, in which the soles of the couple's boots are stuck forever, making them unable to move forward. This idea of crushed optimism is reinforced in lines 36 through 40, in which the couple's relationship is compared to an insect preserved in amber and a burnt matchstick stuck into coalesced beeswax. Rather than moving forward when the century changes to a new one, this couple are doomed to continue with their unhappy, emotionally drained life.

Style

Syllabic Verse

"Portrait of a Couple at Century's End" has little noticeable consistency for readers who try to examine it line by line. The poem does not follow a set rhyme scheme, and the lines within each stanza do not resemble each other in rhythm or length. Santos does, however, use rhythmic consistency in this poem by repeating the pattern of line lengths in each stanza. The first line of each stanza has five syllables; the second lines all have eleven syllables; all but one—line 13—of the third lines have seven syllables; the fourth lines have ten syllables; and the fifth lines have four syllables. Poetry in which lines are measured by the number of syllables in a line, rather than by the rhythm of stressed and unstressed syllables in the line, is called syllabic verse.

Syllabic verse is more common in languages other than English. Japanese, French, and Spanish are examples of languages that are syllable timed. Their syllables are approximately the same length. English, by contrast, is a stress-timed language, which means that it flows rhythmically. Syllable-timed languages are more likely to organize verse around counting syllables, and stress-timed languages are inclined to focus on the pattern created by stressed and unstressed syllables.

Extended Metaphor

Throughout the poem's early stanzas, Santos uses rain to imply an ominous sense of discontent pervading modern culture. In the first stanza, the rush-hour traffic is slowed by the rain. In the second and third stanzas, lines 6 through 15, it is raining in the country being covered on the television news. The couple inside their house are aware of the rain, which drives them to take themselves back to the summer in their conversation. The rain defines the mood of the entire poem.

In the seventh stanza, lines 31 through 35, Santos refers to the rain obliquely when he mentions boots that are "pressed forever in our century's mud." The rain that is everywhere, representing grim oppression, will not go away. The mud that results from the rain will trap the people in this poem in that same oppression. By altering the reference only a little, Santos carries the metaphorical rain to its logical conclusion, mud.

Historical Context

The Approaching Millennium

"Portrait of a Couple at Century's End" was published in the late 1990s, when the world was looking forward to the approach of the twenty-first century. Many cultures around the world celebrate New Year's Day each year as a time of promise, when old troubles can be left behind and a better life can begin. The interest in the change of the calendar is intensified at the turn of each century, with the beginning of another hundred-year cycle. In 1999, that effect was made more significant by the fact that it represented the start of a new millennium, an event that had not occurred since the year 999, well before the Georgian calendar, which is common throughout the Western world, was introduced in 1582.

Because of the end of the millennium, expectations were raised as the year 2000 approached. Some evangelical Christians, for example, their expectations piqued by strict readings of the book of Revelation in the Bible, claimed that the end of the millennium would signify the long-awaited Second Coming, the return of Jesus Christ on the last day of the world. Some people believed that the turn of the century would bring with it earthquakes, plagues, and catastrophe. Their predictions were based on ancient texts they believed foretold the start of the new millennium as a time of apocalypse.

The U.S. government had reason for more practical concerns. Evidence had been uncovered that the al Qaeda terrorist organization was planning public attacks during New Year's celebrations around the world that would injure or kill dozens if not hundreds of people. On December 14, 1999, an Algerian citizen named Ahmed Ressam, traveling with a false Canadian passport, was caught driving into the United States at Port Angeles, Washington, with one hundred pounds of explosives in the trunk of his car. After his arrest, it was determined that Ressam had been trained by al Qaeda and that he was planning to blow up a terminal at Los Angeles International Airport. In early January 2000, U.S. government officials went public with information that they had disrupted terrorist plans in eight countries where attacks had been planned. The approach of the new millennium raised concerns about the sort of terror attacks that would later strike Washington, D.C., and New York City in 2001, Madrid in 2004, and London in 2005.

Neither celestial prophecy nor terrorist attack was the biggest concern as the new century approached. The years and months before the event brought increasing international concern about a credible problem with computer systems worldwide. Called the Y2K bug, or millennium bug, this problem threatened to do widespread and lasting damage. The bug stemmed from the fact that since the 1960s, computer programmers had used two digits rather than four for the year in date codes.

As the turn of the century approached, companies realized that their computers might not be able to correctly read dates after December 31, 1999, that 2000 might be read as 1900. The resulting problem in continuity was predicted to create widespread havoc—that automatic teller machines would refuse to dispense cash; that air and ground traffic control programs would shut down at midnight on December 31, 1999; that electrical, water, and gas utilities would fail. During the last half of the 1990s, the Y2K phenomenon became well known, and public anxiety about the pending calamity grew. Corporations and governments devoted millions of dollars to hiring teams of programmers to go over their computer systems and ensure that they were Y2K compliant. In the end, relatively little damage occurred. The few problems that did happen, such as a brief railway shutdown in Denmark and the temporary blinding of a U.S. spy satellite, were isolated and did not have the cascading effect that was expected to cause life-threatening social collapse on an unprecedented scale.

Critical Overview

Santos has long been admired by critics as a poet of impressive style and vision. Reviewing Santos's second collection, *The Southern Reaches* (1989), Christopher Buckley writes in the *New Leader*, "it has been a very long time since I have read a work of poetry as consciously and deftly orchestrated. . . . Santos' mastery of his craft, of form, sound and music, is astounding." Santos's next book, *The City of Women* (1993), impresses critics for its ability to string together poetry and fiction in an extended meditation on a single theme. "His book is a sustained series of shimmering, shape-shifting meditations on the ways the self is one's story and one's story is always one's self," writes Deborah Pope in the *Southern Review*. *Publishers Weekly* declares that the same collection "makes sense of the vast canvas of remembered love" and that "Santos's greatest accomplishment here is not that he provides answers for the unanswerable, but that he convinces readers that love creates 'words whose syllables we are laved in, / Whose meanings keep endlessly coming to pass.'"

The Pilot Star Elegies, in which "Portrait of a Couple at Century's End" appears, was met in 1999 with critical enthusiasm. Ann K. van Buren writes in *Library Journal* that "Santos brings thoughtfulness and wisdom to subjects like suicide, war, and extinction. His poems avoid stating the obvious and strip tragedies bare of their most hideous details." The book centers on the extended poem "Elegy for My Sister," written after Santos's sister committed suicide. In the *Washington Post*, Rafael Campo writes that the book is not one of laments, noting that "this poet seems most concerned with salving our common flaws and recognizing how beautifully human it is simply to need."

Floyd Collins directly addresses "Portrait of a Couple at Century's End" in his review of the collection in the *Gettysburg Review*. Regarding the book, Collins notes that "Santos encompasses the myriad contingencies of loss in lyrics." Collins realizes the sadness of the poem and the gentleness with which Santos has written about it. "Although youthful emotions appear transient within the larger context of the century's upheaval," Collins writes, "the charred match-end that once blossomed into flame, however briefly, betokens an innocence and passion long spent."

Criticism

David Kelly

David Kelly is an instructor of creative writing and literature. In this essay, he examines the ways that Santos balances misery with banality.

Poetry in general can be looked at as a balance between ideas, which are insubstantial, and the imagery used to tether them. There is no way to tell in advance what the proper balance will be. For some poems, being heavy on ideas is the way to go, but other poems reach maximum effectiveness with a series of images that require readers to use their interpretive skills to piece together meanings. It would be a mistake to say that a poem has the right style before knowing what ideas are being conveyed. As the rule for writers states, form should serve the piece's function, not dictate it.

A poem like Santos's "Portrait of a Couple at Century's End" is effective because it establishes its own balance, even among the chaos of the subjects and images it presents. As indicated in the title, which situates the couple under discussion as poised between one historical epoch and the next, the poem is frozen, pulled neither toward its worldly elements nor toward its conceptual ones. It is a poem in which humanity's deepest and darkest emotions, the horror and existential weight that come from nothing more than from being, are

balanced against a familiar domestic situation that, described in another setting, may seem so common as to be forgettable. The huge is balanced against the small and the profound balanced against the mundane with such deft accuracy that the poem seems to gravitate motionlessly. In some poems, it would seem as if the writer is too little involved in his subject, but in Santos's poem the balance is appropriate.

The important ideas in "Portrait of a Couple at Century's End" are pain, sorrow, regret, and loss. These concepts are hinted at in the early, rain-soaked stanzas, but Santos does more than simply imply these ideas. Near the end of the poem, he states them outright. In lines 26 through 35, Santos refers to the sinister "shadow-life," the "industry of pain," and the "Ho- / ly Spirit of / everything that's been / taken away." "Portrait of a Couple at Century's End" is a grim poem about the aspects of life that most people would rather avoid thinking about, as the couple described here does. Santos even evokes an unidentified "us," which brings reader and writer into the conspiracy of avoidance, marking the ideas as being so dark that most people, like the couple, would rather suppress knowledge of them.

Although the mood is somber, one would not characterize this poem as fatalistic. Santos pulls it away from the depths of absolute misery not only with the images that he uses (which are in themselves bleak) but also with the way that he conveys both ideas and images. Santos does not say much that is good. The most uplifting idea in the poem is a mention of "buried longings," which in any context but this one would not be stretched into a ray of hope. The cumulative effect of the dark imagery and the even darker proclamations is more buoyant than any of the parts.

Santos chooses words in his descriptions that, although not positive, are at least not gloomy. The net effect is that the words tend to elevate the mood of the poem. The details of Santos's images are important. Traffic in the rain does not sound simply like paper tearing but specifically like construction paper tearing, a sound most people associate with childhood and school projects. Using the image of construction paper conjures up thoughts of white paste and safety scissors being used to make collages and dioramas. Inside the couple's house, the walls sound as if they hold not simply a hundred thousand flies but specifically "bottle-flies." These flies are the ones associated not with clustering on the dead but with the harmless domesticity of screen doors and cooling pies. The walls themselves are

What Do I Read Next?

- Santos has written one book of prose, a collection of essays titled *A Poetry of Two Minds* (2000). The essays are pertinent to poetry in the late twentieth and early twenty-first centuries, but readers curious about Santos's style will be particularly interested in "Writing the Poet, Unwriting the Poem: Notes Toward an *Ars Poetica*."

- Santos's collection *The Perishing: Poems* (2003) is both mournful and political, reflecting the changed world after September 11, 2001.

- C. K. Williams's poem "Elegy for Paul Zweig" has been compared with Santos's writing at about the time he wrote "Portrait of a Couple at Century's End," both in subject matter and in

treatment. It is found in Williams's *Selected Poems* (1994).

- One of Santos's elegies in *The Pilot Star Elegies* is dedicated to the critic M. L. Rosenthal. Rosenthal's book *Poetry and the Common Life* (1974) is an influence on Santos's style.

- The year that Santos was a finalist for the National Book Award for Poetry, that prize was awarded to Ai for her collection *Vice: New and Selected Poems* (1999). The poets' styles could hardly be farther apart. Santos is dry and academic, and Ai is a populist, weaving figures from modern culture—Marilyn Monroe, O. J. Simpson, murderers, and rapists—to write a new kind of poetry for the twenty-first century.

---

made of "clapboards," a word seldom used in the early twenty-first century but familiar to earlier generations. The use of this word reminds readers of more than the boundary-setting function of walls, taking them back to older building materials with a mild case of nostalgia. When discussing the destruction caused by mortar fire in the middle of an urban war zone, Santos softens the harshness of reality by mentioning a "terrace." These reminders of the genteel world in the middle of a poem about misery can be seen as an exercise in irony, but the more important accomplishment is that they keep the poem from falling entirely into despair.

The details go beyond the poet's usual responsibility of evoking images with specificity. The details in "Portrait of a Couple at Century's End" poem are more domestic than they need to be. As a result, the objects—walls, flies, traffic sounds, even a bombed-out café—enforce the poem's domestic, everyday side. They ground the poem in the familiar, the nonthreatening, and buy the reader's patience for later, when the poem digs in with flat-out anger.

Although the familiarity of the imagery helps to take the edge off the unpleasantness of the ideas expressed, Santos achieves much the same effect

by hyphenating words. Two of the hyphenated compound words in the poem are "bottle-flies" and "shadow-life." The complexity that Santos gives to these ordinary, simple words serves to numb the senses, overloading readers with the opposite of the effect they would get from punchy, snappy terms. Similarly, although the poem uses "boot- / soles" where "boots" would suffice, the extended form surrounds a simple concept with a dreamy fog. "Boot-soles" is a more specific description than "boots," which makes it stronger writing, but the word itself, like "clapboard," sounds antiquated, like a throwback to an earlier, more manageable time. For this reason, it lacks immediacy. If Santos's purpose had been to keep things compelling or lively, then slowing down the poem this way would be a flaw. As it is, though, this poem works best when excess wording slows it down. As a word, "boot-soles" is mired in the poem's language as much as the boots in the poem are mired in mud. Breaking the word in two, stretching it out with a hyphen, makes it slow and lazy. Carrying the word over to the next line makes the concept of boots plodding and domestic.

The effect of carrying a word into the next line is used in an even more eye-catching way when

> *These reminders of the genteel world in the middle of a poem about misery can be seen as an exercise in irony, but the more important accomplishment is that they keep the poem from falling entirely into despair."*

Santos spans the short, four-letter word "holy" across the break between lines 34 and 35. This stylistic maneuver is the most unusual one in the poem and is telling about the poet's method. The oversimplified explanation for why Santos does not keep the two syllables of "holy" together is that keeping the word intact would violate the syllabic pattern of the poem. The fourth line of each stanza has ten syllables, and line 34 reaches that total with "Ho-." This argument is too easy. The poet has control of the words he uses, and Santos could have easily avoided the interruption by using a shorter word for "industry" earlier in the line.

To divide the word "holy," dragging it out the way the poem does, is to diminish the idea that it represents. In presenting the word in its parts, the poem requires readers to pay more attention to the word itself than to its meaning. If the reference was really to the Holy Spirit of Christian dogma, this technique might be irreverent or blasphemous. Santos, however, is using this phrase in a personal way when he writes "the Ho- / ly Spirit of / everything that's been / taken away." The central idea of the poem is ultimate loss, and the words "Holy Spirit" add a religious dimension. The overall expression would not work if the poem did not negate the power of its effect by reminding readers that they are involved in reading a poem.

Although much poetry is about balance—between form and idea, thought and substance, implication and assertion—it is even more crucial for a piece like "Portrait of a Couple at Century's End" to stay between the extremes, to not give too much attention to any of the aspects of the poem at the expense of others. Santos's poetry has a melancholy edge, a willingness to look at the harshness just under the surface of everyday life. In this poem, much is stated about the harshness, and much is implied about quiet suffering. If this mood dominated by "darker crimes" were not contrasted by word choice and style, it would seem to present a vision of unendurable gloom, and that in itself would not be reality. The situation described in the poem is complex. The one thing that Santos cannot say about the situation is that it may change. That is the point of the poem. With no chance of even hoping for hope, the poem has to find other ways to oppose its own misery.

Source: David Kelly, Critical Essay on "Portrait of a Couple at Century's End," in *Poetry for Students*, Thomson Gale, 2006.

James Rother

In the following review of The Pilot Star Elegies *from the online website* Contemporary Poetry Review, *Rother calls the collection "astonishing" and remarks on the "higher reaches of statement" attained compared with Santos's previous volumes.*

With *The Pilot Star Elegies,* his fourth collection of poems and a National Book Award finalist, Sherod Santos shows convincingly that whatever suspicions his earlier volumes might have aroused that here was just one more *New Yorker*–style poet specializing in poser-cat's cradles for the highly strung, his work—to paraphrase Ezra Pound—is that of a purveyor of news likely to stay news and not the preciosities of some warm-up act for the Post-PoMo Follies. Which is not to say that his earlier volumes of verse—*The City of Women, The Southern Reaches* and *Accidental Weather*—lack *gravitas* or substance. It is just that the higher reaches of statement attained in this latest book (most formidably in its centerpiece "Elegy for My Sister," a poem in 25 parts) are of an elevation barely glimpsed in Santos's prior writings. There is discernment, finely turned lathework, the business of language on view with undoctored books—but there is not, at least to these eyes, the recombinant vitality of lines like these, from the opening to "Elegy":

> It was late in the day, as I recall,
> her pinking winter-white shoulders bent
> over the backyard flower beds, soggy still
> from the snowmelt that week
> loaded underground, at body heat, in April . . .

Or this concluding stanza, from the all too brief "Abandoned Railway Station":

> The silence of thousands of last goodbyes.
> A dried ink pad. Stanchioned ceiling.

And a cognate, terra-cotta dust over
everything, with the on-tiptoe atmosphere
of a *boule-de-neige* before it's shaken.

This is verse that is content to do the work of figuration done by fine prose before it agonizes tremulously over how it's doing as *poetry,* which is why its ligatures bind without showing where phrase was stuffed into clause or image bound onto after-image in a not very inspired attempt to gild natural ineptitude with inspired clumsiness. More than just a few lines of Santos's verse need to be under one's belt before it becomes apparent that his prevailing unit of composition is the line rather than some prosodic subparticle. Not, it should be noted, a line reminiscent of a printed circuit board, with transistorized energy nodes pulsing out regularized rhythmical patterns in the form of stresses which recur with only minor variations throughout the length of a poem. Santos now seems to be of the opinion that for a poem to really be a poem its poetry must be generated out of the words that constitute its forward motion and not those that self-regardingly thrust *themselves* forward against momentum's perpendicularizing grain. Poets with tin ears—and there are more of them out there, duly subsidized with grants and academic sinecures, than you might think— seldom luck into such realizations, and even when by some quirk of fortuity they do, inadequate technique brings the chatterbox of weights and counterweights crashing down. Santos, unlike them, is blessed with a truly remarkable ear. He can negotiate curves of sound, catching waves of rhythmic energy on the fly as though a poem of his couldn't complete its course without a version of rack-and-pinion steering and the tightest of front-end alignments. Watch how this is done in the singularly compact (and stanzaless) "Pilot Stars," where a woman, having returned to her parental home to visit her father, a retired Air Force pilot diagnosed with cancer, lies in bed and recalls the childhood experience of having sat in his lap staring at the cockpit lights of a plane cruising at 10,000 feet:

> . . . And it's on her skin
> as she's lying there, the salt and shine
> of leaning into him through the tight half-circle
> of that moonward bend, then leveling it out,
> leveling the world in one loosening turn
> for a girl lightheaded at the prospect of a life
> taken up somehow on the scattered narratives
> of all those names, those heart-logged syllables
> by which her father found a way
> (*o, how far the fall from childhood seems*)
> to chart his passage between heaven and earth . . .

This is verse as effortlessly maintained aloft as its progress is kept free of bumps, grinds, and other

> *He can negotiate curves of sound, catching waves of rhythmic energy on the fly as though a poem of his couldn't complete its course without a version of rack-and-pinion steering and the tightest of front-end alignments.*"

distentions of rhythmic plaque non-stanzaic verse is heir to. The "heart-logged syllables" alluded to are the names of constellations—Lyra, Cygnus, Aquila—her father steered his course by, and which now are lodged in her mind as compass settings of the mortal illness that would soon take his life.

Now, none of this would be of any poetic value were Santos's tracking ability, which is to say his control of *story,* not equal to the stabilizing effects of his inner gyroscope which keeps everything from capsizing into doggerel. And what that story culminates in is the daughter's realization that the sound of footsteps that she hears pacing back and forth in the bedroom above her own is the sound of her father's "slow, / incessant, solitary dying"

> that would go on
> another eighteen months, and by which it seemed
> some terrible mourning had already begun
> to extinguish the light-points one by one,
> until the dark like the dark she fell through then
> was suddenly storyless, boundless and blank.

Cancer, too, is a constellation, and the celestial crustacean it inscribes among the stars signals, within the earthly microcosm of human cells, the extinguishment of pilot lights. As approaching death snuffs them out one by one we are left, like the woman in the poem, weightless in a storyless dark as boundless as the space separating sidereal flickers and cytological meltdowns. But it is to Santos's credit that his poem never generates the emotional mildew that ponderings of mortality come home to roost can all too easily give rise to. He lets the reader liberate whatever coruscations his rebus-in-verse might have trapped between its lines. There's no moralizing before or after the fact.

Nor is there any in what is unquestionably Santos's finest poetic achievement to date, "Elegy for My Sister," which is less about suicide and its aftermath than about the alien presence we inherit from the moment death's will is read and the mysteries such presences weave about our lives:

> . . . But I begin this for another reason as well,
> a more urgent and perhaps more selfish reason,
> to answer that question which day by day
> I fear I'm growing less able to answer:
> Who was she whose death now made her
> A stranger to me? As though the problem
> Were not that she had died, and how was I
> To mourn her, but that some stalled memory
> Now kept her from existing, and that she
> Could only begin to exist, to take her place
> In the future, when all of our presuppositions
> About her, all of those things that identified
> The woman we'd buried, were finally swept aside . . .

But more than incidentally Santos's poem diagrams the haphazard "phaseology" of madness and its symmetrically disturbing observation by a sibling who cannot help reading her whole life backwards as an epiphany whose unpacking yields up knots of randomness but no loose ends to tie together. For madness never lacks for order, being steeped in its own dehydrated dreams of drowning, its own deep-sea soundings of heaven's gate. And when it is finally overtaken by the darkness it has courted for so long, it gathers up (in a parody of posterity) whatever remains might have been left behind in the form of *materia poetica* to be seized upon by anyone who, like the poet, is intent on stripping the stranger in his midst of all disquieting *Unheimlichkeit*. Sometimes these turn up unbidden and posthumously in the shape of personal oddments, even bits of cosmetic detritus:

> . . . Shortly after her death,
> we discovered in her closet a large box containing
> countless bottles of lotions, powders, lipsticks,
> and oils. Many of them had never been opened,
> still others had barely been used at all.
> Sorting through the contents it occurred to me
> The box contained some version of herself,
> Some representation of who she was—
> A stronger, more serene, more independent self?—
> That she'd never had the chance to become . . .

His sister, he tells us, never believed her own name to be designative of anything real or self-authorizing. Not able ever to feel at home on the ground of being she had difficulty grasping just who it was that could claim squatter's rights to a name, or what agency of mulled delirium could assure a proper noun of its propriety:

> Thus all her life she felt her name referred to a presence
> outside herself, a presence which sought to enclose

that self which separated her from who they were. Thus all her life she was never quite sure who it was
> people summoned whenever they called her by her name.

The quest for the means to sustain a narrative whereby his sister's long encystment of dying might be acceptably familiarized—or at least made divinable as a spelling of sibyline leaves—persists to the very exhaustion of memory, at which point it subsides into the valedictory terminalizing of italics. All energy thus spent, memorability circles back on itself and the subject of the poet's elegy is free to enter the golden promise of her journey of journeys—

> A warm spring night. A streetlamp beyond an open window.
> Beneath the sill: a girl's hushed voice exhorting itself in whispers.
> One morning, she leaves the house before dawn.
> She doesn't take the car.
> By noon she finds herself in the business district of the city
> a taxi is waiting, the driver is holding the door, and she sees that now,
> after all these years, she's about to take the great journey of her life.

Sherod Santos's *The Pilot Star Elegies* is, at the very least, an astonishing book.

Source: James Rother, "A Star to Pilot By," in http://www.cprw.com/members/Rother/star.htm, 2001, pp. 1–5.

Sherod Santos and James Rother

In the following interview from the online website Contemporary Poetry Review, *Santos comments on his collections and their relation to each other, and the lyric quality of his poetry.*

Poet and essayist Sherod Santos is the author of four books of poetry, *Accidental Weather* (Doubleday, 1982), *The Southern Reaches* (Wesleyan, 1989), *The City of Women* (W. W. Norton, 1993), and, most recently, *The Pilot Star Elegies* (W. W. Norton, 1999), which was both a National Book Award Finalist and one of five nominees for The *New Yorker* Book Award. Mr. Santos' poems appear regularly in such journals as The *New Yorker*, The *Paris Review*, The *Nation*, *Poetry*, and The *Yale Review*. His essays have appeared in *American Poetry Review*, The *New York Times Book Review*, The *Kenyon Review* and *Parnassus*, and a collection of those essays, *A Poetry of Two Minds*, has just been released (University of Georgia Press, 2000). His awards include the Delmore Schwartz Memorial Award, the Discovery/The *Nation* Award, the Oscar

Blumenthal Prize from *Poetry,* a Pushcart Prize in both poetry and the essay, and the 1984 appointment as Robert Frost Poet at the Frost house in Franconia, New Hampshire. He has received fellowships from the Ingraim Merrill and Guggenheim foundations, and the National Endowment for the Arts. From 1990–1997, Mr. Santos served as external examiner and poet-in-residence at the Poets' House in Portmuck, Northern Ireland, and in 1999 he received an Award for Literary Excellence from the American Academy of Arts and Letters. He is currently professor of English at the University of Missouri–Columbia.

[*James Rother*]: *The way books of poetry acquire their titles is often curious and fascinating. What led you to choose* The Pilot Star Elegies *as its title?*

[Sherod Santos]: In the navigational world there are such things called pilot stars, those stars in the firmament which, at any given time of year, one might fix on to establish one's location on the earth. This interested me both for literal and metaphorical reasons, and of course I felt those reasons served, however obliquely, the tonal structure of the collection overall.

Do you feel that The Pilot Star Elegies *represents a departure from your three earlier books of poetry,* Accidental Weather, The Southern Reaches, *and* The City of Women?

I think there is something of a departure in both *The City of Women* and *The Pilot Star Elegies,* though that has less to do with any purposeful design on my part, at least as I began writing those books, than it does with the varying demands of the books themselves. The first is concerned with erotic and romantic love, the second with death, so it seems natural that they'd acquire somewhat different ways of speaking.

In this latest collection you seem less preoccupied with objects and situations shimmering in suspended time, as in (to cite the term you use in "Abandoned Railway Station") a boule-de-neige, than with a more worldly engagement with people and places thrown together in a time-sharing of exile and loss?

What you describe by way of the *boule de neige* is, essentially, the lyric poem, and it's fair to say that in these last two books I have worked within a much larger temporal framework. Still, my ambition was always to approach that framework through the moment of the lyric, by arranging those moments, somewhat in the manner of a stained glass window, into a composition that's not contained in

> *Read everything, avoid thinking you're a genius, don't settle too early on for what kind of poetry you want to write, and be willing and able to give up everything for the work without expecting anything whatsoever in return."*

any of those moments individually. This provides, I hope, the illusion both of time past and of time in the process of passing, just as sunlight through a stained glass window provides the illusion of wholeness and coherence.

We asked you earlier about the relationship of The Pilot Star Elegies *to your earlier collections. How do you feel your work has grown over the four volumes? Have particular themes and concerns tended to emerge, without your immanent knowledge or consent, as dominant shapers of the way you write poetry?*

As for the first part of your question, I couldn't really say. As for the second part, I can say yes, absolutely. You see, I still harbor the rather quaint idea that poems have things to teach me, and one of the things they have to teach is how to write a poem. Because of that, I tend to try, as much as possible, to let the poem have the reins. Of course, there are unavoidable tics and mannerisms in any poet, but I'm less interested in refining those characteristics into some fixed idea of a style than I am in finding out what elements of style will best draw out the inner workings of my subject.

Many of your poems have a deceptively prosaic character: they are built with lines 12–14 syllables long, they have slant rhymes, and prose responsibilities. How did you come to this style? (Is this, in other words, a response to the Whitmanic tradition of long lines, an Englishing of the French alexandrine, or an attempt to break the English pentameter by extending it a foot or two?)

You're speaking of course about the last two books, and again the subject of those poems dictated the forms in which they were written. In "Elegy for My Sister", for example, I was struggling with a very complicated set of issues, not the least of which was: To what extent is my writing about my sister's suicide an appropriation of her suffering for my art? At the simplest level, who was this elegy really for? My sister or me? And what did I hope to gain by writing it? To eulogize her? To console myself and our family? To bring some sort of closure to her life, her death? To create a more socially acceptable portrait of her for posterity's sake? As you might imagine, I was horrified by those possibilities. And so, to answer your question, circumstances demanded, or seemed to demand, the least possible artfulness or flourish in the writing, a subordination of all those things that draw one's attention back to the writer. I wanted a certain transparency in the writing. I wanted a reader to look past, or through, the words themselves. At the same time I wanted them to be significant, to be mediated through the refining instrument of poetry, for words are, after all, our only real connection to the dead.

A number of your poems, it seems to me, appear to lend themselves to musical settings of the sort the art song composer Ned Rorem does so well. The first numbered lyric in "Elegy for My Sister" stands out particularly in this regard. Are you aware of some of your poems veering off, despite their deceptively prosaic prosody, and resembling a species of meditative lieder, as it were, in which variations on themes are conceived as much musically as poetically?

I'm not knowledgeable enough about musical settings to answer this question very thoroughly, though I do feel a certain kinship with the notion of a meditative lieder, as both a form and a process of composition. One of the things that I admire in Ned Rorem's compositions is the scale to which they adapt themselves, their refusal of what he calls—if I'm remembering correctly—"the masterpiece syndrome." And here, too, it seems to me that we're back in the terrain of the lyric, and, as such, I'm not sure I make the same distinction you do at the end of your question. To conceive a poem poetically" means, to my mind, to conceive of it "musically."

While no precise count was kept of the times the theme and/or motif of "backlighting" is alluded to in your latest volume, its recurrence would suggest that things perceived as "backlit" figure rather prominently in your lexicon of images. Does *this have particular meaning for you, or is it something that has more coincidental than real significance in your work?*

This hadn't occurred to me, though of course that doesn't mean it's either coincidental or insignificant. I suppose memory is, by nature, "backlit"—at least insomuch as it poses what's recollected in the soft- or hard-edged light of the past—and because it's elegiac, the poetry of memory is going to have something of that backlit character.

What are your views on creative writing programs, and their influence on contemporary poetry? Of late, as you are probably aware, critics have begun to blame these programs for (what they see as) a loss of individuality in American verse.

A loss of individuality in American verse? Who are they kidding? Has there ever been a more individuated poetry in the history of the world? To think that our poetry can somehow be characterized, for better or worse, by reference to "creative writing programs" is either culturally naïve or intellectually irresponsible. From the Black Aesthetics of Askia Muhammad Touré to the Steinian poetics of Charles Bernstein, from the engagé of Adrienne Rich to the dégagé of John Ashbery, from the canonical authority of the *Harpers Anthology of 20th Century Native American Poetry* to the defensive neo-classicism of the New Formalists, from Miguel Algarin's *Voices from the Nuyorican Poets' Café* to the Cowboy traditions of Howard "Jack" Thorp and Bruce Kiskaddon, from the hip-hop rhythms of rap to the haphazard rhythms of the poetry slam. . . . It may be more accurate to call it, not "contemporary American poetry" at all, but "contemporary American poetries." I'm of course familiar with the kinds of complaints you mention—I've responded to them at length in *A Poetry of Two Minds,* in an essay entitled "In a Glass Darkly, Darkly"—but perhaps you can tell me why it is such unsupported claims are granted such automatic credence. You say, "Of late . . . critics have begun," but the truth is that these complaints have been around for years, and regardless of how scrupulously and thoughtfully and variously they've been addressed, you can rest assured that in a very short while they'll surface again, exactly as before, delivered to a welcoming audience with the wide-eyed fervor of some journalist uncovering a senatorial tryst. Why is that, do you suppose?

Can serious poetry regain the common readers it once had?

Yes, of course it can, and it has, and anyone who hasn't noticed that is just not paying attention.

Not only has the mainstream begun to open its doors to a widening range of marginalized poets, but the last two decades have seen an unprecedented burst of poetry activities, from White House celebrations hosted by the President and First Lady to the formation of a national poetry month; from billboards in Los Angeles filled with poems by contemporary poets to the inclusion of a poetry book as a standard feature with all new Volkswagens shipped in April; from cross-country book giveaways inspired by Joseph Brodsky's claim that poetry should be as available as the Gideon Bible to the distribution by tollbooth operators in New Jersey of free copies of Whitman's "Leaves of Grass." Added to that we've seen a huge proliferation of poetry awards, web sites, spoken arts recordings, open mike nights, and public radio and television specials. All this couldn't have happened without the interest and enthusiasm of the common reader.

What advice would you offer to the young poet? What would you have him do or read for his poetic education?

Oh, I don't know. Read everything, avoid thinking you're a genius, don't settle too early on for what kind of poetry you want to write, and be willing and able to give up everything for the work without expecting anything whatsoever in return.

Source: James Rother, "Sherod Santos: The Refining Instrument of Poetry (An Interview)," in http://www.cprw .com/members/Rother/santos.htm, 2001, pp. 1–5.

Floyd Collins

In the following essay excerpt, Collins describes the attributes of lyric poetry and places Santos's works, including "Portrait of a Couple at Century's End," within a framework of transience and elegy.

I

Thanks to court intrigue and the vacillation of Mary Tudor, half-sister to the late Edward VI, the English crown adorned the head of seventeen-year-old Lady Jane Grey for nine days in 1563. Eventually she was led to the executioner's block to have that head lopped off. When the Tower warden ransacked her cell later, he found a sheet of parchment riddled with pinpricks. When held to the light, the tiny perforations formed verses she had composed shortly before her death. That Lady Jane contrived a solar dot matrix system to record her final meditations seems, in retrospect, less important than her mode of expression, the lyric, the haunting qualities of which Mark Strand has described: "Lyric

> *Although youthful emotions appear transient within the larger context of the century's upheaval, the charred match-end that once blossomed into flame, however briefly, betokens an innocence and passion long spent."*

poetry reminds us that we live in time. It tells us that we are mortal. It celebrates or recognizes moods, ideas, events only as they exist in passing.... Lyric poetry is a long memorial, a valedictory to all our moments on earth." In medieval lyric, the ubi sunt motif emphasizes the transitoriness of life and implies the decadence of the current epoch by invoking an idyllic past. The carpe diem theme of the Renaissance lyric exhorts young lovers to "seize the day" and embodies the spirit of "Let us eat and drink, for tomorrow we shall die." And yet the temporal aspects of the lyric also embody a singular paradox, inasmuch as words betoken absence, the absence of the objects and images that they describe. Indeed, the amorous sonneteer of the late sixteenth century claimed the power to confer immortality on both himself and his "cruel fair."

The lyric typically eschews the strictly linear development essential to epic and dramatic verse, but this does not divest the form of a remarkable range of moods. It may be meditative (Thomas Gray's "Elegy in a Country Churchyard"), admonitory (Percy Shelley's "Ozymandias"), elegiac (John Keats's "Ode to a Nightingale"), apocalyptic (William Butler Yeats's "The Second Coming"), celebratory (Dylan Thomas's "Poem in October"), or iconoclastic (Sylvia Plath's "Daddy"). Because the lyric derives from the personal emotions of the poet, its themes may be exalted or quaint or both (as in Richard Witbur's "Death of a Toad"). Most importantly, it draws cogency and force from the poet's facility with language, relying on rhythm, syntax, diction, image, and metaphor to engage the reader. Some critics would even argue that lyricism is not so much a form as a manner of writing, and a second glance at Thomas Mann's *Death in Venice,* James Joyce's *Ulysses,* F. Scott Fitzgerald's *The Great Gatsby,* or Djuna Barnes's *Nightwood* compels assent.

On the threshold of the millennium, the lyric remains an astonishingly versatile and vital form, as rich in potential and as accessible as it must have been for Lady Jane Grey. Indeed, one might say that the lyric offers a particularly appropriate vehicle for expressing both the joys and discontinuities of modern life. The three poets considered here have sedulously adapted the lyric to their own needs. What emerges from their work, however, is not a pose or a fashionable despair, but rather a keen awareness, both of the transience of life and the ways in which transience is embedded in the lyric form. . . .

In *The Pilot Star Elegies,* Sherod Santos explores a wide variety of subjects; inevitably, however, loss is the overriding theme, a brooding presence that shadows nearly every poem in the volume. For Santos, elegy is the purest form of lyric, an apt medium for capturing the ephemerality of human existence and confronting grief. In "Elegy for My Sister," the poet draws heavily on memory as he seeks to come to terms with the suicide of his elder sibling: "Each step seems drawn out endlessly, and echoes / so in memory that I almost think I can feel—in her—/ that earth-bound, raw, quicksilvered weight / a life takes on in that moment it coarses to be a life." But if transience is a dominant motif in *The Pilot Star Elegies,* Santos also celebrates resilience: the tenacity of a sea turtle cruelly tethered and left to die, the exile of the current Dalai Lama "blessed with the common sense / to survive himself," and the abiding love of a married couple whose shared memory of a quarrel years before awakens "buried longings." In poetry as rhythmically precise as [David] Baker's and as mythically charged as [Sydney] Wade's, Santos forges an aesthetic commensurate with what J. D. McClatchy has called "the world's grief, the soul's despair.". . .

IV

In his fourth book-length collection, *The Pilot Star Elegies,* Sherod Santos encompasses the myriad contingencies of loss in lyrics as richly allusive as Wade's and as musically adept as Baker's. In the centerpiece of his volume, "Elegy for My Sister," Santos shuns the traditional approach of translating bereavement into consolation, preferring instead to delve into the psychological and confessional dimensions of grief. In the prologue to this

long poem (to which I shall return for fuller discussion), Santos relies on memory to illuminate the tragedy of a sibling who eventually took her own life: "Her vine- / borne flowering marginalia (flowering now // in the ever-widening margins of memory)." But the book contains other meditations equally striking in rhythm, syntax, diction, image, and metaphor, on subjects from a dying hawksbill turtle to the exiled Dalai Lama. Transience is the touchstone of Santos's aesthetic, as these lines from "Abandoned Railway Station" reveal: "Large empty walls, and a water stain, / ultramarine, like a fresco of Perseus, / head in hand, fleeing the golden falchion."

Occasionally Santos's lyrics depict transience within the context of apparently cruel and gratuitous behavior. Here are the first eleven lines of "Sea Turtle":

> Out of a ripple in the sea grass,
> two unhoused fiddler crabs
> sidestep past the almost-dead
> hawksbill turtle turned over
> on the beach and left there
> staked with a length of broom-
> stick and baling wire. The squared,
> inquiring head upstraining,
> the plastron split, and the sun-
> dazed eyes that will not weep
> for such incongruities as these.

Aptly tethered to the left-hand margin by trochaic inversion throughout stanzas one and two, these truncated lines nevertheless betray a rhythmic lilt in the repetition of "ripple" and "fiddler," evoking the frenzied grace of the danse macabre in the consonative phrase "sidestep past." The hierarchy of images allows a spatial structuring that juxtaposes the "unhoused fiddler crabs" with the "turtle turned over," thus asserting the incongruity of a seagoing carnivore become ballast to its own massive heart. Other than the poet's metrical dexterity, the only human presence is the malevolent contrivance of stake and "baling wire." The sun beats down, and the horny plates of the hawksbill's underbelly fracture along the grain, the fissure accentuated by the plosives and sibilants of "plastron split." Despite its torpor and helplessness, the aquatic reptile's eye is moistened by no rheum: "Faced into the current of an on- // shore breeze, the once-buoyant / cradle of its shell closes like / a trench around its breathing." Notwithstanding the metaphor "cradle of its shell," Santos resists the impulse toward pathetic fallacy and elegiac apotheosis. Transience, especially mortality, is in the order of things; moreover, the sea appears hardly less capricious than the malign intelligence that stranded the turtle at the margins of its natural habitat:

Now anchored to the earth,
it founders in the slipstream
of a mild, inverted sea,
and labors toward it still, its little
destiny undisturbed by acts
of forgiveness or contrition.

No amount of rectitude or penance can alter the tortoise's fate as it struggles to survive beyond our reckoning. For all its sedulous craftsmanship and lyric intricacy, "Sea Turtle" calls to mind the Nietzschean weltanschauung that obsessed Robinson Jeffers in his mature years. We should not be surprised, therefore, to come across a poem titled "Jeffers Country":

Bay leaves season the air
along Ocean Avenue, which dips down
to the beach, that cypress-lined, granite-faced
allegory he worried into something more
inhuman than a paradise of sticks and stones.

Unlike Jeffers, Santos does not espouse a nihilistic philosophy or yearn for "life purged of its ephemeral accretions." Only in his manner of revolving words and cadences, his desire to capture the grandeur of the phenomenal universe, does Santos pay homage to the poet of the Monterey coast mountains: "He imagined the strophe and antistrophe, / the steelhead nosing at the riverbank."

Perhaps the most disarming and portentous lyric in *The Pilot Star Elegies,* "The Dalai Lama" focuses on a single flower, a memento mori pressed by the young Tibetan god-king between the pages of D'Aulaire's Norse Gods and Giants:

the five clean-cut crenelate petals
of a flower almost alchemical
in its papery
likeness to what
it was: a sign conspired
to preserve some tremor in an adolescent's
heart, to round out phyla in a science
notebook kept for school,
or perhaps, in fear,
to summon the wandering
Valkyries whose muraled lives
are marked for good by the cinnabar
leached off its cells.

Santos's speaker describes the dessicated fibers of a once-living talisman as "clean-cut" and "crenelate," a meticulous arrangement of sound and imagery that evokes what is now the mere simulacrum of beauty or remembrance. Scarcely the palpable, full-blooded rose of the Renaissance love lyric, the petaled husk molders to quintessence, "cinnabar" rouging the "muraled lives" of Odin's daughters. But the exotic transmutation proves only another form of transience: "a dead / metaphor carrying on long / past its paradigm // of human need."

Indeed, the flower "faces into the future / freed of our small demands on it, / like the exiled Tibetan god-king / blessed with the common sense / to survive himself." Santos's closure conceals a double meaning. In Tibetan lore, each Dalai Lama is the reincarnation of his predecessor; thus he survives down the ages. On the other hand, Tenzin Gyatso, the current holder of the title, fled his homeland for India rather than submit to arrest by the Chinese Communists in 1959. He put aside a temporal realm once as secure as Asgard, forsaking his stronghold in the mountains of Tibet so that he might continue to discharge his spiritual obligations. Possibly the frail "crenelate petals" remind him that the Norse gods are themselves subject to time and fate; in the words of the Elder Edda, "the gods are doomed and the end is death."

"Portrait of a Couple at Century's End" initially looks upon transience with a jaded eye, summoning a fin de siècle ambience from the routine of getting through a day: "Impatient for home, / the after-work traffic fanning out along / the wet streets." However, what waits at the house unnerves the speaker more than the rapid-fire assonance of radials on wet asphalt: "a CNN foreign correspondent tells / how a single Serb mortar shell / just leveled the crowded terrace of a / Tuzla café." Ignoring this contemporary drama, the protagonist and his wife prefer to find refuge in the past, recalling a dispute by candlelight years earlier: "how they quarrelled / one night in Iowa. The buried longings / such memories stir." Obviously, the argument arose from a sexual jealousy that seems refreshingly vital in retrospect:

So forget for a moment
the future of their monogamous hearts,
forget the rain,
the traffic, the boot-
soles pressed forever in our century's mud,
for it's all there, whatever
they'd say, the industry of pain, the
Holy Spirit of everything that's been
taken away, it's all there in the burnt match-
head preserved into amber
by a beeswax candle pooling beside
their dinnerware.

Although youthful emotions appear transient within the larger context of the century's upheaval, the charred match-end that once blossomed into flame, however briefly, betokens an innocence and passion long spent.

"Elegy for My Sister," a cycle of twenty-five lyric vignettes that accrue meaning layer by layer, represents Santos's most ambitious effort to date. Despite narrative elements, its progression is nonlinearly elliptical, relying on image and metaphor to engage the reader. Santos's basic tone is at once confessional and noncompensatory, and the poem begins by offering a traditional disclaimer—"I can already feel her slipping beyond / the reach of words"—that is almost immediately belied by a passage of astonishing visual and linguistic clarity:

> Bolstered by pillows, I'd stayed inside,
> my headcold clearing in the camphored room,
> though I wasn't simply imagining things
> when I watched a field rat bore back out
> from the mulch pile tumbled behind her;
> or when, sinking her pitchfork into the banked
> hay bales, a blacksnake speared by the tines
> wound up like a caduceus along the handle.

Santos conjures an incident from his childhood, as he remembers his sister doing yardwork in late spring. Embedded within a rich texture of language, the poet's images presage his sibling's unhappy fate. While the rat connotes but ill luck and pestilence, the blacksnake "wound up like a caduceus" suggests a number of meanings. The caduceus is the wand belonging to the divine messenger Hermes who, in Greek mythology, doubles as the psychopompos, the guide of souls to the underworld. Did Santos receive a premonition of his sister's suicide? The irony deepens when we realize that the caduceus also symbolizes the physicians who unwittingly collaborated in her death. Moreover, the very transience of Santos's vision lends it a numinous aura: "there she is, made over again / by my own deliberate confusions: bare- / shouldered, burning, imperiled in the yard."

Sometimes Santos's elegy lapses into a linguistic mediation between the quick and the dead, an apologia for his sister's mental and emotional instability: "that darkening shape-shift she could feel / was somehow, through her, handed down, / mother-to-daughter, daughter-to-child." But more often, he evokes her "unabated spiritual yearning," which renders so poignant the Danteesque phantasmagoria of section twenty-two:

> A lead-colored hoarfrost solders the grass
> to the staked, transplanted cedars along
> the new "park walk" on the hospital grounds,
> where a patient empurpled like a fake
> carnation nods toward the thousand-
> windowed front. It's just past ten, the first
> of Sunday's visiting hours, and now,
> in broken files, past ghosted, rainbow-
> coded signs, the families come forward
> from the parking lots ... which to her
> still seem some vast frontier the healthy
> into exile cross: dogged, downcast,
> hunkered into the cold, drawn in caravan
> from the smoke-filled feudal towns beyond.

Santos's blank verse sonnet could serve as a microcosm of the poem as a whole, which in dramatic terms resembles the medieval psychomachia or "soul battle." The poet sets the tone in the first line, his rolling o and r sounds slowed to an ineffable dolor by the repetition of d in "lead-colored" and "solders." No frost fires crackle on the lawn, but a dull fume rises, as from a soldering iron. Even the pungent, uprooted cedars are staked fast to the frozen ground. The hospital as an institution had its inception in the Church during the Middle Ages, but in lieu of the stained-glass radiance of cathedral windows, we now have luminescent "ghosted, rainbow- / coded signs." Indeed, few ravishments greet the eye in this purgatorial setting, as families and other visitors move like penitents in "caravan" from "smoke-filled feudal towns." But transience is inherent, both here and elsewhere: visitors and convalescents transgress invisible "frontiers" every day. Santos never attains formal solace in "Elegy for My Sister," but in detailing Sarah's escape from the dismal home of her childhood, he achieves transcendence, albeit metaphorical:

> A warm spring night. A streetlamp beyond an open window. Beneath the sill: a girl's hushed voice exhorting itself in whispers.
>
> One morning, she leaves the house before dawn. She doesn't take the car. By noon she finds herself in the business district of the city—a taxi is waiting, the driver is holding the door, and she sees that now, after all these years, she's about to take the great journey of her life.

Like Baker and Wade, Santos celebrates the tenuous and transient nature of being through the felt rhythms and vivid figurations of the lyric form. Each of these poets has devised a personal aesthetic of startling resonance and exceptional power.

Source: Floyd Collins, "Transience and the Lyric Impulse," in *Gettysburg Review*, Vol. 12, No. 4, Winter 1999, pp. 702–19.

Sources

Buckley, Christopher, Review of *The Southern Reaches*, in the *New Leader*, Vol. 73, No. 1, January 8, 1990, pp. 15–18.

Campo, Rafael, "Poetry," in the *Washington Post*, March 21, 1999, final edition, p. X03.

Collins, Floyd, "Transience and the Lyric Impulse," in *Gettysburg Review*, Vol. 12, No. 4, Winter 1999, pp. 702–19.

Pope, Deborah, Review of *The City of Women: A Sequence of Prose and Poems*, in the *Southern Review*, Vol. 29, No. 4, Autumn 1993, pp. 808–19.

Review of *The City of Women: A Sequence of Prose and Poems*, in *Publishers Weekly*, Vol. 240, No. 9, March 1, 1993, p. 43.

Santos, Sherod, "Portrait of a Couple at Century's End," in *The Pilot Star Elegies*, W. W. Norton, 1999, pp. 30–31.

van Buren, Ann K., Review of *The Pilot Star Elegies,* in *Library Journal*, Vol. 124, No. 10, June 1, 1999, p. 120.

Further Reading

Baker, David, "The Push on Reading," in *Heresy and the Ideal: On Contemporary Poetry*, University of Arkansas Press, 2000.
    In his examination of academic poetry, Baker links Santos to his fellow poets Jorie Graham, Carol Muske-Dukes, and A. R. Ammons.

Berg, Steven L., and Paul S. Shoup, *The War in Bosnia-Herzegovina: Ethnic Conflict and International Intervention*, M. E. Sharpe, 2000.

When Santos mentions the shelling of Tuzla, he is alluding to the frightening moral complexity of the world in the era before September 11, 2001. This book explores the war in detail, explaining the realities of a conflict that most Americans became aware of only periodically through scattered news reports.

Paley, Morton D., *Apocalypse and Millennium in English Romantic Poetry*, Oxford University Press, 2000.
    Santos's style has been described as neo-Romantic. Paley writes about poets who preceded Santos by hundreds of years, but his points are relevant about the expectations people hold and the ways in which poets address them.

Yenser, Stephen, "Sensuous and Particular: Sherod Santos, Rosanna Warren, Richard Kenny," in *A Boundless Field: American Poetry at Large*, University of Michigan Press, 2002, pp. 160–75.
    A prominent critic looks at the works of Santos and of other writers and points out their place in recent American literature.

The Room

Conrad Aiken
1930

Conrad Aiken's "The Room," collected in *John Deth and Other Poems* and published in 1930, symbolically remembers and transforms Aiken's parents' deaths. It focuses on the dark and troubled struggle between chaos and order that was, for Aiken, the source of his creativity, and it proclaims his conviction (as quoted by Catharine F. Seigel in her article for *Literature and Medicine*) that "death and birth [are] inseparably interlocked." The poem also reflects the intellectual currents of its time. It presents aspects of psychological phenomena described in Freudian literature, like repression and displacement, and it uses mythic, or archetypal, imagery and a theory of recurrent cycles like those that were explored by the Swiss psychologist Carl Jung. Aiken represents emotional states and psychic phenomena using images that suggest those states. "The Room" is available in Aiken's *Collected Poems* (1953; 2nd ed., 1970), published by Oxford University Press.

Author Biography

Conrad Aiken was born in Savannah, Georgia, on August 5, 1889, the eldest of four children. When Aiken was eleven, his father, a physician and a poet, murdered his wife and then turned the pistol on himself. Seeing the blood-soaked bodies, Aiken went to the police station for help. After their parents' burial, the children were separated. Aiken was

Conrad Aiken   The Library of Congress

sent to Massachusetts to live with his father's sister's family.

When Aiken entered Harvard in 1907, he had already begun writing poetry; in 1911 he was named Class Poet. At Harvard he met T. S. Eliot (1885–1965). Together they edited the *Advocate*, a magazine of poetry and criticism. The friendship begun at Harvard, despite a period of estrangement when Eliot embraced Anglicanism and distanced himself from those who did not, lasted throughout their lives. Aiken was a contributing editor to Eliot's magazine the *Dial* between 1917 and 1919.

In 1912, Aiken married Jessie McDonald; the couple had three children. In 1917, his first book of poems, *Nocturne of Remembered Spring*, was published. *The Charnel Rose* followed in 1918. In 1919, the Aikens left Cambridge, Massachusetts, and moved to South Yarmouth, England. In 1920, Aiken published *House of Dust: A Symphony*. In 1921, the family moved to London. There Aiken became the U.S. correspondent for the *Athenaeum* and the *London Mercury*. In 1924, he bought a house in Winchelsea, a village in East Sussex, England, which he kept until 1947. Aiken returned to Boston in 1926 without his family. There he met Clarissa Lorenz, who became his second wife, after he divorced Jessie McDonald in 1929. In 1927, his first novel, partly autobiographical, *Blue Voyage*,

appeared, and he became a tutor in English at Harvard.

In 1929, Aiken received the Shelley Memorial Award and, in 1930, the Pulitzer Prize for his *Selected Poems*. That same year, he published *John Deth and Other Poems*, in which "The Room" first appeared. In 1930, too, Aiken returned to London with Clarissa. He attempted suicide by turning on the gas in his flat in 1932, but Clarissa, returning home from the movies early, rescued him. From 1933 through 1936, Aiken was the London correspondent for the *New Yorker*. In 1936, he met Mary Hoover, a painter, and married her in 1937, immediately after his divorce from Clarissa. In England, they ran a summer school for writers and painters.

Toward the end of September 1939, with the outbreak of World War II in Europe, the Aikens sailed for New York and settled in Brewster, Massachusetts, on Cape Cod. From 1950 to 1952, Aiken was a Fellow in American Letters and occupied the Chair of Poetry at the Library of Congress. In 1952, his autobiographical novel *Ushant* appeared. In 1953, his *Collected Poems* was published and won the National Book Award. In 1956, he garnered the Bollingen Prize for poetry. He received the Gold Medal in Poetry from the American Academy of Arts and Letters in 1958 and the National Medal for Literature in 1969. In his lifetime he published more than fifty volumes of poetry, fiction, and criticism. In 1962, Aiken returned to Savannah and lived there in the house next door to his childhood home and, during most summers, in Brewster, Massachusetts, until his death in Savannah on August 17, 1973, at the age of eighty-four.

Poem Summary

Lines 1–5

"The Room" begins with the speaker telling of a past struggle, which took place in a particular but unidentified room. As if pointing, he says, "Through that window . . . I saw the struggle"—a "struggle / Of darkness against darkness" in which the darkness "turned and turned" and "dived downward." Everything besides the speaker and the window now is gone, "all else being extinct / Except itself [the window] and me." No reason is given for the struggle or its origin, history, or circumstances.

The insight the speaker gains from seeing the struggle is that he "saw / How order might—if chaos wished—become"—that is, how order can come into being out of chaos. Chaos is depicted as having potential: order might come into existence "if chaos wished."

Lines 6–11

In this section, the speaker traces the way chaos is transformed into order. He "saw the darkness crush upon itself, / Contracting powerfully." The energy that had been diffuse in struggle draws in upon itself and by contraction becomes concentrated. Contraction is a kind of suicide filled with pain: "It was as if / It killed itself, slowly: and with much pain. / Pain. The scene was pain, and nothing but pain." Only pain is left to the speaker from the struggle. Then comes the insight and a miraculous gift: "What else" can there be but pain "when chaos draws all forces inward / To shape a single leaf?" The leaf appears as abruptly and surprisingly in the poem as it does in the room.

Destruction is a dynamic struggle of dark forces spiraling downward and imploding; creation is presented as an image resulting from that struggle: a leaf. The potential energy of the struggle, concentrated by contraction, is converted to kinetic energy, to energy in motion, by the will of the speaker, exercised in pain, and bursts into something structured: "a single leaf."

Lines 12–18

Beginning with the image of the single, unattached leaf, the speaker presents the creative process as deriving a structure from an idea or a vision. Destruction is represented by implosion; creation is described as a process of uniting parts until an encompassing and order-giving whole is achieved. The leaf does not grow on a tree rising from a seed. It appears as a free-floating vision that the speaker has to work from to create a complete structure. "After a while," from that leaf, "the twig" that connects the leaf to the bough "shot downward from it." And then "from the twig a bough; and then the trunk, / Massive and coarse; and last the one black root." Anchoring comes last: creation, the process of opening outward after implosion, is delicate and tentative. Reversing the contraction, this process of expansion breaks the boundaries of the room, goes beyond the speaker's boundaries: "The black root cracked the walls. Boughs burst the window / The great tree took possession."

Lines 19–25

The final section of the poem confronts the new chaos. "Tree of trees!" the speaker cries in triumph, as if it were the very tree of life he has created. But, he continues, warning, "Remember

(when time comes) how chaos died / To shape the shining leaf." As Aiken wrote later in a letter to a friend, "death and birth [are] inseparably interlocked." Life and death, order and chaos are embedded in each other and change into each other. After order, chaos returns.

With restored life comes time and, thus, memory. Memory forces the speaker beyond the bounds of the newly ordered present back to the chaos of the struggle. Memory renews the pain of grief. Earlier, in line 9, the speaker had avoided experiencing grief by attributing pain to "the scene" rather than experiencing it as his own response. Now he accepts it. Addressing the tree, which he describes in a humanized form and, therefore, as an embodiment of himself, he says, "Then turn, have courage, / Wrap arms and roots together, be convulsed / With grief, and bring back chaos out of shape." Let order, he is saying, show as much of a will in confronting chaos as he had earlier attributed to chaos when he wrote that "order might ... become" "if chaos wished" it. The cycle continues.

The speaker ends with a vow that he will keep an awareness of the partiality of each phase, chaos and order, for neither by itself is the unity. The whole is composed of both. "I will be watching then," when chaos returns, he says, "as I watch now. / I will praise darkness now," at a time of brightness, not forgetting darkness. "But then," when chaos is come again, remembering the role of chaos in creation, he will praise "the leaf" and thereby not succumb to chaos.

Themes

Memory

The power of memory and the nature of memory are underlying themes of "The Room." The poem begins with a recollection that represents both active and repressed memory, a memory the speaker has pushed down into unconsciousness. "Through that window ... I saw," the speaker begins. He is recounting something that happened but that has remained in his memory only as a mythic image of "the struggle / Of darkness against darkness." The work of the poem involves the speaker in freeing himself through the act of creation from the weight of the memory he has pushed down. In creating, he can experience the emotion attached to that buried memory. Even after succeeding, the speaker reminds himself not to forget either the grief he has experienced or the process of creation

Topics For Further Study

- In "The Room," Aiken suggests that destruction necessarily precedes creation—that in order for something to be created, something first must be destroyed. Does this make sense to you? Can you think of instances where this might apply? Make a table of ten items. In the left-hand column, list destructive acts. In the right-hand column, list the creative acts they have given or could give rise to. Then, for each item, write a short explanation. Choose from personal, historical, mythological, religious, emotional, geological or meteorological, and cultural events.

- Arrange individual interviews with four to six people and discuss a traumatic experience in their lives, finding out what the experience was, how they responded to it at the time, how it affected them later, and what weight it bears in their lives now. Remember to be cautious, sensitive, and respectful in your approach, since you may be dealing with delicate material and calling forth painful memories. Immediately after each interview, while the conversation is still fresh in your mind, write out a case history. After you have compiled all your histories, write a short essay describing the points of similarity in the several stories you have gathered.

- Choose an important event in your life. Write a matter-of-fact prose summary of that event, describing its effect on you, its consequences, and what you learned from it. Then thinking of the same event, write a poem in which you offer the same narrative but in disguise, never referring to the actual event but instead relating it in other terms, that is, symbolically.

- Write a short story whose outcome is that the main character undergoes the kind of experience that would result in his or her writing "The Room."

---

he has accomplished. "Remember," he says to himself, "how chaos died / To shape the shining leaf."

Repression

In "The Room," the speaker emphasizes the intensity of the pain involved in the event he is recalling by an insistent repetition of the word "pain." He does not say, "The scene was painful to me." Instead, he says, "Pain. The scene was pain, and nothing but pain." Nevertheless, the event that caused so much pain is never remembered specifically but only as it has been converted into a mythic "struggle / Of darkness against darkness." Transforming the memory of the situation into abstract, dreamlike images allows the speaker to recognize emotion without actually experiencing it. Acknowledging the existence of emotion without experiencing the emotion directly or attaching it to a specific event suggests the psychological process of repression. Repression can result when a situation is too overwhelming to be kept in conscious awareness but too strong to be entirely forgotten and ignored. The result is what Aiken describes. An intense feeling can be represented by an image, but no corresponding reason can be given for that feeling.

Chaos and Order

In "The Room," Aiken claims that chaos and order, while seeming to be opposites, actually depend upon each other and are phases of a recurring cycle. Each contains within it the seeds of the other. Aiken presents chaos as a contraction of dark energy in a death struggle with itself. He also shows that the force of that struggle releases creative energy and results in the development of a new order. By giving chaos volition, or the power of choice, in line 5 ("if chaos wished"), the poet gives chaos a human attribute, personifies it and makes it, thus, an attribute of himself. He then ascribes his wish to chaos. Consequently, he gains the power to fashion order, as a poet, out of chaos. The sudden presence of the leaf in the room, in line 11, represents the mysterious way creation happens.

The poem arises in the speaker's mind in the same way from its terrible source. The painful, destructive contraction of struggling dark energy explodes in creation, described in line 17. "The black root cracked the walls. Boughs burst the window." The poem itself bursts the order the speaker created for himself in composing it and brings a new threat of chaos by restoring the full memory of the event it memorializes. That order, as it fulfills its potential, overflows its boundaries and reintroduces chaos. As in nature, there is a continuous shift back and forth between birth and death. Each is necessary for the other.

Courage

Emotion is experienced as something dangerous in "The Room" because it is associated with a struggle that is painful for the speaker to remember. Nevertheless, he pushes himself through a recollection of the experience, even though he has translated it into mythic, or archetypal, terms. The reward is that the experience becomes his to use creatively rather than the source of an emotion that torments him. After he has created the poem, which is represented by the leaf and the tree that follows it, he understands that he will still have to encounter the grief he had tried to avoid. When he does so, he will again be cast into chaos. But he presses himself to have courage, and he defines what courage is. It is the ability to endure the situation that confronts him, and to rejoice in it, no matter what—to praise darkness during periods of order and to praise order during periods of chaos. He calls upon himself to have the courage to be rooted in time by experience and to transcend time through art.

The Craft of Poetry

The craft of poetry itself is an implicit theme of "The Room." By writing the poem, the speaker confronts a buried experience, excavates it, and transforms the raw material of chaos into a work of art. The poem, like the leaf that symbolizes it, is the consequence of a terrible event and serves as a memorial to that event and to the speaker's ability to bring order to a chaotic event that threatened to destroy him. The leaf is an image for the poem itself, which the poet drew from the chaos. A leaf, besides being the green growth on a tree, is also a sheet of paper. Written down upon a sheet of paper the poem is given tangible and enduring form. The speaker-as-poet's art is both the symbol of the enlightenment he drew from the darkness he encountered and the means of drawing it.

Style

Blank Verse

"The Room" is written in blank verse, meaning that there is no fixed rhyme scheme. Most of the lines do not rhyme at all, but they all are pentameter lines, meaning that they are made up of five feet, and each foot has two beats to it. Usually, as is common in English, the rhythm of each foot is iambic, or made up of iambs, meaning that the stress in each foot falls on the second beat. But Aiken's use of iambic pentameter is not absolute. Look at the first line for an example of five varied feet (with the capitalization indicating the stress): "through THAT / WINdow / all ELSE / Being / exTINCT." The second and fourth feet reverse the pattern, giving an emphasis to the words. They are in a meter called trochaic, which is made up of trochees. A trochee is composed of one stressed syllable followed by an unstressed one.

Although the verse of "The Room" is unrhymed, the last words of each line carry a significant amount of weight. Consider the final words of the first five lines: "extinct," "struggle," "room," "saw," and "become." These words are central to the situation the poem recounts. An *extinct struggle*, which the speaker *saw* in a *room* (the title of the poem), is at the root of what will *become*. Lines 8 and 9 set the all-important word "pain" to rhyme with itself. But the rhyme becomes more like the pounding of tympani when the word "pain" appears twice again before the rhyme closes. Three lines later, at the end of line 12, which is an extension of a shortened line 11, the word "pain" is echoed by the word "came," an inexact rhyming, called a slant rhyme. In the next line, slant rhyming continues with the word "room" again. From "pain" to "came" to "room" the rhyming traces the process the poem celebrates, the transformation in the room of painful chaos into a leaf. In the last section, once again, the words at the end of each line recapitulate and illuminate the text of the poem.

Imagism

In 1912, the American poet Ezra Pound introduced the term "imagism" to describe a kind of poetry that he characterized as being fashioned out of precise and concrete visual images. Instead of stating directly an idea or a feeling, by the use of images a poet could suggest ideas and feelings, which readers could discover and experience for themselves. Rather than having the grandeur, sonority, and scope of Victorian poetry, imagism sought to have the poet present precise subject matter, briefly and sharply defined through appropriate corresponding images and plain language. Aiken, along with Marianne Moore, Wallace Stevens, D. H. Lawrence, and T. S. Eliot, was influenced by imagism and incorporated its aesthetic into his poetry. In "The Room," Aiken uses imagist techniques, representing states of mind and emotional conditions through particular images presented in unadorned language. Brutal conflict is seen, for example, as the struggle of two darknesses in a room. Similarly, order and creation are represented by the appearance of a single leaf and the parts of a tree.

Historical Context

Sigmund Freud and Psychoanalysis

In 1934, Aiken was asked whether he had been influenced by Sigmund Freud (1857–1939), the Viennese physician and founder of psychoanalysis, and how he regarded him. He responded (as Catharine F. Seigel quotes in her article for *Literature and Medicine*), "Profoundly, . . . I decided very early . . . that Freud, and his co-workers and rivals and followers, were making the most important contribution of the century to the understanding of man and his consciousness." With the formulation of psychoanalytic theory, Freud changed the map of human understanding. Drawing on the story of Oedipus, the Theban king who unwittingly murdered his father and married his mother, Freud constructed a model of the human psyche that proposed that consciousness was only the surface aspect of a person's mental apparatus. Freud identified and charted a realm beneath conscious awareness that he called the unconscious. The unconscious is the realm in which great residues of the events that people experience, but that are no longer available to them, are buried. Freud often compared the unconscious to the hidden, historic layers of a city, like Rome, which can be uncovered only through archaeological digs.

This buried material can affect a person in a disturbing way, for it has a tendency to reappear. Rather than affecting someone directly, it makes its existence felt indirectly through what Freud called symptoms. Symptoms are distorted expressions of the buried material, material of which the person has become unaware through a process of forgetting Freud called repression. When those symptoms are properly understood—that is, correctly interpreted—they reveal the repressed material. Repressed material is composed of experiences that have been too painful to hold in consciousness. When that repressed material is recovered and revealed for what it is and the painful emotions associated with it are fully experienced, Freud argued, the symptoms disappear.

Archetypal Myths

One of Freud's most important early followers, Carl Jung (1875–1961), a Swiss psychoanalyst, broke with Freud and became the head of what is often seen as a rival school of psychoanalysis. One of Jung's major theories and one that is of interest to Aiken's readers is the concept of archetypes, or original patterns, models, or myths. Jung believed that there are eternal images and processes built into the human psyche that constantly reappear in literary and cultural forms. These archetypes are representations in images of both individual events in a person's lifetime and shared psychic functions and beliefs in what Jung called a collective unconscious, which links all of humankind together at the deepest level.

The idea of the interdependency of order and chaos is one of these archetypes, or original patterns. So are the related archetypes of expansion and contraction and of birth and death. These interconnections are seen not only in the natural cycle of the seasons, in the vegetation cycle, in the rhythm of the breath, or in the phenomenon of childbirth, but they are also seen in such a mythic figure as the phoenix, the firebird that burns itself to ashes every five hundred years and then springs to life again from those ashes. Ideas of death and resurrection, of life emerging from death, as well as death following life, are also central to the Christian story. The myth of the dying and reviving god is a widely held belief in many religions that preceded Christianity. Stories of sacrifice that assure the continuation of life or the soothing of nature are also widespread. Many folktales tell of the yearly sacrifice of chosen youths to a monster to ensure the continuing safety of a community. Many early peoples practiced actual or symbolic sacrifices in order to ensure good harvests or good hunting. These all embody the archetypal connection between chaos and order, destruction and creation, and life and death.

Modernism

The literary movement called modernism, which emerged in the first decades of the twentieth century and of which Aiken was a part, shifted emphasis from the external world that the writer perceived to the internal process of perception and,

Compare & Contrast

- **1920s:** Reacting to nineteenth-century poetry, which often was highly emotional and narrative in style and strongly reflected the personality of the poet, modernist poets of the first decades of the twentieth century produce detached, intellectually complex, usually unrhymed, and obscure poetry characterized by fragmented imagery.

  Today: Through rap and hip-hop and in poetry slams, young poets of the early twenty-first century, continuing the rebellion begun in the 1950s by beat generation poets against academic and modernist poetry, write and perform poetry using everyday and sometimes even obscene speech in heavily rhymed verse concerned with social problems and highlighting the opinions, adventures, and personalities of the poets themselves.

- **1920s:** While the influence of psychoanalytic thought creates a climate that allows some writers like Aiken, James Joyce, and Henry Roth to explore and express emotional vulnerability, other writers, like Ernest Hemingway, still insist on taking a tough stand and work to project the image of a man who never lets down his guard no matter how deeply injured he may feel.

Today: Because of the continuing influence of psychoanalytic thought and the influence of the gay liberation and women's movements on the culture as a whole, it has become much more culturally acceptable for men to express their emotions openly and to admit their vulnerability, as is evident in the work of writers like David Sedaris and Garrison Keillor.

- **1920s:** Poets like Aiken and novelists like Marcel Proust, under the influence of the psychologists of their day—among them, Freud and Jung—explore the effect of memory on present experience, believing that in order to understand and be at peace in the present, it is necessary to come to terms with the traumatic past.

  Today: Although some professionals still think that reprocessing events that haunt us is useful, among some schools of psychiatry and psychology, there is a belief that exploration of the past through memory only keeps people bound to that past and that the use of psychotropic drugs rather than sifting through memory is the way to overcome traumatic experience. Rather than sifting through memories, writers like John Falk, Kay Redfields Jamison, and William Styron write memoirs describing their use of psychotropic drugs to deal with mental distress.

---

consequently, to the psyche of the writer. The literature produced was less concerned with logical form, organization, and structure, all of which were characteristic of nineteenth-century writing, than with the spontaneous images that impressed themselves upon the writer's imagination. Explaining modernist technique through an analysis of the writing of James Joyce, the author of *Ulysses*, Virginia Woolf (1882–1941), herself a great modernist, wrote, "Joyce ... is concerned at all costs to reveal the flickerings of that innermost flame which flashes its message through the brain, and in order to preserve it he disregards ... whatever to him seems adventitious, whether it be probability,

or coherence or any other of the signposts which for generations have served to support the imagination of the reader."

Critical Overview

According to Catharine F. Seigel, writing in "Conrad Aiken and the Seduction of Suicide," "one would be hard pressed to name another U.S. writer of the first half of the twentieth century [besides Aiken] who so nearly satisfied T. S. Eliot's famous conditions for literary greatness: abundance, variety, and complete competence." Yet Aiken is more esteemed by poets and critics than he is popular among readers. As Seigel says, Louis Untermeyer wrote an article in the *Saturday Review* in 1967 titled "Conrad Aiken: Our Best Known Unread Poet." Fifteen years before that, Seigel also says, the critic Mark Schorer, writing in the *Nation*, called the critical neglect of Aiken's work "a conspiracy of silence."

Perhaps the main reason for this is that Aiken has been out of step with one of the fundamental aesthetic principles that governed poetry in the twentieth century, as formulated by T. S. Eliot in his essay "Tradition and the Individual Talent": "The progress of an artist is a continual self-sacrifice, a continual extinction of personality." All of Aiken's work, quite to the contrary, is a continuous, even obsessive, combing through and exploitation of the harrowing primal events of his life. He constantly attempts to find universals in his own particulars and to transform his personal trauma into literature. Yet Aiken, despite his poetry's concern with autobiography, always remained behind his poetry. He did not have the temperament to be a celebrity poet.

Writing in the *Atlantic Monthly*, R. P. Blackmur says Aiken's "work [is] in a continuous relation to the chaos of [his] sensibilit[y] . . . and each separate poem issues with a kind of random spontaneity." Writing in the *Georgia Review* shortly after Aiken's death, Calvin S. Brown pays tribute to Aiken and also touches upon what makes his poetry sometimes difficult: "This poetry exhibits an astonishing variety of forms and types. Beginning with narrative verse, he soon reduced the narrative element to a mere scaffolding—often perilously flimsy—to support an investigation of the minds and inner lives of his characters."

Criticism

Neil Heims

Neil Heims is a writer and teacher living in Paris. In this essay, he discusses the problem of how to use a poet's biography in the interpretation of his work.

A recurring problem for anyone who reads poetry and wants to understand it is the problem of determining what information about a poem is useful in the interpretation of the poem and where the information might come from. In the opening decades of the twentieth century, an aesthetic of depersonalization, meaning a belief that the poet should be removed from the poem, dominated theories about how to write poetry. For example, T. S. Eliot not only was one of the century's major English poets, he also set the critical values and standards that would be used to judge poetry and determine the way poetry ought to be interpreted. Writing in 1920, he says in "Tradition and the Individual Talent," a classic of twentieth-century criticism, "The progress of an artist is a continual self-sacrifice, a continual extinction of personality." This implies that in trying to understand a poem, nothing about the poet's life, thought, or environment may be introduced.

I. A. Richards, whose influence was as important as Eliot's in shaping the way people, especially readers in universities, think about English poetry, published *Practical Criticism* nine years later, in 1929. In it, he solidifies a position he had been working on through the 1920s. Simply stated, Richards argues for an approach to poetry that regards each poem as a hermetic object, meaning that it is impervious to outside interference or influence. It exists in its own independence, isolated and separate from everything but itself, even from other poems. A poem's meaning can be found only from closely reading the words of the poem itself and reflecting on their relation to nothing else but each other. Requirements of reading this way are to accept that meaning might, in fact, be elusive and to recognize ambiguity as an inherent and inescapable part of knowing and understanding.

At the same time that this self-enclosed idea of reading was establishing itself, another wave, as strong and as influential, arose. In 1893, two physicians, Joseph Breuer and Sigmund Freud, published *Studies in Hysteria*, a series of case histories of patients who were plagued with incapacitating conditions that were not the result of physical problems but were apparently mental or emotional in origin. These conditions, the doctors argued, would go into remission when the sufferers could think about and interpret their symptoms based on associations they brought forth when they let themselves say whatever came into their minds—that is, by "free association." In 1900, Freud published *The Interpretation of Dreams* (first English translation, 1913), which used his psychoanalytic method of free association to penetrate the surface of dreams, or the "manifest" content, and uncover the hidden meaning of dreams, their "latent" or underlying content. This method of interpretation is the opposite of the critical method proposed by Eliot and Richards. They turn interpretation back upon the object being interpreted (the

What Do I Read Next?

- *Collected Poems* (1953) offers a rich survey of Aiken's poetry. Presenting Aiken's poetry in chronological order, this volume enables readers to see the development of recurrent themes, images, and concerns and the way Aiken varies and transforms them.

- In *Jacob's Room* (1922), a short novel about a young man killed in World War I, Virginia Woolf attempts to tell the story of his life through a series of scenes presented as if viewed from outside and without the help of an organizing and orienting narrator.

- In "The Love Song of J. Alfred Prufrock," published in *Prufrock and Other Observations* in 1917, T. S. Eliot gives his sense of the devitalized nature of early-twentieth-century sensibility by creating a portrait of a character with a listless personality, portrayed through a series of images.

- Henry Roth's *Call It Sleep* (1934) is an autobiographical novel recounting his brutal and traumatic childhood and his parents' terrible marriage. He combined traditional narrative with the stream-of-consciousness technique introduced by James Joyce.

- After writing *Call It Sleep*, Roth was silent for the next sixty years until, between 1994 and 1998, he published a four-volume continuation of that novel (*A Star Shines over Morris Park* [1994], *A Diving Rock on the Hudson* [1995], *From Bondage* [1996], and *Requiem for Harlem* [1998]), a tribute to memory titled collectively *Mercy of a Rude Stream*. It traces the growth of his artistic and emotional sensibility through the 1920s, juxtaposes it with his experience through the 1990s, and combines stream-of-consciousness and traditional narrative techniques.

- "Counterparts," one of the stories in *Dubliners* (1914), by James Joyce, draws its emotional force through the use of a series of painful images that dramatize the vain, empty, and cruel life of a beaten man.

poem on the page) and exclude from consideration the person and the personal (the poet's biography) or any outside event. Freud allows interpretation to roam freely and welcomes any association, however far-fetched it might appear. A poem, from a psychoanalytic perspective—being the product of a highly charged mental state—can be seen as a kind of dream. Like dreams, poems offer, according to Freud, surface or manifest content, which must be interpreted by uncovering the hidden or latent content. Reaching that original content and meaning becomes a matter of associating freely from the given to the hidden.

As opposed as these two approaches seem to be, they share the assumption that interpretation is necessary. The need for interpretation indicates that there is a meaning to be decoded from a set of words, a meaning that the words themselves are concealing until they are somehow made to reveal it. Both approaches assume that something is hidden. However, those who forbid the use of any outside information to interpret a poem are guided by the fear that such interpretation, instead of illuminating the poem, will distort it and make it express something imposed upon it by a reader. The poem becomes, under such conditions, a vehicle to reinforce ideas, emotions, sentiments, and responses that the reader already has. Consequently, the poem and the work of the poet will be debased. Rather than challenging the reader to new awareness, the poem becomes a reflection of the reader's notions and prejudices, a recapitulation of what already is, rather than a bearer of something new.

This is not an idle concern, yet it is one that risks causing too great a removal of poetry from the human sphere. The concern can become a justification for denying the worth of a poet who creates poetry to express overcharged emotion in order to gain relief from it by sharing fundamental human experience with a community of readers.

Readers, too, can be deprived of experiencing highly charged, humanly grounded emotions that elate, purge, and enlighten. Traditionally, poets—either in their own person, like Dante, William Blake, and William Wordsworth, or through characters serving as their surrogates, like Virgil, Homer, Shakespeare, and John Milton—have been heroes who have gone through hell, seen visions of heaven, and returned to tell about it. Moreover, poetry can explore the limits of psychic and emotional experience and cross the borders of what is judged acceptable by social, moral, or religious standards. It can strive to reach levels of perception beyond those of the five senses. Consequently, poetry can be an art associated with external environments and extrinsic purposes and not only with the act of creating hermetic, self-enclosed, self-enclosing artifacts.

The problem remains, then, what associations are to be deemed admissible—only those found within the poem or those free associations the poem suggests when its author's biography and its originating conditions are recognized? The problem is, perhaps, a problem only when one attempts to impose a rule from outside and from above. Each poem may offer a solution to the problem by demonstrating which method most richly reveals its own riches most fully. If outside information is acceptable in formulating the meanings of a poem, it follows, too, that advances in biographical, historical, and cultural scholarship can change readers' understanding of what a poem is saying.

In the case of Aiken's "The Room," the problem the reader faces is this: Does the poem benefit from the reader's awareness of the circumstances of Aiken's childhood and if it does, how? Were Aiken called upon to answer the question about the admissibility of an author's biography for the understanding of his poetry, it is clear from his writing that he would think its exclusion indefensible and damaging. That is obvious from his mocking criticism (found in his essay "A Basis for Criticism," quoted in Catharine Seigel's article "Conrad Aiken and the Seduction of Suicide") against the proponents of exclusion:

> We have heard, we still hear savage outcries against [the autobiographical] method—it is by the idolators of art considered a despicable sort of espionage, this ruffianly pillaging of the great man's archives and arcana, this wholly unwarranted detective-work in his kitchen or sleeping-quarters. . . . Simple-minded certainly is the cry of these zealots today that the artist's "life" is not of the smallest importance, that his work is everything, and that if indeed there is any demonstrable relationship between the two—a fact

> *Were Aiken called upon to answer the question about the admissibility of an author's biography for the understanding of his poetry, it is clear from his writing that he would think its exclusion indefensible and damaging.*"

considered by some extremely dubious—it at any rate sheds no light.

Aiken believed, as quoted in Seigel, that the poet "must make his experience articulate for the benefit of others, he must be, in the evolving consciousness of man, the servant-example, and in fact he has little choice in the matter." Knowing the details of Aiken's childhood—his father's suicide after murdering his wife—it is fair to seek in "The Room" the experience represented by "the struggle / Of darkness against darkness." That struggle refers to an experience of the poet narrator, and he is impelled to tell the reader about it and thus about himself, as the opening words of the poem indicate, with a haunting passion for memorializing, "Through that window . . . / . . . I saw the struggle."

To refer to a "struggle / Of darkness against darkness" is to indicate nothing that can be seen. "Darkness" itself may represent a metaphor. The seventeenth-century English poet John Milton, for example, in his epic poem *Paradise Lost*, describes hell's indescribability, its alternate dimensionality, by comparing hell to "A Dungeon horrible," which "on all sides round / As one great Furnace flam'd, yet from those flames / No light, but rather darkness visible." Hell is without light, but the darkness can be seen there. Darkness is an attribute of hell. That resonance may serve to deepen the anguish in "The Room," but the darkness is presented as something itself, not as an attribute of something else. If it is an attribute of something else, it is an attribute of something omitted from the poem. Thus darkness as an image obscures rather than illuminates whatever is being represented. If nothing is being represented but darkness itself, these questions must arise: Why is darkness so terrible? How does an attribute like darkness come to be divided into two? What makes darkness represent a struggle that is nothing but pain?

Intuitively, one might guess that the answer to the last of those questions is the wish to avoid looking at the source of that pain directly. The questions as a whole yield a convincing answer, and the intuition seems to be confirmed once the facts are known. Aiken heard the argument preceding the suicide and murder, heard the pistol shots, and saw the bleeding bodies on the bed and on the floor in his mother's bedroom. He responded with an uncanny calmness, with a suppression of self. As Seigel's article points out, it was "with a degree of calmness and self-possession beyond his years and that under the tragic circumstances was almost weird," the *Savannah Morning News* on February 28, 1901, reported, that "the lad indicated the room of his mother" to a police officer. Most telling: the first thing the police officer saw when he opened the door to the room was *darkness*. Here is a description of the room from the same newspaper account, as provided by the police officer: "The room was in almost total darkness, as it was then scarcely broad daylight, and the shutters of the windows were closed."

To ignore these facts and exclude their association when considering the image of "the struggle / Of darkness with darkness" suggests doctrinal stubbornness and critical negligence rather than interpretive rigor. The echo of the suicidal struggle between his parents and within his father, which spilled over into his own psychic constitution (as a knowledge of Aiken's lifelong obsession with suicide and his several unsuccessful attempts underscores) is suggested not only by "the struggle / Of darkness against darkness" but also by the fact that that struggle is described as "crush[ing] upon itself, / Contracting powerfully . . . as if / It killed itself."

Expressing the suicidal struggle of his father by "the struggle / Of darkness against darkness" transforms a specific biographical event that contributed to robbing life of meaning and the boy of his ability to feel. It endows the event with mythic dimension and makes one suicide and murder an instance of an archetypal process, a cosmic struggle of terrible forces engaged not only in destruction but also in an essential preliminary stage of creation. Likewise, the association endows the archetype with an emotional depth and force that gives it resonance and shows it to be not just an intellectual exercise but a universal expression of actual experience. In the poem itself,

the manifest and the latent contents of each term resonate inside each other, until the poem vibrates in the reader's mind like a complex experience.

Source: Neil Heims, Critical Essay on "The Room," in *Poetry for Students*, Thomson Gale, 2006.

Sources

Aiken, Conrad, *Collected Poems*, Oxford University Press, 1953; 2nd ed., 1970, pp. 460–61.

Blackmur, R. P., "Conrad Aiken: The Poet," in the *Atlantic Monthly*, Vol. 192, No. 6, December 1953, p. 77.

Breuer, Joseph, and Sigmund Freud, *Studies in Hysteria*, Beacon Press, 1964.

Brown, Calvin S., "The Achievement of Conrad Aiken," in the *Georgia Review*, Vol. 27, No. 4, Winter 1973, pp. 477–88.

Eliot, T. S., "Tradition and the Individual Talent," in *The Sacred Wood: Essays on Poetry and Criticism*, Methuen, 1922.

Heims, Neil, "Recomposing Reality: An Introduction to the Work of Virginia Woolf," in *Virginia Woolf: Bloom's Bio-Critiques*, Chelsea House Publishers, 2005, p. 69.

Milton, John, *Complete Poems and Major Prose*, edited by Merritt Y. Hughes, Oxford University Press, 1957, p. 213.

Richards, I. A., *Practical Criticism: A Study of Literary Judgment*, Routledge, 2001.

Seigel, Catharine F., "Conrad Aiken and the Seduction of Suicide," in *Literature and Medicine*, Vol. 18, No. 1, Spring 1999, pp. 82–99.

Sugars, Cynthia C., *The Letters of Conrad Aiken and Malcolm Lowry, 1929–1954*, ECW Press, 1992.

Further Reading

Aiken, Conrad, *Ushant*, Little, Brown, 1952.
 In *Ushant*, an autobiographical novel, Aiken describes his struggles with despair and his own suicidal impulses resulting from the childhood trauma of his parents' death. The book also chronicles his many friendships with poets such as T. S. Eliot and Ezra Pound and traces his career and the development of his thought.

Jung, C. G., *The Basic Writings of C. G. Jung*, edited by Violet Staub de Laszlo, Modern Library, 1993.
 This anthology of Jung's writings provides an excellent introduction to his thought and includes selections on symbols, archetypes, and the collective unconscious.

Lorenz, Clarissa, *Lorelei Two: My Life with Conrad Aiken*, University of Georgia Press, 1983.
 This book is an account of life with Aiken in the late 1920s and early 1930s, written by his second wife.

Spivey, Ted R., *Time's Stop in Savannah*, Mercer University Press, 1997.
 In an examination of the body of Aiken's work, Spivey, who conducted many interviews with Aiken toward the end of his life, combines biography with literary analysis.

Seeing You

Jean Valentine

1990

Jean Valentine's "Seeing You" was first published in the 1990 January/February issue of *American Poetry Review*. Subsequently, the poem was included in Valentine's 1992 collection of poetry called *The River at Wolf* and then republished in the collection *Door in the Mountain: New and Collected Poems, 1965–2003* (2004).

Valentine often writes about her mother and her lovers. "Seeing You" combines these two subjects in an effort to show that the experience of getting to know one's mother and the intimacy of that relationship are similar to the experience of one's relationship with a lover. In particular, revelations of understanding—of truly "seeing" the mother or lover physically and emotionally—are much the same astounding turning points in life.

Valentine discusses in this poem a child's dependency on its mother for life and nurture as well as the realization that, despite her love, the mother has fears arising from the challenges of parenting. The resulting appreciation of the commitment of the mother deepens the relationship and brings joy to the child. There is also joy in falling in love, in getting to know another person who is absolutely a glorious wonder. As Valentine expresses in "Seeing You," when one is in love, one wants to know everything there is to know about the other person, and so the impulse is to plunge into getting to know the beloved, much as one plunges into a lake and is immersed. The revelations are many, including the experience of ultimate intimacy, of seeing each other unclothed, literally and emotionally. "Seeing

You" is a poem about that moment of revelation and realization that brings tremendous growth and happiness in a loving relationship.

Author Biography

Born in Chicago, Illinois, on April 27, 1934, to Jean Purcell and John W. Valentine, Jean Valentine went to Milton Academy from 1949 to 1952 and then received a bachelor's degree from Radcliffe College (of Harvard University) in 1956. Valentine has lived most of her life in New York City, teaching at Sarah Lawrence College, the Graduate Writing Program of New York University, Columbia University, and the 92nd Street Y in Manhattan. She has also taught many poetry workshops at various universities. Valentine married James Chace in 1957. They had two daughters, Sarah and Rebecca, but were divorced in 1968. For nearly eight years, from 1989 to 1996, Valentine lived in Ireland with Barrie Cooke, an English painter, but returned to the United States when that relationship dissolved. Some of her poetry, however, reflects her time in Ireland.

There was also a period from 1982 to 1987 when Valentine did not write at all because of alcoholism. She had stopped drinking at age forty-seven in 1981, but she suffered so much from the trauma of withdrawal that she could not write. She entered a recovery program in 1985 and eventually found that writing again helped her to regain her life. A Catholic convert, Valentine also made progress in her recovery through the effects of her volunteer work for her church during that time. Her religious affiliation is on again, off again, however. Valentine is also attracted to Buddhism.

Valentine's poetry has evolved through slightly different themes and techniques over the years, but she is best known for a dreamlike quality in poems that describe real life with passionate and intimate images. This combination of the invisible and the visible, the personal yet secretive, often makes her poetry difficult to understand. Consequently, her audience, which includes many contemporary poets, is small but astute in its appreciation of her use of language and syntax, which allows her narrator to pass from one image to another as if in a dream.

"Seeing You" is a poem that Valentine originally published in *American Poetry Review* in early 1990 and then in her collection of poetry called *The River at Wolf* in 1992. This poem appears again in the collection that won the 2004 National Book Award for Poetry, *Door in the Mountain: New and Collected*

Jean Valentine © AP/Wide World

Poems, 1965–2003, a volume that contains all her poetry from other books as well as seventy previously unpublished poems. Among Valentine's awards are the Yale Younger Poets Prize in 1965 for her first book, *Dream Barker and Other Poems*, a National Endowment for the Arts Grant (1972), a Guggenheim Fellowship (1976), and awards from the Bunting Institute, the Rockefeller Foundation, the New York State Council on the Arts, the New York Foundation for the Arts, the Teasdale Poetry Prize, and the Poetry Society of America's Shelley Memorial Award (2000). Her other books include *Pilgrims* (1969), *Ordinary Things* (1974), *The Messenger* (1979), *Home Deep Blue: New and Selected Poems* (1989), *The Under Voice: Selected Poems* (1995), *Growing Darkness, Growing Light* (1997), *The Cradle of the Real Life* (2000), and *The Lighthouse Keeper: Essays on the Poetry of Eleanor Ross Taylor* (2001).

Poem Text

1. Mother

I was born under the mudbank
and you gave me your boat.

For a long time
I made my home in your hand:

5

your hand was empty, it was made
of four stars, like a kite;   5

you were afraid, afraid, afraid, afraid,
I licked it from your finger-spaces

and wanted to die.
Out of the river sparks rose up: 10

I could see you, your fear and your love.
I could see you, brilliance magnified.

That was the original garden:
seeing you.

2. Lover

Your hand was empty, it was made   15
of four stars, like a kite;

blessed I stood my fingers
in your blue finger-space, my eyes' light in

your eyes' light,
we drank each other in.   20

I dove down my mental lake fear and love:
first fear then under it love:

I could see you,
Brilliance, at the bottom. Trust you
                                                                    25
stillness in the last red inside place.
Then past the middle of the earth it got light again.

Your tree. Its heavy green sway. The bright male
      city.
Oh that was the garden of abundance, seeing you.

Media Adaptations

- A thirty-minute VHS video is available from the Poetry Center and American Poetry Archives at www.sfsu.edu, showing Valentine reading her poetry at San Francisco State University on November 29, 1979.

- A thirty-one-minute VHS video is available from the Poetry Center and American Poetry Archives at www.sfsu.edu, showing Valentine reading from *Home Deep Blue* and *Growing Darkness, Growing Light* at San Francisco State University on October 15, 1997.

- A 1989 audiotape of *The Resurrected*, produced by Watershed, is available from the Writer's Center of Bethesda, Maryland, at www.writer.org/index.asp.

- A number of Valentine's poems are available in audio form on her official website: www.jean valentine.com.

Poem Summary

Mother

In this first section of the two-section poem, the narrator, "I," describes being born as coming out from under a mudbank and being given a boat. The care provided by the mother is compared to being given a home in the mother's hand, but the hand is empty. Perhaps the hand is empty because, ultimately, all a parent can do is give a child life; after that, even with the parent's guiding hand, the child is on its own to make something of that life. The idea behind the further description of the hand as being made of four stars, like a kite, is perhaps that of the future. A child has its mother's protection when held in her hand, but that safe place cannot last forever. The child must fly out of the nest of its mother's hand, perhaps clinging to a kite, but the future could be as bright as the four stars that give structure to the kite.

The narrator's tone throughout the poem is one of wonder and awe. By the fourth stanza, the child can sense the mother's fears and trepidations as palpably as the child is able to lick the fear from between the fingers of the mother's cradling hand. The fear is everywhere. This fear is enough to frighten the child into wanting to die, but the mother's role is to encourage and inspire, so sparks arise out of the river, symbolizing the mother, upon which the child's boat has been afloat. These sparks reflect the brilliance of the mother's love as well as her fear, but with her love dominating, and the child is able to truly see the mother in this light.

Lover

The second part of "Seeing You" starts by repeating the third stanza from the first part of the poem, about the mother. The two parts are linked through similar descriptions of the mother and the lover. The lover's hand, like the mother's, will also be empty at first, but there is a future in what the relationship will bring. The narrator feels blessed to have found love. This time, instead of seeing the emotion in the finger spaces, the narrator shares emotion by intertwining fingers with the lover.

The child looks at the mother as the authority figure, but the narrator and the lover look at each other, drinking each other in, as they try to learn as much as they can about each other.

The narrator continues the imagery of water by comparing the experience of immersing oneself in the lover to that of diving into a lake. The mother was a river, but the lover is a lake, and there are the same emotions of fear and love. Once again, the narrator notices the fear first, the fear of what the future holds with this person, the fear of losing identity when giving so much of oneself to another, the fear of all the changes and new experiences that come with a romantic relationship. However, once again, the narrator gets past the fear to find the love. The brilliance here is not seen as sparks rising from the river but is seen instead at the bottom of the lake. Emerging from the plunge into the soul of the lover, the narrator finds an illuminating light. With this light, the narrator is able to see the lover, in all his maleness, and the new world of experience that being with him will bring. His garden is one of abundance, with many fruits to taste.

Themes

Repeated Patterns

"Seeing You" is about repeated patterns in relationships. In particular, Valentine wants to suggest that what is learned from one's first teachers, one's parents, is something one will learn again with a lover. Often in her poetry, Valentine seems to evaluate her romantic loves according to the standard of maternal love. Correspondingly, she finds similarities between the way she feels about a lover and the way she feels about her mother. Will one find subsequent gardens to be the same as the "original garden," or will there be different landscaping? Will other gardens be as akin to Eden as was the garden of her mother? Will the feeling of coming out of her mother's mudbank be the same as emerging from the lake of her lover? Valentine's narrator is seeking reassurance that her man's love will be as caring as her mother's love at the same time that she is reveling in the added dimensions of the new experience. There are also questions about dependency and independence. A child is dependent on its mother but must eventually strike out on his or her own. In a romantic relationship, there is an emotional dependence that must be balanced with staying true to oneself.

To symbolize these relationship patterns, Valentine creates patterns in the words and structure of the poem. There is, of course, significance in the words that are chosen for repetition: fear, love, brilliance, and gardens. Perhaps they are the four stars. They definitely form the skeleton upon which the poem is fleshed out. Repetition also occurs in the whole structure of the poem. Each verse is only two lines. Stanza 3 of the first part is repeated as stanza 1 of the second part. The two subjects, the mother and the lover, are each described with water imagery, with the mother as a river and the lover as a lake. With each person, there is a garden and a moment of revelation when the narrator feels that she is finally really "seeing" the other person in the sense of understanding the other.

Fear and Love

Fear and love are not separate themes in "Seeing You." The theme is the relationship of fear and love. Valentine first homes in on the fears that the mother has, the kind of fears that every mother has about the challenges of child rearing. Across her works, one of Valentine's themes is departure, but usually in the negative sense of divorce or death. In "Seeing You," the departure of the child from the mother's womb is a natural occurrence, although it is a fearful experience for the mother, who suffers great pain in childbirth, and a fearful experience for the child, who must leave the protective, cozy atmosphere of the womb for the cold, cruel world. Mother and child fear separation, psychological as well as physical, throughout their lifetimes but also fear the loss of individual identity. The child must develop an identity of his or her own, and the mother must maintain her own identity as a person other than just "Mom." For the mother, this identity struggle is one of the fears that comes from the enormous responsibility of parenting. However, uppermost are the concerns about caring for the child, providing food, clothing, shelter, a good education, a good example, a healthy environment, and so on. Valentine, the mother of two, emphasizes the extent of a mother's fear by repeating the word "afraid" four times. These anxieties can be relayed to a sensitive child, who may respond with such distress that she "want[s] to die." Perhaps the child feels that her death will relieve the mother of her burden. However, "out of the river" of the mother, "sparks rose up" to give the child encouragement and confirm that love will conquer the fears. The darkness of fear is contrasted to the "brilliance" of the light from the mother's love.

Topics For Further Study

- Valentine considers her fellow poets Fanny Howe, Jane Cooper, Sharon Olds, C. D. Wright, and Adrienne Rich to be her friends and models. Write a brief biography for each of these American women, including a capsule description of her work. Summarize your research with a comparison of these poets.

- Valentine's *Door in the Mountain* is a collection of all of her previous publications as well as several new poems. Investigate this practice of reprinting previously published works that is so common among poets. Why are previous collections "recycled"? Write a report on the answer, which should be an insight into the publishing industry and the reading public. Information relating to this topic may be found in the introductions to the collections of various poets.

- Valentine has spent most of her life as a college professor. Check on the professions of a number of other famous modern writers in the fields of poetry, fiction, and nonfiction and list them. Are most or many involved in teaching? If so,

conduct a discussion with a group of your classmates about why you think that is or is not the case.

- "Seeing You" is a poem that describes the poet's mother as being afraid. Why do you think she is afraid? What are the fears that all mothers (and fathers) share? Write a composition on this subject, perhaps interviewing various parents about their challenges and feelings.

- Valentine has spent most of her life in the New York City area, which is the publishing center of the United States. Investigate the publishing industry, including publishing houses, agents, and authors. List some of the major publishing houses located in New York City and comment in a group discussion on why you think so many are in New York City or close to each other.

- Valentine is often compared to Emily Dickinson and Louise Bogan. Choose one of these two poets and then write a paragraph identifying her followed by a paragraph comparing her work to that of Valentine.

With regard to the lover, fear comes first as the narrator plunges into the relationship, but then, under the fear, the narrator reaches love. The message is that one has to get past one's fears to be able to find love. The fear starts with the awkwardness of a first date and leads to many questions: Will he like me? Will he break my heart? Will this last forever? Taking the first steps into a romantic relationship is quite frightening when one does not know where it will all end or what one will find out about the other. The narrator dives to the very core of the other person, as if going down to the core of the earth. At the bottom is the brilliance, the light of the true self of the lover, and there is then the trust that is essential to the success of the relationship. Once this epiphany of love and trust has occurred, the narrator can commit completely to her lover, physically and emotionally.

Style

Free Verse and Repetition

Using short, usually irregular line lengths and a controlled rhythm, free verse lacks the regular stress pattern, metric feet, and rhyme of traditional verse. Instead of a recurrent beat, the rhythmic effect depends on repetition, balance, and variation of phrases. A poet using free verse may suspend ordinary syntax and increase the control of pace, pauses, and timing. Poets noted for their use of free verse are Walt Whitman, T. S. Eliot, Ezra Pound, William Carlos Williams, and e. e. cummings, among many others. In "Seeing You," Valentine uses irregular line lengths and a controlled rhythm, sometimes unexpectedly stopping the reader once or twice in a line ("Brilliance, at the bottom. Trust you"), while at other times racing through a line, omitting punctuation in places where prose would demand punctuation ("I dove down my mental lake fear and love"). Repetition is the most obvious tool, with stanza 3 of the first section being identical to stanza 1 of the second; the repetition of the phrases "finger-spaces" and "seeing you"; and the repetition of the words "brilliance," "garden," "fear," and "love." In addition, the first part, "Mother," has seven two-line stanzas, and the second, "Lover," has seven two-line stanzas.

Imagery

The major feature of Valentine's poetry is imagery, vividly yet simply presented in a moment of intensity. In the first line, "mudbank," a bank of mud that is fully or partially submerged along a river, is the image Valentine uses to represent her mother's womb. Many of Valentine's poems are about her mother, and she often uses womb imagery to associate with the maternal.

In stanza 4 of the second half of the poem, the image of her mind as a "mental lake," into which she can dive and swim through the emotions of fear and love, is striking. She carries the image to the bottom of the lake, which is so deep that it goes all the way to the middle of the earth, where she passes through to the other side of the world. Valentine loves movies that are dreamlike and heavy with symbolism, and this admiration is reflected in her poetic style. According to Valentine, in an interview with Michael Klein, diving down through the lake is an image that comes from a scene in the 1988 movie *The Navigator*, in which the main character goes down through the earth and comes out in Auckland, New Zealand.

Poetic imagery, as descriptive language, normally appeals to multiple senses. In "Seeing You," however, the appeal is to only one sense, that of sight, in keeping with the title of the poem. All the images are things the reader sees with the mind's eye: a mudbank, a boat, a hand, stars, a kite, fingers, a river, sparks, eyes, a lake, and the colors blue, red, and green. The colors appear only in the second stanza, perhaps signifying how a person grows and blossoms when in love and experiencing new dimensions in life.

Poetic imagery, as figurative language, often uses metaphors to stand for the actual object. In the final stanza of "Seeing You," Valentine avoids a graphic description of her lover's private parts by calling his genitalia "Your tree." She extends the metaphor to describe the "heavy green sway" of the tree. She then offers a new metaphor for the same

thing by equating the genitalia to a "bright male city." Seeing her mother for who she really is, with all her fears and love, equates with the "original garden." Seeing her lover in a sexual context becomes a "garden of abundance," perhaps signifying the physical and emotional sensations of love that he will bring to her.

Fragments and Caesuras

In an interview with Richard Jackson, Valentine was asked about the fragments upon which her poetry seems to be based. She replied: "These 'fragments' . . . are very often what I sense and feel; they are how I 'get' this time and place and the currents of my private and public life and the lives around me." She compares these fragments to newspaper clippings or scenes from a movie. In other words, she uses the fragments like pictures in her mind, flashing images that she grabs and puts together to communicate a whole idea.

Free verse varies line length to control the flow of the thought and emphasize meaning. In "Seeing You," few stanzas have lines of equal length, and thoughts are broken between stanzas. Within the lines as well, Valentine may use one or two caesuras, or strong pauses, to break up the thought into fragments or slow down the reading. Caesuras are used to emphasize meaning, such as strong contrasts or close relationships between ideas. For example, a comma is placed between "four stars" and "like a kite," which might get the reader to place the image of the four stars firmly in the mind before going on to connect those four stars into a kite shape. Furthermore, there is a difference of emphasis and meaning between "I could see your brilliance magnified" and what Valentine wrote, "I could see you, brilliance magnified." Valentine's way makes the brilliance more outstanding and equates brilliance with the mother as if it were her whole being and not just a quality she possesses. Valentine's caesuras, therefore, are a result of the fragmented nature of her imagination.

Historical Context

Feminist Poetry

Feminist poetry is not the same thing as poetry written by women. Women often write poetry in traditional and formulaic ways. However, a distinctive kind of poetry is feminist poetry, born out of the women's movement in the 1970s and coming to maturity in the following decade, 1980–1990. Feminist

Compare & Contrast

- **1990:** As their children's protectors and teachers, parents are encouraged to focus on building their children's self-esteem. Parents are challenged to teach their children how to handle such modern issues as body image, drug and alcohol abuse, peer pressure, crime, and rapidly changing technology. Many parents regard the world as an unfriendly place for their children, and they struggle with fear for them. Friends are often a stronger influence over children than their parents are.

  Today: Parents are still encouraged to build their children's self-esteem, but new challenges make this task increasingly difficult. Violence among children is on the rise, and the consequences are more serious than ever. Technology can represent as much danger as benefit to children, and parents must be vigilant in monitoring Internet and cell-phone activity. Childhood obesity and eating disorders pose unique early challenges to self-esteem. Friends continue to be extremely influential in children's lives, forcing mothers and fathers to work harder to be effective in their parenting. As the issues facing children become more difficult and more serious, parents often find themselves fearful as they strive to protect their children.

- **1990:** Most of the well-known women literary writers are novelists, such as Amy Tan, Toni Morrison, Louise Erdrich, and Margaret Atwood. The poetry of such popular writers as Maya Angelou is gaining widespread exposure. A woman has not won the Nobel Prize in Literature since 1966 (Nelly Sachs) but has been awarded the Pulitzer Prize for Poetry as recently as 1987 (Rita Dove).

  Today: Most of the popular women writers are still novelists, many of whom have proved their staying power. Toni Morrison, Amy Tan, and Margaret Atwood continue to enjoy a large readership, as do newer writers, such as Anita Shreve. Women are capturing more elite literary awards. Four women have been awarded the Nobel Prize in Literature in the past fifteen years (Nadine Gortimer, Toni Morrison, Wislawa Szymborska, and Elfriede Jelinek) and four have earned the Pulitzer Prize for Poetry (Mona Van Duyn, Louise Gluck, Jorie Graham, and Lisel Mueller).

- **1990:** American poetry is generally personal in nature. Poets tend to use poetry to express political opinions (especially at poetry slams, where poets perform their work before audiences in competition) or as a way to relate their personal experiences. Some scholars have reached the conclusion that American poetry has become too academic and is written more for a small segment of the publishing industry than for the general public. Despite these claims that poetry is marginalized among American readers, creative writing programs and workshops have become increasingly popular and well attended.

  Today: American poetry is still characterized by personal expression. Many poets still use poetry as a way to express opinions about politics and social issues. Poetry slams have declined in popularity, although organized slams are still held all over the country. The public's interest in poetry continues to decline; in 2002, only 12 percent of American adults read poetry. This figure is almost one-fourth of the number of people who read novels and short fiction.

---

poetry bears a resemblance to the antiwar poetry and some of the beat poetry of the 1960s in its consciousness-raising and political goals. What distinguishes feminist poetry is its experimentation with the function of language in poetry and its themes and imagery based on the unique experiences of women. These two characteristics are evident in "Seeing You," when Valentine employs free verse, with her trademark fragments, combined with the imagery of a woman's relationship with her mother and her lover.

Furthermore, feminist poetry has both subjective and collective stories to tell. While the poem may be or seem to be about the poet's private life, it is at the same time intended to express the experiences of many women. The worldview is no longer strictly male but has a female perspective. Valentine, as a rule, does not use herself literally; her narrator is not necessarily herself but one who is meant to draw upon the personal feelings and experiences of the reader. Thus, the poetry remains personal in its ability to capture each reader's intimate thoughts and portray universal experiences. This revealing of the personal and intimate has upset many mainstream American poets and critics, who find such revelations embarrassing and inappropriate. The American Academy of Poets gave its prestigious Lamont Prize in 1990 to Minnie Bruce Pratt, known for her explicitly personal poetry, yet reportedly there was some uneasiness with her work. Thus, feminist poetry has remained somewhat outside the American poetry establishment while nonetheless garnering a supportive audience among readers and critics.

Exceptions to the separation of feminist poetry and the mainstream have been the careers of Adrienne Rich and Sylvia Plath, perhaps because of the impact of their outspoken literary criticism. Rich is one of Valentine's closest friends and influences, and Valentine's work has been compared to Plath's. It could be said that feminist poetry runs alongside the mainstream in that it has been stripping language and form to its rawest elements to express the previously hidden and secret lives of women, including their views on sexuality, since the 1970s. In various interviews, Valentine has indicated that she wants to get past the secrets and the myths to the truths of women's lives. She achieves this goal in the sexual intimacy, the fears, and the emotions of loves that she describes in "Seeing You." Another theme that recurs in interviews with Valentine is her admiration of women political poets and their efforts to speak out on issues that matter. As long as there is oppression based on gender and an elitism in poetry that prefers personal and political detachment, there will be a place for feminist poets such as Valentine.

Critical Overview

Because "Seeing You" has been published twice in book-length collections by Valentine, it is appropriate to look at the critical reaction to both books.

The River at Wolf was called "daring" in the *Virginia Quarterly Review*, which goes on to state that the poems "succeed by not giving in to melodrama or sentimentality; they focus on details of great clarity." The reviewer for the *Virginia Quarterly Review* adds that many of the poems, such as "Seeing You," "repeat lines, with a resonant echoing effect," observing that "occasionally the repetition drowns out the poem, and sometimes the resistance to the maudlin is so great that the narration sounds harsh." The poet David Rivard, in a critique of *The River at Wolf* for *Ploughshares*, says that Valentine "faces head-on the most serious mysteries of desire and death." Rivard describes the poems in this volume as "intense, calligraphic lyricism," "epics of the inner life," and "militantly non-narrative."

The awarding of the National Book Award to Valentine for *Door in the Mountain* was for many readers, among them Barbara Hoffert writing for the *Library Journal*, an affirmation that Valentine is "one of the best [poets] at work in America today." Hoffert finds Valentine's work "beautifully precise—as in music, there's as much here in the silence as there is in the sound—and radiant with the pain of being in the world." The critic John Freeman, in the *Seattle Times*, writes that Valentine displays "a sensibility unlike any other in American letters" and that her style "gives the reader a chance to indulge a heightened awareness in the natural world, the passage of time and the aural quality of language."

In general, critics praise Valentine for a unique talent, although some complain that her dreamlike images wander into the inexplicable. Nonetheless, the number of her awards, the admiration of fellow poets, and the longevity of her career testify to the quality of her poetry and the value to be found in studying it.

Criticism

Lois Kerschen

Lois Kerschen is a school district administrator and freelance writer. In this essay, she discusses understanding a Valentine poem through a knowledge of her methods and influences.

Poetry is often a part of English class that students dread, because they do not have a clue about how to read a poem or what it means. For the general reading public, the problem is much the same.

Learning the elements of poetry and having an ear for the sounds of language that are so important to the genre will help a reader understand a poem. It also helps to know something about the poet, influences on the poet, and the characteristic style of the poet. Certainly, in the case of poetry by Valentine, it is useful to understand something about her mental process and intentions as she writes. Interviews with Valentine herself and analysis by experts who know her work provide this information.

Readers might be in the best position to understand a Valentine poem if they bring to mind how they feel during a dream or when just waking from a dream. It is from this viewpoint of dream logic that a Valentine poem makes the most sense. "Seeing You" first appeared in the collection *The River at Wolf*, published in 1992. In an article for *Poetry* magazine that reviewed that book, Steven Cramer comments: "A poem by Jean Valentine travels in two directions—inward toward the recesses of self and outward toward the reaches of otherness—via a single route: the dream." For Valentine, Cramer surmises, dreams provide not only insight but also revelation. Indeed, in an interview with Michael Klein in 1991, the year after the first publication of "Seeing You" in the *American Poetry Review*, Valentine says, "I feel more and more as if my poems are almost all from dreams, or written as if from dreams." She adds that the way "another poet might write from an outward experience is the same way that I would write from a dream."

In a review of *Door in the Mountain* (2004), which also contains "Seeing You," the poet and Rutgers University professor Alicia Ostriker, writing for *American Book Review*, describes Valentine's dream poems as "poems of profound imagination, delicate and sensual, fearless and magical," much like those of John Keats and Wallace Stevens. Ostriker quotes Valentine's fellow poet and close friend Adrienne Rich as saying that delving into a Valentine poem:

> is like looking into a lake: you can see your own outline, and the shapes of the upper world, reflected among rocks, underwater life, glint of lost bottles, drifted leaves. The known and familiar become one with the mysterious and half-wild, at the place where consciousness and the subliminal meet. . . . It lets us into spaces and meanings we couldn't approach in any other way.

This description from Rich is especially helpful when reading "Seeing You," since this poem actually uses the imagery not only of looking into a lake but also of diving into one's mental lake of

. . . Valentine says that she often writes poems that she herself does not understand, so she has to rely on the sound of the language to judge the success of the poem."

fear and love and finding brilliance at the bottom. To use Rich's description, the known and familiar emotions of fear and love become one with the mysterious brilliance at the bottom. The conscious and subliminal, or what is below consciousness, meet in the person of the lover. This meeting of two parts of the mind defies "rationality in ways that help us break through to another dimension of the real," concludes Ostriker.

The critic Carol Muske, writing in the *Nation*, feels that readers should recognize this new dimension from their own dreams as one in which "there are no unessential details—everything is given equal moral and aesthetic weight." Cramer adds that Valentine's "compact lyrics inhabit the *thought* of the unconscious . . . hard-edged in detail but elusive in total effect. . . . as if the poet were simply taking notes." Ostriker agrees when she notes that Valentine writes with "an impulse toward the ardently and intensely chaste," in an austere and cryptic style in which "poems strike like the arrows of a Zen archer." H. Susskind, writing for *Choice*, says that Valentine's bone-sharp accuracy of detail is often combined with the personal. This combination results in "images enough to conjure up like memories for her readers," because, though her message may be elusive, her images are down to earth. That is the effect that Valentine herself says she seeks. In an interview with Richard Jackson for *Acts of Mind: Conversations with Contemporary Poets*, she says that the voices or narrators are not autobiographical. Rather, she is "trying to move into an other, into others; to move out of the private self into an imagination of everyone's history, into the public world." To Klein, she says that "our dreams are universal; our emotional and spiritual life is universal. Because of that, it's just

What Do I Read Next?

- At the age of seventy-five, Jane Cooper, who befriended Valentine when her first book came out, published *The Flashboat: Poems Collected and Reclaimed* (2000), a complete collection of her work, which is known mostly for its insightful and compassionate political views.

- Valentine is an admirer of Fanny Howe, whose *On the Ground: Poems* (2004) is a set of short sequences that reflect her intense interest in politics and social justice and express her belief that love can light the way.

- Sharon Olds, whose collection of her best poems from seven other books was published in 2004 as *Strike Sparks: Selected Poems, 1980–2002*, is another poet whom Valentine admires. Olds has a style that connects immediately with audiences, making her one of the most widely read of modern poets.

- Adrienne Rich, who is an icon of feminist poets and a close friend of Valentine's, coedited *Adrienne Rich's Poetry and Prose* (1993) with Albert and Barbara Charlesworth Gelpi.

- Showing a style akin to Emily Dickinson's, Valentine's *Home Deep Blue: New and Selected Poems* (1989) is a collection of lyrical verse that displays her strength in the use of language and sound.

- Valentine's eighth book, *The Cradle of the Real Life* (2000), has a long sequence merging Irish and feminist themes as well as poems of Valentine's usual trademark brevity.

- Valentine enjoys reading the poetry of the southern-born poet C. D. Wright, whose tenth book, *Steal Away: Selected and New Poems* (2003), exhibits enticing and diverse multicultural subjects and experimental forms.

- *The Extraordinary Tide: New Poetry by American Women* (2001), edited by Susan Alzenberg, Erin Belieu, and Jeremy Countryman, is an anthology of 400 poems by 118 female American poets, including 7 by Valentine.

---

as much a communication, from one person to another, as if you were describing a landscape."

Susskind notes in his review of *The River at Wolf* that Valentine's "skill is in the manner in which she touches on passion without giving everything away." Klein, too, makes note of this element and tells Valentine in his interview with her that what makes her poems so luminous to him is that he does not "miss not having the whole story." He appreciates that the sparseness of her language creates poems of "essences" that give the reader the sense that nothing is missing from them, because the essence becomes the reader's own history. The process allows the reader to live his or her own life subconsciously in the poem. The idea is that the essence draws out the reader's personal history, communicates a connection to the world as a whole, and results in an examination of the reader's subconscious.

Since she is working with the unconscious or subconscious, Valentine says that she often writes poems that she herself does not understand, so she has to rely on the sound of the language to judge the success of the poem. If she thinks it sounds good, it does not matter to her that she does not understand it. However, if her friends do not understand it either, to the point of not liking it, she reworks the poem or discards it. If her friends do not understand it but like it anyway, then she trusts that she has written a poem of value, something deep and alive, like the poetry of Emily Dickinson or Elizabeth Bishop, whose poetry Valentine admires because it makes her feel as if she could always go deeper.

All of this complexity can make a poem quite mysterious. However, Valentine has no objection to mystery. In fact, Klein asks Valentine in his interview, "How much do you feel you have to give readers in order for them to understand what you are saying?" She replies, "I think I do everything I can to be understood but after a point there's nothing more I can do." Rather than lose the poetic qualities of the work, Valentine says she "would hold out for mystery. . . . I don't have any liking at all for obscurity, but I do love mystery."

Muske thinks that Valentine manages to communicate in what appears to be an overly cryptic and mysterious style because "her mastery of the form, the deep image" enables the words to expand and become rich with meaning. It is, therefore, a style that requires being able to read between the lines, where so much seems to be stored. Valentine writes about the invisible, so the white spaces signify the unspoken and the unseen. Lee Upton, in *The Muse of Abandonment*, interprets Valentine's white spaces as creating "tenuous psychological states" through the appearance of the poem floating in the white spaces "as if about to be lifted from the page. . . . lightening and diffusing her sense of corporeality, rendering an ethereal poetry that revolts against the materiality of the body and the text and their combined gravity."

This ethereal nature may be attributed to the influence of the spiritual in Valentine's life and beliefs. A religious person, Valentine devotes time to prayer and meditation. Naturally, then, there is a sense in her poetry of a curiosity about God and another world. In her interview with Michael Klein, she says, "I feel that all poetry is prayer, it's just as simple as that. Who else would we be talking to?" Valentine adds later in the interview that "the cry of the heart of modern poetry, for the most part, is more like prayer." Perhaps that is because Valentine sees prose as where one learns history, that is to say, the what and how of life, while poetry, she thinks, tries to give meaning to life. This element of the spiritual relates to the dreams that influence her poetry in that they are both dimensions which are not rational. Both work with the unseen but emotionally undeniable.

The advice students do not want to hear is that the best way to understand poetry is to read lots of poetry. When trying to understand the works of one poet in particular, such as Valentine, it is valuable to read a number of her works. How else could one know if a particular poem, "Seeing You," for instance, is a continuation of typical themes for Valentine or is a departure into a new message or structure? It is also very helpful to read other poets who have influenced her writing or to whose work her own works are similar.

Valentine is often compared to Louise Bogan, an American poet who is considered one of the best critics of poetry in the mid-twentieth century.

Bogan's lyrics are also brief and limited mostly to two themes for which Valentine is noted: love and grief. Bogan's two favorite poets are also favorites of Valentine's: William Butler Yeats of Ireland and Rainer Maria Rilke of Germany. Yeats is also skilled at finding imagery that would fix a moment of experience in the memory, and Valentine's works are quite similar to Rilke's, in that his poetry also conveys a sense of something hidden and beyond, of a reality that escapes us just as it is grasped at, of mystery and the mystical.

Valentine is called a poet's poet. That is a title that is also given to Bogan and to Elizabeth Bishop, with whom Valentine identifies closely. Bishop, too, has a talent for small poetic structures and descriptive detail, using sharp-edged language and images that are precise and true to life. The same could be said of Emily Dickinson, who quickly comes to mind when reading Valentine. In fact, Valentine has said that Dickinson is in her blood. Consequently, when studying a particular poem, reading more poetry by the same author and by others opens up the mind and adds colors to the literary palette to a point that not only makes interpretation easier but also makes poetry more enjoyable. It is an investment of time that will pay dividends in the delight that language can bring and the tremendous breadth of the world that poetic expression opens.

Source: Lois Kerschen, Critical Essay on "Seeing You," in *Poetry for Students*, Thomson Gale, 2006.

Jennifer Bussey

Jennifer Bussey holds a master's degree in interdisciplinary studies and a bachelor's degree in English literature and is an independent writer specializing in literature. In the following essay, she explores water imagery in "Seeing You."

Valentine's use of water imagery in "Seeing You" provides continuity and meaning to the poet's reflections on love. With water imagery, she taps into a tradition that has been sustained throughout literature. As far back as Homer's *Odyssey*, readers find water as symbolic of movement, possibility, danger, and journeying. Mark Twain used the river in *The Adventures of Huckleberry Finn* to stand for the journey of life, where one encounters things that can be controlled and others that cannot. The deep, mysterious ocean in Herman Melville's *Moby-Dick* represents danger, fate, and the unknown. In F. Scott Fitzgerald's novel *The Great Gatsby*, water imagery symbolizes continuity and calm in contrast to the chaos and superficiality of

"In this highly visual poem, Valentine incorporates numerous layers of literary symbolism and psychological exploration in her use of water imagery."

the lives of his characters. These are just a few well-known examples of water imagery, but the incidence of its use throughout world literature attests to its rich symbolic possibilities. The analytical psychologist Carl Jung also recognized the importance of water imagery and employed it to symbolize the unconscious, both personal and collective. Jung saw water as representative of the life cycle.

In this highly visual poem, Valentine incorporates numerous layers of literary symbolism and psychological exploration in her use of water imagery. In the first section of the poem, the speaker addresses her mother and comments on the love they shared. She writes that she was "born under the mudbank," which describes a place that contains water but is only in proximity to an entire body of water. It is murky and a bit shapeless. It actually represents a mix of earth and water. These are the conditions in which the speaker entered the world, and the reader recognizes the presence of water as an element not yet defined. Readers may also note that water is often associated with the womb and birth, so this seems a fitting introduction to Valentine's poem. In the second line, the speaker recalls to her mother, "you gave me your boat." Her mother gave her the ability to go forth into the water safely and navigate it. Here, Valentine uses the water to symbolize life experiences and venturing into the world. It also points to the mother's sacrifice. That the mother made the speaker feel safe is expressed in line 4: "I made my home in your hand."

Valentine first introduces the idea of water as only one of four elements: water, air, earth, and fire. Many writers and thinkers also characterize air as wind or sky. The idea of the four elements was

first held by the ancient Greeks but continues to be held by modern thinkers. In line 6, the speaker says that her mother's hand is made of "four stars, like a kite." These two references are to the air (or sky) and bring in a sense of contrast to the water. The speaker's emotional maturity and gradual loss of innocence are expressed in line 7, when the speaker recalls that her mother was "afraid, afraid, afraid, afraid" and that she tried to give her mother some temporary comfort from the fear. The two are taking care of each other against a background of fear; first, the mother gave her daughter the boat to make her feel safe in the water, and then the daughter tries to remove the mother's relentless fear. Another element arrives in line 10: "Out of the river sparks rose up." Fire imagery provides contrast in the form of an unexpected burst of sparks from the water, signaling change.

The next two lines describe the mother's reaction to the change. She has both fear and love, and the speaker recalls seeing her "brilliance magnified." This is a subtle reinforcement of the importance of water in the mother-daughter relationship. The speaker sees her mother's brilliance magnified, as if in a drop of water or as a reflection of bright light on still water. The section ends with the speaker telling her mother that seeing her was the "original garden," her first experience of a love relationship.

The second section deals with a romantic love, and the speaker addresses a lover. Like the mother, the lover has an empty hand made of "four stars, like a kite." This repeated imagery relates the two loves in the speaker's mind. She sees something familiar in the lover that she recalls from her mother, and it makes her feel comfortable enough to go forward with the relationship. It also reinforces the use of the air element as a balance to the recurring water imagery. But here the empty hand does not symbolize fear and neediness. The lover's empty hand is a place where the speaker can simply stand and feel blessed and enjoy gazing into her lover's eyes. Where her mother kept fear in her "finger-spaces," the lover has blue, the color of water, in his. Water in this poem represents love, possibility, and growth; Valentine invokes water imagery surrounding the empty hand of the lover to create a thematically consistent picture. Blue is also the color of the sky, which has been present in both the mother's and the lover's hands. When she says, "my eyes' light in / your eyes' light" (lines 18 and 19), the speaker is expressing her sense of love and her belonging in the "blue finger-spaces" (line 18). Line 20 takes the significance of water a step further: "we drank each other in." Valentine uses the fact that water is quenching and life-sustaining to illustrate the mutual love the speaker shares with her lover.

The speaker symbolically abandons the boat her mother gave her when she decides, in line 21, to immerse herself fully in the water and seek its depths. She writes, "I dove down my mental lake fear and love: / first fear then under it love." Feeling safe and fulfilled by romantic love, she finds herself anxious to see what is at the bottom of her lake. She is not just curious; she also feels empowered and capable of asserting her will to see what her mental lake holds. The lake is herself, her abilities, and her purpose. Although she first encounters fear (which is not at all surprising, given what she described in the first section), she faces the fear to see what is past it. There she finds love. Valentine suggests that fear is motivated by love. A mother's fear for her children is generally driven by her love for them and desire for them to be happy and safe. In romantic love, people are often fearful of having their hearts broken. When the speaker discovers this fear within herself, she is really discovering something about human nature in general.

The speaker's decision to dive into the water is rewarded when she finds her lover at the bottom of her lake. The unknown has become known, and it is safe and trustworthy. She depicts her lover as "brilliance" (line 24), just as she had described her mother. Having experienced her journey through the water, she can trust her lover. In line 26, Valentine brings back the earth element: "Then past the middle of the earth it got light again." This is the first time in the poem she refers to earth as its own element; early in the poem she referred to the mudbank of her birth, but the mud was a blend of water and earth. In line 26, late in the poem, earth is an element unto itself. She has gone past the water in her journey and into the earth, seemingly without fear, and she finds light at the end of the journey. She has embraced herself and love, and her courage has been rewarded with peace and security. The poem ends with her characterizing her lover as "the garden of abundance" (line 28). Where her mother was the "original garden," the first love, the lover is abundant love.

In drenching "Seeing You" in water imagery, Valentine joins a rich literary tradition that reaches back to the beginnings of literary expression. Water is such an integral part of the human experience that it is readily understood and valued by readers. Valentine uses water to represent possibility, reflection, commonality, uncertainty, and movement. She also uses water to demonstrate the contrasts of life and death, peace and turmoil. By combining the universality of water imagery with the universal themes of familial and romantic loves, Valentine offers readers a poem that is both complex and relevant.

Source: Jennifer Bussey, Critical Essay on "Seeing You," in *Poetry for Students*, Thomson Gale, 2006.

Joyce Hart

Joyce Hart is a published author and former writing instructor. In this essay, she takes the poet's advice to feel the poem rather than to figure out its meaning.

In several interviews, Valentine, author of the poem "Seeing You," has stated that the point of writing or of reading poetry is not to be able to explain it but rather to feel it. Valentine has said that there are many times when she herself does not know precisely what her poems are about. She senses the emotions behind them, however, and hopes that she is able to transfer these emotions to her audience. With this idea is mind, this essay investigates the emotions behind "Seeing You."

People who have studied creativity, whether they are artists involved in the process or theorists interested in the topic, talk about the flow of the creative process. Metaphors used to explain this flow include rivers or beams of light or forces of energy. The artist, whether working with words, clay, or paint, thus becomes the vehicle through which this creativity flows. The artist must be open, focused, disciplined, and experienced in a particular medium. With these skills in place, the artist is equipped and ready to accept creative inspiration. Artists trust this flow of inspiration to bring new ideas to the imagination. Because artists have trained themselves in a medium, they are capable of interpreting the creative thoughts and transposing them into their chosen art forms. This may be what Valentine is referring to. She opens herself to the flow of creativity, which enlightens her as to how to express a feeling she has. She translates the energy that flows through her into words that create images that she and her readers can grasp. Artists such as Valentine are so open to and trusting of this flow of creative thoughts that they do not unduly censor it with rational thinking. She implies that she does not try to make these creative thoughts fit into a presubscribed language. Valentine does not stop the flow of words to ask what the words mean. Rather, she accepts the words, because they create a vessel into which she can pour her feelings.

> *Valentine does not stop the flow of words to ask what the words mean. Rather, she accepts the words, because they create a vessel into which she can pour her feelings."*

Looking more specifically at the poem "Seeing You," readers will note that the first section of the poem is focused on the word "mother." It would not be taking too much liberty here to assume that the poet is thinking of her own mother. The words that flow from the concept "mother" must represent, according to the poet's own description of her writing, her feelings (or at least some feelings) that she has concerning her mother. The title of the poem provides the sense that the speaker is looking at her mother from the distance of time, as if she is trying to understand her relationship with her mother; from this distance, she is finally "seeing" her.

The speaker conveys these feelings through abstract concepts. She uses a metaphoric language that offers images that the reader can interpret through his or her personal experience. For example, in the first stanza, the speaker refers to having been born "under the mudbank." What feeling does this convey? This birth can be felt in a variety of ways. To be born under a mudbank might be suffocating. How could anyone breathe under a mudbank? But, then, no one breathes while in the womb. It is possible that the slimy feel of mud is one that the speaker relates to the slimy feel of uterine fluids that surround an unborn child. "Mudbank" could also make one think of a primordial field of creation, from which much of life has evolved.

After mentioning this birth in the mudbank, the poet then writes that her mother gives her a boat. A boat can be looked upon as a vessel. It is not necessary to decipher whether this is a metaphor for the mother's womb. The feeling behind the phrase is that this child who was born under a mudbank has, in some way, been rescued and protected. The boat presents itself as a safety zone, something that lifts the child out of the suffocating mud and carries it.

The speaker of this poem then switches the metaphor. The mother, who was at first seen as a boat, is now referred to as a hand. These images are not so different from each other. A cupped hand looks much like the bowed hull of a boat. The hand also works in much the same way as a boat, at least in this poem. This child, who was the speaker at one time, was carried in both the boat and the hand. The feeling between the two metaphors is therefore somewhat similar up to this point; the only difference might be a sense of perspective. A boat is something large that floats on water; a hand is much smaller and more personal. Being carried in the mother's hand as opposed to having been given the mother's boat brings a sensation of warmth to the poem, at least momentarily. In the next stanza, this feeling changes.

The mother's hand is empty, the speaker states, and it is made "like a kite." Whereas the image of a hand suggests warmth, the kite, with its angular points and inanimate and somewhat flimsy construction, offers no such warmth. It is airy and, like the boat, is removed from the child. The speaker may have felt cuddled by the mother at one point, but this was only a transitional period. So far we have been told that the child was saved by the mother's boat and lived a long time in her hand, but then that hand became kitelike and empty. This transition of feelings is better explored with reference to the following stanza, in which the speaker informs her readers that the mother was filled with fear. The speaker does not state the source of the mother's fear, but she uses a metaphor to explain how her mother's fear affected her: "I licked it from your finger-spaces / and wanted to die." This could easily be the strongest emotion of the poem. The mother's fear was fed to the child, who became, literally, scared to death by it.

The speaker mentions love, a few lines later, but she couples it with this fear. "I could see you, your fear and your love." This is not a comfortable feeling. There is confusion here. Fear makes the speaker think of death, but love draws her in despite the terror. And this, the speaker declares, "was the original garden." In other words, the sense at this point of the poem is that these were the feelings that helped to sculpt the person the speaker would become.

The second section of the poem is titled "Lover." The speaker appears to use the previous section of the poem to provide her first, or original, experiences and definitions of love: from whom she gained it, what it meant to her, and how it felt. In the second section, the speaker refers to a time when she is grown up and has found a lover. How have her feelings about love changed? How do they remain the same?

The speaker begins the second section almost in the same way that she began the first. She is not born of this lover, but there is a similar feeling that she experiences. Like the mother, the lover has an empty hand that is also made like a kite, but the speaker's experience with that empty hand feels so much healthier. She does not lick fear from the lover's fingers as she had with her mother's fingers. Rather, for some unspoken reason, she feels blessed for having been offered this empty hand. She states, "I stood my fingers / in your blue finger-spaces." Sucking from the mother's fingers brings the notion of the mother's having given nourishment to the child, but that nourishment was tainted. The mother was, in some way, superior to the child, who was dependent on her, and her love was polluted with fear. In the speaker's adult relationship with a lover, she is an equal. She does not put her mouth to the lover's fingers but rather places her own fingers there. Her fingers fit with the lover's, intertwining where the fingers are not (in the spaces between). This feels so much more like a healthy relationship compared with the one with the mother. The poet expands on this feeling of equality when she writes "my eyes' light in / your eyes' light, / we drank each other in."

The remaining stanzas of the poem feel equally more healthy, as the speaker dives past the fear that she had inherited from her relationship with her mother and finds the love, the "brilliance, at the bottom." Without even knowing the meanings for the "mental lake," the "last red inside place," the "middle of the earth," and the many other metaphors that the poet uses to conclude her poem, readers can feel the changes in the speaker—her happiness, her exaltation—that come about from having seen, and felt, the other side of love.

Source: Joyce Hart, Critical Essay on "Seeing You," in *Poetry for Students*, Thomson Gale, 2006.

Alicia Ostriker

Ostriker is a noted poet. In the following review of Door in the Mountain, *she calls Valentine "a poet's poet" and praises her poems for striking "like the arrows of a Zen archer."*

She belongs to no school but the school, if one dares to mention it, of high art. She is a poet's poet, which means that she creates beauty, and has no objection to mystery. In the era covered by her

> " *Jean Valentine has not turned, ever, from the purity of an art that cedes nothing to fashion. Yet she is as beloved as any poet writing today.*"

work, as poetry has turned increasingly toward the popular and populist, toward accessibility and theatricality, Jean Valentine has not turned, ever, from the purity of an art that cedes nothing to fashion. Yet she is as beloved as any poet writing today.

Born in Chicago, Valentine studied at Radcliff College, has lived in New York for most of her life, and has taught at Sarah Lawrence, NYU, Columbia University, and the 92nd St. Y in Manhattan, among other places, earning the devotion of generations of students. She won the Yale Younger Poets Award for her eccentrically-titled first book, *Dream Barker,* in 1965 (compare Adrienne Rich's *A Change of World,* which won the same prize a generation earlier, in 1951), and while publishing eight other books she has received numerous other awards. Most recently, *Door in the Mountain* received the 2004 National Book Award for poetry.

With this history, you might think "mainstream." But Valentine's title poem will give you a provocative taste of a voice like no other:

> Never ran this hard through the valley
> never ate so many stars
>
> I was carrying a dead deer
> tied on to my neck and shoulders
>
> deer legs hanging in front of me
> heavy on my chest
>
> People are not wanting
> to let me in
>
> Door in the mountain
> let me in.

Part of the magic here is that we cannot tell if that last line is a beseeching request for something that has not happened and may never happen—solace, acceptance, renewal—or if it is a declaration of something that has happily, against all odds, happened. It can be either. And we must guess for ourselves, by our own interior experiences of despair and hope, what that mountain is, what that door is, what blocks us, what allows us entry. We may be reminded of Hart Crane's poignant "Permit me voyage, love, into your hands," or of Galway Kinnell's "The Bear," two poems of vision quest, though Valentine's diction is the more spare.

This is one of Jean Valentine's many dream poems, poems of profound imagination, delicate and sensual, fearless and magical, poems that often seem to make her the heir of John Keats and of Wallace Stevens. Her language is haunting in ways it would be hard to explain. I don't know why I want to say a line like "The snow is over and the sky is light," over and over like a mantra, but I do. "Looking into a Jean Valentine poem," Adrienne Rich says,

> is like looking into a lake: you can see your own out-
> line, and the shapes of the upper world, reflected
> among rocks, underwater life, glint of lost bottles,
> drifted leaves. The known and familiar become one
> with the mysterious and half-wild, at the place where
> consciousness and the subliminal meet. . . . it lets as
> into spaces and meanings we couldn't approach in
> any other way.

Yes, I agree, and then again, looking into Valentine's poetry is also like playing chess with a master—you might think you know what's happening on the board, how the game is developing, and suddenly the other player's bishop skids along a border, a knight twists before your very eyes and lands someplace you never thought of, a queen sails majestically through your frail defenses. In "The Messenger," for instance,

> Now I want to live forever
> Now I could scatter my body easily
> if it was any use
>
> now that the earth
> has rained through us
> green white
> green green grass

Did you expect that stanza closure? No, you didn't. Is it beautiful, is it mysterious? Yes, it is. Does something within you, seldom touched, feel touched by it? I hope so.

For there is no standard Valentine poem, no predictable Valentine move. She writes hot love poems and tender elegies. She writes short-line free verse and long prose poems. She writes brilliantly and painfully of dysfunctional family life and of the life of the spirit; she can write about mental breakdown, alcoholism, AIDS, and desire with the accuracy of a scalpel and the sweetness of a flute. One sequence of poems, "Her Lost Book," contains poems as devastating as anything written at the

height of fiminist rage, though the tone is utterly controlled:

> I was dark and silent.
> The therapist said.
> "Why don't you wear lipstick?"
> To J: "Does she lie on top?" To J:
> "Don't *play her role.*
> Don't give the children their baths
> or feed them."

Another sequence is about visiting a friend in prison. Another is about the death of her mother. She is unafraid to ask unanswerable questions like "why are we in this life" or to cry "God break me out / of this stiff life I've made." She is part Catholic, part Buddhist, she prays and she meditates, she sees herself sometimes as a horse, she sees the soul sometimes as a boat, she describes the process of writing as *listening*. Often there is a koan-like quality to the poems, defying rationality in ways that help us break through to another dimension of the real. Often she makes me think of a poem by the great Japanese poet Basho: "The barn burned down. Now I can see the moon."

In the new poems of *Door in the Mountain,* Valentine continues an impulse toward the ardently and intensely chaste, writing in a style more austere and cryptic than ever. Yet the poems strike like the arrows of a Zen archer. Here is one more. "To the Bardo," that shifts before our gaze from loss and confusion to illumination, the scarf up the magician's sleeve, the trick we might all want to learn:

> I dreamed I finally got through to C on the
> phone
> he was whispering
> I couldn't make out the words
>
> he had been in the hospital
> and then in a home
> M was sick too
>
> You know how in dreams you are everyone:
> awake too you are everyone:
> I am listening breathing your ashy breath
>
> old Chinese poet:
> fire:
> to see the way.

Source: Alicia Ostriker, "Seeing the Way," in *American Book Review*, Vol. 26, No. 4, May–June 2005, p. 16.

D. H. Tracy

In the following review of Door in the Mountain, *Tracy calls Valentine's poems "disquieting" in their progression from "abundance to their fleeting and attenuated meaning."*

Door in the Mountain collects Valentine's eight previous books (including *Dream Barker,* selected for the Yale Younger Poets series in 1965) and several dozen new poems. You could say that *Dream Barker* was her best book, but it was really the only one that cared how it sounded, and she subsequently lost even that limited appetite for Plath-like musical lavishness:

> How deep we met in the sea, my love,
> My double, my Siamese heart, my whiskery,
> fish-belly, glue-eyed prince, my dearest black nudge
>
> —From "First Love"

She writes in this book with a three-quarters profile that enables certain voicings—her passing indictment of Cambridge, for example ("Every public place in this city / Is a sideshow of souls swordswallowing pity"), is better than Cummings's. But the stance is made in part of disengagement, and you sense that, although her poetics faces the daylight world of a readership, the poet herself would rather not. In subsequent collections, the poet prevails by degrees. Valentine goes from some form in *Dream Barker* (1965) to none in *Pilgrims* (1969). The poems begin to feel reactive and momentary, and solitude becomes a condition which they can explore but not ameliorate. In *Ordinary Things* (1974) she prays, "God break me out / of this stiff life I've made." In her translations from the Dutch of Huub Oosterhuis, she is attracted to the theme of blurrings and dissolving markings: chalk lines on a floor rubbed off, footprints in the snow blown over, sand rubbed into eyes. Somewhere around *The River at Wolf* (1992) the poems on the page begin to seem like footprints of the poems in her head, and mistrust of surfaces has gone from a secondary consideration to a constrictive condition.

What's disquieting is that this progression seems to have no proximate cause. She never expresses revulsion at public language, and no single private tragedy or crisis undoes her (though recently someone close, I think a young man, is in prison). Lately, the poems have little evident patterning, although even in their privacy and dream logic they bemoan their own aphasia. The last five lines of the book are true, in their ephemera, to the means Valentine has arrived at:

> Snow falling
> off the Atlantic
> out towards strangeness
> you
> a breath on a coal
>
> —From "Home"

But it is wrenching to see a poet erode herself in this way, and, even with all the evidence of the poems before you, be unable to reconstruct the route they took from abundance to their fleeting and attenuated meaning.

Source: D. H. Tracy, Review of *Door in the Mountain: New and Collected Poems, 1965–2003*, in *Poetry*, Vol. 186, No. 3, June 2005, pp. 257–59.

Jean Valentine and Richard Jackson

In the following interview with Richard Jackson of Poetry Miscellany, *Valentine discusses what the interviewer calls her "fragmentary vision" and her relationship to the narrative voices in her poems.*

[*Poetry Miscellany*]: *Your poetry is unique in the way it presents itself; it seems to be based upon fragments, shifts in perspective, traces, frayings. As you say in "Twenty Days' Journey," it is a world of things "almost visible," of "The blown away footstep / in the snow." Could we begin by talking about the nature of the vision, this world, where often, it seems, "it was like touching the center and therefore losing it, emptying it of what you might have been able to hold on to" ("February 9th"). It seems a world of deferrals, discontinuities, differences, gaps.*

[Jean Valentine]: I can only respond to your first sentence here, very simply: that when I'm most attentive, these "fragments," etc., are very often what I sense and feel; they are how I "get" this time and place and the currents of my private and public life and the lives around me. To try to clarify this—not to compare—I think of, for instance, Paul Klee's painting, certain newspaper photos or documentary film scenes, or certain intricately plotted mysteries.

In *The Lives Around Me* I include the work of someone like Huub Oosterhuis (you quote next from my version of his long poem *Twenty Days' Journey,* made with the Dutch poet Judith Herzberg). To try a version of this poem, I had to feel very close to it. There are still mysteries in the poem for me, but I make out this much: a vision of both personal and worldwide suffering of loss and anguish, in which a personal and/or an Everyman "I" undertakes a journey: a journey in search of God, who is both present and absent in the poem, and who also suffers loss and anguish. (I should say clearly here that I haven't had the chance to talk with either Herzberg or Oosterhuis about this, and I could be very far off.) The experience of that journey is something I could only have known or approached at all through Oosterhuis's poem: but

"
I think the relationship between me and my voices, narrators, is the common one: I am trying to move into an other, into others; to move out of the private self into an imagination of everyone's history, into the public world."

to return to your question, the poem seems fragmented as its subject seems to demand.

Your second quotation, from "February 9th" (from *The Messenger*) came to me in a letter from a friend and spoke wonderfully to me of one negative side of naming: I think Robert Coles said this somewhere, though I can't remember his exact words: "Name it, and it is so." Just the opposite, of course, of the creating or the hallowing powers of naming, this would be the destructive use of language to lie, to deny, to erase life. In the quotation, it would be the violent or intrusive use of touch.

Your sense of timing seems predicated upon this same fragmentary vision. For example, "This Minute" portrays the moment as being continually undercut as the filmstrip keeps running again and again, presencing future, present, and past in the one moment. Or take "Here Now," where "The sky is the same changing / colors as the farthest snow"—here the moment gets defined by all the possibilities that range beyond it. Could you sketch out, then, how you feel time is at work in the poems as a theme, as a principle of structuring?

I don't think the use of time in "This Minute" is trying to do anything more than to present a nightmare, in which time does not move naturally, historically, but is fixed, distorted.

About how time is at work in the poems in general, again I can only say simply that this awareness of past and present and future "in the one moment" seems to me how time is experienced, when one is most alive, most attentive—except perhaps

for extraordinary moments when only the present is there.

I don't really see time as a "theme" in my own poems, except in the most ordinary and universal ways. As a "principle of structuring"—our thoughts do range all over time, and in lots of poems I am trying to catch the way someone might think, or "think out loud" in a quiet talk with some close friend, or say in a letter.

In the context of this fragmentary vision, it often seems that the processes of writing, collecting, locating, comparing, absenting become themselves part of the subject of the poems. That is, there often seems a way in which the process itself is the subject, not the fact of the finished poem. I perceive a sense that the poem is always emerging, even in its last line—this holds especially true for the poems in The Messenger. *I think of Stevens's ideal that all poems comprise or refer to an ideal, always unwritten poem. Do you have this sense of your work? I think of the last poem in* The Messenger *that is also a sort of collecting of images from earlier in the book.*

If this "sense that the poem is always emerging" is working successfully, that is, if the poem is accessible, I'd be very content. I have this wish, right now anyhow, to catch our experience "on the fly," so to speak: a pull against the poem as a sort of finished, well-wrought statement—much as I admire and love that kind of poem by certain other poets.

Yes, like Stevens, I certainly do imagine how one is writing along underneath some one "ideal, always unwritten poem" all one's life—I like very much Anne Sexton's notion that this ideal poem is being written by everyone all the time, a sort of communal poem being written by all the poets alive. Though with Stevens again, I would imagine this poem as "an ideal, always unwritten." Being "written after," maybe.

In the last poem in *The Messenger*, "March 21st," I'm sure there are images collected that I wasn't conscious of; but in that piece I was consciously trying to bring in sense-echoes from the various sections of the sequence, "Solitudes," trying to get to a moment of gathering-in, there.

There is a double movement in the poems—in "Sanctuary," for instance, there is a "scattering of life" that is counterpointed by the movement along "the thread you have to keep finding, over again, to / follow it back to life." Could you describe your sense of this movement? It seems as if the farther you go out into things, into the world, the more you find yourself intact; an escape from the self to find the self. In psychology, at least that of Jacques

Lacan, this movement tends to suggest an otherness we seek; we always seek to know ourselves in, identify with, the Other a double.

What you say is very good, and it ought to be included. But I have nothing to add because you really answer it yourself.

How do you see yourself figured in the poems? In other words, what is the relationship between you and your voices, narrators? Sometimes your perspective changes in a single poem, such as "Susan's Photograph," where you are razor, wrist, photographer, the friend, and so on. Ultimately, then, this is a question about voice, its varieties and modulations, about the ways you throw yourself, aspects of your self that are real or imagined, into the poems.

One thing I feel sure of about the use of the self is that while there are poems that may use the "I" with very little of the "real self" in them, there are no poems that present the "real self" precisely, "as is," as one would try to in, say, an autobiography.

I think the relationship between me and my voices, narrators, is the common one: I am trying to move into an other, into others; to move out of the private self into an imagination of everyone's history, into the public world. This is what I most want to do—maybe what every lyric poet most wants to do. This effort in no way means to exclude the eccentric, but to enlarge what is human. (Here Emily Dickinson and Whitman both come to mind and the wonderful southern poet of our own time, Eleanor Ross Taylor.)

What is the nature of the "messenger"? It seems a sort of metamorphic entity. I think, for example, of "Beka, 41," where you tell the girl that the messenger is like her brother,

like the penguin
who sits on the nest of pebbles, and the one
who brings home pebbles, to the nest's edge in his
beak,
one at a time, and also like the one
who is lying there, warm, who is going to break
out soon:
becoming yourself; the messenger is growing . . .

I think also of "Turn (2): After Years," where the name of the absent friend is presenced at the end by uttering the two words "other" and "thou" almost as if to bring them together, as if to presence the absent other, to bring the messenger close. Could we talk, then, about the "messenger" and the "you"?

Yes, in *"Beka, 14,"* the messenger is a metamorphic figure: I tried to use the changing figures as messengers coming, gradually, to call the fourteen-year-old child to her adult life, including, at the end

of the poem, her leaving home to go her own way. A series of callings. Whether the "messenger" is thought of as internal (as it becomes, halfway through this particular poem), or as an external figure, doesn't matter, I don't think: what matters to me in the poem is the figuring of the person's coming into possession of his or her own strongest desires—something which Father William E Lynch, S.J., writes so clearly and so healingly of in his book *Images of Hope.*

In "Turn (2): After Years," I hadn't thought consciously of a messenger figure, but I do feel the absent friend "present at the end" of the poem, yes. The two words *Other* and *thou* are trying to express closeness and the redemption of a harmful past. In this way, the poem is (maybe like many poems) part recognition and part talk, real or imagined, to another person.

Your poems, especially in The Messenger, *defy paraphrase perhaps as well as any I know. Yet there is a certain "path of saying," as Heidegger calls it, that can be followed in poems. For him, this sort of movement is an undercurrent or underplot that must be participated in and that goes below the surface of the words. It is something like a "gesture" of language. I think that all the things we have been talking about so far are the elements of this underplot. Could you speak to how this works in poems or something like it that you might have experienced?*

I like Heidegger's notion and his phrase for it. I'm more familiar with the process you bring up here as a teacher than in my own writing: to try to *hear* a poem with students, rather than to encourage a kind of structured puzzling out of the poet's "meaning," which ends up being reductive. But this can be a tricky business, because in the poems I most value, there is meaning, and very precise meaning, at that.

Barthes called texts "infinite cipher" because for him their ultimate meanings were unresolvable, unfathomable. Would you say that a poem should strive for this (from your own point of view), and that the techniques of fragmentation, shifting perspectives, and so on that we discussed earlier are means of achieving the character of an infinite cipher? How much of what goes on beyond the words is the poet aware of? to what extent?

I haven't read Barthes, but from what you tell me here, I'd go on with my last sentence, in the previous question, to disagree with his idea of a poem as an "infinite cipher," etc. For myself, I'd always want a poem to have mystery, yes, but also to be very clear. That tension matters as much as anything to me in a poem—as much as the music of its language, say.

As to how aware the poet is of "what goes on beyond the words," I just don't know. Sometimes a reader will see a lot in a poem of mine that I never say; but I do always hope absolutely that what I *did* see will be very clear, very precise. And when a reader misses what I'm up to, well, then I know I've missed getting it down.

More and more, I revere poets who are both simple and endlessly resonant with meaning: Elizabeth Bishop, Tomas Transtroömer, to think of just a couple. Their poems remind me of a phrase of Frost's, about thought being "a feat of association." And their thought is always grounded in the real: there's a real bridge, a real gas station, and so forth.

Barthes also talked about literature's subversive activity. That is, for him, literature subverts by undermining the ordinary ways we perceive and think about the world. For him, as for, say, Susan Sontag, literature ought to be unsettling. It ought to provide new categories of thought. Do you see anything like this working in your own poems? Your "ordinary things," to steal one of your titles, become very extraordinary in your poems.

"New categories of thought"—well, the writing we remember does bring us something new, does in that sense trouble our sleeping selves, keep us from settling down in whatever we thought last year, or last month; and that's one thing writing seems to be for, yes.

But my wish in using the title *"Ordinary Things"* was not so much to be ironic as to look as attentively as I could at the ordinary, at the sort of feelings and events that are part of everyone's daily life in this time and place. It was a high ambition which I still have (and which many writers must have): an attempt at what Martin Buber calls "the hallowing of the everyday."

Source: Jean Valentine and Richard Jackson, "The Hallowing of the Everyday," in *Acts of Mind: Conversations with Contemporary Poets*, Unversity of Alabama, 1983, pp. 27–31.

Sources

Cramer, Steven, "Self-defense—*The River at Wolf* by Jean Valentine / *Meetings with Time* by Carl Dennis / *Apocrypha* by Eric Pankey / and Others," in *Poetry*, Vol. 161, No. 3, December 1992, p. 161.

Freeman, John, Review of *Door in the Mountain: New and Selected Poems, 1965–2003*, in the *Seattle Times*, November 28, 2004, Section K, p. 7.

Hoffert, Barbara, "Best Poetry of 2004," in *Library Journal*, Vol. 130, No. 7, April 15, 2005, p. 94.

Jackson, Richard, "The Hallowing of the Everyday," in *Acts of Mind: Conversations with Contemporary Poets*, University of Alabama Press, 1983, pp. 27, 29.

Klein, Michael, "Jean Valentine: An Interview," in *American Poetry Review*, Vol. 20, No. 4, July/August 1991, pp. 39–44.

Muske, Carol, "Growing Darkness, Growing Light," in the *Nation*, Vol. 265, No. 3, July 21, 1997, pp. 36, 37.

Ostriker, Alicia, "Seeing the Way," in *American Book Review*, Vol. 26, No. 4, May/June 2005, p. 16.

Review of *The River at Wolf*, in the *Virginia Quarterly Review*, Vol. 69, No. 3, Summer 1993, p. SS101.

Rivard, David, Review of *The River at Wolf*, in *Ploughshares*, Vol. 19, No. 2, Fall 1993, p. 246.

Susskind, H., Review of *The River at Wolf*, in *Choice*, Vol. 30, No. 5, January 1993, p. 798.

Upton, Lee, *The Muse of Abandonment: Origin, Identity, Mastery in Five American Poets*, Bucknell University Press, 1998, pp. 76, 77, 90–91.

Further Reading

Howe, Florence, ed., *No More Masks!: An Anthology of Twentieth-Century American Women Poets*, Perennial, 1993.

Originally published in 1973, this book is an important collection of women's poetry that portrays the themes of individual identity and roles in society as women have asked for justice and nonviolence across the decades.

Middlebrook, Diane Wood, and Marilyn Yalom, eds., *Coming to Light: American Women Poets in the Twentieth Century*, University of Michigan Press, 1985.

The Center for Research on Women at Stanford University collected sixteen essays for this book on the relationship of the American literary tradition and women poets. The volume includes bibliographies.

Rankine, Claudia, and Julia Spahr, eds., *American Women Poets in the 21st Century: Where Lyric Meets Language*, Wesleyan University Press, 2002.

This volume explores the influence of gender on contemporary poetry with statements on aesthetics and identity by the ten featured poets. The book includes a critical essay on each poet and a bibliography of works.

Zook, Amy Jo, and Wauneta Hackleman, eds., *The Study and Writing of Poetry by American Women Poets*, 2nd rev. ed., Whitston Publishing Company, 1996.

Designed for high school and college students, this handbook provides explanations by fifty contemporary American women poets about the techniques used in writing poetry.

Three To's and an Oi

Heather McHugh
1999

"Three To's and an Oi" is in Heather McHugh's 1999 poetry collection, *The Father of the Predicaments*. The title of the book comes from a line in "Not a Prayer," one of the other poems in the collection: "The father of the / predicaments, wrote Aristotle's translator, is being." In "Three To's and an Oi," McHugh focuses on death and language, referring to the story of Cassandra, the woman to whom the god Apollo grants the power to see the future but then curses with the burden of never having her accurate predictions believed. The play *Agamemnon*, by the Greek dramatist Aeschylus (525–456 B.C.E.), depicts Cassandra as knowing that she is about to be murdered and wailing "*ototototoi*." The title "Three To's and an Oi" refers to words that do not seem to be in the poem, but they appear in this focal word, "*ototototoi*." The presence of the "to's" and the "oi" is obscured because the "oi" is broken up, so that its *o* comes at the start of the poem and its *i* comes at the end. The poem questions why translators felt the need to render this cry "woe is me," when it is clearly just the sort of emotional outburst, or "baby talk," that people use when meaningful words are not adequate.

For years, McHugh has been one of America's most celebrated poets, with a list of major honors and awards that few poets could ever approach. In "Three To's and an Oi," as in most of her poetry, McHugh combines a rich sense of language and culture with a sly sense of humor, working a basic premise and its ramifications while more and more associations come to light. Using a delicate and deliberate style, McHugh takes the poem from dread to love, from infancy to maturity, from Aeschylus to the Bible, and from emotion to definition, all within a few short lines.

Author Biography

Heather McHugh was born on August 20, 1948, in San Diego, California. She was raised in rural Virginia, where she was a shy child who began writing poetry at the age of five. She was also a natural scholar, breezing through high school and graduating early with academic honors. She entered Radcliffe College at age sixteen. While she was at Radcliffe, the *New Yorker* accepted one of her poems for publication. McHugh graduated from Radcliffe in 1970 and received her master of arts degree in English literature from the University of Denver two years later. Financial support from a MacDowell Colony fellowship and a grant from the National Endowment for the Arts enabled McHugh to work on her first poetry collection, *Dangers*, which was published in 1977. Several collections of poetry followed. "Three To's and an Oi" is from McHugh's 1999 collection, *The Father of the Predicaments*.

In 1976, McHugh took a position as associate professor of English at the State University of New York, Binghamton, where she stayed until 1982. At the time, she was in her early thirties and having her work published regularly in such showcases as the *New Yorker*, the *Nation*, the *Atlantic*, and the *Paris Review*. McHugh moved to Seattle, where she became professor of English at the University of Washington in 1983 and was teaching as of 2005. She also became a Milliman Distinguished Writer-in-Residence at the University of Washington.

McHugh became a chancellor of the American Academy of Poets and a member of the American Academy of Arts and Sciences. Among her numerous awards were a Guggenheim Fellowship, grants from the Rockefeller Foundation and Yaddo artists' community, a Lila Wallace–Reader's Digest Writers' Award, several Pushcart Prizes, and the PEN/Voelcker Award. McHugh was a finalist for the 1994 National Book Award for Poetry for *Hinge and Sign: Poems, 1968–1993*, which won the Boston Book Review Bingham Poetry Prize and the Daniel A. Pollack–Harvard Review Prize. McHugh's collection *Eyeshot* (2003) was a finalist for the Pulitzer Prize in 2004. In addition to her work as a poet, McHugh

earned critical praise for her work as a translator, working sometimes with her husband, the scholar Nikolai Popov.

Poem Text

Cassandra's kind
of crying was

otototoi . . . They translate it
o woe is me, but really it's

less graspable than that—it isn't Greek for   5
nothing, all that stuttering in tones . . . When things
            get bad,

we baby-talk. In throes of terror in the night,
when dreads cannot be turned aside

by presences with promises, or dronings of a long
erroneous lullaby, or shorter story lines—   10

of which the lines themselves
have given rise to fear—we wake up

in Cassandra's kind
of quandary. There's been

some terrible mistake.   15
We're all about to die.

Each whiplash of a girl, each eddy of a boy
comes reeling back from too much sheer

towardness—clarity from cataract—only to be
drawn in, again: 20

into tomorrow by today,
into the tune by gondolier,

into the two by two who turn
the bow toward torrents of *veyz mir.*

Poem Summary

Lines 1–2

"Three To's and an Oi" starts by mentioning Cassandra, a figure from ancient Greek mythology. Cassandra is the daughter of Priam, the king of Troy. Apollo is in love with her and gives her the gift of foretelling the future. Cassandra rejects Apollo, however, and he condemns her to always having her prophesies misunderstood by the people to whom she tells them.

Lines 3–4

The poem refers to Cassandra's cry in *Agamemnon*. In the play, Agamemnon, the leader of the Greek army, returns to Atreus, his father, after the conquest of Troy, bringing Cassandra as his concubine, a battle prize. As soon as she steps into Agamemnon's palace, Cassandra knows that she will die there. Agamemnon's wife, Clytemnestra, is already plotting to kill him. Cassandra cries out in fear, but the chorus interprets her fear as caused by not understanding the Greek language and her agony as grief for those she has lost in the war. Although it sometimes is translated "woe is me," Cassandra's cry also has been written "Aieeeeee!" Because Aeschylus wrote in ancient Greek, translations are left to the discretion of the translator and often are inexact.

Lines 5–6

In lines 5 and 6, McHugh gets to the point of the poem—the duality of language. She points out that the meaning of Cassandra's expression is not as specific as "woe is me"; it is "less graspable than that." At the same time, though, her cry is not meaningless: "it isn't Greek for / nothing." That the sound Cassandra makes is not rich in meaning should not be thought to indicate that it is entirely meaningless.

Lines 7–8

The poem explains situations under which speaking with phonetic sounds rather than identifiable words might be expected. In times of "terror" and "dreads," for instance, one cannot be expected to form ideas into rational thought. People revert to childhood at such times, which the poem generalizes as times when things go bad, and speak in baby talk, or the half-formed language that relies as much on sound as on meaning.

Lines 9–10

"Presences with promises" are those that have no current meaning themselves but are important because of what they imply. McHugh uses the word "promises" rather than "implications" to indicate that the emotion hidden behind the sound is important and worth delving into. Mentioning a lullaby refers to the baby talk of the previous stanza. It reinforces the idea that the unstructured language of adults in crisis is the same as the language a baby tries to form out of emotion and sound. In this case, though, the language is not a startled exclamation but a soothing one, like a parent singing a lullaby to calm a baby while knowing full well that the child cannot understand the meanings of the words. With "shorter story lines," the poem moves away from sound and toward meaning. The lines of a story are combinations of words and sentences, but they have to be held back from being too complex.

Lines 11–12

The "story lines" referred to in line 10 are not short by their nature. They have been abbreviated by fear, cut down from what they would naturally have been. Line 12 mentions waking up, returning the thought to the direction in which it starts in line 7, setting the situation for these feelings as occurring in the middle of the night, when one's logical defenses are at their weakest.

Lines 13–14

To be in a "quandary" is to be poised in an uncertain position with no clear course of action presenting itself. The quandary refers to Cassandra's inability to find words sufficient to express the horror that she knows is coming. Although the cause of Cassandra's predicament is clearly identified in ancient myth, McHugh notes that the problem is not simply one of a legendary person. Myths tend to resonate to modern times because they describe the human condition. Mirroring the earlier mention of shorter story lines, the lines of the poem become noticeably narrower starting with lines 13 and 14 and continuing with the next two lines.

Lines 15–16

McHugh ends the poem's first section with two bluntly stated, dire pronouncements. The first one indicates the type of complex situation that usually deserves discussion. That there has been a mistake raises questions such as how the error happened, who caused it, and what things would be like if the mistake had not occurred. The second statement leads into the poem's section break with an air of finality. Just as Cassandra knows that her death is unavoidable, all people know that there is no escape from death. The poem uses such drastic phrasing because, unlike Cassandra, most people do not recognize the seriousness of the end they are faced with. They know about it logically, but they do not feel it.

Lines 17–18

In the beginning of the second section, McHugh refers to humanity in general in terms of boys and girls. Mentioning girls, she uses the term "whiplash," implying a violent reaction in the opposite direction. In this case, it is a revolt against the certainty of death that ends the first section of the poem. When she speaks of boys, McHugh uses the word "eddy," which is a motion contrary to the prevailing current. Both words show that people, particularly young people, push back against the fates they know are coming.

Lines 19–20

The distinction between male and female made in lines 17 and 18 is used in lines 19 and 20 to hint at human closeness, and possibly even love, with the phrases "towardness" and "drawn in." The poem not only is talking about the struggle against inevitable death but also is asserting that this struggle against hopelessness creates the illusion of hope. A cataract is, by definition, an opaque spot on the eye that cannot be seen through, but McHugh claims that through this unclear spot, in the struggle against it, clarity can be found.

Lines 21–22

The possibility of hopefulness continues in lines 21 and 22 as the poem says that even after realizing the certainty of death, the grimness of today will lead one to focus attention on tomorrow. Line 22 takes a more poetic approach. In Venice, gondoliers have traditionally been known for singing for their passengers while navigating the canals. Although this image is in itself romantic, McHugh implies sinister undertones. First is the issue of the passengers, paying attention only to the song and failing to notice where the boat is going. Second, the image is an implied reference to Charon, the ferryman of Greek myth who transports people across the river of death to the afterlife.

Lines 23–24

The "two by two" reference brings the poem back to the division of boys and girls mentioned in line 17. Pairing off into couples is a distraction from the inevitability of death. Being distracted is not necessarily a bad thing. The poem shows that people in couples are willing to head right into death's finality, implying that bonding with another is a way of gaining the courage that language fails to give.

The last line uses the Yiddish term "*veyz mir*," which also is rendered "*vei iz mihr*" and "*vai iz mir*." Yiddish is a Germanic language written in Hebrew and spoken by Jews of Central and Eastern European origin as well as by their descendants. Like the expression from ancient Greek that begins the poem, this phrase is usually translated with the words that translators ascribe to Cassandra: "woe is me."

Themes

Language and Meaning

In "Three To's and an Oi," McHugh explores the inability of language to express the feelings that human beings have at their most vulnerable moments, the moments "when things get bad" and the awareness of death is inevitable. At such moments, she says, the complex language that people, even poets, use to surround themselves is useless. McHugh examines the similarities between the language used in times of crisis and the language used by babies first learning to talk. Both types of language rely more on sounds, "dronings," than they do on meanings, and both use the simplest, shortest phrases.

That the sounds of words are more important to people under duress than are their meanings implies that the sounds have relevance unto themselves. When they turn their attention away from what words mean, people find that the words still hold some importance to them. In this way, the poem shows that meaning and sound are not opposites but are parts of the same system. The poem uses the song sung by a gondolier to illustrate this point. Although the logical purpose of a gondola ride is to get from one point to another, the trip is made different by the song, and it is the song that travelers remember.

To show the shortcomings of language, McHugh refers to Cassandra, the Greek mythological figure

Topics For Further Study

- Find two different translations of Aeschylus's play *Agamemnon* and point out five or more differences in the translations. For each, write a paragraph explaining which you think is more appropriate and why.

- Do a search of news stories from the past year. Compile cases in which the word "Cassandra" has been used to refer to a person whose truthful predictions have been ignored. On the basis of your findings, nominate a figure in the news who you think will be the next Cassandra.

- Child development experts differ in their opinions of how language develops in babies. Form

teams to debate two theories about when infant language begins to take on meaning.

- The last two words of "Three To's and an Oi," *veyz mir*, are Yiddish words that are presented without translation. Look for poems that use words or phrases from other languages, and compile them along with their meanings. See if you can compose a found poem made entirely of foreign words taken from other poems.

- McHugh refers to the tunes sung by gondoliers. Listen to or read the lyrics of Gilbert and Sullivan's light opera *The Gondoliers* (1889), and write your own gondola song specifically meant to distract people from the idea of death.

who is blessed with the gift of prophecy but later cursed with being unable to convince anyone that her predictions are true. At a moment of crisis, Cassandra shouts out a nonsense sound, *"otototoi,"* which translators, in their drive to ascribe meaning to her words, have written as "woe is me." McHugh contends that "woe is me" is not the meaning, that the sound Cassandra is said to make in *Agamemnon* does not have any translation at all. That the sound cannot be converted to meaningful words, however, does not make the expression of emotion any less true or important.

Fatalism

One of the basic premises of "Three To's and an Oi" is that death is inevitable and that humans spend their lives trying, not always successfully, to forget that basic truth. This idea is introduced into the poem with the story of Cassandra, who is able to see her own death looming as she arrives at the palace of Agamemnon. Faced with her own certain death, Cassandra lets out a cry of nonsensical stuttering. To translate her sheer, unspeakable horror as a simple "woe is me" diminishes the depth of Cassandra's fear.

McHugh goes beyond Cassandra's story to remind readers that the situation is not Cassandra's

alone but is one faced by all people. McHugh points out that people wake in the night in terror, aware that death is at hand and knowing that death is approaching with the same certainty that Cassandra must feel. After driving home this point by implication—by association with Cassandra and by mention of a situation that people find familiar—the poem states the point bluntly and flatly with no room for equivocation: "We're all about to die."

Youth

The second part of "Three To's and an Oi" recedes from the knowledge of death to explore young people who are just coming into that knowledge. McHugh breaks the human race into sexes, but she makes her examples of each sex young: "a girl" and "a boy." Starting from youth enables the poet to trace the ways in which humans build their defenses against the crippling knowledge of death. She has the girl "whiplash" and the boy "eddy," although these actions can easily be reversed. The main thing is that youth responds violently against mortality. McHugh also implies that these strong, violent backlashes are a result of too much "towardness." Youth sometimes leans in toward death, examining it with a curiosity that those with more experience do not feel.

Introspection

The point of "Three To's and an Oi" is to make readers think about the truths that they carry within themselves. When, at the midway point, McHugh states directly that "we're all about to die," she has earned the right to cut through illusions by examining the illusions that surround this unequivocal statement. Because the medium of poetry is language, the poet is as destructive of her own illusions as she is of those of others when she points out that the attempt to give coherent meaning to Cassandra's anguished cry is pointless.

The second part of the poem depicts how people proceed from youth, alone or in couples, building systems to distract themselves from the thought of death. When it begins to seem that human intellect can overcome primal fear, however, McHugh explains that the journey of distraction drives people to the very attitude of "woe is me" ("*veyz mir*") that translators have tried to impose on Cassandra's anguish, implying that such a verbal twisting of raw emotion, even when one is aware of it, is inevitable.

Style

Short Stanzas

In most poems, the individual lines are clustered into stanzas, or groups of lines. The most common stanza length is the quatrain, or four-line grouping, although the lengths of stanzas can vary from poem to poem and sometimes even within a poem, producing a free-form style, also called "open form." "Three To's and an Oi" is a mix of stanzaic formality with open-form structure. The poem is formal in that McHugh uses two-line stanzas consistently, from start to end. Although the number of lines in each stanza stays the same, the lengths of the lines vary widely throughout the poem, and there is no set meter or rhyme scheme. The consistency of the stanzas gives the poem a measured feel, which indicates the author's control. The lack of other formal elements has the opposite effect, reinforcing the poem's idea of underlying dread, as if the poet is not able to stay with any prolonged sequence of thought owing to an awareness of the futility of logic.

The mention of "shorter story lines" in line 10 echoes the poem's use of two-line stanzas, with each stanza ending almost as soon as it begins. What keeps the poem from seeming abrupt or halting is the lack of end-stopping: most of the stanzas do not end with punctuation, allowing thoughts to carry over from one stanza to the next. On the page, the two-line stanzas of "Three To's and an Oi" make the poem look as if it will be composed of many diverse ideas, but listeners who hear the poem read aloud would not be as aware of the individual stanzas and would therefore focus more on the coherency of the ideas.

Literary Allusion

An allusion is a reference to an event in history or literature. It can be overtly stated or merely implied. "Three To's and an Oi" contains both types of allusion. The reference to Cassandra is clearly announced in the first word. Readers who are familiar with the story or who look it up when they see it mentioned in the poem can see how the events of Cassandra's life apply to the issues being discussed. It would be difficult to make sense of the first section of the poem without knowing that Cassandra has the ability to foretell her own death and that she cries out in anguish when she knows death is looming.

The last stanza, lines 23 and 24, contains an allusion to the biblical story of Noah and the ark and the flood that destroys the world. "Two by two" is a phrase associated with the way Noah gathers the animals of the earth, assuring that there is a male and a female of each species so that they can reproduce. When this phrase appears with the word "torrents," it is clearly meant to remind readers of the story of the ark. Readers can understand the poem without being reminded of the story from the Bible, but knowing how the story relates to the poem's subject of death and the will to survive makes reading the poem a richer experience.

Historical Context

Academic Poetry

With its references to ancient Greek drama and languages other than English, "Three To's and an Oi" is considered typical of McHugh's intellectual style of poetry. Good poetry has always been built on references to things outside of itself, whether they are references to well-known classical literature or to universal emotions. Readers sometimes feel, however, that having a degree in literature might be useful, if not necessary, in reading a poem such as this one. The connection between higher education and poetry has grown in recent decades. By the end of the twentieth century, it had become rare for poets to support themselves financially with writing alone. Most modern poets work at other jobs for their income. Some may dabble in writing as a hobby, but those who are serious about writing as their life's work manage to hold down two jobs at once—one that pays and one that does not. Most of those poets make their livings through teaching.

The number of would-be poets and fiction writers expanded toward the end of the twentieth century, as did the number of places where they can teach. Colleges and universities have offered creative writing classes as part of their English programs since the 1800s. Although they have helped some young writers find their creative voice, these individual classes have done little to help writers find a career. Nationally recognized literary figures often have held teaching appointments or honorary professorships at universities. At least until the 1950s in the United States, poetry writing was considered a separate entity from academics.

The Writers' Workshop at the University of Iowa is considered the first successful college program focusing strictly on creative writing, that is, poetry and fiction. Started in 1936, in the following decade the workshop was a magnet for famous writers, who came to teach for a semester or to give a lecture. A list of the writers who have been involved with the Iowa Writers' Workshop is practically reproduced in the table of contents of any modern literature textbook, from Robert Frost, Flannery O'Connor, and John Berryman in the early days to Susan Wheeler and Jonathan Franzen later. Graduates of the Writers' Workshop have gone on to create similar programs in creative writing at other institutions.

At the same time that creative writing was growing as a college-level field of study, there was a population explosion in academics. In the years after World War II, college attendance, which had once been limited to people of the upper income brackets, became democratized through the GI Bill of Rights, which paid for the college educations of tens of thousands of veterans who had fought in the war. University English departments expanded, as did the availability of extension sites and community colleges. The influx of new students meant that colleges were able to hire instructors with varied backgrounds. Poets who had not been widely known found employment as college instructors.

Another landmark in the connection between academia and creative writing took place in 1967 with the formation of the Association of Writers and Writing Programs. Founded by fifteen writers who were themselves graduates of writing programs, the association has grown to include 22,000 teachers, writers, and students and 330 college and university writing programs. Based on a philosophy that the practitioners of an art are best suited to teach that art, the Association of Writers and Writing Programs has encouraged the recognition of creative writing as an important part of English programs, which once focused on literature and rhetoric. One result has been the dominance of intellectual poetry such as McHugh's, which draws from academic source material as naturally as it does from other parts of human experience.

Critical Overview

McHugh has been one of the most important American poets for nearly thirty years. Her 1994 compilation, *Hinge and Sign: Poems, 1968–1993*, a collection of works published in her first twenty-five years as a poet as well as new poems, was nominated for a National Book Award and a Pulitzer Prize. Peter Turchi notes in *Ploughshares* that the book "demonstrates depth well beyond the early virtuosity, as well as humility, evidence of a writer who is still listening, still learning." "Three To's and an Oi" comes from McHugh's next collection, *The Father of the Predicaments*, which was welcomed by critics as yet another masterly work. Jane Satterfield, in the *Antioch Review*, calls the book a "welcome fourth compilation" noting that in it "incidents of dramatic and seemingly random stature implode to reveal surprising insights."

To the extent that there has been any critical negativity toward McHugh's writing, it is that it is sometimes too complex and not always accessible to the common reader. As Doris Lynch points out in her review of *The Father of the Predicaments* in *Library Journal*, "McHugh is a modernist and an extremely cerebral poet, so these poems will not please everyone, but readers interested in language poetry will find poems of interest here." Lynch points out that her remarks are not a poor reflection on the poetry but are simply a warning that the book may be better placed in "academic collections and libraries where McHugh has a following."

The Father of the Predicaments has been held in high regard by important publications. As an unsigned review in the Briefly Noted column of the *New Yorker* explains, the book is considered an "accomplished volume of poems, which illuminates how the contradictions and dualities concealed in language both betray and redeem us."

Criticism

David Kelly

David Kelly is an instructor of creative writing and literature. In this essay, he examines how McHugh's specific sense of organization helps the poem explore diverse and even contradictory ideas.

Reading McHugh's work can make one's head spin. Her poetic vision allows her to recognize the contradictions in life that often escape notice, and she is clearly comfortable with accepting these contradictions. As a writer, McHugh has the fluidity with words' inventiveness to present life's paradoxes as naturally as another poet might describe the petals of a flower. The frustrating thing about reading McHugh's poetry is that it *does* encompass paradoxes—at times it seems that McHugh is changing subjects, changing directions, or even taking up the position opposite the one in the preceding stanza. McHugh's control of poetic style is so strong and sure that the average reader is compelled to keep up with her despite the shifts in tone and subject. It may be a trying experience to mentally follow along with McHugh's poetic range, but it is by no means impossible.

"Three To's and an Oi" argues persuasively in a few lines that life is a futile quest to suppress the dread of impending, unavoidable death. The poem suggests that people struggle with themselves throughout their lives to see the truth but also that they struggle equally hard to avoid it. These thoughts are not contradictory, but neither do they provide the harmonious continuity that most readers expect of one continuous poem. The imagery ranges from waking with night dread to floating along on a river listening to the song of a gondolier, and the language ranges from Greek to English to Yiddish. Organization is what makes it possible for all of these variables to coexist in the service of one central idea.

This poem about contradictions is physically divided into two parts, which makes it easy for readers to identify the binary nature of McHugh's inquiry—even the least curious reader should be able to see that because it is split in two, this poem must have two points—and to determine what the two ideas may be. The first eight stanzas, lines 1

through 16, explain the poem's stark view of existence. It begins with Cassandra, the clairvoyant of Greek legend who knows that her death is at hand and that there is nothing she can do about it. The first part continues through deeds and mistakes, ending with the horrible but undeniable idea "We're all about to die."

While pushing the idea of death at the reader, the poem's first section then splits apart into two even smaller ideas, each following naturally from the contemplation of death. The first regards the way in which language breaks down during times of crisis, devolving from the sort of thing that can give intellectual comfort once it is realized that there is no comfort to be had. There is a futility that makes complexity of language (ironically, the kind of language this poem is made of) worthless. Following from the idea of language breakdown is the idea that to avoid the finality of death, humans tend to assign meaning to meaningless expressions of emotion—meaningless not in that they lack value but in that they convey no particular ideas. McHugh objects to translating Cassandra's cry of grief as if she means to express the idea "woe is me," because there is no particular thought meant by *"otototoi,"* just pure emotion.

The foregoing discussion of the three main concepts of the first part of "Three To's and an Oi"—knowledge of death, breakdown of meaning, and the use of meaningless expressions—proceeds in the order in which the concepts derive from one another. In the poem, however, the concepts appear in the reverse order. McHugh goes from language to meaning to dread to obliteration with her early reference to Cassandra, a reference loaded with associations. Readers come into the poem with thoughts already flowing. The more important aspect, though, is that McHugh dissects these ideas methodically and with a calm, even pace. By limiting her stanzas to two lines each, McHugh feeds thoughts to readers in manageable bites. Stringing the ideas together as the poet does helps readers follow the logical implications from one step to the next.

The second part of the poem is less methodical than the first. Ideas bounce around and double over on one another, presenting variations on one theme. This discussion by implication is what readers usually expect of poetry. The second part of "Three To's and an Oi" can stand as a poem on its own, albeit a much more obscure one without the discussion that precedes it.

The main subject of the second part of the poem is "towardness," an idea not even raised in the first part. The second section starts not with to-wardness but with its opposite, with boys and girls "reeling back" from one another after being close, evoking a visual after-passion scene more graphic than anything in the first section. After this dramatic opening, with people snapping back like rubber bands, the rest of the poem follows the slow, mesmeric way with which the world lulls humanity toward the comfort that is rejected in the poem. Music and two-by-two coupling are the examples given for the sorts of things that can make people forget their moments of clarity.

The second part of the poem, like the first, is characterized by opposition. Not only are there boys and girls jumping away from one another, but there is also the contrast of language. The section that begins with "whiplash," "eddy," and "reeling" ends passively with "turn" and "bow." Tomorrow is placed in opposition to today; the gondolier is separated from the tune. After the first part of the poem differentiates preverbal awareness of death and the intellect's struggle to bury that awareness with words, the second part puts the opposition into motion, and suppression always wins. It is not until the last line that the poem brings back the third main idea from the first section—that expressions such as "woe is me" exist in a middling state. These expressions acknowledge the misery of the human condition but acknowledge it with a cliché. *Veyz mir* is often expressed as the hackneyed *oy vey*, which means roughly the same thing as *veyz mir* but has come to be so overused that it has less to do with real woe than with the slightest of discomforts. The expression has no meaning, nor is it an expression, as "*otototoi*" is, of pre-meaning emotion. At least this faint echo brings the poem back to the lament from Cassandra that it starts with.

The other outstanding technique that helps McHugh pack so many complex ideas into "Three To's and an Oi" is her sense of wordplay. Poetry is always about playing with words, but there are not many poets who piece ideas, sounds, and meanings together with as much glee as McHugh does. Readers must always be on the lookout for references that when explored lead the poem into new areas of significance. An example is the use of the word "cataract" in the phrase "clarity from cataract." The word is most often associated with a condition of the eye in which the lens becomes cloudy or opaque, making it difficult to see through. Insisting that one can gain clarity from such a situation is to imply that sight itself is misleading and that one understands more from lack of sight, as the first part of the poem makes a case that one

> *As a writer, McHugh has the fluidity with words' inventiveness to present life's paradoxes as naturally as another poet might describe the petals of a flower."*

understands more from lack of meaning. "Cataract" has a second meaning, though, that is less often applied: a waterfall. This meaning fits perfectly into the water imagery of the second part of the poem, from "eddy" to "gondolier" to "torrents."

Another wording easy to miss is the phrase "it isn't Greek for nothing." The poem is saying primarily that the expression in question, "*otototoi*," does not mean "nothing" in Greek. But McHugh writes the word "nothing" without the quotation marks that would identify it as a definition. This technique opens up the phrase to another meaning. If the meaning of "Greek" as in the common phrase "It's all Greek to me"—in which the word is used to signify something that is unintelligible and cannot be understood—is applied, the poem says, "It isn't unintelligible for nothing." The meaning is that something requires "*otototoi*" to actually be unintelligible, that there is a good reason to say translating the cry as "woe is me" misses the mark.

The title "Three To's and an Oi" is conspicuous because it refers to words that do not actually appear in the poem. One has to look for them. The first place they are found is in the focal word "*otototoi*." The presence of the "to's" and the "oi" is obscured because the "oi" is broken up, so that its "o" comes at the start of Cassandra's expression and its "i" comes at the end. Strained as it is, this interpretation of the title is the more literal one. The more fanciful interpretation entails reading the last stanza, lines 23 and 24, closely. The "to's" are really the "into's" that begin lines 22 through 24, showing the mind being sucked from primordial understanding to intellectual complacence. The *oi* is implied in the phrase *veyz mir*, referring to a standard complaint when things go wrong, *oy vey*. It mirrors and mocks the seriousness of Cassandra's situation, putting her fear of death on the level of

What Do I Read Next?

- The death of Cassandra is only one of the subjects of *Agamemnon* (458 B.C.E.), by the ancient Greek dramatist Aeschylus. The main story concerns the plot by Agamemnon's wife, Clytemnestra, to murder him after he returns from the Trojan War. She takes revenge because Agamemnon has sacrificed their daughter, Iphigenia, for the cause of war.

- McHugh's understanding of the deeper meaning of Greek mythology serves her well in her 2001 translation of *Cyclops*, by Euripides. It is the only Greek satyr play still existing, and McHugh adds to it a sense of wordplay and wit.

- McHugh's poetry has been compared to that of many other contemporary poets. One of the most frequently mentioned is Louise Glück. Readers can get to know Glück's style through poems such as "Parados," which is included in her collection *Ararat* (1994).

- McHugh's style has also been linked to that of the poet Richard Hugo. Readers can learn about the theory behind a poet who works as McHugh does by reading Hugo's *The Triggering Town: Essays and Lectures on Poetry and Writing* (1979).

- The novelist Christa Wolf retells the story of the Trojan War through the eyes of Cassandra in *Cassandra: A Novel and Four Essays* (1984).

any number of other complaints that a person may bemoan.

"Three To's and an Oi" is an example of poetry at its intellectual best. It tackles a philosophical subject always lingering on the edges of human awareness and layers onto one basic truth multiple implications. A less-skilled hand would not be able to pack so much inquiry into the small space that this poem occupies, but McHugh does so with a smoothness and certainty that make it all seem natural. Much in the poem deserves exploration, but much is revealed without great effort. The poem works on so many levels that it has something to say to everyone.

Source: David Kelly, Critical Essay on "Three To's and an Oi," in *Poetry for Students*, Thomson Gale, 2006.

Bruce F. Murphy

In the following review excerpt, Murphy places McHugh within a group of poets who mix prose and poetry in their poems and praises her precision.

More than half a century ago Edmund Wilson argued in the essay "Is Verse a Dying Technique?" that "the technique of prose is inevitably tending more and more to take over the material which had

formerly provided the subjects for compositions in verse." Still timely is Wilson's comment that "the two techniques of writing are beginning to appear, side by side or combined, in a single work," and that "recently the techniques of prose and verse have been getting mixed up at a bewildering rate—with the prose technique steadily gaining."

Heather McHugh is one of those contemporary poets who have written poems that mix prose with poetry—as opposed to writing "prose poems," which are supposed to be prose entirely, while being poetry at the same time. Suffice it to say that McHugh's new book begins with the longish poem, "Not a Prayer," a beautiful work about the death of a woman who seems to be in the final stages of Alzheimer's Disease. The poem is moving partly because of the scenes it contains, such as the moment when "she is lifting one hand / up toward her mouth to take / a great big bite from—ah!—an apple: / very gesture of good health," but there is no apple there, her hand is empty and she "bites down hard" and cannot understand why she fails. On another level, McHugh is interested in the short circuiting of the language centers of the sufferer, the jumbled phrases that, "if anybody / listens long enough," reveal "something terribly intelligible." Yet there's nothing clinical, or removed, or clever about these linguistic observations; it's just the way it is, for this group of people watching this beloved person go out of existence. It also prepares you for the most wrenching moment of the poem, which is not the moment of death, but a farewell to a dear friend in which the shattered mind musters itself for a final leap into intelligibility:

> the voice of Martha in the cellphone saying tinnily:
> "We love you, dearest friend; we love your love of
> life,"
> and leaning back I saw upon that listening face
> some wild emotions, efforts, tearings of intent,
> attempts to speak—and then
> there burst out from her voicebox
> words—or rather, one word cried
> three times—so loud
> the others all came running from
> their rooms: GOODBYE
> GOODBYE GOODBYE

Phrases like "tearings of intent" and the linebreak that creates a hesitation just before "words" in the second stanza show McHugh's hallmark: precision. If, as Wilson said, the "work of the imagination" is "the recreation, in the harmony and logic of words, of the cruel confusion of life," then this is work of a high order.

It is interesting to see why, when she uses prose passages, McHugh's language remains under pressure, powerful. The sentence "We talked our time away around her figure in the silent chair, we missed our Madame Raconteuse," is obviously iambic, and could be rewritten as decasyllabic lines. This is even true of later poems in the book, where McHugh falls back into her usual conceptual mode, for example, "Nano-Knowledge," whose opening, "There, a little right / of Ursus Major, is / the Milky Way," is chopped up on the page but strikes the ear as—dare one say it?—quite regular verse.

Source: Bruce F. Murphy, "Verse Versus Poetry," in *Poetry*, Vol. 177, No. 3, January 2001, pp. 279–86.

Peter Turchi

In the following essay, Turchi provides background on McHugh's life and career and examines her "stress-testing of our language" in her poetry.

Heather McHugh is wired. She is also wireless (see laptop, below), wry, and webbed (spondee .com). She speaks in passionate flurries, seriocomic riffs that only begin to reflect her speed of thought. She annotates as she speaks, offering first and second answers, embellishing and revising and punning. Words are her sparks and her flame.

> *Words are her sparks and her flame."*

"As the world's shyest child" she has written, "I was the one who never spoke in school but who registered, with uncalled-for intensity, every twist of tone and talk; who, at home, went directly to her room to write, because writing proposed a fellow listener, though things seemed quite unspeakable."

Listening to McHugh, one has the sense that she must constantly slow herself down for the sake of others, or, more often, leave her words behind for readers and audiences to unpack. Asked about her earliest ambitions and expectations, she replies: "Ambitions and expectations are different creatures entirely. I expected to be a writer for five years; then, starting at age five, I was a writer. Ambition comes, if I'm not losing my etymological marbles, from going around. I never went around. I went straight, even when stoned."

Born to Canadian parents in San Diego in 1948, McHugh was raised in "rural saltwater Virginia." The writing produced at age five was poetry, which the author bound with ribbon and cardboard covers. Soon after, she attended a four-room primary school (complete with outhouse), then a parochial school. One imagines a young McHugh in the back of the room, intellectual motor revving, barely contained by anything so conventional as a classroom, but she claims otherwise: "Suffice it to say it sometimes seems I am the only writer in America who loved the nuns." She confesses that one of her early influential teachers was "Sister Cletus, who, in her innocence and love of grammar, and despite all snickerers, persisted in her use of the term 'suspended period: We preferred to think of suspended periods as resembling those asterisks in Victorian literature that were followed— nine months later—by babies." From there, McHugh went to a suburban high school that did, in fact, fail to contain her. When a ninth-grade geography teacher advised her against anything so presumptuous as applying to Radcliffe, she determined to get in, ASAP. With near-perfect SATs, she entered the college at age sixteen and graduated cum laude.

At about the same time, The *New Yorker's* Howard Moss "saw something to like" in a poem she had written. She says, "My bet is this: to that early acceptance I owe the whole trail of professional fortuities that followed. The grad-school admissions people [at the University of Denver] loved The *New Yorker* acceptance and put me in a classroom. I learned as I taught. Galassi at Houghton Mifflin liked the inference of forms in my perversities, and didn't mind The *New Yorker* credential, either. I was lucky. Sending something over the transom is like entering a lottery." Soon after graduation from Denver in 1972, she was awarded a MacDowell Colony fellowship and the first of three NEA fellowship grants, which allowed her to complete the book Jonathan Galassi published in 1977.

Dangers featured on its cover a photo of the twenty-nine-year-old poet, who with her high cheekbones and dark coat might have stepped out of a European thriller, standing at the edge of a manhole, and was dedicated "For my lovers." The epigraph, from Browning, is "Our interest's on the dangerous edge of things . . . ," and that focus on the dangerous, the threatening, the unspoken and nearly unspeakable, continues. Although McHugh spends many of her days standing in the front of a classroom, she sometimes sounds like the wicked wit of the back row, the bad girl you'd dare yourself to sit beside.

Just four years after her first collection came her second, *A World of Difference* (Houghton, 1981). One sign of difference was in the acknowledgments: McHugh recognized her mother and her aunts, the source of her "strong will and sense of independence," and her father, a marine biologist, for passing down "his passion for work." Not yet thirty-five, she was publishing regularly in the *New Yorker, APR,* the *Paris Review,* the *Atlantic Monthly,* the *Nation,* and a host of literary journals, including *Ploughshares;* she was also being anthologized. James Tate called her "a wickedly astute critic of our times," while Richard Howard noted that her poems contained "a compassion that is more nearly perfect for it has nothing to do with pity." What keeps McHugh's work from being merely brilliant in its linguistic dexterity and wit is that she marries criticism with compassion and self-reproach; she is no cynic, no simply clever quipper. In the poem "Unspeakable" she moves from observing the death of a close friend to the potentially exotic distraction of a circus, in which an elephant defecates voluminously:

> . . . half the audience, by turns,
> is treated to the sight
> of how the stuff emerges,
> where it lands. The snickers

> are the language of
> the animal the animal offends,
> the one that thinks
> it's different. We can't
> contain ourselves: the laughs
> burst out in spatters from the stands . . .

McHugh is one of our most honored writers, a Chancellor of the Academy of American Poets, a member of the American Academy of Arts and Sciences, recipient of a Guggenheim Fellowship, a Lila Wallace–*Reader's Digest* Writing Award, the PEN/Voelcker Award, and the Folger Library's O. B. Hardison Prize for a poet excelling in teaching. She has received The *Boston Book Review's* Bingham Poetry Prize and the Pollack–Harvard Review Prize and has been a finalist for the National Book Award. She has done service as board member of AWP, panelist selecting the New York State poet, and judge for prizes and awards from the National Poetry Series and Laughlin Prize to, this year, the first Electronic Literature Organization Poetry Prize.

She is also one of our most prolific writers. In addition to her six books of poems, a collection of essays (and another completed), a collaboration with collage artist Tom Phillips, and four volumes of translation—including last year's *Glottal Stop: IO Poems of Paul Celan,* co-translated with her husband, Nikolai Popov, and this year's *Euripides' Cyclops,* co-translated with David Konstan—she is one of the great literary correspondents. Her faxes look like ransom notes, with capitalizations and boldface, exuberant arrows and illustrations, and her e-mails are legendary. "I'll send her a message;" one of her many correspondents recently said, "and I have an answer two minutes later. One day we must have exchanged twenty messages." McHugh claims, "I'm a hermit. I'd rather send an e-mail than myself, but poetry readings pay me more than e-mail does." She is a poet of the twenty-first century, more likely to give a reading from her laptop than from the printed page, but she is also an old-fashioned woman of letters, deeply interested in the world around her, quick to discuss McDonald's (where she often writes) and etymology, orgasms and Epictetus.

When she needs seclusion, she retreats to an island oasis in Maine. Otherwise, she is very much in the world. In addition to her ongoing appointment as Milliman Distinguished Writer-in-Residence at the University of Washington in Seattle, she is a core faculty member of the low-residency M.F.A. Program for Writers at Warren Wilson College, and a visitor to other writing programs around the country. Last summer, she wowed the crowds at the Dodge Poetry Festival. She is a frequent crowd-wower (and received the International Poetry Forum's Charity Randall citation for excellence at public reading), thanks to her verbal agility and wit, her passionate delivery, and her generosity. While she might easily pay the bills lecturing and giving readings, she truly teaches, reading and responding to hundreds of student poems each year, with kindness and modesty born, perhaps, of wariness. Asked about the pros and cons of teaching, she says, "No pro at all. That's not to tout the con. I don't mind fessing. It's prefixing I hate. One of the Waughs, if I remember rightly, is said to have said that the natural enemy of any subject is the professor thereof."

Her new and selected poems, *Hinge & Sign* (Wesleyan, 1994), demonstrates depth well beyond the early virtuosity, as well as humility, evidence of a writer who is still listening, still learning, still, as McHugh says, "finding life strange (this is the extent, and intent, of spirituality in me)." The first of that book's new poems tells of traveling as a Famous Poet in Italy, speaking glibly, and being sobered by the story of Giordano Bruno, "famous / for his eloquence," burned in an iron mask so that he could not speak.

Forced muteness, and the loss of speech and thought that comes with death, is chronicled even more chillingly in the extraordinary first poem of McHugh's most recent collection, *The Father of the Predicaments* (Wesleyan, 1999). "Not a Prayer" tells the story of the death of cellist Raya Garbousova, whom McHugh has called her "soul's mother." Here, the unspeakable takes on new meaning, as Raya loses the ability to communicate, and her family and closest friends lose the ability to understand.

The struggle against the inevitable muting of the individual voice inspires McHugh's stress-testing of our language; and the limitations of words lead her, increasingly, to examinations of the spirit. The keys to both are intelligence, honesty, and precise expression.

"There's a nice story I heard somewhere about Samuel Beckett attending a performance of one of his pieces," McHugh says. "The stage manager was nervously trying to be precise about all the details, desperate to please the famously exacting author. In view of one particular stage direction about a door (that it should be 'imperceptibly ajar'), he was fussing with the aperture, moving the door a half-inch this way, a half-inch that, when he felt the shadow of the master fall across his shoulder. It

was Beckett who had walked up behind him and was watching his exertions. Said Beckett, 'The door should be shut:'

> The stage manager stammered, "But the stage direction says 'ajar.'"
>
> "Yes," replied Beckett, "but it also says 'imperceptibly.'"

This exquisite moment amounts, paradoxically, rather to a confidence in, than a correction of, the hapless manager. For as an act of language within the script of a play, an act in which the adverb effectively erases the adjective, that stage direction was a secret gift to be delivered only to readers (stage managers themselves, among others): it will never be heard aloud in the theatrical performance, nor is it manifest in the object-life of the stage, except as a double negative (the absence of an aperture!).

"That's the kind of language-love I want to be in as long as I can work, a love in which passion and precision conspire, and in which a quiet thrill is communicated from one witting reader to another."

Source: Peter Turchi, "About Heather McHugh," in *Ploughshares*, Vol. 27, No. 1, Spring 2001, pp. 210–16.

Jane Satterfield

In the following review, Satterfield finds the poems in The Father of Predicaments *to be "rooted in a wealth of wit and etymological musings."*

"I have a secret theory," said Heather McHugh, speaking of Ezra Pound's "The Lake Isle" to fellow poets in a recent *Harper's* Forum on poetry, "that most poets, at one time or another, write into their poems their own self-criticism." Much of what McHugh finds worthy in this fractious forebear, "high reference and low irreverence" (for McHugh the "great conjunction" in Pound), is apparent also in her verse. Poetry as secret theory, poetry as self-criticism, poetry as linguistic feast—all are central to McHugh's most recent collection. In this welcome fourth compilation, incidents of dramatic and seemingly random stature implode to reveal surprising insights. Whatever their triggering subject— a loved one's last days spent in a hospital room fluttering in and out of consciousness, a mother who "propels a babystroller," loss, love, doubt, the workings of mind and spirit—the poems are rooted in a wealth of wit and etymological musings; they upend linguistic bedrock, moving toward "radical rewrite, therootretort." The poem as map, then, a tracery of language's historicity. Once the triggering subjects have "plunged beyond" her viewpoint, the poet, "the brooder on / the bench" is prompted to wonder about her relation to the observed world, "a starscape cast / about my minor part" in which definitions and favored assumptions are always under siege. McHugh's deliberations with ancient, unanswerable questions—the predicaments of being alive and staying alive—emerge anew in streetslang and idiom, the "binding / stitcheries of syntax" and "linking mechanisms," which demonstrate McHugh's conviction that words are indeed the engine of perception.

Source: Jane Satterfield, Review of *Father of the Predicaments*, in *Antioch Review*, Vol. 58, No. 2, Spring 2000, p. 247.

Sources

Lynch, Doris, Review of *The Father of the Predicaments*, in *Library Journal*, Vol. 124, No. 13, September 1999, p. 98.

McHugh, Heather, "Three To's and an Oi," in *The Father of the Predicaments*, University Press of New England, 1999, pp. 28–29.

Review of *The Father of the Predicaments*, in the *New Yorker*, November 29, 1999, p. 124.

Satterfield, Jane, Review of *The Father of the Predicaments*, in the *Antioch Review*, Vol. 28, No. 2, Spring 2004, p. 247.

Turchi, Peter, "About Heather McHugh," in *Ploughshares*, Vol. 27, No. 1, Spring 2001, p. 216.

Further Reading

Becker, Robin, "The Poetics of Engagement," in *American Poetry Review*, Vol. 30, No. 6, November/December 2001, pp. 11–15.

In this article, Becker reviews books by eight American women poets, including McHugh, and points out the similarities of the times.

Harvey, Matthea, "Heather McHugh," in *Bomb*, Summer 2005, pp. 82–88.

This interview brings up matters of style and method in McHugh's works that reflect directly on "Three To's and an Oi."

Murphy, Bruce F., "Verse Versus Poetry," in *Poetry*, Vol. 177, No. 3, January 2001, pp. 279–86.

An analysis of prose poetry, a form that McHugh often uses, includes discussion of her overall technique and reputation.

Schapira, Laurie Layton, *The Cassandra Complex: Living with Disbelief*, Inner City Books, 1988.

Schapira takes a Jungian psychological approach to the Cassandra story, looking at how its meaning has changed through age and cultures.

Glossary of Literary Terms

A

Abstract: Used as a noun, the term refers to a short summary or outline of a longer work. As an adjective applied to writing or literary works, abstract refers to words or phrases that name things not knowable through the five senses.

Accent: The emphasis or stress placed on a syllable in poetry. Traditional poetry commonly uses patterns of accented and unaccented syllables (known as feet) that create distinct rhythms. Much modern poetry uses less formal arrangements that create a sense of freedom and spontaneity.

Aestheticism: A literary and artistic movement of the nineteenth century. Followers of the movement believed that art should not be mixed with social, political, or moral teaching. The statement "art for art's sake" is a good summary of aestheticism. The movement had its roots in France, but it gained widespread importance in England in the last half of the nineteenth century, where it helped change the Victorian practice of including moral lessons in literature.

Affective Fallacy: An error in judging the merits or faults of a work of literature. The "error" results from stressing the importance of the work's effect upon the reader—that is, how it makes a reader "feel" emotionally, what it does as a literary work—instead of stressing its inner qualities as a created object, or what it "is."

Age of Johnson: The period in English literature between 1750 and 1798, named after the most prominent literary figure of the age, Samuel Johnson. Works written during this time are noted for their emphasis on "sensibility," or emotional quality. These works formed a transition between the rational works of the Age of Reason, or Neoclassical period, and the emphasis on individual feelings and responses of the Romantic period.

Age of Reason: See *Neoclassicism*

Age of Sensibility: See *Age of Johnson*

Agrarians: A group of Southern American writers of the 1930s and 1940s who fostered an economic and cultural program for the South based on agriculture, in opposition to the industrial society of the North. The term can refer to any group that promotes the value of farm life and agricultural society.

Alexandrine Meter: See *Meter*

Allegory: A narrative technique in which characters representing things or abstract ideas are used to convey a message or teach a lesson. Allegory is typically used to teach moral, ethical, or religious lessons but is sometimes used for satiric or political purposes.

Alliteration: A poetic device where the first consonant sounds or any vowel sounds in words or syllables are repeated.

Allusion: A reference to a familiar literary or historical person or event, used to make an idea more easily understood.

Amerind Literature: The writing and oral traditions of Native Americans. Native American literature was originally passed on by word of mouth, so it consisted largely of stories and events that were easily memorized. Amerind prose is often rhythmic like poetry because it was recited to the beat of a ceremonial drum.

Analogy: A comparison of two things made to explain something unfamiliar through its similarities to something familiar, or to prove one point based on the acceptedness of another. Similes and metaphors are types of analogies.

Anapest: See *Foot*

Angry Young Men: A group of British writers of the 1950s whose work expressed bitterness and disillusionment with society. Common to their work is an antihero who rebels against a corrupt social order and strives for personal integrity.

Anthropomorphism: The presentation of animals or objects in human shape or with human characteristics. The term is derived from the Greek word for "human form."

Antimasque: See *Masque*

Antithesis: The antithesis of something is its direct opposite. In literature, the use of antithesis as a figure of speech results in two statements that show a contrast through the balancing of two opposite ideas. Technically, it is the second portion of the statement that is defined as the "antithesis"; the first portion is the "thesis."

Apocrypha: Writings tentatively attributed to an author but not proven or universally accepted to be their works. The term was originally applied to certain books of the Bible that were not considered inspired and so were not included in the "sacred canon."

Apollonian and Dionysian: The two impulses believed to guide authors of dramatic tragedy. The Apollonian impulse is named after Apollo, the Greek god of light and beauty and the symbol of intellectual order. The Dionysian impulse is named after Dionysus, the Greek god of wine and the symbol of the unrestrained forces of nature. The Apollonian impulse is to create a rational, harmonious world, while the Dionysian is to express the irrational forces of personality.

Apostrophe: A statement, question, or request addressed to an inanimate object or concept or to a nonexistent or absent person.

Archetype: The word archetype is commonly used to describe an original pattern or model from which all other things of the same kind are made. This term was introduced to literary criticism from the psychology of Carl Jung. It expresses Jung's theory that behind every person's "unconscious," or repressed memories of the past, lies the "collective unconscious" of the human race: memories of the countless typical experiences of our ancestors. These memories are said to prompt illogical associations that trigger powerful emotions in the reader. Often, the emotional process is primitive, even primordial. Archetypes are the literary images that grow out of the "collective unconscious." They appear in literature as incidents and plots that repeat basic patterns of life. They may also appear as stereotyped characters.

Argument: The argument of a work is the author's subject matter or principal idea.

Art for Art's Sake: See *Aestheticism*

Assonance: The repetition of similar vowel sounds in poetry.

Audience: The people for whom a piece of literature is written. Authors usually write with a certain audience in mind, for example, children, members of a religious or ethnic group, or colleagues in a professional field. The term "audience" also applies to the people who gather to see or hear any performance, including plays, poetry readings, speeches, and concerts.

Automatic Writing: Writing carried out without a preconceived plan in an effort to capture every random thought. Authors who engage in automatic writing typically do not revise their work, preferring instead to preserve the revealed truth and beauty of spontaneous expression.

Avant-garde: A French term meaning "vanguard." It is used in literary criticism to describe new writing that rejects traditional approaches to literature in favor of innovations in style or content.

B

Ballad: A short poem that tells a simple story and has a repeated refrain. Ballads were originally intended to be sung. Early ballads, known as folk ballads, were passed down through generations, so their authors are often unknown. Later ballads composed by known authors are called literary ballads.

Baroque: A term used in literary criticism to describe literature that is complex or ornate in style or diction. Baroque works typically express tension, anxiety, and violent emotion. The term "Baroque Age" designates a period in Western European literature beginning in the late sixteenth century and ending about one hundred years later.

Works of this period often mirror the qualities of works more generally associated with the label "baroque" and sometimes feature elaborate conceits.

Baroque Age: See *Baroque*

Baroque Period: See *Baroque*

Beat Generation: See *Beat Movement*

Beat Movement: A period featuring a group of American poets and novelists of the 1950s and 1960s—including Jack Kerouac, Allen Ginsberg, Gregory Corso, William S. Burroughs, and Lawrence Ferlinghetti—who rejected established social and literary values. Using such techniques as stream-of-consciousness writing and jazz-influenced free verse and focusing on unusual or abnormal states of mind—generated by religious ecstasy or the use of drugs—the Beat writers aimed to create works that were unconventional in both form and subject matter.

Beat Poets: See *Beat Movement*

Beats, The: See *Beat Movement*

Belles-lettres: A French term meaning "fine letters" or "beautiful writing." It is often used as a synonym for literature, typically referring to imaginative and artistic rather than scientific or expository writing. Current usage sometimes restricts the meaning to light or humorous writing and appreciative essays about literature.

Black Aesthetic Movement: A period of artistic and literary development among African Americans in the 1960s and early 1970s. This was the first major African American artistic movement since the Harlem Renaissance and was closely paralleled by the civil rights and black power movements. The black aesthetic writers attempted to produce works of art that would be meaningful to the black masses. Key figures in black aesthetics included one of its founders, poet and playwright Amiri Baraka, formerly known as LeRoi Jones; poet and essayist Haki R. Madhubuti, formerly Don L. Lee; poet and playwright Sonia Sanchez; and dramatist Ed Bullins.

Black Arts Movement: See *Black Aesthetic Movement*

Black Comedy: See *Black Humor*

Black Humor: Writing that places grotesque elements side by side with humorous ones in an attempt to shock the reader, forcing him or her to laugh at the horrifying reality of a disordered world.

Black Mountain School: Black Mountain College and three of its instructors—Robert Creeley, Robert Duncan, and Charles Olson—were all influential in projective verse. Today poets working in projective verse are referred to as members of the Black Mountain school.

Blank Verse: Loosely, any unrhymed poetry, but more generally, unrhymed iambic pentameter verse (composed of lines of five two-syllable feet with the first syllable accented, the second unaccented). Blank verse has been used by poets since the Renaissance for its flexibility and its graceful, dignified tone.

Bloomsbury Group: A group of English writers, artists, and intellectuals who held informal artistic and philosophical discussions in Bloomsbury, a district of London, from around 1907 to the early 1930s. The Bloomsbury Group held no uniform philosophical beliefs but did commonly express an aversion to moral prudery and a desire for greater social tolerance.

Bon Mot: A French term meaning "good word." A *bon mot* is a witty remark or clever observation.

Breath Verse: See *Projective Verse*

Burlesque: Any literary work that uses exaggeration to make its subject appear ridiculous, either by treating a trivial subject with profound seriousness or by treating a dignified subject frivolously. The word "burlesque" may also be used as an adjective, as in "burlesque show," to mean "striptease act."

C

Cadence: The natural rhythm of language caused by the alternation of accented and unaccented syllables. Much modern poetry—notably free verse—deliberately manipulates cadence to create complex rhythmic effects.

Caesura: A pause in a line of poetry, usually occurring near the middle. It typically corresponds to a break in the natural rhythm or sense of the line but is sometimes shifted to create special meanings or rhythmic effects.

Canzone: A short Italian or Provencal lyric poem, commonly about love and often set to music. The *canzone* has no set form but typically contains five or six stanzas made up of seven to twenty lines of eleven syllables each. A shorter, five- to ten-line "envoy," or concluding stanza, completes the poem.

Carpe Diem: A Latin term meaning "seize the day." This is a traditional theme of poetry, especially lyrics. A *carpe diem* poem advises the reader or the person it addresses to live for today and enjoy the pleasures of the moment.

Catharsis: The release or purging of unwanted emotions—specifically fear and pity—brought about by exposure to art. The term was first used by the Greek philosopher Aristotle in his *Poetics* to refer to the desired effect of tragedy on spectators.

Celtic Renaissance: A period of Irish literary and cultural history at the end of the nineteenth century. Followers of the movement aimed to create a romantic vision of Celtic myth and legend. The most significant works of the Celtic Renaissance typically present a dreamy, unreal world, usually in reaction against the reality of contemporary problems.

Celtic Twilight: See *Celtic Renaissance*

Character: Broadly speaking, a person in a literary work. The actions of characters are what constitute the plot of a story, novel, or poem. There are numerous types of characters, ranging from simple, stereotypical figures to intricate, multifaceted ones. In the techniques of anthropomorphism and personification, animals—and even places or things—can assume aspects of character. "Characterization" is the process by which an author creates vivid, believable characters in a work of art. This may be done in a variety of ways, including (1) direct description of the character by the narrator; (2) the direct presentation of the speech, thoughts, or actions of the character; and (3) the responses of other characters to the character. The term "character" also refers to a form originated by the ancient Greek writer Theophrastus that later became popular in the seventeenth and eighteenth centuries. It is a short essay or sketch of a person who prominently displays a specific attribute or quality, such as miserliness or ambition.

Characterization: See *Character*

Classical: In its strictest definition in literary criticism, classicism refers to works of ancient Greek or Roman literature. The term may also be used to describe a literary work of recognized importance (a "classic") from any time period or literature that exhibits the traits of classicism.

Classicism: A term used in literary criticism to describe critical doctrines that have their roots in ancient Greek and Roman literature, philosophy, and art. Works associated with classicism typically exhibit restraint on the part of the author, unity of design and purpose, clarity, simplicity, logical organization, and respect for tradition.

Colloquialism: A word, phrase, or form of pronunciation that is acceptable in casual conversation but not in formal, written communication. It is considered more acceptable than slang.

Complaint: A lyric poem, popular in the Renaissance, in which the speaker expresses sorrow about his or her condition. Typically, the speaker's sadness is caused by an unresponsive lover, but some complaints cite other sources of unhappiness, such as poverty or fate.

Conceit: A clever and fanciful metaphor, usually expressed through elaborate and extended comparison, that presents a striking parallel between two seemingly dissimilar things—for example, elaborately comparing a beautiful woman to an object like a garden or the sun. The conceit was a popular device throughout the Elizabethan Age and Baroque Age and was the principal technique of the seventeenth-century English metaphysical poets. This usage of the word conceit is unrelated to the best-known definition of conceit as an arrogant attitude or behavior.

Concrete: Concrete is the opposite of abstract, and refers to a thing that actually exists or a description that allows the reader to experience an object or concept with the senses.

Concrete Poetry: Poetry in which visual elements play a large part in the poetic effect. Punctuation marks, letters, or words are arranged on a page to form a visual design: a cross, for example, or a bumblebee.

Confessional Poetry: A form of poetry in which the poet reveals very personal, intimate, sometimes shocking information about himself or herself.

Connotation: The impression that a word gives beyond its defined meaning. Connotations may be universally understood or may be significant only to a certain group.

Consonance: Consonance occurs in poetry when words appearing at the ends of two or more verses have similar final consonant sounds but have final vowel sounds that differ, as with "stuff" and "off."

Convention: Any widely accepted literary device, style, or form.

Corrido: A Mexican ballad.

Couplet: Two lines of poetry with the same rhyme and meter, often expressing a complete and self-contained thought.

Criticism: The systematic study and evaluation of literary works, usually based on a specific method or set of principles. An important part of literary studies since ancient times, the practice of criticism has given rise to numerous theories, methods, and "schools," sometimes producing conflicting, even contradictory, interpretations of literature in general as well as of individual works. Even such basic issues as what constitutes a poem or a novel have been the subject of much criticism over the centuries.

D

Dactyl: See *Foot*

Dadaism: A protest movement in art and literature founded by Tristan Tzara in 1916. Followers of the movement expressed their outrage at the destruction brought about by World War I by revolting against numerous forms of social convention. The Dadaists presented works marked by calculated madness and flamboyant nonsense. They stressed total freedom of expression, commonly through primitive displays of emotion and illogical, often senseless, poetry. The movement ended shortly after the war, when it was replaced by surrealism.

Decadent: See *Decadents*

Decadents: The followers of a nineteenth-century literary movement that had its beginnings in French aestheticism. Decadent literature displays a fascination with perverse and morbid states; a search for novelty and sensation—the "new thrill"; a preoccupation with mysticism; and a belief in the senselessness of human existence. The movement is closely associated with the doctrine Art for Art's Sake. The term "decadence" is sometimes used to denote a decline in the quality of art or literature following a period of greatness.

Deconstruction: A method of literary criticism developed by Jacques Derrida and characterized by multiple conflicting interpretations of a given work. Deconstructionists consider the impact of the language of a work and suggest that the true meaning of the work is not necessarily the meaning that the author intended.

Deduction: The process of reaching a conclusion through reasoning from general premises to a specific premise.

Denotation: The definition of a word, apart from the impressions or feelings it creates in the reader.

Diction: The selection and arrangement of words in a literary work. Either or both may vary depending on the desired effect. There are four general types of diction: "formal," used in scholarly or lofty writing; "informal," used in relaxed but educated conversation; "colloquial," used in everyday speech; and "slang," containing newly coined words and other terms not accepted in formal usage.

Didactic: A term used to describe works of literature that aim to teach some moral, religious, political, or practical lesson. Although didactic elements are often found in artistically pleasing works, the term "didactic" usually refers to literature in which the message is more important than the form. The term may also be used to criticize a work that the critic finds "overly didactic," that is, heavy-handed in its delivery of a lesson.

Dimeter: See *Meter*

Dionysian: See *Apollonian and Dionysian*

Discordia concours: A Latin phrase meaning "discord in harmony." The term was coined by the eighteenth-century English writer Samuel Johnson to describe "a combination of dissimilar images or discovery of occult resemblances in things apparently unlike." Johnson created the expression by reversing a phrase by the Latin poet Horace.

Dissonance: A combination of harsh or jarring sounds, especially in poetry. Although such combinations may be accidental, poets sometimes intentionally make them to achieve particular effects. Dissonance is also sometimes used to refer to close but not identical rhymes. When this is the case, the word functions as a synonym for consonance.

Double Entendre: A corruption of a French phrase meaning "double meaning." The term is used to indicate a word or phrase that is deliberately ambiguous, especially when one of the meanings is risque or improper.

Draft: Any preliminary version of a written work. An author may write dozens of drafts which are revised to form the final work, or he or she may write only one, with few or no revisions.

Dramatic Monologue: See *Monologue*

Dramatic Poetry: Any lyric work that employs elements of drama such as dialogue, conflict, or characterization, but excluding works that are intended for stage presentation.

Dream Allegory: See *Dream Vision*

Dream Vision: A literary convention, chiefly of the Middle Ages. In a dream vision a story is presented as a literal dream of the narrator. This device was commonly used to teach moral and religious lessons.

E

Eclogue: In classical literature, a poem featuring rural themes and structured as a dialogue among shepherds. Eclogues often took specific poetic forms, such as elegies or love poems. Some were written as the soliloquy of a shepherd. In later centuries, "eclogue" came to refer to any poem that was in the pastoral tradition or that had a dialogue or monologue structure.

Edwardian: Describes cultural conventions identified with the period of the reign of Edward VII of England (1901–1910). Writers of the Edwardian Age typically displayed a strong reaction against the propriety and conservatism of the Victorian Age. Their work often exhibits distrust of authority in religion, politics, and art and expresses strong doubts about the soundness of conventional values.

Edwardian Age: See *Edwardian*

Electra Complex: A daughter's amorous obsession with her father.

Elegy: A lyric poem that laments the death of a person or the eventual death of all people. In a conventional elegy, set in a classical world, the poet and subject are spoken of as shepherds. In modern criticism, the word elegy is often used to refer to a poem that is melancholy or mournfully contemplative.

Elizabethan Age: A period of great economic growth, religious controversy, and nationalism closely associated with the reign of Elizabeth I of England (1558–1603). The Elizabethan Age is considered a part of the general renaissance—that is, the flowering of arts and literature—that took place in Europe during the fourteenth through sixteenth centuries. The era is considered the golden age of English literature. The most important dramas in English and a great deal of lyric poetry were produced during this period, and modern English criticism began around this time.

Empathy: A sense of shared experience, including emotional and physical feelings, with someone or something other than oneself. Empathy is often used to describe the response of a reader to a literary character.

English Sonnet: See *Sonnet*

Enjambment: The running over of the sense and structure of a line of verse or a couplet into the following verse or couplet.

Enlightenment, The: An eighteenth-century philosophical movement. It began in France but had a wide impact throughout Europe and America. Thinkers of the Enlightenment valued reason and believed that both the individual and society could achieve a state of perfection. Corresponding to this essentially humanist vision was a resistance to religious authority.

Epic: A long narrative poem about the adventures of a hero of great historic or legendary importance. The setting is vast and the action is often given cosmic significance through the intervention of supernatural forces such as gods, angels, or demons. Epics are typically written in a classical style of grand simplicity with elaborate metaphors and allusions that enhance the symbolic importance of a hero's adventures.

Epic Simile: See *Homeric Simile*

Epigram: A saying that makes the speaker's point quickly and concisely.

Epilogue: A concluding statement or section of a literary work. In dramas, particularly those of the seventeenth and eighteenth centuries, the epilogue is a closing speech, often in verse, delivered by an actor at the end of a play and spoken directly to the audience.

Epiphany: A sudden revelation of truth inspired by a seemingly trivial incident.

Epitaph: An inscription on a tomb or tombstone, or a verse written on the occasion of a person's death. Epitaphs may be serious or humorous.

Epithalamion: A song or poem written to honor and commemorate a marriage ceremony.

Epithalamium: See *Epithalamion*

Epithet: A word or phrase, often disparaging or abusive, that expresses a character trait of someone or something.

Erziehungsroman: See *Bildungsroman*

Essay: A prose composition with a focused subject of discussion. The term was coined by Michel de Montaigne to describe his 1580 collection of brief, informal reflections on himself and on various topics relating to human nature. An essay can also be a long, systematic discourse.

Existentialism: A predominantly twentieth-century philosophy concerned with the nature and perception of human existence. There are two major strains of existentialist thought: atheistic and Christian. Followers of atheistic existentialism believe that the individual is alone in a godless universe and that the basic human condition is one of suffering and loneliness. Nevertheless, because there are no fixed values, individuals can create their own characters—indeed, they can shape themselves—through the exercise of free will. The atheistic strain culminates in and is popularly associated with the works of Jean-Paul Sartre. The Christian existentialists, on the other hand, believe that only in God may people find freedom from life's anguish. The two strains hold certain beliefs in common: that existence cannot be fully understood or described through empirical effort; that anguish is a universal element of life; that individuals must bear responsibility for their actions; and that there is no common standard of behavior or perception for religious and ethical matters.

Expatriates: See *Expatriatism*

Expatriatism: The practice of leaving one's country to live for an extended period in another country.

Exposition: Writing intended to explain the nature of an idea, thing, or theme. Expository writing is often combined with description, narration, or argument. In dramatic writing, the exposition is the introductory material which presents the characters, setting, and tone of the play.

Expressionism: An indistinct literary term, originally used to describe an early twentieth-century school of German painting. The term applies to almost any mode of unconventional, highly subjective writing that distorts reality in some way.

Extended Monologue: See *Monologue*

F

Feet: See *Foot*

Feminine Rhyme: See *Rhyme*

Fiction: Any story that is the product of imagination rather than a documentation of fact. Characters and events in such narratives may be based in real life but their ultimate form and configuration is a creation of the author.

Figurative Language: A technique in writing in which the author temporarily interrupts the order, construction, or meaning of the writing for a particular effect. This interruption takes the form of one or more figures of speech such as hyperbole, irony, or simile. Figurative language is the opposite of literal language, in which every word is truthful, accurate, and free of exaggeration or embellishment.

Figures of Speech: Writing that differs from customary conventions for construction, meaning, order, or significance for the purpose of a special meaning or effect. There are two major types of figures of speech: rhetorical figures, which do not make changes in the meaning of the words; and tropes, which do.

Fin de siecle: A French term meaning "end of the century." The term is used to denote the last decade of the nineteenth century, a transition period when writers and other artists abandoned old conventions and looked for new techniques and objectives.

First Person: See *Point of View*

Folk Ballad: See *Ballad*

Folklore: Traditions and myths preserved in a culture or group of people. Typically, these are passed on by word of mouth in various forms—such as legends, songs, and proverbs—or preserved in customs and ceremonies. This term was first used by W. J. Thoms in 1846.

Folktale: A story originating in oral tradition. Folktales fall into a variety of categories, including legends, ghost stories, fairy tales, fables, and anecdotes based on historical figures and events.

Foot: The smallest unit of rhythm in a line of poetry. In English-language poetry, a foot is typically one accented syllable combined with one or two unaccented syllables.

Form: The pattern or construction of a work which identifies its genre and distinguishes it from other genres.

Formalism: In literary criticism, the belief that literature should follow prescribed rules of construction, such as those that govern the sonnet form.

Fourteener Meter: See *Meter*

Free Verse: Poetry that lacks regular metrical and rhyme patterns but that tries to capture the cadences of everyday speech. The form allows a poet to exploit a variety of rhythmical effects within a single poem.

Futurism: A flamboyant literary and artistic movement that developed in France, Italy, and Russia from 1908 through the 1920s. Futurist theater and poetry abandoned traditional literary forms. In their place, followers of the movement attempted to achieve total freedom of expression through bizarre imagery and deformed or newly invented words. The Futurists were self-consciously modern artists who attempted to incorporate the appearances and sounds of modern life into their work.

G

Genre: A category of literary work. In critical theory, genre may refer to both the content of a given work—tragedy, comedy, pastoral—and to its form, such as poetry, novel, or drama.

Genteel Tradition: A term coined by critic George Santayana to describe the literary practice of certain late nineteenth-century American writers, especially New Englanders. Followers of the Genteel

Tradition emphasized conventionality in social, religious, moral, and literary standards.

Georgian Age: See *Georgian Poets*

Georgian Period: See *Georgian Poets*

Georgian Poets: A loose grouping of English poets during the years 1912–1922. The Georgians reacted against certain literary schools and practices, especially Victorian wordiness, turn-of-the-century aestheticism, and contemporary urban realism. In their place, the Georgians embraced the nineteenth-century poetic practices of William Wordsworth and the other Lake Poets.

Georgic: A poem about farming and the farmer's way of life, named from Virgil's *Georgics.*

Gilded Age: A period in American history during the 1870s characterized by political corruption and materialism. A number of important novels of social and political criticism were written during this time.

Gothic: See *Gothicism*

Gothicism: In literary criticism, works characterized by a taste for the medieval or morbidly attractive. A gothic novel prominently features elements of horror, the supernatural, gloom, and violence: clanking chains, terror, charnel houses, ghosts, medieval castles, and mysteriously slamming doors. The term "gothic novel" is also applied to novels that lack elements of the traditional Gothic setting but that create a similar atmosphere of terror or dread.

Graveyard School: A group of eighteenth-century English poets who wrote long, picturesque meditations on death. Their works were designed to cause the reader to ponder immortality.

Great Chain of Being: The belief that all things and creatures in nature are organized in a hierarchy from inanimate objects at the bottom to God at the top. This system of belief was popular in the seventeenth and eighteenth centuries.

Grotesque: In literary criticism, the subject matter of a work or a style of expression characterized by exaggeration, deformity, freakishness, and disorder. The grotesque often includes an element of comic absurdity.

H

Haiku: The shortest form of Japanese poetry, constructed in three lines of five, seven, and five syllables respectively. The message of a *haiku* poem usually centers on some aspect of spirituality and provokes an emotional response in the reader.

Half Rhyme: See *Consonance*

Harlem Renaissance: The Harlem Renaissance of the 1920s is generally considered the first significant movement of black writers and artists in the United States. During this period, new and established black writers published more fiction and poetry than ever before, the first influential black literary journals were established, and black authors and artists received their first widespread recognition and serious critical appraisal. Among the major writers associated with this period are Claude McKay, Jean Toomer, Countee Cullen, Langston Hughes, Arna Bontemps, Nella Larsen, and Zora Neale Hurston.

Hellenism: Imitation of ancient Greek thought or styles. Also, an approach to life that focuses on the growth and development of the intellect. "Hellenism" is sometimes used to refer to the belief that reason can be applied to examine all human experience.

Heptameter: See *Meter*

Hero/Heroine: The principal sympathetic character (male or female) in a literary work. Heroes and heroines typically exhibit admirable traits: idealism, courage, and integrity, for example.

Heroic Couplet: A rhyming couplet written in iambic pentameter (a verse with five iambic feet).

Heroic Line: The meter and length of a line of verse in epic or heroic poetry. This varies by language and time period.

Heroine: See *Hero/Heroine*

Hexameter: See *Meter*

Historical Criticism: The study of a work based on its impact on the world of the time period in which it was written.

Hokku: See *Haiku*

Holocaust: See *Holocaust Literature*

Holocaust Literature: Literature influenced by or written about the Holocaust of World War II. Such literature includes true stories of survival in concentration camps, escape, and life after the war, as well as fictional works and poetry.

Homeric Simile: An elaborate, detailed comparison written as a simile many lines in length.

Horatian Satire: See *Satire*

Humanism: A philosophy that places faith in the dignity of humankind and rejects the medieval perception of the individual as a weak, fallen creature. "Humanists" typically believe in the perfectibility of human nature and view reason and education as the means to that end.

Humors: Mentions of the humors refer to the ancient Greek theory that a person's health and personality were determined by the balance of four basic fluids in the body: blood, phlegm, yellow bile, and black bile. A dominance of any fluid would cause extremes in behavior. An excess of blood created a sanguine person who was joyful, aggressive, and passionate; a phlegmatic person was shy, fearful, and sluggish; too much yellow bile led to a choleric temperament characterized by impatience, anger, bitterness, and stubbornness; and excessive black bile created melancholy, a state of laziness, gluttony, and lack of motivation.

Humours: See *Humors*

Hyperbole: In literary criticism, deliberate exaggeration used to achieve an effect.

I

Iamb: See *Foot*

Idiom: A word construction or verbal expression closely associated with a given language.

Image: A concrete representation of an object or sensory experience. Typically, such a representation helps evoke the feelings associated with the object or experience itself. Images are either "literal" or "figurative." Literal images are especially concrete and involve little or no extension of the obvious meaning of the words used to express them. Figurative images do not follow the literal meaning of the words exactly. Images in literature are usually visual, but the term "image" can also refer to the representation of any sensory experience.

Imagery: The array of images in a literary work. Also, figurative language.

Imagism: An English and American poetry movement that flourished between 1908 and 1917. The Imagists used precise, clearly presented images in their works. They also used common, everyday speech and aimed for conciseness, concrete imagery, and the creation of new rhythms.

In medias res: A Latin term meaning "in the middle of things." It refers to the technique of beginning a story at its midpoint and then using various flashback devices to reveal previous action.

Induction: The process of reaching a conclusion by reasoning from specific premises to form a general premise. Also, an introductory portion of a work of literature, especially a play.

Intentional Fallacy: The belief that judgments of a literary work based solely on an author's stated or implied intentions are false and misleading. Critics who believe in the concept of the intentional fallacy typically argue that the work itself is sufficient matter for interpretation, even though they may concede that an author's statement of purpose can be useful.

Interior Monologue: A narrative technique in which characters' thoughts are revealed in a way that appears to be uncontrolled by the author. The interior monologue typically aims to reveal the inner self of a character. It portrays emotional experiences as they occur at both a conscious and unconscious level. Images are often used to represent sensations or emotions.

Internal Rhyme: Rhyme that occurs within a single line of verse.

Irish Literary Renaissance: A late nineteenth- and early twentieth-century movement in Irish literature. Members of the movement aimed to reduce the influence of British culture in Ireland and create an Irish national literature.

Irony: In literary criticism, the effect of language in which the intended meaning is the opposite of what is stated.

Italian Sonnet: See *Sonnet*

J

Jacobean Age: The period of the reign of James I of England (1603–1625). The early literature of this period reflected the worldview of the Elizabethan Age, but a darker, more cynical attitude steadily grew in the art and literature of the Jacobean Age. This was an important time for English drama and poetry.

Jargon: Language that is used or understood only by a select group of people. Jargon may refer to terminology used in a certain profession, such as computer jargon, or it may refer to any nonsensical language that is not understood by most people.

Journalism: Writing intended for publication in a newspaper or magazine, or for broadcast on a radio or television program featuring news, sports, entertainment, or other timely material.

K

Knickerbocker Group: A somewhat indistinct group of New York writers of the first half of the nineteenth century. Members of the group were linked only by location and a common theme: New York life.

Kunstlerroman: See *Bildungsroman*

L

Lais: See *Lay*

Lake Poets: See *Lake School*

Lake School: These poets all lived in the Lake District of England at the turn of the nineteenth century. As a group, they followed no single "school" of thought or literary practice, although their works were uniformly disparaged by the *Edinburgh Review*.

Lay: A song or simple narrative poem. The form originated in medieval France. Early French *lais* were often based on the Celtic legends and other tales sung by Breton minstrels—thus the name of the "Breton lay." In fourteenth-century England, the term "lay" was used to describe short narratives written in imitation of the Breton lays.

Leitmotiv: See *Motif*

Literal Language: An author uses literal language when he or she writes without exaggerating or embellishing the subject matter and without any tools of figurative language.

Literary Ballad: See *Ballad*

Literature: Literature is broadly defined as any written or spoken material, but the term most often refers to creative works.

Lost Generation: A term first used by Gertrude Stein to describe the post-World War I generation of American writers: men and women haunted by a sense of betrayal and emptiness brought about by the destructiveness of the war.

Lyric Poetry: A poem expressing the subjective feelings and personal emotions of the poet. Such poetry is melodic, since it was originally accompanied by a lyre in recitals. Most Western poetry in the twentieth century may be classified as lyrical.

M

Mannerism: Exaggerated, artificial adherence to a literary manner or style. Also, a popular style of the visual arts of late sixteenth-century Europe that was marked by elongation of the human form and by intentional spatial distortion. Literary works that are self-consciously high-toned and artistic are often said to be "mannered."

Masculine Rhyme: See *Rhyme*

Measure: The foot, verse, or time sequence used in a literary work, especially a poem. Measure is often used somewhat incorrectly as a synonym for meter.

Metaphor: A figure of speech that expresses an idea through the image of another object. Metaphors suggest the essence of the first object by identifying it with certain qualities of the second object.

Metaphysical Conceit: See *Conceit*

Metaphysical Poetry: The body of poetry produced by a group of seventeenth-century English writers called the "Metaphysical Poets." The group includes John Donne and Andrew Marvell. The Metaphysical Poets made use of everyday speech, intellectual analysis, and unique imagery. They aimed to portray the ordinary conflicts and contradictions of life. Their poems often took the form of an argument, and many of them emphasize physical and religious love as well as the fleeting nature of life. Elaborate conceits are typical in metaphysical poetry.

Metaphysical Poets: See *Metaphysical Poetry*

Meter: In literary criticism, the repetition of sound patterns that creates a rhythm in poetry. The patterns are based on the number of syllables and the presence and absence of accents. The unit of rhythm in a line is called a foot. Types of meter are classified according to the number of feet in a line. These are the standard English lines: Monometer, one foot; Dimeter, two feet; Trimeter, three feet; Tetrameter, four feet; Pentameter, five feet; Hexameter, six feet (also called the Alexandrine); Heptameter, seven feet (also called the "Fourteener" when the feet are iambic).

Modernism: Modern literary practices. Also, the principles of a literary school that lasted from roughly the beginning of the twentieth century until the end of World War II. Modernism is defined by its rejection of the literary conventions of the nineteenth century and by its opposition to conventional morality, taste, traditions, and economic values.

Monologue: A composition, written or oral, by a single individual. More specifically, a speech given by a single individual in a drama or other public entertainment. It has no set length, although it is usually several or more lines long.

Monometer: See *Meter*

Mood: The prevailing emotions of a work or of the author in his or her creation of the work. The mood of a work is not always what might be expected based on its subject matter.

Motif: A theme, character type, image, metaphor, or other verbal element that recurs throughout a single work of literature or occurs in a number of different works over a period of time.

Motiv: See *Motif*

Muckrakers: An early twentieth-century group of American writers. Typically, their works exposed the wrongdoings of big business and government in the United States.

Muses: Nine Greek mythological goddesses, the daughters of Zeus and Mnemosyne (Memory). Each muse patronized a specific area of the liberal arts and sciences. Calliope presided over epic poetry, Clio over history, Erato over love poetry, Euterpe over music or lyric poetry, Melpomene over tragedy, Polyhymnia over hymns to the gods, Terpsichore over dance, Thalia over comedy, and Urania over astronomy. Poets and writers traditionally made appeals to the Muses for inspiration in their work.

Myth: An anonymous tale emerging from the traditional beliefs of a culture or social unit. Myths use supernatural explanations for natural phenomena. They may also explain cosmic issues like creation and death. Collections of myths, known as mythologies, are common to all cultures and nations, but the best-known myths belong to the Norse, Roman, and Greek mythologies.

N

Narration: The telling of a series of events, real or invented. A narration may be either a simple narrative, in which the events are recounted chronologically, or a narrative with a plot, in which the account is given in a style reflecting the author's artistic concept of the story. Narration is sometimes used as a synonym for "storyline."

Narrative: A verse or prose accounting of an event or sequence of events, real or invented. The term is also used as an adjective in the sense "method of narration." For example, in literary criticism, the expression "narrative technique" usually refers to the way the author structures and presents his or her story.

Narrative Poetry: A nondramatic poem in which the author tells a story. Such poems may be of any length or level of complexity.

Narrator: The teller of a story. The narrator may be the author or a character in the story through whom the author speaks.

Naturalism: A literary movement of the late nineteenth and early twentieth centuries. The movement's major theorist, French novelist Emile Zola, envisioned a type of fiction that would examine human life with the objectivity of scientific inquiry. The Naturalists typically viewed human beings as either the products of "biological determinism," ruled by hereditary instincts and engaged in an endless struggle for survival, or as the products of "socioeconomic determinism," ruled by social and economic forces beyond their control. In their works, the Naturalists generally ignored the highest levels of society and focused on degradation: poverty, alcoholism, prostitution, insanity, and disease.

Negritude: A literary movement based on the concept of a shared cultural bond on the part of black Africans, wherever they may be in the world. It traces its origins to the former French colonies of Africa and the Caribbean. Negritude poets, novelists, and essayists generally stress four points in their writings: One, black alienation from traditional African culture can lead to feelings of inferiority. Two, European colonialism and Western education should be resisted. Three, black Africans should seek to affirm and define their own identity. Four, African culture can and should be reclaimed. Many Negritude writers also claim that blacks can make unique contributions to the world, based on a heightened appreciation of nature, rhythm, and human emotions—aspects of life they say are not so highly valued in the materialistic and rationalistic West.

Negro Renaissance: See *Harlem Renaissance*

Neoclassical Period: See *Neoclassicism*

Neoclassicism: In literary criticism, this term refers to the revival of the attitudes and styles of expression of classical literature. It is generally used to describe a period in European history beginning in the late seventeenth century and lasting until about 1800. In its purest form, Neoclassicism marked a return to order, proportion, restraint, logic, accuracy, and decorum. In England, where Neoclassicism perhaps was most popular, it reflected the influence of seventeenth-century French writers, especially dramatists. Neoclassical writers typically reacted against the intensity and enthusiasm of the Renaissance period. They wrote works that appealed to the intellect, using elevated language and classical literary forms such as satire and the ode. Neoclassical works were often governed by the classical goal of instruction.

Neoclassicists: See *Neoclassicism*

New Criticism: A movement in literary criticism, dating from the late 1920s, that stressed close textual analysis in the interpretation of works of literature. The New Critics saw little merit in historical and biographical analysis. Rather, they aimed to examine the text alone, free from the question of how external events—biographical or otherwise—may have helped shape it.

New Journalism: A type of writing in which the journalist presents factual information in a form usually used in fiction. New journalism emphasizes description, narration, and character development to bring readers closer to the human element of the story, and is often used in personality profiles and in-depth feature articles. It is not compatible with "straight" or "hard" newswriting, which is generally composed in a brief, fact-based style.

New Journalists: See *New Journalism*

New Negro Movement: See *Harlem Renaissance*

Noble Savage: The idea that primitive man is noble and good but becomes evil and corrupted as he becomes civilized. The concept of the noble savage originated in the Renaissance period but is more closely identified with such later writers as Jean-Jacques Rousseau and Aphra Behn.

O

Objective Correlative: An outward set of objects, a situation, or a chain of events corresponding to an inward experience and evoking this experience in the reader. The term frequently appears in modern criticism in discussions of authors' intended effects on the emotional responses of readers.

Objectivity: A quality in writing characterized by the absence of the author's opinion or feeling about the subject matter. Objectivity is an important factor in criticism.

Occasional Verse: Poetry written on the occasion of a significant historical or personal event. *Vers de societe* is sometimes called occasional verse although it is of a less serious nature.

Octave: A poem or stanza composed of eight lines. The term octave most often represents the first eight lines of a Petrarchan sonnet.

Ode: Name given to an extended lyric poem characterized by exalted emotion and dignified style. An ode usually concerns a single, serious theme. Most odes, but not all, are addressed to an object or individual. Odes are distinguished from other lyric poetic forms by their complex rhythmic and stanzaic patterns.

Oedipus Complex: A son's amorous obsession with his mother. The phrase is derived from the story of the ancient Theban hero Oedipus, who

unknowingly killed his father and married his mother.

Omniscience: See *Point of View*

Onomatopoeia: The use of words whose sounds express or suggest their meaning. In its simplest sense, onomatopoeia may be represented by words that mimic the sounds they denote such as "hiss" or "meow." At a more subtle level, the pattern and rhythm of sounds and rhymes of a line or poem may be onomatopoeic.

Oral Tradition: See *Oral Transmission*

Oral Transmission: A process by which songs, ballads, folklore, and other material are transmitted by word of mouth. The tradition of oral transmission predates the written record systems of literate society. Oral transmission preserves material sometimes over generations, although often with variations. Memory plays a large part in the recitation and preservation of orally transmitted material.

Ottava Rima: An eight-line stanza of poetry composed in iambic pentameter (a five-foot line in which each foot consists of an unaccented syllable followed by an accented syllable), following the *abababcc* rhyme scheme.

Oxymoron: A phrase combining two contradictory terms. Oxymorons may be intentional or unintentional.

P

Pantheism: The idea that all things are both a manifestation or revelation of God and a part of God at the same time. Pantheism was a common attitude in the early societies of Egypt, India, and Greece—the term derives from the Greek *pan* meaning "all" and *theos* meaning "deity." It later became a significant part of the Christian faith.

Parable: A story intended to teach a moral lesson or answer an ethical question.

Paradox: A statement that appears illogical or contradictory at first, but may actually point to an underlying truth.

Parallelism: A method of comparison of two ideas in which each is developed in the same grammatical structure.

Parnassianism: A mid nineteenth-century movement in French literature. Followers of the movement stressed adherence to well-defined artistic forms as a reaction against the often chaotic expression of the artist's ego that dominated the work of the Romantics. The Parnassians also rejected the moral, ethical, and social themes exhibited in the works of French Romantics such as Victor Hugo. The aesthetic doctrines of the Parnassians strongly influenced the later symbolist and decadent movements.

Parody: In literary criticism, this term refers to an imitation of a serious literary work or the signature style of a particular author in a ridiculous manner. A typical parody adopts the style of the original and applies it to an inappropriate subject for humorous effect. Parody is a form of satire and could be considered the literary equivalent of a caricature or cartoon.

Pastoral: A term derived from the Latin word "pastor," meaning shepherd. A pastoral is a literary composition on a rural theme. The conventions of the pastoral were originated by the third-century Greek poet Theocritus, who wrote about the experiences, love affairs, and pastimes of Sicilian shepherds. In a pastoral, characters and language of a courtly nature are often placed in a simple setting. The term pastoral is also used to classify dramas, elegies, and lyrics that exhibit the use of country settings and shepherd characters.

Pathetic Fallacy: A term coined by English critic John Ruskin to identify writing that falsely endows nonhuman things with human intentions and feelings, such as "angry clouds" and "sad trees."

Pen Name: See *Pseudonym*

Pentameter: See *Meter*

Persona: A Latin term meaning "mask." *Personae* are the characters in a fictional work of literature. The *persona* generally functions as a mask through which the author tells a story in a voice other than his or her own. A *persona* is usually either a character in a story who acts as a narrator or an "implied author," a voice created by the author to act as the narrator for himself or herself.

Personae: See *Persona*

Personal Point of View: See *Point of View*

Personification: A figure of speech that gives human qualities to abstract ideas, animals, and inanimate objects.

Petrarchan Sonnet: See *Sonnet*

Phenomenology: A method of literary criticism based on the belief that things have no existence outside of human consciousness or awareness. Proponents of this theory believe that art is a process that takes place in the mind of the observer as he or she contemplates an object rather than a quality of the object itself.

Plagiarism: Claiming another person's written material as one's own. Plagiarism can take the form of direct, word-for-word copying or the theft of the substance or idea of the work.

Platonic Criticism: A form of criticism that stresses an artistic work's usefulness as an agent of social engineering rather than any quality or value of the work itself.

Platonism: The embracing of the doctrines of the philosopher Plato, popular among the poets of the Renaissance and the Romantic period. Platonism is more flexible than Aristotelian Criticism and places more emphasis on the supernatural and unknown aspects of life.

Plot: In literary criticism, this term refers to the pattern of events in a narrative or drama. In its simplest sense, the plot guides the author in composing the work and helps the reader follow the work. Typically, plots exhibit causality and unity and have a beginning, a middle, and an end. Sometimes, however, a plot may consist of a series of disconnected events, in which case it is known as an "episodic plot."

Poem: In its broadest sense, a composition utilizing rhyme, meter, concrete detail, and expressive language to create a literary experience with emotional and aesthetic appeal.

Poet: An author who writes poetry or verse. The term is also used to refer to an artist or writer who has an exceptional gift for expression, imagination, and energy in the making of art in any form.

Poete maudit: A term derived from Paul Verlaine's *Les poetes maudits (The Accursed Poets)*, a collection of essays on the French symbolist writers Stephane Mallarme, Arthur Rimbaud, and Tristan Corbiere. In the sense intended by Verlaine, the poet is "accursed" for choosing to explore extremes of human experience outside of middle-class society.

Poetic Fallacy: See *Pathetic Fallacy*

Poetic Justice: An outcome in a literary work, not necessarily a poem, in which the good are rewarded and the evil are punished, especially in ways that particularly fit their virtues or crimes.

Poetic License: Distortions of fact and literary convention made by a writer—not always a poet—for the sake of the effect gained. Poetic license is closely related to the concept of "artistic freedom."

Poetics: This term has two closely related meanings. It denotes (1) an aesthetic theory in literary criticism about the essence of poetry or (2) rules prescribing the proper methods, content, style, or diction of poetry. The term poetics may also refer to theories about literature in general, not just poetry.

Poetry: In its broadest sense, writing that aims to present ideas and evoke an emotional experience in the reader through the use of meter, imagery, connotative and concrete words, and a carefully constructed structure based on rhythmic patterns. Poetry typically relies on words and expressions that have several layers of meaning. It also makes use of the effects of regular rhythm on the ear and may make a strong appeal to the senses through the use of imagery.

Point of View: The narrative perspective from which a literary work is presented to the reader. There are four traditional points of view. The "third person omniscient" gives the reader a "godlike" perspective, unrestricted by time or place, from which to see actions and look into the minds of characters. This allows the author to comment openly on characters and events in the work. The "third-person" point of view presents the events of the story from outside of any single character's perception, much like the omniscient point of view, but the reader must understand the action as it takes place and without any special insight into characters' minds or motivations. The "first person" or "personal" point of view relates events as they are perceived by a single character. The main character "tells" the story and may offer opinions about the action and characters which differ from those of the author. Much less common than omniscient, third person, and first person is the "second-person" point of view, wherein the author tells the story as if it is happening to the reader.

Polemic: A work in which the author takes a stand on a controversial subject, such as abortion or religion. Such works are often extremely argumentative or provocative.

Pornography: Writing intended to provoke feelings of lust in the reader. Such works are often condemned by critics and teachers, but those which can be shown to have literary value are viewed less harshly.

Post-Aesthetic Movement: An artistic response made by African Americans to the black aesthetic movement of the 1960s and early 1970s. Writers since that time have adopted a somewhat different tone in their work, with less emphasis placed on the disparity between black and white in the United States. In the words of post-aesthetic authors such as Toni Morrison, John Edgar Wideman, and Kristin Hunter, African Americans are portrayed as looking inward for answers to their own questions, rather than always looking to the outside world.

Postmodernism: Writing from the 1960s forward characterized by experimentation and continuing to apply some of the fundamentals of modernism, which included existentialism and alienation. Postmodernists have gone a step further in the rejection of tradition begun with the modernists by also rejecting traditional forms, preferring the antinovel over the novel and the antihero over the hero.

Pre-Raphaelites: A circle of writers and artists in mid nineteenth-century England. Valuing the pre-Renaissance artistic qualities of religious symbolism, lavish pictorialism, and natural sensuousness, the Pre-Raphaelites cultivated a sense of mystery and melancholy that influenced later writers associated with the Symbolist and Decadent movements.

Primitivism: The belief that primitive peoples were nobler and less flawed than civilized peoples because they had not been subjected to the corrupt influence of society.

Projective Verse: A form of free verse in which the poet's breathing pattern determines the lines of the poem. Poets who advocate projective verse are against all formal structures in writing, including meter and form.

Prologue: An introductory section of a literary work. It often contains information establishing the situation of the characters or presents information about the setting, time period, or action. In drama, the prologue is spoken by a chorus or by one of the principal characters.

Prose: A literary medium that attempts to mirror the language of everyday speech. It is distinguished from poetry by its use of unmetered, unrhymed language consisting of logically related sentences. Prose is usually grouped into paragraphs that form a cohesive whole such as an essay or a novel.

Prosopopoeia: See *Personification*

Protagonist: The central character of a story who serves as a focus for its themes and incidents and as the principal rationale for its development. The protagonist is sometimes referred to in discussions of modern literature as the hero or antihero.

Proverb: A brief, sage saying that expresses a truth about life in a striking manner.

Pseudonym: A name assumed by a writer, most often intended to prevent his or her identification as the author of a work. Two or more authors may work together under one pseudonym, or an author may use a different name for each genre he or she publishes in. Some publishing companies maintain "house pseudonyms," under which any number of authors may write installations in a series. Some authors also choose a pseudonym over their real names the way an actor may use a stage name.

Pun: A play on words that have similar sounds but different meanings.

Pure Poetry: poetry written without instructional intent or moral purpose that aims only to please a reader by its imagery or musical flow. The term pure poetry is used as the antonym of the term "didacticism."

Q

Quatrain: A four-line stanza of a poem or an entire poem consisting of four lines.

R

Realism: A nineteenth-century European literary movement that sought to portray familiar characters, situations, and settings in a realistic manner. This was done primarily by using an objective narrative point of view and through the buildup of accurate detail. The standard for success of any realistic work depends on how faithfully it transfers common experience into fictional forms. The realistic method may be altered or extended, as in stream of consciousness writing, to record highly subjective experience.

Refrain: A phrase repeated at intervals throughout a poem. A refrain may appear at the end of each stanza or at less regular intervals. It may be altered slightly at each appearance.

Renaissance: The period in European history that marked the end of the Middle Ages. It began in Italy in the late fourteenth century. In broad terms, it is usually seen as spanning the fourteenth, fifteenth, and sixteenth centuries, although it did not reach Great Britain, for example, until the 1480s or so. The Renaissance saw an awakening in almost every sphere of human activity, especially science, philosophy, and the arts. The period is best defined by the emergence of a general philosophy that emphasized the importance of the intellect, the individual, and world affairs. It contrasts strongly with the medieval worldview, characterized by the dominant concerns of faith, the social collective, and spiritual salvation.

Repartee: Conversation featuring snappy retorts and witticisms.

Restoration: See *Restoration Age*

Restoration Age: A period in English literature beginning with the crowning of Charles II in 1660 and running to about 1700. The era, which was characterized by a reaction against Puritanism, was the first great age of the comedy of manners. The finest literature of the era is typically witty and urbane, and often lewd.

Rhetoric: In literary criticism, this term denotes the art of ethical persuasion. In its strictest sense, rhetoric adheres to various principles developed since classical times for arranging facts and ideas in a clear, persuasive, appealing manner. The term is also used to refer to effective prose in general and theories of or methods for composing effective prose.

Rhetorical Question: A question intended to provoke thought, but not an expressed answer, in the reader. It is most commonly used in oratory and other persuasive genres.

Rhyme: When used as a noun in literary criticism, this term generally refers to a poem in which words sound identical or very similar and appear in parallel positions in two or more lines. Rhymes are classified into different types according to where they fall in a line or stanza or according to the degree of similarity they exhibit in their spellings and sounds. Some major types of rhyme are "masculine" rhyme, "feminine" rhyme, and "triple" rhyme. In a masculine rhyme, the rhyming sound falls in a single accented syllable, as with "heat" and "eat." Feminine rhyme is a rhyme of two syllables, one stressed and one unstressed, as with "merry" and "tarry." Triple rhyme matches the sound of the accented syllable and the two unaccented syllables that follow: "narrative" and "declarative."

Rhyme Royal: A stanza of seven lines composed in iambic pentameter and rhymed *ababbcc*. The name is said to be a tribute to King James I of Scotland, who made much use of the form in his poetry.

Rhyme Scheme: See *Rhyme*

Rhythm: A regular pattern of sound, time intervals, or events occurring in writing, most often and most discernably in poetry. Regular, reliable rhythm is known to be soothing to humans, while interrupted, unpredictable, or rapidly changing rhythm is disturbing. These effects are known to authors, who use them to produce a desired reaction in the reader.

Rococo: A style of European architecture that flourished in the eighteenth century, especially in

France. The most notable features of *rococo* are its extensive use of ornamentation and its themes of lightness, gaiety, and intimacy. In literary criticism, the term is often used disparagingly to refer to a decadent or overly ornamental style.

Romance: A broad term, usually denoting a narrative with exotic, exaggerated, often idealized characters, scenes, and themes.

Romantic Age: See *Romanticism*

Romanticism: This term has two widely accepted meanings. In historical criticism, it refers to a European intellectual and artistic movement of the late eighteenth and early nineteenth centuries that sought greater freedom of personal expression than that allowed by the strict rules of literary form and logic of the eighteenth-century Neoclassicists. The Romantics preferred emotional and imaginative expression to rational analysis. They considered the individual to be at the center of all experience and so placed him or her at the center of their art. The Romantics believed that the creative imagination reveals nobler truths—unique feelings and attitudes—than those that could be discovered by logic or by scientific examination. Both the natural world and the state of childhood were important sources for revelations of "eternal truths." "Romanticism" is also used as a general term to refer to a type of sensibility found in all periods of literary history and usually considered to be in opposition to the principles of classicism. In this sense, Romanticism signifies any work or philosophy in which the exotic or dreamlike figure strongly, or that is devoted to individualistic expression, self-analysis, or a pursuit of a higher realm of knowledge than can be discovered by human reason.

Romantics: See *Romanticism*

Russian Symbolism: A Russian poetic movement, derived from French symbolism, that flourished between 1894 and 1910. While some Russian Symbolists continued in the French tradition, stressing aestheticism and the importance of suggestion above didactic intent, others saw their craft as a form of mystical worship, and themselves as mediators between the supernatural and the mundane.

S

Satire: A work that uses ridicule, humor, and wit to criticize and provoke change in human nature and institutions. There are two major types of satire: "formal" or "direct" satire speaks directly to the reader or to a character in the work; "indirect" satire relies upon the ridiculous behavior of its char-

acters to make its point. Formal satire is further divided into two manners: the "Horatian," which ridicules gently, and the "Juvenalian," which derides its subjects harshly and bitterly.

Scansion: The analysis or "scanning" of a poem to determine its meter and often its rhyme scheme. The most common system of scansion uses accents (slanted lines drawn above syllables) to show stressed syllables, breves (curved lines drawn above syllables) to show unstressed syllables, and vertical lines to separate each foot.

Second Person: See *Point of View*

Semiotics: The study of how literary forms and conventions affect the meaning of language.

Sestet: Any six-line poem or stanza.

Setting: The time, place, and culture in which the action of a narrative takes place. The elements of setting may include geographic location, characters' physical and mental environments, prevailing cultural attitudes, or the historical time in which the action takes place.

Shakespearean Sonnet: See *Sonnet*

Signifying Monkey: A popular trickster figure in black folklore, with hundreds of tales about this character documented since the nineteenth century.

Simile: A comparison, usually using "like" or "as," of two essentially dissimilar things, as in "coffee as cold as ice" or "He sounded like a broken record."

Slang: A type of informal verbal communication that is generally unacceptable for formal writing. Slang words and phrases are often colorful exaggerations used to emphasize the speaker's point; they may also be shortened versions of an often-used word or phrase.

Slant Rhyme: See *Consonance*

Slave Narrative: Autobiographical accounts of American slave life as told by escaped slaves. These works first appeared during the abolition movement of the 1830s through the 1850s.

Social Realism: See *Socialist Realism*

Socialist Realism: The Socialist Realism school of literary theory was proposed by Maxim Gorky and established as a dogma by the first Soviet Congress of Writers. It demanded adherence to a communist worldview in works of literature. Its doctrines required an objective viewpoint comprehensible to the working classes and themes of social struggle featuring strong proletarian heroes.

Soliloquy: A monologue in a drama used to give the audience information and to develop the speaker's character. It is typically a projection of the speaker's innermost thoughts. Usually delivered while the speaker is alone on stage, a soliloquy is intended to present an illusion of unspoken reflection.

Sonnet: A fourteen-line poem, usually composed in iambic pentameter, employing one of several rhyme schemes. There are three major types of sonnets, upon which all other variations of the form are based: the "Petrarchan" or "Italian" sonnet, the "Shakespearean" or "English" sonnet, and the "Spenserian" sonnet. A Petrarchan sonnet consists of an octave rhymed *abbaabba* and a "sestet" rhymed either *cdecde, cdccdc,* or *cdedce.* The octave poses a question or problem, relates a narrative, or puts forth a proposition; the sestet presents a solution to the problem, comments upon the narrative, or applies the proposition put forth in the octave. The Shakespearean sonnet is divided into three quatrains and a couplet rhymed *abab cdcd efef gg.* The couplet provides an epigrammatic comment on the narrative or problem put forth in the quatrains. The Spenserian sonnet uses three quatrains and a couplet like the Shakespearean, but links their three rhyme schemes in this way: *abab bcbc cdcd ee.* The Spenserian sonnet develops its theme in two parts like the Petrarchan, its final six lines resolving a problem, analyzing a narrative, or applying a proposition put forth in its first eight lines.

Spenserian Sonnet: See *Sonnet*

Spenserian Stanza: A nine-line stanza having eight verses in iambic pentameter, its ninth verse in iambic hexameter, and the rhyme scheme *ababbcbcc.*

Spondee: In poetry meter, a foot consisting of two long or stressed syllables occurring together. This form is quite rare in English verse, and is usually composed of two monosyllabic words.

Sprung Rhythm: Versification using a specific number of accented syllables per line but disregarding the number of unaccented syllables that fall in each line, producing an irregular rhythm in the poem.

Stanza: A subdivision of a poem consisting of lines grouped together, often in recurring patterns of rhyme, line length, and meter. Stanzas may also serve as units of thought in a poem much like paragraphs in prose.

Stereotype: A stereotype was originally the name for a duplication made during the printing process; this led to its modern definition as a person or thing that is (or is assumed to be) the same as all others of its type.

Stream of Consciousness: A narrative technique for rendering the inward experience of a character. This technique is designed to give the impression of an ever-changing series of thoughts, emotions, images, and memories in the spontaneous and seemingly illogical order that they occur in life.

Structuralism: A twentieth-century movement in literary criticism that examines how literary texts arrive at their meanings, rather than the meanings themselves. There are two major types of structuralist analysis: one examines the way patterns of linguistic structures unify a specific text and emphasize certain elements of that text, and the other interprets the way literary forms and conventions affect the meaning of language itself.

Structure: The form taken by a piece of literature. The structure may be made obvious for ease of understanding, as in nonfiction works, or may obscured for artistic purposes, as in some poetry or seemingly "unstructured" prose.

Sturm und Drang: A German term meaning "storm and stress." It refers to a German literary movement of the 1770s and 1780s that reacted against the order and rationalism of the enlightenment, focusing instead on the intense experience of extraordinary individuals.

Style: A writer's distinctive manner of arranging words to suit his or her ideas and purpose in writing. The unique imprint of the author's personality upon his or her writing, style is the product of an author's way of arranging ideas and his or her use of diction, different sentence structures, rhythm, figures of speech, rhetorical principles, and other elements of composition.

Subject: The person, event, or theme at the center of a work of literature. A work may have one or more subjects of each type, with shorter works tending to have fewer and longer works tending to have more.

Subjectivity: Writing that expresses the author's personal feelings about his subject, and which may or may not include factual information about the subject.

Surrealism: A term introduced to criticism by Guillaume Apollinaire and later adopted by Andre Breton. It refers to a French literary and artistic movement founded in the 1920s. The Surrealists sought to express unconscious thoughts and feelings in their works. The best-known technique used for achieving this aim was automatic writing—transcriptions of spontaneous outpourings from the unconscious. The Surrealists proposed to unify the contrary levels of conscious and unconscious, dream and reality, objectivity and subjectivity into a new level of "super-realism."

Suspense: A literary device in which the author maintains the audience's attention through the buildup of events, the outcome of which will soon be revealed.

Syllogism: A method of presenting a logical argument. In its most basic form, the syllogism consists of a major premise, a minor premise, and a conclusion.

Symbol: Something that suggests or stands for something else without losing its original identity. In literature, symbols combine their literal meaning with the suggestion of an abstract concept. Literary symbols are of two types: those that carry complex associations of meaning no matter what their contexts, and those that derive their suggestive meaning from their functions in specific literary works.

Symbolism: This term has two widely accepted meanings. In historical criticism, it denotes an early modernist literary movement initiated in France during the nineteenth century that reacted against the prevailing standards of realism. Writers in this movement aimed to evoke, indirectly and symbolically, an order of being beyond the material world of the five senses. Poetic expression of personal emotion figured strongly in the movement, typically by means of a private set of symbols uniquely identifiable with the individual poet. The principal aim of the Symbolists was to express in words the highly complex feelings that grew out of everyday contact with the world. In a broader sense, the term "symbolism" refers to the use of one object to represent another.

Symbolist: See *Symbolism*

Symbolist Movement: See *Symbolism*

Sympathetic Fallacy: See *Affective Fallacy*

T

Tanka: A form of Japanese poetry similar to *haiku*. A *tanka* is five lines long, with the lines containing five, seven, five, seven, and seven syllables respectively.

Terza Rima: A three-line stanza form in poetry in which the rhymes are made on the last word of each line in the following manner: the first and third lines of the first stanza, then the second line of the first stanza and the first and third lines of the second stanza, and so on with the middle line of any

stanza rhyming with the first and third lines of the following stanza.

Tetrameter: See *Meter*

Textual Criticism: A branch of literary criticism that seeks to establish the authoritative text of a literary work. Textual critics typically compare all known manuscripts or printings of a single work in order to assess the meanings of differences and revisions. This procedure allows them to arrive at a definitive version that (supposedly) corresponds to the author's original intention.

Theme: The main point of a work of literature. The term is used interchangeably with thesis.

Thesis: A thesis is both an essay and the point argued in the essay. Thesis novels and thesis plays share the quality of containing a thesis which is supported through the action of the story.

Third Person: See *Point of View*

Tone: The author's attitude toward his or her audience may be deduced from the tone of the work. A formal tone may create distance or convey politeness, while an informal tone may encourage a friendly, intimate, or intrusive feeling in the reader. The author's attitude toward his or her subject matter may also be deduced from the tone of the words he or she uses in discussing it.

Tragedy: A drama in prose or poetry about a noble, courageous hero of excellent character who, because of some tragic character flaw or *hamartia*, brings ruin upon him- or herself. Tragedy treats its subjects in a dignified and serious manner, using poetic language to help evoke pity and fear and bring about catharsis, a purging of these emotions. The tragic form was practiced extensively by the ancient Greeks. In the Middle Ages, when classical works were virtually unknown, tragedy came to denote any works about the fall of persons from exalted to low conditions due to any reason: fate, vice, weakness, etc. According to the classical definition of tragedy, such works present the "pathetic"—that which evokes pity—rather than the tragic. The classical form of tragedy was revived in the sixteenth century; it flourished especially on the Elizabethan stage. In modern times, dramatists have attempted to adapt the form to the needs of modern society by drawing their heroes from the ranks of ordinary men and women and defining the nobility of these heroes in terms of spirit rather than exalted social standing.

Tragic Flaw: In a tragedy, the quality within the hero or heroine which leads to his or her downfall.

Transcendentalism: An American philosophical and religious movement, based in New England from around 1835 until the Civil War. Transcendentalism was a form of American romanticism that had its roots abroad in the works of Thomas Carlyle, Samuel Coleridge, and Johann Wolfgang von Goethe. The Transcendentalists stressed the importance of intuition and subjective experience in communication with God. They rejected religious dogma and texts in favor of mysticism and scientific naturalism. They pursued truths that lie beyond the "colorless" realms perceived by reason and the senses and were active social reformers in public education, women's rights, and the abolition of slavery.

Trickster: A character or figure common in Native American and African literature who uses his ingenuity to defeat enemies and escape difficult situations. Tricksters are most often animals, such as the spider, hare, or coyote, although they may take the form of humans as well.

Trimeter: See *Meter*

Triple Rhyme: See *Rhyme*

Trochee: See *Foot*

U

Understatement: See *Irony*

Unities: Strict rules of dramatic structure, formulated by Italian and French critics of the Renaissance and based loosely on the principles of drama discussed by Aristotle in his *Poetics.* Foremost among these rules were the three unities of action, time, and place that compelled a dramatist to: (1) construct a single plot with a beginning, middle, and end that details the causal relationships of action and character; (2) restrict the action to the events of a single day; and (3) limit the scene to a single place or city. The unities were observed faithfully by continental European writers until the Romantic Age, but they were never regularly observed in English drama. Modern dramatists are typically more concerned with a unity of impression or emotional effect than with any of the classical unities.

Urban Realism: A branch of realist writing that attempts to accurately reflect the often harsh facts of modern urban existence.

Utopia: A fictional perfect place, such as "paradise" or "heaven."

Utopian: See *Utopia*

Utopianism: See *Utopia*

V

Verisimilitude: Literally, the appearance of truth. In literary criticism, the term refers to aspects of a work of literature that seem true to the reader.

Vers de societe: See *Occasional Verse*

Vers libre: See *Free Verse*

Verse: A line of metered language, a line of a poem, or any work written in verse.

Versification: The writing of verse. Versification may also refer to the meter, rhyme, and other mechanical components of a poem.

Victorian: Refers broadly to the reign of Queen Victoria of England (1837–1901) and to anything with qualities typical of that era. For example, the qualities of smug narrowmindedness, bourgeois materialism, faith in social progress, and priggish morality are often considered Victorian. This stereotype is contradicted by such dramatic intellectual developments as the theories of Charles Darwin, Karl Marx, and Sigmund Freud (which stirred strong debates in England) and the critical attitudes of serious Victorian writers like Charles Dickens and George Eliot. In literature, the Victorian Period was the great age of the English novel, and the latter part of the era saw the rise of movements such as decadence and symbolism.

Victorian Age: See *Victorian*

Victorian Period: See *Victorian*

W

Weltanschauung: A German term referring to a person's worldview or philosophy.

Weltschmerz: A German term meaning "world pain." It describes a sense of anguish about the nature of existence, usually associated with a melancholy, pessimistic attitude.

Z

Zarzuela: A type of Spanish operetta.

Zeitgeist: A German term meaning "spirit of the time." It refers to the moral and intellectual trends of a given era.

Cumulative Author/Title Index

A

Accounting (Alegría): V21
Ackerman, Diane
  On Location in the Loire Valley:
  V19
Acosta, Teresa Palomo
  My Mother Pieced Quilts: V12
Address to the Angels (Kumin): V18
The Afterlife (Collins): V18
An African Elegy (Duncan): V13
Ah, Are You Digging on My Grave?
  (Hardy): V4
Ai
  Reunions with a Ghost: V16
Aiken, Conrad
  The Room: V24
Air for Mercury (Hillman): V20
Akhmatova, Anna
  Midnight Verses: V18
Alabama Centennial (Madgett): V10
The Alchemy of Day (Hébert): V20
Alegría, Claribel
  Accounting: V21
Alexander, Elizabeth
  The Toni Morrison Dreams: V22
All I Was Doing Was Breathing
  (Mirabai): V24
All It Takes (Phillips): V23
Allegory (Bang): V23
Always (Apollinaire): V24
American Poetry (Simpson): V7
Amichai, Yehuda
  Not like a Cypress: V24
Ammons, A. R.
  The City Limits: V19
An Arundel Tomb (Larkin): V12
Anasazi (Snyder): V9

And What If I Spoke of Despair
  (Bass): V19
Angelou, Maya
  Harlem Hopscotch: V2
  On the Pulse of Morning: V3
Angle of Geese (Momaday): V2
Annabel Lee (Poe): V9
Anniversary (Harjo): V15
Anonymous
  Barbara Allan: V7
  Go Down, Moses: V11
  Lord Randal: V6
  The Seafarer: V8
  Sir Patrick Spens: V4
  Swing Low Sweet Chariot: V1
Anorexic (Boland): V12
Answers to Letters (Tranströmer):
  V21
Any Human to Another (Cullen): V3
A Pièd (McElroy): V3
Apollinaire, Guillaume
  Always: V24
Apple sauce for Eve (Piercy): V22
Arnold, Matthew
  Dover Beach: V2
Ars Poetica (MacLeish): V5
The Arsenal at Springfield
  (Longfellow): V17
The Art of the Novel (Sajé): V23
Arvio, Sarah
  Memory: V21
As I Walked Out One Evening
  (Auden): V4
Ashbery, John
  Paradoxes and Oxymorons: V11
Astonishment (Szymborska): V15
At the Bomb Testing Site (Stafford):
  V8

At the Cancer Clinic (Kooser): V24
Atwood, Margaret
  Siren Song: V7
Auden, W. H.
  As I Walked Out One Evening:
  V4
  Funeral Blues: V10
  Musée des Beaux Arts: V1
  The Unknown Citizen: V3
Aurora Leigh (Browning): V23
Auto Wreck (Shapiro): V3
Autumn Begins in Martins Ferry,
  Ohio (Wright): V8

B

Ballad of Orange and Grape
  (Rukeyser): V10
Baraka, Amiri
  In Memory of Radio: V9
Barbara Allan (Anonymous): V7
Barbie Doll (Piercy): V9
Ballad of Birmingham (Randall): V5
Bang, Mary Jo
  Allegory: V23
Barrett, Elizabeth
  Sonnet 43: V2
The Base Stealer (Francis): V12
Bashō, Matsuo
  Falling Upon Earth: V2
  The Moon Glows the Same: V7
  Temple Bells Die Out: V18
Bass, Ellen
  And What If I Spoke of Despair:
  V19
Baudelaire, Charles
  Hymn to Beauty: V21

The Bean Eaters (Brooks): V2

Because I Could Not Stop for Death (Dickinson): V2

Bedtime Story (MacBeth): V8

Behn, Robin
  Ten Years after Your Deliberate Drowning: V21

La Belle Dame sans Merci (Keats): V17

The Bells (Poe): V3

Beowulf (Wilbur): V11

Beware: Do Not Read This Poem (Reed): V6

Beware of Ruins (Hope): V8

Bialosky, Jill
  Seven Seeds: V19

Bidwell Ghost (Erdrich): V14

Biele, Joelle
  Rapture: V21

Birch Canoe (Revard): V5

Birches (Frost): V13

Birney, Earle
  Vancouver Lights: V8

A Birthday (Rossetti): V10

Bishop, Elizabeth
  Brazil, January 1, 1502: V6
  Filling Station: V12

Blackberrying (Plath): V15

Black Zodiac (Wright): V10

Blake, William
  The Lamb: V12
  A Poison Tree: V24
  The Tyger: V2

A Blessing (Wright): V7

Blood Oranges (Mueller): V13

The Blue Rim of Memory (Levertov): V17

Blumenthal, Michael
  Inventors: V7

Bly, Robert
  Come with Me: V6
  Driving to Town Late to Mail a Letter: V17

Bogan, Louise
  Words for Departure: V21

Boland, Eavan
  Anorexic: V12
  It's a Woman's World: V22

The Boy (Hacker): V19

Bradstreet, Anne
  To My Dear and Loving Husband: V6

Brazil, January 1, 1502 (Bishop): V6

Bright Star! Would I Were Steadfast as Thou Art (Keats): V9

Brooke, Rupert
  The Soldier: V7

Brooks, Gwendolyn
  The Bean Eaters: V2
  The Sonnet-Ballad: V1
  Strong Men, Riding Horses: V4
  We Real Cool: V6

Brouwer, Joel
  Last Request: V14

Browning, Elizabeth Barrett
  Aurora Leigh: V23
  Sonnet 43: V2
  Sonnet XXIX: V16

Browning, Robert
  My Last Duchess: V1
  Porphyria's Lover: V15

Burns, Robert
  A Red, Red Rose: V8

Business (Cruz): V16

The Bustle in a House (Dickinson): V10

But Perhaps God Needs the Longing (Sachs): V20

Butcher Shop (Simic): V7

Byrne, Elena Karina
  In Particular: V20

Byron, Lord
  The Destruction of Sennacherib: V1
  She Walks in Beauty: V14

C

The Canterbury Tales (Chaucer): V14

Cargoes (Masefield): V5

Carroll, Lewis
  Jabberwocky: V11

Carson, Anne
  New Rule: V18

Carver, Raymond
  The Cobweb: V17

Casey at the Bat (Thayer): V5

Castillo, Ana
  While I Was Gone a War Began: V21

Cavafy, C. P.
  Ithaka: V19

Cavalry Crossing a Ford (Whitman): V13

Celan, Paul
  Late and Deep: V21

The Chambered Nautilus (Holmes): V24

The Charge of the Light Brigade (Tennyson): V1

Chaucer, Geoffrey
  The Canterbury Tales: V14

Chicago (Sandburg): V3

Childhood (Rilke): V19

Chocolates (Simpson): V11

The Cinnamon Peeler (Ondaatje): V19

Cisneros, Sandra
  Once Again I Prove the Theory of Relativity: V19

The City Limits (Ammons): V19

Clifton, Lucille
  Climbing: V14
  Miss Rosie: V1

Climbing (Clifton): V14

The Cobweb (Carver): V17

Coleridge, Samuel Taylor
  Kubla Khan: V5
  The Rime of the Ancient Mariner: V4

Colibrí (Espada): V16

Collins, Billy
  The Afterlife: V18

Come with Me (Bly): V6

The Constellation Orion (Kooser): V8

Concord Hymn (Emerson): V4

The Conquerors (McGinley): V13

The Continuous Life (Strand): V18

Cool Tombs (Sandburg): V6

The Country Without a Post Office (Shahid Ali): V18

Courage (Sexton): V14

The Courage That My Mother Had (Millay): V3

Crane, Stephen
  War Is Kind: V9

The Creation (Johnson): V1

Creeley, Robert
  Fading Light: V21

The Cremation of Sam McGee (Service): V10

The Crime Was in Granada (Machado): V23

Cruz, Victor Hernandez
  Business: V16

Cullen, Countee
  Any Human to Another: V3

cummings, e. e.
  i was sitting in mcsorley's: V13
  l(a: V1
  maggie and milly and molly and may: V12
  old age sticks: V3
  somewhere i have never travelled,gladly beyond: V19

The Czar's Last Christmas Letter. A Barn in the Urals (Dubie): V12

D

The Darkling Thrush (Hardy): V18

Darwin in 1881 (Schnackenberg): V13

Dawe, Bruce
  Drifters: V10

Daylights (Warren): V13

Dear Reader (Tate): V10

The Death of the Ball Turret Gunner (Jarrell): V2

The Death of the Hired Man (Frost): V4

Death Sentences (Lazić): V22

Deep Woods (Nemerov): V14

Dennis, Carl
  The God Who Loves You: V20

The Destruction of Sennacherib (Byron): V1

Dickey, James
   The Heaven of Animals: V6
   The Hospital Window: V11
Dickinson, Emily
   *Because I Could Not Stop for
      Death:* V2
   The Bustle in a House: V10
   *"Hope" Is the Thing with
      Feathers:* V3
   I felt a Funeral, in my Brain: V13
   *I Heard a Fly Buzz—When I
      Died—:* V5
   Much Madness Is Divinest Sense:
      V16
   *My Life Closed Twice Before Its
      Close:* V8
   A Narrow Fellow in the Grass:
      V11
   *The Soul Selects Her Own
      Society:* V1
   There's a Certain Slant of Light:
      V6
   This Is My Letter to the World:
      V4
Digging (Heaney): V5
Dobyns, Stephen
   It's like This: V23
*Do Not Go Gentle into that Good
    Night* (Thomas): V1
Donne, John
   Holy Sonnet 10: V2
   *A Valediction: Forbidding
      Mourning:* V11
Dove, Rita
   Geometry: V15
   This Life: V1
Dover Beach (Arnold): V2
Dream Variations (Hughes): V15
Drifters (Dawe): V10
A Drink of Water (Heaney): V8
Drinking Alone Beneath the Moon
    (Po): V20
*Driving to Town Late to Mail a
    Letter* (Bly): V17
Drought Year (Wright): V8
Dubie, Norman
   *The Czar's Last Christmas Letter.
      A Barn in the Urals:* V12
Du Bois, W. E. B.
   The Song of the Smoke: V13
Duncan, Robert
   An African Elegy: V13
Dugan, Alan
   How We Heard the Name: V10
Dulce et Decorum Est (Owen): V10
Dunn, Stephen
   The Reverse Side: V21
Duration (Paz): V18

E

The Eagle (Tennyson): V11
Early in the Morning (Lee): V17

Easter 1916 (Yeats): V5
Eating Poetry (Strand): V9
*Elegy for My Father, Who is Not
    Dead* (Hudgins): V14
*Elegy Written in a Country
    Churchyard* (Gray): V9
*An Elementary School Classroom in
    a Slum* (Spender): V23
Eliot, T. S.
   Journey of the Magi: V7
   *The Love Song of J. Alfred
      Prufrock:* V1
   The Waste Land: V20
Emerson, Ralph Waldo
   Concord Hymn: V4
   The Rhodora: V17
Erdrich, Louise
   Bidwell Ghost: V14
Espada, Martín
   Colibrí: V16
   *We Live by What We See at
      Night:* V13
Ethics (Pastan): V8
The Exhibit (Mueller): V9

F

Facing It (Komunyakaa): V5
Fading Light (Creeley): V21
Falling Upon Earth (Bashō): V2
A Far Cry from Africa (Walcott): V6
A Farewell to English (Hartnett):
    V10
Farrokhzaad, Faroogh
   A Rebirth: V21
Fenton, James
   The Milkfish Gatherers: V11
Fern Hill (Thomas): V3
Fiddler Crab (Jacobsen): V23
Fifteen (Stafford): V2
Filling Station (Bishop): V12
Fire and Ice (Frost): V7
The Fish (Moore): V14
*For a New Citizen of These United
    States* (Lee): V15
For An Assyrian Frieze (Viereck):
    V9
*For Jean Vincent D'abbadie, Baron
    St.-Castin* (Nowlan): V12
For Jennifer, 6, on the Teton (Hugo):
    V17
For the Sake of Strangers (Laux):
    V24
For the Union Dead (Lowell): V7
*For the White poets who would be
    Indian* (Rose): V13
*The Force That Through the Green
    Fuse Drives the Flower*
    (Thomas): V8
Forché, Carolyn
   The Garden Shukkei-en: V18
The Forest (Stewart): V22
Four Mountain Wolves (Silko): V9

Francis, Robert
   The Base Stealer: V12
Frost, Robert
   Birches: V13
   The Death of the Hired Man: V4
   Fire and Ice: V7
   Mending Wall: V5
   Nothing Gold Can Stay: V3
   Out, Out—: V10
   The Road Not Taken: V2
   *Stopping by Woods on a Snowy
      Evening:* V1
   The Wood-Pile: V6
Funeral Blues (Auden): V10

G

Gacela of the Dark Death (García
    Lorca): V20
Gallagher, Tess
   I Stop Writing the Poem: V16
García Lorca, Federico
   Gacela of the Dark Death: V20
The Garden Shukkei-en (Forché):
    V18
Geometry (Dove): V15
Ghazal (Spires): V21
Ginsberg, Allen
   A Supermarket in California: V5
Gioia, Dana
   The Litany: V24
Giovanni, Nikki
   Knoxville, Tennessee: V17
Glück, Louise
   The Gold Lily: V5
   The Mystery: V15
Go Down, Moses (Anonymous): V11
The God Who Loves You (Dennis):
    V20
The Gold Lily (Glück): V5
A Grafted Tongue (Montague): V12
Graham, Jorie
   The Hiding Place: V10
   Mind: V17
Gray, Thomas
   *Elegy Written in a Country
      Churchyard:* V9
The Greatest Grandeur (Rogers):
    V18
Gregg, Linda
   A Thirst Against: V20
Grennan, Eamon
   Station: V21
Gunn, Thom
   The Missing: V9

H

H.D.
   Helen: V6
Hacker, Marilyn
   The Boy: V19

Hahn, Kimiko
  Pine: V23
Hall, Donald
  Names of Horses: V8
Hardy, Thomas
  *Ah, Are You Digging on My
    Grave?:* V4
  The Darkling Thrush: V18
  The Man He Killed: V3
Harjo, Joy
  Anniversary: V15
Harlem (Hughes): V1
Harlem Hopscotch (Angelou): V2
Hartnett, Michael
  A Farewell to English: V10
Hashimoto, Sharon
  *What I Would Ask My Husband's
    Dead Father:* V22
Having a Coke with You (O'Hara):
  V12
Having it Out with Melancholy
  (Kenyon): V17
Hawk Roosting (Hughes): V4
Hayden, Robert
  Those Winter Sundays: V1
Heaney, Seamus
  Digging: V5
  A Drink of Water: V8
  Midnight: V2
  The Singer's House: V17
Hébert, Anne
  The Alchemy of Day: V20
Hecht, Anthony
  "More Light! More Light!": V6
The Heaven of Animals (Dickey): V6
Helen (H.D.): V6
Herbert, Zbigniew
  Why The Classics: V22
Herrick, Robert
  *To the Virgins, to Make Much of
    Time:* V13
The Hiding Place (Graham): V10
High Windows (Larkin): V3
The Highwayman (Noyes): V4
Hillman, Brenda
  Air for Mercury: V20
Hirsch, Edward
  Omen: V22
Hirshfield, Jane
  *Three Times My Life Has
    Opened:* V16
His Speed and Strength (Ostriker):
  V19
Hoagland, Tony
  Social Life: V19
Holmes, Oliver Wendell
  The Chambered Nautilus: V24
  Old Ironsides: V9
Holy Sonnet 10 (Donne): V2
Hope, A. D.
  Beware of Ruins: V8
Hope Is a Tattered Flag (Sandburg):
  V12

"Hope" Is the Thing with Feathers
  (Dickinson): V3
The Horizons of Rooms (Merwin): V15
The Hospital Window (Dickey): V11
Housman, A. E.
  To an Athlete Dying Young: V7
  When I Was One-and-Twenty: V4
How We Heard the Name (Dugan):
  V10
Howe, Marie
  What Belongs to Us: V15
Hudgins, Andrew
  *Elegy for My Father, Who is Not
    Dead:* V14
Hugh Selwyn Mauberley (Pound): V16
Hughes, Langston
  Dream Variations: V15
  Harlem: V1
  Mother to Son: V3
  The Negro Speaks of Rivers: V10
  Theme for English B: V6
Hughes, Ted
  Hawk Roosting: V4
  Perfect Light: V19
Hugo, Richard
  For Jennifer, 6, on the Teton: V17
Hunger in New York City (Ortiz): V4
Huong, Ho Xuan
  Spring-Watching Pavilion: V18
Hurt Hawks (Jeffers): V3
Hymn to Aphrodite (Sappho): V20
Hymn to Beauty (Baudelaire): V21

I

I felt a Funeral, in my Brain
  (Dickinson): V13
I Go Back to May 1937 (Olds): V17
I Hear America Singing (Whitman):
  V3
I Heard a Fly Buzz—When I Died—
  (Dickinson): V5
I Stop Writing the Poem (Gallagher):
  V16
i was sitting in mcsorley's
  (cummings): V13
The Idea of Order at Key West
  (Stevens): V13
If (Kipling): V22
In a Station of the Metro (Pound): V2
In Flanders Fields (McCrae): V5
In Memory of Radio (Baraka): V9
In Particular (Byrne): V20
In the Land of Shinar (Levertov): V7
In the Suburbs (Simpson): V14
Incident in a Rose Garden (Justice):
  V14
Inventors (Blumentha): V7
An Irish Airman Foresees His Death
  (Yeats): V1
Island of the Three Marias (Ríos):
  V11
Ithaka (Cavafy): V19

It's a Woman's World (Boland): V22
It's like This (Dobyns): V23

J

Jabberwocky (Carroll): V11
Jacobsen, Josephine
  Fiddler Crab: V23
Jarrell, Randall
  *The Death of the Ball Turret
    Gunner:* V2
Jeffers, Robinson
  Hurt Hawks: V3
  Shine Perishing Republic: V4
Johnson, James Weldon
  The Creation: V1
Jonson, Ben
  Song: To Celia: V23
Journey of the Magi (Eliot): V7
Justice, Donald
  Incident in a Rose Garden: V14

K

Keats, John
  La Belle Dame sans Merci: V17
  *Bright Star! Would I Were
    Steadfast as Thou Art:* V9
  Ode on a Grecian Urn: V1
  Ode to a Nightingale: V3
  *When I Have Fears that I May
    Cease to Be:* V2
Kelly, Brigit Pegeen
  The Satyr's Heart: V22
Kenyon, Jane
  Having it Out with Melancholy:
    V17
  *"Trouble with Math in a One-
    Room Country School":* V9
Kilroy (Viereck): V14
Kim, Sue (Suji) Kwock
  Monologue for an Onion: V24
Kindness (Nye): V24
King James Bible
  Psalm 8: V9
  Psalm 23: V4
Kinnell, Galway
  Saint Francis and the Sow: V9
Kipling, Rudyard
  If: V22
Kizer, Carolyn
  To an Unknown Poet: V18
Knoxville, Tennessee (Giovanni): V17
Koch, Kenneth
  Paradiso: V20
Komunyakaa, Yusef
  Facing It: V5
  Ode to a Drum: V20
Kooser, Ted
  At the Cancer Clinic: V24
  The Constellation Orion: V8
Kubla Khan (Coleridge): V5

Kumin, Maxine
  Address to the Angels: V18
Kunitz, Stanley
  The War Against the Trees: V11
Kyger, Joanne
  September: V23

L

l(a (cummings): V1
The Lady of Shalott (Tennyson):
  V15
Lake (Warren): V23
The Lake Isle of Innisfree (Yeats):
  V15
The Lamb (Blake): V12
Lament for the Dorsets (Purdy): V5
Landscape with Tractor (Taylor):
  V10
Lanier, Sidney
  Song of the Chattahoochee: V14
Larkin, Philip
  An Arundel Tomb: V12
  High Windows: V3
  Toads: V4
The Last Question (Parker): V18
Last Request (Brouwer): V14
Late and Deep (Celan): V21
Laux, Dorianne
  For the Sake of Strangers: V24
Lawrence, D. H.
  Piano: V6
Layton, Irving
  A Tall Man Executes a Jig: V12
Lazić, Radmila
  Death Sentences: V22
Leda and the Swan (Yeats): V13
Lee, Li-Young
  Early in the Morning: V17
  *For a New Citizen of These
    United States:* V15
  The Weight of Sweetness: V11
Lepidopterology (Svenbro): V23
Levertov, Denise
  The Blue Rim of Memory: V17
  In the Land of Shinar: V7
Leviathan (Merwin): V5
Levine, Philip
  Starlight: V8
The Litany (Gioia): V24
Longfellow, Henry Wadsworth
  The Arsenal at Springfield: V17
  Paul Revere's Ride: V2
  A Psalm of Life: V7
Lord Randal (Anonymous): V6
Lorde, Audre
  What My Child Learns of the Sea:
    V16
Lost in Translation (Merrill): V23
Lost Sister (Song): V5
The Love Song of J. Alfred Prufrock
  (Eliot): V1

Lowell, Robert
  For the Union Dead: V7
  *The Quaker Graveyard in
    Nantucket:* V6
Loy, Mina
  Moreover, the Moon: V20

M

MacBeth, George
  Bedtime Story: V8
Machado, Antonio
  The Crime Was in Granada:
    V23
MacLeish, Archibald
  Ars Poetica: V5
Madgett, Naomi Long
  Alabama Centennial: V10
maggie and milly and molly and may
  (cummings): V12
Malroux, Claire
  Morning Walk: V21
The Man He Killed (Hardy): V3
Marlowe, Christopher
  *The Passionate Shepherd to His
    Love:* V22
A Martian Sends a Postcard Home
  (Raine): V7
Marvell, Andrew
  To His Coy Mistress: V5
Masefield, John
  Cargoes: V5
Maternity (Swir): V21
Matsuo Bashō
  Falling Upon Earth: V2
  The Moon Glows the Same: V7
  Temple Bells Die Out: V18
Maxwell, Glyn
  The Nerve: V23
McCrae, John
  In Flanders Fields: V5
McElroy, Colleen
  A Pièd: V3
McGinley, Phyllis
  The Conquerors: V13
  *Reactionary Essay on Applied
    Science:* V9
McHugh, Heather
  Three To's and an Oi: V24
McKay, Claude
  The Tropics in New York: V4
Meeting the British (Muldoon): V7
Memoir (Van Duyn): V20
Memory (Arvio): V21
Mending Wall (Frost): V5
Merlin Enthralled (Wilbur): V16
Merriam, Eve
  Onomatopoeia: V6
Merrill, James
  Lost in Translation: V23
Merwin, W. S.
  The Horizons of Rooms: V15
  Leviathan: V5

Metamorphoses (Ovid): V22
Midnight (Heaney): V2
Midnight Verses (Akhmatova): V18
The Milkfish Gatherers (Fenton): V11
Millay, Edna St. Vincent
  *The Courage That My Mother
    Had:* V3
  Wild Swans: V17
Milosz, Czeslaw
  Song of a Citizen: V16
Milton, John
  [On His Blindness] Sonnet 16: V3
  *On His Having Arrived at the Age
    of Twenty-Three:* V17
Mind (Graham): V17
Mirabai
  All I Was Doing Was Breathing:
    V24
Mirror (Plath): V1
Miss Rosie (Clifton): V1
The Missing (Gunn): V9
Momaday, N. Scott
  Angle of Geese: V2
  *To a Child Running With
    Outstretched Arms in Canyon
    de Chelly:* V11
Monologue for an Onion (Kim):
  V24
Montague, John
  A Grafted Tongue: V12
Montale, Eugenio
  On the Threshold: V22
The Moon Glows the Same (Bashō):
  V7
Moore, Marianne
  The Fish: V14
  Poetry: V17
"More Light! More Light!" (Hecht):
  V6
Moreover, the Moon (Loy): V20
Morning Walk (Malroux): V21
Mother to Son (Hughes): V3
Much Madness Is Divinest Sense
  (Dickinson): V16
Muldoon, Paul
  Meeting the British: V7
  Pineapples and Pomegranates:
    V22
Mueller, Lisel
  Blood Oranges: V13
  The Exhibit: V9
Musée des Beaux Arts (Auden): V1
Music Lessons (Oliver): V8
Muske-Dukes, Carol
  Our Side: V24
My Father's Song (Ortiz): V16
My Last Duchess (Browning): V1
*My Life Closed Twice Before Its
  Close* (Dickinson): V8
My Mother Pieced Quilts (Acosta):
  V12
My Papa's Waltz (Roethke): V3
The Mystery (Glück): V15

N

Names of Horses (Hall): V8
A Narrow Fellow in the Grass
    (Dickinson): V11
The Negro Speaks of Rivers
    (Hughes): V10
Nemerov, Howard
    Deep Woods: V14
    The Phoenix: V10
Neruda, Pablo
    Tonight I Can Write: V11
The Nerve (Maxwell): V23
New Rule (Carson): V18
Not like a Cypress (Amichai): V24
Not Waving but Drowning (Smith):
    V3
Nothing Gold Can Stay (Frost): V3
Nowlan, Alden
    For Jean Vincent D'abbadie,
        Baron St.-Castin: V12
Noyes, Alfred
    The Highwayman: V4
Nye, Naomi Shihab
    Kindness: V24
The Nymph's Reply to the Shepherd
    (Raleigh): V14

O

O Captain! My Captain! (Whitman):
    V2
Ode on a Grecian Urn (Keats): V1
Ode to a Drum (Komunyakaa): V20
Ode to a Nightingale (Keats): V3
Ode to the West Wind (Shelley): V2
O'Hara, Frank
    Having a Coke with You: V12
    Why I Am Not a Painter: V8
old age sticks (cummings): V3
Old Ironsides (Holmes): V9
Olds, Sharon
    I Go Back to May 1937: V17
Oliver, Mary
    Music Lessons: V8
    Wild Geese: V15
Omen (Hirsch): V22
On Freedom's Ground (Wilbur): V12
[On His Blindness] Sonnet 16
    (Milton): V3
On His Having Arrived at the Age of
    Twenty-Three (Milton): V17
On Location in the Loire Valley
    (Ackerman): V19
On the Pulse of Morning (Angelou):
    V3
On the Threshold (Montale): V22
Once Again I Prove the Theory of
    Relativity (Cisneros): V19
Ondaatje, Michael
    The Cinnamon Peeler: V19
    To a Sad Daughter: V8
One Is One (Ponsot): V24

Onomatopoeia (Merriam): V6
Ordinary Words (Stone): V19
Ortiz, Simon
    Hunger in New York City: V4
    My Father's Song: V16
Ostriker, Alicia
    His Speed and Strength: V19
Our Side (Muske-Dukes): V24
Out, Out— (Frost): V10
Overture to a Dance of Locomotives
    (Williams): V11
Ovid, (Naso, Publius Ovidius)
    Metamorphoses: V22
Owen, Wilfred
    Dulce et Decorum Est: V10
Oysters (Sexton): V4

P

Paradiso (Koch): V20
Paradoxes and Oxymorons
    (Ashbery): V11
Parker, Dorothy
    The Last Question: V18
The Passionate Shepherd to His Love
    (Marlowe): V22
Pastan, Linda
    Ethics: V8
Paul Revere's Ride (Longfellow): V2
Pavese, Cesare
    Two Poems for T.: V20
Paz, Octavio
    Duration: V18
Perfect Light (Hughes): V19
Phillips, Carl
    All It Takes: V23
The Phoenix (Nemerov): V10
Piano (Lawrence): V6
Piercy, Marge
    Apple sauce for Eve: V22
    Barbie Doll: V9
Pine (Hahn): V23
Pineapples and Pomegranates
    (Muldoon): V22
Pinsky, Robert
    Song of Reasons: V18
Plath, Sylvia
    Blackberrying: V15
    Mirror: V1
A Psalm of Life (Longfellow): V7
Po, Li
    Drinking Alone Beneath the
        Moon: V20
Poe, Edgar Allan
    Annabel Lee: V9
    The Bells: V3
    The Raven: V1
Poetry (Moore): V17
A Poison Tree (Blake): V24
Ponsot, Marie
    One Is One: V24
Pope, Alexander
    The Rape of the Lock: V12

Porphyria's Lover (Browning): V15
Portrait of a Couple at Century's
    End (Santos): V24
Pound, Ezra
    Hugh Selwyn Mauberley: V16
    In a Station of the Metro: V2
    The River-Merchant's Wife: A
        Letter: V8
Practice (Voigt): V23
Proem (Tennyson): V19
Psalm 8 (King James Bible): V9
Psalm 23 (King James Bible): V4
Purdy, Al
    Lament for the Dorsets: V5
    Wilderness Gothic: V12

Q

The Quaker Graveyard in Nantucket
    (Lowell): V6
Queen-Ann's-Lace (Williams): V6

R

Raine, Craig
    A Martian Sends a Postcard
        Home: V7
Raleigh, Walter, Sir
    The Nymph's Reply to the
        Shepherd: V14
Randall, Dudley
    Ballad of Birmingham: V5
The Rape of the Lock (Pope): V12
Rapture (Biele): V21
The Raven (Poe): V1
Reactionary Essay on Applied
    Science (McGinley): V9
A Rebirth (Farrokhzaad): V21
A Red, Red Rose (Burns): V8
The Red Wheelbarrow (Williams):
    V1
Reed, Ishmael
    Beware: Do Not Read This Poem:
        V6
Remember (Rossetti): V14
Reunions with a Ghost (Ai): V16
Revard, Carter
    Birch Canoe: V5
The Reverse Side (Dunn): V21
The Rhodora (Emerson): V17
Rich, Adrienne
    Rusted Legacy: V15
Richard Cory (Robinson): V4
Rilke, Rainer Maria
    Childhood: V19
The Rime of the Ancient Mariner
    (Coleridge): V4
Ríos, Alberto
    Island of the Three Marias: V11
The River-Merchant's Wife: A Letter
    (Pound): V8
The Road Not Taken (Frost): V2

Robinson, E. A.
Richard Cory: V4
Roethke, Theodore
My Papa's Waltz: V3
Rogers, Pattiann
The Greatest Grandeur: V18
The Room (Aiken): V24
Rose, Wendy
For the White poets who would be Indian: V13
Rossetti, Christina
A Birthday: V10
Remember: V14
Rukeyser, Muriel
Ballad of Orange and Grape: V10
Rusted Legacy (Rich): V15

S

Sachs, Nelly
But Perhaps God Needs the Longing: V20
Sailing to Byzantium (Yeats): V2
Saint Francis and the Sow (Kinnell): V9
Sajé, Natasha
The Art of the Novel: V23
Salter, Mary Jo
Trompe l'Oeil: V22
Sandburg, Carl
Chicago: V3
Cool Tombs: V6
Hope Is a Tattered Flag: V12
Santos, Sherod
Portrait of a Couple at Century's End: V24
Sappho
Hymn to Aphrodite: V20
The Satyr's Heart (Kelly): V22
Schnackenberg, Gjertrud
Darwin in 1881: V13
The Seafarer (Anonymous): V8
The Second Coming (Yeats): V7
Seeing You (Valentine): V24
September (Kyger): V23
Service, Robert W.
The Cremation of Sam McGee: V10
Seven Seeds (Bialosky): V19
Sexton, Anne
Courage: V14
Oysters: V4
Shahid Ali, Agha
The Country Without a Post Office: V18
Shakespeare, William
Sonnet 18: V2
Sonnet 19: V9
Sonnet 29: V8
Sonnet 30: V4
Sonnet 55: V5
Sonnet 116: V3
Sonnet 130: V1

Shapiro, Karl
Auto Wreck: V3
She Walks in Beauty (Byron): V14
Shelley, Percy Bysshe
Ode to the West Wind: V2
Shine, Perishing Republic (Jeffers): V4
Silko, Leslie Marmon
Four Mountain Wolves: V9
Story from Bear Country: V16
Simic, Charles
Butcher Shop: V7
Simpson, Louis
American Poetry: V7
Chocolates: V11
In the Suburbs: V14
The Singer's House (Heaney): V17
Sir Patrick Spens (Anonymous): V4
Siren Song (Atwood): V7
60 (Tagore): V18
Small Town with One Road (Soto): V7
Smart and Final Iris (Tate): V15
Smith, Stevie
Not Waving but Drowning: V3
Snyder, Gary
Anasazi: V9
True Night: V19
Social Life (Hoagland): V19
The Soldier (Brooke): V7
somewhere i have never travelled,gladly beyond (cummings): V19
Song, Cathy
Lost Sister: V5
Song of a Citizen (Milosz): V16
Song of Reasons (Pinsky): V18
Song of the Chattahoochee (Lanier): V14
The Song of the Smoke (Du Bois): V13
Song: To Celia (Jonson): V23
Sonnet 16 [On His Blindness] (Milton): V3
Sonnet 18 (Shakespeare): V2
Sonnet 19 (Shakespeare): V9
Sonnet 30 (Shakespeare): V4
Sonnet 29 (Shakespeare): V8
Sonnet XXIX (Browning): V16
Sonnet 43 (Browning): V2
Sonnet 55 (Shakespeare): V5
Sonnet 116 (Shakespeare): V3
Sonnet 130 (Shakespeare): V1
The Sonnet-Ballad (Brooks): V1
Soto, Gary
Small Town with One Road: V7
The Soul Selects Her Own Society (Dickinson): V1
Southbound on the Freeway (Swenson): V16
Spender, Stephen
An Elementary School Classroom in a Slum: V23

Spires, Elizabeth
Ghazal: V21
Spring-Watching Pavilion (Huong): V18
Stafford, William
At the Bomb Testing Site: V8
Fifteen: V2
Ways to Live: V16
Starlight (Levine): V8
Station (Grennan): V21
Stevens, Wallace
The Idea of Order at Key West: V13
Sunday Morning: V16
Stewart, Susan
The Forest: V22
Stone, Ruth
Ordinary Words: V19
Stopping by Woods on a Snowy Evening (Frost): V1
Story from Bear Country (Silko): V16
Strand, Mark
The Continuous Life: V18
Eating Poetry: V9
Strong Men, Riding Horses (Brooks): V4
Sunday Morning (Stevens): V16
A Supermarket in California (Ginsberg): V5
Svenbro, Jesper
Lepidopterology: V23
Swenson, May
Southbound on the Freeway: V16
Swing Low Sweet Chariot (Anonymous): V1
Swir, Anna
Maternity: V21
Szymborska, Wislawa
Astonishment: V15

T

Tagore, Rabindranath
60: V18
A Tall Man Executes a Jig (Layton): V12
Tate, James
Dear Reader: V10
Smart and Final Iris: V15
Taylor, Henry
Landscape with Tractor: V10
Tears, Idle Tears (Tennyson): V4
Teasdale, Sara
There Will Come Soft Rains: V14
Temple Bells Die Out (Bashō): V18
Ten Years after Your Deliberate Drowning (Behn): V21
Tennyson, Alfred, Lord
The Charge of the Light Brigade: V1
The Eagle: V11
The Lady of Shalott: V15

Proem: V19
Tears, Idle Tears: V4
Ulysses: V2
Thayer, Ernest Lawrence
    Casey at the Bat: V5
Theme for English B (Hughes): V6
There's a Certain Slant of Light
    (Dickinson): V6
There Will Come Soft Rains
    (Teasdale): V14
A Thirst Against (Gregg): V20
This Life (Dove): V1
Thomas, Dylan
    Do Not Go Gentle into that Good
       Night: V1
    Fern Hill: V3
    The Force That Through the
       Green Fuse Drives the
       Flower: V8
Those Winter Sundays (Hayden): V1
Three Times My Life Has Opened
    (Hirshfield): V16
Three To's and an Oi (McHugh):
    V24
Tintern Abbey (Wordsworth): V2
To a Child Running With
    Outstretched Arms in Canyon
    de Chelly (Momaday): V11
To a Sad Daughter (Ondaatje): V8
To an Athlete Dying Young
    (Housman): V7
To an Unknown Poet (Kizer): V18
To His Coy Mistress (Marvell): V5
To His Excellency General
    Washington (Wheatley): V13
To My Dear and Loving Husband
    (Bradstreet): V6
To the Virgins, to Make Much of
    Time (Herrick): V13
Toads (Larkin): V4
Tonight I Can Write (Neruda): V11
The Toni Morrison Dreams
    (Alexander): V22
Tranströmer, Tomas
    Answers to Letters: V21
Trompe l'Oeil (Salter): V22
The Tropics in New York (McKay):
    V4
True Night (Snyder): V19
Two Poems for T. (Pavese): V20
The Tyger (Blake): V2

U

Ulysses (Tennyson): V2
Ungaretti, Giuseppe
    Variations on Nothing: V20
The Unknown Citizen (Auden): V3

V

A Valediction: Forbidding Mourning
    (Donne): V11
Valentine, Jean
    Seeing You: V24
Van Duyn, Mona
    Memoir: V20
Vancouver Lights (Birney): V8
Variations on Nothing (Ungaretti):
    V20
Viereck, Peter
    For An Assyrian Frieze: V9
    Kilroy: V14
Voigt, Ellen Bryant
    Practice: V23

W

Walcott, Derek
    A Far Cry from Africa: V6
The War Against the Trees (Kunitz):
    V11
War Is Kind (Crane): V9
Warren, Rosanna
    Daylights: V13
    Lake: V23
The Waste Land (Eliot): V20
Ways to Live (Stafford): V16
We Live by What We See at Night
    (Espada): V13
We Real Cool (Brooks): V6
The Weight of Sweetness (Lee): V11
What Belongs to Us (Howe): V15
What I Would Ask My Husband's
    Dead Father (Hashimoto):
    V22
What My Child Learns of the Sea
    (Lorde): V16
Wheatley, Phillis
    To His Excellency General
       Washington: V13
When I Have Fears That I May
    Cease to Be (Keats): V2

When I Heard the Learn'd
    Astronomer (Whitman): V22
When I Was One-and-Twenty
    (Housman): V4
While I Was Gone a War Began
    (Castillo): V21
Whitman, Walt
    Cavalry Crossing a Ford: V13
    I Hear America Singing: V3
    O Captain! My Captain!: V2
    When I Heard the Learn'd
       Astronomer: V22
Why I Am Not a Painter (O'Hara):
    V8
Why The Classics (Herbert): V22
Wilbur, Richard
    Beowulf: V11
    Merlin Enthralled: V16
    On Freedom's Ground: V12
Wild Geese (Oliver): V15
Wild Swans (Millay): V17
Wilderness Gothic (Purdy): V12
Williams, William Carlos
    Overture to a Dance of
       Locomotives: V11
    Queen-Ann's-Lace: V6
    The Red Wheelbarrow: V1
The Wood-Pile (Frost): V6
Words for Departure (Bogan): V21
Wordsworth, William
    Lines Composed a Few Miles
       above Tintern Abbey: V2
Wright, Charles
    Black Zodiac: V10
Wright, James
    A Blessing: V7
    Autumn Begins in Martins Ferry,
       Ohio: V8
Wright, Judith
    Drought Year: V8

Y

Yeats, William Butler
    Easter 1916: V5
    An Irish Airman Foresees His
       Death: V1
    The Lake Isle of Innisfree: V15
    Leda and the Swan: V13
    Sailing to Byzantium: V2
    The Second Coming: V7

Cumulative Nationality/Ethnicity Index

Acoma Pueblo

Ortiz, Simon
  Hunger in New York City: V4
  My Father's Song: V16

African American

Ai
  Reunions with a Ghost: V16
Angelou, Maya
  Harlem Hopscotch: V2
  On the Pulse of Morning: V3
Baraka, Amiri
  In Memory of Radio: V9
Brooks, Gwendolyn
  The Bean Eaters: V2
  The Sonnet-Ballad: V1
  Strong Men, Riding Horses: V4
  We Real Cool: V6
Clifton, Lucille
  Climbing: V14
  Miss Rosie: V1
Cullen, Countee
  Any Human to Another: V3
Dove, Rita
  Geometry: V15
  This Life: V1
Giovanni, Nikki
  Knoxville, Tennessee: V17
Hayden, Robert
  Those Winter Sundays: V1
Hughes, Langston
  Dream Variations: V15
  Harlem: V1
  Mother to Son: V3
  The Negro Speaks of Rivers: V10
  Theme for English B: V6

Johnson, James Weldon
  The Creation: V1
Komunyakaa, Yusef
  Facing It: V5
  Ode to a Drum: V20
Lorde, Audre
  What My Child Learns of the Sea: V16
Madgett, Naomi Long
  Alabama Centennial: V10
McElroy, Colleen
  A Pièd: V3
Phillips, Carl
  All It Takes: V23
Randall, Dudley
  Ballad of Birmingham: V5
Reed, Ishmael
  Beware: Do Not Read This Poem: V6

American

Ackerman, Diane
  On Location in the Loire Valley: V19
Acosta, Teresa Palomo
  My Mother Pieced Quilts: V12
Ai
  Reunions with a Ghost: V16
Aiken, Conrad
  The Room: V24
Alegría, Claribel
  Accounting: V21
Alexander, Elizabeth
  The Toni Morrison Dreams: V22
Ammons, A. R.
  The City Limits: V19

Angelou, Maya
  Harlem Hopscotch: V2
  On the Pulse of Morning: V3
Ashbery, John
  Paradoxes and Oxymorons: V11
Arvio, Sarah
  Memory: V21
Auden, W. H.
  As I Walked Out One Evening: V4
  Musée des Beaux Arts: V1
  The Unknown Citizen: V3
Bang, Mary Jo
  Allegory: V23
Bass, Ellen
  And What If I Spoke of Despair: V19
Behn, Robin
  Ten Years after Your Deliberate Drowning: V21
Bialosky, Jill
  Seven Seeds: V19
Biele, Joelle
  Rapture: V21
Bishop, Elizabeth
  Brazil, January 1, 1502: V6
  Filling Station: V12
Blumenthal, Michael
  Inventors: V7
Bly, Robert
  Come with Me: V6
  Driving to Town Late to Mail a Letter: V17
Bogan, Louise
  Words for Departure: V21
Bradstreet, Anne
  To My Dear and Loving Husband: V6
Brooks, Gwendolyn
  The Bean Eaters: V2

The Sonnet-Ballad: V1
Strong Men, Riding Horses: V4
We Real Cool: V6
Brouwer, Joel
Last Request: V14
Byrne, Elena Karina
In Particular: V20
Carver, Raymond
The Cobweb: V17
Castillo, Ana
While I Was Gone a War Began: V21
Cisneros, Sandra
Once Again I Prove the Theory of Relativity: V19
Clifton, Lucille
Climbing: V14
Miss Rosie: V1
Collins, Billy
The Afterlife: V18
Crane, Stephen
War Is Kind: V9
Creeley, Robert
Fading Light: V21
Cruz, Victor Hernandez
Business: V16
Cullen, Countee
Any Human to Another: V3
cummings, e. e.
i was sitting in mcsorley's: V13
l(a: V1
maggie and milly and molly and may: V12
old age sticks: V3
somewhere i have never travelled,gladly beyond: V19
Dennis, Carl
The God Who Loves You: V20
Dickey, James
The Heaven of Animals: V6
The Hospital Window: V11
Dickinson, Emily
Because I Could Not Stop for Death: V2
The Bustle in a House: V10
"Hope" Is the Thing with Feathers: V3
I felt a Funeral, in my Brain: V13
I Heard a Fly Buzz—When I Died—: V5
Much Madness Is Divinest Sense: V16
My Life Closed Twice Before Its Close: V8
A Narrow Fellow in the Grass: V11
The Soul Selects Her Own Society: V1
There's a Certain Slant of Light: V6
This Is My Letter to the World: V4

Dobyns, Stephen
It's like This: V23
Dove, Rita
Geometry: V15
This Life: V1
Dubie, Norman
The Czar's Last Christmas Letter. A Barn in the Urals: V12
Du Bois, W. E. B.
The Song of the Smoke: V13
Dugan, Alan
How We Heard the Name: V10
Duncan, Robert
An African Elegy: V13
Dunn, Stephen
The Reverse Side: V21
Eliot, T. S.
Journey of the Magi: V7
The Love Song of J. Alfred Prufrock: V1
Emerson, Ralph Waldo
Concord Hymn: V4
The Rhodora: V17
Erdrich, Louise
Bidwell Ghost: V14
Espada, Martín
Colibrí: V16
We Live by What We See at Night: V13
Forché, Carolyn
The Garden Shukkei-En: V18
Francis, Robert
The Base Stealer: V12
Frost, Robert
Birches: V13
The Death of the Hired Man: V4
Fire and Ice: V7
Mending Wall: V5
Nothing Gold Can Stay: V3
Out, Out—: V10
The Road Not Taken: V2
Stopping by Woods on a Snowy Evening: V1
The Wood-Pile: V6
Gallagher, Tess
I Stop Writing the Poem: V16
Ginsberg, Allen
A Supermarket in California: V5
Gioia, Dana
The Litany: V24
Giovanni, Nikki
Knoxville, Tennessee: V17
Glück, Louise
The Gold Lily: V5
The Mystery: V15
Graham, Jorie
The Hiding Place: V10
Mind: V17
Gregg, Linda
A Thirst Against: V20
Gunn, Thom
The Missing: V9

H.D.
Helen: V6
Hacker, Marilyn
The Boy: V19
Hahn, Kimiko
Pine: V23
Hall, Donald
Names of Horses: V8
Harjo, Joy
Anniversary: V15
Hashimoto, Sharon
What I Would Ask My Husband's Dead Father: V22
Hayden, Robert
Those Winter Sundays: V1
Hecht, Anthony
"More Light! More Light!": V6
Hillman, Brenda
Air for Mercury: V20
Hirsch, Edward
Omen: V22
Hirshfield, Jane
Three Times My Life Has Opened: V16
Hoagland, Tony
Social Life: V19
Holmes, Oliver Wendell
The Chambered Nautilus: V24
Old Ironsides: V9
Howe, Marie
What Belongs to Us: V15
Hudgins, Andrew
Elegy for My Father, Who is Not Dead: V14
Hughes, Langston
Dream Variations: V15
Harlem: V1
Mother to Son: V3
The Negro Speaks of Rivers: V10
Theme for English B: V6
Hugo, Richard
For Jennifer, 6, on the Teton: V17
Jarrell, Randall
The Death of the Ball Turret Gunner: V2
Jeffers, Robinson
Hurt Hawks: V3
Shine, Perishing Republic: V4
Johnson, James Weldon
The Creation: V1
Justice, Donald
Incident in a Rose Garden: V14
Kelly, Brigit Pegeen
The Satyr's Heart: V22
Kenyon, Jane
Having it Out with Melancholy: V17
"Trouble with Math in a One-Room Country School": V9
Kim, Sue (Suji) Kwock
Monologue for an Onion: V24
Kinnell, Galway
Saint Francis and the Sow: V9

Kizer, Carolyn
  To An Unknown Poet: V18
Koch, Kenneth
  Paradiso: V20
Komunyakaa, Yusef
  Facing It: V5
  Ode to a Drum: V20
Kooser, Ted
  At the Cancer Clinic: V24
  The Constellation Orion: V8
Kumin, Maxine
  Address to the Angels: V18
Kunitz, Stanley
  The War Against the Trees: V11
Kyger, Joanne
  September: V23
Lanier, Sidney
  Song of the Chattahoochee: V14
Laux, Dorianne
  For the Sake of Strangers: V24
Lee, Li-Young
  Early in the Morning: V17
  *For a New Citizen of These
    United States:* V15
  The Weight of Sweetness: V11
Levertov, Denise
  The Blue Rim of Memory: V17
  In the Land of Shinar: V7
Levine, Philip
  Starlight: V8
Longfellow, Henry Wadsworth
  The Arsenal at Springfield: V17
  Paul Revere's Ride: V2
  A Psalm of Life: V7
Lorde, Audre
  What My Child Learns of the Sea:
    V16
Lowell, Robert
  For the Union Dead: V7
  *The Quaker Graveyard in
    Nantucket:* V6
Loy, Mina
  Moreover, the Moon: V20
MacLeish, Archibald
  Ars Poetica: V5
Madgett, Naomi Long
  Alabama Centennial: V10
McElroy, Colleen
  A Pièd: V3
McGinley, Phyllis
  The Conquerors: V13
  *Reactionary Essay on Applied
    Science:* V9
McHugh, Heather
  Three To's and an Oi: V24
McKay, Claude
  The Tropics in New York: V4
Merriam, Eve
  Onomatopoeia: V6
Merrill, James
  Lost in Translation: V23
Merwin, W. S.
  The Horizons of Rooms: V15
  Leviathan: V5

Millay, Edna St. Vincent
  *The Courage that My Mother
    Had:* V3
  Wild Swans: V17
Momaday, N. Scott
  Angle of Geese: V2
  *To a Child Running With
    Outstretched Arms in Canyon
    de Chelly:* V11
Montague, John
  A Grafted Tongue: V12
Moore, Marianne
  The Fish: V14
  Poetry: V17
Mueller, Lisel
  The Exhibit: V9
Muske-Dukes, Carol
  Our Side: V24
Nemerov, Howard
  Deep Woods: V14
  The Phoenix: V10
Nye, Naomi Shihab
  Kindness: V24
O'Hara, Frank
  Having a Coke with You: V12
  Why I Am Not a Painter: V8
Olds, Sharon
  I Go Back to May 1937: V17
Oliver, Mary
  Music Lessons: V8
  Wild Geese: V15
Ortiz, Simon
  Hunger in New York City: V4
  My Father's Song: V16
Ostriker, Alicia
  His Speed and Strength: V19
Parker, Dorothy
  The Last Question: V18
Pastan, Linda
  Ethics: V8
Phillips, Carl
  All It Takes: V23
Piercy, Marge
  Apple sauce for Eve: V22
  Barbie Doll: V9
Pinsky, Robert
  Song of Reasons: V18
Plath, Sylvia
  Blackberrying: V15
  Mirror: V1
Poe, Edgar Allan
  Annabel Lee: V9
  The Bells: V3
  The Raven: V1
Ponsot, Marie
  One Is One: V24
Pound, Ezra
  Hugh Selwyn Mauberley: V16
  In a Station of the Metro: V2
  *The River-Merchant's Wife: A
    Letter:* V8
Randall, Dudley
  Ballad of Birmingham: V5

Reed, Ishmael
  Beware: Do Not Read This Poem:
    V6
Revard, Carter
  Birch Canoe: V5
Rich, Adrienne
  Rusted Legacy: V15
Ríos, Alberto
  Island of the Three Marias: V11
Robinson, E. A.
  Richard Cory: V4
Roethke, Theodore
  My Papa's Waltz: V3
Rogers, Pattiann
  The Greatest Grandeur: V18
Rose, Wendy
  *For the White poets who would be
    Indian:* V13
Rukeyser, Muriel
  Ballad of Orange and Grape:
    V10
Salter, Mary Jo
  Trompe l'Oeil: V22
Sandburg, Carl
  Chicago: V3
  Cool Tombs: V6
  Hope Is a Tattered Flag: V12
Santos, Sherod
  *Portrait of a Couple at Century's
    End:* V24
Schnackenberg, Gjertrud
  Darwin in 1881: V13
Sexton, Anne
  Courage: V14
  Oysters: V4
Shapiro, Karl
  Auto Wreck: V3
Silko, Leslie Marmon
  Four Mountain Wolves: V9
  Story from Bear Country: V16
Simic, Charles
  Butcher Shop: V7
Simpson, Louis
  American Poetry: V7
  Chocolates: V11
  In the Suburbs: V14
Snyder, Gary
  Anasazi: V9
  True Night: V19
Song, Cathy
  Lost Sister: V5
Soto, Gary
  Small Town with One Road: V7
Spires, Elizabeth
  Ghazal: V21
Stafford, William
  At the Bomb Testing Site: V8
  Fifteen: V2
  Ways to Live: V16
Stevens, Wallace
  The Idea of Order at Key West:
    V13
  Sunday Morning: V16

Stewart, Susan
  The Forest: V22
Stone, Ruth
  Ordinary Words: V19
Strand, Mark
  The Continuous Life: V18
Swenson, May
  Southbound on the Freeway:
    V16
Tate, James
  Dear Reader: V10
  Smart and Final Iris: V15
Taylor, Henry
  Landscape with Tractor: V10
Teasdale, Sara
  There Will Come Soft Rains: V14
Thayer, Ernest Lawrence
  Casey at the Bat: V5
Valentine, Jean
  Seeing You: V24
Van Duyn, Mona
  Memoir: V20
Viereck, Peter
  For An Assyrian Frieze: V9
  Kilroy: V14
Voigt, Ellen Bryant
  Practice: V23
Warren, Rosanna
  Daylights: V13
  Lake: V23
Wheatley, Phillis
  *To His Excellency General
    Washington:* V13
Whitman, Walt
  Cavalry Crossing a Ford: V13
  I Hear America Singing: V3
  O Captain! My Captain!: V2
  *When I Heard the Learn'd
    Astronomer:* V22
Wilbur, Richard
  Beowulf: V11
  Merlin Enthralled: V16
  On Freedom's Ground: V12
Williams, William Carlos
  *Overture to a Dance of
    Locomotives:* V11
  Queen-Ann's-Lace: V6
  The Red Wheelbarrow: V1
Wright, Charles
  Black Zodiac: V10
Wright, James
  A Blessing: V7
  *Autumn Begins in Martins Ferry,
    Ohio:* V8

Asian American

Hahn, Kimiko
  Pine: V23
Hashimoto, Sharon
  *What I Would Ask My Husband's
    Dead Father:* V22
Kim, Sue (Suji) Kwok
  Monologue for an Onion: V24

Australian

Dawe, Bruce
  Drifters: V10
Hope, A. D.
  Beware of Ruins: V8
Wright, Judith
  Drought Year: V8

Canadian

Atwood, Margaret
  Siren Song: V7
Birney, Earle
  Vancouver Lights: V8
Carson, Anne
  New Rule: V18
Hébert, Anne
  The Alchemy of Day: V20
Jacobsen, Josephine
  Fiddler Crab: V23
Layton, Irving
  A Tall Man Executes a Jig: V12
McCrae, John
  In Flanders Fields: V5
Nowlan, Alden
  *For Jean Vincent D'abbadie,
    Baron St.-Castin:* V12
Purdy, Al
  Lament for the Dorsets: V5
  Wilderness Gothic: V12
Strand, Mark
  Eating Poetry: V9

Canadian, Sri Lankan

Ondaatje, Michael
  The Cinnamon Peeler: V19
  To a Sad Daughter: V8

Chilean

Neruda, Pablo
  Tonight I Can Write: V11

Chinese

Po, Li
  *Drinking Alone Beneath the
    Moon:* V20

Egyptian

Cavafy, C. P.
  Ithaka: V19

English

Alleyn, Ellen
  A Birthday: V10

Arnold, Matthew
  Dover Beach: V2
Auden, W. H.
  As I Walked Out One Evening:
    V4
  Funeral Blues: V10
  Musée des Beaux Arts: V1
  The Unknown Citizen: V3
Blake, William
  The Lamb: V12
  A Poison Tree: V24
  The Tyger: V2
Bradstreet, Anne
  *To My Dear and Loving
    Husband:* V6
Brooke, Rupert
  The Soldier: V7
Browning, Elizabeth Barrett
  Aurora Leigh: V23
  Sonnet XXIX: V16
  Sonnet 43: V2
Browning, Robert
  My Last Duchess: V1
  Porphyria's Lover: V15
Byron, Lord
  The Destruction of Sennacherib:
    V1
  She Walks in Beauty: V14
Carroll, Lewis
  Jabberwocky: V11
Chaucer, Geoffrey
  The Canterbury Tales: V14
Coleridge, Samuel Taylor
  Kubla Khan: V5
  The Rime of the Ancient Mariner:
    V4
Donne, John
  Holy Sonnet 10: V2
  *A Valediction: Forbidding
    Mourning:* V11
Eliot, T. S.
  Journey of the Magi: V7
  *The Love Song of J. Alfred
    Prufrock:* V1
  The Waste Land: V20
Fenton, James
  The Milkfish Gatherers: V11
Gray, Thomas
  *Elegy Written in a Country
    Churchyard:* V9
Gunn, Thom
  The Missing: V9
Hardy, Thomas
  *Ah, Are You Digging on My
    Grave?:* V4
  The Darkling Thrush: V18
  The Man He Killed: V3
Herrick, Robert
  *To the Virgins, to Make Much of
    Time:* V13
Housman, A. E.
  To an Athlete Dying Young: V7
  When I Was One-and-Twenty: V4

Hughes, Ted
  Hawk Roosting: V4
  Perfect Light: V19
Jonson, Ben
  Song: To Celia: V23
Keats, John
  La Belle Dame sans Merci: V17
  Bright Star! Would I Were
    Steadfast as Thou Art: V9
  Ode on a Grecian Urn: V1
  Ode to a Nightingale: V3
  When I Have Fears that I May
    Cease to Be: V2
Kipling, Rudyard
  If: V22
Larkin, Philip
  An Arundel Tomb: V12
  High Windows: V3
  Toads: V4
Lawrence, D. H.
  Piano: V6
Levertov, Denise
  The Blue Rim of Memory: V17
Loy, Mina
  Moreover, the Moon: V20
Marlowe, Christopher
  The Passionate Shepherd to His
    Love: V22
Marvell, Andrew
  To His Coy Mistress: V5
Masefield, John
  Cargoes: V5
Maxwell, Glyn
  The Nerve: V23
Milton, John
  [On His Blindness] Sonnet 16:
    V3
  On His Having Arrived at the Age
    of Twenty-Three: V17
Noyes, Alfred
  The Highwayman: V4
Owen, Wilfred
  Dulce et Decorum Est: V10
Pope, Alexander
  The Rape of the Lock: V12
Raine, Craig
  A Martian Sends a Postcard
    Home: V7
Raleigh, Walter, Sir
  The Nymph's Reply to the
    Shepherd: V14
Rossetti, Christina
  A Birthday: V10
  Remember: V14
Service, Robert W.
  The Cremation of Sam McGee:
    V10
Shakespeare, William
  Sonnet 18: V2
  Sonnet 19: V9
  Sonnet 30: V4
  Sonnet 29: V8
  Sonnet 55: V5
  Sonnet 116: V3

  Sonnet 130: V1
Shelley, Percy Bysshe
  Ode to the West Wind: V2
Smith, Stevie
  Not Waving but Drowning: V3
Spender, Stephen
  An Elementary School Classroom
    in a Slum: V23
Tennyson, Alfred, Lord
  The Charge of the Light Brigade:
    V1
  The Eagle: V11
  The Lady of Shalott: V15
  Proem: V19
  Tears, Idle Tears: V4
  Ulysses: V2
Williams, William Carlos
  Queen-Ann's-Lace: V6
  The Red Wheelbarrow: V1
Wordsworth, William
  Lines Composed a Few Miles
    above Tintern Abbey: V2
Yeats, W. B.
  Easter 1916: V5
  An Irish Airman Forsees His
    Death: V1
  The Lake Isle of Innisfree:
    V15
  Leda and the Swan: V13
  Sailing to Byzantium: V2
  The Second Coming: V7

French

Apollinaire, Guillaume
  Always: V24
Baudelaire, Charles
  Hymn to Beauty: V21
Malroux, Claire
  Morning Walk: V21

German

Amichai, Yehuda
  Not like a Cypress: V24
Blumenthal, Michael
  Inventors: V7
Erdrich, Louise
  Bidwell Ghost: V14
Mueller, Lisel
  Blood Oranges: V13
  The Exhibit: V9
Rilke, Rainer Maria
  Childhood: V19
Roethke, Theodore
  My Papa's Waltz: V3
Sachs, Nelly
  But Perhaps God Needs the
    Longing: V20
Sajé, Natasha
  The Art of the Novel: V23

Ghanaian

Du Bois, W. E. B.
  The Song of the Smoke: V13

Greek

Cavafy, C. P.
  Ithaka: V19
Sappho
  Hymn to Aphrodite: V20

Hispanic

Castillo, Ana
  While I Was Gone a War Began:
    V21
Cruz, Victor Hernandez
  Business: V16
Espada, Martín
  Colibrí: V16

Indian

Mirabai
  All I Was Doing Was Breathing:
    V24
Shahid Ali, Agha
  Country Without a Post Office:
    V18
Tagore, Rabindranath
  60: V18

Indonesian

Lee, Li-Young
  Early in the Morning: V17
  For a New Citizen of These
    United States: V15
  The Weight of Sweetness: V11

Iranian

Farrokhzaad, Faroogh
  A Rebirth: V21

Irish

Boland, Eavan
  Anorexic: V12
  It's a Woman's World: V22
Grennan, Eamon
  Station: V21
Hartnett, Michael
  A Farewell to English: V10
Heaney, Seamus
  Digging: V5
  A Drink of Water: V8
  Midnight: V2
  The Singer's House: V17
Muldoon, Paul
  Meeting the British: V7

Pineapples and Pomegranates:
V22
Yeats, William Butler
Easter 1916: V5
*An Irish Airman Foresees His
Death:* V1
The Lake Isle of Innisfree: V15
Leda and the Swan: V13
Sailing to Byzantium: V2
The Second Coming: V7

Israeli
Amichai, Yehuda
Not like a Cypress: V24

Italian
Apollinaire, Guillaume
Always: V24
Montale, Eugenio
On the Threshold: V22
Pavese, Cesare
Two Poems for T.: V20
Ungaretti, Giuseppe
Variations on Nothing: V20

Jamaican
McKay, Claude
The Tropics in New York: V4
Simpson, Louis
In the Suburbs: V14

Japanese
Ai
Reunions with a Ghost: V16
Bashō, Matsuo
Falling Upon Earth: V2
The Moon Glows the Same: V7
Temple Bells Die Out: V18

Jewish
Blumenthal, Michael
Inventors: V7
Espada, Martín
Colibrí: V16
*We Live by What We See at
Night:* V13
Hirsch, Edward
Omen: V22
Piercy, Marge
Apple sauce for Eve: V22
Barbie Doll: V9
Sachs, Nelly
*But Perhaps God Needs the
Longing:* V20

Shapiro, Karl
Auto Wreck: V3

Kiowa
Momaday, N. Scott
Angle of Geese: V2
*To a Child Running With
Outstretched Arms in Canyon
de Chelly:* V11

Lithuanian
Milosz, Czeslaw
Song of a Citizen: V16

Mexican
Paz, Octavio
Duration: V18
Soto, Gary
Small Town with One Road: V7

Native American
Ai
Reunions with a Ghost: V16
Erdrich, Louise
Bidwell Ghost: V14
Harjo, Joy
Anniversary: V15
Momaday, N. Scott
Angle of Geese: V2
*To a Child Running With
Outstretched Arms in Canyon
de Chelly:* V11
Ortiz, Simon
Hunger in New York City: V4
My Father's Song: V16
Revard, Carter
Birch Canoe: V5
Rose, Wendy
*For the White poets who would be
Indian:* V13
Silko, Leslie Marmon
Four Mountain Wolves: V9
Story from Bear Country: V16

Osage
Revard, Carter
Birch Canoe: V5

Polish
Herbert, Zbigniew
Why The Classics: V22
Milosz, Czeslaw
Song of a Citizen: V16

Swir, Anna
Maternity: V21
Szymborska, Wislawa
Astonishment: V15

Roman
Ovid (Naso, Publius Ovidius)
Metamorphoses: V22

Romanian
Celan, Paul
Late and Deep: V21

Russian
Akhmatova, Anna
Midnight Verses: V18
Levertov, Denise
In the Land of Shinar: V7
Merriam, Eve
Onomatopoeia: V6
Shapiro, Karl
Auto Wreck: V3

St. Lucian
Walcott, Derek
A Far Cry from Africa: V6

Scottish
Burns, Robert
A Red, Red Rose: V8
Byron, Lord
The Destruction of Sennacherib:
V1
MacBeth, George
Bedtime Story: V8

Senegalese
Wheatley, Phillis
*To His Excellency General
Washington:* V13

Serbian
Lazić, Radmila
Death Sentences: V22

Spanish
García Lorca, Federico
Gacela of the Dark Death:
V20

Machado, Antonio
The Crime Was in Granada:
V23
Williams, William Carlos
The Red Wheelbarrow: V1

Swedish

Sandburg, Carl
Chicago: V3
Svenbro, Jesper
Lepidopterology: V23

Tranströmer, Tomas
Answers to Letters: V21

Vietnamese

Huong, Ho Xuan
Spring-Watching Pavilion: V18

Welsh

Levertov, Denise
In the Land of Shinar: V7

Thomas, Dylan
*Do Not Go Gentle into that Good
Night:* V1
Fern Hill: V3
*The Force That Through the
Green Fuse Drives the
Flower:* V8

Yugoslavian

Lazić, Radmila
Death Sentences: V22

Cumulative Nationality/Ethnicity Index

Subject/Theme Index

A

Abandonment
The Chambered Nautilus: 53–54
Monologue for an Onion: 121, 123
Adventure and Exploration
Always: 14, 16–18, 22–24
Alcoholism, Drugs, and Drug Addiction
Kindness: 83, 89–90
American Midwest
At the Cancer Clinic: 40
American Northeast
The Litany: 110–112
American West
At the Cancer Clinic: 40–41
Angels
One Is One: 174
Anger
One Is One: 159–162
A Poison Tree: 196–198, 200
Apathy
Always: 27
The Artistic Impulse
The Litany: 103
Asia
Monologue for an Onion: 119, 123–124
Our Side: 179, 182–183

B

Balancing Opposites
Kindness: 87
Beauty
The Chambered Nautilus: 62–64

The Litany: 118
Our Side: 179, 189
Black Arts Movement
Seeing You: 249
Bourgeois Life
Portrait of a Couple at Century's End: 217

C

Capitalism
A Poison Tree: 206, 209–210
Chaos and Order
The Room: 235
Christianity
The Chambered Nautilus: 58–59
Classicism
The Litany: 118
Not like a Cypress: 139, 147
Compassion
At the Cancer Clinic: 38
Confusion
Our Side: 181
Contrast and Contradiction
Always: 16
Control
One Is One: 161
Couplet
Our Side: 187–188
A Poison Tree: 196–197, 199
Courage
At the Cancer Clinic: 37–38, 40
The Room: 236
The Craft of Poetry
The Room: 236

Creativity
Always: 14, 16–18, 20, 22–24, 30–32, 34
Seeing You: 255
Three To's and an Oi: 269
Crime and Criminals
A Poison Tree: 197–198, 200
Cruelty
Kindness: 83, 87, 89–90
Monologue for an Onion: 125–127
Not like a Cypress: 146
A Poison Tree: 204–205
Cubism
Always: 14, 16, 18–19, 28, 30–31
The Cultivation of Anger
A Poison Tree: 198
Cynicism
Always: 19
Not like a Cypress: 143–144, 146

D

Dadaism
Always: 17, 19–20
Dance
All I Was Doing Was Breathing: 8
Death
All I Was Doing Was Breathing: 1, 6–7
Always: 24–27, 29–30, 32–34
The Chambered Nautilus: 53–56
For the Sake of Strangers: 76–78
Kindness: 86–87, 90
The Litany: 100, 102–104, 106–107, 113–116

Not like a Cypress: 134, 137–138, 142–143, 145–148

Our Side: 176, 178–188

Portrait of a Couple at Century's End: 227–230

The Room: 232, 234–237, 239

Three To's and an Oi: 263, 265–268

Death and the Afterlife

The Chambered Nautilus: 55

Deceit

A Poison Tree: 195–196, 198, 203–205, 208–209

Depression and Melancholy

Always: 29, 31–33

Portrait of a Couple at Century's End: 220–222

Description

At the Cancer Clinic: 36–37

The Chambered Nautilus: 53–54, 56

The Litany: 106–107

Despair

For the Sake of Strangers: 66, 68–69

Determination

Monologue for an Onion: 122

Development and Mobility

The Chambered Nautilus: 54

Dialogue

A Poison Tree: 207, 211

Dictatorship

The Chambered Nautilus: 58–59

Dignity

At the Cancer Clinic: 38

Disease

At the Cancer Clinic: 36–39

Drama

Always: 25–28

Dreams and Visions

Always: 14, 17–24, 28, 30–32

A Poison Tree: 203–205

Seeing You: 251, 253

E

Elusiveness of Truth

Monologue for an Onion: 121

Emotional Healing

For the Sake of Strangers: 69

Emotions

All I Was Doing Was Breathing: 12

Always: 28, 31–32

At the Cancer Clinic: 38

The Chambered Nautilus: 63

For the Sake of Strangers: 66, 68, 70, 72–73, 75, 80–81

Kindness: 91, 94

The Litany: 104–105, 111

Monologue for an Onion: 119, 123–124, 130

Not like a Cypress: 145–146, 149, 152

One Is One: 157–166

Our Side: 178–180, 183–188

A Poison Tree: 196, 201, 209

Portrait of a Couple at Century's End: 213, 216–218, 220, 227, 229–230

The Room: 232, 234–238

Seeing You: 243, 245–248, 250–251, 253–256

Three To's and an Oi: 263–265, 267–268, 270–271

Empathy

Portrait of a Couple at Century's End: 216

Eternity

At the Cancer Clinic: 45–46

A Poison Tree: 203–204

Europe

Always: 18–20

Not like a Cypress: 144–145, 147

A Poison Tree: 200–202

Evil

A Poison Tree: 194, 197–198, 200–201, 203–205

Exile

The Chambered Nautilus: 61–63, 65

Exploration

Always: 16

F

Fatalism

Three To's and an Oi: 267

Fate and Chance

Portrait of a Couple at Century's End: 228–230

Three To's and an Oi: 266–268

Fear and Love

Seeing You: 246

Fear and Terror

Seeing You: 245–249, 254–257

Three To's and an Oi: 264–265, 267–268

Feminism

Seeing You: 248–250

G

Ghost

Always: 16, 18

Our Side: 183

God

All I Was Doing Was Breathing: 1–6, 8–10, 12

The Litany: 106–107

Not like a Cypress: 144–145, 147, 149–152, 154

A Poison Tree: 197–198, 200, 202–205

Grace

At the Cancer Clinic: 39

Grief and Sorrow

For the Sake of Strangers: 66–70, 72–76

Kindness: 84–87, 89–91, 93–95

Our Side: 180, 184–188

The Room: 234, 236

Three To's and an Oi: 263, 265–268, 270–271

H

Happiness and Gaiety

Not like a Cypress: 150, 153

One Is One: 159–161, 166

A Poison Tree: 206, 208, 211

Hatred

Monologue for an Onion: 125–127

Not like a Cypress: 144–145, 147, 149, 152–154

A Poison Tree: 196–197, 201

Heaven

The Chambered Nautilus: 51, 54, 56

Hell

The Room: 241

Heritage and Ancestry

Kindness: 95–98

A Poison Tree: 206, 208, 211

Heroism

Not like a Cypress: 147

History

The Litany: 114–116

Not like a Cypress: 150–154

A Poison Tree: 200, 202

Honor

All I Was Doing Was Breathing: 7

Hope

Always: 24, 26, 29, 33–34

For the Sake of Strangers: 66, 68–69, 71–73

Our Side: 178, 180–181, 183

Portrait of a Couple at Century's End: 216, 218

Hope and Support

For the Sake of Strangers: 68

Human Kindness

Kindness: 87

Humor

Always: 25–27

The Chambered Nautilus: 62, 64

Monologue for an Onion: 119, 123–124

Not like a Cypress: 151, 153

Hypocrisy

A Poison Tree: 198

I

Illness
  At the Cancer Clinic: 38
Imagery and Symbolism
  Always: 16–17, 20, 29–32
  At the Cancer Clinic: 46
  The Chambered Nautilus: 51, 53–56, 58–59
  Kindness: 85–86, 88–89, 93–94
  The Litany: 106–107
  Monologue for an Onion: 125–126, 129–130
  Not like a Cypress: 136, 141, 144, 146–147, 149, 151–155
  One Is One: 158, 161–163
  Our Side: 178–180, 182, 187–188
  A Poison Tree: 196–200, 205, 207, 209
  Portrait of a Couple at Century's End: 217–218, 220–221, 227–230
  The Room: 232, 236–238
  Seeing You: 245–246, 248–249, 253–257
Imagination
  Always: 17–18, 21–22, 28–34
  A Poison Tree: 202–203, 205
  Seeing You: 255
Imagism
  Always: 18, 20
  The Room: 236–237
Immigrants and Immigration
  Not like a Cypress: 140
Impatience
  At the Cancer Clinic: 37–39
Imprisonment
  One Is One: 160
Influence of the Past
  The Litany: 103
Insanity
  All I Was Doing Was Breathing: 8, 10
Introspection
  Three To's and an Oi: 268
Irony
  Always: 17–18
  The Litany: 115–116
  Monologue for an Onion: 123
  Not like a Cypress: 143–145, 147, 149–150, 153
  One Is One: 161
Islamism
  All I Was Doing Was Breathing: 6–7

J

Judaism
  Not like a Cypress: 136, 138–140, 143–145, 147, 149–154

K

Killers and Killing
  All I Was Doing Was Breathing: 5–7
  The Litany: 116
  The Room: 234, 242
Kindness
  For the Sake of Strangers: 66, 68–69, 75–76
  Kindness: 83, 85–89, 91–96, 98
Knowledge
  Always: 28
  The Chambered Nautilus: 59–60
  Monologue for an Onion: 129–130

L

Landscape
  All I Was Doing Was Breathing: 3–6
  At the Cancer Clinic: 40
  The Chambered Nautilus: 51, 53–55, 58
  Our Side: 178–183
  Portrait of a Couple at Century's End: 228–230
  Seeing You: 243, 245–246, 248, 253–255
Language and Meaning
  Three To's and an Oi: 266
Law and Order
  A Poison Tree: 197, 200–201
Literary Criticism
  At the Cancer Clinic: 40
  Not like a Cypress: 139
  One Is One: 162
  Seeing You: 250
Loneliness
  The Litany: 108, 110–111, 113
Longing
  Our Side: 180
Love
  One Is One: 159
  Our Side: 180
Love and Passion
  All I Was Doing Was Breathing: 1–7, 11–12
  Always: 14, 16–20, 22–23, 25–27
  The Chambered Nautilus: 61–64
  For the Sake of Strangers: 80–82
  The Litany: 100, 102–105, 108–113, 115–116
  Monologue for an Onion: 129–130
  Not like a Cypress: 144–146, 148–155
  One Is One: 159–163
  Our Side: 176, 178–186, 188–189
  A Poison Tree: 195, 197–198, 200, 203–205

Portrait of a Couple at Century's End: 227–229
Seeing You: 243–249, 251–257
Three To's and an Oi: 273–275
Loyalty
  All I Was Doing Was Breathing: 1, 3–12

M

Marriage
  Our Side: 189–191
Memory
  The Room: 234
Memory and Reminiscence
  The Litany: 113–117
  Portrait of a Couple at Century's End: 228–229
  The Room: 234–236, 238
Middle Class
  A Poison Tree: 206–207, 210–211
  Portrait of a Couple at Century's End: 217
Middle East
  All I Was Doing Was Breathing: 6–7
  Kindness: 95–97
  Not like a Cypress: 136, 138–141, 143–149, 151, 153–155
Modernism
  Always: 20–21
  Not like a Cypress: 146–147, 150–152
  The Room: 237–238
Monarchy
  For the Sake of Strangers: 78
  Not like a Cypress: 136, 138–143
Money and Economics
  The Chambered Nautilus: 59–60
  Kindness: 85–86, 89–90
Monologue
  Monologue for an Onion: 123, 127–128
Mood
  Portrait of a Couple at Century's End: 220, 222
Morals and Morality
  The Chambered Nautilus: 58–60
  A Poison Tree: 195–198, 200–201, 204–206, 208–211
Murder
  The Litany: 114–115, 117
Music
  All I Was Doing Was Breathing: 5, 7, 10–12
  Always: 16, 19, 20–21
  For the Sake of Strangers: 76–78, 80–81
  The Litany: 104–106, 108, 111–113, 117
  A Poison Tree: 202
  Three To's and an Oi: 265–266

Mystery and Intrigue
At the Cancer Clinic: 45–46
The Chambered Nautilus: 61–65
One Is One: 159–161, 163
Seeing You: 251–253
Myths and Legends
Always: 14, 16–18
The Chambered Nautilus: 53–54, 56
Portrait of a Couple at Century's End: 228–230
The Room: 232, 234–237
Three To's and an Oi: 263–267

N

Narration
At the Cancer Clinic: 35–40
A Poison Tree: 209–210
The Room: 238–239
Seeing You: 245–247, 250, 260–261
Nature
Always: 25, 29–32
At the Cancer Clinic: 46
The Chambered Nautilus: 51, 53, 63–65
Kindness: 83, 86–87
The Litany: 100, 103–104, 106–107
Not like a Cypress: 138, 146–147
A Poison Tree: 205
Portrait of a Couple at Century's End: 227, 230
Seeing You: 248–249
North America
The Chambered Nautilus: 56–57
Monologue for an Onion: 124

O

Optimism
Portrait of a Couple at Century's End: 218

P

Painting
Always: 14, 18–20, 28, 30–32
The Chambered Nautilus: 61–62, 64–65
Patience
At the Cancer Clinic: 35, 37–38, 40
Perception
For the Sake of Strangers: 66, 68, 70–71
Monologue for an Onion: 121–123
The Room: 233–235, 237
Permanence
Monologue for an Onion: 123–124

Portrait of a Couple at Century's End: 217
Persecution
Always: 25–27
Monologue for an Onion: 128
Personal Identity
Seeing You: 246
Personification
The Chambered Nautilus: 54, 56
Kindness: 86, 89, 93–95
The Litany: 109, 112
One Is One: 160–162
The Room: 234–235, 237
Philosophical Ideas
The Chambered Nautilus: 51, 56–58
One Is One: 162–163
Plants
At the Cancer Clinic: 45–46
Not like a Cypress: 136–139
Poetry
All I Was Doing Was Breathing: 1–5, 7–12
Always: 14, 16–33
At the Cancer Clinic: 35–50
The Chambered Nautilus: 51, 53–56, 58–65
For the Sake of Strangers: 66–82
Kindness: 83, 85–98
The Litany: 100, 102–117
Monologue for an Onion: 119, 121–131
Not like a Cypress: 134, 136–139, 141–155
One Is One: 157–175
Our Side: 176, 178–184, 187–192
A Poison Tree: 194–199, 201–202, 204–211
Portrait of a Couple at Century's End: 213, 215–230
The Room: 232, 234–242
Seeing You: 243–262
Three To's and an Oi: 263–275
Point of View
Always: 16, 18–19
Politicians
The Chambered Nautilus: 61, 64
Politics
The Chambered Nautilus: 56–57, 62, 64
Kindness: 83, 89–90
Monologue for an Onion: 119, 123–124
Not like a Cypress: 138, 140, 145, 147
A Poison Tree: 200–201, 205–207, 210–211
Powerlessness and Weakness
For the Sake of Strangers: 68
Pride
A Poison Tree: 209–211
The Process of Interpretation
Always: 17

Prophecy
Always: 30–34
Three To's and an Oi: 263, 267–268
Psychology and the Human Mind
The Litany: 115
A Poison Tree: 207, 210
The Room: 232, 235, 237–238
Seeing You: 246, 248

R

Rebirth
Not like a Cypress: 137
Religion
Not like a Cypress: 138
Religion and Religious Thought
All I Was Doing Was Breathing: 1, 6, 7, 10
The Chambered Nautilus: 54, 59–60
The Litany: 100, 102–104, 106–107
Not like a Cypress: 138–139, 141, 144, 147, 150–152
Our Side: 178
A Poison Tree: 194–195, 197–198, 200, 202–205
Portrait of a Couple at Century's End: 229
Religious Works
Not like a Cypress: 136, 138, 140
A Poison Tree: 203, 205
Repeated Patterns
Seeing You: 246
Repression
The Room: 235

S

Saints
All I Was Doing Was Breathing: 7
Science and Technology
Always: 16, 17–18, 20–22, 28–32, 34
Portrait of a Couple at Century's End: 219
Search for Knowledge
Not like a Cypress: 144–145
Self-Confidence
At the Cancer Clinic: 38–39
Self-Insight
Not like a Cypress: 138
Sentimentality
Our Side: 184–185
Setting
A Poison Tree: 202
Sex and Sexuality
Not like a Cypress: 149, 151, 152, 154

Sickness
  At the Cancer Clinic: 35–40, 44
  Kindness: 90
Slavery
  The Chambered Nautilus: 56–58
Social Order
  Kindness: 89–90
  Portrait of a Couple at Century's End: 217
Socialism
  A Poison Tree: 205–207, 211
Solitude
  The Litany: 110
Soothsayer
  Three To's and an Oi: 263–268, 270–271
Soul
  The Chambered Nautilus: 51, 54, 56, 58–59
  Our Side: 178, 182
South America
  Kindness: 83, 89–90
Space Exploration and Study
  Always: 14, 16–18
  Seeing You: 245–246, 248
Spiritual Devotion
  All I Was Doing Was Breathing: 3
Spiritual Life Versus Worldly Life
  All I Was Doing Was Breathing: 4
Spirituality
  The Litany: 100, 102–104, 106–107
  Not like a Cypress: 149, 151–153
Storms and Weather Conditions
  All I Was Doing Was Breathing: 2–3
  The Litany: 102–104
  Not like a Cypress: 136–138, 141–143
  Portrait of a Couple at Century's End: 215–216, 218
Stream of Consciousness
  For the Sake of Strangers: 70

Strength
  At the Cancer Clinic: 35–36, 38, 40
Structure
  The Room: 234, 238
  Seeing You: 245–246
The Sublime
  The Chambered Nautilus: 63–64
Suicide
  The Room: 241–242
Supernatural
  Our Side: 183
Suppression Versus Expression
  A Poison Tree: 198
Surrealism
  Always: 17, 19–20, 24–25, 28, 30–33

T

Time and Change
  A Poison Tree: 203, 205
Tone
  Always: 18, 25–26, 28
  For the Sake of Strangers: 66, 70
  Not like a Cypress: 139, 141, 151, 153
  A Poison Tree: 208
Transcendentalism
  The Chambered Nautilus: 59–60
Trust
  Seeing You: 247

U

Uncertainty
  The Room: 232–237, 239
Understanding
  A Poison Tree: 202, 204, 210
Unification
  One Is One: 161
Utopianism
  A Poison Tree: 194, 197–198, 200, 206–207, 210–211

V

Victory
  Always: 17

W

War, the Military, and Soldier Life
  Always: 18–19, 21, 24, 26–28, 30, 32–33
  For the Sake of Strangers: 68, 70–71
  Kindness: 89
  Monologue for an Onion: 119, 123–124, 130–133
  Not like a Cypress: 134, 136–137, 139–141, 144–145, 147, 149–151, 153–154
  Portrait of a Couple at Century's End: 213, 215, 217, 219
Western Hemisphere
  Kindness: 90
Wisdom
  A Poison Tree: 196, 200, 202
World War I
  Always: 18–20
The Wrathfulness of the Old Testament God
  A Poison Tree: 198

Y

Yearning
  All I Was Doing Was Breathing: 2, 5
  Our Side: 176, 178–181, 184–186
Youth
  Three To's and an Oi: 267

Z

Zionism
  Not like a Cypress: 143–145, 147

Subject/Theme Index

Cumulative Index of
First Lines

1

1. Mother I was born under the mudbank (Seeing You) V24:244–245

A

A brackish reach of shoal off Madaket,— (The Quaker Graveyard in Nantucket) V6:158

"A cold coming we had of it (Journey of the Magi) V7:110

A few minutes ago, I stepped onto the deck (The Cobweb) V17:50

A gentle spring evening arrives (Spring-Watching Pavilion) V18:198

A line in long array where they wind betwixt green islands, (Cavalry Crossing a Ford) V13:50

A narrow Fellow in the grass (A Narrow Fellow in the Grass) V11:127

A pine box for me. I mean it. (Last Request) V14: 231

A poem should be palpable and mute (Ars Poetica) V5:2

A stone from the depths that has witnessed the seas drying up (Song of a Citizen) V16:125

A tourist came in from Orbitville, (Southbound on the Freeway) V16:158

A wind is ruffling the tawny pelt (A Far Cry from Africa) V6:60

a woman precedes me up the long rope, (Climbing) V14:113

About me the night moonless wimples the mountains (Vancouver Lights) V8:245

About suffering they were never wrong (Musée des Beaux Arts) V1:148

Across Roblin Lake, two shores away, (Wilderness Gothic) V12:241

After the double party (Air for Mercury) V20:2–3

After the party ends another party begins (Social Life) V19:251

After you finish your work (Ballad of Orange and Grape) V10:17

Again I've returned to this country (The Country Without a Post Office) V18:64

"Ah, are you digging on my grave (Ah, Are You Digging on My Grave?) V4:2

All Greece hates (Helen) V6:92

All my existence is a dark sign a dark (A Rebirth) V21:193–194

All night long the hockey pictures (To a Sad Daughter) V8:230

All over Genoa (Trompe l'Oeil) V22:216

All winter your brute shoulders strained against collars, padding (Names of Horses) V8:141

Also Ulysses once—that other war. (Kilroy) V14:213

Always (Always) V24:15

Among the blossoms, a single jar of wine. (Drinking Alone Beneath the Moon) V20:59–60

Anasazi (Anasazi) V9:2

"And do we remember our living lives?" (Memory) V21:156

And God stepped out on space (The Creation) V1:19

And what if I spoke of despair—who doesn't (And What If I Spoke of Despair) V19:2

Animal bones and some mossy tent rings (Lament for the Dorsets) V5:190

Any force— (All It Takes) V23:15

April is the cruellest month, breeding (The Waste Land) V20:248–252

As I perceive (The Gold Lily) V5:127

As I walked out one evening (As I Walked Out One Evening) V4:15

As virtuous men pass mildly away (A Valediction: Forbidding Mourning) V11:201

As you set out for Ithaka (Ithaka) V19:114

At noon in the desert a panting lizard (At the Bomb Testing Site) V8:2

Ay, tear her tattered ensign down! (Old Ironsides)
V9:172

B

Back then, before we came (On Freedom's Ground)
V12:186

Bananas ripe and green, and ginger-root (The Tropics in
New York) V4:255

Because I could not stop for Death— (Because I Could
Not Stop for Death) V2:27

Before the indifferent beak could let her drop? (Leda and
the Swan) V13:182

Before you know what kindness really is (Kindness)
V24:84–85

Be happy if the wind inside the orchard (On the
Threshold) V22:128

Bent double, like old beggars under slacks, (Dulce et
Decorum Est) V10:109

Between my finger and my thumb (Digging) V5:70

Beware of ruins: they have a treacherous charm (Beware
of Ruins) V8:43

Bright star! would I were steadfast as thou art— (Bright
Star! Would I Were Steadfast as Thou Art)
V9:44

But perhaps God needs the longing, wherever else should
it dwell, (But Perhaps God Needs the Longing)
V20:41

By the rude bridge that arched the flood (Concord Hymn)
V4:30

By way of a vanished bridge we cross this river (The
Garden Shukkei-en) V18:107

C

Cassandra's kind of crying was (Three To's and an Oi)
V24:264

Celestial choir! enthron'd in realms of light, (To His
Excellency General Washington V13:212

Come with me into those things that have felt his despair
for so long— (Come with Me) V6:31

Complacencies of the peignoir, and late (Sunday Morning)
V16:189

Composed in the Tower, before his execution ("More
Light! More Light!") V6:119

D

Darkened by time, the masters, like our memories, mix
(Black Zodiac) V10:46

Death, be not proud, though some have called thee (Holy
Sonnet 10) V2:103

Devouring Time, blunt thou the lion's paws (Sonnet 19)
V9:210

Disoriented, the newly dead try to turn back, (Our Side)
V24:177

Do not go gentle into that good night (Do Not Go Gentle
into that Good Night) V1:51

Do not weep, maiden, for war is kind (War Is Kind)
V9:252

Don Arturo says: (Business) V16:2

Drink to me only with thine eyes, (Song: To Celia)
V23:270–271

(Dumb, (A Grafted Tongue) V12:92

E

Each day the shadow swings (In the Land of Shinar) V7:83

Each morning the man rises from bed because the
invisible (It's like This) V23:138–139

Each night she waits by the road (Bidwell Ghost) V14:2

F

Face of the skies (Moreover, the Moon) V20:153

Falling upon earth (Falling Upon Earth) V2:64

Far far from gusty waves these children's faces. (An
Elementary School Classroom in a Slum)
V23:88–89

Five years have past; five summers, with the length
(Tintern Abbey) V2:249

Flesh is heretic. (Anorexic) V12:2

For a long time the butterfly held a prominent place in
psychology (Lepidopterology) V23:171–172

For three years, out of key with his time, (Hugh Selwyn
Mauberley) V16:26

Forgive me for thinking I saw (For a New Citizen of
These United States) V15:55

From my mother's sleep I fell into the State (The Death
of the Ball Turret Gunner) V2:41

G

Gardener: Sir, I encountered Death (Incident in a Rose
Garden) V14:190

Gather ye Rose-buds while ye may, (To the Virgins, to
Make Much of Time) V13:226

Gazelle, I killed you (Ode to a Drum) V20:172–173

Go down, Moses (Go Down, Moses) V11:42

Gray mist wolf (Four Mountain Wolves) V9:131

H

"Had he and I but met (The Man He Killed) V3:167

Had we but world enough, and time (To His Coy
Mistress) V5:276

Half a league, half a league (The Charge of the Light
Brigade) V1:2

Having a Coke with You (Having a Coke with You)
V12:105

He clasps the crag with crooked hands (The Eagle) V11:30

He was found by the Bureau of Statistics to be (The
Unknown Citizen) V3:302

He was seen, surrounded by rifles, (The Crime Was in
Granada) V23:55–56

Hear the sledges with the bells— (The Bells) V3:46

Heart, you bully, you punk, I'm wrecked, I'm shocked
(One Is One) V24:158

Her body is not so white as (Queen-Ann's-Lace) V6:179

Her eyes were coins of porter and her West (A Farewell
to English) V10:126

Here they are. The soft eyes open (The Heaven of
Animals) V6:75

His speed and strength, which is the strength of ten (His Speed and Strength) V19:96

Hog Butcher for the World (Chicago) V3:61

Hold fast to dreams (Dream Variations) V15:42

Hope is a tattered flag and a dream out of time. (Hope is a Tattered Flag) V12:120

"Hope" is the thing with feathers— (Hope Is the Thing with Feathers) V3:123

How do I love thee? Let me count the ways (Sonnet 43) V2:236

How shall we adorn (Angle of Geese) V2:2

How soon hath Time, the subtle thief of youth, (On His Having Arrived at the Age of Twenty-Three) V17:159

How would it be if you took yourself off (Landscape with Tractor) V10:182

Hunger crawls into you (Hunger in New York City) V4:79

I

I am not a painter, I am a poet (Why I Am Not a Painter) V8:258

I am the Smoke King (The Song of the Smoke) V13:196

I am silver and exact. I have no preconceptions (Mirror) V1:116

I am trying to pry open your casket (Dear Reader) V10:85

I became a creature of light (The Mystery) V15:137

I cannot love the Brothers Wright (Reactionary Essay on Applied Science) V9:199

I don't mean to make you cry. (Monologue for an Onion) V24:120–121

I felt a Funeral, in my Brain, (I felt a Funeral in my Brain) V13:137

I gave birth to life. (Maternity) V21:142–143

I have just come down from my father (The Hospital Window) V11:58

I have met them at close of day (Easter 1916) V5:91

I haven't the heart to say (To an Unknown Poet) V18:221

I hear America singing, the varied carols I hear (I Hear America Singing) V3:152

I heard a Fly buzz—when I died— (I Heard a Fly Buzz—When I Died—) V5:140

I know that I shall meet my fate (An Irish Airman Foresees His Death) V1:76

I leant upon a coppice gate (The Darkling Thrush) V18:74

I lie down on my side in the moist grass (Omen) v22:107

I looked in my heart while the wild swans went over. (Wild Swans) V17:221

I prove a theorem and the house expands: (Geometry) V15:68

I see them standing at the formal gates of their colleges, (I go Back to May 1937) V17:112

I sit in the top of the wood, my eyes closed (Hawk Roosting) V4:55

I thought wearing an evergreen dress (Pine) V23:223–224

I'm delighted to see you (The Constellation Orion) V8:53

I've known rivers; (The Negro Speaks of Rivers) V10:197

I was angry with my friend; (A Poison Tree) V24:195–196

I was born too late and I am much too old, (Death Sentences) V22:23

I was born under the mudbank (Seeing You) V24:244–245

I was sitting in mcsorley's. outside it was New York and beautifully snowing. (i was sitting in mcsorley's) V13:151

I will arise and go now, and go to Innisfree, (The Lake Isle of Innisfree) V15:121

If all the world and love were young, (The Nymph's Reply to the Shepard) V14:241

If ever two were one, then surely we (To My Dear and Loving Husband) V6:228

If I should die, think only this of me (The Soldier) V7:218

If you can keep your head when all about you (If) V22:54–55

"Imagine being the first to say: *surveillance*," (Inventors) V7:97

Impatient for home, (Portrait of a Couple at Century's End) V24:214–215

In 1790 a woman could die by falling (The Art of the Novel) V23:29

In 1936, a child (Blood Oranges) V13:34

In a while they rose and went out aimlessly riding, (Merlin Enthralled) V16:72

In China (Lost Sister) V5:216

In ethics class so many years ago (Ethics) V8:88

In Flanders fields the poppies blow (In Flanders Fields) V5:155

In India in their lives they happen (Ways to Live) V16:228

In May, when sea-winds pierced our solitudes, (The Rhodora) V17:191

In the bottom drawer of my desk . . . (Answers to Letters) V21:30–31

In the groves of Africa from their natural wonder (An African Elegy) V13:3

In the Shreve High football stadium (Autumn Begins in Martins Ferry, Ohio) V8:17

In the sixty-eight years (Accounting) V21:2–3

In Xanadu did Kubla Khan (Kubla Khan) V5:172

Ink runs from the corners of my mouth (Eating Poetry) V9:60

Is it the boy in me who's looking out (The Boy) V19:14

It is a cold and snowy night. The main street is deserted. (Driving to Town Late to Mail a Letter) V17:63

It is an ancient Mariner (The Rime of the Ancient Mariner) V4:127

It is in the small things we see it. (Courage) V14:125

It little profits that an idle king (Ulysses) V2:278

It looked extremely rocky for the Mudville nine that day (Casey at the Bat) V5:57

It must be troubling for the god who loves you (The God Who Loves You) V20:88

It seems vainglorious and proud (The Conquerors) V13:67

It starts with a low rumbling, white static, (Rapture) V21:181

It was in and about the Martinmas time (Barbara Allan) V7:10

It was many and many a year ago (Annabel Lee) V9:14

Its quick soft silver bell beating, beating (Auto Wreck) V3:31

J

Januaries, Nature greets our eyes (Brazil, January 1, 1502) V6:15

Just off the highway to Rochester, Minnesota (A Blessing) V7:24

just once (For the White poets who would be Indian) V13:112

L

l(a (l(a) V1:85
Let me not to the marriage of true minds (Sonnet 116)
 V3:288
Let us console you. (Allegory) V23:2–3
Listen, my children, and you shall hear (Paul Revere's
 Ride) V2:178
Little Lamb, who made thee? (The Lamb) V12:134
Long long ago when the world was a wild place (Bedtime
 Story) V8:32

M

maggie and milly and molly and may (maggie & milly &
 molly & may) V12:149
Mary sat musing on the lamp-flame at the table (The
 Death of the Hired Man) V4:42
Men with picked voices chant the names (Overture to a
 Dance of Locomotives) V11:143
"Mother dear, may I go downtown (Ballad of
 Birmingham) V5:17
Much Madness is divinest Sense— (Much Madness is
 Divinest Sense) V16:86
My black face fades (Facing It) V5:109
My father stands in the warm evening (Starlight) V8:213
My heart aches, and a drowsy numbness pains (Ode to a
 Nightingale) V3:228
My heart is like a singing bird (A Birthday) V10:33
My life closed twice before its close— (My Life Closed
 Twice Before Its Close) V8:127
My mistress' eyes are nothing like the sun (Sonnet 130)
 V1:247
My uncle in East Germany (The Exhibit) V9:107

N

Nature's first green is gold (Nothing Gold Can Stay) V3:203
No easy thing to bear, the weight of sweetness (The
 Weight of Sweetness) V11:230
Nobody heard him, the dead man (Not Waving but
 Drowning) V3:216
Not like a cypress, (Not like a Cypress) V24:135
Not marble nor the gilded monuments (Sonnet 55) V5:246
Not the memorized phone numbers. (What Belongs to Us)
 V15:196
Now as I was young and easy under the apple boughs
 (Fern Hill) V3:92
Now as I watch the progress of the plague (The Missing)
 V9:158
Now I rest my head on the satyr's carved chest, (The
 Satyr's Heart) V22:187
Now one might catch it see it (Fading Light) V21:49

O

O Captain! my Captain, our fearful trip is done (O
 Captain! My Captain!) V2:146
O Lord our Lord, how excellent is thy name in all the
 earth! who hast set thy glory above the heavens
 (Psalm 8) V9:182
O my Luve's like a red, red rose (A Red, Red Rose)
 V8:152

O what can ail thee, knight-at-arms, (La Belle Dame sans
 Merci) V17:18
"O where ha' you been, Lord Randal, my son? (Lord
 Randal) V6:105
O wild West Wind, thou breath of Autumn's being (Ode
 to the West Wind) V2:163
Oh, but it is dirty! (Filling Station) V12:57
old age sticks (old age sticks) V3:246
On either side the river lie (The Lady of Shalott) V15:95
On the seashore of endless worlds children meet. The
 infinite (60) V18:3
Once upon a midnight dreary, while I pondered, weak and
 weary (The Raven) V1:200
Once some people were visiting Chekhov (Chocolates)
 V11:17
One day I'll lift the telephone (Elegy for My Father, Who
 Is Not Dead) V14:154
One foot down, then hop! It's hot (Harlem Hopscotch)
 V2:93
one shoe on the roadway presents (A Piéd) V3:16
Out of the hills of Habersham, (Song of the
 Chattahoochee) V14:283
Out walking in the frozen swamp one gray day (The
 Wood-Pile) V6:251
Oysters we ate (Oysters) V4:91

P

Pentagon code (Smart and Final Iris) V15:183
Poised between going on and back, pulled (The Base
 Stealer) V12:30

Q

Quinquireme of Nineveh from distant Ophir (Cargoes)
 V5:44

R

Recognition in the body (In Particular) V20:125
Red men embraced my body's whiteness (Birch Canoe)
 V5:31
Remember me when I am gone away (Remember) V14:255

S

Shall I compare thee to a Summer's day? (Sonnet 18)
 V2:222
She came every morning to draw water (A Drink of
 Water) V8:66
She sang beyond the genius of the sea. (The Idea of Order
 at Key West) V13:164
She walks in beauty, like the night (She Walks in Beauty)
 V14:268
Side by side, their faces blurred, (An Arundel Tomb)
 V12:17
Since the professional wars— (Midnight) V2:130
Since then, I work at night. (Ten Years after Your
 Deliberate Drowning) V21:240
S'io credesse che mia risposta fosse (The Love Song of
 J. Alfred Prufrock) V1:97
Sky black (Duration) V18:93

Sleepless as Prospero back in his bedroom (Darwin in 1881) V13:83

so much depends (The Red Wheelbarrow) V1:219

So the man spread his blanket on the field (A Tall Man Executes a Jig) V12:228

So the sky wounded you, jagged at the heart, (Daylights) V13:101

Softly, in the dark, a woman is singing to me (Piano) V6:145

Some say it's in the reptilian dance (The Greatest Grandeur) V18:119

Some say the world will end in fire (Fire and Ice) V7:57

Something there is that doesn't love a wall (Mending Wall) V5:231

Sometimes walking late at night (Butcher Shop) V7:43

Sometimes, a lion with a prophet's beard (For An Assyrian Frieze) V9:120

Sometimes, in the middle of the lesson (Music Lessons) V8:117

somewhere i have never travelled,gladly beyond (somewhere i have never travelled,gladly beyond) V19:265

South of the bridge on Seventeenth (Fifteen) V2:78

Stop all the clocks, cut off the telephone, (Funeral Blues) V10:139

Strong Men, riding horses. In the West (Strong Men, Riding Horses) V4:209

Such places are too still for history, (Deep Woods) V14:138

Sundays too my father got up early (Those Winter Sundays) V1:300

Swing low sweet chariot (Swing Low Sweet Chariot) V1:283

T

Take heart, monsieur, four-fifths of this province (For Jean Vincent D'abbadie, Baron St.-Castin) V12:78

Tears, idle tears, I know not what they mean (Tears, Idle Tears) V4:220

Tell me not, in mournful numbers (A Psalm of Life) V7:165

Temple bells die out. (Temple Bells Die Out) V18:210

That is no country for old men. The young (Sailing to Byzantium) V2:207

That negligible bit of sand which slides (Variations on Nothing) V20:234

That time of drought the embered air (Drought Year) V8:78

That's my last Duchess painted on the wall (My Last Duchess) V1:165

The apparition of these faces in the crowd (In a Station of the Metro) V2:116

The Assyrian came down like the wolf on the fold (The Destruction of Sennacherib) V1:38

The broken pillar of the wing jags from the clotted shoulder (Hurt Hawks) V3:138

The bud (Saint Francis and the Sow) V9:222

The Bustle in a House (The Bustle in a House) V10:62

The buzz saw snarled and rattled in the yard (Out, Out—) V10:212

The courage that my mother had (The Courage that My Mother Had) V3:79

The Curfew tolls the knell of parting day (Elegy Written in a Country Churchyard) V9:73

The fiddler crab fiddles, glides and dithers, (Fiddler Crab) V23:111–112

The force that through the green fuse drives the flower (The Force That Through the Green Fuse Drives the Flower) V8:101

The grasses are light brown (September) V23:258–259

The green lamp flares on the table (This Life) V1:293

The ills I sorrow at (Any Human to Another) V3:2

The instructor said (Theme for English B) V6:194

The king sits in Dumferling toune (Sir Patrick Spens) V4:177

The land was overmuch like scenery (Beowulf) V11:2

The last time I saw it was 1968. (The Hiding Place) V10:152

The Lord is my shepherd; I shall not want (Psalm 23) V4:103

The man who sold his lawn to standard oil (The War Against the Trees) V11:215

The moon glows the same (The Moon Glows the Same) V7:152

The old South Boston Aquarium stands (For the Union Dead) V7:67

The others bent their heads and started in ("Trouble with Math in a One-Room Country School") V9:238

The pale nuns of St. Joseph are here (Island of Three Marias) V11:79

The Phoenix comes of flame and dust (The Phoenix) V10:226

The plants of the lake (Two Poems for T.) V20:218

The rain set early in to-night: (Porphyria's Lover) V15:151

The river brought down (How We Heard the Name) V10:167

The rusty spigot (Onomatopoeia) V6:133

The sea is calm tonight (Dover Beach) V2:52

The sea sounds insincere (The Milkfish Gatherers) V11:111

The slow overture of rain, (Mind) V17:145

The Soul selects her own Society—(The Soul Selects Her Own Society) V1:259

The time you won your town the race (To an Athlete Dying Young) V7:230

The way sorrow enters the bone (The Blue Rim of Memory) V17:38

The whiskey on your breath (My Papa's Waltz) V3:191

The white ocean in which birds swim (Morning Walk) V21:167

The wind was a torrent of darkness among the gusty trees (The Highwayman) V4:66

There are strange things done in the midnight sun (The Cremation of Sam McGee) V10:75

There have been rooms for such a short time (The Horizons of Rooms) V15:79

There is a hunger for order, (A Thirst Against) V20:205

There is no way not to be excited (Paradiso) V20:190–191

There is the one song everyone (Siren Song) V7:196

There's a Certain Slant of Light (There's a Certain Slant of Light) V6:211

There's no way out. (In the Suburbs) V14:201

There will come soft rains and the smell of the ground, (There Will Come Soft Rains) V14:301

There you are, in all your innocence, (Perfect Light) V19:187

These open years, the river (For Jennifer, 6, on the Teton) V17:86

They eat beans mostly, this old yellow pair (The Bean Eaters) V2:16

they were just meant as covers (My Mother Pieced Quilts) V12:169

They said, "Wait." Well, I waited. (Alabama Centennial) V10:2

This girlchild was: born as usual (Barbie Doll) V9:33

This is a litany of lost things, (The Litany) V24:101–102

This is my letter to the World (This Is My Letter to the World) V4:233

This is the Arsenal. From floor to ceiling, (The Arsenal at Springfield) V17:2

This is the black sea-brute bulling through wave-wrack (Leviathan) V5:203

This is the ship of pearl, which, poets feign, (The Chambered Nautilus) V24:52–53

This poem is concerned with language on a very plain level (Paradoxes and Oxymorons) V11:162

This tale is true, and mine. It tells (The Seafarer) V8:177

Thou still unravish'd bride of quietness (Ode on a Grecian Urn) V1:179

Three times my life has opened. (Three Times My Life Has Opened) V16:213

Time in school drags along with so much worry, (Childhood) V19:29

to fold the clothes. No matter who lives (I Stop Writimg the Poem) V16:58

To weep unbidden, to wake (Practice) V23:240

Tonight I can write the saddest lines (Tonight I Can Write) V11:187

Toni Morrison despises (The Toni Morrison Dreams) V22:202–203

tonite, *thriller* was (Beware: Do Not Read This Poem) V6:3

Turning and turning in the widening gyre (The Second Coming) V7:179

'Twas brillig, and the slithy toves (Jabberwocky) V11:91

Two roads diverged in a yellow wood (The Road Not Taken) V2:195

Tyger! Tyger! burning bright (The Tyger) V2:263

W

wade (The Fish) V14:171

Wanting to say things, (My Father's Song) V16:102

We are saying goodbye (Station) V21:226–227

We could be here. This is the valley (Small Town with One Road) V7:207

We met the British in the dead of winter (Meeting the British) V7:138

We real cool. We (We Real Cool) V6:242

Well, son, I'll tell you (Mother to Son) V3:178

What dire offense from amorous causes springs, (The Rape of the Lock) V12:202

What happens to a dream deferred? (Harlem) V1:63

What of the neighborhood homes awash (The Continuous Life) V18:51

What thoughts I have of you tonight, Walt Whitman, for I walked down the sidestreets under the trees with a headache self-conscious looking at the full moon (A Supermarket in California) V5:261

Whatever it is, it must have (American Poetry) V7:2

When Abraham Lincoln was shoveled into the tombs, he forgot the copperheads, and the assassin . . . in the dust, in the cool tombs (Cool Tombs) V6:45

When I consider how my light is spent ([On His Blindness] Sonnet 16) V3:262

When I have fears that I may cease to be (When I Have Fears that I May Cease to Be) V2:295

When I heard the learn'd astronomer, (When I Heard the Learn'd Astronomer) V22:244

When I see a couple of kids (High Windows) V3:108

When I see birches bend to left and right (Birches) V13:14

When I was born, you waited (Having it Out with Melancholy) V17:98

When I was one-and-twenty (When I Was One-and-Twenty) V4:268

When I watch you (Miss Rosie) V1:133

When, in disgrace with Fortune and men's eyes (Sonnet 29) V8:198

When the mountains of Puerto Rico (We Live by What We See at Night) V13:240

When the world was created wasn't it like this? (Anniversary) V15:2

When they said *Carrickfergus* I could hear (The Singer's House) V17:205

When you consider the radiance, that it does not withhold (The City Limits) V19:78

Whenever Richard Cory went down town (Richard Cory) V4:116

While I was gone a war began. (While I Was Gone a War Began) V21:253–254

While my hair was still cut straight across my forehead (The River-Merchant's Wife: A Letter) V8:164

While the long grain is softening (Early in the Morning) V17:75

While this America settles in the mould of its vulgarity, heavily thickening to empire (Shine, Perishing Republic) V4:161

While you are preparing for sleep, brushing your teeth, (The Afterlife) V18:39

Who has ever stopped to think of the divinity of Lamont Cranston? (In Memory of Radio) V9:144

Whose woods these are I think I know (Stopping by Woods on a Snowy Evening) V1:272

Why should I let the toad *work* (Toads) V4:244

Y

You are small and intense (To a Child Running With Out-stretched Arms in Canyon de Chelly) V11:173

You do not have to be good. (Wild Geese) V15:207

You should lie down now and remember the forest, (The Forest) V22:36–37

You stood thigh-deep in water and green light glanced (Lake) V23:158

You were never told, Mother, how old Illya was drunk (The Czar's Last Christmas Letter) V12:44

Cumulative Index of Last Lines

A

. . . a capital T in the endless mass of the text. (Answers to Letters) V21:30–31

a fleck of foam. (Accounting) V21:2–3

A heart that will one day beat you to death. (Monologue for an Onion) V24:120–121

A heart whose love is innocent! (She Walks in Beauty) V14:268

a man then suddenly stops running (Island of Three Marias) V11:80

A perfect evening! (Temple Bells Die Out) V18:210

a space in the lives of their friends (Beware: Do Not Read This Poem) V6:3

A sudden blow: the great wings beating still (Leda and the Swan) V13:181

A terrible beauty is born (Easter 1916) V5:91

About my big, new, automatically defrosting refrigerator with the built-in electric eye (Reactionary Essay on Applied Science) V9:199

about the tall mounds of termites. (Song of a Citizen) V16:126

Across the expedient and wicked stones (Auto Wreck) V3:31

affirming its brilliant and dizzying love. (Lepidopterology) V23:171

Ah, dear father, graybeard, lonely old courage-teacher, what America did you have when Charon quit poling his ferry and you got out on a smoking bank and stood watching the boat disappear on the black waters of Lethe? (A Supermarket in California) V5:261

All losses are restored and sorrows end (Sonnet 30) V4:192

Amen. Amen (The Creation) V1:20

Anasazi (Anasazi) V9:3

and all beyond saving by children (Ethics) V8:88

and all the richer for it. (Mind) V17:146

And all we need of hell (My Life Closed Twice Before Its Close) V8:127

And, being heard, doesn't vanish in the dark. (Variations on Nothing) V20:234

and changed, back to the class ("Trouble with Math in a One-Room Country School") V9:238

And Death shall be no more: Death, thou shalt die (Holy Sonnet 10) V2:103

and destruction. (Allegory) V23:2–3

And drunk the milk of Paradise (Kubla Khan) V5:172

and fear lit by the breadth of such calmly turns to praise. (The City Limits) V19:78

And Finished knowing—then— (I Felt a Funeral in My Brain) V13:137

And gallop terribly against each other's bodies (Autumn Begins in Martins Ferry, Ohio) V8:17

and go back. (For the White poets who would be Indian) V13:112

And handled with a Chain—(Much Madness is Divinest Sense) V16:86

And has not begun to grow a manly smile. (Deep Woods) V14:139

And his own Word (The Phoenix) V10:226

And I am Nicholas. (The Czar's Last Christmas Letter) V12:45

And I was unaware. (The Darkling Thrush) V18:74

And in the suburbs Can't sat down and cried. (Kilroy) V14:213

And it's been years. (Anniversary) V15:3

and joy may come, and make its test of us. (One Is One) V24:158

and leaving essence to the inner eye. (Memory) V21:156

And life for me ain't been no crystal stair (Mother to Son) V3:179

And like a thunderbolt he falls (The Eagle) V11:30

And makes me end where I begun (A Valediction: Forbidding Mourning) V11:202

And 'midst the stars inscribe Belinda's name. (The Rape of the Lock) V12:209

And miles to go before I sleep (Stopping by Woods on a Snowy Evening) V1:272

and my father saying things. (My Father's Song) V16:102

And no birds sing. (La Belle Dame sans Merci) V17:18

And not waving but drowning (Not Waving but Drowning) V3:216

And oh, 'tis true, 'tis true (When I Was One-and-Twenty) V4:268

And reach for your scalping knife. (For Jean Vincent D'abbadie, Baron St.-Castin) V12:78

and retreating, always retreating, behind it (Brazil, January 1, 1502) V6:16

And settled upon his eyes in a black soot ("More Light! More Light!") V6:120

And shuts his eyes. (Darwin in 1881) V13: 84

And so live ever—or else swoon to death (Bright Star! Would I Were Steadfast as Thou Art) V9:44

and strange and loud was the dingoes' cry (Drought Year) V8:78

and stride out. (Courage) V14:126

and sweat and fat and greed. (Anorexic) V12:3

And that has made all the difference (The Road Not Taken) V2:195

And the deep river ran on (As I Walked Out One Evening) V4:16

And the midnight message of Paul Revere (Paul Revere's Ride) V2:180

And the mome raths outgrabe (Jabberwocky) V11:91

And the Salvation Army singing God loves us. . . . (Hope is a Tattered Flag) V12:120

and these the last verses that I write for her (Tonight I Can Write) V11:187

and thickly wooded country; the moon. (The Art of the Novel) V23:29

And those roads in South Dakota that feel around in the darkness . . . (Come with Me) V6:31

and to know she will stay in the field till you die? (Landscape with Tractor) V10:183

and two blankets embroidered with smallpox (Meeting the British) V7:138

and waving, shouting, *Welcome back.* (Elegy for My Father, Who Is Not Dead) V14:154

And—which is more—you'll be a Man, my son! (If) V22:54–55

and whose skin is made dusky by stars. (September) V23:258–259

And would suffice (Fire and Ice) V7:57

And yet God has not said a word! (Porphyria's Lover) V15:151

and you spread un the thin halo of night mist. (Ways to Live) V16:229

And Zero at the Bone— (A Narrow Fellow in the Grass) V11:127

(answer with a tower of birds) (Duration) V18:93

Around us already perhaps future moons, suns and stars blaze in a fiery wreath. (But Perhaps God Needs the Longing) V20:41

As any She belied with false compare (Sonnet 130) V1:248

As ever in my great Task-Master's eye. (On His Having Arrived at the Age of Twenty-Three) V17:160

As far as Cho-fu-Sa (The River-Merchant's Wife: A Letter) V8:165

As the contagion of those molten eyes (For An Assyrian Frieze) V9:120

As they lean over the beans in their rented back room that is full of beads and receipts and dolls and clothes, tobacco crumbs, vases and fringes (The Bean Eaters) V2:16

aspired to become lighter than air (Blood Oranges) V13:34

at home in the fish's fallen heaven (Birch Canoe) V5:31

away, pedaling hard, rocket and pilot. (His Speed and Strength) V19:96

B

Back to the play of constant give and change (The Missing) V9:158

Before it was quite unsheathed from reality (Hurt Hawks) V3:138

before we're even able to name them. (Station) V21:226–227

behind us and all our shining ambivalent love airborne there before us. (Our Side) V24:177

Black like me. (Dream Variations) V15:42

Bless me (Hunger in New York City) V4:79

bombs scandalizing the sanctity of night. (While I Was Gone a War Began) V21:253–254

But, baby, where are you?" (Ballad of Birmingham) V5:17

But be (Ars Poetica) V5:3

but it works every time (Siren Song) V7:196

but the truth is, it is, lost to us now. (The Forest) V22:36–37

But there is no joy in Mudville—mighty Casey has "Struck Out." (Casey at the Bat) V5:58

But we hold our course, and the wind is with us. (On Freedom's Ground) V12:187

by a beeswax candle pooling beside their dinnerware. (Portrait of a Couple at Century's End) V24:214–215

by good fortune (The Horizons of Rooms) V15:80

C

Calls through the valleys of Hall. (Song of the Chattahoochee) V14:284

chickens (The Red Wheelbarrow) V1:219

clear water dashes (Onomatopoeia) V6:133

Columbia. (Kindness) V24:84–85

come to life and burn? (Bidwell Ghost) V14:2

Comin' for to carry me home (Swing Low Sweet Chariot) V1:284

crossed the water. (All It Takes) V23:15

D

Dare frame thy fearful symmetry? (The Tyger) V2:263

"Dead," was all he answered (The Death of the Hired Man) V4:44

deep in the deepest one, tributaries burn. (For Jennifer, 6, on the Teton) V17:86

Delicate, delicate, delicate, delicate—now! (The Base Stealer) V12:30

Die soon (We Real Cool) V6:242

Do what you are going to do, I will tell about it. (I go Back to May 1937) V17:113

Down in the flood of remembrance, I weep like a child for the past (Piano) V6:145

Downward to darkness, on extended wings. (Sunday Morning) V16:190

Driving around, I will waste more time. (Driving to Town Late to Mail a Letter) V17:63

dry wells that fill so easily now (The Exhibit) V9:107

dust rises in many myriads of grains. (Not like a Cypress) V24:135

E

endless worlds is the great meeting of children. (60) V18:3

Eternal, unchanging creator of earth. Amen (The Seafarer) V8:178

Eternity of your arms around my neck. (Death Sentences) V22:23

even as it vanishes—were not our life. (The Litany) V24:101–102

every branch traced with the ghost writing of snow. (The Afterlife) V18:39

F

fall upon us, the dwellers in shadow (In the Land of Shinar) V7:84

Fallen cold and dead (O Captain! My Captain!) V2:147

filled, never. (The Greatest Grandeur) V18:119

Firewood, iron-ware, and cheap tin trays (Cargoes) V5:44

Fled is that music:—Do I wake or sleep? (Ode to a Nightingale) V3:229

For I'm sick at the heart, and I fain wad lie down." (Lord Randal) V6:105

For nothing now can ever come to any good. (Funeral Blues) V10:139

forget me as fast as you can. (Last Request) V14:231

from one kiss (A Rebirth) V21:193–194

G

going where? Where? (Childhood) V19:29

H

Had anything been wrong, we should certainly have heard (The Unknown Citizen) V3:303

Had somewhere to get to and sailed calmly on (Mus,e des Beaux Arts) V1:148

half eaten by the moon. (Dear Reader) V10:85

hand over hungry hand. (Climbing) V14:113

Happen on a red tongue (Small Town with One Road) V7:207

Has no more need of, and I have (The Courage that My Mother Had) V3:80

Hath melted like snow in the glance of the Lord! (The Destruction of Sennacherib) V1:39

He rose the morrow morn (The Rime of the Ancient Mariner) V4:132

He says again, "Good fences make good neighbors." (Mending Wall) V5:232

He writes down something that he crosses out. (The Boy) V19:14

here; passion will save you. (Air for Mercury) V20:2–3

Has set me softly down beside you. The Poem is you (Paradoxes and Oxymorons) V11:162

History theirs whose languages is the sun. (An Elementary School Classroom in a Slum) V23:88–89

How at my sheet goes the same crooked worm (The Force That Through the Green Fuse Drives the Flower) V8:101

How can I turn from Africa and live? (A Far Cry from Africa) V6:61

How sad then is even the marvelous! (An Africian Elegy) V13:4

I

I am black. (The Song of the Smoke) V13:197

I am going to keep things like this (Hawk Roosting) V4:55

I am not brave at all (Strong Men, Riding Horses) V4:209

I could not see to see— (I Heard a Fly Buzz—When I Died—) V5:140

I didn't want to put them down. (And What If I Spoke of Despair) V19:2

I have just come down from my father (The Hospital Window) V11:58

I cremated Sam McGee (The Cremation of Sam McGee) V10:76

I hear it in the deep heart's core. (The Lake Isle of Innisfree) V15:121

I never writ, nor no man ever loved (Sonnet 116) V3:288

I romp with joy in the bookish dark (Eating Poetry) V9:61

I see Mike's painting, called SARDINES (Why I Am Not a Painter) V8:259

I shall but love thee better after death (Sonnet 43) V2:236

I should be glad of another death (Journey of the Magi) V7:110

I stand up (Miss Rosie) V1:133

I stood there, fifteen (Fifteen) V2:78

I take it you are he? (Incident in a Rose Garden) V14:191

I turned aside and bowed my head and wept (The Tropics in New York) V4:255

I'll be gone from here. (The Cobweb) V17:51

I'll dig with it (Digging) V5:71

If Winter comes, can Spring be far behind? (Ode to the West Wind) V2:163

In a convulsive misery (The Milkfish Gatherers) V11:112

In balance with this life, this death (An Irish Airman Foresees His Death) V1:76

in earth's gasp, ocean's yawn. (Lake) V23:158

In Flanders fields (In Flanders Fields) V5:155

In ghostlier demarcations, keener sounds. (The Idea of Order at Key West) V13:164

In hearts at peace, under an English heaven (The Soldier) V7:218

In her tomb by the side of the sea (Annabel Lee) V9:14

in the family of things. (Wild Geese) V15:208

in the grit gray light of day. (Daylights) V13:102

In the rear-view mirrors of the passing cars (The War Against the Trees) V11:216

In these Chicago avenues. (A Thirst Against) V20:205

in this bastion of culture. (To an Unknown Poet) V18:221

iness (l(a) V1:85

Into blossom (A Blessing) V7:24

Is Come, my love is come to me. (A Birthday) V10:34

is love—that's all. (Two Poems for T.) V20:218

is safe is what you said. (Practice) V23:240

is still warm (Lament for the Dorsets) V5:191

It asked a crumb—of Me (Hope Is the Thing with Feathers) V3:123

It is our god. (Fiddler Crab) V23:111–112

it is the bell to awaken God that we've heard ringing. (The Garden Shukkei-en) V18:107

It rains as I write this. Mad heart, be brave. (The Country Without a Post Office) V18:64

It was your resting place." (Ah, Are You Digging on My Grave?) V4:2

it's always ourselves we find in the sea (maggie & milly & molly & may) V12:150

its bright, unequivocal eye. (Having it Out with Melancholy) V17:99

It's the fall through wind lifting white leaves. (Rapture) V21:181

its youth. The sea grows old in it. (The Fish) V14:172

J

Judge tenderly—of Me (This Is My Letter to the World) V4:233

Just imagine it (Inventors) V7:97

L

Laughing the stormy, husky, brawling laughter of Youth, half-naked, sweating, proud to be Hog Butcher, Tool Maker, Stacker of Wheat, Player with Railroads and Freight Handler to the Nation (Chicago) V3:61

Learn to labor and to wait (A Psalm of Life) V7:165

Leashed in my throat (Midnight) V2:131

Leaving thine outgrown shell by life's un-resting sea (The Chambered Nautilus) V24:52–53

Let my people go (Go Down, Moses) V11:43

life, our life and its forgetting. (For a New Citizen of These United States) V15:55

Life to Victory (Always) V24:15

like a shadow or a friend. *Colombia.* (Kindness) V24:84–85

Like Stone— (The Soul Selects Her Own Society) V1:259

Little Lamb, God bless thee. (The Lamb) V12:135

Look'd up in perfect silence at the stars. (When I Heard the Learn'd Astronomer) V22:244

love (The Toni Morrison Dreams) V22:202–203

M

'Make a wish, Tom, make a wish.' (Drifters) V10: 98

make it seem to change (The Moon Glows the Same) V7:152

midnight-oiled in the metric laws? (A Farewell to English) V10:126

Monkey business (Business) V16:2

More dear, both for themselves and for thy sake! (Tintern Abbey) V2:250

My foe outstretchd beneath the tree. (A Poison Tree) V24:195–196

My love shall in my verse ever live young (Sonnet 19) V9:211

My soul has grown deep like the rivers. (The Negro Speaks of Rivers) V10:198

N

never to waken in that world again (Starlight) V8:213

Nirvana is here, nine times out of ten. (Spring-Watching Pavilion) V18:198

No, she's brushing a boy's hair (Facing It) V5:110

no—tell them *no*— (The Hiding Place) V10:153

Noble six hundred! (The Charge of the Light Brigade) V1:3

nobody,not even the rain,has such small hands (somewhere i have never travelled,gladly beyond) V19:265

Not even the blisters. Look. (What Belongs to Us) V15:196

Not of itself, but thee. (Song: To Celia) V23:270–271

Nothing gold can stay (Nothing Gold Can Stay) V3:203

Nothing, and is nowhere, and is endless (High Windows) V3:108

Now! (Alabama Centennial) V10:2

nursing the tough skin of figs (This Life) V1:293

O

O Death in Life, the days that are no more! (Tears, Idle Tears) V4:220

O Lord our Lord, how excellent is thy name in all the earth! (Psalm 8) V9:182

O Roger, Mackerel, Riley, Ned, Nellie, Chester, Lady Ghost (Names of Horses) V8:142

Of all our joys, this must be the deepest. (Drinking Alone Beneath the Moon) V20:59–60

of gentleness (To a Sad Daughter) V8:231

of love's austere and lonely offices? (Those Winter Sundays) V1:300

of peaches (The Weight of Sweetness) V11:230

Of the camellia (Falling Upon Earth) V2:64

Of the Creator. And he waits for the world to begin (Leviathan) V5:204

Of what is past, or passing, or to come (Sailing to Byzantium) V2:207

Oh that was the garden of abundance, seeing you. (Seeing You) V24:244–245

Old Ryan, not yours (The Constellation Orion) V8:53

On the dark distant flurry (Angle of Geese) V2:2

On the look of Death— (There's a Certain Slant of Light) V6:212

On your head like a crown (Any Human to Another) V3:2

One could do worse that be a swinger of birches. (Birches) V13:15

Or does it explode? (Harlem) V1:63

Or help to half-a-crown." (The Man He Killed) V3:167

or last time, we look. (In Particular) V20:125

or nothing (Queen-Ann's-Lace) V6:179

or the one red leaf the snow releases in March. (Three Times My Life Has Opened) V16:213

ORANGE forever. (Ballad of Orange and Grape) V10:18

our every corpuscle become an elf. (Moreover, the Moon) V20:153

outside. (it was New York and beautifully, snowing . . . (i was sitting in mcsorley's) V13:152

owing old (old age sticks) V3:246

P

patient in mind remembers the time. (Fading Light) V21:49

Perhaps he will fall. (Wilderness Gothic) V12:242

Petals on a wet, black bough (In a Station of the Metro) V2:116

Plaiting a dark red love-knot into her long black hair (The Highwayman) V4:68

Powerless, I drown. (Maternity) V21:142–143

Pro patria mori. (Dulce et Decorum Est) V10:110

R

Rage, rage against the dying of the light (Do Not Go Gentle into that Good Night) V1:51

Raise it again, man. We still believe what we hear. (The Singer's House) V17:206

Remember the Giver fading off the lip (A Drink of Water) V8:66

rise & walk away like a panther. (Ode to a Drum) V20:172–173

Rises toward her day after day, like a terrible fish (Mirror) V1:116

S

Shall be lifted—nevermore! (The Raven) V1:202

Shantih shantih shantih (The Waste Land) V20:248–252

Shuddering with rain, coming down around me. (Omen) v22:107

Simply melted into the perfect light. (Perfect Light) V19:187

Singing of him what they could understand (Beowulf) V11:3

Singing with open mouths their strong melodious songs (I Hear America Singing) V3:152

slides by on grease (For the Union Dead) V7:67

Slouches towards Bethlehem to be born? (The Second Coming) V7:179

So long lives this, and this gives life to thee (Sonnet 18) V2:222

So prick my skin. (Pine) V23:223–224

Somebody loves us all. (Filling Station) V12:57

spill darker kissmarks on that dark. (Ten Years after Your Deliberate Drowning) V21:240

Stand still, yet we will make him run (To His Coy Mistress) V5:277

startled into eternity (Four Mountain Wolves) V9:132

Still clinging to your shirt (My Papa's Waltz) V3:192

Stood up, coiled above his head, transforming all. (A Tall Man Executes a Jig) V12:229

Surely goodness and mercy shall follow me all the days of my life: and I will dwell in the house of the Lord for ever (Psalm 23) V4:103

syllables of an old order. (A Grafted Tongue) V12:93

T

Take any streetful of people buying clothes and groceries, cheering a hero or throwing confetti and blowing tin horns . . . tell me if the lovers are losers . . . tell me if any get more than the lovers . . . in the dust . . . in the cool tombs (Cool Tombs) V6:46

Than from everything else life promised that you could do? (Paradiso) V20:190–191

Than that you should remember and be sad. (Remember) V14:255

That then I scorn to change my state with Kings (Sonnet 29) V8:198

That when we live no more, we may live ever (To My Dear and Loving Husband) V6:228

That's the word. (Black Zodiac) V10:47

the bigger it gets. (Smart and Final Iris) V15:183

The bosom of his Father and his God (Elegy Written in a Country Churchyard) V9:74

the bow toward torrents of *veyz mir.* (Three To's and an Oi) V24:264

The crime was in Granada, his Granada. (The Crime Was in Granada) V23:55–56

The dance is sure (Overture to a Dance of Locomotives) V11:143

The eyes turn topaz. (Hugh Selwyn Mauberley) V16:30

The garland briefer than a girl's (To an Athlete Dying Young) V7:230

The guidon flags flutter gayly in the wind. (Cavalry Crossing a Ford) V13:50

The hands gripped hard on the desert (At the Bomb Testing Site) V8:3

The holy melodies of love arise. (The Arsenal at Springfield) V17:3

the knife at the throat, the death in the metronome (Music Lessons) V8:117

The Lady of Shalott." (The Lady of Shalott) V15:97

The lightning and the gale! (Old Ironsides) V9:172

the long, perfect loveliness of sow (Saint Francis and the Sow) V9:222

The Lord survives the rainbow of His will (The Quaker Graveyard in Nantucket) V6:159

The man I was when I was part of it (Beware of Ruins) V8:43

the quilts sing on (My Mother Pieced Quilts) V12:169

The red rose and the brier (Barbara Allan) V7:11

The self-same Power that brought me there brought you. (The Rhodora) V17:191

The shaft we raise to them and thee (Concord Hymn) V4:30

The sky became a still and woven blue. (Merlin Enthralled) V16:73

The spirit of this place (To a Child Running With Out-stretched Arms in Canyon de Chelly) V11:173

The town again, trailing your legs and crying! (Wild Swans) V17:221

the unremitting space of your rebellion (Lost Sister) V5:217

The woman won (Oysters) V4:91

their guts or their brains? (Southbound on the Freeway) V16:158

their dinnerware. (Portrait of a Couple at Century's End) V24:214–215

There is the trap that catches noblest spirits, that caught—
they say—God, when he walked on earth
(Shine, Perishing Republic) V4:162

there was light (Vancouver Lights) V8:246

They also serve who only stand and wait." ([On His
Blindness] Sonnet 16) V3:262

They are going to some point true and unproven.
(Geometry) V15:68

They rise, they walk again (The Heaven of Animals) V6:76

They think I lost. I think I won (Harlem Hopscotch)
V2:93

This is my page for English B (Theme for English B)
V6:194

This Love (In Memory of Radio) V9:145

Tho' it were ten thousand mile! (A Red, Red Rose)
V8:152

Though I sang in my chains like the sea (Fern Hill) V3:92

Till human voices wake us, and we drown (The Love
Song of J. Alfred Prufrock) V1:99

Till Love and Fame to nothingness do sink (When I Have
Fears that I May Cease to Be) V2:295

To every woman a happy ending (Barbie Doll) V9:33

to glow at midnight. (The Blue Rim of Memory) V17:39

to its owner or what horror has befallen the other shoe
(A Pièd) V3:16

To live with thee and be thy love. (The Nymph's Reply to
the Shepherd) V14:241

To strive, to seek, to find, and not to yield (Ulysses)
V2:279

To the moaning and the groaning of the bells (The Bells)
V3:47

To the temple, singing. (In the Suburbs) V14:201

U

Undeniable selves, into your days, and beyond. (The
Continuous Life) V18:51

until at last I lift you up and wrap you within me. (It's
like This) V23:138–139

Until Eternity. (The Bustle in a House) V10:62

unusual conservation (Chocolates) V11:17

Uttering cries that are almost human (American Poetry)
V7:2

W

War is kind (War Is Kind) V9:253

watching to see how it's done. (I Stop Writing the Poem)
V16:58

Went home and put a bullet through his head (Richard
Cory) V4:117

Were not the one dead, turned to their affairs. (Out,
Out—) V10:213

Were toward Eternity— (Because I Could Not Stop for
Death) V2:27

What will survive of us is love. (An Arundel Tomb)
V12:18

When I died they washed me out of the turret with a
hose (The Death of the Ball Turret Gunner)
V2:41

when they untie them in the evening. (Early in the
Morning) V17:75

when you are at a party. (Social Life) V19:251

When you have both (Toads) V4:244

Where deep in the night I hear a voice (Butcher Shop)
V7:43

Where ignorant armies clash by night (Dover Beach)
V2:52

Which Claus of Innsbruck cast in bronze for me! (My
Last Duchess) V1:166

Which for all you know is the life you've chosen. (The
God Who Loves You) V20:88

which is not going to go wasted on me which is why I'm
telling you about it (Having a Coke with You)
V12:106

which only looks like an *l*, and is silent. (Trompe l'Oeil)
V22:216

white ash amid funereal cypresses (Helen) V6:92

Who are you and what is your purpose? (The Mystery)
V15:138

Wi' the Scots lords at his feit (Sir Patrick Spens) V4:177

Will always be ready to bless the day (Morning Walk)
V21:167

will be easy, my rancor less bitter . . . (On the Threshold)
V22:128

Will hear of as a god." (How we Heard the Name)
V10:167

Wind, like the dodo's (Bedtime Story) V8:33

With gold unfading, WASHINGTON! be thine. (To His
Excellency General Washington) V13:213

with my eyes closed. (We Live by What We See at Night)
V13:240

With the slow smokeless burning of decay (The Wood-
Pile) V6:252

With what they had to go on. (The Conquerors) V13:67

Without cease or doubt sew the sweet sad earth. (The
Satyr's Heart) V22:187

Would scarcely know that we were gone. (There Will
Come Soft Rains) V14:301

Y

Ye know on earth, and all ye need to know (Ode on a
Grecian Urn) V1:180

You live in this, and dwell in lovers' eyes (Sonnet 55)
V5:246

You may for ever tarry. (To the Virgins, to Make Much
of Time) V13:226

you who raised me? (The Gold Lily) V5:127

you'll have understood by then what these Ithakas mean.
(Ithaka) V19:114